"How Much Can I Make?"

Actual Sales and Profit Potential for Your Small Business

9th Edition

Robert E. Bond
Publisher

Blair Cavagrotti
Senior Editor

Basant Singh Sanghera
Editor

Sarah Hwang
Editor

Tiffany Han
Editor

Source Book Publications
Serving the Franchising Industry

1814 Franklin St., Suite 603
Oakland, CA 94612
800.841.0873

ISBN-10: 1-887137-68-8
ISBN-13: 978-1-887137-68-3

DISCLAIMER

The Financial Performance Representations/Earnings Claims Statements in *"How Much Can I Make?"* are based on data submitted by the franchisors themselves to various state and/or federal regulatory agencies. The franchisor profiles are based on information submitted to Source Book Publications by the franchisors themselves. Every reasonable effort has been made to ensure that the information presented accurately reflects the original data submitted. Although the publisher and Source Book Publications feel confident that the information submitted is accurate and complete, they have not independently verified or corroborated the information. Accordingly, neither the publisher, Source Book Publications nor the World Franchising Network assume any responsibility for errors or omissions. They strongly encourage any prospective franchisee to conduct an aggressive independent investigation into the sales and income potential of the franchises being considered. Readers should keep in mind that some of the franchisors may have terminated their franchising efforts since the submission of the original data. Others may have superseded the information contained herein with more current financial performance representations.

It is the intent of the author and publisher to periodically update *"How Much Can I Make?"* To the extent that any franchisor making a Financial Performance Representation wishes to be included in subsequent editions, please forward a current copy of your FDD or Item 19 to Source Book Publications, 1814 Franklin St., Suite 603, Oakland, CA 94612.

This publication is designed to provide its readers with accurate and authoritative information with regard to the subject matter covered. It is sold with the understanding that neither the author nor the publisher is engaged in rendering legal, accounting or other professional services. If legal advice or other expert assistance is required, the services of a competent professional person should be sought.

From a Declaration of Principles jointly adopted by a Committee of the American Bar Association and a Committee of Publishers.

Cover Design by Joyce Coffland, Artistic Concepts.

ISBN-10: 1-887137-68-8
ISBN-13: 978-1-887137-68-3

Printed in the United States of America.
10 9 8 7 6 5 4 3 2 1
"How Much Can I Make?" is available at special discounts for bulk purchase. Special editions or book excerpts can also be created to specifications. For details, contact Source Book Publications, 1814 Franklin St., Suite 603, Oakland, CA 94612. Phone: (800) 841-0873 or (510) 839-5471; Fax: (510) 839-2104.

Preface

As a prospective franchisee, the single most important task ahead of you is to get an accurate and reliable sense of a business's potential sales, expenses and profits. Without this analysis, you will have only a faint idea of how much you are going to earn as a result of your investment and considerable efforts.

Keep in mind that, in acquiring a franchise, or any business for that matter, you are making an investment that has long-term responsibilities and consequences that are potentially far reaching. If you find out 12 months after starting your business that you didn't properly project the negative cash flows that would occur during the start-up phase, or didn't appreciate the magnitude of advertising/promotion costs or assumed that revenues would be 30% higher than they actually are, then shame on you. At that point, you can't re-negotiate your franchise contract. If you can't make the business work financially, the fact that you really enjoy being your own boss, really like the franchisor's management team and its vision and really believe in the product/service is of secondary importance. If, six months after starting the business, you find yourself financially strapped, your options are severely limited. You can continue to limp along operating the business, working even harder, and most likely hating what you are doing. You can borrow more money in the hopes of generating increased revenues. Or you can sell the business, most likely for substantially less than you invested.

Do yourself a favor. Take whatever time is necessary to do your homework. You will no doubt be under an inordinate amount of pressure to start your new business as soon as possible. Resist the temptation to do so until you are completely conversant with all facets of the particular business in which you are investing and the dynamics of the industry itself. Spend the extra time and money to ensure that no stones are left unturned. In addition to the required due diligence, make sure you fully understand what cash flow statements are about, the distinction between fixed and variable costs and what industry operating standards are. Know where to go to get industry data. Call as many existing (and former) franchisees as are required to corroborate your projections. They will be able to tell you if your assumptions are either too optimistic or too pessimistic. Keep in mind that the existing franchisee base represents your best source of information on the business. You will only get one chance to perform your due diligence.

Given these alarmist warnings, it is incumbent on you to thoroughly research all aspects of the industry you are considering prior to making an irreversible investment. The risks are high. Your failure could well result in the loss of your investment, as well as any other property you may have pledged, your marriage (to the extent that your spouse was not equally committed to franchising and the inherent risks involved) and, possibly most important, your self-esteem. Contrary to much of the hype surrounding the industry, there are no guarantees. To think that you can simply pay a franchise fee and automatically step into a guaranteed money machine is naive at best and fatal at worst. There is absolutely no substitute for extensive due diligence. The burden is on you to do your homework and ensure that the choice is fully researched. Only you can maximize the chances of success and minimize the chances of failure or unfulfilled expectations.

"How Much Can I Make?" contains 93 financial performance representations/earnings claims statements in their entirety. The roster of franchisors runs from large, well-established operations like Burger King and McDonald's to newer, smaller franchises with only a handful of operating units. Keep in mind that the financial data presented below is based on actual, verifiable operating results that the franchisors must be able to document. Understanding these financial statements is only one step in a long and tedious process. They nevertheless provide an invaluable source of critical background information that you will not find in any other source.

One of the most important exercises you can do is to rigorously determine what the net earnings from your investment will be. Realize that you have an "opportunity cost" associated with your investment in the business. If you invest $100,000 of equity, that money could probably earn a minimum of 6% if deployed elsewhere and with considerably less risk. Accordingly, the first $6,000 earned is not really a profit, but a return on your investment. Does the remaining "adjusted net cash flow" adequately reward you for the stress and strain of running your own business: putting in long, hard hours at work, wearing 10 hats at a time, living with financial uncertainty and giving up much of your discretionary time? On the other side of the ledger are the advantages of owning your own business: the pride and independence of running your own show, the chance to start something from scratch and sell it 5–10 years later at a multiple of your original investment, and the opportunity to take full advantage of your management, sales and people skills. Clearly there is a balance, but make sure that you have a strong sense of how realistic your expectations are and if they have a solid chance of being achieved.

Although the level of detail and applicability to your own investment differs substantially among the various financial performance representations/earnings claims statements, you can, nevertheless, learn a great deal by reviewing the data presented. Just because a financial performance representation/earnings claims statement is not in the same industry you are considering, don't assume that you shouldn't read it. Reviewing a wide range of actual operating results provides an invaluable chance to become acquainted with basic accounting practices— how to get from gross sales to net income, how to differentiate between fixed expenses (such as rent, equipment rental and utilities) and variable expenses (direct labor, shipping and percentage rent) and how to determine a break-even point. Consider how various aspects of a totally different type of business might apply to your business. This is a great chance to avoid saying six months from now, "Why wasn't I aware of that expense?" Devoting even a minimal amount of time and energy will provide invaluable insights.

Presuming that you are committed to maximizing your chances for success, you have a great deal of work ahead of you. Because it is tedious, many people will opt for the easy way out and do only a modest amount of homework. Many of these will ultimately regret their slothfulness and, accordingly, their investment decision. Others will be happy with the decision to enter franchising, but will wish they had joined another franchise system. Still others will go out of business. I strongly recommend that you commit the next several months to learning everything you can about the franchising industry in general, the specific industry you are considering in particular, all of the franchise opportunities within that industry and, most importantly, the individual franchise you ultimately select.

You have a great deal at risk, and you don't get a second chance. Your cheapest form of insurance is the time you put in investigating a business before you invest. Take full advantage of the tools available to you. Do your homework.

Good luck and Godspeed.

4

Table of Contents

30-Minute Overview | 1

There are three stages to the franchise selection process: the investigation, the evaluation and the negotiation stages. This book is intended to assist the reader in the first two stages by providing a framework for developing reasonable financial guidelines upon which to make a well-researched and properly-documented investment decision.

Understand at the outset that the entire franchise selection process should take many months and can involve a great deal of frustration. I suggest that you set up a realistic timeline for signing a franchise agreement and that you stick to that schedule. There will be a lot of pressure on you to prematurely complete the selection and negotiation phases. Resist the temptation. The penalties are too severe for a seat-of-the-pants attitude. A decision of this magnitude clearly deserves careful consideration.

Before starting the selection process, briefly review the areas covered below.

Franchise Industry Structure

The franchising industry is made up of two distinct types of franchises. The first, and by far the larger, includes product and trade name franchising. Included in this group are automotive and truck dealers, soft drink bottlers and gasoline service stations. For the most part, these are essentially distributorships.

The second group encompasses business format franchisors. This book only includes information on this latter category.

Layman's Definition of Franchising

Business format franchising is a method of market expansion by which one business entity expands the distribution of its products and/or services through independent, third-party operators. Franchising occurs when the operator of a concept or system (the franchisor) grants an independent businessperson (the franchisee) the right to duplicate its entire business format at a particular location and for a specified period, under terms and conditions set forth in the contract (franchise agreement). The franchisee has full access to all of the trademarks, logos, marketing techniques, controls, and systems that have made the franchisor successful. In effect, the franchisee acts as a surrogate for a company-owned store in the distribution of the franchisor's goods and/or services. It is important to keep in mind that the franchisor and the franchisee are separate legal entities.

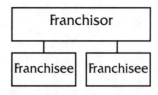

Classic Business Format Model

6

In return for a front-end franchise fee — which usually ranges from $15,000–35,000 — the franchisor is obligated to "set up" the franchisee in business. This generally includes assistance in selecting a location, negotiating a lease, obtaining financing, building and equipping a site and providing the necessary training, operating manuals and start-up assistance. Once the training is completed and the store is open, the new franchisee should have a carbon copy of other units in the system and enjoy the same benefits they do, whether they are company-owned or not.

Business format franchising is unique because it is a long-term relationship characterized by an on-going, mutually beneficial partnership. On-going services include research and development, marketing strategies, advertising campaigns, group buying, periodic field visits, training updates, and whatever else is required to make the franchisee competitive and profitable. In effect, the franchisor acts as the franchisee's "back office" support organization. To reimburse the franchisor for this support, the franchisee pays the franchisor an on-going royalty fee, generally 4–8% of gross sales. In many cases, franchisees also contribute an advertising fee to reimburse the franchisor for expenses incurred in maintaining a national or regional advertising campaign.

To work to maximum advantage, both the franchisor and the franchisees should share common objectives and goals. Both parties must accept the premise that their fortunes are mutually intertwined and that they are each better off working in a co-operative effort rather than toward self-serving goals. Unlike the parent/child relationship that has dominated franchising over the past 30 years, franchising is now becoming a true relationship of partners.

The Players

Franchisors

Source Book Publications routinely tracks approximately 3,000+ U.S. and Canadian franchisors. We believe this represents the number of legitimate, active franchisors in North America at any point in time. Profiles of these franchisors can be found in *Bond's Franchise Guide*, published annually by Source Book Publications. Copies of this 530+ page directory, which is considered the definitive

directory in the field, are available for $34.95 plus $8.50 for shipping and handling ($45.50 + $12.00 in Canada). Call (800) 841-0873 or (510) 839-5471 or fax (510) 839-2104 to place a credit card order, or send a check to Source Book Publications, 1814 Franklin St., Suite 603, Oakland, CA 94612. There is an order form at the end of Chapter 4.

While you may already have your sights on a particular franchise opportunity, it would be short-sighted not to find out as much as you can about both the direct and indirect competition. You might discover that other franchises have similar products or services, but offer superior training and support, a reduced royalty fee or vastly superior financing options. I strongly encourage you to read either *Bond's Franchise Guide* or one of the other franchise directories to fully explore the options open to you.

The Regulatory Agencies

The offer and sale of franchises are regulated at both the federal and state levels. Federal requirements cover all 50 states. In addition, certain states have adopted their own requirements.

In 1979, after many years of debate, the Federal Trade Commission (FTC) implemented Rule 436. This Rule requires that franchisors provide prospective franchisees with a disclosure statement (called an offering circular) containing specific information about a company's franchise offering. The Rule has two objectives: to ensure that potential franchisees have sufficient background information to make an educated investment decision and to provide them with adequate time to do so.

The Franchise Rule was substantially updated (and improved) on July 1, 2008 as the FTC tried to make the disclosure document more consistent with various state regulations. Among other things, the Uniform Franchise Offering Circular (UFOC) became the Franchise Disclosure Document (FDD) and Item 19 of the new FDD morphed from an Earnings Claims Statement to a Financial Performance Representation. Overall the revisions were positive and resulted in considerably more and better information being available to the prospective franchisee. Unfortunately, the revisions did not <u>require</u> all franchisors to provide a Financial Performance Representation from which potential franchisees could better determine the overall profitability of their potential investments.

Certain "registration states" require additional safeguards to protect potential franchisees. Their requirements are generally more stringent than the FTC's requirements. These states include California, Florida, Hawaii, Illinois, Indiana, Maryland, Michigan, Minnesota, New York, North Dakota, Oregon, Rhode Island, South Dakota, Virginia, Washington and Wisconsin. Separate registration is also required in the province of Alberta.

The regulations require that the franchisor provide a prospective franchisee with the required information at their first face-to-face meeting or at least 14 days prior to the signing of the franchise agreement, whichever is earlier. Required information includes:

1. The franchisor and any predecessors.
2. Identity and business experience of persons affiliated with the franchisor.
3. Litigation.
4. Bankruptcy.
5. Franchisee's initial fee or other initial payments.
6. Other fees.
7. Franchisee's initial investment.
8. Obligations of franchisee to purchase or lease from designated sources.
9. Obligations of franchisee to purchase or lease in accordance with specifications or from approved suppliers.
10. Financing arrangements.
11. Obligations of the franchisor; other supervision, assistance or services.
12. Exclusive area or territory.
13. Trademarks, service marks, trade names, logotypes and commercial symbols.
14. Patents and copyrights.
15. Obligations of the participant in the actual operation of the franchise business.
16. Restrictions on goods and services offered by franchisee.
17. Renewal, termination, repurchase, modification and assignment of the franchise agreement and related information.
18. Arrangements with public figures.
19. Actual, average, projected or forecasted franchise sales, profits or earnings.
20. Information regarding franchises of the franchisor.
21. Financial statements.
22. Contracts.
23. Acknowledgment of receipt by respective franchisee.

If you live in a registration state, make sure that the franchisor you are evaluating is, in fact, registered to sell franchises there. If not, and the franchisor has no near-term plans to register in your state, you should consider other options.

Keep in mind that neither the FTC nor any of the states has reviewed the disclosure document to determine whether the information submitted is true and accurate or not. They merely require that the franchisor make representations based upon a prescribed format. If the information provided is false, franchisors are subject to civil penalties. You should also be aware of the reality that neither the FTC nor the individual states have the staff or budget necessary to pursue a lengthy battle over possible misrepresentations. If you run into problems, your only real option is to retain an attorney and battle a franchisor who may have an in-house legal staff and a bottomless war chest. While you might win the battle, you would most likely lose the war.

It is up to you to read and thoroughly understand all elements of the disclosure document and to take full advantage of the documentation that is available to you. Know exactly what you can expect from the franchisor and what your own obligations are. Under what circumstances can the relationship be unilaterally terminated by the franchisor? What is your protected territory? What are the terms of a renewal? Can you expand within your territory? While there is no question that the FDD is tedious reading, it, nevertheless, provides invaluable information. The penalties for not doing your homework are severe. You will have no one to blame but yourself. Hedge your bet by having a professional also review the FDD.

The Trade Associations

The **International Franchise Association** (IFA) was established in 1960 as a non-profit trade association to promote franchising as a responsible method of doing business. The IFA currently represents over 1,200 franchisors in the U.S. and around the world. It is recognized as the leading spokesperson for the industry. For most of its 40+ years, the IFA has represented the interests of franchisors only. In recent years, however, it has initiated an aggressive campaign to recruit franchisees into its membership and to represent their interests as well. The IFA's offices are located at 1501 K St., Suite 350, Washington, DC 20005. (202) 628-8000; FAX (202) 628-0812; www.franchise.org.

The **Canadian Franchise Association** (CFA), which has some 250+ members, is the Canadian equivalent of the IFA. Information on the CFA can be obtained by writing the group at 5399 Eglinton Ave. West, # 116, Toronto, ON M9C 5K6, Canada. (800) 665-4232 or (416) 695-2896; FAX (416) 695-1950; www.CFA.ca.

What Makes a Winning Franchise

Virtually every writer on the subject of franchising has his or her own idea of what determines a winning franchise. I believe there are five primary factors.

1. A product or service with clear advantages over the competition. These advantages may include brand recognition, a unique, proprietary product or service, or 30 years of proven experience.

2. A standardized franchise system that has been time-tested. A company that has operated numerous units, both company-owned and franchised, has usually worked out most of the bugs in the system. By the time a system has 30 or more operating units, it should be thoroughly tested.

3. Exceptional franchisor support. This includes not only the initial training program, but the on-going support (Research & Development, refresher training, [800] help-lines, field representatives who provide on-site training, annual meetings, advertising and promotion, central purchasing, etc.).

4. The financial wherewithal and management experience to carry out any announced growth plans without short-changing its franchisees. Sufficient depth of management is often lacking in younger, high-growth franchises.

5. A strong mutuality of interest between franchisor and franchisees. Unless both parties realize that their relationship is one of long-term partners, the system will probably never achieve its full potential. A few telephone calls to existing and former franchisees can easily determine whether the necessary rapport between franchisor and franchisees exists.

The Negotiation Process

Once you have narrowed your options down to your two or three top choices, you now have to negotiate the best deal you can with the franchisor. In most cases, the franchisor will tell you that the franchise agreement cannot be changed. Think twice before you accept the statement that the contract is non-negotiable. Notwithstanding the legal requirement that all of a franchisor's agreements be substantially the same at any point in time, there are usually a number of variables that are flexible. If the franchisor truly wants you as a franchisee, it may be willing to make concessions not available to the next applicant.

Will the franchisor take a short-term note for all or part of the franchise fee? Can you expand from your initial unit after you have proven yourself? If so, can the franchise fee on a second unit be eliminated or reduced? Can you get a right of first refusal on adjacent territories? Can the term of the agreement be extended from 10 to 15 years? Can you include a franchise cancellation right if the training and/or initial support don't meet your expectations or the franchisor's promises? The list goes on ad infinitum.

To successfully negotiate, you must have a thorough knowledge of the industry, the franchise agreement you are negotiating (and agreements of competitive franchise opportunities) and access to experienced professional advice. This can be a lawyer, an accountant or a franchise consultant. Above all else, he or she should have proven experience in negotiating franchise agreements. Franchising is a unique method of doing business. Don't pay someone $100+ per hour to learn the industry. Make him or her demonstrate that he or she has been through the process several times before. Negotiating a long-term agreement of this type is extremely tricky and fraught with pitfalls. The risks are extremely high. Don't think that you can handle the negotiations yourself, or that you can't afford outside counsel. In point of fact, you can't afford not to employ an experienced professional advisor.

The 4 R's of Franchising

At a young age we're taught that the three R's of reading, 'riting, and 'rithmetic are critical to our scholastic success. Success in franchising depends on four R's — realism, research, reserves and resolve.

Realism

At the outset of your investigation, be realistic about your strengths, weaknesses, goals and capabilities. I strongly recommend you take the time necessary to do a personal audit — possibly with the help of outside professionals — before investing your life's savings in a franchise.

Franchising is not a money machine. It involves hard work, dedication, set-backs and long hours. Be realistic about the nature of the business you are buying. What traits will ultimately determine your success? Do you have them? If it is a service-oriented business, will you be able to keep smiling when you know the client is a fool? If it is a fast-food business, will you be able to properly manage a minimum-wage staff? How well will you handle the uncertainties that will invariably arise? Can you make day-to-day decisions based on imperfect information? Can you count on the support of your partner after you have gone through all of your working capital reserves and the future looks increasingly cloudy?

Be equally realistic about your franchise selection process. Have you thoroughly evaluated all of the alternatives? Have you talked with everyone you can, leaving no stone unturned? Have you carefully and realistically assessed the advantages and disadvantages of the system offered, the unique demographics of your territory, the near-term market trends and the financial projections? The selection process is tiring. It is easy to convince yourself that the franchise opportunity in your hand is really the best one for you before you've done all your homework. The penalties for such laziness, however, are extreme.

Research

There is no substitute for exhaustive research!

Bond's Franchise Guide contains over 900 franchise listings, broken into 29 distinct business categories. This represents a substantial number of options from which to choose. Other directories also cover the industry to varying degrees of thoroughness and accuracy. Spend the time required to come up with an optimal selection. At a minimum, you will probably be in the business for five years. More likely, you will be in it for 10 years or more. Given the long-term commitment, allow yourself the necessary time to ensure you won't regret your decision. Research is a tedious, boring process, but doing it carefully and thoroughly can greatly reduce your risk and exposure. The benefits are immeasurable.

First, determine which industry groups hold your interest. Don't arbitrarily limit yourself to a particular industry in which you have first-hand experience. Next, request information from all of the companies that participate in those industries. The incremental cost of mailing (or calling) an additional 15 or 20 companies for information is insignificant in the big picture. Based on personal experience, you may feel you already know the best franchise. Step back. Assume there is a competing franchise out there with a comparable product or service, comparable management, etc., but which charges a royalty fee of sales that is 2% lower than your intuitive choice. Over a 10-year period, that could add up to a great deal of money. It certainly justifies your requesting initial information.

A thorough analysis of the literature you receive should allow you to reduce the list of prime candidates to six or eight companies. Aggressively evaluate each firm. Talking with current and former franchisees is the single best source of information you can get. Where possible, visit franchise sites. My experience is that franchisees tend to be candid in their level of satisfaction with the franchisor. However, since they don't know you, they may be less candid about their sales, expenses and income. *"How Much Can I Make?"* should be of some assistance in filling this void. Go to the library and get studies that forecast industry growth, market saturation, industry problems, technical break-throughs, etc. Don't find out a year after becoming a franchisee of a coffee company that readily available reports suggested that the coffee market was over-saturated or that coffee was linked to some obscure form of colon cancer in rats.

Reserves

Like any new business, franchising is replete with uncertainty, uneven cash flows and unforeseen problems. It is an imperfect world that might not bear any relation to the clean pro formas you prepared to justify getting into the business. Any one of these unforeseen contingencies could cause a severe drain on your cash reserves. At the same time, you will have fixed and/or contractual payments that must be met on a current basis regardless of sales: rent, employee salaries, insurance, etc.

Adequate back-up reserves may be in the form of savings, commitments from relatives, bank loans, etc. Just make certain that the funds are available when, and if, you need them. To be absolutely safe, I suggest that you double the level of reserves recommended by the franchisor.

Keep in mind that the most common cause of business failure is inadequate working capital. Plan properly so you don't become a statistic.

Resolve

Let's assume for the time being that you have demonstrated exceptional levels of realism, thoroughly researched your options and lined up ample capital reserves. You have picked an optimal franchise that takes full advantage of your strengths. You are in business and bringing in enough money to achieve a positive cash flow. The future looks bright. Now the fourth R — resolve — comes into play. Remember why you chose franchising in the first place: to take full advantage of a system that had been time-tested in the marketplace. Remember also what makes franchising work so well: that the franchisor and franchisees maximize their respective success by working within the system for the common good. Invariably, two obstacles arise.

The first is the physical pain associated with writing that monthly royalty check. Annual sales of $250,000 and a 6% royalty fee result in a monthly royalty check of $1,250 that must be sent to the franchisor. Every month. As a franchisee, you may look for any justification to reduce this sizable monthly outflow. Resist the temptation. Accept the fact that royalty fees are simply another cost of doing business. They are also a legal obligation that you willingly agreed to pay when you signed the franchise agreement. In effect, they are the dues you agreed to pay to belong to the club.

Although there may be an incentive, don't look for loopholes in the contract that might allow you to sue the franchisor or get out of the relationship. Don't report lower sales than actual in an effort to reduce royalties. If you have received the support that you were promised, continue to play by the rules. Honor your commitment. Let the franchisor enjoy the rewards it has earned from your success.

The second obstacle is the desire to change the system. You need to honor your commitment to be a "franchisee" and to live within the franchise system. What makes franchising successful as far as your customers are concerned is uniformity and consistency of appearance, product/service quality and corporate image. The most damaging thing an individual franchisee can do is suddenly and unilaterally introduce changes into a proven system. While these modifications may work in one market, they only serve to diminish the value of the system as a whole. Imagine what would happen to the national perception of your franchise if every franchisee had the latitude to make unilateral changes in his or her operations. Accordingly, any ideas you have on improving the system should be submitted directly to the franchisor for its evaluation. Accept the franchisor's decision on whether or not to pursue an idea.

If you suspect that you have a penchant for being an entrepreneur, for unrestrained experimenting and tinkering, you are probably not cut out to be a good franchisee. Seriously consider this question before you get into a relationship, instead of waiting until you are locked into an untenable situation.

Summary

I hope that I have been clear in suggesting that the selection of an optimal franchise is both time and energy-consuming. Done properly, the process may take six to nine months and involve the expenditure of several thousand dollars. The difference between a hasty, gut-feel investigation and an exhaustive, well-thought-out investigation may mean the difference between finding a poorly-conceived, or even fraudulent, franchise and an exceptional one.

There is a strong correlation between the efforts put into the investigative process and the ultimate degree of success you enjoy as a franchisee. The process is to investigate, evaluate and negotiate. Don't try to bypass any one of these elements.

Financial Performance Representations/ Earnings Claims Statements | 2

The harsh reality is that you cannot tell—much less guarantee—how much you might make from a specific investment. Even the most successful business model, whether a franchise or not, simply cannot be replicated by someone who isn't prepared to run the business the way it should be run. Area demographics, such as population, disposable per capita income and education, are critical. For a retail business, a heavily trafficked location is critical. Adequate capital is critical. Management and decision-making skills are critical. Hard work is critical. The list goes on. It is up to you to ensure that all of these factors are optimized. If any one of these critical factors is missing or marginal, chances are the business will not meet your expectations.

This compendium of financial performance representations/earnings claims statements is meant to provide prospective franchisees with a better sense of what they might earn from their efforts. Without a sure understanding of potential sales, expenses and profits, an investor is inviting disappointment at best and failure at worst. I strongly encourage you to take whatever time is required to review carefully the following financial performance representations/earnings claims statements. Some are easy reading, others tedious and detail-oriented. But the better versed you are on the actual, historical operating results of the 93 companies included, however, the better positioned you will be to make an optimal franchise selection. You will be able to ask franchisors intelligent, penetrating questions when evaluating them. You will be better prepared to compare franchises within similar industries. You will have more credibility seeking the insights of existing franchisees. If you take the time to develop your own financial projections, you will not have to rely as heavily on expensive outside accountants and financial advisers. Most importantly, you will have a real understanding of the business before you commit your financial resources and your life. If your objective is to maximize your bottom line, taking full advantage of the financial performance representations/ earnings claims statements in this book is an important start.

The Average Franchisee

The only in-depth study of actual franchisee earnings and satisfaction was conducted several years ago by Franchise Times Magazine. Based on answers from more than 1,000 franchisees, the Second Annual Franchisee Survey found that the average franchisee owned 3.5 units, had been in franchising for 8.9 years and enjoyed net pre-tax earnings of $171,000, or roughly $50,000 per unit. Total annual household income before taxes averaged $118,000 for all franchisees. The median income, however, was $81,000. The initial start-up cost was $151,000 and the average loan size was $196,000, with a median of $88,000. Three-quarters of those surveyed answered that they were either "very" or "somewhat" satisfied with franchising. Just over 15% were "not too" satisfied, while only 9.8% were "not at all" satisfied. If you think that franchising is an automatic pot of gold, you should temper your enthusiasm with the facts of life brought out in the survey.

Whether these averages satisfy or alarm you, most prospective franchisees will probably be surprised to learn that even after 8+ years in the business, the average franchisee has pre-tax earnings of less than $50,000 per unit. Keep in mind, however, that the above statistics are only that—statistics. How well your earnings compare with those of the average franchisee is what counts. Yet if you hope to make $100,000 per year with your initial unit, you will have to be markedly more successful than the average franchisee. Picking up the right franchise in the right market is the first step.

The Market Void

The single most important factor in buying any business is calculating a realistic and verifiable projection of sales, expenses and profits. Specifically, how much can you expect to earn after working 65 hours a week for 52 weeks a year? A prospective franchisee clearly does not have the experience to sit down and determine what his or her sales and profits will be over the next five years, especially if he or she has no applied experience in that particular business. The only source in a position to supply accurate information about a franchise opportunity is the franchisor itself.

It is unfortunate that all franchisors are not required to supply prospective franchisees with operating results. At a minimum, franchisors have information regarding net sales by all of their franchised units and certainly they have complete accounting information from any company-owned units. Similarly, if they have any sophistication, they must have developed computer models for outlets in various geographic and retail environments.

The sad reality, however, is that franchisors are not required to share this information, and roughly 80% do not. The likelihood that any such requirement will be implemented within the next 2 or so years is slim, leaving the franchisee to his or her own devices.

"How Much Can I Make?" has located and published 93 of these documents for your review. Nowhere else can a potential franchisee find such a wealth of financial information on the industry.

Any serious prospective investor would be short-sighted not to fully exploit this extraordinary resource.

General Disclosure Background

In 1979, the Federal Trade Commission adopted the "FTC Rule," which regulates the franchising industry. Titled "Disclosure Requirements and Prohibitions Concerning Franchising and Business Opportunities Ventures," the rule requires all franchisors to prepare and distribute a disclosure document or offering circular according to a format prescribed by the FTC. The document must be delivered to a prospective franchisee at either the first personal meeting or at least 14 days prior to the signing of any contract or the payment of any consideration, whichever is earlier. In addition, 15 states have adopted their own disclosure laws that are generally more demanding than the FTC's requirements. Chapter 1 provides more information about the requirements of both the FTC and the 15 "registration" states.

Financial Performance Representations/ Earnings Claims Statements Defined

Financial performance representations/earnings claims statements are covered under Item 19 of both the FTC and the state Franchise Disclosure Document (FDD) requirements. As defined by the FTC Rule, a financial performance representation is "any oral, written, or visual representation to a prospective franchisee, including a representation disseminated in the general media and Internet, that states or suggests a specific level or range of potential or actual sales, income, gross profits, or net profits. A chart, table, or mathematical calculation that demonstrates possible results based upon a combination of variables is a financial performance representation."

In their broadest sense, financial performance representations/earnings claims are defined as estimates or historical figures detailing the level of sales, expenses and/or income a prospective franchisee might realize as the owner of a particular franchise.

However, it is important to remember that neither the FTC nor the state regulatory agencies check financial performance representations/earnings claims statements for accuracy or completeness. The document is voluntary and unverified, and the information's format and level of detail is left completely to each company's discretion.

The only requirement for any Item 19 is that the franchisor has a "reasonable basis" for the financial performance representation/earnings claim at the time the statement is prepared. The franchisor is merely required to deliver the document to the franchisee before the franchise can be sold. Although franchisors suggest that you should let them know if something is amiss, they often do not have the manpower or budget to pursue any but the most flagrant and obvious violations. For the most part, you are on your own. In the next chapter, we will show you how to put financial performance representations/earnings claims statements and other related resources to good use.

Setting Realistic Expectations

You can learn a great deal by reviewing financial performance representations/earnings claims statements. Identifying the sales and costs that would be relevant to your own business, as well as to your skills and your experience, is invaluable. Do not be swayed by the profit margin alone, as you should also consider the cost of sales, payrolls, operating expenses, and rent and occupancy. Furthermore, you should also note that the historical data used as the basis for the claims do not apply to every geographic region, individual location or franchisee, whose experience and business acumen may vary.

There is no universal way to measure and report on those variables. If you are evaluating how variations in revenue and expenses could affect your bottom line, then you are putting financial performance representations/earnings claims statements to good use. At best, these documents help you set realistic expectations. But, in reality, the actual earnings of any franchise will vary from individual to individual. Does the actual net cash flow adequately reward you for the stress and strain of running your own business, putting in long hours, wearing 10 hats at a time, living with financial uncertainty and giving up much of your discretionary time?

On the other side of the ledger are the advantages of business ownership: the pride and independence of running the show, the chance to start something from scratch and sell it 5–10 years later for a multiple of your original investment and the opportunity to take full advantage of your management, sales and people skills. Clearly there is a balance, but make sure that you have a strong sense of how realistic your expectations are and if they have a solid chance of being achieved.

Presuming that you are committed to maximizing your chances for success, you have a great deal of work ahead of you. It is important to review a wide range of financial performance representations/earnings claims statements, including ones outside the industry you are considering. A sampling of financial performance representations/earnings claims statements will acquaint you with basic accounting practices—how to calculate net income from gross sales, how to differentiate between fixed expenses (rent, equipment rental and utilities) and variable expenses (direct labor, shipping and percentage rent) and how to determine a break-even point. Devoting even a minimal amount of time and energy to this research will provide invaluable insights and serve you well when making an investment decision.

How Can I Research A Franchise?

In addition to the financial performance representations/earnings claims statements in this book, there are a number of sources for information on franchisors and franchise offerings.

1. Franchise Disclosure Documents (FDDs)
Although FDDs are public documents, many companies consider the information contained within them proprietary, thus, they do not make them readily accessible to the public. If you contact franchisors directly to request copies of FDDs, chances are they will not respond to your request or they will wait weeks before granting it. Alternatively, you may purchase FDDs from the state (if the company has registered in that state) or submit a request through a service such as Franchise.com's Franchise E-Disclosure service, which notifies a company of your desire to receive an FDD. If the company decides to share its disclosure document with you, you will receive an electronic copy.

The easiest and quickest way to obtain FDDs and historical UFOCs, however, is to purchase them directly from companies that sell them. Among the various websites that sell FDDs directly online, one of the most popular is UFOCs.com. Offering over 20,000 FDDs and UFOCs for roughly 3,000 North American franchisors, UFOCs.com is the most comprehensive and up-to-date database of current FDD filings, as well as historical UFOCs dating back to 1997. In addition, UFOCs.com makes every effort to provide all available financial performance representations/earnings claim statements (Item 19s), in their entirety, to the public; as a result, over 500 financial performance representations/earnings claims are available on UFOCs.com, either as pre-selected packages or as individual statements.

All FDDs, historical UFOCs, earnings claims and earnings claim packages are available in PDF format and are delivered via email, CD-ROM or hardcopy. Current year FDD orders are typically processed in less than 24 hours. Prior year or unique orders may take 1-7 days to complete.

Price: Entire FDD/UFOC - $220 per statement; Partial FDD/UFOC - $150 per statement; Franchise Agreement - $100 per statement; Item 19 - $40 per statement; Item 20 - $100 per statement; Item 21 - $100 per statement; Food-Service Industry Package (89 earnings claims) - $250; Lodging Industry Package (29 earnings claims) - $90; Retail Industry Package (33 earnings claims) - $100; Service-Based Industry Package (143 earnings claims) - $350. Website: www.UFOCs.com.

2. Current and Former Franchisees

Without doubt, the most meaningful information that you can obtain on a particular franchise comes from existing franchisees, who tend to be very candid about their level of satisfaction with the franchisor, but less candid about their sales, expenses and income. Depending on how well you have done your homework and your ability to ask meaningful questions that show a solid understanding of the basic business and its underlying economics, other franchisees should be willing to respond to your questions about: the major cost elements of the cash flow statement, the biggest surprises they encountered when they started their business, whether to buy supplies from the franchisor or from a third-party supplier, potential lenders, negotiable points in the franchise agreement and more. In reviewing finances, pay particular attention to the major expense items and see if there are any expense

categories that you may have left out. Spend some time at a franchised unit to get a feel for the day-to-day operations of the business.

The FDD should include a list of current franchisees, as well as franchisees who left the system within the last year. Past UFOCs list franchisees that may no longer be in the system. Don't call only the franchisees specifically recommended by the franchisor. Contact as many as you can until you feel comfortable that you are hearing a consensus. You should also talk with as many former franchisees as you can. It is up to you to separate the truth from the fiction as to why they left the system. Too many disenchanted former franchisees should be a strong warning to be exceedingly cautious in your investigation and analysis.

3. State Franchise Regulators

If you are in a state with franchise registration requirements (see the section on Regulatory Agencies in Chapter 1), the state franchise regulators can tell you whether a franchisor is in good standing. They may also be able to tell you whether there are any pending complaints against a franchisor. The North American Securities Administrators Association, Inc. website (www.nasaa.org) contains a directory of each state's franchise regulators.

You can contact state franchise regulators to request a copy of the financial performance representation/earnings claims statement from any franchisor registered to do business in the state. Unfortunately, most of these state agencies cannot accommodate your request unless you are physically at their offices. The best bet is to call to learn your options. Some states are more helpful than others in providing access to their library of offering circulars.

4. SEC

If a franchise is a publicly traded company, it is required to file certain information with the U.S. Securities and Exchange Commission. These filings are available online at www.edgar.gov.

5. *Bond's Franchise Guide*

The 2008 (19th) Edition of *Bond's Franchise Guide* provides detailed profiles of over 1,000 North American franchisors resulting from an exhaustive 45-point questionnaire. The book also provides detailed profiles on leading franchise attorneys, consultants and service providers. The data represents the most up-to-date, comprehensive and reliable information about the franchising industry.

The franchisor profiles are divided into 29 distinct industry categories and include the following:

• Background — number of operating units, geographic distribution and detailed description of the business.
• Capital requirements — initial cash investment and total investment, on-going royalty and advertising fees, staffing levels, space needs, etc.
• Initial training and start-up assistance provided, as well as on-going services.
• Franchisee evaluation criteria.
• Specific areas of geographic expansion: U.S., Canada and International.
• And much more…

6. Business and Industry Publications

The next best source of information is provided by various publications that compile general operating statistics on industries broken down by Standard Industrial Classification (SIC) codes. Three of the best-known annual industry surveys are 1) the RMA Annual Statement Studies, published by Robert Morris Associates of Philadelphia, PA, 2) the Almanac of Business and Industrial Financial Ratios, edited by Leo Troy and published by Prentice Hall and 3) the Industry Norms and Key Business Rations, published by Dun & Bradstreet Information Services. Although none of these publications provide detailed expense data, each is extremely helpful in determining industry averages/norms and key financial ratios. Based on actual tax returns for the entire spectrum of business categories (manufacturing, wholesaling, agriculture, service and retailing), the composite financial data reflect actual operating results for major SIC code industries.

7. Franchise Attorneys

Franchising is a highly specialized field, and you should hire legal experts with experience representing franchisees or franchisors. FranchisingAttorney.com has a searchable directory that provides 25 fields of information about each attorney listed. Visit www.findlegalhelp.org, a site sponsored by the American Bar Association, to learn about referral services and issues you should address when consulting with a lawyer. Another source for examining an attorney's cre-

dentials is www.martindale.com. The franchise associations below may also provide referrals to experienced franchise attorneys.

8. Franchise Consultants and Service Providers

If you are using a franchise consultant or service provider, they can likely assist you with your franchisor research. FranchisingSuppliers.com includes listings of hundreds of firms that provide goods and services to the franchising community. These goods and services are designed to help franchisors and franchisees alike and include advertising, consulting, translation and Internet services.

9. Your Local Library

Industry trade associations publish composite financial statistics, usually on an annual basis. Consult the Directory of Trade Associations at your local business library for the address of the relevant trade association(s). Be prepared to pay reasonable fees to obtain as much industry-specific information as possible. Keep in mind that these statistics are made up solely of like-minded businesses that have similar expenses and competitive pressures.

Most industries are covered by one or more research houses that sell studies pertaining to the future of that industry. These cover new technology, industry trends, competitive trends, financial projections for various sales levels and more. Even if these studies are somewhat outdated, it may be a worthwhile to gather as much data as possible about an industry rather than risk your life savings based on incomplete information.

Your Own Cash Flow Projections

What Items Are in an FDD?

Every FDD contains the following 23 items:

Item 1 - The Franchisor, and any Parents, Predecessors and Affiliates
Item 2 - Business Experience
Item 3 - Litigation
Item 4 - Bankruptcy
Item 5 - Initial Fees
Item 6 - Other Fees
Item 7 - Estimated Initial Investment
Item 8 - Restrictions On Sources Of Products And Services

Item 9 - Franchisee's Obligations
Item 10 - Financing
Item 11 - Franchisor's Assistance, Advertising, Computer Systems and Training
Item 12 - Territory
Item 13 - Trademarks
Item 14 - Patents, Copyrights and Proprietary Information
Item 15 - Obligation To Participate In The Actual Operation Of The Franchise Business
Item 16 - Restrictions On What The Franchisee May Sell
Item 17 - Renewal, Termination, Transfer And Dispute Resolution
Item 18 - Public Figures
Item 19 - Financial Performance Representations
Item 20 - Outlets and Franchisee Information
Item 21 - Financial Statements
Item 22 - Contracts
Item 23 - Receipts

Armed with financial performance representations/earnings claims statements, industry operating statistics and the information gathered from conversations with existing and former franchisees, as well as input from trusted colleagues and consultants, you can now prepare your own financial projections. This exercise is the most critical step in the process of evaluating and selecting a franchise. Without a solid understanding of the financial aspects of the business, you may be throwing your time and money away. Investors who don't do their homework because they say they do not understand an income statement or they aren't a "numbers person" may soon regret their lack of motivation.

A number of well-written books about preparing financial projections are available. Most are written for the layman who has little or no formal understanding of the process. (Some are even written by laymen with little or no formal understanding of the process themselves.) Purchase a few of these books and become proficient in the rudiments of accounting and finance. Remember, you are playing with your own money and livelihood. Don't put yourself in a position where you have to pay your accountant $100+ per hour every time you have a question. Learn the distinction

between income statements and cash flow statements. Realize that you have an "opportunity cost" associated with your investment, and that you must receive an annual return on this investment, as well as the return of the investment itself, before a true net profit can be determined. Put a value on the psychic income earned by being your own boss. This is especially important when comparing your near-term hourly income with what you might earn working for someone else. Ask yourself if you would invest in the business if you were an investor rather than an owner/operator. Alternatively, would you loan money to the business if you were a banker?

If you don't know how to develop a pro forma cash flow model on a computer, have someone help you. Perform "what if" calculations to see what would happen under best- and worst-case scenarios. This represents the cheapest insurance you can buy to fully understand the dynamics of your new business. You will probably be sorely handicapped in the operation of your business unless you are "computerized." Learn the basics of operating a computer before you have made your investment. Your discretionary time is likely to be minimal during the start-up phase of your new business.

Although the process of generating realistic cash flow statements may seem daunting without any prior business management experience, it is easier than you think. With a little common sense, you can learn it quickly.

To provide a starting point for your own financial projections, plug some numbers into the following tables. These tables are by no means complete and do not attempt to represent all possible scenarios. Each industry will have its own unique investment requirements and related operating expenses.

Table 1 lists Total Investment Requirements. In the second column, you should place the appropriate expenses listed by the franchisor in Item 9 of the offering circular. In the third column, you should place your own well-researched estimate of what that expense or service will cost in your market. The sum of these various expenses represents the non-recurring expenses you will incur when starting the business. Some of the expenses, such as land and improvements, may not be appropriate if you can lease your space at an acceptable market rate over the term of your investment. Consult your financial advisor about the appropriate figures to include if you lease rather than purchase various expense items.

Table 2 is a Pro Forma Cash Flow Statement. The objective of a pro forma is to project monthly and annual sales over the next five years and deduct the corresponding operating expenses. The result is the pre-tax operating cash flow. From this number, deduct the non-cash items—depreciation and amortization—to determine pre-tax income. Further additions and subtractions determine net cash flow before taxes. It is worthwhile to construct a computer model that includes all of the items that will impact your business.

Hopefully, when the time comes, you can negotiate an agreement with a franchisor that allows you to extend the contract for successive 5–15 year periods, presuming you have performed satisfactorily. Over the next 7–15 years, you may attempt to build your business to its maximum potential. At some point, you may want to retire or try something else. The market value of your business will be a function of how much cash flow the business generates. Based on the current earnings potential, the prospective buyer will most likely use one of two valuation models. The first, and more simplistic, involves multiplying the current cash flow by some multiple (say 3 to 5 times) to arrive at a purchase price. The more sophisticated buyer will develop a 5–10 year cash flow statement, put in his or her own liquidation value and discount the annual cash flows at a rate that properly reflects the inherent risk of achieving those cash flows. As an example, if your business generates a legitimate cash flow of $150,000 after 10 years, you should be able to sell the business for $450,000–750,000. If you have done well selecting and managing the franchise, the real payoff will most likely come when you sell the business.

Recommendations Regarding Mandatory Financial Performance Representations/Earnings Claims Statements

Virtually everyone agrees that the information included in a financial performance representation/earnings claims statement can be exceedingly helpful to a potential franchisee. Unfortunately, there are many reasons why franchisors don't willingly make their actual results available to the public. Many franchisors feel that prospective investors will be turned off if they have access to actual operating results and prefer to let them draw their own conclusions.

Other franchisors are understandably afraid of being sued for "misrepresentation." When publishing financial performance representations/earnings claims statements, franchisors face a considerable risk that it will be interpreted as a "guarantee" of sales or income for new units. Given today's highly litigious society and the propensity of courts to award large settlements to the little guy, it's not surprising that few franchisors provide the information.

Notwithstanding the potential problems, franchisors should be required to provide prospective franchisees with some form of earnings projection. To the extent that they are able to substantiate their claims, franchisors should be protected from frivolous and potentially devastating lawsuits filed by failed franchisees. Everyone should realize that the historical data used as the basis for the claims do not apply to every geographic region, individual location or franchisee. Clearly, there is no universal methodology that covers all the variables. All parties involved—the franchisors, the franchisees, the regulatory agencies and the legal system—should rely on common business sense.

As it now stands, a franchisor is liable if it misrepresents its financial performance representation/earnings claims statement, or any other items in the disclosure document. Normally, one would interpret this to mean that someone goes to jail if it is proven that he or she intentionally misled the prospective investor. Unfortunately, neither the FTC nor any registration state has the budget, manpower or technical expertise to enforce such a punishment. Unless a violation is particularly flagrant, there is little chance that a franchisor will be severely penalized. Accordingly, you should not assume that anyone is going to protect or support you if you decide that you have been misled.

However, if there are mandatory requirements, there must be some corresponding penalties for fraudulent financial performance representations/earnings claims. Specifically, franchisees must have a "right of action" that would give regulatory bodies the budget and staff to aggres-

19

	Franchisor's Item IX	Actual in Your Area
TABLE 1		
FRONT-END INVESTMENT REQUIREMENTS		
	Franchisor's Item IX	Actual in Your Area
Initial Franchise Fee	$	$
Land & Improvements		
Leasehold Improvements		
Architectural/Engineering Fees		
Furniture & Fixtures		
Vehicles Purchased		
Initial Inventory		
Initial Signage		
Initial Advertising Commitment		
Initial Training Fees		
Travel/Lodging/Etc. for Initial Training		
Rent Deposits		
Utility Deposits		
Telephone Deposits		
Initial Insurance		
In-Store Graphics		
Yellow Page Advertising		
Initial Office Supplies		
Prepaid Sales Taxes		
Initial Business Permits/Fees		
Office Equipment:		
Computer Hardware		
Computer Software		
Computer Installation		
Computer Training		
Point-of-Sales Computer		
Answering Machine		
Fax Machine		
Postage Meter		
Telephone System (Including Installation)		
Copier		
Security System		
Initial Loan Fees		
Due Diligence Expenses		
Attorney Fees		
Accounting Fees		
Consultant Fees		
Book Purchases/Courses/Etc.		
Travel Expenses		
Telephone/Mailing Expenses		
Total Non-Recurring Expenses	$	$
Working Capital Requirements		
FRONT-END INVESTMENT REQUIREMENTS	$	$

	Month	Month	Month	Month	Month	Month
TABLE 2						
PRO FORMA CASH FLOW STATEMENT						
	1	2	3	4	- - - - ->	12
Gross Sales	$	$	$	$	$	$
Less Returns and Allowances						
Net Sales						
Less Cost of Goods Sold						
Gross Profit						
Gross Profits As A % Of Sales	%	%	%	%	%	%
Operating Expenses:						
Payroll:						
Direct Labor						
Indirect Labor						
Employee Benefits						
Payroll Taxes						
Owner Salary & Benefits						
Rent & Common Area Maintenance						
Equipment Rental/Lease Payments						
Advertising Fund Payments To Franchisor						
Yellow Page & Local Advertising						
Insurance						
Utilities:						
Telephone/Fax						
Gas & Electric						
Water						
Janitorial Expense						
Trash Removal						
Security						
Travel & Lodging						
Meals & Entertainment						
Delivery Charges						
Printing Expense						
Postage						
Operating Supplies						
Office Supplies						
Vehicle Expense						
Equipment Maintenance						
Uniforms & Laundry						
Professional Fees:						
Accounting						
Legal						
Consulting						
Repairs & Maintenance						
Business Licenses/Fees/Permits						
Dues & Subscriptions						

Property Taxes						
Business Taxes						
Bad Debt/Theft						
Bank Charges & Credit Card Fees						
Royalties to Franchisor						
Interest Expense						
Total Operating Expenses						
Pre-Tax Operating Cash Flow	$	$	$	$	$	$
Operating Cash Flow As A & Of Sales	%	%	%	%	%	%

ADJUSTMENT TO PRE-TAX NET CASH FLOW						
Pre-Tax Operating Cash Flow	$	$	$	$	$	$
Less Depreciation/Amortization						
Pre-Tax Income						
Plus Depreciation/Amortization						
Less Principal Payments						
Less Capital Expenditures						
Pre-Tax Net Cash Flow	$	$	$	$	$	$

ADJUSTMENT TO "REAL" CASH FLOW						
Pre-Tax Net Cash Flow						
Less Return On Invested Capital @ x%						
Pre-Tax "Real" Cash Flow						

sively police fraud and deception. And this funding should come from the registration fees paid by the franchisors themselves. Alternatively, a portion of the initial franchise fee paid by franchisees could also pad the super agency's budget.

At some point, registration states and the FTC (or its successor) will find common ground upon which to merge their efforts and require the filing of a single disclosure document/offering circular acceptable to all parties. This will go a long way toward reducing the expense, effort and frustration built into the now largely redundant registration process. At that time, mandatory financial performance representations/earnings claims statements should be instituted along with general, common sense guidelines for their preparation, substantiation and presentation. Equally important is a standard set of rules for documenting and penalizing fraud and deception.

Required Item 19 Preamble

The Federal Trade Commission requires that Financial Performance Representations begin with the following paragraph. This paragraph has been removed from all individual statements in this book in order to avoid redundancy.

The FTC's Franchise Rule permits a franchisor to provide information about the actual or potential financial performance of its franchised and/or franchisor-operated outlets, if there is a reasonable basis for the information, and if the information is included in the disclosure document. Financial performance information that differs from that included in this Item 19 may be given only if: (1) a franchisor provides the actual records of an existing outlet you are considering buying; or (2) a franchisor supplements the information provided in this Item 19, for example, by providing information about possible performance at a particular location or under particular circumstances.

How to Use the Data | 3

This book contains 93 financial performance representations/earnings claim statements that are categorized into food-service, lodging, retail and service-based industries. The data at the beginning of each company's earnings data is the result of a 45-point questionnaire sent out annually to the franchising community. This information is intended as a brief overview of the company; the text that follows provides a more in-depth analysis of the company's requirements and advantages.

In some cases, an answer has been abbreviated to conserve room and to facilitate the comparison of different companies. When no answer was provided to an item within the profile, "NR" is used to signify "No Response."

Please take a few minutes to acquaint yourself with the composition of the questionnaire data. Supplementary comments have been added where some interpretation of the franchisor's response is required.

EXPRESS EMPLOYMENT PROFESSIONALS
8516 NW Expressway
Oklahoma City, OK 73162-5145
Tel: (877) 652-6400 (405) 840-5000
Fax: (405) 717-5665
E-Mail: franchising@expresspros.com
Web Site: www.expressfranchising.com
Ms. Diane Carter, Manager of Franchise Admin.

Express franchise offices provide a full range of business-to-business staffing and HR services. The franchise includes all three service lines in one agreement: temporary/contract staffing, professional search/direct hire, and HR services. Express offers new franchise owners the unique chance to earn money by helping people grow their careers and businesses while impacting the local community. For established staffing business owners, we provide the opportunity to grow your business and advance the services provided. Independent staffing owners that have teamed with Express have benefited from our network of support, allowing them to keep up in this fast paced business.

BACKGROUND: IFA MEMBER

Established: 1983	1st Franchised: 1985
Franchised Units:	592
Company-Owned Units:	4
Total Units:	596
Dist.:	US-554; CAN-27; O'seas-15
North America:	49 States, 3 Provinces
Density:	55 in TX, 49 in CA, 34 in OK
Projected New Units (12 Months):	50
Qualifications:	4, 4, 3, 4, 4, 4
Registered:	CA,FL,HI,IL,IN,MD,MI,MN,NY,ND,OR,RI, SD,VA,WA,WI,DC

FINANCIAL/TERMS:

Cash Investment:	$130-170K
Total Investment:	$129.15-166.5K
Minimum Net Worth:	$100K
Fees:	Franchise — $35K
	Royalty — 8-9%; Ad. — 0.6%
Earnings Claim Statement:	Yes
Term of Contract (Years):	5/5
Avg. # Of Employees:	3 FT
Passive Ownership:	Not Allowed
Encourage Conversions:	Yes
Area Develop. Agreements:	No
Sub-Franchising Contracts:	No
Expand In Territory:	Yes

Space Needs:	1,000-1,200 SF; SF, SC	On-Going Support:	A,C,D,E,G,H,I
		Training:	2 Weeks in Oklahoma City, OK;
SUPPORT & TRAINING PROVIDED:			1 Week in Certified Training Office (In Field).
Financial Assistance Provided:	No		
Site Selection Assistance:	Yes	**SPECIFIC EXPANSION PLANS:**	
Lease Negotiation Assistance:	Yes	US:	Yes, All United States
Co-Operative Advertising:	Yes	Canada:	Yes, All Except Quebec
Franchisee Assoc./Member:	No	Overseas:	Yes, South Africa
Size Of Corporate Staff:	200		

Address/Contact

1. **Company name, address, telephone and fax numbers.**

Comment: All of the data published in the book was current at the time the completed questionnaire was received or upon subsequent verification by phone. Over a 12-month period between annual publications, 10–15% of the addresses and/or telephone numbers become obsolete for various reasons. If you are unable to contact a franchisor at the address/telephone number listed, please call Source Book Publications at (510) 839-5471 or fax us at (510) 839-2104 and we will provide you with the current address and telephone number.

2. **(877) 652-6400 (405) 840-5000.** In many cases, you may find that you cannot access the (800) number from your area. Do not conclude that the company has gone out of business. Simply call the local number.

Comment: An (800) number serves two important functions. The first is to provide an efficient, no-cost way for potential franchisees to contact the franchisor. Making the prospective franchisee foot the bill artificially limits the number of people who might otherwise make the initial contact. The second function is to demonstrate to existing franchisees that the franchisor is doing everything it can to efficiently respond to problems in the field as they occur. Many companies have a restricted (800) line for their franchisees that the general public cannot access. Since you will undoubtedly be talking with the franchisor's staff on a periodic basis, determine whether an (800) line is available to franchisees.

3. **Contact.** You should honor the wishes of the franchisor and address all initial correspondence to the contact listed. It would be counter-productive to try to reach the president directly if the designated contact is the director of franchising.

Comment: The president is the designated contact in approximately half of the company profiles in this book. The reason for this varies among franchisors. The president is the best spokesperson for his or her operation, and no doubt it flatters the franchisee to talk directly with the president, or perhaps there is no one else around. Regardless of the justification, it is important to determine if the operation is a one-man show in which the president does everything or if the president merely feels that having an open line to potential franchisees is the best way for him or her to sense the "pulse" of the company and the market. Convinced that the president can only do so many things well, I would want assurances that, by taking all incoming calls, he or she is not neglecting the day-to-day responsibilities of managing the business.

Description of Business

4. **Description of Business:** The questionnaire provides franchisors with adequate room to differentiate their franchise from the competition. In a minor number of cases, some editing was required.

Comment: In instances where franchisors show no initiative or imagination in describing their operations, you must decide whether this is symptomatic of the company or simply a reflection on the individual who responded to the questionnaire.

Background

5. **IFA.** There are two primary affinity groups associated with the franchising industry — the International Franchise Association (IFA) and the Canadian Franchise Association (CFA). Both the IFA and the CFA are described in Chapter One.

6. **Established: 1983.** Express Employment Professionals was founded in 1983, and, accordingly, has 25 years of experience in its primary business. It should be intuitively obvious that a firm that has been in existence for over 25 years has a greater likelihood of being around five years from now than a firm that was founded only last year.

7. **1st Franchised: 1985.** 1985 was the year that Express Employment Professionals' first franchised unit(s) were established.

Comment: Over ten years of continuous operation, both as an operator and as a franchisor, is compelling evidence that a firm has staying power. The number of years a franchisor has been in business is one of the key variables to consider in choosing a franchise. This is not to say that a new franchise should not receive your full attention. Every company has to start from scratch. Ultimately, a prospective franchisee has to be convinced that the franchise has 1) been in operation long enough, or 2) its key management personnel have adequate industry experience to have worked out the bugs normally associated with a new business. In most cases, this experience can only be gained through on-the-job training. Don't be the guinea pig that provides the franchisor with the experience it needs to develop a smoothly running operation.

8. **Franchised Units: 592.** As of 5/28/09, Express Employment Professionals had 592 franchisee-owned and operated units.

9. **Company-Owned Units: 4.** As of 5/28/09, Express Employment Professionals had 4 company-owned or operated units.

Comment: A younger franchise should prove that its concept has worked successfully in several company-owned units before it markets its "system" to an inexperienced franchisee. Without company-owned prototype stores, the new franchisee may well end up being the "testing kitchen" for the franchise concept itself.

If a franchise concept is truly exceptional, why doesn't the franchisor commit some of its resources to take advantage of the investment opportunity? Clearly, a financial decision on the part of the franchisor, the absence of company-owned units should not be a negative in and of itself. This is especially true of proven franchises, which may have previously sold their company-owned operations to franchisees.

Try to determine if there is a noticeable trend in the percentage of company-owned units. If the franchisor is buying back units from franchisees, it may be doing so to preclude litigation. Some firms also "churn" their operating units with some regularity. If the sales pitch is compelling, but the follow-through is not competitive, a franchisor may sell a unit to a new franchisee, wait for him or her to fail, buy it back for $0.60 cents on the dollar, and then sell that same unit to the next unsuspecting franchisee. Each time the unit is resold, the franchisor collects a franchise fee, plus the negotiated discount from the previous franchisee.

Alternatively, an increasing or high percentage of company-owned units may well mean the company is convinced of the long-term profitability of such an approach. The key is to determine whether a franchisor is building new units from scratch or buying them from failing and/or unhappy franchisees.

10. **Total Units: 596.** As of 5/28/09, Express Employment Professionals had a total of 596 operating units.

Comment: Like a franchisor's longevity, its experience in operating multiple units offers considerable comfort. Those franchisors with over 15–25 operating units have proven that their system works and have probably encountered and overcome most of the problems that plague a new operation. Alternatively, the management of franchises with less than 15 operating units may have gained considerable industry experience before joining the current franchise. It is up to the franchisor to convince you that it is providing you with as risk-free an operation as possible. You don't want to be providing a company with its basic experience in the business.

11. **Distribution: US-554; CAN-27; O'seas-15.** As of 5/28/09, Express Employment Professionals had 554 operating units in the U.S., 27 in Canada and 15 Overseas.

12. **Distribution: North America: 49 States, 3 Provinces.** As of 5/28/09, Express Employment

Professionals had operations in 49 states and 3 Canadian provinces.

Comment: It should go without saying that the wider the geographic distribution, the greater the franchisor's level of success. For the most part, such distribution can only come from a large number of operating units. If, however, the franchisor has operations in 15 states, but only 18 total operating units, it is unlikely that it can efficiently service these accounts because of geographic constraints. Other things being equal, a prospective franchisee would vastly prefer a franchisor with 15 units in New York to one with 15 units scattered throughout the U.S., Canada and overseas.

13. **Distribution: Density: TX, CA, OK.** The franchisor was asked "what three states/provinces have the largest number of operating units." As of 5/28/09, Express Employment Professionals had the largest number of units in Texas, California and Oklahoma.

Comment: For smaller, regional franchises, geographic distribution could be a key variable in deciding whether to buy. If the franchisor has a concentration of units in your immediate geographic area, it is likely you will be well-served.

For those far removed geographically from the franchisor's current areas of operation, however, there can be problems. It is both time consuming and expensive to support a franchisee 2,000 miles away from company headquarters. To the extent that a franchisor can visit four franchisees in one area on one trip, there is no problem. If, however, your operation is the only one west of the Mississippi, you may not receive the on-site assistance you would like. Don't be a missionary who has to rely on his or her own devices to survive. Don't accept a franchisor's idle promises of support. If on-site assistance is important to your ultimate success, get assurances in writing that the necessary support will be forthcoming. Remember, you are buying into a system, and the availability of day-to-day support is one of the key ingredients of any successful franchise system.

14. **Projected New Units (12 Months): 50.** Express Employment Professionals plans to establish 50 new units over the course of the next 12 months.

Comment: In business, growth has become a highly visible symbol of success. Rapid growth is generally perceived as preferable to slower, more controlled growth. I maintain, however, that the opposite is frequently the case. For a company of Express Employment Professionals' size, adding 50 new units over a 12-month period is both reasonable and achievable. It is highly unlikely, however, that a new franchise with only five operating units can successfully attract, screen, train and bring multiple new units on-stream in a 12-month period. If it suggests that it can, or even wants to, be properly wary. You must be confident a company has the financial and management resources necessary to pull off such a Herculean feat. If management is already thin, concentrating on attracting new units will clearly diminish the time it can and should spend supporting you. It takes many months, if not years, to develop and train a second level of management. You don't want to depend upon new hires teaching you systems and procedures they themselves know little or nothing about.

15. **Qualifications: 4,4,3,4,4,4.** This question was posed to determine which specific evaluation criteria were important to the franchisor. The franchisor was asked the following: "In qualifying a potential franchisee, please rank the following criteria from Unimportant (1) to Very Important (5)." The responses should be self-explanatory:

Financial Net Worth (Rank from 1–5)
General Business Experience (Rank from 1–5)
Specific Industry Experience (Rank from 1–5)
Formal Education (Rank from 1–5)
Psychological Profile (Rank from 1–5)
Personal Interview(s) (Rank from 1–5)

16. **Registered** refers to the 16 states that require specific formal registration at the state level before the franchisor may offer franchises in that state. State registration and disclosure to the Federal Trade Commission are separate issues that are discussed in Chapter 1.

Capital Requirements/Rights

17. **Cash Investment: $130-170K.** On average, an Express Employment Professionals franchisee will have made a cash investment of $130,000–170,000 by the time he or she finally opens the initial operating unit.

Comment: It is important that you be realistic about the amount of cash you can comfortably invest in a business. Stretching beyond your means can have grave and far-reaching consequences. Assume that you will encounter periodic set-backs and that you will have to draw on your reserves. The demands of starting a new business are harsh enough without adding the uncertainties associated with inadequate working capital. Trust the franchisor's recommendations regarding the suggested minimum cash investment. If anything, there is an incentive for setting the recommended level of investment too low, rather than too high. The franchisor will want to qualify you to the extent that you have adequate financing. No legitimate franchisor wants you to invest if there is a chance that you might fail because of a shortage of funds.

Keep in mind that you will probably not achieve a positive cash flow before you've been in business more than six months. In your discussions with the franchisor, be absolutely certain that its calculations include an adequate working capital reserve.

18. **Total Investment: $129.15-166.5K.** On average, Express Employment Professionals franchisees will invest a total of $129,150-166,500, including both cash and debt, by the time the franchise opens its doors.

Comment: The total investment should be the cash investment noted above plus any debt that you will incur in starting up the new business. Debt could be a note to the franchisor for all or part of the franchise fee, an equipment lease, building and facilities leases, etc. Make sure that the total includes all of the obligations that you assume, especially any long-term lease obligations.

Be conservative in assessing what your real exposure is. If you are leasing highly specialized equipment or if you are leasing a single-purpose building, it is naive to think that you will recoup your investment if you have to sell or sub-lease those assets in a buyer's market. If there is any specialized equipment that may have been manufactured to the franchisor's specifications, determine if the franchisor has any form of buy-back provision.

19. **Minimum Net Worth: $100K.** In this case,

Express Employment Professionals feels that a potential franchisee should have a minimum net worth of $100,000. Although net worth can be defined in vastly different ways, the franchisor's response should suggest a minimum level of equity that the prospective franchisee should possess. Net worth is the combination of both liquid and illiquid assets. Again, don't think that franchisor-determined guidelines somehow don't apply to you.

20. **Fees (Franchise): $35K.** Express Employment Professionals requires a front-end, one-time-only payment of $35,000 to grant a franchise for a single location. As noted in Chapter One, the franchise fee is a payment to reimburse the franchisor for the incurred costs of setting the franchisee up in business — from recruiting through training and manuals. The fee usually ranges from $15,000–30,000. It is a function of competitive franchise fees and the actual out-of-pocket costs incurred by the franchisor.

Depending upon the franchisee's particular circumstances and how well the franchisor thinks he or she might fit into the system, the franchisor may finance all or part of the franchise fee. (See Section 32 below to see if a franchisor provides any direct or indirect financial assistance.)

The franchise fee is one area in which the franchisor frequently provides either direct or indirect financial support.

Comment: Ideally, the franchisor should do no more than recover its costs on the initial franchise fee. Profits come later in the form of royalty fees, which are a function of the franchisee's sales. Whether the franchise fee is $5,000 or $35,000, the total should be carefully evaluated. What are competitive fees and are they financed? How much training will you actually receive? Are the fees reflective of the franchisor's expenses? If the fees appear to be non-competitive, address your concerns with the franchisor.

Realize that a $5,000 differential in the one-time franchise fee is a secondary consideration in the overall scheme of things. You are in the relationship for the long-term.

By the same token, don't get suckered in by an extremely low fee if there is any doubt about the franchisor's ability to follow through. Franchisors need to collect reasonable fees to cover their actual costs. If they don't recoup these costs, they cannot recruit and train new franchisees on whom your own future success partially depends.

21. **Fees (Royalty): 8-9%** means that eight to nine percent of gross sales (or other measure, as defined in the franchise agreement) must be periodically paid directly to the franchisor in the form of royalties. This on-going expense is your cost for being part of the larger franchise system and for all of the "back-office" support you receive. In a few cases, the amount of the royalty fee is fixed rather than variable. In others, the fee decreases as the volume of sales (or other measure) increases (i.e., 8% on the first $200,000 of sales, 7% on the next $100,000 and so on). In others, the fee is held at artificially low levels during the start-up phase of the franchisee's business, then increases once the franchisee is better able to afford it.

Comment: Royalty fees represent the mechanism by which the franchisor finally recoups the costs it has incurred in developing its business. It may take many years and many operating units before the franchisor is able to make a true operating profit.

Consider a typical franchisor who might have been in business for three years. With a staff of five, rent, travel, operating expenses, etc., assume it has annual operating costs of $300,000 (including reasonable owner's salaries). Assume also that there are 25 franchised units with average annual sales of $250,000. Each franchise is required to pay a 6% royalty fee. Total annual royalties under this scenario would total only $375,000. The franchisor is making a $75,000 profit. Then consider the personal risk the franchisor took in developing a new business and the initial years of negative cash flows. Alternatively, evaluate what it would cost you, as a sole proprietor, to provide the myriad services included in the royalty payment.

In assessing various alternative investments, the amount of the royalty percentage is a major on-going expense. Assuming average annual sales of $250,000 per annum over a 15 year period, the total royalties at 5% would be $187,500. At 6%, the cumulative fees would be $225,000. You have to be fully convinced that the $37,500 differential is justified. While this is clearly a mean-ingful number, what you are really evaluating is the quality of management and the competitive advantages of the goods and/or services offered by the franchisor.

22. **Fees (Advertising): 0.6%.** Most national or regional franchisors require their franchisees to contribute a certain percentage of their sales (or other measure, as determined in the franchise agreement) into a corporate advertising fund. These individual advertising fees are pooled to develop a corporate advertising/marketing effort that produces great economies of scale. The end result is a national or regional advertising program that promotes the franchisor's products and services. Depending upon the nature of the business, this percentage usually ranges from 2–6% and is in addition to the royalty fee.

Comment: One of the greatest advantages of a franchised system is its ability to promote, on a national or regional basis, its products and services. The promotions may be through television, radio, print medias or direct mail. The objective is name recognition and, over time, the assumption that the product and/or service has been "time-tested." An individual business owner could never justify the expense of mounting a major advertising program at the local level. For a smaller franchise that may not yet have an advertising program or fee, it is important to know when an advertising program will start, how it will be monitored and its expected cost.

23. **Earnings Claims Statement: Yes** means Express Employment Professionals provides a financial performance representation/earnings claims statement to potential franchisees. Unfortunately, only approximately 18-22% of franchisors provide a financial performance representation/earnings claims statement in their Franchise Disclosure Document (FDD). The franchising industry's failure to require earnings claims statements does a serious disservice to the potential franchisee. See Chapter Two for comments on the financial performance representation/earnings claims statement.

24. **Term of Contract (Years): 5/5.** Express Employment Professionals' initial franchise period runs for five years. The first renewal period runs for an additional five years. Assuming that the franchisee operates within the terms of the franchise

agreement, he or she has ten years within which to develop and, ultimately, sell the business.

Comment: The potential (discounted) value of any business (or investment) is the sum of the operating income that is generated each year plus its value upon liquidation. Given this truth, the length of the franchise agreement and any renewals are extremely important to the franchisee. It is essential that he or she has adequate time to develop the business to its full potential. At that time, he or she will have maximized the value of the business as an on-going concern. The value of the business to a potential buyer, however, is largely a function of how long the franchise agreement runs. If there are only two years remaining before the agreement expires, or if the terms of an extension(s) are vague, the business will be worth only a fraction of the value assigned to a business with 15 years to go. For the most part, the longer the agreement and the subsequent extension, the better. (The same logic applies to a lease. If your sales are largely a function of your location and traffic count, then it is important that you have options to extend the lease under known terms. Your lease should never be longer than the remaining term of your franchise agreement, however.)

Assuming the length of the agreement is acceptable, be clear under what circumstances renewals might not be granted. Similarly, know the circumstances under which a franchise agreement might be prematurely and unilaterally canceled by the franchisor. I strongly recommend you have an experienced lawyer review this section of the franchise agreement. It would be devastating if, after spending years developing your business, there were a loophole in the contract that allowed the franchisor to arbitrarily cancel the relationship.

25. **Avg. # of Employees: 3 FT.** The question was asked "Including the owner/operator, how many employees are recommended to properly staff the average franchised unit?" In Express Employment Professionals' case, three full-time employees are required.

Comment: Most entrepreneurs start a new business based on their intuitive feel that it will be "fun" and that their talents and experience will be put to good use. They will be doing what they enjoy and what they are good at. Times change.

Your business prospers. The number of employees increases. You are spending an increasing percentage of your time taking care of personnel problems and less and less on the fun parts of the business. In Chapter One, the importance of conducting a realistic self-appraisal was stressed. If you found that you really are not good at managing people, or you don't have the patience to manage a large minimum wage staff, cut your losses before you are locked into doing just that.

26. **Passive Ownership: Not Allowed.** Depending on the nature of the business, many franchisors are indifferent as to whether you manage the business directly or hire a full-time manager. Others are insistent that, at least for the initial franchise, the franchisee be a full-time owner/operator. Express Employment Professionals does not allow franchisees to hire full-time managers to run their outlets.

Comment: Unless you have a great deal of experience in the business you have chosen or in managing similar businesses, I feel strongly that you should initially commit your personal time and energies to make the system work. After you have developed a full understanding of the business and have competent, trusted staff members who can assume day-to-day operations, then consider delegating these responsibilities. Running the business through a manager can be fraught with peril unless you have mastered all aspects of the business and there are strong economic incentives and sufficient safeguards to ensure the manager will perform as desired.

27. **Conversions Encouraged: Yes.** This section pertains primarily to sole proprietorships or "mom and pop" operations. To the extent that there truly are centralized operating savings associated with the franchise, the most logical people to join a franchise system are sole practitioners who are working hard but only eking out a living. The implementation of proven systems and marketing clout could significantly reduce operating costs and increase profits.

Comment: The franchisor has the option of 1) actively encouraging such independent operators to become members of the franchise team, 2) seeking out franchisees with limited or no applied experience or 3) going after both groups. Concerned that it will be very difficult to break independent operators of the bad habits they have picked up over the years, many only choose course two. "They will continue to do things their way. They won't, or can't, accept corporate direction," they might say to themselves. Others are simply selective in the conversions they allow. In many cases, the franchise fee is reduced or eliminated for conversions.

28. **Area Development Agreements: No** means that Express Employment Professionals does not offer an area development agreement. Area development agreements are more fully described in Chapter One. Essentially, they allow an investor or investment group to develop an entire area or region. The schedule for development is clearly spelled out in the area development agreement. (Note: "Var." means varies and "Neg." means negotiable.)

Comment: Area development agreements represent an opportunity for the franchisor to choose a single franchisee or investment group to develop an entire area. The franchisee's qualifications should be strong and include proven business experience and the financial depth to pull it off. An area development agreement represents a great opportunity for an investor to tie up a large geographical area and develop a concept that may not have proven itself on a national basis. Keep in mind that this is a quantum leap from making an investment in a single franchise and is relevant only to those with development experience and deep pockets.

29. **Sub-Franchising Contracts: No.** Express Employment Professionals does not grant sub-franchising agreements. (See Chapter One for a more thorough explanation.) Like area development agreements, sub-franchising allows an investor or investment group to develop an entire area or region. The difference is that the sub-franchisor becomes a self-contained business, responsible for all relations with franchisees within its area, from initial training to on-going support. Franchisees pay their royalties to the sub-franchisor, who in turn pays a portion to the master franchisor.

Comment: Sub-franchising is used primarily by smaller franchisors who have a relatively easy concept and who are prepared to sell a portion of the future growth of their business to someone for some front-end cash and a percentage of the future royalties they receive from their franchisees.

30. **Expand in Territory: Yes.** Under conditions spelled out in the franchise agreement, Express Employment Professionals will allow its franchisees to expand within their exclusive territory.

Comment: Some franchisors define the franchisee's exclusive territory so tightly that there would never be room to open additional outlets within an area. Others provide a larger area in the hopes that the franchisee will do well and have the incentive to open additional units. There are clearly economic benefits to both parties from having franchisees with multiple units. There is no question that it is in your best interest to have the option to expand once you have proven to both yourself and the franchisor that you can manage the business successfully. Many would concur that the real profits in franchising come from managing multiple units rather than being locked into a single franchise in a single location. Additional fees may or may not be required with these additional units.

31. **Space Needs: 1,000-1,200 SF; SF, SC.** The average Express Employment Professionals retail outlet will require 1,000-1,200 square feet in a Storefront (SF) or Strip Center (SC). Other types of leased space might be a Free-Standing (FS) building, Convenience Store (C-store) location, Executive Suite (ES), Home-Based (HB), Industrial Park (IP), Kiosk (KI), Office Building (OB), Power Center (PC), Regional Mall (RM) or Warehouse (WH).

Comment: Armed with the rough space requirements, you can better project your annual occupancy costs. It should be relatively easy to get comparable rental rates for the type of space required. As annual rent and related expenses can be as high as 15% of your annual sales, be as accurate as possible in your projections.

Franchisor Support and Training Provided

32. **Financial Assistance Provided: No** notes that Express Employment Professionals does not provide financial assistance. Indirect assistance (I) might include making introductions to the franchisor's financial contacts, providing financial

templates for preparing a business plan or actually assisting in the loan application process. In some cases, the franchisor becomes a co-signer on a financial obligation (equipment lease, space lease, etc.). Other franchisors are (D) directly involved in the process. In this case, the assistance may include a lease or loan made directly by the franchisor. Any loan would generally be secured by some form of collateral. A very common form of assistance is a note for all or part of the initial franchise fee. Yes (B) indicates that the franchisor provides both direct and indirect financial assistance. The level of assistance will generally depend upon the relative strengths of the franchisee.

Comment: The best of all possible worlds is one in which the franchisor has enough confidence in the business and in you to co-sign notes on the building and equipment leases and allow you to pay off the franchise fee over a specified period of time. Depending upon your qualifications, this could happen. Most likely, however, the franchisor will only give you some assistance in raising the necessary capital to start the business. Increasingly, franchisors are testing a franchisee's business acumen by letting him or her assume an increasing level of personal responsibility in securing financing. The objective is to find out early in the process how competent a franchisee really is.

33. **Site Selection Assistance: Yes** means that Express Employment Professionals will assist the franchisee in selecting a site location. While the phrase "location, location, location" may be hackneyed, its importance should not be discounted, especially when a business depends upon retail traffic counts and accessibility. If a business is home- or warehouse-based, assistance in this area is of negligible or minor importance.

Comment: Since you will be locked into a lease for a minimum of three, and probably five, years, optimal site selection is absolutely essential. Even if you were somehow able to sub-lease and extricate yourself from a bad lease or bad location, the franchise agreement may not allow you to move to another location. Accordingly, it is imperative that you get it right the first time.

If a franchisor is truly interested in your success, it should treat your choice of a site with the same care it would use in choosing a company-owned site. Keep in mind that many firms provide excellent demographic data on existing locations at a very reasonable cost.

34. **Lease Negotiations Assistance: Yes.** Once a site is selected, Express Employment Professionals will be actively involved in negotiating the terms of the lease.

Comment: Given the complexity of negotiating a lease, an increasing number of franchisors are taking an active role in lease negotiations. There are far too many trade-offs that must be considered — terms, percentage rents, tenant improvements, pass-throughs, kick-out clauses, etc. This responsibility is best left to the professionals. If the franchisor doesn't have the capacity to support you directly, enlist the help of a well-recommended broker. The penalties for signing a bad long-term lease are very severe.

35. **Co-operative Advertising: Yes.** This refers to the existence of a joint advertising program in which the franchisor and franchisees each contribute to promote the company's products and/ or services (usually within the franchisee's specific territory).

Comment: Co-op advertising is a common and mutually-beneficial effort. By agreeing to split part of the advertising costs, whether for television, radio or direct mail, the franchisor is not only supporting the franchisee, but guaranteeing itself royalties from the incremental sales. A franchisor that is not intimately involved with the advertising campaign — particularly when it is an important part of the business — may not be fully committed to your overall success.

36. **Franchisee Assoc./Member: No.** This response notes that the Express Employment Professionals system does not include an active association made up of Express Employment Professionals franchisees and that, consequently, the franchisor is not a member of any such franchisee association.

Comment: The empowerment of franchisees has become a major rallying cry within the industry over the past three years. Various states have recently passed laws favoring franchisee rights, and the subject has been widely discussed in congressional staff hearings. Political groups even represent franchisee rights on a national basis. Similarly, the IFA is now actively courting franchisees to become active members. Whether they are equal members remains to be seen.

Franchisees have also significantly increased their clout with respect with the franchisor. If a franchise is to grow and be successful in the long term, it is critical that the franchisor and its franchisees mutually agree they are partners rather than adversaries.

37. Size of Corporate Staff: 200. Express Employment Professionals has 200 full-time employees on its staff to support its 596 operating units.

Comment: There are no magic ratios that tell you whether the franchisor has enough staff to provide the proper level of support. It would appear, however, that Express Employment Professionals' staff of 200 is adequate to support 596 operating units. Less clear is whether a staff of three, including the company president and his wife, can adequately support 15 fledgling franchisees in the field.

Many younger franchises may be managed by a skeleton staff, assisted by outside consultants who perform various management functions during the start-up phase. From the perspective of the franchisee, it is essential that the franchisor have actual in-house franchising experience, and that the franchisee not be forced to rely on outside consultants to make the system work. Whereas a full-time, salaried employee will probably have the franchisee's objectives in mind, an outside consultant may easily not have the same priorities. Franchising is a unique form of business that requires specific skills and experience — skills and experience that are markedly different from those required to manage a non-franchised business. If you are thinking about establishing a long-term relationship with a firm just starting out in franchising, you should insist that the franchisor prove that it has an experienced, professional team on board and in place to provide the necessary levels of support to all concerned.

38. On-Going Support: A,C,D,E,G,H,I. Like initial training, the on-going support services provided by the franchisor are of paramount importance. Having a solid and responsive team

behind you can certainly make your life much easier and allow you to concentrate your energies on other areas. As is noted below, the franchisors were asked to indicate their support for nine separate on-going services:

Service Provided	Included in Fees	At Add'l. Cost	NA
Central Data Processing	A	a	NA
Central Purchasing	B	b	NA
Field Operations Evaluation	C	c	NA
Field Training	D	d	NA
Initial Store Opening	E	e	NA
Inventory Control	F	f	NA
Franchisee Newsletter	G	g	NA
Regional or National Meetings	H	h	NA
800 Telephone Hotline	I	i	NA

If the franchisor provides the service at no additional cost to the franchisee (as indicated by letters A–I), a capital letter was used to indicate this. If the service is provided, but only at an additional cost, a lower case letter was used. If the franchisor responded with a NA, or failed to note an answer for a particular service, the corresponding letter was omitted from the data sheet.

39. Training: 2 Weeks in Oklahoma City, OK; 1 Week in Certified Training Office (In Field).

Comment: Assuming that the underlying business concept is sound and competitive, adequate training and on-going support are among the most important determinants of your success as a franchisee. The initial training should be as lengthy and as "hands-on" as necessary to allow the franchisee to operate alone and with confidence. Obviously, every potential situation cannot be covered in any training program. But the franchisee should come away with a basic understanding of how the business operates and where to go to resolve problems when they come up. Depending on the business, there should be operating manuals, procedural manuals, company policies, training videos, (800) help-lines, etc. It may be helpful at the outset to establish how satisfied recent franchisees are with a company's training. I would also have a clear understanding about how often the company updates its manuals and training programs, the cost of sending additional employees through training, etc.

Remember, you are part of an organization that

you are paying (in the form of a franchise fee and on-going royalties) to support you. Training is the first step. On-going support is the second step.

Specific Expansion Plans

40. **U.S.: Yes, All United States.** Express Employment Professionals is currently focusing its growth on the entire United States. Alternatively, the franchisor could have listed particular states or regions into which it wished to expand.

41. **Canada: Yes, All Except Quebec.** Express Employment Professionals is currently seeking additional franchisees in all Canadian provinces except for Quebec. Specific markets or provinces could have also been indicated.

42. **Overseas: Yes, South Africa.** Express Employment Professionals is currently expanding overseas with a focus on South Africa.

Comment: You will note that many smaller companies with less than 15 operating units suggest that they will concurrently expand throughout the U.S., Canada and internationally. In many cases, these are the same companies that foresee a 50+% growth rate in operating units over the next 12 months. The chances of this happening are negligible. As a prospective franchisee, you should be wary of any company that thinks it can expand throughout the world without a solid base of experience, staff and financial resources. Even if adequate financing is available, the demands on existing management will be extreme. New management cannot adequately fill the void until they are able to fully understand the system and absorb the corporate culture. If management's end objective is expansion for its own sake rather than by design, the existing franchisees will suffer.

Note: The statistics noted in the profiles preceding each company's analysis are the result of data provided by the franchisors themselves by way of a detailed questionnaire. Similarly, the data in the summary comparisons in the Introduction Chapter were taken from the company profile data. The figures used throughout each company's analysis, however, were generally taken from the FDDs. In many cases, the FDDs, which are only printed annually, contain information that is somewhat out of date. This is especially true with regard to the number of operating units and the current level of investment. A visit to our website at www.worldfranchising.com should provide current data.

శు

If you have not already done so, please invest some modest time to read Chapter 1 — 30-Minute Overview.

Recommended Reading | 4

My strong sense is that every potential franchisee should be well-versed in the underlying fundamentals of the franchising industry before he or she commits to the way of life it involves. The better you understand the industry, the better prepared you will be to take maximum advantage of the relationship with your franchisor. There is no doubt that it will also place you in a better position to negotiate the franchise agreement — the conditions of which will dictate every facet of your life as a franchisee for the term of the agreement. The few extra dollars spent on educating yourself could well translate into tens of thousand of dollars to the bottom line in the years ahead.

In addition to general franchising publications, we have included several special interest books that relate to specific, but critical, parts of the start-up and on-going management process— site selection, hiring and managing minimum wage employees, preparing accurate cash flow projections, developing comprehensive business and/or marketing plans, etc.

We have also attempted to make the purchasing process easier by allowing readers to purchase the books directly from Source Book Publications, either via our 800-line or our website at www.sourcebookpublications.com. All of the books are currently available in inventory and are generally sent the same day an order is received. A 15% discount is available on all orders over $100.00. See page 38 for an order form. Your complete satisfaction is 100% guaranteed on all books.

Background/Evaluation

The Franchise Fraud: How to Protect Yourself Before and After You Invest, Purvin, Jr., BookSurge Publishing. 332 pp. 2008. $18.95

A primer on the promises and perils of franchising. It's big business, accounting for one-third of America's retail revenue. But franchising is still a risky proposition—at least for the franchisee. This resource exposes the frauds and abuses too many companies perpetrate on their franchisees—everything from unfulfilled pledges of promotional support to oversaturating the market with outlets. It helps potential franchise owners avoid being victimized by explaining, in specific detail, what to look for, what questions to ask, and what agreements to make before signing a contract. Robert Purvin also reveals how to identify and take advantage of the worthwhile franchising opportunities available today.

Grow to Greatness: How to Build a World-Class Franchise System Faster, 2nd edition, Olson, Franchise Update Media Group. 237 pp. 2008. $29.95

This breakthrough book, Grow to Greatness, has instantly become the must-read, essential guide on how to build a world-class franchise system--faster! This book contains advice and proven, step-by-step systems and processes for emerging and established franchisors, as well as for anyone considering franchising a business.

Franchise Times Guide to Selecting, Buying and Owning a Franchise, Bennett, Babcock, Hamburger, Sterling. 2008. 352 pp.

Buying a franchise can be a handy shortcut to the American dream of owning your own business. But there are dangerous pitfalls—and possible drawbacks to even the best franchise deals. Here, for every prospective franchisee, is authoritative advice from a trustworthy source. The experts of Franchise Times offer their picks of the top 200 franchises and 100 up-and-comers, complete with contact information, financial requirements, fees, and more. There are practical tips on everything from hiring and marketing to financing your franchise, leasing a retail space (or setting up a home office), and deciding if you should buy or run a franchise with your spouse. With anecdotes and advice from current franchisees and franchisors, this is a book every would-be entrepreneur should read before signing a contract.

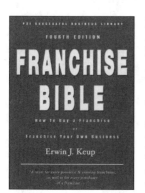

Franchise Bible: A Comprehensive Guide, 4th Edition, Keup, Oasis Press. 2000. 318 pp. $27.95.

This recently updated classic is equally useful for prospective franchisees and franchisors alike. The comprehensive guide and workbook explain in detail what the franchise system entails and the precise benefits it offers. The book features the new franchise laws that became effective January, 1995. To assist the prospective franchisee in rating a potential franchisor, Keup provides necessary checklists and forms. Also noted are the franchisor's contractual obligations to the franchisee and what the franchisee should expect from the franchisor in the way of services and support.

Tips & Traps When Buying a Franchise, Revised 2nd Edition, Tomzack, Source Book Publications. 1999. 236 pp. $19.95.

Many a green franchisee is shocked to discover that the road to success in franchising is full of hidden costs, inflated revenue promises, reneged marketing support and worse. In this candid, hard-hitting book, Tomzack steers potential franchisees around the pitfalls and guides them in making a smart, lucrative purchase. Topics include: matching a franchise with personal finances and lifestyle, avoiding the five most common pitfalls, choosing a prime location, asking the right questions, etc.

Databases

Franchisor Database, Source Book Publications. (800) 841-0873/(510) 839-5471.

Listing of over 2,400 active North American franchisors. 29 fields of information per company: full address, telephone/800/fax numbers, Internet address, email address, contact/title/salutation, president/title/salutation, # of franchised units, # of company-owned units, # total units, IFA/CFA Member, etc. 48 industry categories. Unlimited use. Guaranteed deliverability — $0.50 rebate for any returned mailings. $1,500 for initial database, $150 per quarter for updates.

Directories

Bond's Franchise Guide — 2008 Edition, Bond/Kimmel, Source Book Publications, 2008. 528 pp. $34.95.

This annual directory offers the prospective franchisee a detailed profile of over 1,000 franchises, as well as listings of franchise attorneys, consultants and service providers. The companies are divided into 45 distinct business categories for easy comparison. The data represents the most up-to-date, comprehensive and reliable information about this dynamic industry.

Minority Franchise Guide — 2006 Edition, Bond/Hinh/Kimmel, Source Book Publications, 2006. 353 pp. $19.95.

The only minority franchising directory! Contains detailed profiles and company logos of over 550 forward-looking franchisors that encourage and actively support the inclusion of minority franchisees. It also includes a listing of resources available to prospective minority franchisees.

Franchise Rankings

Bond's Top 100 Franchises — 2009 Edition, Bond/Cavagrotti, Source Book Publications, 2009. 384 pp. $24.95.

In response to the constantly asked question, *"What are the best franchises?"*, Bond's new book focuses on the top 100 franchises broken down into four major segments — food-service, lodging, retail and service-based franchises. Within each group, a rigorous, in-depth analysis was performed on over 500 systems. Many of the companies selected are household names. Others are rapidly growing, mid-sized firms that are also strong national players. Still others are somewhat smaller systems that demonstrate sound concepts, exceptional management and an aggressive expansion system. Companies were analyzed on the basis of historical performance, brand identification, market dynamics, franchisee satisfaction, the level of training and on-going support, financial stability, etc. Includes detailed four to five page profiles on each company, as well as key statistics and industry overview. All companies are proven performers and most have a national presence.

Other

The Economics of Franchising, Blair/ Lafontaine, Cambridge University Press. 2005. 338 pp. $45.00.

The Economics of Franchising describes how and why franchising works. It also analyses the economic tensions that contribute to conflict in the franchisor-franchisee relationship. The treatment includes a great deal of empirical evidence on franchising, its importance in various segments of the economy, the terms of franchise contracts, and what we know about how all these have evolved over time, especially in the US market. The economic analysis of the franchisor-franchisee relationship begins with the observation that for franchisors, franchising is a contractual alternative to vertical integration. Subsequently, the tensions that arise between a franchisor and its franchisees, who in fact are owners of independent businesses, are examined in turn. In particular the authors discuss issues related to product quality control, tying arrangements, pricing, location and territories, advertising, and termination and renewals.

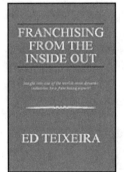

Franchising From the Inside Out, Teixeira. 2005. 177 pp. $19.95.

"Franchising From The Inside Out" is a valuable resource for those people interested in buying a franchise. This book contains an in-depth explanation of the entire franchise process including how to choose and evaluate a franchise opportunity and detailing the important questions to ask before making that final decision. There are also chapters for franchisees and franchisors currently involved in the franchise industry. The chapters on "Negotiating The Franchise Agreement," "The Laws of Franchising" and "The Secrets to Success" represent examples of the practical advice this book contains.

From Ice Cream to the Internet, Shane. 2005. 256 pp. $29.95.

Franchising can offer businesses a powerful new source of growth and improved financial performance. Now, Dr. Scott A. Shane helps businesses systematically assess the pros and cons of franchising, and offers proven best practices for building a successful system. *From Ice Cream to the Internet* focuses squarely on the strategic issues and challenges faced by franchisors. Shane answers key questions such as: What do the winners do differently? How does franchising affect your ability to compete with firms that don't? Shane then presents proven principles for every facet of franchising success: designing the system, recruiting, selecting, managing and supporting franchisees; establishing territories and pricing; managing expansion; and more.

Earnings Claims Packages

2008 Food-Service Earnings Claims Package. $250.00.

The 2008 Food-Service Earnings Claims Package includes 89 recent earnings claims, inlcuding Arby's, Baskin-Robbins, El Pollo Loco, Famous Dave's, Great Harvest Bread Co., Mrs. Fields Cookies, Pizza Patron, Pizzeria Uno, Quiznos and TCBY.

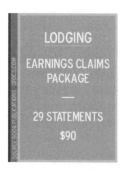

2008 Lodging Earnings Claims Package. $90.00.

The 2008 Lodging Earnings Claims Package includes 29 recent earnings claims, including Clarion Hotels, Holiday Inns, Motel 6, Quality Inns, Ramada, Studio 6 and Suburban Lodges.

2008 Retail Earnings Claims Package. $100.00.

The 2008 Retail Earnings Claims Package includes 33 recent earnings claims, including 7-Eleven, Aaron's Sales and Lease Ownership, Color Me Mine, Pearle Vision, Relax The Back, Snap-On Tools and Verlo Mattress Factory Stores.

2008 Service-Based Earnings Claims Package. $350.00.

The 2008 Service-Based Earnings Claims Package includes 143 recent earnings claims, including Allegra Network, Aussie Pet Mobile, Children's Orchard, ComForcare Senior Services, Epcon Communities, FasTracKids, Great Clips, Huntington Learning Centers, Keller Williams Realtors, Link Staffing, Money Mailer, Mr. Rooter, Postal Annex+, Thrifty Car Sales, Weed Man and WSI.

2008 Complete Earnings Claims Package. $525.00.

The 2008 Complete Earnings Claims Package includes 295 recent earnings claims -- 89 Food-Service Earnings Claims, 29 Lodging Earnings Claims, 33 Retail Earnings Claims and 143 Service-Based Earnings Claims.

For more detailed information on the contents of the earnings claims packages, please visit either www.sourcebookpublications.com or www.UFOCs.com.

The Franchise Bookstore
Order Form

Call (800) 841-0873 or (510) 839-5471; or FAX (510) 839-2104

Item #	Title	Price	Qty.	Total

Basic postage (1 Book)	$8.50
Each additional book add $4.00	
California tax (if CA resident)	
Total due in U.S. dollars	
Deduct 15% if total due is over $100.00	
Net amount due in U.S. dollars	

Please include credit card number and expiration date for all charge card orders! Checks should be made payable to Source Book Publications. All prices are in U.S. dollars.

Mailing Information: All books shipped by USPS Priority Mail (2nd Day Air). Please print clearly and include your phone number in case we need to contact you. Postage and handling rates are for shipping within the U.S. Please call for international rates.

Name: _____

Company: _____

Address: _____

City: _____

☐ Check enclosed or

Charge my:

☐ American Express ☐ MasterCard ☐ VISA

Card #: _____

Expiration Date: _____

Signature: _____

Security Code: _____

Title: _____

Telephone No.: (___) _____

State/Prov.: _____ Zip: _____

Please send order to:
Source Book Publications
1814 Franklin St., Ste. 603, Oakland, CA 94612
Satisfaction Guaranteed. If not fully satisfied, return for a prompt, 100% refund.

Food-Service Franchises | 5

AuntieAnne's
PRETZEL PERFECT

AUNTIE ANNE'S HAND-ROLLED SOFT PRETZELS

48-50 W. Chestnut St. # 200

Lancaster, PA 17603

Tel: (717) 442-4766

Fax: (717) 442-4139

E-Mail: lindae@auntieannesinc.com

Web Site: www.auntieannes.com

Ms. Linda Engels, Franchise Support Rep.

Auntie Anne's, Inc. is a franchise organization with a commitment to exceeding our customers' expectations. We've built our company on the quality of our products and strong support for our franchisees, nurturing relationships for the long-term growth of the franchise system. That approach continues to drive our growth. We provide our customers with pretzels, dips, and drinks which are mixed, twisted, and baked to a golden brown in full view of our customers. Each and every one of our pretzels comes with the Pretzel Perfect Guarantee - we guarantee you'll love your pretzel or we'll replace it with one that you do.

BACKGROUND: IFA MEMBER

Established: 1988;   1st Franchised: 1989

Franchised Units: 929

Company-Owned Units: 10

Total Units: 939

Dist.:   US-744; CAN-0; O'seas-195

  North America: 43 States, 0 Provinces

  Density: 59 in CA, 48 in FL, 74 in PA

Projected New Units (12 Months):	50
Qualifications:	4, 2, 2, 2, 3, 5
Registered:	CA,HI,IL,IN,MD,MI,MN,ND,NY,RI,SD,VA, WA,WI

FINANCIAL/TERMS:

Cash Investment:	$198-441K
Total Investment:	$198-441K
Minimum Net Worth:	$400K
Fees: Franchise -	$30K
Royalty - 7%;	Ad. - 1%
Earnings Claims Statement:	Yes
Term of Contract (Years):	20/Variable
Avg. # Of Employees:	4 FT, 4 PT
Passive Ownership:	Allowed
Encourage Conversions:	NA
Area Develop. Agreements:	No
Sub-Franchising Contracts:	No
Expand In Territory:	No
Space Needs:	400-600 SF; RM, Lifestyle Centers, Airports, Outlet Centers

SUPPORT & TRAINING:

Financial Assistance Provided:	Yes (I)
Site Selection Assistance:	Yes
Lease Negotiation Assistance:	Yes
Co-Operative Advertising:	Yes
Franchisee Assoc./Member:	Yes/Member
Size Of Corporate Staff:	150
On-Going Support:	C,D,E,G,H,I
Training:	2 Weeks Gap, PA

SPECIFIC EXPANSION PLANS:

US:	Yes, All United States
Canada:	Yes
Overseas:	Yes, All Countries

ITEM 19 FINANCIAL PERFORMANCE REPRESENTATIONS

Except for the analyses provided below, we do not furnish or authorize our officers, directors, employees or any salespersons to furnish any oral or written information concerning the actual or potential sales, costs, income or profits of any Auntie Anne's franchise. Actual results will vary from franchise to franchise and we cannot estimate the results of any particular franchise. We have specifically instructed our officers, directors, employees and salespersons that except for the sales analyses provided below, they are not permitted to make claims or statements as to earnings, sales or profits or prospects or chances of success, nor are they authorized to represent or estimate dollar figures as to any particular Auntie Anne's franchise or Auntie Anne's franchises in general.

WARNING: Please note the net sales, average net sales, average expenses and average net operating income figures shown in the following tables are based on unaudited actual reported results from franchises for the period January 1 through December 31, 2006. There is no assurance that future sales will correspond to historical sales. These figures should not be considered as the actual or potential net sales, expenses or net operating income that will be realized by any franchisee. Auntie Anne's does not represent that any franchisee can expect to attain these sales, expenses or net operating income. A new franchisee's individual financial results are likely to differ from the results stated below.

The following tables present net sales or average net sales, average expenses and average net operating income figures for the fiscal year ending December 31, 2006 for a majority of Auntie Anne's franchises that operated under the same ownership for the entire year, obtained from the profit and loss statements submitted by Auntie Anne's franchises. All of the Auntie Anne's franchisees report financial information based upon a uniform reporting system. The Notes which follow each table apply to that table and should be read in conjunction with the information contained in the table. As used throughout the following tables, Net Sales are the sales after taxes, discounts and allowances.

Table 1
Net Sales Range 2006 Fiscal Year — Systemwide - All Venues

2006	Enclosed Malls	Airports	Outlet Centers	Wal-Marts	Alternative Locations	Train Stations
Sample Size	434	17	15	21	31	5
High Sales	$1,836,758.00	$1,426,129.00	$706,863.00	$487,868.00	$650,628.00	$1,042,198.00
Low Sales	$152,659.00	$331,740.00	$177,242.00	$123,297.00	$101,873.00	$344,230.00
Average Sales	$470,768.17	$671,690.18	$390,435.67	$299,813.71	$314,123.55	$678,268.40
% of Stores at or Above Average	43.09%	41.18%	46.67%	42.86%	38.71%	40.00%
# of Stores at or Above Average	187	7	7	9	12	2
Median Sales	$432,356.00	$607,173.00	$355,994.00	$280,982.00	$295,618 00	$642,940.00
# of Stores at or Above Median	217	9	8	11	16	3
Total Number	451	17	16	23	32	5
Percent Included in Sample	96.23%	100.00%	93.75%	91.30%	96.88%	100.00%

Approximately 80% of Auntie Anne's franchises are located in enclosed malls. The remaining tables relate only to Auntie Anne's franchises operated in enclosed malls.

Table 2
Net Sales of Franchises In Operation For All 12 Months Of 2006

by Sales Range — Systemwide - Enclosed Malls

Sales Range	Low	High	Number of Franchisees
1	$700,000	and up	54
2	$550,000	$699,999	60
3	$400,000	$549,999	138
4	$250,000	$399,999	140
5	up to	$249,999	42

Average Net Sales $470,768 (187 franchises, or 43.09%, were at or above this figure)
Median Net Sales $432,356 (217 franchises were at or above this figure)

Notes to Table 2:
1. The total number of franchises included in Table 2 is 434. These franchises are located throughout the United States in enclosed mall locations.
The total number of franchises throughout the United States in enclosed mall locations that operated under the same ownership for all of 2006 is 451.
The total number of franchises included in Table 2 represent 96.23% of the total number of franchises in enclosed mall locations that operated under the same ownership for all of 2006.
2. Some reasons why a franchise's reported financial information is not included in Table 2 include the franchisee submitting the information late, incomplete, illegible or in an unacceptable format.

Table 3
Average Net Sales and Net Operating Income as a percentage of Average Net Sales for 2006 Fiscal Year— Systemwide — Enclosed Malls

ALL REGIONS	Average	% of Gross Sales	% of Stores at or Above Average	# of Stores at or Above Average
Gross Sales	**$470,768.17**	**100.00%**	**43.09%**	**187**
Cost of Goods Sold	$87,331.95	18.55%	58.76%	255
Gross Profit	**$383,436.22**	**81.45%**	**41.24%**	**179**
Operating Expenses				
Labor	$129,363.05	27.48%	64.29%	279
Rent	$ 69,102.95	14.68%	64.29%	279
Other Expenses	$ 77,347.21	16.43%	64.52%	280
Total Expenses	**$275,844.99**	**58.59%**	**64.29%**	**279**
Net Operating Income	**$107,617.60**	**22.86%**	**46.77%**	**203**

Average Net Sales $470,768 (187 franchises, or 43.09%, were at or above this figure)
Median Net Sales $432,356 (217 franchises were at or above this figure)

Notes to Table 3:
1.   The total number of franchises included in Table 3 is 434. These franchises are located throughout the United States in enclosed mall locations.
The total number of franchises throughout the United States in enclosed mall locations that operated under the same ownership for all of 2006 is 451.
The total number of franchises included in Table 3 represent 96.23% of the total number of franchises

in enclosed mall locations that operated under the same ownership for all of 2006.
2. Some reasons why a franchise's reported financial information is not included in Table 3 include the franchisee submitting the information late, incomplete, illegible or in an unacceptable format.

Table 4
MID-ATLANTIC REGION
Average Net Sales and Net Operating Income as a percentage of Average Net Sales for 2006 Fiscal Year - Enclosed Malls

MID ATLANTIC REGION	Average	% of Gross Sales	% of Stores at or Above Average	# of Stores at or Above Average
Gross Sales	$512,567.37	100.00%	41.57%	37
Cost of Goods Sold	$100,666.21	19.64%	46.07%	41
Gross Profit	$411,901.16	80.36%	53.93%	48
Operating Expenses				
Labor	$133,924.03	26.13%	57.30%	51
Rent	$ 69,059.19	13.47%	62.92%	56
Other Expenses	$ 82,933.40	16.18%	64.04%	57
Total Expenses	$285,903.84	55.78%	60.67%	54
Net Operating Income	$125,997.33	24.58%	39.33%	35

Average Net Sales $512,567 (37 franchises, or 41.57%, were at or above this figure)
Median Net Sales $474,121 (45 franchises were at or above this figure)

Notes to Table 4:
1.   The total number of franchises included in Table 4 is 89.
The total number of franchises that operated in enclosed mall locations under the same ownership in the Mid Atlantic Region for all of 2006 is 92.
The total number of franchises included in Table 4 represent 96.74% of the total number of franchises that operated in enclosed mall locations under the same ownership for all of 2006 in the Mid Atlantic Region.
2.   Some reasons why a franchise's reported financial information is not included in Table 4 include the franchisee submitting the information late, incomplete, illegible or in an unacceptable format.

Table 5
NORTH EAST REGION
Average Net Sales and Net Operating Income as a percentage of Average Net Sales for 2006 Fiscal Year - Enclosed Malls

NORTH EAST REGION	Average	% of Gross Sales	% of Stores at or Above Average	# of Stores at or Above Average
Gross Sales	$573,018.07	100.00%	34.48%	20
Cost of Goods Sold	$104,862.31	18.30%	36.21%	21
Gross Profit	$468,155.76	81.70%	63.79%	37

Operating Expenses				
Labor	$167,902.21	29.30%	55.17%	32
Rent	$85,142.78	14.86%	60.34%	35
Other Expenses	$ 97,312.65	16.98%	43.10%	25
Total Expenses	**$350,326.88**	**61.14%**	**50.00%**	**29**
Net Operating Income	**$117,812.51**	**20.56%**	**41.38%**	**24**

Average Net Sales $573,018 (20 franchises, or 34.48%, were at or above this figure)
Median Net Sales $487,680 (29 franchises were at or above this figure)

Notes to Table 5:
1. The total number of franchises included in Table 5 is 58.
The total number of franchises in enclosed mall locations that operated under the same ownership for all of 2006 in the North East Region is 62. The total number of franchises included in Table 5 represent 93.55% of the total number of franchises in enclosed mall locations that operated under the same ownership for all of 2006 in the North East Region.
2. Some reasons why a franchise's reported financial information is not included in Table 5 include the franchisee submitting the information late, incomplete, illegible or in an unacceptable format.

Table 6
SOUTH EAST REGION
Average Net Sales and Net Operating Income as a percentage of Average Net Sales for 2006 Fiscal Year - Enclosed Malls

SOUTH EAST REGION	Average	% of Gross Sales	% of Stores at or Above Average	# of Stores at or Above Average
Gross Sales	**$425,460.09**	**100.00%**	**38.67%**	**29**
Cost of Goods Sold	$ 76,436.66	17.97%	72.00%	54
Gross Profit	**$349,023.43**	**82.03%**	**28.00%**	**21**
Operating Expenses				
Labor	$116,810.43	27.46%	72.00%	54
Rent	$66,496.74	15.63%	54.67%	41
Other Expenses	$69,988.19	16.45%	66.67%	50
Total Expenses	**$253,316.81**	**59.54%**	**54.67%**	**41**
Net Operating Income	**$ 95,706.62**	**22.49%**	**45.33%**	**34**

Average Net Sales $425,460 (29 franchises, or 38.67%, were at or above this figure)
Median Net Sales $370,472 (38 franchises were at or above this figure)

Notes to Table 6:
1.   The total number of franchises included in Table 6 is 75.
The total number of franchises that operated in enclosed mall locations under the same ownership for all of 2006 in the South East Region is 80.
The total number of franchises included in Table 6 represent 93.75% of the total number of franchises that operated in enclosed mall locations under the same ownership for all of 2006 in the South East

Region.
2.   Some reasons why a franchise's reported financial information is not included in Table 6 include the franchisee submitting the information late, incomplete, illegible or in an unacceptable format.

Table 7
MID WEST REGION
Average Net Sales and Net Operating Income as a percentage of Average Net Sales for 2006 Fiscal Year - Enclosed Malls

MID WEST REGION	Average	% of Gross Sales	% of Stores at or Above Average	# of Stores at or Above Average
Gross Sales	$444,742.63	100.00%	44.26%	54
Cost of Goods Sold	$ 81,364.13	18.29%	72.95%	89
Gross Profit	$363,378.50	81.71%	27.05%	33
Operating Expenses				
Labor	$120,078.03	27.00%	42.62%	52
Rent	$ 65,896.33	14.82%	60.66%	74
Other Expenses	$ 69,459.07	15.62%	41.80%	51
Total Expenses	$255,460.17	57.44%	42.62%	52
Net Operating Income	$107,945.07	24.27%	31.97%	39

Average Net Sales $444,742 (54 franchises, or 44.26%, were at or above this figure)
Median Net Sales $422,184 (61 franchises were at or above this figure)

Notes to Table 7:
1. The total number of franchises included in Table 7 is 122.
The total number of franchises that operated in enclosed mall locations under the same ownership for all of 2006 in the Mid West Region is 123.
The total number of franchises included in Table 7 represent 99.19% of the total number of franchises that operated in enclosed mall locations under the same ownership for all of 2006 in the Mid West Region.
2. Some reasons why a franchise's reported financial information is not included in Table 7 include the franchisee submitting the information late, incomplete, illegible or in an unacceptable format.

Table 8
WESTERN REGION
Average Net Sales and Net Operating Income as a percentage of Average Net Sales for 2006 Fiscal Year - Enclosed Malls

WESTERN REGION	Average	% of Gross Sales	% of Stores at or Above Average	# of Stores at or Above Average
Gross Sales	$436,574.80	100.00%	47.78%	43
Cost of Goods Sold	$ 80,014.63	18.33%	54.44%	49
Gross Profit	$356,560.17	81.67%	45.56%	41

44

Operating Expenses				
Labor	$123,063.25	28.19%	54.44%	49
Rent	$65,328.04	14.96%	45.56%	41
Other Expenses	$75,949.63	17.40%	44.44%	40
Total Expenses	**$264,340.92**	**60.55%**	**45.56%**	**41**
Net Operating Income	**$ 92,219.25**	**21.12%**	**54.44%**	**49**

Average Net Sales $436,574 (43 franchises, or 47.78%, were at or above this figure)
Median Net Sales $418,362 (45 franchises)

Notes to Table 8:
1.   The total number of franchises included in Table 8 is 90.
The total number of franchises in enclosed mall locations that operated under the same ownership for all of 2006 in the Western Region is 94.
The total number of franchises in enclosed mall locations included in Table 8 represent 95.74% of the total number of franchises that operated under the same ownership for all of 2006 in the Western Region.
2.   Some reasons why a franchise's reported financial information is not included in Table 8 include the franchisee submitting the information late, incomplete, illegible or in an unacceptable format.

<u>WARNING:</u> **As stated previously, please note the net sales, average net sales, average expenses and average net operating income figures shown in the above tables are based on unaudited actual reported results from franchises for the period January 1 through December 31, 2006. There is no assurance that future sales will correspond to historical sales. These figures should not be considered as the actual or potential net sales, expenses or net operating income that will be realized by any franchisee. Auntie Anne's does not represent that any franchisee can expect to attain these sales, expenses or net operating income. A new franchisee's individual financial results are likely to differ from the results stated above.**

Your sales will be affected by your own operational ability, which may include your experience with managing a business, your capital and financing (including working capital), continual training of you and your staff, customer service orientation, product quality, your business plan, and the use of experts, e.g., an accountant, to assist you with your business plans.

Your sales may be affected by franchise location and site criteria, including traffic count, local household income, residential and/or daytime populations, ease of ingress and egress, parking, visibility of your sign, physical condition of premises, number and type of other businesses around your location, competition, inflation, economic conditions, seasonal conditions (particularly in colder climates), inclement weather (e.g., hurricanes), changes in the Homeland Security threat level, etc.

We will make available for your inspection substantiation of the data used in preparing these tables and cost claims at our headquarters in Lancaster, Pennsylvania, upon reasonable request and notice.

We encourage you to consult with your own accounting, business, and legal advisors to assist you to prepare your budgets and projections, and to assess the likely or potential financial performance of your franchise. We also encourage you to contact existing franchisees to discuss their experiences with the system and their franchise business. Notwithstanding the information set forth in this earnings claim, existing franchisees of Auntie Anne's are your best source of information about franchise operations.

45

BASKIN-ROBBINS

130 Royall St.
Canton, MA 02021
Tel: (800) 777-9983 (818) 996-9361
Fax: (818) 996-5163
E-Mail: franchiseinfo@dunkinbrands.com
Web Site: www.dunkinbrandsfranchising.com
Mr. James Franks, Director of Franchising

BASKIN-ROBBINS develops, operates and franchises retail stores that sell ice cream, frozen yogurt and other approved services. In some markets, BASKIN-ROBBINS, together with TOGO'S and/ or DUNKIN' DONUTS, offers multiple brand combinations of the three brands. TOGO'S, BASKIN-ROBBINS and DUNKIN' DONUTS are all subsidiaries of Dunkin' Brands, Inc.

BACKGROUND: IFA MEMBER

Established: 1950;	1st Franchised: 1950
Franchised Units:	4700
Company-Owned Units:	0
Total Units:	4700
Dist.:	US-2286; CAN-620; O'seas-1594
North America:	41 States, 0 Provinces
Density:	554 in CA, 195 in IL, 181 in NY
Projected New Units (12 Months):	27
Qualifications:	NR
Registered:	CA,DC,FL,HI,IL,IN,MD,MI,MN,ND,NY,OR,RI,SD,

VA,WA,WI

FINANCIAL/TERMS:

Cash Investment:	$100K
Total Investment:	$145.7-527.8K
Minimum Net Worth:	$300K
Fees: Franchise -	$40K
Royalty - 5-5.9%;	Ad. - 5%
Earnings Claims Statement:	Yes
Term of Contract (Years):	20
Avg. # Of Employees:	NA FT, 0 PT
Passive Ownership:	Allowed
Encourage Conversions:	No
Area Develop. Agreements:	Yes
Sub-Franchising Contracts:	No
Expand In Territory:	Yes
Space Needs:	NR SF; FS,SF,SC,RM

SUPPORT & TRAINING:

Financial Assistance Provided:	Yes (D)
Site Selection Assistance:	NA
Lease Negotiation Assistance:	Yes
Co-Operative Advertising:	No
Franchisee Assoc./Member:	Yes/Member
Size Of Corporate Staff:	NR
On-Going Support:	B,C,D,G,H,I
Training:	51 Days Randolph, MA; 3.5 Days Another Location

SPECIFIC EXPANSION PLANS:

US:	Yes, All Regions
Canada:	Yes, All Canada
Overseas:	Yes, All Countries

Item 19: Financial Performance Representations

Please note that a new franchisee's individual financial results may differ from the results stated in the financial performance representations in this Item 19.

We will make written substantiation for the financial performance representations in this Item 19 available to prospective franchisees upon reasonable request.

The following tables should be read together with the notes that follow in this Item 19.

BASKIN-ROBBINS *STANDALONE* STORES: The following financial performance representations are historical based on information from all existing *Baskin-Robbins Standalone* stores (exclusive of Combo Stores, Non-Traditional Outlets and Stores Operating under Territorial Franchises) for the prior fiscal year, DECEMBER 31, 2006 THROUGH DECEMBER 29, 2007.

Table A: Total number of Stores included in calculations for Table A is 935.

BASKIN-ROBBINS STORES (Excluding Combo Stores, Non-Traditional Outlets and Stores under Territorial Franchises. See Note 1)	Average Sales Per Store	Percent of all Stores that Meet or Exceed the Average Figure	Percentile Benchmarks (See Note 2)			
			25th	50th	75th	100th
Total Continental U.S.	$319,852	47.2%	$251,651	$313,134	$378,375	$951,031

BASKIN-ROBBINS *STANDALONE* STORES REMODELED TO NEW B31R IMAGE IN FISCAL YEAR 2006: The following financial performance representations are historical based on information from all existing *Baskin-Robbins Standalone* stores (exclusive of Combo Stores, Non-Traditional Outlets and Stores Operating under Territorial Franchises) that were remodeled to the new B31R Image during 2006 for the prior fiscal year, DECEMBER 31, 2006 THROUGH DECEMBER 29, 2007.

Table B: Total number of Stores included in calculations for Table B is <u>244.</u>

BASKIN-ROBBINS STORES (Excluding Combo Stores, Non-Traditional Outlets and Stores under Territorial Franchises. See Note 1)	Average Sales Per Store	Percent of all Stores that Meet or Exceed the Average Figure	Percentile Benchmarks (See Note 2)			
			25th	50th	75th	100th
Total Continental U.S.	$367,719	45.1%	$297,321	$350,299	$412,275	$951,031

BASKIN-ROBBINS *STANDALONE* STORES OPENED IN FISCAL YEAR 2006: The following financial performance representations are historical based on information from all existing *Baskin-Robbins Standalone* stores (exclusive of Combo Stores, Non-Traditional Outlets and Stores Operating under Territorial Franchises) that were initially opened for business under the new B31R Image during 2006 for the prior fiscal year, DECEMBER 31, 2006 THROUGH DECEMBER 29, 2007.

Table C: Total number of Stores included in calculations for Table C is 21.

BASKIN-ROBBINS STORES (Excluding Combo Stores, Non-Traditional Outlets and Stores under Territorial Franchises. See Note 1)	Average Sales Per Store	Percent of all Stores that Meet or Exceed the Average Figure	Percentile Benchmarks (See Note 2)			
			25th	50th	75th	100th
Total Continental U.S.	$323,740	57.14%	$277,800	$326,891	$348,459	$453,505

NOTES:

(1)   The stores used to provide the data listed in Tables B and C are subsets of the total stores used to provide the data in Table A. The sales data listed above includes average sales and the percentage of stores that meet or exceed the average. The percentage of stores that meet or exceed the average are based on stores that were opened for business during the entire year and actually attained or surpassed the stated average. This sales data does not include sales tax. The vast majority of the stores that comprise this data are franchised, although we may have a small number of company owned stores at any given time (see Item 20). The data listed in Tables A, B and C exclude data from (a) stores built in combination with our other affiliated concepts ("Combos"), (b) Alternative Points of Distribution ("APODs") (also known as Non-Traditional Outlets) and (c) stores sold under Territorial Franchise Agreements ("TFAs"), which may not follow the standard prototype for a traditional standalone store. APOD locations may be found within sports arenas, airports, schools, hospitals, military bases, service stations, transportation centers, home improvement stores, supermarkets and other non-traditional venues. Stores operating under a TFA include some, but not all stores located in the States of Arkansas, Georgia, Idaho, Kansas, Missouri, Mississippi, Montana, Nebraska, Oklahoma, Oregon, Tennessee and Washington.

(2)   "Percentile Benchmarks" show the highest sales figure in each quartile and means the following:

25th percentile means that 25% of the stores included in the Table are less than (or equal to) the stated amount and 75% are greater (or equal to) the stated amount.

50th percentile means that 50% of the stores included in the Table are less than (or equal to) the stated amount and 50% are greater (or equal to) the stated amount.

75th percentile means that 75% of the stores included in the Table are less than (or equal to) the stated amount and 25% are greater (or equal to) the stated amount.

The 100th percentile sales figure refers to the highest sales figure in the Table.

(3)   The sales figures from franchised stores are compiled by using sales that are reported to us by franchisees. We have not audited or verified the reports nor have franchisees confirmed that their reports are prepared in accordance with generally accepted accounting principles.

(4)   In some states or regions, sales volume may be significantly different for many reasons, such as areas where there is already a higher concentration of stores that have been in operation for a substantial period of time (which tend to have higher sales per store than stores located in states or regions with a lower concentration of stores that have been in operation for a shorter period of time). Stores operating in these higher concentration areas significantly increase the

overall average due to both their higher sales and their larger numbers. Therefore, the sales performance of stores outside of these higher concentration areas may not be commensurate with the overall average sales on a nationwide basis. Please see Item 20 of this FDD for the number of stores per state. We have not been able to draw conclusions regarding the role longevity may have played in achieving preeminence in a market, or whether the lack of longevity in a market may be a barrier to achieving preeminence. For example, competitors' customers may resist changing their buying habits. It is possible that preeminence may not be achieved in some higher concentration areas due to other reasons. When you have settled upon an area in which you wish to operate a store, please visit our offices and carefully review the substantiating sales data that we have for that region to get a better idea of sales volume in the area of most interest to you. Of course, we also encourage you to speak about sales volumes with franchisees that already operate stores in that region.

(5)   Many of the stores included in this data in Table A have been open and operating for several years. These franchisees have achieved their level of sales after spending many years building customer goodwill at a particular location.

(6)   Your sales will be affected by your own operational ability, which may include your experience with managing a business, your capital and financing (including working capital), continual training of you and your staff, customer service orientation, product quality, your business plan, and the use of experts (e.g., an accountant) to assist in your business plan.

(7)   Your sales may be affected by store location and site criteria, including traffic count and which side of the street your store is located on, local household income, residential and/or daytime populations, ease of ingress and egress, seating, parking, the physical condition of your store, the size of your site, and the visibility of your exterior sign(s). Your sales may be negatively affected by not adhering to our standards and system, including the above, and proper equipment layout, design and construction criteria, customer queuing and flow, and local store marketing.

(8)   Individual locations may have layouts and seating capacities that vary from the typical location.

(9)   Other factors that could have an affect upon your sales may include competition (national and local), inflation, local construction and its impact on traffic patterns, and reports on the health effects of consuming food similar to that served in the stores, as well as the impact of federal, state and local government regulations.

(10) Your sales may be affected by changes in the menu and regional differences in products including whether there are products not available to you or your region but sold in other regions. Menus are continually being revised, both adding and discontinuing products and product line extensions. Not all stores may have these new products. New products may not be successful for all stores. Marketing activity associated with new products may be at higher than normal levels and, therefore, sales increases may not be maintained after this temporary marketing activity is completed.

(11) Sales may be affected by fluctuations due to seasonality (particularly in colder climates), weather and periodic marketing and advertising programs. Inclement weather may cause temporary store closings in some areas.

(12) The store with the highest sales for the applicable category may have characteristics that are not available to you.

(13) The above data reflects historical sales. There is no assurance that future sales will correspond to historical sales.

(14) There are numerous factors that may affect sales at your store. The factors listed above and below are not an all-inclusive list of those factors.

THE DATA IN THE TABLES ABOVE RELATE ONLY TO SALES, AND DO NOT REFLECT COSTS, SUCH AS THE COST OF SALES, OPERATING EXPENSES (INCLUDING, FOR EXAMPLE, ROYALTIES, ADVERTISING FEES AND EXPENSES, SALARIES), OR OTHER COSTS OR EXPENSES THAT MUST BE DEDUCTED FROM THE GROSS REVENUE OR GROSS SALES FIGURES TO OBTAIN NET INCOME OR PROFIT. YOU SHOULD CONDUCT AN INDEPENDENT INVESTIGATION NOT ONLY OF POTENTIAL SALES VOLUMES, BUT ALSO ALL OF THE COSTS AND EXPENSES THAT YOU MAY INCUR IN OPERATING YOUR FRANCHISED BUSINESS. FRANCHISEES OR FORMER FRANCHISEES, WHO ARE LISTED IN THE DISCLOSURE DOCUMENT, MAY BE ONE SOURCE OF THIS INFORMATION. (PLEASE NOTE THAT WHILE TABLE C BELOW INCLUDES SOME COST INFORMATION, IT IS NOT MEANT TO PROVIDE INFORMATION ON ALL COSTS THAT YOU ARE LIKELY TO INCUR IN OPERATING A STORE.)

Many *Baskin-Robbins* franchisees actively pursue cake sales opportunities. If you do not, your sales may be negatively affected. Additionally, seasonality and weather may significantly affect sales of ice cream and related products.

DUNKIN' DONUTS/BASKIN-ROBBINS COMBO STORES

We do not make financial performance representations about Dunkin' Donuts/Baskin-Robbins Combo Stores.

We do not make any representations about a franchisee's future financial performance or the past financial performance of company-owned or franchised outlets. We also do not authorize our employees or representatives to make any such representations either orally or in writing. If you are purchasing an existing outlet, however, we may provide you with the actual records of that outlet. If you receive any other financial performance information or projections of your future income, you should report it to the franchisor's management by contacting our General Counsel, Stephen Horn, c/o Dunkin' Donuts/Baskin-Robbins, 130 Royall Street, Canton, MA 02021, 781-737-3000, the Federal Trade Commission, and the appropriate state regulatory agencies.

IF APPLICABLE, HISTORICAL SALES AND PROFIT DATA
FOR EXISTING STORE TO BE SOLD BY US

If the subject store is an existing store being sold by us, we may provide to you unaudited historical sales and profit data for the store. Statements prepared by us are prepared in accordance with generally accepted accounting principals. Statements prepared by past franchisee(s) of the store, if any, were submitted to us by franchisee(s) who we require to prepare statements in accordance with generally accepted accounting principals. We cannot assure you that in all cases they were so prepared.

Historical costs do not correspond to future costs because of such factors as inflation, changes in minimum wage laws, the local labor market, financing, real estate related costs and other variables. For example, actual costs such as rent, taxes, depreciation, amortization interest, insurance, payroll, and utilities may vary from historical costs. Historical sales may also not correspond to future sales because of such factors as the duration, if any, that the store was closed, changes in store management and employees, remodel or refurbishment, if any, over or under reporting of sales, changes in competition and other variables.

Your accountant should develop your own data for these accounts based on your particular financing and other costs. All information should be evaluated in light of current market conditions including such cost and price information as may then be available.

ACTUAL SALES, INCOME, GROSS OR NET PROFIT DATA RELATE TO THE PERFORMANCE OF THE FRANCHISED OR COMPANY-OWNED OPERATION OF THIS STORE DURING THE TIME PERIODS REPORTED AND SHOULD NOT BE CONSIDERED AS THE ACTUAL OR PROBABLE SALES, INCOME, GROSS OR NET PROFITS THAT YOU WILL REALIZE IF YOU PURCHASE AND

OPERATE THE SAME STORE. WE CAN NOT KNOW, AND THEREFORE WE DO NOT REPRESENT, WHETHER YOU WOULD REACH, FALL SHORT OF, OR EXCEED THE REPORTED LEVEL OF SALES, INCOME, GROSS OR NET PROFITS.

BIG APPLE BAGELS

500 Lake Cook Rd., # 475
Deerfield, IL 60015
Tel: (800) 251-6101 (847) 948-7520
Fax: (847) 948-7521
E-Mail: tcervini@babcorp.com
Web Site: www.babcorp.com
Mr. Anthony S. Cervini, Director of Development

Bakery-cafe featuring three brands, fresh-from-scratch Big Apple Bagels and My Favorite Muffin, and freshly roasted Brewster's specialty coffee. Our product offering covers many day parts with a delicious assortment of made-to-order gourmet sandwiches, salads, soups, espresso beverages, and fruit smoothies. Franchisees can develop beyond their stores with corporate catering and gift basket opportunities, as well as wholesaling opportunities within their market area.

BACKGROUND: IFA MEMBER
Established: 1992; 1st Franchised: 1993
Franchised Units: 136
Company-Owned Units: 1
Total Units: 137
Dist.: US-136; CAN-0; O'seas-1
  North America: 21 States, 0 Provinces
  Density: 8 in IL, 37 in MI, 19 in WI
Projected New Units (12 Months): 10

Qualifications: 3, 4, 3, 3, 3, 5
Registered:CA,DC,FL,HI,IL,IN,MD,MI,MN,ND,NY,OR,RI,SD, VA,WA,WI,AB

FINANCIAL/TERMS:
Cash Investment: $60K
Total Investment: $204.8-342.5K
Minimum Net Worth: $250K
Fees: Franchise - $25K
  Royalty - 5%; Ad. - 1%
Earnings Claims Statement: No
Term of Contract (Years): 10/10
Avg. # Of Employees: 3 FT, 11 PT
Passive Ownership: Allowed
Encourage Conversions: Yes
Area Develop. Agreements: Yes
Sub-Franchising Contracts: No
Expand In Territory: Yes
Space Needs: 1,600-1,900 SF; SC

SUPPORT & TRAINING:
Financial Assistance Provided: No
Site Selection Assistance: Yes
Lease Negotiation Assistance: Yes
Co-Operative Advertising: No
Franchisee Assoc./Member: No
Size Of Corporate Staff: 20
On-Going Support: C,D,E,F,G,H,I
Training: 2 Weeks Milwaukee, WI

SPECIFIC EXPANSION PLANS:
US: Yes, All United States
Canada: Yes, All Canada
Overseas: Yes, All Countries

19. <u>FINANCIAL PERFORMANCE REPRESENTATIONS</u>

The information included in the Table below is based on reports submitted to us by 118 fully-reporting franchised BAB Stores located in the United States that were operated for the entire 2007 Fiscal Year. The Franchised Stores include 109 BAB Production Stores and 9 BAB Satellite Stores (collectively the "Franchised Stores"). The Table does not include any company-owned or affiliate-owned stores. Any franchised BAB Store that either opened or closed during the 2007 Fiscal Year, or failed to submit all 52 weeks of reporting during the 2007 Fiscal Year, has been excluded from the information contained in this Table. The information was collected by us, but has not been independently audited or verified.

<u>TABLE</u>

Gross Revenues[1] of BAB Franchised Stores
By Quartile for 2007 Fiscal Year

QUARTILE[2]	GROSS REVENUE RANGE[3]	# FRANCHISEES REP-RESENTED
1st	$472,649 - $746,820	29
2nd	$335,312 - $424,650	30
3rd	$252,252 - $333,614	30
4th	$14,873 - $249,703	29

Notes:

1.   "Gross Revenues" is defined in the Franchise Agreement as the entire amount of all gross sales and business receipts, including direct or indirect barter transactions, catering accounts, proceeds of business interruption insurance policies, wholesale accounts (both on and off premises) arising out of the operation of the Store, or through or by means of the business conducted in connection therewith, whether for cash or credit, but excluding: (1) sales, use, or service taxes collected from customers and paid to the appropriate taxing authority; and (2) all bona fide customer refunds and approved rebates, discounts and allowances.

2.   Quartile. As used herein, "Quartile" refers to the relative performance of the Franchised Stores. Therefore, the "1st Quartile" refers to the top 25% performing Franchised Stores, based on Gross Revenues, the "2nd Quartile" refers to the next highest 25% performing Franchised Stores, and so on.

3.   Gross Revenues Range. The Table combines the Gross Revenues of all of the Franchised Stores for the 2007 Fiscal Year, and lists the high and low end of the Gross Revenues Range for each Quartile. There are 29 Franchised Stores in the 1st Quartile, 30 in the 2nd Quartile, 30 in the 3rd Quartile, and 29 in the 4th Quartile.

Material Bases and Assumptions

The Franchised Stores represented in the Table above are substantially similar to the concept being offered to you.

The Franchised Stores are primarily located in strip shopping centers, with a small percentage in free-standing locations.

The Gross Revenues are <u>NOT</u> net of costs of goods sold or other operating expenses. We have not provided information regarding costs and expenses because we do not regularly collect that data from franchisees and do not operate enough company-owned stores from which we could present reliable figures.

The financial performance representations in this Item 19 do not reflect the cost of sales, operating expenses, or other costs or expenses that must be deducted from the gross revenues figures to obtain your net income or profit. You will incur at least the following expenses, and possibly more: inventory, labor, occupancy costs, pre-opening expenses, depreciation and amortization, taxes, insurance, operating expenses, royalty fees to us, advertising fees to us, other fees to us as set forth in the Franchise Agreement, professional fees, bank charges, telephone, repairs. All of your expenses will affect the operating profit, net income and/or cash flow of your BAB Store and should be carefully considered and evaluated.

These financial performance representations do not necessarily reflect the actual Gross Revenues that you may experience. In addition, your results will vary depending on a number of factors which you should consider carefully in evaluating this information and in making any decision to purchase a franchise. These factors include: business skills, motivation, quality, effort, and effectiveness of the individual franchisee and of the franchisee's staff and management; the quality of your customer service; location of your Store; market conditions; weather and climate conditions; the effectiveness of your marketing efforts; the quality and effectiveness of your staff; income and demographic characteristics in your particular market area; the degree and quality of competition in your market area; number of years of operation; as well as conditions generally prevailing in the local and national economy, and, in particular, in your local market.

You should note that the information contained in these financial performance representations is not intended to express or infer an estimate, projection or forecast of income, sales, profits or earnings to be derived in connection with any particular franchise. We make no representation whether you will derive any specific level of Gross Revenues or profits. The financial performance representations should not be viewed as an assurance that you or any franchisee will attain the results shown above.

PROSPECTIVE FRANCHISEES OR SELLERS OF FRANCHISES SHOULD BE ADVISED THAT NO CERTIFIED PUBLIC ACCOUNTANT HAS AUDITED THESE FIGURES OR EXPRESSED HIS/HER OPINION WITH REGARD TO THEIR CONTENT OR FORM. THE AMOUNTS HAVE NOT BEEN AUDITED OR REVIEWED FOR REASONABLENESS BY INDEPENDENT AUDITORS.

THE RESULTS ABOVE ARE FOR BAB FRANCHISED STORES DURING A SPECIFIC PERIOD OF TIME AND SHOULD NOT BE CONSIDERED AS THE ACTUAL OR PROBABLE RESULTS THAT ANY FRANCHISEE WILL REALIZE. THERE IS NO ASSURANCE THAT FUTURE GROSS REVENUES WILL CORRESPOND TO GROSS REVENUES FROM THOSE REPORTED IN 2007 FISCAL YEAR. WE DO NOT REPRESENT THAT ANY FRANCHISEE CAN EXPECT TO ATTAIN THESE GROSS REVENUES. YOUR INDIVIDUAL RESULTS ARE LIKELY TO DIFFER FROM THE RESULTS SHOWN ABOVE.

YOU SHOULD CONDUCT AN INDEPENDENT INVESTIGATION OF THE COSTS AND EXPENSES YOU WILL INCUR IN OPERATING YOUR BAB STORE. WE ENCOURAGE YOU TO CONSULT WITH YOUR OWN ACCOUNTING, BUSINESS, AND LEGAL ADVISORS TO ASSIST YOU TO PREPARE YOUR BUDGETS AND PROJECTIONS, AND TO ASSESS THE LIKELY OR POTENTIAL FINANCIAL PERFORMANCE OF YOUR BAB STORE. WE ALSO ENCOURAGE YOU TO CONTACT EXISTING BAB STORE OPERATORS TO DISCUSS THEIR EXPERIENCES WITH THE SYSTEM AND THEIR STORE BUSINESS. EXISTING FRANCHISEES ARE YOUR BEST SOURCE OF INFORMATION.

SUBSTANTIATION OF THE DATA WE USED IN PREPARING THIS STATEMENT WILL BE MADE AVAILABLE UPON REASONABLE REQUEST.

EXCEPT FOR THE INFORMATION IN THIS ITEM 19, WE DO NOT FURNISH OR AUTHORIZE OUR SALESPERSONS TO FURNISH ANY ORAL OR WRITTEN INFORMATION CONCERNING THE ACTUAL OR POTENTIAL SALES, COSTS, INCOME OR PROFITS OF A BAB FRANCHISED STORE. ACTUAL RESULTS WILL VARY FROM BUSINESS TO BUSINESS, AND WE CANNOT ESTIMATE THE RESULTS OF ANY PARTICULAR FRANCHISE.

BOJANGLES' FAMOUS CHICKEN 'N BISCUITS

9432 Southern Pine Blvd.
Charlotte, NC 28273-5553
Tel: (800) 366-9921 (704) 527-2675
Fax: (704) 523-6803
E-Mail: cbailey@bojangles.com
Web Site: www.bojanglesfranchise.com
Mr. Chris Bailey, Dir. Franchise Development

BOJANGLES OPERATES DURING ALL 3 DAY-PARTS. Breakfast items are available all day long. Our menu in unique, and flavorful, with chicken prepared either spicy or traditional Southern-style. Restaurants operate in traditional locations and non-traditional locations in convenience stores.

BACKGROUND: IFA MEMBER

Established: 1977;	1st Franchised: 1979
Franchised Units:	263
Company-Owned Units:	147
Total Units:	410
Dist.:	US-402; CAN-0; O'seas-8
North America:	12 States, 0 Provinces
Density:	18 in GA, 130 in NC, 55 in SC
Projected New Units (12 Months):	50
Qualifications:	5, 4, 5, 3, 3, 5
Registered:	FL,IL,MD,VA

FINANCIAL/TERMS:

Cash Investment:	$500K
Total Investment:	$300K-1.5M
Minimum Net Worth:	$1M
Fees: Franchise -	$12-25K
Royalty - 4%;	Ad. - 1%
Earnings Claims Statement:	Yes
Term of Contract (Years):	20/10
Avg. # Of Employees:	20 FT, 25 PT
Passive Ownership:	Allowed, But Discouraged
Encourage Conversions:	Yes
Area Develop. Agreements:	Yes
Sub-Franchising Contracts:	No
Expand In Territory:	Yes
Space Needs: 3,000+ SF; FS, C-Store/Gas station, Airport, Sporting Venue	

SUPPORT & TRAINING:

Financial Assistance Provided:	No
Site Selection Assistance:	Yes
Lease Negotiation Assistance:	No
Co-Operative Advertising:	No
Franchisee Assoc./Member:	Yes/Member
Size Of Corporate Staff:	118
On-Going Support:	C,D,E,F,G,H,I
Training:	5 Weeks Training in Training Units

SPECIFIC EXPANSION PLANS:

US:	Yes, Southeast
Canada:	No
Overseas:	No

ITEM 19
FINANCIAL PERFORMANCE REPRESENTATIONS

The following tables reflect information about the past financial performance of a selected group of our Full-size and Express Restaurants which are franchise-owned and company-operated. This information consists of the sales and expenses shown for Restaurants operated, including those by our affiliate, Bojangles' Restaurants, Inc., continuously throughout our 2007 fiscal year which was January 1, 2007 through December 30, 2007. "Company-operated" Restaurants include (1) Restaurants owned by BJ Restaurant Development, LLC and BJ Georgia, LLC since our affiliate, Bojangles' Restaurants, Inc. operates these restaurants under a management agreement; and (2) Restaurants owned and operated by Bojangles' Restaurants, Inc. directly. Annual sales shown for franchised Restaurants may be based on our fiscal year or the calendar year depending on how a particular franchisee has reported sales. Restaurants outside the United States are not included in any of the disclosures contained in Item 19.

1. Full-Size Restaurants:[1]
Disclosed below is information concerning the gross sales of franchise-owned and company-operated full size Restaurants which were in operation continuously throughout the period January 1, 2007 through December 30, 2007.

2. Express Restaurants:[2]
Disclosed below is information concerning the gross sales of operating, franchised and com-

pany-operated Express Restaurants which were in operation continuously throughout the period January 1, 2007 through December 30, 2007.

"Gross Sales" used in all Tables include revenue received by the applicable Restaurant, but excludes all sales tax and non-cash discounts; or more simply, gross sales are cash sales received from franchise-owned and company-operated Restaurants. All Food and Paper and Direct Labor (including payroll taxes) expenses are shown as a percentage of Gross Sales from company-operated Restaurants.

I. FULL SIZE RESTAURANTS

TABLE A: Annual Gross Sales Range of Restaurants by State

State	Over $3,000,000 Franchise Owned	Over $3,000,000 Company Operated	Between $2,000,000 and $2,999,999 Franchise Owned	Between $2,000,000 and $2,999,999 Company Operated	Between $1,600,000 and $1,999,999 Franchise Owned	Between $1,600,000 and $1,999,999 Company Operated	Between $1,400,000 And $1,599,999 Franchise Owned	Between $1,400,000 And $1,599,999 Company Operated	Between $1,200,000 and $1,399,999 Franchise Owned	Between $1,200,000 and $1,399,999 Company Operated	Between $1,000,000 and $1,199,999 Franchise Owned	Between $1,000,000 and $1,199,999 Company Operated	Between $800,000 and $999,999 Franchise Owned	Between $800,000 and $999,999 Company Operated	Less than $800,000 Franchise Owned	Less than $800,000 Company Operated	Total Number of Restaurants Franchise Owned	Total Number of Restaurants Company Operated
North Carolina	10	0	49	4	21	23	7	19	7	28	8	14	3	7	1	0	106	95
South Carolina	0	0	0	2	1	2	2	5	13	9	4	7	6	7	0	0	26	32
Georgia	0	0	1	0	1	0	9	0	4	1	3	0	0	1	2	2	20	4
Virginia	0	0	1	0	4	0	1	0	1	0	2	0	1	0	2	0	12	0
Pennsylvania	0	0	0	0	0	0	1	0	0	0	0	0	0	0	0	0	1	0
Tennessee	0	0	0	0	0	0	2	0	3	0	4	0	2	0	1	0	12	0
Florida	0	0	0	0	0	0	0	0	1	0	0	0	0	0	0	0	1	0
Maryland	0	0	0	0	0	0	0	0	0	0	0	2	0	3	0	0	0	5
Alabama	0	0	0	0	0	0	0	0	0	0	1	0	0	0	0	0	1	0
Total	10	0	51	6	27	25	22	24	29	38	22	23	12	18	6	2	179	136

55

II. EXPRESS RESTAURANTS

TABLE B: Annual Gross Sales Range of Restaurants by State

State	Over 1,400,000		Between $1,200,000 and $1,399,999		Between $1,000,000 and $1,199,999		Between $800,000 and $999,999		Between $600,000 and $799,999		Less than $600,000		Total Number Of Restaurants	
	Franchise Owned	Company Operated	Franchise Owned	Company Operated	Franchise Owned	Company Operated	Franchise Owned	Company Operated	Franchise Owned	Company Operated	Franchise Owned	Company Operated	Franchise Owned	Company Operated
North Carolina	3	1	0	1	4	0	1	0	2	0	1	1	11	3
South Carolina	0	0	0	0	3	0	3	1	4	0	3	0	13	1
Georgia	0	0	0	0	1	0	2	0	2	0	3	0	8	0
Virginia	2	0	0	0	3	0	1	0	0	0	0	0	6	0
New York	0	0	0	0	0	0	0	0	0	0	1	0	1	0
Total	5	1	0	1	11	0	7	1	8	0	8	1	39	4

OF FRANCHISES SHOULD BE ADVISED THAT NO CERTIFIED PUBLIC ACCOUNTANT HAS AUDITED THESE FIGURES OR EXPRESSED HIS/HER OPINION WITH REGARD TO THE CONTENT OR FORM.

TABLE C: Summary of Gross Sales Ranges of Full-Size Restaurants by Percentage

Gross Sales	Percentage of Franchise-Owned Restaurants	Percentage of Bojangles'-Operated Restaurants	Percentage of All Restaurants
Over $3,000,000	5.60%	0%	3.17%
$2,000,000-$2,999,999	28.49%	4.41 %	18.10%
$1,600,000-$1,999,999	15.08%	18.38%	16.51 %
$1,400,000-$1,599,999	12.29%	17.65%	14.60%
$1,200,000-$1,399,999	16.20%	27.94%	21.27%
$1,000,000-$1,199,999	12.29%	16.91%	14.29%
$800,000-$999,999	6.70%	13.24%	9.52%
Under $800,000	3.35%	1.47%	2.54%

TABLE D: Summary of Gross Sales Ranges of Express Restaurants by Percentage

Gross Sales	Percentage of Franchise-Owned Restaurants	Percentage of Bojangles'-Operated Restaurants	Percentage of All Restaurants
Over $1,400,000	12.82%	25.00%	13.95%
$1,200,000 - $1,399,999	0%	25.00%	2.32%
$1,000,000 - $1,199,999	28.21%	0%	25.58%
$800,000 - $999,999	17.95%	25.00%	18.61%
$600,000 - $799,999	20.51%	0%	18.61%
Under $600,000	20.51%	25.00%	20.93%

TABLE E: Average Gross Sales of Full Size Restaurants

	Arithmetic	Median

Franchise	$1,752,862		$1,544,897
	Number Above Average	74	
	Number Below Average	105	
Company	$1,366,963		$1,333,724
	Number Above Average	60	
	Number Below Average	76	

TABLE F: Gross Sales Range of Full-Size Restaurants

	High	Low
Franchise	$3,764,671	$608,162
Company	$2,748,062	$738,778

TABLE G: Average Gross Sales of Express Restaurants

	Arithmetic		Median
Franchise	$891,600		$893,188
	Number Above Average	20	
	Number Below Average	19	
Company	$1,028,360		$920,207
	Number Above Average	2	
	Number Below Average	2	

TABLE H: Gross Sales Range of Express Restaurants

	High	Low
Franchise	$1,811,441	$93,976
Company	$1,429,279	$387,390

TABLE I: Selected Expenses of Company-Operated Restaurants[4]

Expense Category	Average Cost

Food and Paper	33.13%
Direct Labor (including payroll taxes)	27.58%

THESE FINANCIAL STATEMENTS ARE PREPARED WITHOUT AN AUDIT. PROSPECTIVE FRANCHISEES OR SELLERS OF FRANCHISES SHOULD BE ADVISED THAT NO CERTIFIED PUBLIC ACCOUNTANT HAS AUDITED THESE FIGURES OR EXPRESSED HIS/HER OPINION WITH REGARD TO THE CONTENT OR FORM.

Remarks and footnotes:

1.   The gross sales information from "Full-Size Restaurants" refers to domestic free-standing Restaurants which are 2,400 to 4,800 square feet that were in operation for the full 2007 fiscal year and not operated in connection with another business. We have excluded, in Tables A through I the following:

    a.   One Full-Size Restaurant that was acquired by franchisees from the Company during 2007and five full-size restaurants that were acquired by Company from Franchisees during 2007.

    b.   One Full-Size company-operated Restaurant and twenty-four Full-Size franchise-owned Restaurants that were not open a full year in 2007.

    c.   One Full-Size franchise-owned Restaurant that was closed during 2007.

2.   The gross sales information from "Express Restaurants" refers to restaurants operated and attached to another business such as a convenience store or a grocery store, generally 2,200 to 3,800 square feet, in operation for the full 2007 fiscal year. Also included in "Express Restaurants" are small unit Restaurants operated as part of a food court (one franchise- owned Restaurant and one company-operated Restaurant) and "drive-thru-only" Restaurants without interior seating (three franchise-owned Restaurants and one company-operated Restaurant). We have excluded in Tables A through I the following:

    a.   Three Express franchise-owned Restaurants that were closed during 2007.

3.   We relied on the royalty reports submitted by franchisees for their franchise-owned Restaurants and the internal reports prepared by company personnel for company-operated Restaurants, when preparing the information appearing in these tables. These results are unaudited, but we have no reason to question the accuracy of the reports submitted to us.

4.   The information concerning expenses of company-operated Restaurants that appears in Table I reflects the 2007 results of the 140 company-operated Restaurants whose results are reflected in Tables A through H. Both Full Size and Express company-operated Restaurants are included in Table I. No franchise results are contained in this chart. Food costs include costs of all food and food components, paper sold and condiments given at retail level, but excludes costs of supplies and uniforms. "Direct Labor (including payroll taxes)" includes the combined costs of management and crew labor, including payroll taxes, but excluding all other fringe benefits such as workers' compensation insurance premiums, health and insurance benefits, 401(k) and other retirement plans. Also excluded from "Direct Labor (including payroll taxes)" is the cost of multi-unit Restaurant supervision above store level. You will incur other costs in addition to this selected expense category described in Table I. We strongly recommend that you consult with your accountant and other business advisors to properly analyze and budget for your Restaurant's revenues and expenses. This chart contains information from Full-Size and Express Restaurants.

5.   The information contained in this Item 19 refers to specific franchise-owned and company-operated Restaurants, and should not be considered as the actual or potential sales or

costs that will be achieved by your Restaurant.

6.   We have written substantiation in our possession to support the information appearing in this Item 19. This substantiation will be made available by us to all prospective franchisees upon reasonable request.

7.   Except for the information contained in this Disclosure Document, we do not furnish or authorize our sales persons to furnish any oral or written information concerning the actual, average, projected or forecasted sales, income or profits of a company-operated or franchise-owned Full-Size Restaurant or Express Restaurant.

8.   Restaurants outside the United States are not included in any of the disclosures contained in Item 19.

BREADSMITH

BREADSMITH
HAND MADE. HEARTH BAKED.

BREADSMITH
409 E. Silver Spring Dr.
Whitefish Bay, WI 53217
Tel: (888) BREADS-1 (414) 962-1965
Fax: (414) 962-5888
E-Mail: lynn@breadsmith.com
Web Site: www.breadsmith.com
Ms. Lynn Pavlic, Support Specialist

Award-winning, European, hearth-bread bakery, featuring fresh-from-scratch crusty breads, scones, muffins, gourmet jams and oils. Open kitchen concept reveals a six-ton, stone hearth oven imported from Europe used to bake the hand-crafted loaves each morning. BREADSMITH has been ranked by Bon Appetit, Best in 11 cities across the country.

BACKGROUND: IFA MEMBER
Established: 1993;   1st Franchised: 1994
Franchised Units: 35
Company-Owned Units: 1
Total Units: 36
Dist.: US-36; CAN-0; O'seas-0
  North America: 10 States, 0 Provinces
  Density: 7 in IL, 10 in MI
Projected New Units (12 Months): 5
Qualifications: 4, 4, 2, 4, 4, 5

Registered: CA,FL,IL,IN,MI,MN,NY,OR,SD,VA,WA,WI

FINANCIAL/TERMS:
Cash Investment: $100-250K
Total Investment: $200-400K
Minimum Net Worth: $500K
Fees: Franchise - $30K
  Royalty - 7/6/5%; Ad. - 0%
Earnings Claims Statement: Yes
Term of Contract (Years): 15/15
Avg. # Of Employees: 6 FT, 12 PT
Passive Ownership: Not Allowed
Encourage Conversions: NA
Area Develop. Agreements: Yes
Sub-Franchising Contracts: No
Expand In Territory: Yes
Space Needs: 1,800 SF; FS,SF,SC

SUPPORT & TRAINING:
Financial Assistance Provided: Yes (D)
Site Selection Assistance: Yes
Lease Negotiation Assistance: Yes
Co-Operative Advertising: No
Franchisee Assoc./Member: Yes/Member
Size Of Corporate Staff: 10
On-Going Support: C,D,E,F,G,H,I
Training: 4 Weeks Corporate Store;
1 Week Franchisee Store

SPECIFIC EXPANSION PLANS:
US: Yes, All United States
Canada: Yes, All Canada
Overseas: No

Item 19
FINANCIAL PERFORMANCE REPRESENTATIONS
Statement of Actual Earnings

The following is an example of the actual sales, expenses and net income achieved by our affiliated company owned store in 2006. We selected this store because we believe that the sales level, retail and wholesale revenue ratios, and expense levels are representative of our system as a whole. We are not saying that you can expect to achieve these sales or profits in your first year, or at any time. Your revenues and expenses will vary significantly depending on a number of factors, including the location of your store and how you operate your business. In addition, this store is run by professionals in our company that have significant retail bakery experience. This store opened in 1998. It has approximately 2,250 square feet and is located in a strip center.

The revenues and expenses shown are actual numbers from this store, but we did not include expenses for royalties because our company owned store does not pay royalties. We also did not include expenses for interest, depreciation, amortization, income taxes, and owner's draw. However, we did include expenses for payroll for the store's managers and other employees.

A NEW FRANCHISEE'S INDIVIDUAL FINANCIAL RESULTS MAY SIGNIFICANTLY DIFFER FROM THE RESULTS STATED BELOW.

Revenues[1]			
Retail Sales	$	343,318	45.9%
Wholesale/Bulk Sales[2]	$	404,706	54.1%
Total Sales[3]	$	748,024	100.0%
Cost of Goods Sold			
Raw Materials	$	177,540	23.7%
Finished Goods	$	8,592	1.1%
Total Costs of Goods Sold	$	186,132	24.8%
Gross Profit	$	561,892	75.1%
Expenses			
Advertising & Promotion[4]	$	7,760	1.0%
Insurance	$	11,504	1.5%
Professional Fees	$	4,726	0.6%
Royalties[5]	$	-	0.0%
Office Supplies	$	1,045	0.1%
Management Payroll	$	41,478	5.5%
Shop Payroll [6]	$	247,784	33.1%
Payroll Taxes	$	24,627	3.3%
Employee Benefits	$	21,283	2.8%
Equipment Maintenance	$	2,279	0.3%
Bakery Maintenance	$	7,726	1.0%
Utilities	$	24,755	3.3%
Bakery Supplies	$	1,711	0.2%
Rent	$	50,099	6.7%
Property Taxes	$	577	0.1%
Vehicle[7]	$	7,509	1.0%
Telephone	$	1,756	0.2%
Trash	$	2,262	0.3%
Total Expenses[8]	$	491,242	65.7%

Net Income Before Royalties, interest, depreciation, amortization, and income Taxes	$ 70,650	9.5%

(1)   Because this store is a mature store, it has significant revenues from the sale of products at bulk and wholesale. While this store's performance did not place it in the top quartile among all our system stores for total revenue, it was higher than both mean and median store revenue performance.

(2)   A typical store performing at this level would expect to have approximately 50% of its sales from retail sales. Your store should not expect to have any bulk or wholesale revenues for at least the first 3 months you operate.

(3)   There are approximately 37,000 households located within 3 miles of this store. The average annual income of households within 3 miles of this store was approximately $100,000. This figure is higher than average. However, we believe that as long as the average household income surrounding a BREADSMITH bakery is equal to or higher than the average household income in the United States, the fact that one neighborhood may have a higher average income level than another will not materially affect store revenues.

(4)   We recommend you spend 2% of your sales for advertising and promotion. The store represented by this example spent less than we recommend. However, this store's advertising and promotional expenses were reduced by joint advertising within the Milwaukee market and these expenses equaled the recommended level.

(5)   Because the store is company owned, it does not pay royalties. You will initially pay a royalty of 7% on most items, but 5% on pre-packaged non-bakery items and on bulk and wholesale accounts. In the second year of operation, your 7% royalty decreases to 6% (and in the following year to 5%).

(6)   Payroll reflects wages paid to management and staff. The manager's salary was $37,000. Typically, our franchisees assume management responsibilities and the owner's salary is paid from any net income at the end of the year.

(7)   Initially, you should not need a vehicle in your business. Once you begin delivering bulk and wholesale orders, you will need a vehicle. Some franchisees use their personal vehicle, and therefore do not incur this expense. However, as sales increase, it is more likely you will need a separate vehicle for this business.

(8)   The total expenses do not include non-cash expenses such as depreciation or amortization. It also does not include interest and debt service payments because each store's interest and debt service costs will vary depending on how they finance their initial investment.

The following chart shows the actual sales ranges (including bulk and wholesale sales) for the 27 full service BREADSMITH bakery stores that were operating through all of 2007.

	Under $300*	$300*-$399	$400*-$499	$500*-$599	$600*-$699	$700*-$799	$800*-$899	$900*-$999	$1.0**-$1.09	$1.1**-$1.19	$1.2*-$1.59	$1.6**-and up
Percentage Of Stores In Range	11.11%	14.81%	14.81%	11.11%	7.41%	11.11%	7.41%	0.00%	3.70%	11.11%	3.70%	3.70%
Number of Stores In Range	3	4	4	3	2	3	2	0	1	3	1	1

* In thousands

** In millions

All of the information provided in the chart above was taken from unaudited financial reports provided to us by our individual franchise owners. We are not aware of any reason this information is not accurate, but we have not checked the information for accuracy. We recommend a particular accounting method or system to you. This system is consistent with generally accepted accounting principles. To the best of our knowledge, each of the stores that reported to us used this accounting method or system. Most of the stores in our system offer the same products as those you will offer in your store. However, there are stores that, with our consent, have added additional products.

If you want substantiation of any of the data or information we used in preparing the numbers in this Item 19, we will make it available to you upon reasonable request.

THESE STATEMENTS OF SALES, INCOME, GROSS OR NET PROFITS ARE BASED ON HISTORICAL RESULTS AND SHOULD NOT BE CONSTRUED AS THE ACTUAL OR PROBABLE SALES, INCOME, GROSS OR NET PROFITS THAT WILL BE REALIZED BY ANY FRANCHISEE. INDEED, SALES, INCOME, GROSS AND NET PROFITS CAN VARY SIGNIFICANTLY AMONG VARIOUS LOCATIONS. WE DO NOT REPRESENT THAT ANY FRANCHISEE CAN EXPECT TO ATTAIN ANY SPECIFIC LEVEL OF SALES, INCOME, GROSS OR NET PROFITS.

SEE ADDITION INFORMATION REGARDING THE EARNINGS CLAIMS IN THE ADDENDUM ATTACHED TO THIS DISCLOSURE DOCUMENT.

BRUEGGER'S

159 Bank St.
Burlington, VT 05401
Tel: (866) 660-4104 (802) 660-4020
Fax: (802) 660-4034
E-Mail: franchise@brueggers.com
Web Site: www.brueggers.com
Mr. Holly Ryan, Franchise Development Assistant

Our mission is to be the dominant, first choice, neighborhood bagel bakery in all markets where we operate.

BACKGROUND: IFA MEMBER
Established: 1983;   1st Franchised: 1993
Franchised Units: 103
Company-Owned Units: 155
Total Units: 258
Dist.:   US-258; CAN-0; O'seas-0
 North America: 18 States, 0 Provinces
 Density: 29 in MA, 35 in NY, 25 in OH
Projected New Units (12 Months):   25
Qualifications: 4, 3, 5, 1, 4, 5
Registered: CA,FL,IN,MD,MI,MN,ND,NY,RI,SD,VA,WA,WI

FINANCIAL/TERMS:

Cash Investment:	$100K
Total Investment:	$330.4K-559.4K
Minimum Net Worth:	$400K
Fees: Franchise -	$25K
Royalty - 5%;	Ad. - 2-4%
Earnings Claims Statement:	Yes
Term of Contract (Years):	10/5
Avg. # Of Employees:	FT, 0 PT
Passive Ownership:	Not Allowed
Encourage Conversions:	Yes
Area Develop. Agreements:	Yes
Sub-Franchising Contracts:	No
Expand In Territory:	Yes
Space Needs:	1,500-2,200 SF; RM

SUPPORT & TRAINING:

Financial Assistance Provided:	No
Site Selection Assistance:	Yes
Lease Negotiation Assistance:	No
Co-Operative Advertising:	No
Franchisee Assoc./Member:	No
Size Of Corporate Staff:	20
On-Going Support:	a,b,C,D,E,f,G,H
Training:	NR

SPECIFIC EXPANSION PLANS:

US:	Yes, All United States
Canada:	No
Overseas:	No

ITEM 19
FINANCIAL PERFORMANCE REPRESENTATIONS

In this Item we provide information about the actual operating results of franchised and Company- owned Bakeries. Table 1 provides average Bakery revenue information for franchised and Company-owned Bakeries during fiscal year 2007. "Bakery revenue" means Gross Sales (as defined in Item 6) plus the dollar value of coupons redeemed at the Bakery and the dollar value of other sales discounts given by the Bakery. Table 2 presents selected cost information, for Company-owned Bakeries only, during fiscal year 2007.

TABLE 1 - AVERAGE BAKERY REVENUE FOR THE 52-WEEK PERIOD ENDING DECEMBER 26, 2007

Average for 146 Company-owned Bakeries	$699,296
Average for 95 Franchised Bakeries	$714,603

The figures in Table 1 are the mean averages of the reported annual Bakery revenue of 146 Company- owned Bakeries and 95 Franchised Bakeries open during the entire 52-week reporting period ending December 26, 2007. We have excluded from this calculation 12 Company-owned bakeries that were either not open for the full year or were acquired by BEI during the year. We also excluded 10 Franchised Bakeries that were not open for the full year. The 146 Company-owned Bakeries had 2007 Bakery revenue ranging from $299,114 to $1,320,831, and 71 of them (49%) attained or surpassed the average of $683,450 in Bakery revenue. The 95 Franchised Bakeries had Bakery revenue ranging from $268,503 to $1,301,422 and 48 of them (50%) attained or surpassed the average of $714,603 in Bakery revenue.

The figures in Tables 1 reflects average Bakery revenue and not profits. Revenue is not necessarily indicative of profits.

TABLE 2 - SELECTED AVERAGE COSTS FOR 146 COMPANY-OWNED BAKERIES FOR 52-WEEK PERIOD ENDING DECEMBER 25, 2007

Table 2 presents selected average costs of 146 Company-owned Bakeries during the fiscal year ending December 25, 2007, presented both as a dollar average and as a percentage of average Bakery revenue. The table excludes 12 Company-owned Bakeries that we either opened or acquired during the year.

The results incorporated in Table 2 are the arithmetic average result of all 146 Company-owned Bakeries. The Bakeries whose financial data are incorporated in Table 2 have been open for an average of more than 12 years; none has been open less than one year. In our experience, Bakeries that have been open more than a year perform better than Bakeries that have been open less than a year.

Company-owned Bakery Financial Data (1) For the Fiscal Year Ending December 25, 2007			
	See Note:	Average Amount per Bakery	% of average bakery revenue
Bakery Revenue		699,296	100.0%
COGS	(2)	191,824	27.4%
Payroll Operating	(3)	198,424	28.4%

Expenses	(4)	74,685	10.7%
Margin to Point	(5)	234,363	33.5%

1.   The data shown are limited to the 2007 results of Company-owned Bakeries that were open for the full fiscal year ending December 25, 2007. The table excludes 9 Company-owned Bakeries that opened during the year and 3 that were acquired from a franchisee. Although we know of no material differences between the operations of Company-owned Bakeries and Bakeries owned by franchisees, no franchisee Bakeries are included in Table 2.

2.   Cost of Goods Sold (COGS) represents food, beverage and paper products used when serving guests. As noted in Item 8, the Company-owned Bakeries purchase certain food, beverage, and paper products for their Bakeries from commissaries that BEI operates. In order to more accurately reflect the COGS, the financial results of operation of the commissaries were added to COGS. The allocation is of the commissary's operating gain or loss before interest, depreciation, amortization, and state and federal income taxes.

As noted in Item 8, we have negotiated contracts with vendors of certain products under which Company- owned Bakeries and franchisees' Bakeries may qualify for volume discounts based on total purchases by our franchise system. There is no assurance that these discounts will continue to be available. Without these discounts, the COGS in Table 4 would have been higher. The cost of items that must be purchased locally, such as fresh produce, will vary according to the location of the Bakery.

3.   Payroll includes the actual salaries, wages, and related expenses incurred by Company-owned Bakeries included in Table 2. This includes the costs of the general manager, assistant managers, crew, payroll taxes, vacation benefits, the employer portion of group health benefits, workers' compensation expenses, and bonuses for Bakery personnel. Salaries, wages and related payroll expenses vary substantially depending on the geographic location of the Bakery, demands on the local labor pool, state and federally mandated minimum wage laws, and the level of benefits (i.e., medical insurance, vacation and bonuses) provided.

4.   Operating Expenses include costs of utilities (e.g. gas, electric and telephone), restaurant supplies, repairs and maintenance, uniforms, smallwares, security, and outside service contracts (e.g., trash collection, equipment service, music rental, cleaning supplies, and janitorial and linen services). These costs are subject to local market conditions and vary depending on the geographic location of the Bakery. The figures do not include $798,900 of expenses we incurred for the grand openings of 13 acquired and new Company-owned Bakeries in 2007.

5.   "Margin to Point" means the excess of average Bakery revenue over average COGS, Payroll, and Operating Expenses (as those terms are defined in footnotes 3, 4, and 5 above), before taking into account additional costs that you will incur. These additional expenses include, among other things, initial franchise fees and franchise royalties; NAC contributions and local marketing expenses and costs of promotional discounts; grand opening expenses; rent and related occupancy charges; depreciation and amortization; interest expense; equipment leasing costs; allocation of corporate and regional overhead; non-Bakery payroll and related expenses; accounting and legal fees; general insurance; and federal and state income taxes. We strongly encourage you to consult with your financial advisors in estimating the categories and amount of additional expenses that you will incur. We currently require you to spend 3.25% of Gross Sales on Marketing Expenses, which consists of 2% for local Bakery marketing and 1.25% for your contribution to the NAC. You will incur occupancy costs which will vary depending upon your specific circumstances, e.g., whether you rent or own and the size of your Bakery.

THE INFORMATION IN TABLES 1 AND 2 SHOULD NOT BE CONSIDERED. TO BE THE ACTUAL OR PROBABLE RESULTS THAT YOU WILL REALIZE. YOUR RESULTS WILL LIKELY DIFFER FROM THESE RESULTS. WE DO NOT REPRESENT THAT YOU WILL ATTAIN COMPA-

RABLE RESULTS.

We obtained the Bakery revenue data for the Company-owned Bakeries in Tables 1 and 2 from BEI's internal operating records. We obtained the Bakery revenue data for the Franchised Bakeries from the financial reports submitted by the franchisees for the purpose of computing royalties. We have not independently verified the information furnished to us by the franchisees for use in Table 1. Neither the information furnished to us nor the figures in Tables 1 and 2 have been audited. You may wish to consult a financial advisor or an accountant to help you determine how to interpret the information contained in this Item. The raw data that we used in preparing Tables 1 and 2 is available to you upon reasonable request; however, we reserve the right to delete identifying information in order to protect the confidentiality of the franchisees involved.

Except for the information presented above, we do not make information available to prospective franchisees concerning actual, average, projected, or forecasted sales, costs, profits, or earnings. We specifically instruct our sales personnel, agents, employees, and officers that, other than as set forth in this Item, they are not permitted to make any claims or statements as to the sales, costs, or profits, or prospects or chances of success, nor are they authorized to represent or estimate dollar figures as to your operation.

Actual operating results are dependent on a variety of internal and external factors, some of which neither we nor you can estimate, including competition, taxes, the availability of financing, general economic climate, demographics, and changing consumer preferences. Sales can very significantly between locations and regions.

Actual operating costs and expenses for a Bakery may vary considerably and be different from those disclosed above as a result of higher food and distribution costs, labor shortages, and competitive real estate markets, among other factors. Additionally, distribution costs in those areas of the country not currently serviced by a commissary, approved suppliers or distributors may be higher.

We recommend that you make your own independent investigation to determine whether or not the franchise may be profitable. We urge you to discuss our business with existing franchisees and consult with an attorney and other advisors before executing any agreement.

BURGER KING CORPORATION

5505 Blue Lagoon Dr.
Miami, FL 33126
Tel: (866) 546-4252
Fax: (305) 378-7721
E-Mail: franchiseinquiry@whopper.com
Web Site: www.burgerking.com
Ms. Silvie Jordan, VP Franchise Development

Our Vision: We proudly serve the best burgers in the business, plus a variety of real, authentic foods - all freshly prepared - just the way you want it! BURGER KING® Corporation operates more than 11,220 restaurants in all 50 states and in 60 countries around the world. 90% of the BURGER KING® restaurants are owned and operated by independent franchisees, many of them family-owned operations that have been in business for decades.

BACKGROUND:	IFA MEMBER
Established: 1954;	1st Franchised: 1961
Franchised Units:	10144
Company-Owned Units:	1079
Total Units:	11223
Dist.:	US-7679; CAN-460; O'seas-3084
North America:	50 States, 9 Provinces
Density:	NR
Projected New Units (12 Months):	NR
Qualifications:	NA
Registered:CA,DC,FL,HI,IL,IN,MD,MI,MN,NY,ND,OR,RI,SD,	
	VA,WA,WI,AB

FINANCIAL/TERMS:

Cash Investment:	Varies
Total Investment:	$294K-2.8M
Minimum Net Worth:	$1.5MM

Fees: Franchise -	$50K	Financial Assistance Provided:	Yes (D)
Royalty - 4.5%;	Ad. - 4%	Site Selection Assistance:	Yes
Earnings Claims Statement:	Yes	Lease Negotiation Assistance:	Yes
Term of Contract (Years):	20	Co-Operative Advertising:	No
Avg. # Of Employees:	15 FT, 35 PT	Franchisee Assoc./Member:	Yes/Member
Passive Ownership:	Allowed	Size Of Corporate Staff:	928
Encourage Conversions:	Yes	On-Going Support:	B,C,D,E,F,H
Area Develop. Agreements:	0	Training:	400 Hours Restaurant;
Sub-Franchising Contracts:	No		300 Hours Classroom
Expand In Territory:	Yes	**SPECIFIC EXPANSION PLANS:**	
Space Needs:	3,600 SF; FS,SF,RM	US:	Yes, All United States
		Canada:	Yes, All Canada
SUPPORT & TRAINING:		Overseas:	Yes, All Countries

Item 19
FINANCIAL PERFORMANCE REPRESENTATIONS

This Item includes certain information about (a) gross sales of franchised and BKC-operated BURGER KING Restaurants during the 12-month period ended June 30, 2008 ("Sales Distributions"), and (b) selected cost factors for certain BKC-operated BURGER KING Restaurants during that period ("Cost Factors"). Sales Distributions are provided separately for "Traditional Restaurants," "Non-Traditional Restaurants," and four types of "Fuel Co-Branded Restaurants," as those terms are used for purposes of this Item. Cost Factors are provided only for BKC-owned "Traditional Restaurants." For purposes of this Item, "Non-Traditional Restaurants" include the following types of BURGER KING Restaurants:

(1) Limited menu in-line facilities;
(2) Restaurants or food courts at institutional locations (such as airports, military facilities, colleges, schools, hospitals, office buildings, retail stores, tourist locations, and turnpikes; see Item 1);
(3) Conversion Restaurant facilities;
(4) Double drive-thru facilities;
(5) Mall location facilities; and
(6) Mobile restaurant units (buses/trailers).

For purposes of this Item, "Traditional Restaurants" are all Restaurants other than those included as "Non- Traditional Restaurants". There were 5,666 Burger King franchised restaurants and 739 BKC-operated Burger King Restaurants during the 12-month period ended June 30, 2008.

The Sales Distributions and Cost Factors presented here do not reflect the sales distributions or cost factors of all the varying facility types or sizes or facility locations.

The Sales Distributions and Cost Factors should be read together with all of the related information about the factual bases and material assumptions underlying them. BKC will make available to you, on reasonable request, data used in preparing the Sales Distributions and Cost Factors, in a form that does not identify any individual franchised Restaurant.

Your individual financial results are likely to differ from the results shown in the Sales Distributions and Cost Factors. In providing the Sales Distributions and Cost Factors, BKC is not making a representation or guarantee that you will or may achieve any level of sales shown in the Sales Distributions or experience costs comparable to those shown in the Cost Factors. BKC does not make any representation or guarantee of future sales, costs, income or profits.

Other than the Sales Distributions and Cost Factors presented in this Item, or as described below in connection with the sale by BKC of a Restaurant, BKC does not furnish, or authorize the furnishing, to prospective Franchisees of any oral or written information of actual, potential, average or projected sales, costs, income or profits of BURGER KING restaurants. If you obtain this information, do not rely on it because it is intended for internal use only by BKC as a basis for BKC's own investment decisions.

You should construct your own pro forma cash flow statement and make your own projections concerning potential sales, operating costs, total capital investment requirements, cash injection, debt, overall potential cash flow, and other financial aspects of operating a BURGER KING Restaurant. You should not rely solely on information provided by BKC, but should conduct your own independent investigation of costs and sales potential for your proposed Restaurant. You should consult an accountant, attorney and existing BURGER KING Franchisees.

The data used in preparing the Sales Distributions and Cost Factors have been prepared on a basis consistent with generally accepted accounting principles to the extent applicable; BKC has not independently confirmed gross sales reported by Franchisees for Franchisee-owned Restaurants, but has relied on gross sales as reported by Franchisees.

THE REVENUE FIGURES IN THIS ITEM 19 DO NOT REFLECT THE COSTS OF SALES, OPERATING EXPENSES, OR OTHER COSTS OR EXPENSES THAT MUST BE DEDUCTED FROM THE GROSS REVENUE OR GROSS SALES FIGURES TO OBTAIN YOUR NET INCOME OR PROFIT. YOU SHOULD CONDUCT AN INDEPENDENT INVESTIGATION OF THE COSTS AND EXPENSES YOU WILL INCUR IN OPERATING YOUR BURGER KING® RESTAURANT. FRANCHISEES OR FORMER FRANCHISEES, LISTED IN THIS DISCLOSURE DOCUMENT, MAY BE ONE SOURCE OF THIS INFORMATION.

<u>Sale of Restaurants Operated by BKC</u>

From time to time BKC may offer certain of its company operated restaurants for sale. In connection with the sale of a BURGER KING Restaurant operated by BKC, BKC gives the prospective purchaser certain historical financial information for the specific Restaurant(s) being sold. This historical financial information is given only to the potential purchaser of that Restaurant. BKC also provides the prospective purchaser with the name and last known address of each owner of the Restaurant during the 5 years preceding the sale.

The following historical financial information is provided on the offered Restaurant(s): (1) 24 months of gross sales of the specific Restaurant (in some cases, the Restaurant may have been operated by a franchisee for part of the 24-month period); and (2) if available, an unaudited operating statement of actual sales and expenses of BKC's own operation of the Restaurant for 13 months or a shorter period. The operating statement is prepared on a basis consistent with generally accepted accounting principles, except for the following:

> It excludes depreciation, occupancy, general and administrative expenses.
> It is prepared on a pre-tax basis, except for the labor line, which includes any targeted job tax credit.
> Since BKC is primarily a self-insured company, the casualty line may not reflect the fully allocated insurance cost.

ACTUAL SALES ARE OF SPECIFIC COMPANY-OWNED AND OPERATED RESTAURANTS AND FRANCHISED RESTAURANTS AND DO NOT INDICATE THE ACTUAL OR PROBABLE SALES, THAT YOU MAY OR WILL REALIZE. ACTUAL EXPENSES ARE OF SPECIFIC COMPANY-OWNED AND OPERATED RESTAURANTS AND DO NOT REPRESENT THE ACTUAL OR PROBABLE EXPENSES THAT YOU MAY OR WILL INCUR. BKC DOES NOT REPRESENT THAT YOU CAN EXPECT TO GAIN ANY LEVEL OF SALES, EXPENSE, INCOME, OR GROSS OR NET PROFITS.

SALES DISTRIBUTION (1)
"TRADITIONAL" AND "NON-TRADITIONAL" RESTAURANTS
JULY 1, 2007 - JUNE 30, 2008
Percentage of Restaurants at Sales Level

Annual Sales Level - Range	"TRADITIONAL" (2)			"NON-TRADITIONAL" (3)		
	Consolidated	Company*	Franchise	Consolidated	Company*	Franchise
Above $1,500000	23%	22%	24%	21%	32%	20%
$1,300,000 - $1,499,999	18%	19%	18%	10%	5%	10%
$1,100,000 - $1,299,999	24%	27%	23%	10%	21%	10%
$900,000 - $1,099,999	22%	22%	21%	18%	21%	18%
$700,000 - $899,999	11%	8%	11%	17%	11%	17%
$500,000 - $699,999	3%	2%	3%	15%	11%	15%
$300,000 - $499,999	0%	0%	0%	6%	0%	6%
Below $300,000	0%	0%	0%	4%	0%	4%
Total Restaurants in Sample	**6,405**	**739**	**5,666**	**504**	**19**	**485**

* Includes JV data

	Consolidated	Company*	Franchise	Consolidated	Company*	Franchise
Mean Average Sales	$1,222,275	$1,269,305	$1,272,406	$1,159,968	$1,330,243	$1,152,961
Median Average Sales	$1,271,709	$1,231,699	$1,221,334	$981,109	$1,156,704	$973,345
High Annual Sales		$2,617,692	$5,469,466		$2,863,766	$6,367,136
Low Annual Sales		$533,320	$281,496		$637,535	$44,095

The sales levels, sales ranges and median sales shown above reflect the experience of certain franchised and BKC-operated Restaurants and should not be considered as the actual or potential sales that you will realize. BKC does not represent that you can expect to attain any particular sales level.

Notes:

(1)   The information provided in this Sales Distribution excludes Restaurants that have been transferred from/to a Franchisee.

(2)   The information provided in this Sales Distribution is sales information for a total of 6,405 Restaurants treated as "Traditional" Restaurants for purposes of this Item. Of those Restaurants, 5,666 were Franchisee-owned and 739 were BKC-owned as of June 30, 2008. Only those Restaurants with 12 months of actual sales as of June 30, 2008 are reported in this chart.

(3)   The information provided in this Sales Distribution is sales information for a total of 504 Restaurants treated as "Non-Traditional" Restaurants for the purposes of this Item. Of those Restaurants, 485 were operated by Franchisees and 19 were operated by BKC as of June 30, 2008. Only those Restaurants with 12 months of actual sales as of June 30, 2008 are reported in this chart.

Sales Distributions for Fuel Co-Branded Restaurants Basis for Presentation

The Sales Distributions for Fuel Co-Branded BURGER KING Restaurants present certain information about annual gross sales of Fuel Co-Branded Restaurants during the 12 months ended June 30, 2008. For purposes of this presentation, a "Fuel Co-Branded Restaurant" is a BURGER KING Restaurant attached to a branded gas station, other than truck stops and gas stations at travel plazas on interstate highways. In many instances, a convenience store is also located at the Co-Branded Restaurant. Separate Sales Distributions are given for four categories of Fuel Co-Branded Restaurants, distinguished by size and seating capacity. These four categories are as follows:

Category	Approximate Size / Seating Capacity
"Full Size"	2300 square feet and larger; seats 70-130
"Large In-Line"	1500 - 2300 square feet; seats 40-70
"Small In-Line"	1200 - 1500 square feet; seats 30-40
"Kiosk"	200 - 1200 square feet; seats 0 - 30

The Sales Distribution for each category reflects the gross sales of all Restaurants in that category that were open for the full 12 months ended June 30, 2008. All Fuel Co-Branded Restaurants whose gross sales are reflected in the Sales Distributions are franchised Restaurants, and gross sales reflect gross sales as reported by the Franchisees. Such reported gross sales have not been independently verified by BKC.

Sales Distributions
Fuel Co-Branded Restaurants
July 1, 2007 - June 30, 2008

	FULL SIZE		LARGE IN-LINE(1)	
Annual Sales Level-Range	Number of Franchised Restaurants	Percentage of Total	Number of Franchised Restaurants	Percentage of Total
$1,500,000 and above	12	12%	8	8%
$1,300,000 - $1,499,999	14	14%	7	7%
$1,100,000-$1,299,999	21	20%	15	14%
$900,000 - $1,099,999	26	25%	25	24%
$700,000 - $899,999	22	21%	41	39%
$500,000 - $699,999	8	8%	9	8%
Below $500,000	0	0%	1	1%
Total Restaurants in Sample	103	100%	106	100%
Mean Average Sales	$ 1,104,006		$ 988,405	
Median Sales	$ 1,059,568		$ 907,958	
High Annual Sales	$ 2,068,004		$ 1,995,457	
Low Annual Sales	$ 501,413		$ 441,121	

Notes:

(1) Of the 113 Large In-Line Fuel Co-Branded Restaurants opened as of June 30, 2007, 7 were excluded because they were not open for the full 12 months ended June 30, 2008.

Sales Distributions
Fuel Co-Branded Restaurants
July 1, 2007 - June 30, 2008

Annual Sales Level-Range	SMALL IN-LINE		KIOSK (2)	
	Number of Franchised Percentage of Restaurants Total		Number of Franchised Restaurants	Percentage of Total
$1,500,000 and above	0	0%	0	0%
$1,300,000 - $1,499,999	0	0%	3	17%
$1,100,000- $1,299,999	2	12%	2	11%
8900,000 - $1,099,999	6	35%	3	17%
$700,000 - $899,999	3	18%	6	33%
$500,000 - $699,999	6	35%	3	17%
Below $500,000	0	0%	1	6%
Total Restaurants in Sample	17	100%	18	100%
Mean Average Sales	$ 822,574		$ 937,630	
Median Sales	$ 775,442		$ 862,284	
High Annual Sales	$ 1,174,323		$ 1,484,704	
Low Annual Sales	$ 504,927		$ 499,402	

Notes:

(1)   Of the 19 Kiosk Fuel Co-Branded Restaurants opened as of June 30, 2008, 1 was excluded because it was not open for the full 12 months ended June 30, 2008.

Sales Distributions
New Free Standing Restaurant Openings
July 1, 2003 – June 30, 2007

During the fiscal year ended June 30, 2007, 46 Traditional Freestanding BURGER KING restaurants were opened by franchisees and BKC in the United States ("FY07 New Restaurants"). These FY07 New Restaurants had all been opened for at least 12 months as of June 30, 2008. The FY08 average restaurant sales ("ARS") for the FY07 New Restaurants was $1,396,115. Of these FY07 New Restaurants, 18 (or 39%) were above the average. The FY08 ARS for these FY07 New Restaurants is 14.2% higher than the FY08 ARS for all US Traditional BURGER KING restaurants open for at least 12 months as of June 30, 2008. The standard deviation of the average is $383,872.

A total of 109 Traditional Freestanding BURGER KING Restaurants were opened by BKC and our franchisees in the United States between July 1, 2003 and June 30, 2007 (the "New Restaurants"). The FY08 ARS for these New Restaurants for the 12-month period ended June 30, 2007 was $1,468,508. Of these restaurants, 47 (or 43%) had sales above that average. The FY08 ARS for these New Restaurants is 20.1% higher than the FY08 ARS for all US Traditional BURGER KING restaurants open for at least 12 months as of June 30, 2008. The standard deviation of the average is $414,751.

The gross sales average shown above reflects the experience of certain franchised and BKC-operated Restaurants and should not be considered as the actual or potential sales that you will realize. BKC does not represent that you can expect to attain any particular sales level and you should not make any such assumption.

1Standard deviation is the most common method for describing how dispersed or spread out around the mean average a group of data points are. The standard deviations for these sales numbers is high because some of the restaurants had uncommonly high ARS.

Sales Distributions
Scrape and Rebuilds[1]
July 1, 2003 — June 30, 2007

During the fiscal year ended June 30, 2007, 8 BURGER KING BKL Restaurants were scraped and rebuilt in the United States ("FY07 Scrape and Rebuilds"). As of June 30, 2008, these FY07 Scrape and Rebuilds had all been operating for at least 12 months after their scrape and rebuild was completed. When comparing the sales of these restaurants in the 12 months prior to the scrape and rebuild to the sales of these restaurant in the 12 months after the scrape and rebuild, the average sales increase has been 33%. Of these restaurants, 3 (or 37.5%) had a sales increase higher than that average. Of these 8 restaurants, the increases were 15.4%, 19.4%, 23.5%, 25.0%, 32.4%, 35.1%, 36.5%, and 74.6% respectively.

A total of 24 BURGER KING BKL. Restaurants were scraped and rebuilt in the United States between July 1, 2003 and June 30, 2007 (the "Scrape and Rebuild Restaurants"). As of June 30, 2008, these Scrape and Rebuilds had all been operating for at least 12 months after their scrape and their rebuild was completed. When comparing the sales of these restaurants in the 12 months prior to the scrape and rebuild to the sales of these restaurant in the 12 months after the scrape and rebuild, the average sales increase has been 35%. Of these restaurants, 11 (or 45.8%) had a sales increase higher than that average.

[1] A scrape and rebuild is a major remodeling done on a BURGER KING restaurant, typically when it is being successored for a new 20 year franchise term. The restaurant may be scraped to the bare wall or torn down and repositioned on the site before it is remodeled.

Sales Distributions
Remodels[1]
July 1, 2003 —June 30, 2007

During the fiscal year ended June 30, 2007, 16 BURGER KING BKL restaurants were remodeled in the United States ("FY07 Remodels"). As of June 30, 2008, these FY07 Remodels had all been operating for at least 12 months after their remodel was completed. When comparing the sales of these restaurants in the 12 months prior to the remodel to the sales of these restaurants in the 12 months after the remodel, the average sales increase has been 14%. Of these restaurants, 8 (or 33.3%) had a sales increase higher than that average.

A total of 56 BURGER KING BKL Restaurants were remodeled in the United States between July 1, 2003 and June 30, 2007 (the "Remodel Restaurants"). As of June 30, 2008, these Remodel Restaurants had all been operating for at least 12 months after their remodel was completed. When comparing the sales of these restaurants in the 12 months prior to the remodel to the sales of these restaurants in the 12 months after the remodel, the average sales increase has been 15%. Of these restaurants, 19 (or 33.9%) had a sales increase higher than that average.

[1] A Remodel for purposes of this disclosure is defined as any BURGER KING restaurant remodeling project that costs more than $200,000 but is not a scrape and rebuild project (see Scrape and Rebuild above).

Comparable Sales[1]
July 1, 2006-June 30, 2008

At the end of the fiscal year ending June 30, 2007, comparable sales at BURGER KING restaurants in the U.S. were positive 3.7% when compared to the prior fiscal year ending June 30, 2006 ("FY07"). Of the 7,185 restaurants included in the comparison. 3,380 or 47.0% had comparable sales equal to or above the system average. At the end of the fiscal Year ended June 30, 2008, comparable sales at BURGER KING restaurants in the U.S. were positive 5.6% when compared to the prior fiscal year ending June 30, 2007 ("FY08"). Of the 7,146 restaurants included in the comparison 3,543 or 49.6% had comparable sales equal to or above the system average.

[1] Comparable Sales for purposes of this disclosure is determined by comparing the average restaurant sales from one fiscal year to prior fiscal year and using only restaurants that were open at least one full year as of June 30, 2007 with respect to the 2006 - 2007 comparison and as of June 30, 2008 with respect to the 2007 - 2008 comparison.

CERTAIN REPRESENTATIVE COST FACTORS FOR BKC-OPERATED TRADITIONAL RESTAURANTS JULY 1, 2007 - JUNE 30, 2008

TYPE OF EXPENSE/COST[1]	FIXED COST	VARIABLE COST AS % OF GROSS SALES
Food & Paper	$ -	31.5%
Labor Including Fringe Benefits[2]	$ 206,145	14.4%
Repair & Maintenance (Building & Equipment)[3]	$ 21,550	0.7%
Utilities[4]	$ 25,567	3.0%
Other Expenses[5]	$ 23,779	2.2%
Insurance	$ 17,009	N/A
Property Taxes	$ 19,921	N/A
Royalty	N/A	N/A
Advertising	N/A	4.6%

BASIS OF PRESENTATION

The financial information provided in this Cost Factor table is based upon regression analysis of certain actual operating costs for the 12-month period ended June 30, 2008, experienced by 704 "Traditional Restaurants" that were open and operated by BKC for those 12 months. Restaurants sold or acquired by BKC during that time period and Restaurants that were closed for any time during that period are not included in the sample on which the analysis was performed.

Dollar amounts are given in the "Fixed Cost" column for those items with a significant fixed cost component. Variable costs are shown as a representative percentage of gross sales. Certain expense items for which information is provided have both a fixed cost and variable cost component as reflected by the regression analysis.

THESE COST FACTORS ARE BASED UPON THE EXPERIENCE OF BKC-OPERATED TRADITIONAL RESTAURANTS AND SHOULD NOT BE CONSIDERED AS THE ACTUAL OR POTENTIAL COSTS THAT YOU OR ANY FRANCHISEE WILL INCUR FOR THESE TYPES OF EXPENSES.

EXPLANATORY NOTES

1.   These are not the only costs or expenses of operating a BURGER KING Restaurant. Other types of expenses that you will incur include, rent or other occupancy expense (including property taxes); insurance expense; legal and accounting expense; miscellaneous expenses such as operating supplies, uniforms, cleaning expense, laundry and linens, cash shortages, non-capital parts and supplies; non-cash expenses including depreciation and amortization; income taxes; advertising expense; and royalties. As discussed in Item 6 of this Disclosure Document, a Franchisee must pay BKC an advertising contribution based on gross sales, and

may incur other advertising expenses, including investment spending contributions. Additional advertising expenditures typically range from 0.5% to 2.0% of gross sales in addition to the required advertising fund contribution. Item 6 of this Disclosure Document also discusses the royalty payable to BKC by Franchisees. In developing your projections, you should make appropriate allowances for these and other expenses.

2.   Labor and Fringe Benefits: This item includes wages and fringe benefits for salaried Restaurant managers and hourly workers. Labor expense is affected by staffing levels and the level of fringe benefits provided to employees, and by labor market conditions in the areas of the Restaurants and by mandated minimum wage levels. **It does not include wages and fringe benefits for non-restaurant personnel.** Franchisees who elect to provide more limited fringe benefits to employees and who are more conservative in staffing levels may experience lower costs. Franchisees operating in areas with tighter labor markets may experience higher costs.

3.   Repair & Maintenance: The cost of repairs and maintenance of the Restaurant building and equipment can vary with the age and condition of the building. This does not include costs of improvements or remodeling that may be required from time to time.

4.   Utilities: This includes telephone, broadband services, water, gas, electricity and hauling of waste. These costs vary depending upon the region, area and/or government jurisdictions in which the Restaurant is located.

5.   Other Expenses: This includes controllables, taxes and licensing fees, as well as POS related items. These costs vary depending upon the region, area and/or government jurisdictions in which the Restaurant is located.

CAPTAIN D'S

1717 Elm Hill Pike, Suite A-1
Nashville, TN 37210
Tel: (800) 550-4877 (615) 231-2188
Fax: (615) 231-2734
E-Mail: bill_nelson@captainds.com
Web Site: www.captainds.com
Mr. Bill Nelson, VP of Franchise Operations

Captain D's restaurants offer high-quality seafood in a fast food environment. The menu features our signature hand-battered fried fish. We also offer premium-quality grilled, baked, and broiled fish, as well as shrimp, chicken, and home-style side dishes with selected desserts.

BACKGROUND:	IFA MEMBER
Established: 1969;	1st Franchised: 1969
Franchised Units:	260
Company-Owned Units:	291
Total Units:	551
Dist.:	US-549; CAN-0; O'seas-2

North America:	25 States, 0 Provinces
Density:	72 in AL, 102 in GA, 79 in TN
Projected New Units (12 Months):	5
Qualifications:	5, 3, 4, 3, 3, 5
Registered:CA,FL,HI,IL,IN,MD,MI,MN,ND,NY,OR,RI,SD,VA,	
	WA,WI

FINANCIAL/TERMS:	
Cash Investment:	$300K
Total Investment:	$1.3MM
Minimum Net Worth:	$750K
Fees: Franchise -	$25K
Royalty - 4.5%;	Ad. - 5.25%
Earnings Claims Statement:	Yes
Term of Contract (Years):	20/20
Avg. # Of Employees:	3-5 FT, 20 PT
Passive Ownership:	Allowed
Encourage Conversions:	No
Area Develop. Agreements:	Yes
Sub-Franchising Contracts:	No
Expand In Territory:	Yes
Space Needs:	2,300 SF; FS

SUPPORT & TRAINING:	
Financial Assistance Provided:	No
Site Selection Assistance:	Yes
Lease Negotiation Assistance:	No

Co-Operative Advertising:		Yes	**SPECIFIC EXPANSION PLANS:**	
Franchisee Assoc./Member:		No	US:	Yes
Size Of Corporate Staff:		75	Canada:	No
On-Going Support:		C,D,E,h	Overseas:	Yes
Training:	6 Weeks Field training in certified cooperating store			

ITEM 19
FINANCIAL PERFORMANCE REPRESENTATIONS

This Item 19 contains historical gross sales and expense information for certain franchised and company-owned Captain D's restaurants.

Profits in the operation of Captain D's restaurants will vary from franchisee to franchisee and from location to location and will depend on seasonal, local and other factors beyond our control. We do not warrant, represent, promise, predict or guarantee that you can or will attain the same financial results as set forth below. To the contrary, your financial results will vary and probably will vary to a material extent from the results set forth in this Item 19.

The sales and expense information set forth below reflects the operation of our previous Captain D's prototype restaurants. We believe the Captain D's Seafood Kitchen prototype should generate at least an equivalent, if not better, sales and expense history. However, we have no significant history with the new prototype yet and cannot give any assurances in that regard.

Material Factors

You should consider the following material factors in reviewing and determining whether to rely on this data:

1.   The information provided covers our fiscal year ended December 30, 2007 (December 31, 2006, to December 30, 2007).

2.   We based the gross sales information for franchised restaurants set forth below on a total of 252 franchised restaurants in operation during our entire fiscal year ended December 30, 2007. We based the gross sales and expenses for company-owned restaurants set forth below on a total of 290 company-owned restaurants in operation during our entire fiscal year ended December 30, 2007. Those restaurants are substantially similar to the standard and expanded prototype Captain D's restaurants offered by this Offering Circular. The address and date of commencement of operation of those restaurants appear in Exhibit M to this Offering Circular.

3.   In selecting the restaurants identified in Note 2, above, we excluded from all restaurants operating as of the end of our fiscal year ended December 30, 2007, (a) two company-owned restaurants and seven franchised restaurants not open for the full fiscal year, (b) two company-owned restaurants and five franchised restaurants closed for more than one week during the fiscal year, and (c) one company-owned and 10 franchised non-traditional restaurants.

4.   We based the information for end cap and inline restaurants on the following location:

Location	Opening Date
Madison, Indiana (2614 Harry Nichols Drive)	June 21, 2004

5.   We based the gross sales figures for our franchisees reported below on financial information provided to us by our franchisees with respect to franchisee operated Captain D's restaurants. The gross sales figures provided to us by our franchisees are not audited but represent figures on which franchisees pay royalties to us. Therefore, we consider those figures reliable. We based the gross sales and expense figures for our company-owned Captain D's restaurants reported below on

our financial statements.

6.   For purposes of this Item 19, the term "gross sales" means the total revenues derived by a Captain D's restaurant from all sales of all services and merchandise made in, upon or from the Captain D's restaurant, whether for cash, check, credit, barter, exchange or otherwise, less (a) rebates or refunds to customers; (b) the amount of any sales taxes or other similar taxes collected from customers and payable to any federal, state or local tax authority; and (c) the amount of any commissions or fees payable to nonaffiliated third parties of the restaurant not directly employed at the restaurant, or otherwise providing on-going and continuing services to the restaurant, for the services rendered in connection with outside services or goods provided or sold by the restaurant to its customers.

7.   Gross sales and expenses experienced by Captain D's restaurants differ from location to location because of a variety of factors, including (without limitation) differences in menu pricing; competition; demographics; economic conditions; weather conditions; labor conditions and minimum wage laws; commodity, transportation, workers' compensation, insurance and utility costs; real estate acquisition, construction and lease costs; property and sales tax rates; and governmental rules, regulations and interpretations. The expense information set forth below relates only to Captain D's company-owned locations. Expenses in the operation of Captain D's restaurants will vary from franchisee to franchisee and from location to location and will depend on seasonal, local and other factors in addition to those listed above. We make no warranties, representations, predictions, promises or guarantees with respect to the actual expenses you likely will experience.

8.   The expense information set forth below relates only to Captain D's company-owned locations and does not include all of the expenses incurred by the Captain D's restaurants included. It specifically excludes occupancy expenses like rent, depreciation or debt payments for land, building and improvements, as well as property taxes and insurance. The amounts for labor include restaurant-level managers and employees and consist of salaries, wages (net of any job credits), employee benefits, vacation pay, sick pay, performance bonuses, and payroll taxes. Controllable operating expenses consist of utilities, uniforms, laundry, maintenance and repair, and miscellaneous expense. Other operating expenses consist of expenses for taxes, licenses, insurance, advertising, and guest surveys.

9.   The expense information also does not include expenses that you will or may incur as a franchisee of Captain D's but which our company-owned restaurants do not experience. Those expenses include the following items:

(a) Royalty Payments. Your royalty fees for Traditional Locations will equal 4.5% of your gross sales. Your royalty fees for Non-traditional Locations will equal 5% of your gross sales. See Item 6 of this Offering Circular. Our company-owned restaurants do not pay royalties and, therefore, the expense information set forth below does not contain any amounts for royalty payments.

(b) Advertising and Local Restaurant Marketing Fees and Expenses. In most cases, advertising and local restaurant marketing fees and expenses will equal 4.85% of gross sales. That amount consists of an advertising fee of 0.85% of gross sales (which we may increase to a maximum of 1.25%) and local marketing expenses and advertising cooperative contributions of up to an additional 4% of gross sales. See Item 6 of this Offering Circular. Captain D's company-owned restaurants, on average, spent 5.9% of their gross sales on advertising, advertising fees, and local restaurant marketing during our fiscal year ended December 30, 2007. The expense information set forth below includes the amount of expenditures for advertising and local restaurant marketing under the category "other operating expenses."

(c) Legal, Accounting and Other Administrative Expenses. You will incur legal, accounting and other administrative expenses in connection with the operation of your business as a Captain D's franchisee. The expense information set forth below does not contain any amounts for those types of expenditures.

10.   You also may experience additional expenses in connection with the operation of your Captain D's restaurant.

11.   **The following statements of gross sales and expenses reflect the operations of specific franchised and company-owned restaurants. You should not consider them as the actual or probable sales or expenses that you will or may realize. We do not represent, warrant or promise that you can expect to attain the indicated sales or expenses. Your financial results will differ from the results stated in this Item 19. Some franchised Captain D's restaurants have experienced gross sales and some company-owned Captain D's restaurants have experienced gross sales and expenses in the amounts set forth below. We cannot give any assurance that you will do as well. If you rely on our figures, you must accept the risk of not doing as well.**

Number of Restaurants Operating One Year or More	542
Number of Franchised Restaurants	252
Number of Company-owned Restaurants	290

Franchised Restaurants for Fiscal Year Ended December 30, 2007

	Top Third	Middle Third	Bottom Third	Total
Average Gross Sales	$1,237,731	$ 852,907	$ 575,389	$888,675
Number of Restaurants	84	84	84	252
Highest Gross Sales	$1,989,440	$ 991,294	$ 714,398	$ 1,989,440
Lowest Gross Sales	$994,113	$ 715,192	$ 282,517	$ 282,517
Number Above Average	33	37	51	115
Number Below Average	51	47	33	137

For the fiscal year ended December 30, 2007, average gross sales for both franchised and company- owned restaurants equaled $871,082. As shown above, annual gross sales for franchised restaurants averaged $888,675. Annual gross sales for company-owned restaurants averaged $855,795. Of those 290 company- owned restaurants, 128 restaurants exceeded the average and 162 restaurants had annual gross sales below the average.

For the fiscal year ended December 30, 2007, average gross sales for both franchised and company- owned non-traditional restaurants equaled $466,080. Of those 10 non-traditional restaurants, five exceeded the average and five had annual gross sales below the average.

Company-Owned Restaurants for Fiscal Year Ended December 30, 2007

The following table provides the average gross sales and selected expenses for five categories of Captain D's company-owned restaurants based on the amount of annual gross sales experienced by the restaurants during the fiscal year ended December 30, 2007.

	Exceeding $1,200,000		$1,000,000 to $1,200,000		$800,000 to $1,000,000		$600,000 to $800,000		Less Than $600,000	
Average Volume	$1,360,435		$1,076,898		$888,681		$708,947		$558,174	
Number of Restaurants	21		53		80		103		33	
Sales	1,360,435	100.00%	1,076,898	100.00%	888,681	100.00%	708,947	100.00%	558,174	100.00%
Food	421,927	31.01%	335,660	31.17%	280,144	31.52%	223,287	31.50%	176,933	31.70%
Labor	318,253	23.39%	270,876	25.15%	244,119	27.47%	212,296	29.95%	182,554	32.71%
Supplies and Paper	45,621	3.35%	36,936	3.43%	31,059	3.49%	24,967	3.52%	20,308	3.64%
Total Food and Supplies	467,548	34.37%	372,596	34.60%	311,203	35.02%	248,254	35.02%	197,241	35.34%
Total Food, Labor and Supplies	785,801	57.76%	643,472	59.75%	555,322	62.49%	460,550	64.96%	379,795	68.04%
Controllable Operating Expenses	105,126	7.73%	98,509	9.15%	97,305	10.95%	86,127	12.15%	80,109	14.35%
Other Operating Expenses*	108,317	7.96%	91,002	8.45%	80,892	9.10%	67,241	9.48%	56,116	10.05%
Restaurant Level Contribution Before Occupancy	361,190	26.55%	243,915	22.65%	155,162	17.46%	95,030	13.40%	42,154	7.55%
Average	1,360,435		1,076,898		888,681		708,947		558,174	
Percent of Restaurants	7.2%		18.3%		27.6%		35.5%		11.4%	
Number of Restaurants	21		53		80		103		33	
Number of Restaurants Exceeding Average	9		25		36		51		23	
Number of Restaurants Less Than Average	12		28		44		52		10	

* Operating expenses include advertising expenses, fees and contributions of 5.9% of gross sales. Pursuant to the terms of the Franchise Agreement, we may require franchisee advertising expenses, fees and contributions of as much as 5.25% of gross sales. However, we currently do not require our franchisees to spend more than 4.85% of their gross sales for those items. Captain D's company-owned restaurants do not pay royalty fees (currently 4.5% of gross sales). Therefore, the amount for operating expenses set forth above does not include those amounts. See "Material Factors," above.

Gross Sales and Labor Costs, Food Costs, and Supplies and Paper Costs

as a Percentage of Gross Sales for End Cap and Inline Captain D's Restaurants

The following table sets forth the gross sales, labor costs, food costs, and supplies and paper costs as a percentage of gross sales for the one End Cap Captain D's restaurant we operated during our three fiscal years ended December 30, 2007, December 31, 2006, and December 25, 2005.

	52-Weeks Ended 12/25/05	53-Weeks Ended 12/31/06	52-Weeks Ended 12/30/07
Gross Sales	$441,045	$424,244	$504,911
Food Costs	31.70%	31.27%	31.13%
Labor Costs	33.38%	34.90%	29.82%
Supplies and Paper Costs	4.16%	4.49%	4.42%

SUBSTANTIATION OF THE DATA USED IN PREPARING THIS ITEM 19 IS AVAILABLE FROM US UPON REQUEST.

CARL'S JR.

6307 Carpinteria Ave., # A
Carpinteria, CA 93013
Tel: (866) 253-7655 (805) 745-7842
Fax: (714) 780-6320
E-Mail: chopkins@ckr.com
Web Site: www.ckr.com
Mr. Craig Hopkins, VP Franchise Sales

Over the last 60 years Carl's Jr.® has built a reputation as America's premier burger chain, and is known as the place to go for big, juicy, delicious charbroiled burgers. Today, there are more than 1,100 Carl's Jr.® restaurants worldwide, with more than 300 dual-branded Carl's Jr.®/Green Burrito® restaurants.

BACKGROUND: IFA MEMBER
Established: 1961; 1st Franchised: 1984
Franchised Units: 782
Company-Owned Units: 421
Total Units: 1203
Dist.: US-1080; CAN-0; O'seas-123
 North America: 14 States, 0 Provinces
 Density: 62 in AZ, 713 in CA, 44 in OR
Projected New Units (12 Months): NR
Qualifications: 4, 4, 4, 2, 2, 5
Registered: CA,HI,OR,WA

FINANCIAL/TERMS:
Cash Investment: $300K
Total Investment: $1.3-1.8MM
Minimum Net Worth: $1MM
Fees: Franchise - $35K
 Royalty - 4%; Ad. - 5.5%
Earnings Claims Statement: Yes
Term of Contract (Years): 20/5
Avg. # Of Employees: 33 FT, PT
Passive Ownership: Not Allowed
Encourage Conversions: Yes
Area Develop. Agreements: Yes
Sub-Franchising Contracts: No
Expand In Territory: Yes
Space Needs: 2,450 SF; FS,SC,RM, University, Airport (non-trad), Home Improvement

SUPPORT & TRAINING:
Financial Assistance Provided: No
Site Selection Assistance: Yes
Lease Negotiation Assistance: No
Co-Operative Advertising: No
Franchisee Assoc./Member: No
Size Of Corporate Staff: 300
On-Going Support: C,D,E,F,G,H,I
Training: NR

SPECIFIC EXPANSION PLANS:
US: Yes
Canada: Yes
Overseas: Yes

ITEM 19
FINANCIAL PERFORMANCE REPRESENTATIONS

The information presented is unaudited and was prepared using uniform accounting methods consistent with generally accepted accounting practices and on a basis consistent with those included in our annual audited consolidated financial statements. All company-operated Restaurants use the same accounting methods and system.

The information contained in this Item 19 should not be considered to be the actual or probable sales and expenses that you will realize. Your results will likely differ from the results contained in this Item 19. Performance varies from restaurant to restaurant and the information below cannot be used to make estimates related to future performance of any particular restaurant. Your performance will be significantly impacted by your personal business, marketing and management skills, your financial investment capabilities, and your willingness to work hard and follow the Carl's Jr. System. Many factors that may significantly impact financial performance are unique to each restaurant, including location, physical size and layout, market penetration, local market conditions and other factors. CKE does not represent that you will attain these financial results. If you are purchasing the assets of existing company-operated Restaurants, you should not rely on the information set forth below, but should instead review the actual performance of the Restaurants being purchased.

Other than the information set forth below, CKE does not furnish or authorize its employees or affiliates to furnish spoken or written claims regarding financial performance, earnings, revenues or results that you are likely to obtain. CKE specifically instructs its employees and affiliates that they are not permitted to make any such claims, other than the information set forth below, and you may not rely on any such claims if made.

Table 1: Fiscal Year 2008 Financial Performance

The following table represents average Fiscal Year 2008 financial performance for all 391 company-operated domestic Restaurants (including Dual Concept Restaurants) that operated for all 13 periods ending January 28, 2008. Consistent with the audited financial statements attached to this disclosure document, each Fiscal Year will be deemed to end on January 31. While there were 406 company-operated domestic Restaurants (including Dual Concept Restaurants) operating at the end of Fiscal Year 2008, 15 have not been included since they did not operate for the entire 13 periods ending January 31, 2008. The data in Table 1 is grouped into five columns based on average sales performance, with a summary column for all locations.

	Sales > $1.5M 175 Locations		Sales $1.25M to $1.5M 92 Locations		Sales $1M to $1.25M 74 Locations		Sales $750K to $1M 35 Locations		Sales < $750K 15 Locations		All Locations 390	
TOTAL SALES	1,885,764	100.0%	1,377,355	100.0%	1,129,526	100.0%	912,453	100.0%	666,018	100.0%	1,489,096	100.0%
TOTAL MATERIALS	543,745	28.8%	402,559	29.2%	333,491	29.5%	270,878	29.7%	195,003	29.3%	432,930	29.1%
TOTAL LABOR & BENEFITS	472,403	25.1%	379,590	27.6%	331,517	29.4%	292,037	32.0%	233,522	35.1%	398,591	26.8%
TOTAL OPERATING EXPENSE	203,102	10.8%	169,285	12.3%	153,630	13.6%	136,093	14.9%	101,054	15.2%	175,869	11.8%
ADVERTISING	108,579	5.8%	79,736	5.8%	65,404	5.8%	53,617	5.9%	39,461	5.9%	86,090	5.8%
RESTAURANT EBITDAR	557,934	29.6%	346,185	25.1%	245,484	21.7%	159,827	17.5%	96,949	14.6%	395,656	26.6%

NOTES TO TABLE 1

(1)   Variations in Sales

Company-operated Restaurants typically are located in freestanding drive-thru locations. Variations in the sales levels of restaurants may occur due to the foot/vehicular traffic where the restaurants are located, the populations and income of the immediate market area, the retail maturity in the area, the amount of competition in the area and numerous other factors.

(2)   Total Sales

Total sales include sales of all food, beverages and promotional items, net of sales taxes, discounts and coupons.

(3)   Total Materials

Total Materials include all food, paper and distribution costs less supplier rebates. CKE distributes food and other supplies to most Carl's Jr. Restaurants. Any profit derived from the distribution of these items to a company-operated Restaurant is credited back to Total Materials for that company-operated Restaurant's profit and loss statements.

(4)   Total Labor & Benefits

Total Labor & Benefits include wages paid to all hourly and management employees working in the restaurant, as well as all restaurant manager bonuses. Your labor costs could vary depending on the prevailing wage rates in the area of the country in which a restaurant is located and the specific labor laws. Benefits include all employer and payroll taxes, workers' compensation, and expenses for vacation and health insurance. A franchisee's benefits cost will vary depending on the amount of vacation time granted, the amount and type of insurance coverage provided to employees, the size of the franchisee's total employment base and specific local requirements.

(5)   Total Operating Expenses

Total Operating Expenses include cash over and short, supplies, uniforms, repair and maintenance, utilities, telephone, security, armored car services, banking and ATM fees, waste management, certain equipment rental charges, kid's meal toy costs, mileage reimbursement, certain pre-opening costs, property taxes, business insurance, license and permit fees and certain asset retirement charges.

(6)   Advertising

Advertising costs include the cost of developing and executing various marketing programs for the restaurants. This includes development and placement of electronic media, print and outdoor advertising. Advertising also includes the cost of in-restaurant point of purchase materials and local restaurant marketing. Required advertising expenses may vary by DMA. Please refer to Items 6 and 11 of this disclosure document for a description of a franchisee's advertising spending obligations.

(7)   Restaurant EBITDAR

Restaurant EBITDAR equals Restaurant Level Earnings Before Income Taxes, Depreciation, Amortization, and Rent. In addition to those items, this category does not include the following expenses associated with operating a Franchised Restaurant: royalty fees, common area maintenance charges, general and administrative expenses (above the restaurant level) and other miscellaneous expenses a franchisee may incur.

(8)   Royalties

A royalty of 4% of Gross Sales has not been shown since company-operated Restaurants pay no royalties. Please refer to Item 6 of this disclosure document for a description of a franchisee's royalty obligations.

(9)   Legal Expenses and Other Administrative Expenses and Taxes

No amounts have been included for expenses a franchisee may incur for owners' salaries, interest and debt service, legal and accounting fees, income taxes, corporate overhead and similar expenses. To the extent a franchisee expects to incur such expenses, the franchisee's overall expenses would be higher.

Table 2: Historic Average Unit Volume Figures

The data presented in this table represent the average unit volume for all company-operated domestic Restaurants (including Dual Concept Restaurants) that had been open and operating during the designated fiscal year. CKE's fiscal year ends on the last Monday in January each year.

Fiscal Year	Average Unit Volume ($1000's)	Percent Increase Over Previous Fiscal Year	Percent Increase Over Fiscal Year 2002	Number of Units at Close of Fiscal Year	Number of Units Surpassing Average Unit Volume	Percent Surpassing Average Unit Volume
2002	1,135	-	-	443	212	48%
2003	1,152	1.5%	1.5%	440	209	48%
2004	1,187	3.0%	4.6%	426	217	51%
2005	1,301	9.6%	14.6%	428	219	51%
2006	1,341	3.1%	18.1%	428	213	50%
2007	1,440	7.4%	26.9%	393	190	48%
2008	1,493	3.7%	31.5%	406	181	45%

Table 3: Historic Same Store Sales Information

This table presents the increase in same-store sales for all company-operated domestic Restaurants (including Dual Concept Restaurants). The fiscal year same-store sales increase is a cumulative by-period calculation that includes all company-operated domestic Restaurants that had sales for comparable periods during the prior fiscal year. CKE's fiscal year ends on the last Monday in January each year.

Fiscal Year	Same store sales increase
2002	2.9%
2003	0.7%
2004	2.9%
2005	7.7%
2006	2.2%
2007	4.9%
2008	0.9%

*   *   *

Written substantiation of the information used in preparing this statement will be made available to you upon reasonable request. However, we will disclose the identity, revenue or other items of income or expense of any particular company-operated Restaurant only in connection with the sale of that Restaurant.

You are responsible for developing your own business plan for your restaurant, including capital budgets, financial statements, projections and other elements appropriate to your particular circumstances. CKE encourages you to consult with your own accounting, business and legal advisors and to make necessary allowances for changes in financial results to income, expenses or both. You should conduct an independent investigation of the costs and expenses you will incur in operating your restaurant. Franchisees or former franchisees listed in the disclosure document may be one source of this information.

CHESTER'S INTERNATIONAL

3500 Colonade Pkwy. # 325
Birmingham, AL 35213
Tel: (800) 288-1555 (334) 272-3528
Fax: (205) 298-0332
E-Mail: info@chestersinternational.com
Web Site: www.chestersinternational.com
Mr. Ian Byrd, Director of Franchise Development

CHESTER'S offers consumers a high-quality chicken product, cooked to perfection, with a unique taste and style. The Company's secret is a breading recipe and process that has been successful for more than 30 years. CHESTER'S uses only chicken that is specially marinated and offers double-breaded bone-in, tender and potato wedges as well as sandwiches, salads and breakfast. Great opportunity to enter the QSR industry with flexible locations and store design. * 1,449 units are non-franchised.

BACKGROUND: IFA MEMBER
Established: 1952; 1st Franchised: 2002
Franchised Units: 47
Company-Owned Units: 0
Total Units: 47
Dist.: US-47; CAN-225; O'seas-50
 North America: 47 States, 11 Provinces
 Density: NR
Projected New Units (12 Months): 49
Qualifications: 3, 3, 2, 2, 3, 4
Registered:CA,DC,FL,HI,IL,IN,MD,MI,MN,ND,NY,OR,RI,SD, VA,WA,WI,AB

FINANCIAL/TERMS:
Cash Investment: $50K-100K
Total Investment: $60K-400.4K
Minimum Net Worth: $100K
Fees: Franchise - $5-15K
 Royalty - NR; Ad. - NR
Earnings Claims Statement: No
Term of Contract (Years): 7-10/7-10
Avg. # Of Employees: 2 FT, 4 PT
Passive Ownership: Allowed
Encourage Conversions: Yes
Area Develop. Agreements: Yes
Sub-Franchising Contracts: No
Expand In Territory: Yes
Space Needs: 400-1,400 SF; SF,SC,RM, C-Store

SUPPORT & TRAINING:
Financial Assistance Provided: Yes (D)
Site Selection Assistance: Yes
Lease Negotiation Assistance: No
Co-Operative Advertising: No
Franchisee Assoc./Member: No
Size Of Corporate Staff: 13
On-Going Support: C,D,E,H,I
Training: 1 Week Birmingham, AL; 4 Days Franchisee Location.

SPECIFIC EXPANSION PLANS:
US: Yes, All United States
Canada: Yes, All Canada
Overseas: Yes, All Countries

ITEM 19
FINANCIAL PERFORMANCE REPRESENTATIONS

This Item 19 contains information regarding the gross sales reported by franchisees of certain CHESTER'S Restaurants that operated for the full 2007 calendar year. All 14 reporting CHESTER'S Restaurants operated within a convenience store or travel plaza (a convenience store that is on an interstate or major highway that provides services to trucks as well as gas to cars). These CHESTER'S Restaurants are referred to in this Item as "In-Store CHESTER'S Restaurants." As discussed in Item 1, we also offer franchises, through a separate disclosure document, for CHESTER'S Restaurants to be located in food court locations and other traditional strip center locations. This Item does not contain information regarding the 2 CHESTER'S Restaurants falling in the latter category because they have characteristics that differentiate them materially from the CHESTER'S Restaurant you will operate. (For instance, CHESTER'S Restaurants located in food court locations and other traditional strip center locations are much larger than the type of CHESTER'S Restaurant you will operate.) Because we started offering the smaller-sized CHESTER'S CHICKEN ON THE FLY concept only as of this disclosure document's amended issuance date, none of the reporting Restaurants covered by this Item used that trademark. They used only the CHESTER'S trademark.

This Item reports the average daily and annual gross sales (during 2007) for 14 franchised In-Store CHESTER'S Restaurants that were open during all of 2007. These Restaurants were located in the States of Alabama (1), Arizona (4), California (1), Georgia (2), New Mexico (1), South Carolina (2), Tennessee (2), and Texas (1). These 14 CHESTER'S Restaurants were open for an average of 26.8

months as of December 31, 2007. They averaged 700 square feet with a high of 1,200 square feet and a low of 600 square feet.

While these CHESTER'S Restaurants are not concentrated in a particular market area (although 4 of the 14 are in Arizona), you should consider the fact that the greater the number of Restaurants operating in a state or other market area, the greater the goodwill and public recognition of our trademarks in that area are likely to be. The lower the number of Restaurants operating in a state or other market area, the lesser the goodwill and public recognition of our trademarks in that area are likely to be. Positive goodwill and public recognition of trademarks likely will impact sales. You should consider the nature of the area in which you are interested in acquiring a franchise.

The figures below do not reflect the costs of sales, operating expenses, or other costs or expenses that must be deducted from the gross sales figures to obtain your net income or profit. You should conduct an independent investigation of the costs and expenses you will incur in operating your CHESTER'S Restaurant. Franchisees or former franchisees, listed in the disclosure document, may be one source of this information.

As of December 31, 2007, there were 43 franchised CHESTER'S Restaurants open and operating in the United States, 40 In-Store CHESTER'S Restaurants and 3 Chester's Restaurants in food court locations and other traditional strip center locations. There were another 32 franchise agreements signed as of December 31, 2007 for CHESTER'S Restaurants to be operated in the United States that were not yet open as of that date, 27 expected to be In-Store CHESTER'S Restaurants and 5 expected to be Chester's Restaurants in food court locations and other traditional strip center locations. (Because we started offering the smaller-sized CHESTER'S CHICKEN ON THE FLY concept in October 2008, we expect none of these referenced Restaurants to use that trademark.) The gross sales of (a) the franchised In-Store CHESTER'S Restaurants that were not open during all of 2007, and (b) the CHESTER'S Restaurants in food court locations and other traditional strip center locations, are not included in the average daily or annual gross sales information provided in Chart A or Chart B below.

Chart A below relates the average daily gross sales of the 14 franchised In-Store CHESTER'S Restaurants that were open and operating during all of 2007. Gross sales are defined as all revenue the franchisee received from operating the Restaurant but excluding taxes, refunds, credits, and discounts. The average daily gross sales for the one-year period ending December 31, 2007 for these locations ranged from a low of $208 to a high of $2,094 with an average of $895.

CHART A
Average Daily Gross Sales for In-Store CHESTER'S Restaurants
Open During all of 2007

	High	Low	Average	#/% Units Above
Average Daily Gross Sales	$2,094	$208	$895	5/36%

Note: Average daily gross sales are computed based upon the number of days each Restaurant reported to be open during 2007.

Chart B below relates the average annual gross sales of the 14 franchised In-Store CHESTER'S Restaurants that were open and operating during all of 2007. Gross sales are defined as all revenue the franchisee received from operating the Restaurant but excluding taxes, refunds, credits, and discounts. The average annual gross sales for the one-year period ending December 31, 2007 for these locations ranged from a low of $65,940 to a high of $764,171 with an average of $319,571.

CHART B
Average Annual Gross Sales for In-Store CHESTER'S Restaurants
Open During all of 2007

	High	Low	Average	#/% Units Above
Average Annual Gross Sales	$764,171	$65,940	$319,571	5/36%

We will provide to new In-Store CHESTER'S Restaurant franchisees, in our capacity as franchisor, the same services that Chester's LLC provided to the CHESTER'S Restaurants referenced above during 2007. However, we do not provide certain services to franchisees that the owner of a business normally provides, such as financing, accounting, legal, personnel, construction, and management services. The availability of these services to a franchisee, as well as their costs and quality, likely will affect operations. The In-Store CHESTER'S Restaurants referenced above offered the same products to the public as will new In-Store CHESTER'S Restaurants that franchisees will operate under the Franchise Agreement disclosed in this disclosure document. However, the figures presented above are not relevant to, and therefore should not be assessed by, a franchisee who will operate under the CHESTER'S CHICKEN ON THE FLY trademark because, as described in Items 1 and 7 of this disclosure document, the CHESTER'S CHICKEN ON THE FLY concept is a small, self-service "grab 'n go" concept that operates from a modular kiosk-type unit within a retail business's existing space. Its operations are not as expansive as those of a typical In-Store CHESTER'S Restaurant and therefore are not expected the generate comparable revenue levels.

There is no guarantee that any In-Store CHESTER'S Restaurant a prospective franchisee operates will achieve the results reflected above, either during its initial year of operation or afterward. Written substantiation of all financial performance information presented in this Item will be made available to you upon reasonable request. The actual performance of your own CHESTER'S Restaurant will be affected by numerous factors, including amount of time in business; lease terms; financing costs; taxes; labor costs; supply costs; local and regional economic and regulatory conditions; population density; your management skills and business acumen; competition; your ability to promote and market a CHESTER'S Restaurant; how hard you are willing to work; and the degree of adherence to our methods and procedures. While we believe that CHESTER'S Restaurants will have consumer appeal in all geographic areas of the United States as our system grows, the CHESTER'S Restaurant concept has limited operating history. The states in which CHESTER'S Restaurants actually operated for one year or more as of December 31, 2007 are identified above.

Our management prepared this information based on gross sales reported by franchisees but did not independently audit that information.

You should not consider this historical sales information as the actual or potential sales that are realized by franchisees generally or may be realized by you. We do not represent that you can expect to attain these sales. Your financial results are likely to differ from the results stated above. Other than this information, no representations or statements of actual, average, projected, or forecasted sales, earnings, or profits are made to prospective franchisees. Neither our employees nor officers, nor those of any of our affiliates, are authorized to make any claims or statements as to the earnings, sales, profits, or prospects or chances of success that any franchisee can expect or that present or past franchisees have experienced.

This schedule was prepared without an audit. Prospective franchisees or sellers of franchises should be advised that no certified public accountant has audited these figures or expressed his/her opinion with regard to their contents or form.

Other Differentiating Factors

Operating results of the CHESTER'S Restaurants to be operated by franchisees under Franchise Agreements with us also are likely to be affected by the following:

    (a)   Differing rent and related expenses for which the franchisee is obligated;

    (b)   The "CHESTER'S Restaurant" concept is not yet recognized or established in the franchisee's market;

    (c)   Economic conditions in the franchisee's market;

    (d)   Competition from other businesses offering the same, similar, or competitive products;

    (e)   Different leasehold improvement or financing costs;

    (f)   Different levels of employee wages, fringe benefits, and other costs;

    (g)   Different costs on a local basis of obtaining products and supplies; and

    (h)   Different locations.

CHICK-FIL-A

5200 Buffington Rd.
Atlanta, GA 30349-2998
Tel: (800) 232-2677 (404) 765-8000
Fax: (404) 684-8620
E-Mail: martha.lawrence@chick-fil-a.com
Web Site: www.chick-fil-a.com
Ms. LaShawn Cartwright

BACKGROUND:

Established: NR;		1st Franchised: NR
Franchised Units:		1355
Company-Owned Units:		0
Total Units:		1355

Item 19
FINANCIAL PERFORMANCE REPRESENTATIONS

As of December 31, 2007, there were approximately 1,341 domestic Chick-fil-A Restaurants and Licensed Units, including approximately 1,141 domestic Chick-fil-A Restaurants and 200 domestic Chick-fil-A Licensed Units. The domestic Chick-fit-A Licensed Units, which are operated by Chick-fil-A Licensees, and their annual sales volumes are not the subject of these financial performance representations.

As of December 31, 2007, approximately 1,102 of the 1,141 domestic Chick-fil-A Restaurants were being operated by Operators and 39 of the 1,141 domestic Chick-fil-A Restaurants were being operated by Chick-fil-A or its affiliates. Approximately 1,067 of those 1,141 domestic Chick-fil-A Restaurants had been open for at least one full calendar year as of December 31, 2007. Of these 1,067 domestic Chick-fil-A Restaurants, 10 were "Satellite" locations, and their annual sales volumes are not the subject of these financial performance representations. The remaining 1,057 domestic Chick-fil-A Restaurants that had been open for at least one full calendar year as of December 31, 2007, and their annual sales volumes, are the subject of these financial performance representations.

Approximately 372 of the 1,057 domestic Chick-fil-A Restaurants that had been open for at least one full calendar year as of December 31, 2007 were located in malls and approximately 685 of the 1,057 domestic Chick-fil-A Restaurants that had been open for at least one full calendar year as of December 31, 2007 were located in non-mall environments (*e.g.,* Free Standing Units ("FSUs") and Drive-Thru Only Units ("DTOs")).

In 2007, of the approximately 372 domestic Chick-fil-A Restaurants located in malls that were open for at least one year as of December 31, 2007, approximately 32% had annual sales volumes less than $1,000,000; approximately 34% had annual sales volumes between $1,000,000 and $1,300,000; and approximately 34% had annual sales volumes in excess of $1,300,000. In 2007, the average annual sales volume of domestic Chick-fil-A Restaurants located in malls that were open at least one year as of December 31, 2007 was $1,224,835. The highest and lowest annual sales volume for these domestic Chick-fil-A Restaurants located in malls in 2007 was $3,050,994 and $570,522 respectively.

In 2007, of the approximately 685 domestic Chick-fil-A Restaurants located in non-mall environments that were open for at least one year as of December 31, 2007, approximately 32% had annual sales volumes less than $2,400,000; approximately 35% had annual sales volumes between $2,400,000 and $3,100,000; and approximately 33% had annual sales volumes in excess of $3,100,000. In 2007, the average annual sales volume of domestic Chick-fil-A Restaurants located in non-mall environments that were open at least one year was $2,825,576. The highest and lowest sales volume in 2007 for these domestic Chick-fil-A Restaurants located in non-mall environments was $5,479,995 and $1,113,805, respectively.

For purposes of the financial performance representations set forth above, the term "annual sales volume" includes a Chick-fil-A Restaurant's entire gross receipts (excluding only sales taxes levied upon retail sales and payable over to the appropriate governmental authority) from all sales at, from or related to the Chick-fil-A Restaurant during the applicable calendar year, whether for cash or on a charge, credit or time basis, including sales and services (i) where orders originate and/or are accepted at, in or away from the Chick-fil-A Restaurant, or (ii) pursuant to telephone or other similar orders received or filled at or in the Chick-fil-A Restaurant.

The financial performance representations set forth above are based upon a total of 1,057 domestic Chick-fil-A Restaurants that were open for at least one year as of December 31, 2007, of which 372 were located in malls and 685 were located in non-mall environments. Both Chick-fil-A Restaurants located in malls and Chick-fil-A Restaurants located in non-mall environments are similar with respect to their operations and receive similar services from Chick-fil-A. Because Chick-fil-A Restaurants located in malls and Chick-fil-A Restaurants located in non-mall environments achieve generally different levels of financial performance, financial performance representations have been included for each type of restaurant in order to provide information relevant to prospective Operators.

Additionally, the financial performance representations set forth above have been derived from the financial reporting statements of both independent, franchised Operator and company-operated Chick-fil-A Restaurants in order to provide information relevant to a prospective Operator. Both company-operated Chick-fil-A Restaurants and Operator-operated Chick-fil-A Restaurants are similar with respect to their operations, financial performance from an annual sales volume perspective, and receive similar services from Chick-fil-A.

YOU ARE URGED TO CONSULT WITH APPROPRIATE FINANCIAL, BUSINESS AND LEGAL ADVISORS IN CONNECTION WITH THE INFORMATION SET FORTH IN THIS ANALYSIS.

A NEW OPERATOR'S INDIVIDUAL FINANCIAL RESULTS MAY DIFFER FROM THE RESULTS STATED IN THE FINANCIAL PERFORMANCE REPRESENTATIONS FOR THE REASONS STATED BELOW. The computations of all actual and average sales, the range of years in operation, and list of addresses of the Chick-fil-A Restaurants that supplied data used in preparing these financial performance representations will be made available to prospective franchisees upon reasonable request.

THE FINANCIAL PERFORMANCE REPRESENTATIONS DO NOT REFLECT THE COSTS OF SALES OR OPERATING EXPENSES THAT MUST BE DEDUCTED FROM THE GROSS REVENUE OR GROSS SALES FIGURES TO OBTAIN YOUR NET INCOME OR PROFIT. THE BEST SOURCE OF COST AND EXPENSE DATA MAY BE FROM OPERATORS AND FORMER OPERATORS, SOME OF WHOM MAY BE LISTED IN ITEM 20.

THE SALES FIGURES SET FORTH ABOVE ARE AVERAGES OF SPECIFIC FRANCHISED AND COMPANY-OPERATED CHICK-FIL-A RESTAURANTS AND SHOULD NOT BE CONSIDERED AS THE ACTUAL OR POTENTIAL SALES THAT WILL BE REALIZED BY ANY CHICK-FIL-A RESTAURANT OPERATOR. NEITHER CHICK-FIL-A NOR ANY OTHER PERSON CAN GUARANTEE THE SUCCESS OF AN OPERATOR'S RESTAURANT, AND ADMONISHES THAT AN OPERATOR'S RESTAURANT MAY LOSE MONEY OR FAIL. CHICK-FIL-A DOES

NOT REPRESENT, WARRANT, OR PROMISE THAT YOU CAN EXPECT TO ATTAIN THESE SALES. Individual Operators are likely to experience annual sales volume variations. A Chick-fil-A Restaurant's physical location within any particular geographic area, a Chick-fil-A Restaurant's physical location among different geographic areas of the country, the operational skill and the management methods employed by an Operator, and menu price variations may significantly affect the sales realized in any given operation.

Chick-fil-A may provide you with supplemental information relating to the projected sales of a Chick-fil-A Restaurant at a specific location (the "Supplemental Information"). Any such Supplemental Information will be in writing and will explain how it differs from the information contained in this Item 19.

Chick-fil-A specifically instructs its agents, employees, and officers that they are not permitted to make any claims or statements as to the earnings, sales, or profits, or prospects or chances of success, nor are they authorized to represent or estimate dollar figures as to your operation, other than as described in this Item 19 and in any Supplemental Information provided to you, as described above. Chick-fil-A will not be bound by allegations of any unauthorized representations as to earnings, sales, profits, or prospects or chances for success. If you receive any unauthorized information, whether oral or written, concerning the actual, or average, or projected, or forecasted, or potential sales, costs, earnings, or profits, or the prospects or chances of success, or representation or estimated dollar figures as to your operation, you should immediately notify S. Tammy Pearson, Senior Director and Associate General Counsel of Chick-fil-A.

CHURCH'S CHICKEN

980 Hammond Dr. Bldg. 2 # 1100
Atlanta, GA 30328-6161
Tel: (800) 639-3495 (770) 350-3800
Fax: (770) 554-0973
E-Mail: pperry@churchs.com
Web Site: www.churchs.com
Mr. Douglas Pendergast, EVP & Chief Franchise Officer

Founded in San Antonio, Texas, in 1952, Church's Chicken is a highly recognized brand name in the QSR sector and is one of the largest quick-service chicken concepts in the world. Church's Chicken serves freshly prepared, high quality, flavorful chicken and tenders with signature sides and hand-made from scratch biscuits at low prices and differentiates from its competitors in care and attention given in preparation of food, and is positioned as the Value Leader in the Chicken QSR category. As of February 2007, the Church's system had 1,600+ locations worldwide in 18 countries, with system sales exceeding $1 billion.

BACKGROUND: IFA MEMBER

Established: 1952;   1st Franchised: 1967

Franchised Units:	1337
Company-Owned Units:	<u>277</u>
Total Units:	1614
Dist.:	US-1217; CAN-18; O'seas-382
North America:	28 States, 0 Provinces
Density:	74 in CA, 88 in GA, 433 in TX
Projected New Units (12 Months):	111
Qualifications:	5, 5, 4, 3, 3, 5
Registered:	CA,FL,HI,IL,IN,MD,MI,MN,NY,OR,RI,VA,WA,WI

FINANCIAL/TERMS:

Cash Investment:	$300K
Total Investment:	$335-1113.5K
Minimum Net Worth:	$1MM
Fees: Franchise -	$15K
Royalty - 5%;	Ad. - 5%
Earnings Claims Statement:	No
Term of Contract (Years):	20/10
Avg. # Of Employees:	15 FT, 6 PT
Passive Ownership:	Allowed, But Discouraged
Encourage Conversions:	Yes
Area Develop. Agreements:	Yes
Sub-Franchising Contracts:	Yes
Expand In Territory:	Yes
Space Needs:	850-1,850 SF; FS, C-Store, In-Line

SUPPORT & TRAINING:

Financial Assistance Provided:	No
Site Selection Assistance:	Yes

Lease Negotiation Assistance:	No	
Co-Operative Advertising:	Yes	**SPECIFIC EXPANSION PLANS:**
Franchisee Assoc./Member:	Yes/Member	US: Yes, All United States
Size Of Corporate Staff:	157	Canada: Yes, All Canada
On-Going Support:	B,C,D,E,G,H,I	Overseas: Yes, Asia, Middle East, Russia, China
Training:	4 Weeks Regional	

ITEM 19
FINANCIAL PERFORMANCE REPRESENTATIONS

The following four tables present information about the actual sales and expenses of domestic Church's restaurants in our 2007 fiscal year.

Table 1: 2007 Sales by Asset Type (Franchise Restaurants)

Below are average sales for our fiscal year 2007 by type of Church's Restaurant. Only Church's Restaurants which operated at least 50 weeks during fiscal year 2007 are included. Table 1 below includes only franchise restaurants in the United States, and does not include restaurants located in Puerto Rico and U.S. territories. The restaurants in Puerto Rico, all of which are franchised, have higher average annual sales than non-Puerto Rico restaurants; had those restaurants been included, the averages below in Table 1 would have been higher.

2007 Sales (1)	Free Standing		In-Line	C-Store	Co-branded	Other
	With Drive Thru	Without Drive Thru				
Average – domestic franchise	$707,393	$687,239	$645,171	$535,244	$178,661	$507,370
Top quartile - domestic franchise	$817,978	$774,692	$731,147	$640,335	$191,644	$667,620
Restaurant count (2)	555	109	18	130	25	26
Franchised restaurants at or above domestic franchise average	242	61	6	55	10	11
% franchised restaurants at or above domestic franchise average	43.6%	56.0%	33.3%	42.3%	40.0%	42.3%

Notes To Table 1: 2007 Sales By Asset Type (Franchise Restaurants)

1.   "Free-Standing" and "In-Line" units are described in Item 7. "C-Store" means a unit attached to or part of a convenience store or travel plaza. "Co-branded" means a unit which shares operating space with another branded restaurant or business.

2.   We sold 15 company-owned restaurants in Arizona to a franchisee on December 15, 2007. Those restaurants are not included in this table.

Table 2: 2007 Sales by Asset Type (Company Restaurants)

Below are average sales for our fiscal year 2007 by type of Church's Restaurant. Only Church's Restaurants which operated at least 50 weeks during fiscal 2007 are included. Table 2 below includes only company-operated restaurants in the United States.

2007 Sales (1)	Free Standing	
	With Drive Thru	Without Drive Thru

Average – company owned	$907,096	$779,465
Top Quartile - company owned	$1,052,853	$921,467
Restaurant count (2)	209	22

| 2007 Sales (1) | Free Standing | |
	With Drive Thru	Without Drive Thru
Franchise units at or above company-owned average	88	36
% franchise units at or above company owned average	15.9%	33.0%

Notes To Table 2: 2007 Sales By Asset Type (Company Restaurants)

1.   We do not own any in-line, c-store, or co-branded restaurants.

2.   We sold 15 company-owned restaurants in Arizona to a franchisee on December 15, 2007. For this table, those restaurants are considered company restaurants for all of 2007.

Table 3: Sales by New Restaurants

The table below summarizes sales by all new free-standing restaurants built from the ground up in 2006 and open for all of our fiscal year 2007. These restaurants were all built to our "Tower" prototype. The table does not include new restaurants that were opened in existing buildings converted to Church's Restaurants.

2007 Sales	Franchisee	Company Owned
Average	$962,725	$1,205,844
Top Quartile	$1,033,847	n/a
Unit Count	4	1
Franchise units at or above company-owned average	0	n/a
% franchise units at or above company owned average	0%	n/a

Table 4: 2007 Income Statement Summary - By Sales Band (Company Restaurants Only)

Below is an income statement summary for our fiscal year 2007 for restaurants that meet all of the following criteria: (1) owned by Cajun, (2) free-standing (i.e. not part of a convenience store or other non-traditional location), (3) offer both dine-in and drive-thru options, (4) operated continuously for all of fiscal 2007.

The three middle columns (which are divided by 2007 sales amounts) are for company-owned restaurants that conformed to either the "Tower" or "Cloud" corporate images.

The right-hand column contains only company-owned restaurants that conformed to the "Tower" corporate image. Because only 64 stores belonged to this category for all of 2007, we did not divide the results by sales band.

We did not include data from franchisees in the following summary because financial statements provided by franchisees to us are not in a common format, and furthermore they are not audited.

Franchisees will incur other costs not identified below in connection with the operation of Church's Restaurants including, without limitation, occupancy costs (such as rent or mortgage payments), utilities, royalties, advertising and promotional expenses, office expenses, legal and accounting expenses, insurance expenses, and various other general administrative expenses. Expenses in the operation of Restaurants operated by franchisees will differ from Restaurants operated by Cajun and will vary from franchisee to franchisee and from location to location, and are dependant upon seasonal, local and other factors beyond our control, such as the franchisee's efficiency in the utilization of products, the costs of transportation and the fluctuation in market prices for food and other products.

The operating costs information reflected in the following table is based on company financial statements (see Note 1 below).

	2007 Sales "Tower" or "Cloud" image			2007 Sales "Tower" image only
	<$800,000	$800,000 – $1,000,000	>$1,000,000	
Sales	100.0%	100.0%	100.0%	100.0%
Food cost (see Note 2)	34.1%	32.9%	32.4%	31.1%
Labor – Management	7.5%	6.6%	6.3%	5.6%
Labor - Shift Management	3.4%	2.5%	2.0%	1.9%
Labor – Crew	14.1%	12.6%	12.0%	11.0%
Labor – Other	5.0%	4.2%	3.9%	3.7%
Labor – Total (see Note 3)	30.0%	25.9%	24.1%	22.1%
Gross Profit Margin	**35.8%**	**41.2%**	**43.5%**	**46.7%**
Controllables	13.2%	10.7%	8.8%	8.9%
Marketing (see Note 4)	5.0%	5.0%	5.0%	5.0%
Royalty (see Note 5)	5.0%	5.0%	5.0%	5.0%
Controllable Profit Margin	**12.6%**	**20.5%**	**24.7%**	**27.8%**
Non-controllables (see Note 6)	2.0%	1.5%	1.2%	1.5%
Restaurant Operating Profit, pre-tax (Earnings Before Interest, Taxes, Depreciation, Amortization, and Rent)	**10.6%**	**19.0%**	**23.5%**	**26.3%**
Unit Count	86	49	35	46

Notes To Table 4: 2007 Income Statement Summary - By Sales Band

1.   We sold 15 company-owned restaurants in Arizona to a franchisee on December 15, 2007. For this table, those restaurants are considered company restaurants for all of 2007.

2.   Food costs include the delivered cost of food, beverages, paper and promotional items (i.e., limited-time offerings) to the restaurants. Delivered costs include distribution and freight costs. The calculation of food costs is primarily a function of the mix of products sold and the cost of commodities which compromise the products.

3.   Labor costs include unit hourly labor, which is comprised of the average hourly rate and the number of hours worked (a direct correlation to sales volume). The cost of labor will vary from location to location and will be dependent upon factors beyond our control, including, without limitation, local minimum wage laws and local labor market conditions. Labor costs also include the salaries of general and assistant managers. Most company-owned restaurants employ one sala-

ried general manager and one salaried assistant manager. The other components of labor expense are: payroll taxes, health insurance, vacation, wages, sick pay, bonuses and workers' compensation insurance. We make no warranties, representations, predictions, promises or guaranties with respect to the actual labor expenses likely to be experienced by individual franchisees. Also, with respect to labor costs, because a certain number of employees will be necessary to open and operate a restaurant irrespective of its Gross Sales, units that have lower than average Gross Sales probably will experience higher than average labor costs.

4.   The Marketing fee is described as 5.0% because franchisees are required to pay up to 5% of gross income to the Advertising Fund. [See Item 6 and Item 11.] The percentage of income from company-owned stores which is spent on marketing may be higher or lower than 5.0%. You may spend more than 5.0% of gross revenue on marketing.

5.   The Royalty fee is described as 5.0% because franchisees are required to pay 5% of gross income to Cajun. [See Item 6.] Company-owned stores do not pay a royalty fee.

6.   Table 4 excludes occupancy costs, i.e. rent or mortgage payments

Upon reasonable request, written substantiation for the information appearing in these Tables will be made available to you.

Except for the information in this Item 19, we do not furnish or authorize our salespersons to furnish any oral or written information concerning the actual, average, projected, or forecasted sales, costs, income or profits (*i.e.*, earnings capability) of a restaurant. We specifically instruct our sales personnel, agents, and employees that they are not permitted to make any claims or statements concerning a specific franchisee's earnings capability or chances for success.

Your individual financial results are likely to differ from results described in this Item 19. You should conduct an independent investigation of the costs and expenses you will incur in operating your Restaurant. Franchisees or former franchisees indentified in this disclosure document may be one source of information.

CINNABON
200 Glenridge Point Pkwy. # 200
Atlanta, GA 30342
Tel: (800) 227-8353 (404) 255-3250
Fax: (404) 255-4978
E-Mail: spando@focusbrands.com
Web Site: www.cinnabon.com
Mr. D'wayne Tanner, VP Franchise Sales/Develop.

Maker of the world's most famous cinnamon rolls, Cinnabon serves fresh, aromatic, oven-hot cinnamon rolls, as well as a variety of other baked goods and specialty beverages. Cinnabon currently operates more than 600 franchised locations worldwide, primarily in high traffic venues such as shopping malls, airports, train stations, travel plazas, entertainment venues, academic institutions and military bases.

BACKGROUND:
Established: 1985;   IFA MEMBER
                                     1st Franchised: 1986

Franchised Units:	749
Company-Owned Units:	0
Total Units:	749
Dist.:	US-749; CAN-26; O'seas-277
North America:	44 States, 2 Provinces
Density:	129 in CA, 43 in FL, 48 in TX
Projected New Units (12 Months):	10
Qualifications:	5, 5, 5, 4, 4, 5
Registered:	HI,IL,MD,MN,ND,RI,SD,VA,WA,WI

FINANCIAL/TERMS:

Cash Investment:	$100K
Total Investment:	$192.2K-317K
Minimum Net Worth:	$300K
Fees: Franchise -	$30K
Royalty - 6%;	Ad. - 1.5%
Earnings Claims Statement:	Yes
Term of Contract (Years):	20/20
Avg. # Of Employees:	6 FT, 0 PT
Passive Ownership:	Not Allowed
Encourage Conversions:	Yes
Area Develop. Agreements:	Yes
Sub-Franchising Contracts:	No

Expand In Territory:	Yes	Franchisee Assoc./Member:	Yes/Member
Space Needs:	850 SF; RM, Airport, Travel Plaza/venue, Entertainment	Size Of Corporate Staff:	52
		On-Going Support:	E,G
		Training:	2 Weeks CRT Location
SUPPORT & TRAINING:			
Financial Assistance Provided:	NA	**SPECIFIC EXPANSION PLANS:**	
Site Selection Assistance:	Yes	US:	Yes, LA, NY, AL, MS, AR, MO
Lease Negotiation Assistance:	Yes	Canada:	Yes
Co-Operative Advertising:	Yes	Overseas:	Yes, All Countries

ITEM 19
FINANCIAL PERFORMANCE REPRESENTATIONS

The following table presents information about the annual sales, during our fiscal year ended December 31, 2007, of Bakeries in mall locations that were open throughout the entire calendar year.

AMOUNT OF DISTRIBUTION OF ANNUAL SALES
(Mall Locations Only)

Annual Sales (000 omitted)	Consolidated	Number of Franchised Units
$900 and up	3%	7
$800-899	1%	2
$700-799	2%	6
$600-699	6%	14
$500-599	7%	17
$400-499	19%	47
$300-399	27%	66
< $300	35%	87
Total	100.0%	246

Arithmetic Average* Franchised
$388,879

	Sales Range Franchised
High	$1,163,320
Low	$54,272

The following notes form an integral part of the above tables.

Notes:

[1]   The Bakeries whose results are reflected in the tables above were in operation continuously throughout our fiscal year ended December 31, 2007. Results of Bakeries that either opened or closed during this period are not included.

[2]   Results of Bakeries that either opened or closed dining this period are not included. Of

the Bakeries that were open throughout the entire calendar year, (i) there were 246 Bakeries located in the confines of shopping malls and (ii) 186 Bakeries located in other venues. The information in Item 19, is for Bakeries located within the confines of shopping malls, not Bakeries located in any other venues.

[3] As shown in the tables above, sales volumes vary considerably due to a variety of factors, such as demographics of the Bakery trade area; competition from other restaurants in the trade area; traffic and traffic flow accessibility and visibility; mall traffic; economic conditions in the Bakery trade area; advertising and promotional activities; and the business abilities and efforts of the management of the Bakery. Your individual financial results may differ from the results stated in this Item 19.

[4] The results shown for franchise Bakeries have been taken from sales reports submitted by franchisees. We have not audited these sales reports, but have no information or other reason to believe that they are unreliable. This earnings claim also does not include the cost of sales, operating expenses or any other costs that must be deducted from gross revenue or gross sales figures to obtain your net income or profit.

[5] These sales figures are for specific franchise Bakeries and should not be considered as the actual or potential sales that will be achieved by any other franchise Bakery. We do not represent that any franchisee can expect to attain these sales results. Actual results vary from Bakery to Bakery and we cannot estimate the results of any specific Bakery. A new franchisee's results are likely to be lower than the results shown above. We recommend that you make your own independent investigation to determine whether or not the franchise may be profitable, and consult with an attorney or other advisors before signing any Franchise Agreement.

[6] On reasonable request, substantiation for the information appearing in these Tables will be made available to you.

[7] Except for the information in this item, we do not furnish or authorize our salespersons to furnish any oral or written information on the actual, average, projected or forecasted sales, costs, income or profits (the "Earnings Capability") of a Bakery. We specifically instruct our sales personnel, agents and other employees that they are not permitted to make any claims or statements concerning a specific franchisee's Earnings Capability or chances for success.

Please refer to the California Addendum to this Disclosure Document for additional information regarding earnings claims.

DENNY'S

203 E. Main St.
Spartanburg, SC 29319-9912
Tel: (800) 304-0222 (864) 597-8000
Fax: (713) 849-0722
E-Mail: franchisedevelopment@dennys.com
Web Site: www.dennys.com

For over 50 years, Denny's has been the trusted leader in family dining. We enjoy a brand awareness of almost 100%! We cheerfully serve over 26 million customers a month in our 1500+ restaurants worldwide. We are proud to serve America's most loved foods 24 hours a day, 7 days a week. If you are an experienced restaurateur or businessman, we invite you to contact us and learn more about growth opportunities within our great brand.

BACKGROUND: IFA MEMBER

Established: 1953;	1st Franchised: 1963
Franchised Units:	1265
Company-Owned Units:	286
Total Units:	1551
Dist.:	US-1475; CAN-49; O'seas-27
North America:	49 States, 5 Provinces
Density:	404 in CA, 157 in FL
Projected New Units (12 Months):	37
Qualifications:	5, 5, 5, 3, NR, 5

Registered:CA,DC,FL,HI,IL,IN,MD,MI,MN,ND,NY,OR,RI,SD, VA,WA,WI,AB

FINANCIAL/TERMS:

Cash Investment:	$350-$400K	**SUPPORT & TRAINING:**	
Total Investment:	$1M-$2.6M	Financial Assistance Provided:	No
Minimum Net Worth:	$1M	Site Selection Assistance:	Yes
Fees: Franchise -	$40K	Lease Negotiation Assistance:	No
Royalty - 4%;	Ad. - 4%	Co-Operative Advertising:	Yes
Earnings Claims Statement:	Yes	Franchisee Assoc./Member:	Yes/Member
Term of Contract (Years):	20/N/A	Size Of Corporate Staff:	350
Avg. # Of Employees:	50 FT, 25 PT	On-Going Support:	C,D,e,G,I
Passive Ownership:	Allowed, But Discouraged	Training: Up to 10 Weeks, Nearest Training Restaurant to the Franchisee	
Encourage Conversions:	Yes		
Area Develop. Agreements:	Yes	**SPECIFIC EXPANSION PLANS:**	
Sub-Franchising Contracts:	No	US:	Yes, All United States
Expand In Territory:	Yes	Canada:	Yes, All Canada
Space Needs: 4,200 SF; FS,SF,SC, Hotels, Conversions, Endcap		Overseas:	Yes, All Overseas

Item 19
FINANCIAL PERFORMANCE REPRESENTATIONS

The following financial schedule contains information relating to the performance of Denny's restaurants operated by our affiliate, DI. The information is provided for the purpose of helping you evaluate the potential earnings capability of the Restaurant. The information presented does not represent the actual performance of any single restaurant. The notes following the schedule attempt to explain the information and provide the underlying assumptions.

THE NET SALES, GROSS PROFITS, AND EBITDA ARE A COMPILATION OF THE RESULTS OF INDIVIDUAL DENNY'S RESTAURANTS OWNED AND OPERATED BY DI, AND SHOULD NOT BE CONSIDERED AS THE ACTUAL OR PROBABLE NET SALES, GROSS PROFITS, OR EBITDA THAT WILL BE REALIZED BY YOU. WE DO NOT REPRESENT THAT YOU CAN EXPECT TO ATTAIN ANY OF THE RESULTS REFLECTED IN THE SCHEDULE. ACTUAL RESULTS WILL VARY FROM RESTAURANT TO RESTAURANT AND WE CANNOT ESTIMATE OR GUARANTEE THE RESULTS OF ANY SPECIFIC RESTAURANT. IN 2007, DI BEGAN SELLING RESTAURANTS IN A STRATEGIC PROGRAM TO FOCUS ON HIGHER VOLUME RESTAURANTS IN A SMALLER NUMBER OF MARKETS. THE OPERATING RESULTS FOR RESTAURANTS SOLD BY DI DO NOT APPEAR IN THE FOLLOWING TABLE. THE OPERATING PERFORMANCE OF DI'S REMAINING COMPANY RESTAURANTS WHICH WE PRESENT, AND IN PARTICULAR AVERAGE UNIT VOLUMES AND MAJOR EXPENSE CATEGORIES, IS BECOMING INCREASINGLY UNLIKE RESULTS IN FRANCHISE OPERATED UNITS.

ACTUAL SALES AND EARNINGS OF THE RESTAURANT ARE AFFECTED BY MANY FACTORS, INCLUDING YOUR OWN EFFORTS, ABILITY, AND CONTROL OF THE RESTAURANT, AS WELL AS FACTORS OVER WHICH YOU DO NOT HAVE ANY CONTROL.

WE DO NOT REPRESENT THAT THE RESTAURANT WILL BE PROFITABLE.

Denny's
Company Restaurant Operating Performance

	Top Third		Middle Third		Bottom Third	
	$	%	$	%	$	%
Net Sales	2,297	100%	1,697	100%	1,333	100%
Food	523	23%	397	23%	320	24%
Crew Labor	514	22%	397	23%	321	24%

Management Labor	170	7%	148	9%	139	10%
Gross Profit	1,089	47%	755	45%	553	41%
Taxes / Fringe Benefits	170	7%	142	8%	119	9%
Utilities	90	4%	81	5%	74	6%
Repair & Maintenance	40	2%	35	2%	33	2%
Other Expense	126	5%	101	6%	86	6%
EBITDA before Royalties, Advertising, Occupancy Cost and Management Fees	$663	29%	$396	23%	$241	18%

EBITDA defined as Earnings Before Interest. Taxes, Depreciation, and Amortization without considering major capital expenditures. Above numbers reflect a total of 387 stores that were open the entire year, 129 in each Third. All dollar figures in thousands.

NOTES TO FINANCIAL SCHEDULE

A.   The schedule presents the actual operating results with respect to sales and selected costs of 387 Denny's restaurants owned and operated by DI in the United States during the twelve month period beginning December 28, 2006 and ending December 26, 2007, excluding only those restaurants which were open for only part of such period. Each tier is comprised of 129 Denny's restaurants. The schedule is based upon data received from DI's employees at each restaurant who, in the normal course of business, collect such data.

B.   "Net Sales" reflected on the schedule represent all revenue derived from the restaurants, including all sales of food, goods, wares, merchandise, and all services made in, upon, or from the restaurants, including catering services, whether for cash, check, credit, or otherwise, without reserve or deduction for inability to collect same. Net Sales do not include rebates or refunds to customers or the amount of any sales taxes or other similar taxes that restaurants may be required to collect from customers to be paid to any federal, state, or local taxing authority.

C.   We are not able to provide similar information relating to the operation of Denny's restaurants operated by our franchisees because we do not have reliable information relating to costs incurred by franchise operators. However, during the same period (a twelve month period beginning December 28, 2006 and ending December 26, 2007) the average Net Sales of all Denny's restaurants (including both franchised restaurants and restaurants owned and operated by DI) were $1,592,585. This figure excludes any restaurant that was open for only part of such period. See sales information below.

D.   There are no material differences between the operations of the restaurants being franchised by us and the restaurants owned and operated by DI. Both groups of restaurants will operate under the same System, and with similar operating requirements.

E.   The restaurants included in the schedule have been open for periods as short as one year and as long as 49 years. No restaurant has been open for less than twelve months.

F.   The final line of the schedule reflects the restaurant profit before deducting expenses which differ among individual restaurants. These additional expenses, which are likely to be significant, will vary widely among restaurants, and may include, but not necessarily be limited to, the following:

- Royalty fees and advertising contributions
- Occupancy cost
- Management fees
- Interest or financing charges not included in lease payments
- Taxes
- Depreciation on property and equipment
- Any preopening or amortization of organization costs
- Accounting, legal fees, and general administrative expenses

We strongly encourage you to consult with your financial advisors in reviewing the schedule and, in particular, in estimating the categories and amount of additional expenses which you will incur in establishing and operating the Restaurant. The schedule contains only some of the categories in which you may incur expenses.

G. The schedule was prepared from the internal operating records of DI which, in turn, were prepared in accordance with generally accepted accounting principles. The schedule is unaudited. Substantiation for the data set forth in the schedule will be made available by us to all prospective franchisees upon reasonable request.

H. Except for the schedule set forth in this Item, and profit and loss statements which we may provide to you in circumstances in which we sell you an FGI Restaurant (see the section titled, "FGI P&L's," below), we do not make information available to prospective franchisees in this state concerning actual, average, projected, or forecasted sales, costs, income, or profits. You should be aware that the financial performance of any particular restaurant may be affected by a number of factors, including, but not limited to the following:

1. The schedule does not reflect debt service costs. You will incur such costs to the extent you finance the initial franchise fee and the development and construction cost of the Restaurant and the furniture, fixtures, and equipment, or to the extent you borrow funds to acquire the property and build the Restaurant.

2. The Restaurant may face competition from restaurants and food service outlets offering many different types of cuisine. The intensity of this competition will vary depending upon the location of the Restaurant. Further, the tastes of a community or community segment may not be accustomed to the type of products offered by the Restaurant. As such, appreciation for and acceptance of the products offered by the Restaurant may have to be developed to varying degrees depending upon the particular community.

3. You may not have comparable restaurant and food service experience and expertise as found in the Denny's restaurants owned and operated by Dl. While we will provide certain assistance to you (see Item 11), you and the staff of the Restaurant will be primarily responsible for the daily operations of the Restaurant in accordance with the terms of the Franchise Agreement,

4. The quality and effectiveness of your managerial skills will affect, positively or negatively, the sales results of the Restaurant. Decisions with respect to location, additional advertising programs, personnel, cost controls, and other factors may impact the results of the Restaurant.

5. Geographic and socio-economic variations from locality to locality may affect the results of the Restaurant, as well as factors bearing upon business cycles and performance of the national and world economy.

We recommend that you make your own independent investigation to determine whether or not the franchise may be profitable, and consult with an attorney and other advisors prior to executing any agreement.

We require all prospects who have never been Denny's franchisees, as a condition of being approved, to consult with an independent financial advisor and to review with that person operating statements for the restaurants to be acquired or developed and all other terms of the transaction. This review should include current and pro forma P&L's, as applicable. A prospective franchisee with financial expertise, or who has a person with such expertise on its staff, would be excused. Otherwise, the financial advisor would need to be a third party, and not affiliated with any other party to the transaction, including sellers, brokers, lenders or developers.

I. Except for the schedule set forth in this Item, and profit and loss statements which we may provide to you in circumstances in which we sell you an FGI Restaurant (see the section titled, "FGI P&L's," below), we do not furnish, or authorize our salespersons to furnish, any oral or written information concerning the actual, average, projected, or forecasted sales, costs, income, or profits of a Denny's restaurant. Actual results vary from unit to unit, and we cannot estimate the results of any particular restaurant.

Sales of Denny's Restaurants

For 2007, 1363 Denny's restaurants in the US and Canada were open the entire year. We operated 387 restaurants and 976 were franchised. Restaurants open less than one full year have been omitted, of which there were 6 Company-owned and 18 franchised, as well as 130 FGI restaurants. The average sales of the franchised and Company-owned restaurants combined was $1,593,000. Franchised restaurants included in the analysis had average sales of $1,520,000. Company-owned restaurants included in the analysis had average sales of $1,776,000. The range was

Franchised Restaurants:

Sales Range	Number of Franchised Restaurants	Percentage of Franchised Restaurants
Over $2,000,000	132	14%
$1,500,000 to $2,000,000	316	32%
$1,000,000 to $1,500,000	450	46%
Under $1,000,000	78	8%
TOTAL	976	100%

Company-owned Restaurants:

Sales Range	Number of Company-Owned Restaurants	Percentage of Company-Owned Restaurants
Over $2,000,000	87	23%
$1,500,000 to $2,000,000	187	48%
$1,000,000 to $1,500,000	110	28%
Under $1,000,000	3	1%
TOTAL	387	100%

NOTES AND ASSUMPTIONS

1. The size of the restaurants may vary significantly. Over the past few years we had several restaurant plans available, ranging from "Diner" concepts with 101 to 113 seats to classic buildings with 98 to 150 seats.

2. We compiled the figures provided above from our financial statements and from sales reports submitted to us by our franchise operators on a 52 week basis. The sales information provided by our franchise operators has not been audited and, has not necessarily been prepared on a basis consistent with generally accepted accounting principles.

3. The 130 FGI restaurants had an average volume in YE 2006 of $1,510,000.

FGI P&L's

If we sell to you an FGI restaurant, we will share with you information relating to the historical performance of the FGI restaurant. Typically, this information consists of the profit and loss statement (the "P&L") for the FGI restaurant, which is prepared in the normal course of business by DI, the seller of the FGI restaurant. The P&L is prepared in accordance with generally accepted accounting principles, but it is not audited. The P&L does not include royalty payments that you will be required to pay under your Franchise Agreement with us. P&L information will be shared with you only after we have come to some preliminary understandings regarding your purchase of the FGI restaurant, but before you make any binding commitment to purchase the FGI restaurant under the terms of a Purchase Agreement. The information will be subject to a confidentiality agreement. (See Exhibit G.)

In providing to you P&L's for an FGI restaurant, we neither represent nor warrant that the level of sales achieved by DI will be the same as the sales which you may achieve. Moreover, various expenses incurred by DI in the operation of the FGI restaurant will likely differ from the expenses you incur. For example, to the extent you borrow funds to acquire the FGI restaurant, the P&L figures will not reflect debt service costs which you will be required to pay. As a consequence, the results of your operation of the FGI restaurant will not be the same as the results of operation of the FGI restaurant by DI. Therefore, we strongly encourage you to consult with your financial advisors in reviewing P&L's for the FGI restaurant, in particular, in estimating the categories and amount of additional expenses which you will incur in establishing and operating the Restaurant.

DUNKIN' DONUTS

130 Royall St.
Canton, MA 02021
Tel: (877) 938-6546
Fax:
E-Mail: pam.gore@dunkinbrands.com
Web Site: www.dunkinfranchising.com
Ms. Pam Gore, Director of Franchising

Founded in 1950, today Dunkin' Donuts is the number one retailer of coffee-by-the-cup in America, selling 2.7 million cups a day, nearly one billion cups a year. Dunkin' Donuts is also the largest coffee and baked goods chain in the world and sells more donuts, coffee and bagels than any other quick service restaurant in America. Dunkin' Donuts has more than 6,500 shops in 29 countries worldwide. Based in Canton, Massachusetts, Dunkin' Donuts is a subsidiary of Dunkin' Brands, Inc. For more information, visit www.DunkinDonuts.com.

BACKGROUND:	IFA MEMBER
Established: 1950;	1st Franchised: 1955
Franchised Units:	7200
Company-Owned Units:	0
Total Units:	7200
Dist.:	US-4736; CAN-78; O'seas-1856
North America:	39 States, 5 Provinces
Density:	237 in IL, 490 in MA, 359 in NY
Projected New Units (12 Months):	350
Qualifications:	5, 4, 2, 2, 5, 4

Registered: CA,DC,FL,IL,IN,MD,MI,MN,NY,OR,RI,VA,WA,WI

FINANCIAL/TERMS:	
Cash Investment:	$750K
Total Investment:	$240K-1.67MM
Minimum Net Worth:	$1.5MM
Fees: Franchise -	$40-80K
Royalty - 5.9%;	Ad. - 5%
Earnings Claims Statement:	Yes
Term of Contract (Years):	20
Avg. # Of Employees:	NR FT, 0 PT
Passive Ownership:	Allowed
Encourage Conversions:	Yes
Area Develop. Agreements:	Yes
Sub-Franchising Contracts:	No
Expand In Territory:	Yes
Space Needs:	SF; FS,SF,SC,RM

SUPPORT & TRAINING:	
Financial Assistance Provided:	Yes (D)
Site Selection Assistance:	NA
Lease Negotiation Assistance:	Yes
Co-Operative Advertising:	No
Franchisee Assoc./Member:	Yes/Member
Size Of Corporate Staff:	
On-Going Support:	B,C,E,G,H,I
Training:	51 Days Randolph, MA;
	3.5 Days Another Location

SPECIFIC EXPANSION PLANS:	
US:	Yes, All Regions
Canada:	Yes, PQ, ON
Overseas:	Yes, All Countries

Item 19: Financial Performance Representations

Please note that a new franchisee's individual financial results may differ from the results stated in the financial performance representations in this Item 19.

We will make written substantiation for the financial performance representations in this Item 19 available to prospective franchisees upon reasonable request.

All of the tables that follow in this Item 19 should be read together with the notes that follow, also in this Item 19.

DUNKIN' DONUTS STORES: The following financial performance representations are historical based on information from all existing *Dunkin' Donuts* stores for the prior fiscal year, **DECEMBER 31, 2006 THROUGH DECEMBER 29, 2007.**

Region	Average Sales	% at or Above Avg.[1]
Total Continental U.S.	$882,388	42.1%
New England	$962,052	45.0%
Metro NY	$914,992	41.4%
Upstate NY	$889,564	43.8%
Baltimore/ Washington/ Pennsylvania	$811,668	40.4%
Southeast	$673,244	43.2%
Midwest	$607,724	37.1%
Frontier	$646,308	34.9%

Total number of Stores included in calculations for each Region above is as follows:

Total Continental U.S.:	4,398
New England:	2,011
Metro NY:	859
Upstate NY:	276
Baltimore/Washington/ Pennsylvania:	565
Southeast:	345
Midwest:	299
Frontier:	43

DUNKIN' DONUTS ALTERNATIVE POINTS OF DISTRIBUTION: The following financial performance representations are historical based on information from all existing *DUNKIN' DONUTS ALTERNATIVE POINTS OF DISTRIBUTION* stores for the Store type listed below in the prior fiscal year, **DECEMBER 31, 2006 THROUGH DECEMBER 29, 2007.**

Store Type	Average Sales	% at or above Average[1]
Total Continental U.S.	$450,840	30.2%
Airport	$802,100	30.4%
Business/Industry	$540,696	40.0%

100

Hospital/Medical	$571,480	38.9%
Mass Merchandise	$381,576	42.7%
Supermarket	$336,960	42.1%
Travel Center	$712,660	30.6%

Total number of Stores included in calculations for each is as follows:

Total Continental U.S.:	407
Airport:	44
Business/Industry:	18
Hospital/Medical:	18
Mass Merchandise:	82
Supermarket:	195
Travel Center:	50

The annualized sales data for *Dunkin' Donuts* Alternative Points of Distribution is a subset of and included in the annualized sales data for all *Dunkin' Donuts* stores provided above.

For more information regarding the "Regions" used in the Sales Data, refer to Appendix IV at the end of this FDD. The Region descriptions are approximations. Some store locations included in this sales data may not precisely follow the descriptions contained in Appendix IV. (For example, some stores near the boundary of another Region may be included in that other Region's sales data.)

NOTES REGARDING SALES DATA

(1)   We provide you sales data that includes average sales and the percentage of stores reporting who have actually attained or surpassed the stated average. This sales data does not include sales tax. The vast majority of the stores that comprise this data are franchised, although we may have a small number of company owned stores at any given time (see Item 20).

(2)   The sales figures from franchised stores are compiled by using sales that are reported to us by franchisees. We have not audited or verified the reports.

(3)   Sales in states or regions with a higher concentration of stores that have been in operation for a substantial period of time tend to have higher sales than states or regions with a lower concentration of stores that have been in operation for a lesser time period. These higher concentration states or regions significantly increase the overall average due to both their higher sales and their larger numbers. Therefore, the sales performance of stores outside of these higher concentration areas may not be commensurate with the overall average sales. Please see Item 20 of this FDD for the number of stores per state. We have not been able to draw conclusions regarding the role longevity may have played in achieving preeminence in a market, or whether the lack of longevity in a market may be a barrier to achieving preeminence. For example, competitors' customers may resist changing their buying habits. It is possible that preeminence may not be achieved in some higher concentration areas due to other reasons.

(4)   Many of the stores included in this data have been open and operating for several years. These franchisees have achieved their level of sales after spending many years building customer goodwill at a particular location.

(5)   Your sales will be affected by your own operational ability, which may include your

101

experience with managing a business, your capital and financing (including working capital), continual training of you and your staff, customer service orientation, product quality, your business plan, and the use of experts (e.g., an accountant) to assist in your business plan.

(6)   Your sales may be affected by store location and site criteria, including traffic count and which side of the street your store is located on (i.e., whether your store is on the morning drive side or afternoon drive side of traffic), local household income, residential and/or daytime populations, ease of ingress and egress, seating, parking, the physical condition of your store, the size of your site, and the visibility of your exterior sign(s). Additionally, many of the stores included in the sales figures are freestanding stores or located at the end of a strip center, and if your store is not, your sales could be negatively affected. Your sales may be negatively affected by not adhering to our standards and system, including the above, and proper equipment layout, design and construction criteria, customer queuing and flow, and local store marketing.

(7)   Individual locations may have layouts and seating capacities that vary from the typical suburban location.

(8)   Other matters affecting your sales may be competition (national and local), inflation, and federal, state and local government regulations.

(9)   Your sales may be affected by changes in the menu and regional differences in products including whether there are products not available to you or your region but sold in other regions. Menus are continually being revised, both adding and discontinuing products and product line extensions. Not all stores may have these new products. New products may not be successful for all stores. Marketing activity associated with new products may be at higher than normal levels and, therefore, sales increases may not be maintained after this temporary marketing activity is completed.

(10)   Sales may be affected by fluctuations due to seasonality (particularly in colder climates), weather and periodic marketing and advertising programs. Inclement weather may cause temporary store closings in some areas.

(11)   The above data reflects historical sales. There is no assurance that future sales will correspond to historical sales.

(12)   There are numerous factors that may affect sales at your store. The factors listed above and below are not an all-inclusive list of those factors.

THE ABOVE EARNINGS CLAIMS FIGURES RELATE ONLY TO SALES, AND DOES NOT REFLECT THE COSTS OF SALES, OPERATING EXPENSES OR OTHER COSTS OR EXPENSES THAT MUST BE DEDUCTED FROM THE GROSS REVENUE OR GROSS SALES FIGURES TO OBTAIN NET INCOME OR PROFIT. YOU SHOULD CONDUCT AN INDEPENDENT INVESTIGATION OF THE COSTS AND EXPENSES YOU WILL INCUR IN OPERATING YOUR FRANCHISED BUSINESS. FRANCHISEES OR FORMER FRANCHISEES, LISTED IN THE DISCLOSURE DOCUMENT, MAY BE ONE SOURCE OF THIS INFORMATION.

ADDITIONAL NOTES

Stores that have a drive-thru window tend to have higher sales than stores without a drive-thru window. Many of the *Dunkin' Donuts* stores included in the above statistics have a drive-thru window. Some individual stores' sales may include wholesale accounts and other distribution outlets, which may not be available to you. Not all of these opportunities have been successful for all participating franchisees. These opportunities may have been added, expanded, reduced or eliminated from individual reporting stores at varying times during the reporting period. The contracts for such opportunities may have been terminated or expired without renewal in the reported or future periods. Additionally, some products may not be available in your state or region that are included in the reported sales for many of the stores.

The information provided on *Dunkin' Donuts* alternative points of distribution ("APOD") is based upon a relatively small number of stores that are predominantly located in the Northeast Region of the U.S. (New England, Metro NY and Baltimore/Washington/Pennsylvania). Factors such as differences in competition, consumer preferences, execution of the *Dunkin' Donuts* concept, concentration of shops, average sales, among others, may make the experience of *Dunkin' Donuts* APOD shops different than traditional *Dunkin' Donuts* shops.

DUNKIN' DONUTS/BASKIN-ROBBINS COMBO STORES

We do not make financial performance representations about Dunkin' Donuts/Baskin-Robbins Combo Stores

The FTC's Franchise Rule permits a franchisor to provide information about the actual or potential financial performance of its franchise and/or franchisor-owned outlets, if there is a reasonable basis for the information, and if the information is included in the disclosure document. Financial performance information that differs from that included in Item 19 may be given only if: (1) a franchisor provides the actual records of an existing outlet you are considering buying; or (2) a franchisor supplements the information provided in this Item 19, for example, by providing information about possible performance at a particular location or under particular circumstances.

We do not make any representations about a franchisee's future financial performance or the past financial performance of company-owned or franchised outlets. We also do not authorize our employees or representatives to make any such representations either orally or in writing. If you are purchasing an existing outlet, however, we may provide you with the actual records of that outlet. If you receive any other financial performance information or projections of your future income, you should report it to the franchisor's management by contacting our General Counsel, Stephen Horn, c/o Dunkin' Donuts/Baskin-Robbins, 130 Royall Street, Canton, MA 02021, 781-737- 3000, the Federal Trade Commission, and the appropriate state regulatory agencies.

IF APPLICABLE, HISTORICAL SALES AND PROFIT DATA
FOR EXISTING STORE TO BE SOLD BY US

If the subject store is an existing store being sold by us, we may provide to you unaudited historical sales and profit data for the store. Statements prepared by us are prepared in accordance with generally accepted accounting principals. Statements prepared by past franchisee(s) of the store, if any, were submitted to us by franchisee(s) who we require to prepare statements in accordance with generally accepted accounting principals. We cannot assure you that in all cases they were so prepared.

Historical costs do not correspond to future costs because of such factors as inflation, changes in minimum wage laws, the local labor market, financing, real estate related costs and other variables. For example, actual costs such as rent, taxes, depreciation, amortization interest, insurance, payroll, and utilities may vary from historical costs. Historical sales may also not correspond to future sales because of such factors as the duration, if any, that the store was closed, changes in store management and employees, remodel or refurbishment, if any, over or under reporting of sales, changes in competition and other variables.

Your accountant should develop your own data for these accounts based on your particular financing and other costs. All information should be evaluated in light of current market conditions including such cost and price information as may then be available.

SUCH ACTUAL SALES, INCOME, GROSS OR NET PROFITS RELATE TO THE PERFORMANCE OF THE FRANCHISEE(S) OR COMPANY OPERATIONS FOR THIS STORE DURING THE TIME PERIOD(S) REPORTED AND SHOULD NOT BE CONSIDERED AS THE ACTUAL OR PROBABLE SALES, INCOME, GROSS OR NET PROFITS THAT YOU WILL REALIZE. WE DO NOT REPRESENT THAT YOU CAN EXPECT TO ATTAIN SUCH SALES, INCOME, GROSS OR NET PROFITS.

FIGARO'S PIZZA

FIGARO'S PIZZA

1500 Liberty St., S. E.
Salem, OR 97302
Tel: (888) 344-2767 (503) 371-9318
Fax: (503) 363-5364
E-Mail: franchisedev@figaros.com
Web Site: www.figaros.com
Mr. Ron Berger, Chairman/CEO

Take the best pizza anywhere! Make it available to consumers either baked or 'take-and-bake;' for in-store dining, take-out, or delivery; add superior world-class store designs, systems, and marketing, and you have the opportunity Figaro's Pizza offers you today.Be the Boss. Instead of making a lot of money for everyone else, the time is right to make it yourself, building your own assets and equity. You deserve it. And we have just the right vehicle to make the move.

BACKGROUND: IFA MEMBER

Established: 1981;	1st Franchised: 1986
Franchised Units:	89
Company-Owned Units:	0
Total Units:	89
Dist.:	US-87; CAN-0; O'seas-2
North America:	20 States, 0 Provinces
Density:	54 in OR, 12 in WA, 13 in WI
Projected New Units (12 Months):	15
Qualifications:	5, 3, 2, 1, 1, 3

Registered:CA,DC,FL,HI,IL,IN,MI,MN,ND,NY,OR,RI,SD,VA,

WA,WI,AB

FINANCIAL/TERMS:

Cash Investment:	$150K
Total Investment:	$101K-$1338K
Minimum Net Worth:	$150K
Fees: Franchise -	$35K
Royalty - 5%;	Ad. - 3%
Earnings Claims Statement:	Yes
Term of Contract (Years):	5/5
Avg. # Of Employees:	2-3 FT, 8-12 PT
Passive Ownership:	Allowed
Encourage Conversions:	No
Area Develop. Agreements:	Yes
Sub-Franchising Contracts:	Yes
Expand In Territory:	No
Space Needs:	1,100 SF; FS,SC

SUPPORT & TRAINING:

Financial Assistance Provided:	Yes (I)
Site Selection Assistance:	Yes
Lease Negotiation Assistance:	Yes
Co-Operative Advertising:	Yes
Franchisee Assoc./Member:	No
Size Of Corporate Staff:	12
On-Going Support:	B,C,D,E,F,G,H,I
Training:	14 Days Salem, OR and Green Bay, WI

SPECIFIC EXPANSION PLANS:

US:	Yes, All except Maryland
Canada:	Yes, All Canada
Overseas:	Yes, All Countries

19.
FINANCIAL PERFORMANCE REPRESENTATIONS

We do not make any representations about future financial performance or the past financial performance of Master Franchisees or Schmizza or Sargo's operations. We also do not authorize our employees or representatives to make any such representations either orally or in writing. If you are purchasing an existing outlet, however, we may provide you with the actual records of that outlet. If you receive any other financial performance information or projections of your future income, you should report it to the franchisor's management by contacting our President, Ron Berger, c/o Figaro's Italian Pizza, Inc., P.O. Box 12575, Salem, Oregon 97309-0575, (503) 3719318, Ron@Figaros.com, the Federal Trade Commission, and the appropriate state regulatory agencies.

FINANCIAL PERFORMANCE REPRESENTATIONS: INDIVIDUAL UNIT FIGARO'S FRANCHISES

The following table provides average store gross revenues for individual unit Figaro's stores that have been open for at least one year as of December 31, 2007. The average revenues are for the 12 months ended December 31, 2007. The table does not include any financial performance information for any other types of franchises and does not include any stores of any type that had not been open for at least one year on December 31, 2007. See the notes following the table for additional information.

The table provides the average revenues for our top 10% revenue producing stores; our top 25% revenue producing stores (which includes the stores that are in the top 10%); and our second, third and bottom 25% revenue producing stores.

	TOP 10% (8 stores)	TOP 25% (21 stores)	SECOND 25% (21 stores)	THIRD 25% (21 stores)	BOTTOM 25% (21 stores)
AVERAGE GROSS REVENUES (for 12 Months Ended December 31, 2007)	$610,135	$ 506,443	$330,691	$259,047	$178,780

NOTES

As of **December 31, 2007**, there were **101** Unit Franchised Stores (including both Figaro's and Sargo's stores) and no company-owned stores. Of the **101** Franchised Stores, **84** were Figaro's stores that had been open for at least 12 months as of **December 31, 2007**. Of these **84** stores, all reported sufficient financial performance information to be included in this financial performance representation. Of the **84** stores whose financial performance information was used in this table, the following attained or surpassed the stated results:

-     TOP 10%:   **4 or 50%** attained or surpassed the stated results
-     TOP 25%:   **9 or 43%** attained or surpassed the stated results
-     SECOND 25%:   **11 or 52%** attained or surpassed the stated results
-     THIRD 25%:   **12 or 57%** attained or surpassed the stated results
-     BOTTOM 25%:   **12 or 57%** attained or surpassed the stated results

YOUR INDIVIDUAL FINANCIAL RESULTS MAY DIFFER SUBSTANTIALLY FROM THE RESULTS DISCLOSED IN THIS ITEM 19. THESE RESULTS SHOULD NOT BE CONSIDERED AS THE ACTUAL OR POTENTIAL SALES, PROFITS OR EARNINGS THAT WILL BE REALIZED BY ANY FRANCHISE. WE DO NOT REPRESENT THAT ANY FRANCHISEE CAN EXPECT TO ATTAIN THESE SALES, PROFITS OR EARNINGS.

CHARACTERISTICS OF THE INCLUDED FRANCHISED STORES MAY DIFFER SUBSTANTIALLY FROM YOUR STORE DEPENDING ON YOUR PREVIOUS BUSINESS AND MANAGEMENT EXPERIENCE, COMPETITION IN YOUR AREA, LENGTH OF TIME THAT THE INCLUDED STORES HAVE OPERATED AS COMPARED TO YOUR STORE, AND THE SERVICES OR GOODS SOLD AT YOUR STORE AS COMPARED TO THE INCLUDED STORES. THE SALES, PROFITS AND EARNINGS OF AN INDIVIDUAL FRANCHISEE MAY VARY GREATLY DEPENDING ON THESE AND A WIDE VARIETY OF OTHER FACTORS, INCLUDING THE LOCATION OF THE DESIGNATED TERRITORY, POPULATION DEMOGRAPHICS, ECONOMIC AND MARKET CONDITIONS, LABOR AND PRODUCT COSTS, ETC.

Written substantiation for this financial performance representation is available to you upon reasonable request.

We recommend that you make your own independent investigation to determine whether or not the franchise may be profitable, and consult with an attorney and other advisors prior to executing the franchise agreement.

GENGHIS GRILL

4099 McEwen, # 305, The Center, Bldg. 7	
Dallas, TX 75244	**BACKGROUND:** IFA MEMBER
Tel: (888) 436-4447 (214) 744-4240	Established: 1998; 1st Franchised: 2001
Fax: (214) 774-4243	Franchised Units: 9
E-Mail: franchise@genghisgrill.com	Company-Owned Units: 4
Web Site: www.genghisgrill.com	Total Units: 13
Mr. Ron Parikh, Director of Franchising	

ITEM 19
FINANCIAL PERFORMANCE REPRESENTATIONS

The following chart contains historic sales and expense information concerning the six GENGHIS GRILL® Restaurants owned and operated by our affiliates that were open for business during the full calendar year 2007. We derived these figures from our affiliates' unaudited financial statements.

Restaurant	2007 Gross Sales	Avg. Weekly Gross Sales 2007	Approximate Square Footage of Restaurant	Food and Beverage Costs	Hourly Labor, Management, and Payroll Taxes
Addison, TX[1]	$1,652,917.04	$31,786.87	3450	32.3%	25.4%
Dallas, TX[2]	$744,820.49	$14,323.47	2111	33.8%	31.3%
Dallas, TX[3]	$1,293,562.20	$24,876.20	3500	30.6%	27.1%
Plano, TX[4]	$1,736,263.52	$33,389.68	3267	30.5%	26.2%
Hurst, TX[5]	$1,417,699.00	$30,163.81	2911	32.5%	29.0%
McKinney, TX[6]	$1,239,451.20	$23,835.60	3600	31.5%	31.3%

Note 1. This restaurant began operating in 2003.

Note 2. This restaurant began operating in October 2002.

Note 3. This restaurant began operating in January 2003.

Note 4. This restaurant began operating in September 2005.

Note 5. This restaurant began operating in January 2007.

Note 6. This restaurant began operating in July 2006.

AS A NEW FRANCHISEE, YOUR INDIVIDUAL FINANCIAL RESULTS MAY DIFFER FROM THE RESULT STATED IN THIS FINANCIAL PERFORMANCE REPRESENTATION.

Written substantiation for the financial performance representation will be made available to you upon reasonable request.

Except for the information presented above, we do not use or furnish statements of actual, average, projected or forecasted sales, costs, profits or earnings in marketing our franchises. We will not guarantee, nor do we represent, that you will or can expect to attain any specific amount or range of sales, profits or earnings from the operation of your Restaurant. Actual results may vary from Restaurant to Restaurant, and we cannot estimate the results of any franchisee.

Except for the information presented above, we do not authorize any of our officers, employees or sales representatives to make any claims, statements or representations regarding the sales, costs, profits or earnings, or the prospects or chances of success, that you can expect to achieve or that any other franchisee has achieved. We specifically instruct our representatives not to make such claims, statements or representations, and you are cautioned not to rely on any claims, statements or representations any person makes in disregard of these instructions.

HARDEE'S

6307 Carpinteria Ave., # A
Carpinteria, CA 93013
Tel: (866) 253-7655 (805) 745-7842
Fax: (714) 780-6320
E-Mail: chopkins@ckr.com
Web Site: www.ckr.com
Mr. Craig Hopkins, VP Franchise Sales

The Hardee's® brand is one of America's Premier Burger Brands and is the Home of the Thickburger®. Established in 1961, Hardee's® operates or franchises over 1,900 quick service restaurants in 30 U.S. states and 9 countries. The Hardee's® menu consists of charbroiled "Made-to-order" Thickburgers™, Made from Scratch® biscuits. Hand-Scooped Shakes and Malts™, and a distinctive variety of charbroiled and crispy chicken sandwiches.

BACKGROUND: IFA MEMBER

Established: 1961;	1st Franchised: 1962
Franchised Units:	1427
Company-Owned Units:	481
Total Units:	1908
Dist.:	US-1710; CAN-0; O'seas-198
North America:	30 States, 0 Provinces
Density:	238 in NC, 183 in SC, 151 in TN
Projected New Units (12 Months):	NR
Qualifications:	4, 4, 4, 2, 2, 5

Registered:DC,FL,IL,IN,MD,MI,MN,ND,NY,OR,RI,SD,VA,WA,

WI

FINANCIAL/TERMS:

Cash Investment:	$300K
Total Investment:	$1.2-1.6MM
Minimum Net Worth:	$1MM
Fees: Franchise -	$35K
Royalty - 4%;	Ad. - 5% Min.
Earnings Claims Statement:	No
Term of Contract (Years):	20/5
Avg. # Of Employees:	15 FT, PT
Passive Ownership:	Not Allowed
Encourage Conversions:	Yes
Area Develop. Agreements:	No
Sub-Franchising Contracts:	No
Expand In Territory:	Yes
Space Needs:	2,447 SF; FS,SC,RM, University

SUPPORT & TRAINING:

Financial Assistance Provided:	No
Site Selection Assistance:	Yes
Lease Negotiation Assistance:	No
Co-Operative Advertising:	Yes
Franchisee Assoc./Member:	No
Size Of Corporate Staff:	300
On-Going Support:	C,D,E,F,G,H,I
Training:	12 WeeksTraining

SPECIFIC EXPANSION PLANS:

US:	Yes, Midwest/Eastern US
Canada:	No
Overseas:	Yes

ITEM 19
FINANCIAL PERFORMANCE REPRESENTATIONS

The information presented is unaudited and was prepared using uniform accounting methods consistent with generally accepted accounting practices and on a basis consistent with those included in our annual audited consolidated financial statements. All company-operated Restaurants use the same accounting methods and system.

The information contained in this Item 19 should not be considered to be the actual or probable sales and expenses that you will realize. Your results will likely differ from the results contained in this Item 19. Performance varies from restaurant to restaurant and the information below cannot be used to make estimates related to future performance of any particular restaurant. Your performance will be significantly impacted by your personal business, marketing and management skills, your financial investment capabilities, and your willingness to work hard and follow the Hardee's System. Many factors that may significantly impact financial performance are unique to each restaurant, including location, physical size and layout, market penetration, local market conditions and other factors. HFS does not represent that you will attain these financial results. If you are purchasing the assets of existing company-operated Restaurants, you should not rely on the information set forth below, but should instead review the actual performance of the Restaurants being purchased.

Other than the information set forth below, HFS does not furnish or authorize its employees or affiliates to furnish spoken or written claims regarding financial performance, earnings, revenues or results that you are likely to obtain. HFS specifically instructs its employees and affiliates that they are not permitted to make any such claims, other than the information set forth below, and you may not rely on any such claims if made.

Table 1: Fiscal Year 2008 Financial Performance

The following table represents average Fiscal Year 2008 financial performance for 540 company- operated domestic Restaurants (including Dual Concept Restaurants, but excluding 7 Restaurants located on toll roads) that operated for all 13 periods ending January 28, 2008. Consistent with the audited financial statements attached to this disclosure document, each Fiscal Year will be deemed to end on January 31. While there were 560 company-operated domestic Restaurants (including Dual Concept Restaurants) operating at the end of Fiscal Year 2008, 20 have not been included since they either did not operate for the entire 13 periods ending January 31, 2008 or they were located on toll roads. The data in Table 1 is grouped into five columns based on average sales performance, with a summary column for all locations.

	Sales > $1.5M 6 Locations		Sales $1.25M to $1.5M 43 Locations		Sales $1M to $1.25M 144 Locations		Sales $750K to $1M 234 Locations		Sales < $750K 113 Locations		All Locations 540	
TOTAL SALES	1,661,513	100.0%	1,347,003	100.0%	1,105,479	100.0%	879,915	100.0%	658,243	100.0%	939,557	100.0%
TOTAL MATERIALS	486,956	29.3%	397,711	29.5%	328,183	29.7%	259,617	29.5%	198,911	30.2%	278,720	29.7%
TOTAL LABOR & BENEFITS	427,445	25.7%	378,961	28.1%	329,397	29.8%	283,265	32.2%	247,507	37.6%	297,306	31.6%
TOTAL OPERATING EXPENSE	162,430	9.8%	161,304	12.0%	146,572	13.3%	128,628	14.6%	115,061	17.5%	133,552	14.2%
ADVERTISING	77,560	4.7%	76,999	5.7%	66,484	6.0%	54,838	6.2%	43,126	6.6%	57,510	6.1%
RESTAURANT EBITDAR	507,123	30.5%	332,028	24.6%	234,843	21.2%	153,567	17.5%	53,638	8.1%	172,469	18.4%

NOTES TO TABLE 1

(1)   Variations in Sales
Variations in the sales levels of restaurants may occur due to the foot/vehicular traffic where the restaurants are located, the populations and income of the immediate market area, the retail maturity in the area, the amount of competition in the area and numerous other factors.

(2)   Total Sales
Total sales include sales of all food, beverages and promotional items, net of sales taxes, dis-

counts and coupons.

(3)   Total Materials

Total Materials include all food, paper and distribution costs less supplier rebates.

(4)   Total Labor & Benefits

Total Labor & Benefits include wages paid to all hourly and management employees working in the restaurant, as well as all restaurant manager bonuses. Your labor costs could vary depending on the prevailing wage rates in the area of the country in which a restaurant is located and the specific labor laws. Benefits include all employer and payroll taxes, workers' compensation, and expenses for vacation and health insurance. A franchisee's benefits cost will vary depending on the amount of vacation time granted, the amount and type of insurance coverage provided to employees, the size of the franchisee's total employment base and specific local requirements.

(5)   Total Operating Expenses

Total Operating Expenses include cash over and short, supplies, uniforms, repair and mainte- nance, utilities, telephone, security, armored car services, banking and ATM fees, waste management, certain equipment rental charges, kid's meal toy costs, mileage reimbursement, certain pre-open- ing costs, property taxes, business insurance, license and permit fees, and certain asset retirement charges.

(6)   Advertising

Advertising costs include the cost of developing and executing various marketing programs for the restaurants. This includes development and placement of electronic media, print and outdoor advertising. Advertising also includes the cost of in-restaurant point of purchase materials and local restaurant marketing. Required advertising expenses may vary by DMA. Please refer to Items 6 and 11 of this disclosure document for a description of a franchisee's advertising spending obligations.

(7)   Restaurant EBITDAR

Restaurant EBITDAR equals Restaurant Level Earnings Before Income Taxes, Depreciation, Amortization, and Rent. In addition to those items, this category does not include the following expenses associated with operating a Franchised Restaurant: royalty fees, common area maintenance charges, general and administrative expenses (above the restaurant level) and other miscellaneous expenses a franchisee may incur.

(8)   Royalties

A royalty of 4% of Gross Sales has not been shown since company-operated Restaurants pay no royalties. Please refer to Item 6 of this disclosure document for a description of a franchisee's roy- alty obligations.

(9)   Legal Expenses and Other Administrative Expenses and Taxes

No amounts have been included for expenses a franchisee may incur for owners' salaries, interest and debt service, legal and accounting fees, income taxes, corporate overhead and similar expenses. To the extent a franchisee expects to incur such expenses, the franchisee's overall expenses would be higher.

Table 2: Historic Average Unit Volume Figures

The data presented in this table represent the average unit volume for all company-operated domestic Restaurants (including Dual Concept Restaurants and Restaurants located on toll roads) that had been open and operating during the designated fiscal year. HFS' fiscal year ends on the last Monday in January each year.

Fiscal Year	Average Unit Volume ($1000's)	Percent Increase Over Previous Fiscal Year	Percent Increase Over Fiscal Year 2002	Number of Units at Close of Fiscal Year	Number of Units Surpassing Average Unit Volume	Percent Surpassing Average Unit Volume

2002	763	-	-	742	332	45%
2003	763	0.0%	0.0%	730	297	41%
2004	792	3.8%	3.8%	721	310	43%
2005	862	8.8%	13.0%	677	318	47%
2006	874	1.4%	14.5%	663	267	40%
2007	916	4.8%	20.1%	696	285	41%
2008	954	4.1%	25.0%	560	246	44%

NOTE TO TABLE 2

(1)
As reflected in Table No. 4 in Item 20 of this disclosure document, HFS has sold 139 company-operated
Restaurants to franchisees over the last 3 fiscal years.

Table 3: Historic Same Store Sales Information

This table presents the increase in same store sales for all company-operated domestic Restaurants (including Dual Concept Restaurants and Restaurants located on toll roads). The fiscal year same-store sales increase is a cumulative by-period calculation that includes all company-operated domestic Restaurants that had sales for comparable periods during the prior fiscal year. HFS' fiscal year ends on the last Monday in January each year.

Fiscal Year	Same store sales increase (decrease)
2002	0.1%
2003	(2.2%)
2004	2.5%
2005	7.0%
2006	(0.2%)
2007	4.8%
2008	2.0%

Table 4: Breakfast Share

This table shows the average share of sales that are generated during the breakfast day part for company-operated domestic Restaurants (including Dual Concept Restaurants and Restaurants located on toll roads) that had been open and operating for all 13 periods in Fiscal Year 2008. The breakfast day part consists of all sales occurring between 3AM and 11AM.

Breakfast Share	46.6%

*   *   *

Written substantiation of the information used in preparing this statement will be made available to you upon reasonable request. However, we will disclose the identity, revenue or other items of income or expense of any particular company-operated Restaurant only in connection with the sale of that Restaurant.

You are responsible for developing your own business plan for your restaurant, including capital budgets, financial statements, projections and other elements appropriate to your particular circumstances. HFS encourages you to consult with your own accounting, business and legal advisors and to make necessary allowances for changes in financial results to income, expenses or both. You should conduct an independent investigation of the costs and expenses you will incur in operating your restaurant. Franchisees or former franchisees listed in the disclosure document may be one source of this information.

MAID-RITE

2951 86th St.
Des Moines, IA 50322
Tel: (515) 276-5448
Fax: (515) 276-5449
E-Mail: tburt@maid-rite.com
Web Site: www.maid-rite.com
Ms. Tania Burt, Executive VP

Maid-Rite Sandwich Shoppes were founded in 1926 in Iowa. We are famous for our fresh ground beef loose meat sandwiches, seasoned to perfection and served on a warm bun. Our menu also includes Broaster Chicken, Blue Bunny Ice Cream, Godfather's Pizza, and Seattle's Best Coffee. We are an affordable franchise choice that provides franchisee assistance for a turn-key restaurant. We have a training school for franchisees to assist in learning all aspects of restaurant operations and customer service.

BACKGROUND: IFA MEMBER
Established: 1926; 1st Franchised: 1928
Franchised Units: 74
Company-Owned Units: 2
Total Units: 76
Dist.: US-76; CAN-0; O'seas-0
  North America: 10 States, 0 Provinces
  Density: 13 in IL, 47 in IA, 6 in MO
Projected New Units (12 Months): 24
Qualifications: 4, 4, 3, 3, 3, 5

Registered: NR

FINANCIAL/TERMS:
Cash Investment: $50-100K
Total Investment: $125K-300K
Minimum Net Worth: $250K
Fees: Franchise - $35K
  Royalty - 4%; Ad. - 3%
Earnings Claims Statement: No
Term of Contract (Years): 10/Two 10 Additional Term
Avg. # Of Employees: 2 FT, 10 PT
Passive Ownership: Allowed
Encourage Conversions: NA
Area Develop. Agreements: Yes
Sub-Franchising Contracts: Yes
Expand In Territory: Yes
Space Needs: 600-1,800 SF; , Leased Retail End Cap Sites, Companion Stores

SUPPORT & TRAINING:
Financial Assistance Provided: No
Site Selection Assistance: Yes
Lease Negotiation Assistance: Yes
Co-Operative Advertising: No
Franchisee Assoc./Member: No
Size Of Corporate Staff: 40
On-Going Support: B,C,D,E,F,G,H,I
Training: 1-2 Weeks Owner;
  1-2 Weeks Manager; 1 Week On-Site Opening Assistance

SPECIFIC EXPANSION PLANS:
US: Yes, Midwest & FL, CA, CO, NV, AZ, TX
Canada: No
Overseas: No

ITEM 19
FINANCIAL PERFORMANCE REPRESENTATIONS

We encourage and advise you to seek the assistance of a professional accountant or other professional financial advisors as you build your Restaurant financial projections. They will help you determine the impact of customer traffic volume, borrowing funds, taxes, calculating revenues, cost of goods sold and other operating costs. The information provided is not exhaustive and is only provided to you as an example of what could be achieved.

During calendar year 2007, our company-owned restaurants achieved an average of $6.75 per customer ticket at lunchtime, $8.75 per customer ticket for dinner hours and $10.50 for carryout sales. An appropriately-sized restaurant might achieve a customer count of 1.5 turns for lunch hours and 0.75 turns for dinner hours. One "turn" is one customer per seat in the restaurant. For example, a 65 seat restaurant might serve 98 customers (65 seats x 1.5 turns) during an average day's lunch hours. The number customers multiplied by the average ticket would provide an approximation of the income which could be achieved for eat-in revenue. This figure will be approximately 70% of your sales. In addition to eat-in revenue, an estimation of 15% of total gross receipts from drive-thru and 15% from to go or catering revenue. For budgeting purposes, a food cost of thirty percent (30%) of gross receipts and paper costs of two and three-quarters percent (2.75%) of gross receipts could be used. You should note that the pricing structure you implement for your menu items will determine whether you meet or exceed these estimations. We have been able to achieve results within this range at our company-owned restaurants. In addition to this information, you must include your royalty fees of 4% of gross receipts, national advertising fee of 2% of gross receipts (although not currently collected, we reserve the right to impose this fee in the future) and local advertising costs of 1% of gross receipts. Other costs will need to be determined based upon your local conditions.

The above information is derived from three (3) company-owned restaurants that also serve(d) as training centers for Maid-Rite University. The first restaurant was located within a retail strip center located on a well-traveled street in suburban Des Moines, Iowa (Urbandale). The restaurant seated 90 and was in operation for 4 years, although MRC owned this location only since January 31, 2002. The lease on this space expired in May of 2005, and we elected not to renew it. Instead, we opened a new location in suburban Des Moines, Iowa (Northpark) in May, 2005 that seats 76 customers. We also operate a restaurant located in the food court of Merle Hay Mall in Des Moines, Iowa. This location has been in operation since March of 2000, although MRC has owned this location only since January 31, 2002. In August of 2005, MRC opened another new restaurant located on Hwy. 141 in Grimes, Iowa that seats 60 customers. In December of 2007, the Grimes location was sold to a new franchisee who now operates this as a franchisee owned and operated Maid-Rite restaurant. All of these locations serve menu items similar to those we expect our new franchisees to offer, although we may test market items at these locations from time-to-time. Substantially the same services are offered to the company owned restaurants, except that we do not provide financing to franchisees. You should note that these three stores represent only (3 of 76) operating Restaurants. However, MRC does not have adequate information available to base this information on larger numbers of Restaurants. The operating history of other Maid-Rite restaurants may differ. You are encouraged to contact other franchisees to discuss their operations.

The lease rates for these stores are favorable and may vary in different markets. Therefore, the rent expense and operating expenses associated with our locations may be higher or lower depending on the market in which you operate.

The labor costs for your Restaurant may differ depending on the standard of wages for these services in your market. The labor costs will also differ depending on whether your Restaurant is owner- operated or manager-operated. Our calculations assume an owner/manager-operated restaurant. Moreover, if your Restaurant requires more employees than our stores or if you employ more people than we recommend, then your labor costs will exceed those in our stores.

The cost of food will vary somewhat from market to market. The above example uses costs from the Des Moines, Iowa area. Your costs may be higher. Moreover, if your staff does not properly control food portions, product waste, and product shrinkage (due to overcooking), then your costs will be higher. The prices that you charge for your menu items affect the revenue of your restaurant. If your margin is not adequate, then you will not achieve the above results. The quality of service that you provide to your customers creates loyal, repeat customers. The level of service provided will have a great impact on the sales of your restaurant.

The economic conditions in individual markets may substantially affect the sales of your outlet. The sales figures shown are based on the Des Moines, Iowa metropolitan area only.

Your choice of location will also affect your sales. For example, a lack of parking or insufficient traffic will affect your sales.

This information has been prepared by us for use by interested parties in evaluating the prospects of entering into a franchise agreement. In preparing the information, numerous assumptions were made about factors that cannot be predicted with any certainty, including the general business, market and economic conditions in a hypothetical designated area as well as the operating and administrative expenses of a hypothetical franchisee and the level of commitment of a hypothetical franchisee. Although our assumptions on these factors were made on a basis believed to be reasonable, no assurance can be given that these assumptions will ultimately prove to be correct. The differences between the assumptions and actual events could be material.

Some assumptions inevitably will not materialize for any individual franchise and unanticipated events and circumstances will occur subsequent to the date of the forecast. The actual results achieved by any franchisee, particularly a new franchisee, will likely vary from the forecast and the variation may be material. You should not, therefore, rely heavily on the forecast in making a determination whether to invest in a franchise and enter into a franchise agreement.

Substantiation of the information provided above will be made available to prospective franchisees upon reasonable request.

MAUI WOWI HAWAIIAN COFFEES AND SMOOTHIES

5445 DTC Parkway, # 1050
Greenwood Village, CO 80111
Tel: (877) 849-6992 + 130 (303) 781-7800
Fax: (303) 781-2438
E-Mail: info@mauiwowi.com
Web Site: www.mauiwowi.com
Ms. Angela Brazda, Development Coordinator

Ranked as # 175 in Inc 500, with over 350 locations, MAUI WOWI HAWAIIAN is the #1 largest smoothie/coffee franchise in the world. With 24/7 support and extensive training, MAUI WOWI HAWAIIAN offers a simple, profitable and flexible business business model. MAUI WOWI HAWAIIAN has thousands of locations and events throughout the country waiting for a MAUI WOWI HAWAIIAN franchise owner. Because of our flexibility, low investment and variety of business models, MAUI WOWI HAWAIIAN is the fastest-growing franchise.

BACKGROUND: IFA MEMBER

Established: 1983;	1st Franchised: 1997
Franchised Units:	500
Company-Owned Units:	0
Total Units:	500
Dist.:	US-500; CAN-0; O'seas-0
North America:	47 States, 0 Provinces

Density:	NR
Projected New Units (12 Months):	250-300
Qualifications:	2, 2, 1, 1, 1, 5
Registered:CA,DC,FL,HI,IL,IN,MD,MI,MN,ND,NY,OR,RI,SD, VA,WA,WI	

FINANCIAL/TERMS:

Cash Investment:	$50K+
Total Investment:	$75-300K
Minimum Net Worth:	$250K
Fees: Franchise -	$29.5-59.5K
Royalty - 0%;	Ad. - 12%
Earnings Claims Statement:	Yes
Term of Contract (Years):	10
Avg. # Of Employees:	2 FT, 0 PT
Passive Ownership:	Allowed
Encourage Conversions:	Yes
Area Develop. Agreements:	Yes
Sub-Franchising Contracts:	No
Expand In Territory:	Yes
Space Needs:	100 SF; HB, Kiosk

SUPPORT & TRAINING:

Financial Assistance Provided:	Yes (I)
Site Selection Assistance:	Yes
Lease Negotiation Assistance:	Yes
Co-Operative Advertising:	Yes
Franchisee Assoc./Member:	No
Size Of Corporate Staff:	150
On-Going Support:	C,D,E,F,G,H,I
Training:	5 Days Denver, CO

| SPECIFIC EXPANSION PLANS: | | Canada: | Yes, All Canada |
| US: | Yes, All United States | Overseas: | Yes, All Countries |

ITEM 19
FINANCIAL PERFORMANCE REPRESENTATIONS

CAUTION: WHILE THE FIGURES BELOW REPRESENT THE ACTUAL AVERAGE MONTHLY CASE PURCHASES OF MAUI WOWI BLENDS MADE BY THE 40 FRANCHISEES WHO PURCHASED THE MOST CASES OF MAUI WOWI BLENDS DURING CALENDAR YEAR 2007, THE ANNUAL REVENUE NUMBERS IN THE CHART ARE ESTIMATES ONLY AND ARE NOT THE ACTUAL RESULTS OF ANY FRANCHISEE. THEREFORE, THE FOLLOWING DATA SHOULD NOT BE CONSIDERED AS THE ACTUAL, POTENTIAL OR PROBABLE REVENUES THAT WILL BE REALIZED BY YOU OR ANY OTHER FRANCHISEES. WE DO NOT REPRESENT THAT YOU CAN EXPECT TO ATTAIN THESE MAUI WOWI BLENDS PURCHASE LEVELS, REVENUE LEVELS OR ANY INCOME OR PROFIT THAT COULD RESULT FROM OWNING A MAUI WOWI BUSINESS. YOUR FINANCIAL RESULTS ARE LIKELY TO DIFFER FROM THE FIGURES PRESENTED. YOU SHOULD CAREFULLY REVIEW THE ATTACHED EXPLANATORY NOTES.

Top 40 Purchasing Franchisees (See Note 1)				Annual Gross Revenues from Smoothie Sales Before Expenses Based on a Sales Price of ...			
Quartile	Average Time, in Months, Each Franchisee Was in Business Within Each Quartile	Average number of Operating Units per Franchisee in Quartile	Average Number of Cases of MAUI WOWI Blends Purchased by Each Franchisee per Month (Rounded to Nearest Hundredth)	$3.50 per 12-Ounce Smoothie	$4.00 per 12-Ounce Smoothie	$5.00 per 12-Ounce Smoothie	$6.00 per 12-Ounce Smoothie
1st Quartile	48	4.40	103.52	$326,078	$372,660	$465,825	$558,990
2nd Quartile	45	2.40	43.55	$137,183	$156,780	$195,975	$235,170
3rd Quartile	32	2.00	33.10	$104,265	$119,160	$148,950	$178,740
4th Quartile	35	1.60	26.78	$84,341	$96,390	$120,488	$144,585

THE ACCOMPANYING EXPLANATORY NOTES ARE AN INTEGRAL PART OF THIS CHART AND SHOULD BE READ IN THEIR ENTIRETY FOR A FULL UNDERSTANDING OF THE INFORMATION CONTAINED IN THE CHART.

EXPLANATORY NOTES:

1.   The information provided above is based on a subset of franchisees representing the 40 franchisees who purchased the greatest number of cases of MAUI WOW! Blends during calendar year 2007 (the "Top 40 Purchasing Franchisees"). The information is derived from the number of sales of cases of MAUI WOWI Blends by our approved suppliers. These Top 40 Purchasing Franchisees are considered our top performers. Other franchisees of ours do not purchase as many cases of MAUI WOWI Blends. There are 40 total franchisees included in this information out of 320 total franchisees (with 352 total franchise agreements) in the system at the end of calendar year 2007. The Top 40 Purchasing Franchisees were drawn from all of our franchisees, including those who operate their business or particular Operating Units on a less than year-round basis, who add or discontinue Operating Units during the year, who have been in operation for less than 12 months and regardless of the type of Operating Unit(s) they operate. However, these numbers and this information do not

include the results of any DRS franchisees who operate MAUI WOWI Businesses. This information is for calendar year 2007 purchases of MAUI WOWI Blends only and does not include purchases or sales of other MAUI WOWI Products such as bottled waters, Hawaiian coffee and espresso beverages.

2.   The quartiles listed above were derived by sorting the total number of cases purchased during calendar year 2007 by franchisees, in descending value, identifying the Top 40 Purchasing Franchisees, and then splitting these Top 40 Purchasing Franchisees into four equal groups, or quartiles, based on the number of cases of MAUI WOWI Blends purchased by each franchisee. The average months in business, the average number of Operating Units and average monthly purchases of cases of MAUI WOWI Blends were then calculated based on the franchisees in each quartile as outlined herein.

3.   The average months in business for each quartile is based on the franchise agreement date for each franchisee.

4.   The average number of Operating Units for each quartile is calculated by determining the total number of Operating Units for each franchisee, adding the sum of all Operating Units for each franchisee in each quartile and dividing by the number of franchisees in each quartile. The Top 40 Purchasing Franchisees may operate any type or types of Operating Units individually or in any combination. The maximum number of Operating Units that a franchisee is entitled to operate is determined based on the type of franchise acquired by the franchisee. A Single Unit Franchise permits a franchisee to operate one Operating Unit, a Standard Franchise permits a franchisee to operate up to three Operating Units, and an Empire Builder Franchise permits a franchisee to operate up to 10 Operating Units. See Item 1.

5.   The number of 12-ounce smoothies you can expect to make from one case of MAUI WOWI Blends ranges from 75 to 80 depending on various factors including the size of the banana used in each drink, if any, and waste, which varies from franchisee to franchisee. As of the date of this Disclosure Document, our designated supplier charges from $50.96 to $58.80 for each case of MAUI WOWI Blends (this includes the 12 percent Marketing Fee but does not include costs of shipping, distribution, storage, fuel surcharges, minimum order fees, or any other fees that may be charged by suppliers). To make MAUI WOWI smoothies, you may use up to one banana and ice for each 12-ounce smoothie, in addition to the MAUI WOWI Blends. You may purchase bananas and ice from suppliers of your choice who meet all of our specifications and standards.

6.   The MAUI WOWI Blends referenced above are only used to make smoothies. A franchisee will also offer other Maui Wowi proprietary products, including frozen confections, bottled waters, Hawaiian coffee and espresso products. Purchases of and revenues that may be derived from these products are not included in the figures above.

7.   The "Annual Gross Revenues" calculations are based on the average number of cases of MAUI WOWI Blends purchased by each franchisee in each quartile times 75, representing the most conservative estimated number of 12- ounce smoothies that may be made per case of MAUI WOWI Blends, times the variable sales price for a 12-ounce smoothie indicated in the chart ranging from $3.50 to $6.00 per smoothie. The "Annual Gross Revenues" calculations do not take into account any costs or expenses, including the costs of purchasing the MAUI WOWI Blends. See Note 11 below. These "Annual Gross Revenues" calculations also do not consider any additional revenues that may be attained from the sale of MAUI WOWI Products other than smoothies (or any additional expenses that may be incurred related to those other MAUI WOWI Products).

8.   This presentation assumes that only 12-ounce smoothies are sold. You may sell a larger or smaller drink size or multiple sizes. It also assumes that all cases of MAUI WOWI Blends purchased during 2007 were sold during the annual period and that there was little to no waste of smoothie mix. Waste from franchisee to franchisee may vary.

9.   Aside from geographical and demographic differences and managerial emphasis,

there is no material difference in the products, services, training or support offered to any franchisee. Differences in amounts of MAUI WOWI Blends purchased and revenues attained may be attributable to the length of time a MAUI WOWI Business has been open, whether it is operated year round, the type and number of Operating Units operated, the types of venues from which the Operating Units are operated, geographical and demographic differences, and a franchisee's ability and willingness to follow the MAUI WOWI System.

10. The above information was prepared from our approved suppliers' sales records and the reports on prices charged by our approved suppliers for smoothies purchased by each franchisee as reported to our Affiliate. A franchisee pays a Marketing Fee in addition to the purchase price of a case of MAUI WOWI Blends. Based on information provided to us from our franchisees, the price charged by our franchisees for one 12-ounce smoothie ranges from $3.50 to $6.00. You may sell smoothies at a price that may be higher or lower than the price range used in the chart. Sales prices vary between franchisees and may be impacted by competition, contractual requirements, geographical areas, demographics, etc. We recommend that you conduct your own evaluation of sales price or prices that would be acceptable in your own areas of operation.

11. No expenses are shown in this chart. See ITEMS 5, 6 and 7 for information regarding initial investment and other expense considerations. The initial investment and other expenses and costs will vary substantially for each franchisee, and are dependant on different factors particular to each franchisee. Although we have the right to request, inspect and audit certain records related to the expenses of MAUI WOWI Businesses, we have not requested, inspected or audited those records for all MAUI WOWI Businesses, and we therefore do not have knowledge of the expenses or costs incurred by each MAUI WOWI Business disclosed in this ITEM 19. The above purchase figures may not necessarily be predictive of any given MAUI WOWI Business's profitability.

12. This information is based on potential sales of only MAUI WOWI Blends by our approved suppliers to certain franchisees. The estimated revenues should not be considered the actual or probable sales of smoothies which will be achieved by any individual franchisee. We do not represent that any prospective franchisee has or can expect to attain these sales or annual revenue levels. A franchisee's purchases of MAUI WOWI Blends, and its revenues from sales of smoothie drinks, are likely to be lower in its first year of business. We recommend that you conduct your own independent investigation to determine whether or not a franchise may be profitable. We also recommend that you consult with professional advisors before executing any agreement.

13. Actual results may vary from franchise to franchise and depend on a variety of internal and external factors, many of which neither we nor any prospective franchisee can estimate, such as competition, economic climate, demographics, and changing consumer demands and tastes. A franchisee's ability to achieve any level of MAUI WOWI Blends purchases, sales, revenues or net income will depend on these factors and others, including the franchisee's level of expertise, none of which are within our control. Accordingly, we cannot, and do not, estimate the results of any particular franchise.

14. The cost of goods sold (**"COGS"**), expressed as a percentage of the price charged by franchisees for one 12-ounce smoothie, range from 17 percent to 34 percent for MAUI WOWI Blends. These COGS include only the costs of the MAUI WOWI Blends, and do not include costs of bananas, ice, shipping, distribution, storage, fuel surcharges, minimum order fees, Marketing Fees, or any other fees that may be charged by suppliers. Factors affecting COGS include but are not limited to, the types of beverages sold, recipes, drink preparation, sale price, waste, and operator error.

15. The average monthly purchase of cases of MAUI WOWI Blends for the Top 40 Purchasing Franchisees is approximately 51.74 cases. The percentage of the Top 40 Purchasing Franchisees that exceed the average monthly purchase of cases is approximately 22.5% (nine of the 40 franchisees).

Written substantiation for this data is available for inspection at our corporate headquarters and will be provided upon the reasonable request of a prospective franchisee.

EXCEPT FOR THE INFORMATION IN THIS ITEM, WE DO NOT MAKE ANY REPRESENTATIONS ABOUT A FRANCHISEE'S FUTURE FINANCIAL PERFORMANCE OR THE PAST FINANCIAL PERFORMANCE OF COMPANY-OWNED OR FRANCHISED OUTLETS. WE ALSO DO NOT AUTHORIZE OUR EMPLOYEES OR REPRESENTATIVES TO MAKE ANY SUCH REPRESENTATIONS EITHER ORALLY OR IN WRITING. IF YOU ARE PURCHASING AN EXISTING OUTLET, HOWEVER, WE MAY PROVIDE YOU WITH THE ACTUAL RECORDS OF THAT OUTLET. IF YOU RECEIVE ANY OTHER FINANCIAL PERFORMANCE INFORMATION OR PROJECTIONS OF YOUR FUTURE INCOME, YOU SHOULD REPORT IT TO THE FRANCHISOR'S MANAGEMENT BY CONTACTING MICHAEL T. EDWARDS AT 5445 DTC PARKWAY, SUITE 200, GREENWOOD VILLAGE, COLORADO 80111 OR (303) 781-7800, THE FEDERAL TRADE COMMISSION, AND THE APPROPRIATE STATE REGULATORY AGENCIES.

MCDONALD'S

2915 Jorie Blvd.
Oak Brook, IL 60523-2114
Tel: (888) 800-7257 (630) 623-6196
Fax: (630) 623-5658
E-Mail: john.kujawa@us.mcd.com
Web Site: www.mcdonalds.com
Mr. Bob Villa, National Franchise Manager

Quick-service restaurant.

BACKGROUND: IFA MEMBER
Established: 1955; 1st Franchised: 1955
Franchised Units: 25578
Company-Owned Units: 6482
Total Units: 32060
Dist.: US-13898; CAN-1419; O'seas-16743
North America: 50 States, 6 Provinces
Density: 1335 in CA, 840 in FL, 1115 in TX
Projected New Units (12 Months): NR
Qualifications: 3, 5, 3, 3, 4, 4
Registered:CA,DC,FL,HI,IL,IN,MD,MI,MN,ND,NY, OR,RI,SD,VA,WA,WI

FINANCIAL/TERMS:
Cash Investment: $300K
Total Investment: $588K-1.8MM
Minimum Net Worth: NR
Fees: Franchise - $45K
Royalty - 12.5%; Ad. - 4%
Earnings Claims Statement: No
Term of Contract (Years): 20/20
Avg. # Of Employees: FT, 50 PT
Passive Ownership: Not Allowed
Encourage Conversions: NA
Area Develop. Agreements: No
Sub-Franchising Contracts: No
Expand In Territory: Yes
Space Needs: 2,000 SF; FS

SUPPORT & TRAINING:
Financial Assistance Provided: No
Site Selection Assistance: NA
Lease Negotiation Assistance: NA
Co-Operative Advertising: Yes
Franchisee Assoc./Member: Yes/Member
Size Of Corporate Staff: 0
On-Going Support: C,D,E,G,H,I
Training: NR

SPECIFIC EXPANSION PLANS:
US: Yes, All United States
Canada: Yes, All Canada
Overseas: Yes, All Countries

Item 19
Financial Performance Representations

Of the approximately 11,500 domestic traditional McDonald's restaurants opened at least 1 year as of December 31, 2007, approximately 74% had annual sales volumes in excess of $1,800,000; approximately 61% had annual sales volumes in excess of $2,000,000; and approximately 48% had annual sales volumes in excess of $2,200,000 during 2007. The average annual sales volume of domestic traditional McDonald's restaurants open at least 1 year as of December 31, 2007, was $2,218,000 during 2007. The highest and lowest annual sales volume in 2007 for these domestic traditional McDonald's restaurants was $8,410,000 and $339,000, respectively.

The pro forma statements included show annual sales volumes of $1,800,000, $2,000,000, and $2,200,000. These pro forma statements have been derived from independent franchisee traditional restaurant financial statements to provide information relevant to a prospective franchisee (see Note 1). Specific assumptions used in the presentation of these pro forma statements are indicated above and below each statement.

The pro forma statements are based upon a total of 8,762 independent franchisee traditional restaurants open and operated by a franchisee for at least 1 year. **A FRANCHISEE'S INDIVIDUAL FINANCIAL RESULTS MAY DIFFER FROM THE RESULTS STATED IN THE PRO FORMA STATEMENTS FOR THE REASONS DESCRIBED IN THIS ITEM OR FOR OTHER REASONS.** Substantiation of the data used in preparing the earnings claims, including computations of all actual or average profit or earnings, will be made available to prospective franchisees upon reasonable request.

It is anticipated that the information reported in these pro forma statements reflects the operating results before occupancy costs for independent franchisee restaurants open for at least 1 year. However, the operating income before occupancy cost figures appearing below should not be construed as the financial results or "profit" before occupancy costs which might be experienced by a franchisee with a similar sales volume or an indication that any particular sales volume will be obtained. An individual franchisee is likely to experience operating expense variations including, but not limited to, general insurance, legal and accounting fees, labor costs, and store management benefits (life and health insurance, etc.). Additionally, market conditions, operational and management methods employed by a franchisee, different geographic areas of the country, and menu price variations may significantly affect operating results. The nature of these variables makes it difficult to estimate the financial results for any particular franchisee or location.

PRODUCT SALES (see Note 2)	$1,800,000	100.0%	$2,000,000	100.0%	$2,200,000	100.0%
TOTAL COST OF SALES	550,000	30.6%	608,000	30.4%	666,000	30.3%
GROSS PROFIT	1,250,000	69.4%	1,392,000	69.6%	1,534,000	69.7%
OTHER OPERATING EXPENSES (excluding rent, service fees, D&A, interest, and income taxes)*	782,000	43.4%	848,000	42.4%	915,000	41.6%
OPERATING INCOME BEFORE OCCUPANCY COSTS (excluding rent, service fees, D&A, interest, and income taxes) (see Note 3)**	468,000	26.0%	544,000	27.2%	619,000	28.1%

* OTHER OPERATING EXPENSES — Includes, but is not limited to, the following costs: labor, franchisee's salary as manager, payroll taxes, advertising fee (as described in Item 6), promotion, outside services, linen, operating supplies, small equipment, maintenance and repair, utilities, office supplies, legal and accounting fees, insurance, real estate and personal property taxes, business operating licenses, and non-product income or expense. This is a combination of the Total Controllable Expenses and Other Operating Expenses excluding rent, service fees, D&A, and interest included in our typical store financial statements.

** OPERATING INCOME BEFORE OCCUPANCY COSTS — Represents Operating Income excluding rent, service fees, D&A, interest, and income taxes. The rent paid to McDonald's will vary based upon sales and McDonald's investment in land, site improvements, and building costs. Refer to Item 6 for information regarding franchise fees (including rent and service fees paid to McDonald's). D&A and interest will vary based upon the purchase price and required reinvestment of the specific restaurant acquired. Refer to Item 7 for a description of investment costs.

Additionally, organization overhead costs such as salaries and benefits of non-restaurant personnel (if any), cost of an automobile used in the business (if any), and other discretionary expenditures may significantly affect profits realized in any given operation. The nature of these variables makes it difficult to estimate the performance for any particular restaurant with sales of any given volume.

THESE SALES, PROFITS, OR EARNINGS ARE AVERAGES OF SPECIFIC RESTAURANTS AND SHOULD NOT BE CONSIDERED AS THE ACTUAL OR POTENTIAL SALES, PROFITS, OR EARNINGS THAT WILL BE REALIZED BY ANY OTHER FRANCHISEE. McDONALD'S DOES NOT REPRESENT THAT ANY FRANCHISEE CAN EXPECT TO ATTAIN THESE SALES, PROFITS, OR EARNINGS.

Note 1 — Data for McOpCo company restaurants is not included in the pro forma statements because of certain expenses that are typically incurred by a McOpCo-operated restaurant that are not incurred by restaurants franchised to individuals. If data for McOpCo-operated restaurants open 13 or more months were included along with franchised restaurants, the percent of total restaurants in each category would not be statistically different and the range of Operating Income Before Occupancy Costs would be $460,000 to $609,000.

Note 2 — The description of this line, "Product Sales," is to clarify that only product sales are included. Non-product sales and associated costs are included in Other Operating Expenses.

Note 3 — We are not presenting average occupancy costs in the above calculation because a wide variety of rent charts and ownership options exist. In addition, the effective rent paid by a franchisee may be more in any particular month than the stated percent rent indicated in the franchisee's lease because a portion of the rent may be fixed regardless of the sales level for a given month. The range of effective rent percents in 2007 for franchised restaurants was 0% to 32%. Refer to Item 6 for a description of rents.

MRS. FIELDS COOKIES

2855 E. Cottonwood Pkwy., # 400
Salt Lake City, UT 84121-7050
Tel: (800) 343-5377 + 2399
Fax: (801) 736-5936
E-Mail: donl@mrsfields.com
Web Site: www.mrsfields.com
Mr. Don Lewandowski, VP of Development Bakery

Premier retail cookie business with 'uncompromising quality,' 94% brand recognition, easy to operate, flexible designs and store options that operate in traditional and non-traditional venues.

BACKGROUND: IFA MEMBER
Established: 1977;   1st Franchised: 1990
Franchised Units: 300
Company-Owned Units: 300
Total Units: 300
Dist.: US-213; CAN-0; O'seas-77

North America: 43 States, 0 Provinces
Density: 103 in CA, 25 in IL, 30 in MI
Projected New Units (12 Months): 38
Qualifications: 4, 4, 2, 2, 2, 5
Registered:CA,DC,FL,HI,IL,IN,MD,NI,MN,ND,NY,OR,RI,SD, WA,WI,AB

FINANCIAL/TERMS:
Cash Investment: $100K-200K
Total Investment: $179.1-251.1K
Minimum Net Worth: $150K/75K LIQ
Fees: Franchise - $30K
  Royalty - 6%; Ad. - 1%
Earnings Claims Statement: Yes
Term of Contract (Years): 7/7
Avg. # Of Employees: 3 FT, 2 PT
Passive Ownership: Not Allowed
Encourage Conversions: Yes
Area Develop. Agreements: 0
Sub-Franchising Contracts: No
Expand In Territory: Yes
Space Needs: 600-900 SF; SF,SC,RM, Stadium

SUPPORT & TRAINING:
Financial Assistance Provided: No

Site Selection Assistance:	Yes	Training:	Salt Lake City, UT
Lease Negotiation Assistance:	Yes		
Co-Operative Advertising:	No	**SPECIFIC EXPANSION PLANS:**	
Franchisee Assoc./Member:	Yes/Member	US:	Yes, All United States
Size Of Corporate Staff:	100	Canada:	Yes, All Canada
On-Going Support:	A,B,C,D,E,F,G,H,I	Overseas:	NR

ITEM 19. FINANCIAL PERFORMANCE REPRESENTATIONS

Attached as **Exhibit O** to this disclosure document is a Financial Performance Representation, which includes, as qualified in **Exhibit O**, gross revenues by quartile of the 149 fully-reporting franchised Mrs. Fields Cookie Stores located in the United States that were operated for the entire 2007 fiscal year (December 31, 2006 to December 29, 2007). The figures for franchised Mrs. Fields Cookie Stores in Exhibit O do not reflect the cost of sales, operating expenses, or other costs or expense that must be deducted from the gross revenue or gross sales figures to obtain your net income or profit.

You should conduct an independent investigation of the costs and expenses you will incur in operating your Store. Franchisees or former franchisees, listed in this disclosure document may be one source of information.

Your individual results may differ from the information included in **Exhibit O**. There is no assurance that you will do as well. Actual results vary from store to store, and we cannot estimate the results of any particular franchise. Substantiation of all data illustrated in **Exhibit O** will be made available to you upon reasonable request.

EXHIBIT O

MRS. FIELDS COOKIES
FINANCIAL PERFORMANCE REPRESENTATION

The following Table presents unaudited information about the reported gross revenues ("Gross Revenues" as defined by the Mrs. Fields Franchise Agreement)[1] of 149 franchised Mrs. Fields Cookie Stores from which we have collected a full 52 weeks of sales reports for the period from December 31, 2006 through December 29, 2007 (the "**2007 Fiscal Year**").

The franchised store information included in the Table below is based on reports submitted to us by 149 fully-reporting franchised Mrs. Fields Cookie Stores located in the United States that were operated for the entire 2007 Fiscal Year (the "**Franchised Stores**"). The information for the Franchised Stores contained herein does <u>NOT</u> include data for (i) franchised Mrs. Fields Cookie Stores in the United States that opened or closed during the 2007 Fiscal Year; (ii) franchised Mrs. Fields Cookie Stores located outside of the United States; or (iii) franchised Mrs. Fields Cookie Stores that failed to submit sales reports for all 52 weeks of the 2007 Fiscal Year. See Item 20 for information regarding the total number of franchised Mrs. Fields Cookie Stores operating during 2007. The information was collected by us, but has not been independently audited or verified by us. The Franchised Stores are primarily located in regional shopping malls and strip shopping centers, but may also include certain locations within lifestyle centers, theatres and airports.

The financial performance representation figures in this **Exhibit O** do not reflect the cost of sales, operating expenses, or other costs or expenses that must be deducted from the gross revenues or gross sales figures to obtain your net income or profit. You should conduct an independent investigation of the costs and expenses you will incur in operating your Mrs. Fields Cookie Store. Franchisees or former franchisees, listed in this disclosure document, may be one source of this information.

Other than as described this Financial Performance Representation, we do not furnish, or authorize our salespersons (or anyone else) to furnish, and you should not rely on, any oral or written information concerning the actual or potential sales, income, gross profits or net profits of a Mrs. Fields Cookie Store.

TABLE
GROSS REVENUES OF FRANCHISED STORES
BY QUARTILE[2] FOR THE 2007 FISCAL YEAR

QUARTILE	NUMBER OF STORES PER QUARTILE	GROSS REVENUES RANGE[3]
1st	21	$434,410 to $651,580
2nd	29	$337,645 to $431,629
3rd	38	$238,021 to $335,511
4th	62	$102,741 to $235,528[4]

TABLE NOTES:

(1)   As used herein, "Gross Revenues" has the meaning given that term in the Mrs. Fields Franchise Agreement for the 2007 Fiscal Year, which is the aggregate amount of all sales of Mrs. Fields Products, other items, and services made and rendered in connection with the operation a Mrs. Fields Cookie Store, including sales made at or away from the premises of the Mrs. Fields Cookie Store, whether for cash or credits, but excluding all federal, state or municipal sales, use, or service taxes collected from customers and paid to the appropriate taxing authority. Except for these taxes, the Gross Revenues are NOT net of costs of goods sold or other operating expenses.

(2)   Quartile. As used herein, "Quartile" refers to the relative performance of the Franchised Stores. Therefore, a Quartile does not necessary consist of 25% of the total number of Franchised Stores. The "1st Quartile" refers to the top 25% performing Franchised Stores, based on Gross Revenues, the "2nd Quartile" refers to the next highest 25% performing Franchised Stores, and so on. In other words, one Quartile, as used in this Financial Performance Representation, does not necessarily reflect 25% of the total number of Franchised Stores. As you can see, there are less than half the number of Franchised Stores in the top two Quartiles than there are in the bottom two Quartiles.

(3)   Gross Revenues Range. This Table combines the Gross Revenues of all of the Franchised Stores for the 2007 Fiscal Year, and lists the high and low end of the Gross Revenues Range for each Quartile. As further described above, the information relating to the Franchised Stores is based on unaudited Gross Revenues and royalty reports collected by us, but not independently verified.

(4)   Under-performing Franchised Store. We have intentionally left out the reported sales of one underperforming Mrs. Fields Cookie Store located in an office building that is open only five days a week for limited hours. We determined that excluding this uniquely situated underperforming Store from this Financial Performance Representation may present a better cross section of typical Mrs. Fields Cookie Store performance.

Gross Revenues provided for the Franchised Stores may differ widely from any specific franchised location for a number of reasons, including differences in operational experience and ability, capital, financing, training, store location and site criteria, physical condition and size of the Franchised Store, number and type of products sold. For example, of the first Quartile of Franchised Stores, 89% have been open and operating for more than 3 years at their current location. Their Gross Revenues may be much higher than any prospective new development in part because they are well established.

We do not suggest, and we certainly cannot guarantee, that you will succeed in the operation of your Mrs. Fields Cookie Store. The most important factors in the success of any Mrs. Fields Cookie Store, including the one you will operate, are the personal business, marketing, management, judgment and other skills of its owner, and its manager's willingness to work hard and follow the System.

Substantiation of the data presented in this Financial Performance Representation will be made available to you upon reasonable request.

The Gross Revenues in the Table above are based on reported results from the Franchised Stores for the 2007 Fiscal Year. Your individual results may differ. There is no assurance that you will attain any of the Gross Revenues listed in the Table above.

There is no assurance that future sales will correspond to sales from the last fiscal year. These figures should not be considered as the actual or potential revenues or profits that will be realized by any franchisee.

You are responsible for developing your own business plan for your Mrs. Fields Cookie Store, including capital budgets, financial statements, projections and other elements appropriate to your particular circumstances. We encourage you to consult with your own accounting, business, and legal advisors to assist you to identify the expenses you likely will incur in connection with your Mrs. Fields Cookie Store, to prepare your budgets and projections, and to assess the likely or potential financial performance of your Store. We also encourage you to contact existing franchised store operators to discuss their experiences with the System and their store business. Notwithstanding the information set forth in this Financial Performance Representation, our existing franchisees are your best source of information about typical franchised store operations.

In developing the business plan for your Mrs. Fields Cookie Store, you are cautioned to make necessary allowance for changes in financial results to income, expenses or both that may result from operation of your Store during periods of, or in geographic areas suffering from, economic downturns, inflation, unemployment, or other negative economic influences.

As further described above, the figures in the Table above do not reflect the cost of sales, operating expenses, or other costs or expenses that must be deducted from the gross revenues or gross sales figures to obtain your net income or profit. You and your advisors should consider this in your due diligence and preparation of your business plan.

NESTLE TOLLHOUSE CAFÉ BY CHIP

101 W. Renner Rd., # 240
Richardson, TX 75082
Tel: (866) 529-8580 (214) 281-8069
Fax: (214) 853-5347
E-Mail: franchising@nestlecafe.com
Web Site: www.nestlecafe.com
Mr. Scott McIntosh, Business Development

BACKGROUND:	IFA MEMBER
Established: 1998;	1st Franchised: 2000
Franchised Units:	108
Company-Owned Units:	0
Total Units:	108

ITEM 19
FINANCIAL PERFORMANCE REPRESENTATIONS

The following table sets forth by quartile(1) and by mall and non-mall locations the high and low end of the range of the annual Gross Sales(2) during fiscal year 2007 of all full menu Dessert Cafes in the United States operating for at least 12 months as of the end of fiscal year 2007. As of the end of fiscal year 2007, there were 59 full menu Dessert Cafes operating for at least 12 months, of which 44 were located in malls and 15 were not located in malls. We have also included 13 limited menu Dessert Cafes in the United States operating for at least 12 months as of the end of fiscal year 2007 and that are co- branded with another franchise. As of the end of fiscal year 2007, there were 13 limited menu Dessert Cafes co-branded with another franchise. The amounts in the table are based on information reported to us by franchisees in their weekly royalty reports. We have not audited, reviewed or verified this information. If a franchisee failed to submit a weekly royalty report, the prior week's figures were used to estimate the current weeks sales totals.

	Mall	Non-Mall	Co-Brand
1st Quartile	$594,065 to $381,220	$511,540 to $357,063	$499,929 to $356,217
2nd Quartile	$362,483 to $260,439	$298,392 to $210,195	$301,469 to $243,683
3rd Quartile	$250,586 to $201,789	$195,730 to $179,703	$237,400 to $161,148
4th Quartile	$190,584 to $85,363	$170,420 to $113,763	$146,145 to $18,840

(1)   "Quartile" refers to the relative performance of the franchise Cafes. The "1st Quartile" refers to the top 25% performing Cafes based on Gross Sales, the "2nd Quartile" refers to the next highest 25% performing Cafes based on Gross Sales, and so on.

(2)   Gross Sales means the total selling price of all services and products and all income of every other kind and nature related to the Cafes (including, income related to catering and delivery activities, and any sales or orders of food products or food preparation services provided from or related to the Cafe), whether for cash or credit and regardless of collection in the case of credit. Gross Sales excludes the sales and other taxes collected by franchisees in the operation of Cafes.

The Gross Sales attainable by each Café depends on many factors, including geographic differences, competition within the immediate market area, the quality and service provided to customers of the Café, the condition of the Café premises, as well as a franchisee's management skill, experience, business acumen and marketing and sales efforts.

As of the date of this Disclosure Document, 28 Cafes (approximately 25% of total operating Cafes) provided details on their actual food and labor costs. The food cost (Cost of Goods Sold) is inclusive of paper, actual inventory, and food preparation costs and represents the average food cost as a percentage of Gross Sales for the 28 reporting Cafes for fiscal year 2007. The labor costs represent the average labor costs as a percentage of Gross Sales for the 28 reporting Cafes for fiscal year 2007. The amounts in the table are based on information reported to us by franchisees and are not audited. We have not audited, reviewed or verified this information. The numbers are an average only and may not indicate the actual costs associated with your Café.

Average Café Gross Sales	Average Food Cost-COGS	Average Labor Costs
$324,827.63	27.5%	21.9%

YOUR ACTUAL FINANCIAL RESULTS ARE LIKELY TO DIFFER FROM THE FIGURES PRESENTED. THE RANGE OF ANNUAL GROSS SALES PRESENTED ABOVE REPRESENTS GROSS SALES BEFORE DEDUCTIONS FOR ROYALTY AND MARKETING FEES PAYABLE TO US AND ALL OTHER OPERATING EXPENSES. YOU SHOULD CONDUCT AN INDEPENDENT INVESTIGATION OF THE COSTS AND EXPENSES FRANCHISEES WILL INCUR IN OPERATING THEIR CAFES. SEE ITEMS 6 AND 7 OF THIS DISCLOSURE DOCUMENT FOR A PARTIAL LIST OF EXPENSES YOU WILL INCUR. FRANCHISEES AND FORMER FRANCHISEES MAY BE ONE SOURCE OF THIS INFORMATION.

THE RANGE OF ANNUAL GROSS SALES AND FOOD AND LABOR COSTS PRESENTED ABOVE ARE HISTORICAL DATA OF SPECIFIC FRANCHISEES. THIS RANGE SHOULD NOT BE CONSIDERED AS POTENTIAL GROSS SALES OR FOOD OR LABOR COST PERCENTAGES THAT MAY BE REALIZED BY YOU. WE DO NOT REPRESENT THAT YOU CAN EXPECT TO ACHIEVE THESES GROSS SALES OR FOOD OR LABOR COST PERCENTAGES. ACTUAL RESULTS VARY FROM CAFE TO CAFE, AND WE CANNOT MEANINGFULLY ESTIMATE THE RESULTS OF ANY PARTICULAR CAFE OR FRANCHISEE.

SUBSTANTIATION OF THE RANGE OF ANNUAL GROSS SALES IS AVAILABLE TO YOU AT OUR OFFICES IF YOU REQUEST, PROVIDED WE WILL NOT DISCLOSE THE IDENTITY OF ANY CAFE OWNER.

Except for the range of annual Gross Sales and food and labor cost percentages presented above, we do not furnish or authorize our salespersons (or anyone else) to furnish any oral or written information concerning the actual or potential sales, costs, income or profits of a Cafe.

**Better Ingredients.
Better Pizza.**

PAPA JOHN'S INTERNATIONAL

2002 Papa John's Blvd.
Louisville, KY 40299
Tel: (502) 261-4000
Fax: NA
E-Mail: chris_sternberg@papajohns.com
Web Site: www.papajohns.com
Mr. Chris Sternberg, Sr. VP Corporate Communications

Papa John's International, headquartered in Louisville, KY., is the world's third-largest pizza company, owning and franchising over 3,300 restaurants in all 50 states and 29 countries. For nine years running, consumers have rated Papa John's #1 in customer satisfaction among all national pizza chains and #1 seven out of nine years among all national Quick Service Restaurant (QSR) chains in the highly regarded American Customer Satisfaction Index (ACSI).

BACKGROUND:

Established: 1985;	1st Franchised: 1986
Franchised Units:	2683
Company-Owned Units:	649
Total Units:	3332
Dist.:	US-2785; CAN-21; O'seas-526
North America:	50 States, 2 Provinces
Density:	203 in CA, 243 in FL, 218 in TX
Projected New Units (12 Months):	160
Qualifications:	5, 5, 4, 3, 4, 4
Registered:	NR

FINANCIAL/TERMS:

Cash Investment:	Varies
Total Investment:	$110.8-466.6K
Minimum Net Worth:	$250K-2MM
Fees: Franchise -	$25K/Unit
Royalty - 5%;	Ad. - 7%
Earnings Claims Statement:	No
Term of Contract (Years):	10/10
Avg. # Of Employees:	8 FT, 18 PT
Passive Ownership:	Allowed
Encourage Conversions:	NA
Area Develop. Agreements:	Yes
Sub-Franchising Contracts:	No
Expand In Territory:	Yes
Space Needs:	1,200-1,400 SF; SC, Stand-alone; non-trad

SUPPORT & TRAINING:

Financial Assistance Provided:	No
Site Selection Assistance:	Yes
Lease Negotiation Assistance:	No
Co-Operative Advertising:	Yes
Franchisee Assoc./Member:	Yes/Not a Member
Size Of Corporate Staff:	0
On-Going Support:	a,b,C,D,E,G,h,I
Training:	1 Week Papa John's University, Louisville, KY
Mentoring; Varied Location; 5 Weeks Mgmt. Training: Varied	Location

SPECIFIC EXPANSION PLANS:

US:	Yes, All United States
Canada:	Yes, Saskachetwan, Ontario and the Atlantic Provinces
Overseas:	No

Item 19
FINANCIAL PERFORMANCE REPRESENTATIONS

Presented below are average Restaurant-level cash flows of our domestic company-owned Papa John's Restaurants for our fiscal year ended December 30, 2007. At the close of our fiscal year, there were 2,783 total domestic (United States, excluding Alaska and Hawaii) Papa John's Restaurants, 648 of which were company-owned. The following cash flow data is drawn from our financial books and records, which are kept on a basis consistent with Generally Accepted Accounting Principles ("GAAP") in the United States. All information is based on actual historical costs and results. Thus, there are no material assumptions associated with the data, other than the principles of GAAP. However, a number of factors may affect the comparability of this data, which is drawn solely from company-operated Restaurants, to franchised Restaurants and the data's effectiveness as a guide or template for potential operating results of a franchised Restaurant. The most significant of these factors are discussed in the notes following the data. You should carefully consider these factors when reviewing, analyzing considering the data presented below.

Restaurant Cash Flows:		Percent of Sales
Average Sales	$819,210	100.0%
Expenses		
Food Costs	224,668	27.4%
Labor Costs and Taxes	157,896	19.3%
Manager's Labor and Taxes	69,157	8.5%
Mileage	30,867	3.8%
Advertising	76,888	9.4%
Controllables*	56,647	6.9%
Rent and Common Area Maintenance	28,061	3.4%
Other Non Controllables**	40,578	5.0%
Training Costs	4,152	0.5%
Store Bonuses	10,960	1.3%
Pre-Tax Cash Flows***	$119,035	14.5%

*Controllables includes: petty cash, smallwares, repairs and maintenance, commissions, telephone expenses, utilities, cleaning supplies, computer supplies, office supplies, laundry service, uniforms, equipment rental, postage, donations, and special events.

**Other Non-Controllables includes: property taxes, management health insurance, general insurance, credit card charges, bank charges, business licenses, and worker's compensation insurance.

***46.21% of Company-owned Restaurants achieved $119,035 or greater annual pre-tax cash flows.

Key Factors		
Average Weekly Sales ("PSA") Net****		$15,754
Avg Rent and CAM-Monthly		$2,338
Avg Wkly Transactions/Orders		868
Avg Hourly Rate-CREW (pre-tax)	$6.74	
Avg Check	$18.15	
Avg Hourly Hours Worked-CREW	410	
Avg Price Per Pie (Net)	$9.32	
Avg Weekly Management Labor (pretax) 1 General Manager, 1 Assistant GM		$1,219

****$82.85% of Company-owned Restaurants achieved average weekly sales of $15,754 or greater.

Notes and Comments
Historical Performance Data

The foregoing information is drawn from actual historical data from our domestic company-owned Restaurants. Historical information may not be a reliable predictor of future results or experience. Future performance may be affected by many factors at variance from the conditions that yielded past results and experience, including without limitation: volatility of commodity costs (such as cheese, for example); inflation or rising costs in general, especially for labor and energy; general economic upturn or downturn; changing consumer tastes, preferences or sensibilities; and effectiveness of advertising or promotional campaigns. We do not make any representation or guarantee of future sales, costs or profits.

Averages

The data presented is based on averages for our domestic company-owned Restaurants. Many Restaurants have lower sales performance and/or higher costs than the average for all Restaurants. With a data base consisting of more than 600 Restaurants, the lowest performing Restaurants and/or higher cost Restaurants may have performance data that vary significantly from the average. Performance of a particular Restaurant may be affected by many factors, including without limitation: location (whether the Restaurant is in a free-standing building, in-line in a strip center or an end-cap in a strip center; whether the Restaurant is in a high-visibility, high-traffic location); population density in the Restaurant's trade area; business acumen and managerial skills of Restaurant management personnel; prevailing wage rates and quality of the available labor pool; availability and cost of commercial rental property; the presence and aggressiveness of the competition; and utility costs. Consequently, your individual financial results are likely to differ from the results shown in the above data. In providing the above data, Papa John's is not making a representation or guarantee that you can or will achieve a level of sales or profit commensurate with our company-owned Restaurants averages or that you can or will achieve any particular level of sales or profit or experience costs comparable to those of our company-owned Restaurant averages.

Non-Cash Items

The cash flow data does not include depreciation expense or any other non-cash items. Over time, worn-out or obsolete restaurant equipment will have to be replaced and leasehold improvements, signage, computer systems and restaurant furnishings may have to be refurbished, remodeled, upgraded or replaced. The foregoing cash flow data does not include any reserves for funding any of these types of improvements or upgrades.

Royalty

Company-owned Restaurants do not pay a royalty. The expenses incurred by a franchised restaurant will include our standard royalty.

Economies of Scale

Because we operate more than 600 company-owned Restaurants, we are able to achieve certain economies of scale and operational efficiencies that may not be available to a franchisee operating one Restaurant or a limited number of Restaurants, as is the case for the typical franchisee. For example, we have a multi-tiered management hierarchy. At the higher levels of management, we are able to rely on the expertise of management executives with a wealth of experience in the restaurant and food service industries. You may not be able to achieve the same level of management expertise. You will be relying principally on your own business acumen and managerial skills and perhaps that of your Principal Operator. However, the income from our company-owned Restaurants ultimately must bear the costs of our management team and other corporate office overhead. These costs are not reflected in the foregoing cash flow data, which reflect operational cash flows at the Restaurant level, excluding the burden of corporate overhead.

Because of the size of our company-owned operations, we are able to support a marketing department, with personnel dedicated to marketing functions, as well as dedicated cash management, payroll and other administrative functions. You and your Principal Operator will perform most of these functions, although some administrative functions may be out-sourced. Unless you are developing a significant number of Restaurants, you may not be able to have experienced personnel dedicated to specific functions, such as marketing.

We are a publicly-traded company and have raised significant capital through our stock offerings. We typically do not require bank financing for construction or equipping of our Restaurants or for capital improvements or for updating or replacement of worn-out or obsolete equipment in our Restaurants. However, to the extent that we do require financing, we are able to draw on a significant line of credit from our primary bank. It is unlikely that these types of financing efficiencies will be available to you.

We are also able to obtain economies of scale in other areas, such as insurance, that may not be available to franchisees. Because of the size of our operations, insurance risks are spread over a greater number of Restaurants, which enables us to bargain for lower group-rate insurance costs. We are also able to use the size of our operations to achieve volume discounts and other cost savings based on our purchasing power. These cost savings, in areas including telephone services and advertising, may not be available to franchisees operating on a smaller scale.

Restaurant and Market Maturity

Sales of a particular Restaurant may be affected by how long the Restaurant has been in operation and how successfully the surrounding market has been penetrated. Typically, sales "ramp up" as the Restaurant and market develop. New Restaurants (open for less than one year) typically do not operate as efficiently or as profitably as more mature Restaurants. In particular, sales at Restaurants open less than one year are typically lower than more mature Restaurants, as it takes some time to establish consumer recognition and build a customer base in a new trade area. Greater penetration (the greater the number and concentration of Restaurants) in a market also may affect performance. Clusters of Restaurants may be able to pool resources to purchase advertising on local television or radio, which would be prohibitively expensive for a single Restaurant, or even a small cluster of Restaurants in a large media market. The foregoing company-owned Restaurant data represents averages for all of our domestic Restaurants, some of which are long-established in their location and some of which are relatively new. Most of our company-owned Restaurants are in highly developed and highly penetrated markets.

Market Location

Our company-owned Restaurants are typically clustered in and around major metropolitan areas, such as Atlanta, St. Louis and Nashville. Many franchised Restaurants are operated in less densely populated areas, with more limited access to advertising media.

Standard Restaurant Program Only

The foregoing data for company-owned Restaurants refers only to standard Papa John's Restaurants. Performance data for Non-Traditional Restaurants varies widely, depending upon the nature of the non-traditional location, number of events or sales dates and other widely varying factors. Thus, this Item 19 is applicable to standard Papa John's Restaurants only. **With regard to Non-Traditional Restaurants, we do not furnish or authorize our sales persons to furnish any oral or written information concerning the actual or potential sales, costs, income or profits of a Papa John's Non-Traditional Restaurant.**

Other Data

Except as described below, we do not furnish or authorize the furnishing to prospective franchisees of any oral or written information other than the company-owned Restaurant averages data provided above. We may provide to you the actual performance data of a particular Restaurant that you are considering purchasing. Also, we may, but we have no obligation to, provide to you supplemental data consisting of a segmentation or subset of the above data. For example, we may provide company-owned Restaurant averages data for a particular region or individual state. If we do so, that supplemental data will be in writing and will be limited to the types of information set forth in the above data. We do not furnish and do not authorize anyone to furnish supplemental data that is outside the scope of the data provided above. If you obtain any other financial information concerning Papa John's Restaurants, do not rely on it as a representation of Papa John's.

Your Own Due Diligence

You should construct your own *pro forma* cash flow statement and make your own projections concerning potential sales, operating costs, total capital investment requirements, operating cash requirements, debt, cash flow, and other financial aspects of operating a Papa John's Restaurant. You should not rely solely on the information provided by us. You should conduct your own investigation of revenue and expense potential for your proposed Papa John's Restaurant, including consultation with your own attorney, accountant or other adviser and other Papa John's franchisees.

CAUTION

AS A CONSEQUENCE OF THE FACTORS DISCUSSED ABOVE, AND OTHER VARIABLES THAT WE CANNOT ACCURATELY PREDICT, A NEW FRANCHISEE'S INDIVIDUAL FINANCIAL RESULTS ARE LIKELY TO DIFFER FROM THE RESULTS SHOWN IN THE DATA INCLUDED IN THIS ITEM 19.

Substantiation of Data

Substantiation of the data used in preparing the data set forth in this Item 19 will be available to prospective franchisees upon reasonable request.

North America:	34 States, 4 Provinces
Density:	58 in FL, 72 in MN, 57 in PA
Projected New Units (12 Months):	NR
Qualifications:	5, 4, 5, 3, 3, 5
Registered:DC,FL,IL,IN,MD,MI,MN,ND,NY,OR,SD,VA,WA,WI,	
	AB

PERKINS RESTAURANT & BAKERY

6075 Poplar Ave., # 800
Memphis, TN 38119-4717
Tel: (800) 877-7375 (901) 766-6400
Fax: (901) 766-6482
E-Mail: franchise@prkmc.com
Web Site: www.perkinsrestaurants.com
Ms. Linda Jones, Franchise Development

Since 1958, Perkins Restaurant & Bakery has offered quality, tasty, affordable food for breakfast, lunch and dinner. Our brand heritage and ability to adapt to trends make Perkins a leader in the family dining segment. We are seeking experienced restaurants operators to meet our expansion goals in key markets across the country. We provide professional support services in training, design & construction, marketing, operations, quality assurance and R&D.

FINANCIAL/TERMS:

Cash Investment:	$500K
Total Investment:	$1.2-2.6M
Minimum Net Worth:	$1.5M
Fees: Franchise -	$40K
Royalty - 4%;	Ad. - 3%
Earnings Claims Statement:	Yes
Term of Contract (Years):	20
Avg. # Of Employees:	6 FT, 64 PT
Passive Ownership:	Allowed, But Discouraged
Encourage Conversions:	Yes
Area Develop. Agreements:	Yes
Sub-Franchising Contracts:	No
Expand In Territory:	Yes
Space Needs:	5,000 SF; FS,SC

BACKGROUND: IFA MEMBER

Established: 1958;	1st Franchised: 1965
Franchised Units:	324
Company-Owned Units:	163
Total Units:	487
Dist.:	US-308; CAN-16; O'seas-0

SUPPORT & TRAINING:

Financial Assistance Provided:	No
Site Selection Assistance:	Yes
Lease Negotiation Assistance:	Yes
Co-Operative Advertising:	No
Franchisee Assoc./Member:	No

Size Of Corporate Staff:	0	**SPECIFIC EXPANSION PLANS:**	
On-Going Support:	B,C,D,E,F,h,I	US:	1, All except WA, OR, CA, NV, AZ, NM, MA, ME, RI
Training: 8-12 Weeks Management Training at Various Locations		Canada:	Yes, All Canada
		Overseas:	No

FINANCIAL PERFORMANCE REPRESENTATIONS

Item 19

AVERAGE SALES AND SELECTED COSTS OF RESTAURANTS OWNED AND OPERATED BY THE LICENSOR

The first table below of Average Annual Sales Volume (the "Average Sales Table") and the Schedule of Restaurant Financial Data (the "Schedule") discloses the average sales and selected costs of 162 Perkins restaurants owned and operated by PMCI for the entire fiscal year ending December 30, 2007 (referred to as the "Restaurants").

AVERAGE ANNUAL SALES VOLUME

The following table groups the Restaurants into ranges of annual sales volume disclosing the number of Restaurants within each range and further disclosing the average sales volume of each range.

Average Restaurant #	Average Annual Sales Volume	Sales Volume Range of Restaurants Included	# of Restaurants in Range
1	$1,154,785	$879,000 - $1,535,000	54
2	$1,788,253	$1,535,000 - $2,052,000	54
3	$2,478,066	$2,052,000 - $3,752,000	54

The Restaurants are distributed throughout the north central and midwestern United States with the greatest concentrations in Minnesota, Wisconsin, Missouri, Iowa, and Florida. They are located predominantly in metropolitan areas on or near major traffic thoroughfares. The buildings housing the Restaurants are predominantly single-purpose, one story and free-standing, seating from 90 to 250 guests at one time, which are comparable to the restaurants expected to be operated pursuant to the License Agreement.

The location of the Restaurants used to compile the information disclosed in the Average Sales Table and Schedule are categorized by state, as follows:

Average Restaurant No. 1 (54 locations): Colorado-6, Florida-15, Illinois-2, Iowa-3, Kansas-2, Michigan-5, Minnesota-9, Missouri-3, North Dakota-1; Oklahoma-1, Pennsylvania- 1, Tennessee-2, Wisconsin-4

Average Restaurant No. 2 (54 locations): Colorado-2, Florida-12, Illinois-4, Iowa— 6, Kansas— 1, Michigan-2, Minnesota-16, Missouri-1, North Dakota-1, Tennessee-2, Wisconsin-4, Pennsylvania-3

Average Restaurant No. 3 (54 locations): Florida-16, Illinois-1; Iowa-7, Minnesota-14, Missouri- 2, Wisconsin -8, Pennsylvania-2, North Dakota-2, Oklahoma-1.

Substantially the same services were offered by PMCI to the Restaurants as are provided to the licensees; however, PMCI does not provide certain services to licensees which are normally provided by the owner such as financing, accounting (unless the licensee has entered into the Accounting Services Agreement), legal, personnel, management, financial and food and labor cost systems.

The Restaurants offered substantially the same products and services to the public as the restaurants to be operated pursuant to the License Agreement.

The following Schedule was prepared on a basis consistent with generally accepted accounting principles and the same accounting system was used for each Restaurant. The figures used in the Schedule are based on an annual performance.

SUCH SALES, INCOME, GROSS OR NET PROFITS ARE OF SPECIFIC RESTAURANTS OWNED AND OPERATED BY PMCI AND SHOULD NOT BE CONSIDERED AS THE ACTUAL OR PROBABLE SALES, INCOME, GROSS OR NET PROFITS THAT WILL BE REALIZED BY ANY LICENSEE. PMCI DOES NOT REPRESENT THAT ANY LICENSEE CAN EXPECT TO ATTAIN SUCH SALES, INCOME, GROSS OR NET PROFITS. YOUR RESULTS WILL VARY AND SUCH VARIANCES MAY BE MATERIAL AND ADVERSE.

Substantiation of the data used in preparing the Schedule will be made available upon reasonable request.

THE INFORMATION PRESENTED BELOW HAS NOT BEEN AUDITED.

SCHEDULE OF RESTAURANT FINANCIAL DATA
(Dollars in Thousands)

	Average Restaurant No. 1		Average Restaurant No. 2		Average Restaurant No. 3	
	Amount	Percentage of Sales	Amount	Percentage of Sales	Amount	Percentage of Sales
Net Food Sales	1,155	100.0	1,788	100.0	2,478	100
Food Cost	285	24.7	434	24.3	602	24.3
Gross Profit	870	75.3	1,354	75.7	1,876	75.7
Labor:						
Management	99	8.6	136	7.6	166	6.7
Hourly	254	22.0	374	20.9	512	20.7
Total	353	30.6	510	28.5	678	27.4
Benefits:						
Payroll Tax	42	3.7	62	3.5	81	3.3
Vacation/sick	14	1.2	20	1.1	28	1.1
Workers Comp/other	21	1.8	31	1.7	40	1.6
Total	77	6.7	113	6.3	149	6.0
Direct Operating Expenses:						
Supplies	33	2.8	47	2.6	63	2.5
Menus, guest checks, placemats, toys	3	0.3	4	0.3	5	0.2
Uniforms, laundry	4	0.3	5	0.3	5	0.3
Smallwares, others	3	0.1	4	0.1	4	0.1
Total	43	3.5	60	3.3	77	3.1
Repairs & Maintenance	23	2.0	29	1.6	34	1.4
Outside Services	14	1.2	19	1.1	24	1.0
Utilities	71	6.1	88	4.9	102	4.1
Local Store Marketing	20	1.7	27	1.5	34	1.4

Administrative:						
Travel	0	0.0	0	0.0	0	0.0
Classified Advertising	0	0.0	0	0.0	0.0	0.0
Office Supplies	2	0.2	3	0.2	3	0.1
Legal, Bank fees, bad debt	16	1.4	24	1.4	33	1.3
Miscellaneous	3	0.1	3	0.1	4	0.1
Total	21	1.7	30	1.7	40	1.5
Total Operating Expenses	622	53.5	876	48.9	1138	45.9
Total Controllable Income	248	21.8	478	26.8	738	29.8
Non-Controllable Expense:						
Advertising	35	3.0	54	3.0	74	3.0
Property insurance	12	1.0	15	0.9	18	0.7
Property taxes	20	1.7	28	1.6	32	1.3
Employee insurance	13	1.1	21	1.2	30	1.2
Other	23	2.0	9	0.5	21	0.9
Total	103	8.8	127	7.2	175	7.1
Cash Flow from Operations	145	13.0	351	19.6	563	22.7

The average statements shown in the Schedule DO NOT include the following items of expense which have to be calculated and included separately for every restaurant:

a)   Rent.

b)   Royalty Fees consistent with current contractual requirements under the License Agreement (see Item 22).

c)   Depreciation of property and equipment.

d)   Interest or other financing costs for land, buildings, equipment and inventory.

e)   Initial license fee and organization costs (see Item 5).

f)   Any accounting, legal or management fees.

g)   Income taxes.

These excluded items affect the net income and/or cash flow of any restaurant and must be carefully considered and evaluated by any prospective licensee. The actual performance of any restaurant will depend on a number of factors specific to the property including, but not limited to, the above factors.

The Restaurants and restaurants to be operated pursuant to the License Agreement have the following similarities:

a)   Each Restaurant operates under the name "Perkins," including "Perkins Family Restaurant and Bakery" and "Perkins Restaurant and Bakery."

b)   Each Restaurant generally offers the same selection of menu items and many are open 24 hours a day.

Sales and operating results of the Restaurants and the restaurants to be operated pursuant to the License Agreement are affected by the following:

a)   Economic and weather conditions of various geographic areas.

b)   Competition from a variety of other restaurants, including fast food businesses. Some restaurants have greater competition than others.

c)   Different acquisition, development, construction and property costs.

d)   Local property tax rates.

e)   State laws affecting employee costs.

f)   Different traffic counts, accessibility and visibility. The location of each restaurant may have a significant impact on sales and operating income.

g)   Different benefits from advertising. Some Restaurants do not receive the benefits of television advertising. Some Restaurants are not grouped in such a way that local television or other media advertising can be efficiently obtained.

h)   Although each Restaurant has seating and parking, the amount of seating and parking varies among the Restaurants.

i)   All Restaurants have been in business for different periods of time and therefore have experienced varying periods of time to become established in their respective markets.

j)   Each licensee may set its own prices for menu items.

k)   Each Restaurant may experience varying food costs due to geographic area and economies of scale due to the grouping of Restaurants in any single geographic area.

l)   The quality and effectiveness of management of each Restaurant varies.

The following information is based on 315 licensed restaurants and does not include 8 licensed restaurants that opened and 4 that closed during 2007 (it does, however, include one licensed restaurant that did not operate during part of the year due to damage caused by a fire).

a)   To PMCI's knowledge, the number of the licensed restaurants described above that equaled or exceeded the Average Annual Sales Volumes shown in the Average Sales Volume Table are as follows: 119 for Average Restaurant No. 1; 100 for Average Restaurant No. 2; and 76 for Average Restaurant No. 3.

b)   To PMCI's knowledge, the approximate percentage of total sales for the licensed restaurants described above that were in operation during the entire year ending December 30, 2007 that actually fell within the sales ranges shown in the Schedule were: (6.3% were below the sales range of Average Restaurant No. 1) 37.8% for the sales range of Average Restaurant No. 1; 31.7% for the sales range of Average Restaurant No. 2; and 24.1% for the sales range of Average Restaurant No. 3.

c)   PMCI does not have any knowledge of the percentage of licensed restaurants which during the same year actually attained or surpassed the levels of income before royalties, advertising, occupancy costs and taxes as set forth in the Schedule.

d)   Within a range of annual sales volumes from $879,000 to $3,752,000 for Restaurants owned and operated by PMCI, to PMCI's knowledge 93.7% of reporting licensed restaurants that were in operation during the entire year actually fell within such range of sales. Annual sales volumes of all reporting licensed restaurants for the year ending December 30, 2007 ranged from $356,826 (this Restaurant did not operate during part of the year due to damage caused by a fire) to $3,299,275.

Substantiation of the data used in preparing the above statement will be made available upon

132

request. Because PMCI does not require that existing licensed restaurants follow a particular accounting system, PMCI cannot certify that the licensed restaurants follow generally accepted accounting principles. PMCI will not disclose the identity of any specific licensee whose data has been used to compile any information in this item except to the agency(ies) with which this filing is made.

POPEYES CHICKEN & BISCUITS

5555 Glenridge Connector NE, # 300
Atlanta, GA 30342-4759
Tel: (800) 639-3780 (404) 459-4450
Fax: (404) 459-4523
E-Mail: popeyesfranchising@afce.com
Web Site: www.popeyesfranchising.com
Mr. John Feilmeier, Director, New Business Development

POPEYES CHICKEN & BISCUITS, the world's second-largest chicken chain, is owned by AFC Enterprises, Inc., one of the world's largest restaurant parent companies and the winner of the 1997 MUFSO Operator of the Year and Golden Chain awards. POPEYES is famous for its New Orleans-style chicken, buttermilk biscuits and signature side items. The brand name has a presence in 41 states and 20 countries worldwide.

BACKGROUND: IFA MEMBER

Established: 1972;	1st Franchised: 1973
Franchised Units:	1725
Company-Owned Units:	80
Total Units:	1805
Dist.:	US-1490; CAN-12; O'seas-257
North America:	41 States, 2 Provinces
Density:	NR
Projected New Units (12 Months):	120
Qualifications:	5, 4, 5, 3, NR, 3

Registered:CA,DC,FL,HI,IL,IN,MD,MI,MN,NY,ND,OR,RI,SD, VA,WA,WI

FINANCIAL/TERMS:

Cash Investment:	$250-750K
Total Investment:	$1.2-1.5MM
Minimum Net Worth:	$1.2MM
Fees: Franchise -	$20K
Royalty - 5%;	Ad. - 3%
Earnings Claims Statement:	No
Term of Contract (Years):	20/10
Avg. # Of Employees:	15-25 FT, 25 PT
Passive Ownership:	Allowed, But Discouraged
Encourage Conversions:	Yes
Area Develop. Agreements:	Yes
Sub-Franchising Contracts:	No
Expand In Territory:	Yes
Space Needs:	2,200 SF; FS,SC,RM, Airport, University

SUPPORT & TRAINING:

Financial Assistance Provided:	Yes (D)
Site Selection Assistance:	Yes
Lease Negotiation Assistance:	Yes
Co-Operative Advertising:	No
Franchisee Assoc./Member:	Yes/Member
Size Of Corporate Staff:	NR
On-Going Support:	B,C,D,E,F,G,H,I
Training:	4 Weeks Atlanta, GA

SPECIFIC EXPANSION PLANS:

US:	Yes, All United States
Canada:	Yes, All Canada
Overseas:	Yes, All Countries

ITEM 19
FINANCIAL PERFORMANCE REPRESENTATIONS

The following 4 tables present information about the annual sales of Popeyes Restaurants that were open throughout our entire fiscal year ended December 30, 2007.

TABLE I: FREE-STANDING RESTAURANTS

Free-standing Popeyes Restaurants include any type of restaurant other than in-line restaurants, convenience store restaurants, and mall/food court restaurants. 50 company-owned free-standing Popeyes Restaurants and 1,074 franchised free-standing Popeyes Restaurants were continuously operated during the period January 1, 2007 through December 30, 2007. As of December 30, 2007, there were 8 company-owned free-standing Popeyes Restaurants and 60 franchised free-standing Popeyes Restaurants that had not been in continuous operation during the trailing 12-month period. Accordingly, we have not provided any information related to the performance of those free-standing Popeyes Restaurants.

Amount and Distribution of Annual Sales

Annual Sales Levels (In Thousands)	Consolidated	Number of Units	Company-Owned	Number of Units	Franchised	Number of Units
$2MM +	3.6%	40	12.0%	6	3.2%	34
$1500-1999	9.7%	109	26.0%	13	8.9%	96
$1400-1499	3.6%	41	6.0%	3	3.5%	38
$1300-1399	6.0%	68	8.0%	4	6.0%	64
$1200-1299	5.5%	62	4.0%	2	5.6%	60
$1100-1199	7.9%	89	8.0%	4	7.9%	85
$1000-1099	10.1%	114	10.0%	5	10.1%	109
$900-999	10.6%	119	10.0%	5	10.6%	114
$800-899	12.4%	139	8.0%	4	12.6%	135
$700-799	13.3%	149	4.0%	2	13.7%	147
$600-699	8.3%	93	2.0%	1	8.6%	92
$500-599	5.9%	66	2.0%	1	6.1%	65
$400-499	2.4%	27	0.0%	0	2.5%	27
$300-399	0.6%	7	0.0%	0	0.7%	7
< $300	0.1%	1	0.0%	0	0.1%	1
Total	100.0%	1124%	100.0%	50	100.0%	1074

	Consolidated		Company		Franchised	
Arithmetic Average (all restaurants)	$1,049,734		$1,350,638		$1,035,726	
Upper Range Average $1,100 +	$1,477,787		$1,609,923		$1,466,572	
Number of Units		409		32		377
Middle Range Average $800 - 1,099	$943,837		$952,950		$943,480	
Number of Units		372		14		358
Lower Range Average $0 - 799	$654,167		$668,266		$654,000	
Number of Units		343		4		339

	Consolidated	Company	Franchise
High	$3,570,659	$2,484,280	$3,570,659
Low	$288,958	$517,371	$288,958

The notes that follow Table IV are an integral part of Table I.

TABLE II: IN-LINE RESTAURANTS

In-line Popeyes Restaurants are located in traditional "strip style" retail shopping centers. 2 company-owned in-line Popeyes Restaurants and 185 franchised in-line Popeyes Restaurants were continuously operated during the period January 1, 2007 through December 30, 2007. As of December 30, 2007, there were no company-owned in-line Popeyes Restaurants and 29 franchised in-line Popeyes Restaurants that had not been in continuous operation during the trailing 12-month period. Accordingly, we have not provided any information related to the performance of those in-line Popeyes Restaurants.

Amount and Distribution of Annual Sales

Annual Sales Levels (In Thousands)	Consolidated	Number of Units	Company-Owned	Number of Units	Franchised	Number of Units

$2MM +	0.5%	1	0.0%	0	0.5%	1
$1500-1999	5.9%	11	0.0%	0	5.9%	11
$1400-1499	1.6%	3	0.0%	0	1.6%	3
$1300-1399	5.3%	10	0.0%	0	5.4%	10
$1200-1299	4.3%	8	50.0%	1	3.8%	7
$1100-1199	4.8%	9	50.0%	1	4.3%	8
$1000-1099	9.1%	17	0.0%	0	9.2%	17
$900-999	12.3%	23	0.0%	0	12.4%	23
$800-899	11.8%	22	0.0%	0	11.9%	22
$700-799	8.6%	16	0.0%	0	8.6%	16
$600-699	14.4%	27	0.0%	0	14.6%	27
$500-599	15.0%	28	0.0%	0	15.1%	28
$400-499	5.3%	10	0.0%	0	5.4%	10
$300-399	1.1%	2	0.0%	0	1.1%	2
< $300	0.0%	0	0.0%	0	0.0%	0
Total	100.0%	187	100.0%	2	100.0%	185

	Consolidated		Company		Franchised	
Arithmetic Average (all restaurants)	$893,527		$1,198,279		$890,233	
Upper Range Average $1,000 +	$1,292,553		$1,198,279		$1,295,861	
Number of Units		59		2		57
Middle Range Average $700 – 999	$860,073		--		$860,073	
Number of Units		61		0		61
Lower Range Average $0 – 699	$572,605		--		$572,605	
Number of Units		67		0		67

	Consolidated		Company		Franchise	
High	$2,184,398		$1,241,950		$2,184,398	
Low	$393,472		$1,154,609		$393,472	

The notes that follow Table IV are an integral part of Table II.

TABLE III: CONVENIENCE STORE RESTAURANTS

Convenience store Popeyes Restaurants are located within or attached to convenience stores. 1 company-owned convenience store Popeyes Restaurant and 93 franchised convenience store Popeyes Restaurants were continuously operated during the period January 1, 2007 through December 30, 2007. As of December 30, 2007, there were no company-owned convenience store Popeyes Restaurants and 1 franchised convenience store Popeyes Restaurant that had not been in continuous operation during the trailing 12-month period. Accordingly, we have not provided any information related to the performance of those convenience store Popeyes Restaurants.

Amount and Distribution of Annual Sales

Annual Sales Levels (In Thousands)	Consolidated	Number of Units	Company-Owned	Number of Units	Franchised	Number of Units
$2MM +	0.0%	0	0.0%	0	0.0%	0
$1500-1999	2.1%	2	0.0%	0	2.2%	2
$1400-1499	0.0%	0	0.0%	0	0.0%	0

$1300-1399	1.1%	1	100.0%	1	0.0%	0
$1200-1299	2.1%	2	0.0%	0	2.2%	2
$1100-1199	2.1%	2	0.0%	0	2.2%	2
$1000-1099	6.4%	6	0.0%	0	6.5%	6
$900-999	6.4%	6	0.0%	0	6.5%	6
$800-899	12.8%	12	0.0%	0	12.9%	12
$700-799	19.1%	18	0.0%	0	19.4%	18
$600-699	14.9%	14	0.0%	0	15.1%	14
$500-599	18.1%	17	0.0%	0	18.3%	17
$400-499	8.5%	8	0.0%	0	8.6%	8
$300-399	6.4%	6	0.0%	0	6.5%	6
< $300	0.0%	0	0.0%	0	0.0%	0

Total	100.0%	94	100.0%	1	100.0%	93

	Consolidated		Company		Franchised	
Arithmetic Average (all restaurants)	$734,246		$1,328,985		$727,851	
Upper Range Average $800 +	$1,018,332		$1,328,985		$1,007,977	
Number of Units		31		1		30
Middle Range Average $600 - 799	$702,733		-		$702,733	
Number of Units		32		0		32
Lower Range Average $0 - 599	$482,690		-		$482,690	
Number of Units		31		0		31

	Consolidated		Company		Franchise	
High	$1,535,168		$1,328,985		$1,535,168	
Low	$307,229		$1,328,985		$307,229	

The notes that follow Table IV are an integral part of Table III.

TABLE IV: MALL/FOOD COURT RESTAURANTS

Mall/food court Popeyes Restaurants are located within the confines of shopping malls and other food court locations, such as free-standing food court buildings, airports, travel plazas, amusement parks and other retail areas where common seating with other food concepts is used. 1 company-owned mall/food court Popeyes Restaurant and 65 franchised mall/food court Popeyes Restaurants were continuously operated during the period January 1, 2007 through December 30, 2007. As of December 30, 2007, there were no company-owned mall/food court Popeyes Restaurants and 11 franchised mall/food court Popeyes Restaurants that had not been in continuous operation during the trailing 12-month period. Accordingly, we have not provided any information related to the performance of those mall/food court Popeyes Restaurants.

Amount and Distribution of Annual Sales

Annual Sales Levels (In Thousands)	Consolidated	Number of Units	Company-Owned	Number of Units	Franchised	Number of Units
$2MM +	1.5%	1	0.0%	0	1.5%	1
$1500-1999	3.0%	2	0.0%	0	3.1%	2
$1400-1499	4.5%	3	0.0%	0	4.6%	3
$1300-1399	4.5%	3	0.0%	0	4.6%	3

$1200-1299	12.1%	8	0.0%	0	12.3%	8
$1100-1199	1.5%	1	0.0%	0	1.5%	1
$1000-1099	0.0%	0	0.0%	0	0.0%	0
$900-999	6.1%	4	0.0%	0	6.2%	4
$800-899	10.6%	7	0.0%	0	10.8%	7
$700-799	15.2%	10	0.0%	0	15.4%	10
$600-699	13.6%	9	0.0%	0	13.8%	9
$500-599	13.6%	9	0.0%	0	13.8%	9
$400-499	7.6%	5	0.0%	0	7.7%	5
$300-399	6.1%	4	100.0%	1	4.6%	3
< $300	0.0%	0	0.0%	0	0.0%	0
Total	100.0%	66	100.0%	1	100.0%	65

	Consolidated		Company		Franchised	
Arithmetic Average (all restaurants)	$ 867,968		$325,063		$876,320	
Upper Range Average $900 +	$1,338,965		--		$1,338,965	
Number of Units		22		0		22
Middle Range Average $600 – 899	$736,757		--		$736,757	
Number of Units		26		0		26
Lower Range Average $0 – 599	$481,831		$325,063		$491,052	
Number of Units		18		1		17

	Consolidated		Company		Franchise	
High	$2,395,244		$325,063		$2,395,244	
Low	$317,718		$325,063		$317,718	

The notes that follow Table IV in this Item 19 are an integral part of Table IV.

NOTES TO TABLES I THROUGH IV

1. Sales volumes vary considerably due to a variety of factors, such as demographics of the restaurant trade area; competition from other restaurants in the trade area, especially other quick service restaurants; traffic flow; accessibility and visibility; economic conditions in the restaurant trade area; advertising and promotional activities; and the business abilities and efforts of the management of the restaurant.

2. The results shown for franchised restaurants have been taken from royalty reports submitted by franchisees, which represent their actual experience in operating Popeyes Restaurants. We have not audited these royalty reports, but have no reason to believe that they are unreliable. The results shown for company-owned restaurants are taken from reports prepared by company personnel at each restaurant and are unaudited.

3. **These sales figures are for specific franchised and company-owned restaurants and should not be considered as the actual or potential sales that will be achieved by any other franchised restaurant. We do not represent that any franchisee can expect to attain these sales results. Actual results vary from restaurant to restaurant and we cannot estimate the results of any specific restaurant. In addition, these sales figures do not reflect the cost of sales, operating expenses or other expenses that must be deducted from sales to determine net income or profit. We recommend that you make your own independent investigation to determine whether or not the franchise may be profitable (including determining the costs and expenses you will incur while operating the**

Franchised Restaurant), and consult with an attorney and/or other advisors before signing any franchise agreement. Our current and former franchisees identified in Exhibit L may be a source of this information.

4. Substantiation for the information appearing in this Item will be made available to you upon reasonable request.

5. Except for the information set forth in this Item, we do not furnish or authorize our salespersons to furnish any oral or written information concerning the actual, average, projected or forecasted sales, costs, income or profits (collectively, "earnings capability") of a restaurant. We specifically instruct our sales personnel, agents and employees that they are not permitted to make any claims or statements concerning a specific franchisee's earnings capability or chances for success, and we will not be bound by allegations of any unauthorized representations as to earnings capability or chances for success.

6. There were three Louisiana Kitchen restaurants operated that were open at year-end 2007 which are not included in any of the above sales information.

7. There was one additional franchised mobile kitchen restaurant operated by a Popeyes franchisee that had not been in continuous operation during the last trailing twelve month period and therefore is not included in the any of above sales information.

QUIZNOS SUB

1001 17th St., # 200
Denver, CO 80202
Tel: (800) 335-4782 (720) 359-3300
Fax: (720) 359-3393
E-Mail: hhubbell@quiznos.com
Web Site: www.quiznos.com
Ms. Hedi Hubbell, International Brand Expansion Manager

Toasted subs are the key to QUIZNOS SUB's success. QUIZNOS SUB is dedicated to growing the brand by building financially successful franchises and serving the best sub sandwich in the market.

BACKGROUND: IFA MEMBER

Established: 1981;	1st Franchised: 1991
Franchised Units:	1950
Company-Owned Units:	15
Total Units:	1965
Dist.:	US-1965; CAN-310; O'seas-47
North America:	50 States, 9 Provinces
Density:	687 in CA, 311 in TX
Projected New Units (12 Months):	400
Qualifications:	5, 4, 2, 2, 2, 5
Registered:CA,DC,FL,HI,IL,IN,MD,MI,MN,ND,NY,OR,RI,SD,	
	VA,WA,WI

FINANCIAL/TERMS:

Cash Investment:	$70K
Total Investment:	$184.5K-265K
Minimum Net Worth:	$125K
Fees: Franchise -	$25K
Royalty - 7%;	Ad. - 4%
Earnings Claims Statement:	No
Term of Contract (Years):	15
Avg. # Of Employees:	15-20 FT, 0 PT
Passive Ownership:	Allowed, But Discouraged
Encourage Conversions:	Yes
Area Develop. Agreements:	Yes
Sub-Franchising Contracts:	Yes
Expand In Territory:	Yes
Space Needs:	1,200-1,800 SF; FS,SF,SC,RM

SUPPORT & TRAINING:

Financial Assistance Provided:	Yes (I)
Site Selection Assistance:	Yes
Lease Negotiation Assistance:	Yes
Co-Operative Advertising:	Yes
Franchisee Assoc./Member:	Yes/Member
Size Of Corporate Staff:	608
On-Going Support:	E,G,H,I
Training:	1 Week Corporate Office Denver, CO;
	3 Weeks Regional Market

SPECIFIC EXPANSION PLANS:

US:	Yes, All US, Limited in MD and S. CA.
Canada:	Yes, All Canada
Overseas:	Yes, Europe

ITEM 19
FINANCIAL PERFORMANCE REPRESENTATIONS

The following information addresses average per Restaurant sales (including discounts) during fiscal years 2005, 2006 and 2007 at all QUIZNOS Restaurants operating as of December 31, 2005, December 31, 2006 and December 31, 2007, respectively. We and our affiliates obtained the reported information from Franchisees to calculate the average gross sales (including discounts) for Franchisees.

Fiscal Year[1]	2005	2006	2007
Total Number of Restaurants[2]	4,225	4,576	4,636
Total Number of Restaurants open during the entire 12 month period ("Participating Restaurants")[3]	2,596	3,229	3,511
Average Gross Sales for Participating Restaurants[4]	$414,625	$414,574	$404,547
Percentage of Participating Restaurants that Met or Exceeded the Average[5]	43.1%	49.5%	45.4%

Notes:

1.   The information is for fiscal years ended December 31, 2005, December 31, 2006 and December 31, 2007. Neither we, nor our affiliates have undertaken an independent investigation to verify the amounts reported by Franchisees.

2.   This number represents the total number of QUIZNOS Restaurants open in the United States (including non-traditional units) as of the end of each fiscal year. It includes 2 affiliate owned Restaurants as of December 31, 2005 and 3 affiliate owned Restaurants as of December 31, 2006 and December 31, 2007.

3.   This number represents the total number of Restaurants that had been open for business for the entire 12 month period during the relevant fiscal year under the same ownership. It does not include Restaurants that were transferred by a franchisee to another franchisee during the fiscal year.

4.   This is the average gross sales (including discounts) for all Participating Restaurants for the fiscal year.

5.   This is the percentage of Participating Restaurants that had gross sales (including discounts) that met or exceeded the average gross sales (including discounts) for the fiscal year. The Total Number of Restaurants for 2006 does not include 27 Restaurants that were temporarily closed at the end of 2006 for relocation, natural disaster or other extraordinary circumstances.

The products and services offered by each Restaurant, although essentially the same, may vary to some degree based on the individual Franchisee's discretion. The sales volume attainable by each Restaurant depends on many factors, including geographic differences, competition within the immediate market area, the quality and service provided to customers by the Restaurant, as well as its own marketing and sales efforts.

YOUR ACTUAL FINANCIAL RESULTS ARE LIKELY TO DIFFER FROM THE FIGURES PRESENTED. THE AVERAGE GROSS SALES FIGURES PRESENTED ABOVE REPRESENT SALES BEFORE DEDUCTIONS FOR CONTINUING ADVERTISING AND ROYALTY FEES PAYABLE TO THE FRANCHISOR AND ALL OTHER OPERATING EXPENSES. SEE ITEMS 6 AND 7 OF THIS DISCLOSURE DOCUMENT FOR A PARTIAL LIST OF EXPENSES YOU WILL INCUR.

THE SALES FIGURES ABOVE ARE AVERAGES OF HISTORICAL DATA OF SPECIFIC FRANCHISES. THEY SHOULD NOT BE CONSIDERED AS POTENTIAL SALES THAT MAY BE REALIZED BY YOU. WE DO NOT REPRESENT THAT YOU CAN EXPECT TO ACHIEVE THESE SALES LEVELS. ACTUAL RESULTS VARY FROM RESTAURANT TO RESTAURANT, AND WE CANNOT ESTIMATE THE RESULTS OF ANY PARTICULAR FRANCHISE.

SUBSTANTIATION OF THE ABOVE AVERAGES IS AVAILABLE TO YOU AT OUR OFFICES IF YOU REQUEST, PROVIDED IT DOES NOT REQUIRE THE DISCLOSURE OF THE IDENTITY OF ANY RESTAURANT OWNER.

OTHER THAN THE ABOVE INFORMATION, WE DO NOT FURNISH OR AUTHORIZE OUR SALESPERSONS TO FURNISH ANY ORAL OR WRITTEN INFORMATION CONCERNING THE ACTUAL OR POTENTIAL SALES, INCOME, OR PROFITS OF A QUIZNOS RESTAURANT.

RITA'S ITALIAN ICE

1210 North Brook Dr., # 310
Trevose, PA 19053
Tel: (800) 677-7482
Fax: (866) 449-0974
E-Mail: Franchise_sales@ritascorp.com
Web Site: www.ritasice.com
Mr. Mark Mele, Vice President of Franchise Development

Rita's is the largest Italian Ice chain in the nation. With a 25 year proven business model, Rita's offers a variety of frozen treats including its famous Italian Ice, Old Fashioned Frozen Custard, and layered Gelati as well as its signature Misto and Blendini creations.

BACKGROUND:	IFA MEMBER
Established: 1984;	1st Franchised: 1989
Franchised Units:	549
Company-Owned Units:	1
Total Units:	550
Dist.:	US-550; CAN-0; O'seas-0
North America:	23 States, 0 Provinces
Density:	DE, NJ, PA
Projected New Units (12 Months):	30
Qualifications:	3, 3, 3, 3, 3, 5
Registered:	IL,IN,MD,NY,RI,VA

FINANCIAL/TERMS:

Cash Investment:	$75K
Total Investment:	$198.4K-385.4K
Minimum Net Worth:	$250K
Fees: Franchise -	$35K
Royalty - 6.5%;	Ad. - 2.5%
Earnings Claims Statement:	Yes
Term of Contract (Years):	10/10
Avg. # Of Employees:	2 FT, 15 PT
Passive Ownership:	Allowed, But Discouraged
Encourage Conversions:	No
Area Develop. Agreements:	No
Sub-Franchising Contracts:	No
Expand In Territory:	Yes
Space Needs: 1,000-1,200 SF; SC, Transportation Center, University	

SUPPORT & TRAINING:

Financial Assistance Provided:	Yes (I)
Site Selection Assistance:	Yes
Lease Negotiation Assistance:	Yes
Co-Operative Advertising:	Yes
Franchisee Assoc./Member:	No
Size Of Corporate Staff:	80
On-Going Support:	C,D,E,F,G,H,I
Training:	2-4 Days On-Site;6 DaysCorporate Office

SPECIFIC EXPANSION PLANS:

US:	Yes, East of Mississippi
Canada:	No
Overseas:	No

Item 19: Financial Performance Representations

Rita's does not furnish, or authorize its sales persons to furnish, any oral or written information concerning the actual, or average, or projected, or forecasted, or potential sales, costs, earnings or profits of a franchise other than as set forth in this Item.

Included in this Item 19 are Rita's estimates of (1) 2007 average sales of Proprietary Products at franchised Shops ("Average Sales"), described in Section I, below, and (2) 2007 average food costs for ingredients for the Proprietary Products at franchised Shops ("Costs of Goods Sold"), described in Section II, below.

I. 2007 AVERAGE SALES OF PROPRIETY PRODUCTS AT FRANCHISED SHOPS

The following chart represents our estimates of the Average Sales of franchised shops for Italian ice, gelati, frozen custard, Misto shakes, and Blendini in 2007:

	Top Third	Middle Third	Bottom Third
Number of Shops	133	133	133
Range of Sales:			
High	512,746	266,853	203,168
Low	267,374	203,239	61,447
Average	331,838	238,354	157,174

Although Rita's obtained reports from Franchisees as to Gross Sales at franchised Shops for the 2007 season for marketing and research purposes, Rita's is not able to independently verify reported sales. In preparing the Average Sales figure for this Item 19, Rita's estimated Average Sales from franchised Shops. Reported sales were typically lower than estimated Average Sales. As stated in Item 6 of this Disclosure Document, Royalty Fees and Advertising Fees on Proprietary Products are based on estimated sales. Rita's describes below how Rita's estimated the Average Sales contained in this Item 19.

The sales estimates described in this Item 19 represents only the sales by Franchisees of Proprietary Products containing the proprietary Rita's Mixes. These Proprietary Products were Italian ice, gelati, frozen custard, Misto shakes, and Blendini. Not included in the sales calculations described in this Item 19 are any other products sold by Franchisees, such as pretzels and promotional items.

The information in the Chart above is based on Shops that have been open for at least 1 full season. Shops opened less than 1 full season are not included in the calculations. A full season is defined as 1 entire selling season for which Rita's requires operation and the Shop must be opened at least 5 days before Spring. Florida franchised Shops may have been open for as many as 10 to 12 months. Where a Shop was open for a period longer than the selling season, all sales for such Shop were included in Rita's determination of Average Sales.

The Chart divides franchisees into three categories (Top Third, Middle Third, and Bottom Third), based on their sales as compared with the sales for the 399 total Shops considered in arriving at these figures. 52 franchisees or 39 % of the Shops in the Top Third attained or surpassed the average sales for the Top Third, 62 franchisees or 47 % of the Shops in the Middle Third attained or surpassed the average sales for the Middle Third, and 76 franchisees or 57 % of the Shops in the Bottom Third attained or surpassed the average sales for the Bottom Third. The average sales represent the average sales for franchisees within each category. High sales and Low sales represent the Franchisee within each category that attained the highest and lowest sales.

As noted in Item 6 of this disclosure document, each Franchisee must pay to Rita's a Royalty

Fee in the amount of 6 ½ % of the projected sales to be made by a Franchisee based on a Franchisee's purchase of Rita's proprietary Rita's Mixes. In calculating the Royalty Fee, Rita's estimates the projected sales that can be expected to be made from a Franchisee's purchase of Rita's Mixes, based on the amount of Rita's Mixes required for use in Rita's recipes for each product.

In calculating the Average Sales, Rita's estimated Franchisees' Average Sales based on the amount of Rita's Mixes purchased, Franchisees' prices, and the percentage of each type of Proprietary Product sold by Franchisees relative to all Proprietary Products sold (the "Product Percentages"). The historical data from which Rita's calculated the Product Percentages was provided to Rita's by each franchisee via weekly reporting of retail sales figures for each product during the 2007 season. Rita's knows the prices charged by each Franchisee because each Franchisee must notify Rita's of its prices so that Rita's may calculate the Royalty Fee to be paid by such Franchisee.

*   *   *

The Product Percentages for the 2007 season, as determined from Franchisees' franchised Shop register tapes (described in I, above) are described below. The Product Percentages vary based upon a Franchisee's location.

Proprietary Product Percentage of All Proprietary Products Required for Sale

ITALIAN ICE	33.4 %
GELATI	28.5 %
CUSTARD	17.5 %
MISTO SHAKE	10.1 %
BLENDINI	6.0 %
TOPPINGS	1.6 %
MISCELLANEOUS	2.9 %
TOTAL	100.00 %

In calculating the Royalty Fee and Average Sales, Rita's also assumed that some "wastage" would occur. Rita's defines "wastage" as the Rita's Mix that will not be used in Proprietary Products that are sold (e.g., product that will be thrown away or given away in connection with promotions). The Royalty Fee calculation for the 2007 season provided for 7% wastage; accordingly, when Rita's estimated projected sales on which a Franchisee owed Rita's a Royalty Fee, Rita's reduced its projections of sales expected to be made from a given amount of Rita's Mixes by 7%.

II. 2007 COSTS OF GOODS SOLD FOR PROPRIETARY PRODUCTS AT FRANCHISED SHOPS

Rita's estimates that Rita's Franchisees' Costs of Goods Sold represent 19% of Franchisees' revenue from sales of the products. Rita's has calculated the estimated Costs of Goods Sold of 19% based on (1) portions for ingredients required in Rita's proprietary recipes, (2) 2007 prices for such ingredients, (3) the System-wide average selling price in 2007 for each Proprietary Product sold, (4) a weighted average of Proprietary Products sold as determined by Franchisee reports of Product Percentages in 2007 (as defined in Section I, above), and (5) average cost of paper and packaging in 2007. Rita's calculation of Costs of Goods Sold assumes that proper recipes are followed, Franchisees adhere to proper serving sizes for Proprietary Products, and Franchisees maintain product wastage levels of 7%.

Rita's does not obtain reports from Franchisees as to Costs of Goods Sold at franchised Shops. Accordingly, to prepare the Costs of Goods Sold figures in this Item 19 it was necessary for Rita's to estimate the Costs of Goods Sold figures from franchised Shops. Rita's does not know what percentage of Franchisees incurred actual Costs of Goods Sold higher or lower than the estimated Costs of Goods Sold of 19%. Rita's describes below how it estimated the Costs of Goods Sold contained in this Item 19.

The calculation of Costs of Goods Sold contained in this Item 19 represents Costs of Goods Sold only for the products that Rita's requires each Franchisee to sell (i.e., kids, regular, large and quart Italian ice; regular and large gelati; kids, regular and large custard; regular and large Misto shakes; and Blendinis). As described in Section I, above, each franchisee provided its historical data to Rita's via weekly reporting of retail sales figures for each product during the 2007 season. Rita's used this data to estimate the Costs of Goods Sold in the 2007 season. Rita's can estimate the total cost of the ingredients for each Proprietary Product because the recipes for each Proprietary Product are prescribed by Rita's, Franchisees were required in 2007 to purchase the Rita's Mixes from Rita's, and Franchisees may also purchase the remaining ingredients from Rita's. Rita's has used the prices it charged in 2007 to Franchisees for ingredients. Rita's has determined the average selling price (not including sales tax) for each Proprietary Product during the 2007 season based on the prices submitted by Franchisees. In order to approximate the food costs resulting from wastage, in calculating Costs of Goods Sold for this Item 19, Rita's reduced the average selling price for each Proprietary Product by 7%. To determine the total pre-tax sales represented by the register tapes, as adjusted to reflect wastage, Rita's multiplied the adjusted average selling price by the number of units of each Proprietary Product sold (as reflected on the register tapes). Rita's also estimated the total cost of ingredients necessary to produce the total sales represented by the register tapes by multiplying the total number of each Proprietary Product sold by the estimated total costs for the ingredients for each item. Rita's determined estimated total costs for all sales represented by the register tapes by adding the estimated total costs for each Proprietary Product. Rita's determined Costs of Goods Sold by dividing the estimated total costs by the pre-tax adjusted sales. From this calculation, Rita's determined Costs of Goods Sold to be 19% of Franchisees' sales of all Proprietary Products.

As described in Item 6, above, each Franchisee must pay to Rita's a Royalty Fee based upon the amount of Rita's Mixes purchased by the Franchisee. This Royalty Fee has not been included in the calculations to determine Costs of Goods Sold in this Item 19. As a Franchisee, payment of the Royalty Fee would be an additional cost.

The calculations in this Item 19 used in determining Costs of Goods Sold are made under the assumption that Franchisees adhere to Rita's proprietary recipes and serving sizes. Although Rita's has provided each Franchisee with training and support to assist each Franchisee in adhering to these recipes and serving sizes, Rita's Franchisees have indicated to Rita's that an indeterminate number of Franchisees may serve portions to customers larger than those Rita's specifies. However, Rita's strongly encourages Franchisees to adhere to Rita's standards, specifications and portion controls for purposes of System consistency.

Costs of Goods Sold vary depending on store location, menu, Product Percentages, seasonal variances in raw material prices, and Franchisees' ability to effectively control costs. The average new Franchisee generally finds the first year of operation of each franchised Shop to be the most challenging. During the first year of operation a new Franchisee typically experiences higher wastage levels due to sampling, couponing and other promotional programs designed to build brand and product acceptance and due to higher amounts of "throw-aways" resulting from inexperience in planning. Historical costs do not correspond to future costs because of factors such as inflation, changes in menu and market driven changes in raw material costs.

* * * * *

Rita's obtained reports from Franchisees as to Gross Sales at franchised Shops for the 2007 season for marketing and research purposes, but we have not relied on these reports in this Item 19 because we cannot independently verify reported sales. (Reported sales are typically less than estimated Average Sales.) Actual sales and food costs vary from franchise to franchise, and Rita's cannot estimate the sales or food costs for a particular franchise. As stated in Item 6 of this disclosure document, Royalty Fees and Advertising Fees are based on estimated sales. Rita's recommends that you make your own independent investigation to determine whether or not the franchise may be profitable, and consult with an attorney and other advisors prior to executing the Development Agreement or the Franchise Agreement.

THE ESTIMATED SALES AND COSTS CONTAINED IN THIS ITEM 19 ARE ESTIMATES OF THE AVERAGE SALES AND COSTS OF GOODS SOLD OF THE EXISTING FRANCHISES DESCRIBED AND SHOULD NOT BE CONSIDERED AS THE ACTUAL OR PROBABLE AVERAGE SALES OR COSTS OF GOODS SOLD THAT WILL BE REALIZED OR INCURRED BY ANY PROSPECTIVE FRANCHISEE. WE DO NOT REPRESENT THAT ANY FRANCHISEE CAN EXPECT TO ATTAIN SUCH SALES OR TO INCUR SUCH COSTS OF GOODS SOLD. NONE OF THIS INFORMATION IS INTENDED AS A REPRESENTATION OF WHAT AVERAGE SALES YOU CAN EXPECT TO ACHIEVE OR COSTS OF GOODS SOLD YOU CAN EXPECT TO INCUR AT ANY PARTICULAR LOCATION.

NOT ALL FRANCHISED SHOPS HAVE ACHIEVED THESE RESULTS AND INCURRED THESE COSTS. THERE IS NO ASSURANCE THAT YOU WILL DO AS WELL. IF YOU RELY UPON RITA'S FIGURES, YOU MUST ACCEPT THE RISK OF NOT DOING AS WELL.

RITA'S WILL MAKE AVAILABLE TO YOU FOR INSPECTION AND REVIEW PRIOR TO YOUR PURCHASE OF A FRANCHISE THE DATA UTILIZED IN FORMULATING THE INFORMATION CONTAINED IN THIS ITEM 19 UPON REASONABLE REQUEST FROM YOU.

SONIC DRIVE-IN

300 Johnny Bench Dr.
Oklahoma City, OK 73104
Tel: (800) 569-6656 (405) 225-5000
Fax: (405) 225-5963
E-Mail: lcoffman@sonicdrivein.com
Web Site: www.sonicdrivein.com
Mr. David Vernon, VP Franchise Sales

SONIC DRIVE-INS offer made-to-order hamburgers and other sandwiches, and feature signature items, such as extra-long cheese coneys, hand-breaded onion rings, tater tots, fountain favorites, including cherry limeades, slushes and a full ice-cream dessert menu.

BACKGROUND: IFA MEMBER

Established: 1953;	1st Franchised: 1959
Franchised Units:	2850
Company-Owned Units:	625
Total Units:	3475
Dist.:	US-3468; CAN-0; O'seas-7
North America:	37 States, 0 Provinces
Density:	234 in OK, 191 in TN, 739 in TX
Projected New Units (12 Months):	185
Qualifications:	5, 5, 5, 2, 2, 4
Registered:	CA,DC,FL,IL,OR,VA,WA

FINANCIAL/TERMS:

Cash Investment:	$434-545K
Total Investment:	$900K-2.2MM
Minimum Net Worth:	$2MM
Fees: Franchise -	$30K
Royalty - 1-5%;	Ad. - 4%
Earnings Claims Statement:	No
Term of Contract (Years):	20/10
Avg. # Of Employees:	35 FT, 0 PT
Passive Ownership:	Not Allowed
Encourage Conversions:	No
Area Develop. Agreements:	Yes
Sub-Franchising Contracts:	No
Expand In Territory:	Yes
Space Needs:	1,450 SF; FS

SUPPORT & TRAINING:

Financial Assistance Provided:	Yes (I)
Site Selection Assistance:	Yes
Lease Negotiation Assistance:	Yes
Co-Operative Advertising:	Yes
Franchisee Assoc./Member:	Yes/Member
Size Of Corporate Staff:	210
On-Going Support:	B,C,D,E,F,G,H,I
Training:	1 Week Oklahoma City, OK; 11 Weeks Local Market

SPECIFIC EXPANSION PLANS:

US:	Yes, SW, SE, West, Midwest
Canada:	No
Overseas:	Yes, Mexico, Puerto Rico

ITEM 19
FINANCIAL PERFORMANCE REPRESENTATION

This Item 19 contains certain information about (a) Net Sales of Partner Drive-Ins, Franchise

Drive-Ins and New Market Drive-Ins for the 12-month periods ended August 31, 2008 and August 31, 2007; and (b) selected cost factors for Partner Drive-Ins for the 12-month period ended August 31, 2008. Except as described in this Item 19, no representations or statements of actual, average, projected, or forecasted sales, expenses, profits, or earnings of Sonic Drive-Ins are made to prospective franchisees or developers. Our officers and employees are not authorized to make any claims or statements as to sales, expenses, profits, or earnings or prospects or chances of success that you can expect or that have been experienced by us or by present or past Sonic Drive-Ins.

THE PERFORMANCE RESULTS INCLUDED IN THIS ITEM RELATE TO HISTORICAL RESULTS AND ARE NOT THE ACTUAL OR PROBABLE PERFORMANCE RESULTS THAT YOU SHOULD EXPECT TO ACHIEVE THROUGH THE OPERATION OF YOUR SONIC DRIVE-1N. YOU ARE LIKELY TO ACHIEVE RESULTS THAT ARE DIFFERENT, POSSIBLY SIGNIFICANTLY AND ADVERSELY, FROM THE RESULTS SHOWN BELOW.

Statement of Average Net Sales (excluding Non-traditional Sonic Drive-Ins) for the 12-Month Periods Ended August 31, 2008 and August 31, 2007 ($ in thousands)

	August 31, 2008				August 31, 2007	
			Percent of			Percent of
	Number of Drive-Ins in Group	Average Net Sales[1] ($)	Drive-Ins at or above the Average Net Sales	Number of Drive-Ins in Group	Average Net Sales ($)	Drive-Ins at or above the Average Net Sales
Partner Drive-Ins[2]	629	1,012	44	604	1,020	42
Franchise Drive-Ins[3]	2,598	1,156	44	2,496	1,135	44
New Market Drive-Ins[4]	23	1,742	39	5	2,231	60
Total of Partner Drive-Ins and Franchise Drive-Ins	3,227	1,128		3,100	1,113	

[1]Average Net Sales consists of the average of reported Net Sales for the applicable Sonic Drive-Ins for the designated time period. Net Sales include all sales from the Sonic Drive-In, excluding sales tax and discounts, and has the same definition as "Gross Sales" as defined in the License Agreement, Section 1.04 (Exhibit B).

[2]Partner Drive-Ins include those open and operating as Partner Drive-Ins the entire 12-month periods ended August 31, 2008 and August 31, 2007.

[3]Franchise Drive-Ins (which also include New Market Drive-Ins) include those open for the entire 12- month periods ended August 31, 2008 and August 31, 2007. Franchise Drive-Ins also include those drive-ins that changed from a Partner Drive-In to a Franchise Drive-In, or vice versa, during the period.

[4]New Market Drive-Ins include those opened by franchisees in cities where Sonic had no presence prior to September 1, 2005. These New Market Drive-Ins were open for the entire 12-month periods ended August 31, 2008 and August 31, 2007. New Market Drive-Ins opened after September 1, 2005 in the following DMAs:

Cedar Rapid, Waterloo, Iowa City
and Dubuque, IA
Chico-Redding, CA
Dayton, OH
Harrisburg, Lancaster, Lebanon
and York, PA
Medford, OR
Peoria - Bloomington, IL
Philadelphia, PA

Portland, OR
Rapid City, SD
Richmond - Petersburg, VA
Salisbury, MD
Sioux Falls, SD
Spokane, WA
Washington, DC
West Palm Beach — Ft. Pierce, FL

The Statement of Average Net Sales consists of the averages of the reported annual Net Sales of the designated group. Substantiation of the information used in preparing the Statement of Average Net Sales will be made available to you upon reasonable request.

Of the 3,227 Sonic Drive-Ins used for calculating the Average Net Sales for the 12-month period ended August 31, 2008:

(i)   the 629 Partner Drive-Ins had Net Sales that ranged between $435 thousand and $2.33 million, and 274 of those drive-ins attained or surpassed the Average Net Sales of Partner Drive-Ins;

(ii)   the 2,598 Franchise Drive-Ins had Net Sales that ranged between $296 thousand and $3.52 million, and 1,138 of those drive-ins attained or surpassed the Average Net Sales of Franchise Drive-Ins; and

(iii)   the 23 New Market Drive-Ins had Net Sales that ranged between $1.0 million and $2.76 million, and nine of those drive-ins attained or surpassed the Average Net Sales of New Market Drive-Ins.

Of the 3,100 Sonic Drive-Ins used for calculating the Average Net Sales for the 12-month period ended August 31, 2007:

(iv)   the 604 Partner Drive-Ins had Net Sales that ranged between $429 thousand and $2.48 million, and 255 of those attained or surpassed the Average Net Sales of Partner Drive-Ins;

(v)   the 2,496 Franchise Drive-Ins had Net Sales that ranged between $326 thousand and $3.22 million, and 1,091 of those drive-ins attained or surpassed the Average Net Sales of Franchise Drive-Ins; and

(vi)   the five New Market Drive-Ins had Net Sales that ranged between $1.66 million and $2.79 million, and three of those drive-ins attained or surpassed the Average Net Sales of New Market Drive-Ins.

The Average Net Sales of Franchise Drive-Ins, which includes New Market Drive-Ins, was derived from unaudited financial reports submitted by franchisees for the purpose of computing royalty fees. Sonic compiled the Net Sales of Partner Drive-Ins on the basis of generally accepted accounting principles, consistently applied.

The Statement of Average Net Sales and Certain Expenses of Partner Drive-Ins consists of the average of 629 Partner Drive-Ins open and operated for the entire 12-month period ended August 31, 2008. Substantiation of information used in preparing the Statement of Average Sales and Certain Expenses will be made available to you upon reasonable request. The Statement of Average Net Sales and Certain Expenses was prepared in accordance with generally accepted accounting principles, consistently applied. The footnotes are an integral part of the Statement of Average Net Sales and Expenses.

**Statement of Average Net Sales and Certain Expenses of Partner Drive-Ins
for the 12-Month Period Ended August 31, 2008**

	Average ($ in thousands)	Percent of Net Sales	Percent of Stores at or Above Average
Net Sales[1]	1,012	100.0	43.6
Cost of Sales[2]	277	27.4	43.6
Labor[3]			
Direct Labor[4]	238	23.5	44.0
Management Compensation[5]	22	2.2	60.6
Payroll Taxes and Benefits[6]	40	4.0	48.3
Total Labor	300	29.6	43.6
Gross Profit[7]	435	43.0	44.4
Controllable Costs			
Advertising[8]	53	5.2	42.6
Utilities	42	4.2	44.2
Other Controllables[9]	61	6.0	44.8
Total Controllables	156	15.4	44.5
Operating Profit before Occupancy	280	27.7	41.7

Costs (excluding rent, royalty and other fees payable to Sonic, depreciation and amortization, interest, income taxes and legal and administrative expenses)[10]

[1]The term "Net Sales" includes all revenues and excludes sales tax and discounts. Net Sales has the same definition as "Gross Sales" as defined in more detail in the License Agreement, Section 1.04 (Exhibit B).

[2]Cost of Sales includes all food and paper costs, less supplier rebates. You will have the opportunity to take advantage of prices negotiated by Sonic on particular items; however, availability of such prices is generally limited to geographic areas serviced by our approved suppliers and distributors. The cost of items such as produce, which are often purchased locally, may vary according to the Sonic Drive-In's location. Additionally, freight and shipping costs and the mark-up amount imposed by suppliers and distributors will also vary.

[3]Labor for a Sonic Drive-In is generally about 25 employees, including both full-time and part-time workers.

[4]Direct Labor assumes two assistant managers and the drive-ins' hourly employees.

[5]Management Compensation includes one working manager's salary. Additional compensation is distributed to the working manager from the Partner Drive-In's cash flow, for total compensation to a working manager of approximately $55,000 to $60,000.

[6]Payroll Taxes and Benefits includes worker's compensation, group insurance expenses, payroll taxes and vacation pay. The amounts reflect administrative costs and exclude all other general and administrative costs incurred for payroll matters, which are handled by our corporate office. Group medical and dental insurance costs for employees will vary depending on many factors, including the coverage and the group's loss experience. Because the total employee base is much smaller for franchisees than for Sonic, franchisees will likely encounter higher relative costs in providing comparable health benefits.

[7]Gross Profit is calculated by subtracting the Cost of Sales and Labor from Net Sales.

[8]Advertising includes the promotional items included in Wacky Pack® Kid's Meals. Refer to Items 6 and 11 for a description of the advertising amounts you are required to pay.

[9]Other Controllables includes uniforms, laundry, supplies, repair and maintenance, credit card services and accounting and travel expenses.

[10]Occupancy Costs will vary depending on whether you lease or own the site of your Sonic Drive-In and its geographic location. Refer to Item 7 for a description of your estimated investment costs. Depreciation and amortization will vary depending on your investment costs. Interest will vary depending on your financing terms. Refer to Item 6 for a description of royalty fees and other fees payable to Sonic.

This analysis does not include any federal income tax, local income tax or gross profits tax that may be applicable to the jurisdiction in which a drive-in may be located. You are strongly urged to consult with your tax advisor regarding the impact that federal, state and local taxes will have on the amounts shown in this analysis.

Sonic Drive-Ins' sales volumes vary considerably due to a variety of factors, such as the Sonic Drive-Ins': local popularity; competition from other restaurants; traffic flow, accessibility and visibility; economic conditions in the its locality; its age; and the business abilities and efforts of its franchisees. The most important factors in the success of your Sonic Drive-In will be how diligently you follow Sonic's methods and procedures and your business and management skill. Actual results vary from drive-in to drive-in and market to market. We cannot estimate or project the results for any particular Sonic Drive-In.

Operating costs and expenses for your new Sonic Drive-Ins may vary considerably and be different than those disclosed in the foregoing statement as a result of the geographic location of your drive-in, higher food and distribution costs, labor shortages and competitive real estate markets, among other factors. Additionally, distribution costs in those areas of the country not currently served by approved suppliers or distributors may be higher.

This Item 19 is provided as reference information only. We do not intend for it to be used as a statement or forecast of sales, costs or profits that may be achieved by any Sonic Drive-In. We urge you to consult with your financial, accounting and legal advisors about the information contained in this historical analysis.

TERIYAKI EXPERIENCE

700 Kerr St.
Oakville, ON L6K 3W3
Tel: (800) 555-5726 (905) 337-7777
Fax: (905) 337-0331
E-Mail: njurkovic@teriyakiexperience.com
Web Site: www.teriyakiexperience.com
Mr. Nik Jurkovic, VP Internatinal Development

Asian inspired quick service restaurants located in major mall food courts, street fronts, strip centers, airports, universities, hospitals, theme parks, supermarkets and other similar high traffic settings. Healthy, nutritious and delicious meals, prepared fast and fresh before your eyes. Cooked in water, not oil.

BACKGROUND: IFA MEMBER

Established: 1986;	1st Franchised: 1987
Franchised Units:	130
Company-Owned Units:	0
Total Units:	130

Dist.:	US-8; CAN-105; O'seas-21
North America:	9 States, 7 Provinces
Density:	5 in BC, 80 in ON, 14 in QC
Projected New Units (12 Months):	25
Qualifications:	5, 2, 2, 2, 3, 4
Registered:CA,DC,FL,HI,IN,MD,MI,MN,ND,NY,OR,RI,SD,VA,	WA,WI

FINANCIAL/TERMS:

Cash Investment:	$50-100K
Total Investment:	$230-330K
Minimum Net Worth:	$300K
Fees: Franchise -	$25K
Royalty - 6%;	Ad. - 3%
Earnings Claims Statement:	Yes
Term of Contract (Years):	8-10/5-10
Avg. # Of Employees:	3 FT, 6 PT
Passive Ownership:	Allowed, But Discouraged
Encourage Conversions:	Yes
Area Develop. Agreements:	Yes
Sub-Franchising Contracts:	Yes
Expand In Territory:	Yes
Space Needs:	400-1,800 SF; SF,SC,RM, Power Ctrs, Airport, University/College

SUPPORT & TRAINING:		Training:	9-10 Days Store;
Financial Assistance Provided:	Yes (I)	1 Week During your Grand Opening; 3-4 Days Company	
Site Selection Assistance:	Yes		Headquarters
Lease Negotiation Assistance:	Yes	**SPECIFIC EXPANSION PLANS:**	
Co-Operative Advertising:	Yes	US:	Yes, All United States
Franchisee Assoc./Member:	No	Canada:	Yes, All Canada
Size Of Corporate Staff:	40	Overseas:	Yes, All Countries
On-Going Support:	A,B,C,D,E,G,H,I		

Item 19
FINANCIAL PERFORMANCE REPRESENTATIONS

As discussed in Item 1, as of the date of this Disclosure Document, there were 114 Franchised Outlets operating in various countries, including 91 in Canada and 3 in the United States. Of the 3 Franchised Outlets operating in the United States as of the date of this Disclosure Document, 2 did not open until 2008 and 1 was only open for a portion of 2007. This Item only contains information regarding the gross sales reported by franchisees of the 43 Franchised Outlets operating in Canada for at least the entire 3 year period preceding the date of this Disclosure Document (that is, the periods ending December 31, 2005, December 31, 2006, and December 31, 2007). All of these reporting Franchised Outlets are located in shopping malls, strip centers, or free-standing buildings. MIJ also offers franchises to be located in nontraditional locations such as university campuses and hospitals.

This Item reports the average monthly gross sales during 2007 for the 43 reporting Franchised Outlets. The reporting Franchised Outlets all operate in metropolitan areas with higher densities of Made in Japan Teriyaki Experience businesses. You should consider the fact that the greater the number of Made in Japan Teriyaki Experience businesses operating in a state or other market area, the greater the goodwill and public recognition of our trademarks in that area are likely to be. The lower the number of Made in Japan Teriyaki Experience businesses operating in a state or other market area, the lesser the goodwill and public recognition of MIJ's trademarks in that area are likely to be. Positive goodwill and public recognition of trademarks likely will impact sales. You should consider the nature of the area in which you are interested in acquiring a franchise.

The figure below does not reflect the costs of sales, operating expenses, or other costs or expenses that must be deducted from the gross sales figures to obtain your net income or profit. You should conduct an independent investigation of the costs and expenses you will incur in operating your Franchised Outlet. Franchisees listed in this Disclosure Document may be one source of this information.

The chart below relates the average monthly gross sales of the 43 reporting Franchised Outlets during 2007. The average monthly gross sales for the one-year period ending December 31, 2007 for these 43 locations was CAD$435,959.* Gross Sales are defined as the total of all amounts directly or indirectly received or receivable by the Franchised Outlet from the sale of products in the Franchised Outlet, together with all other income generated during that period from all other business of any nature conducted at or originating from the premises of the Franchised Outlet and all proceeds received during that period from any business interruption insurance.

Average Monthly Gross Sales for Certain Franchised Outlets in Canada
Open During all of 2005, 2006 and 2007

	Average	#/% of Outlets Above Average
Average Gross Sales	CAD$435,959*	19/44%

* **This figure is in Canadian dollars. As of the date of this Disclosure Document, the conver-**

sion rate (which can fluctuate on a daily basis) is CAD$1.00 = US$0.98.

MIJ will provide to new franchisees, in its capacity as franchisor, the same services that it provided in the past to the Franchised Outlets referenced above. The Franchised Outlets referenced above offered the same products to the public as will new Franchised Outlets that franchisees will operate under the Franchise Agreement disclosed in this Disclosure Document. However, because the Franchised Outlets referenced above are operated in Canada and the Franchised Outlets that franchisees will operate under the Franchise Agreement disclosed in this Disclosure Document will operate in the United States, there may be differences in the costs and expenses you incur and the gross sales you derive in connection with operating your Franchised Outlet based upon the differences between the Canadian and United States markets.

There is no guarantee that any Franchised Outlet that a prospective franchisee operates will achieve the results reflected above, either during its initial year of operation or afterward. MIJ has written substantiation in our possession to support the information appearing in this Item. Substantiation of all information presented in this Item will be made available to you upon reasonable request. The actual performance of your own Franchised Outlet will be affected by numerous factors, including amount of time in business; lease terms; financing costs; taxes; labor costs; supply costs; local and regional economic and regulatory conditions; population density; your management skills and business acumen; competition; your ability to promote and market a Franchised Outlet; how hard you are willing to work; and the degree of adherence to our methods and procedures. While MIJ believes that Franchised Outlets will have consumer appeal in all geographic areas of the United States as the System grows, the Made in Japan Teriyaki Experience restaurant concept has limited operating history in the United States.

MIJ's management prepared this information based on gross sales reported by franchisees but did not independently audit that information.

YOU SHOULD NOT CONSIDER THIS HISTORICAL SALES INFORMATION AS THE ACTUAL OR POTENTIAL SALES THAT ARE REALIZED BY FRANCHISEES GENERALLY OR MAY BE REALIZED BY YOU. MIJ DOES NOT REPRESENT THAT YOU CAN EXPECT TO ATTAIN THESE SALES. YOUR FINANCIAL RESULTS ARE LIKELY TO DIFFER FROM THE RESULTS STATED ABOVE. OTHER THAN THIS INFORMATION, NO REPRESENTATIONS OR STATEMENTS OF ACTUAL, AVERAGE, PROJECTED, OR FORECASTED SALES, EARNINGS, OR PROFITS ARE MADE TO PROSPECTIVE FRANCHISEES. NEITHER MIJ'S EMPLOYEES NOR OFFICERS, NOR THOSE OF ANY OF MIJ'S AFFILIATES, ARE AUTHORIZED TO MAKE ANY CLAIMS OR STATEMENTS AS TO THE EARNINGS, SALES, PROFITS, OR PROSPECTS OR CHANCES OF SUCCESS THAT ANY FRANCHISEE CAN EXPECT OR THAT PRESENT OR PAST FRANCHISEES HAVE EXPERIENCED.

THIS SCHEDULE WAS PREPARED WITHOUT AN AUDIT. PROSPECTIVE FRANCHISEES OR SELLERS OF FRANCHISES SHOULD BE ADVISED THAT NO CERTIFIED PUBLIC ACCOUNTANT HAS AUDITED THESE FIGURES OR EXPRESSED HIS/HER OPINION WITH REGARD TO THEIR CONTENTS OR FORM.

TIM HORTONS USA	BACKGROUND:	
4150 Tuller Rd., #236	Established: 1964;	1st Franchised: 1964
Dublin, OH 43017	Franchised Units:	3421
Tel: (888) 376-4835	Company-Owned Units:	36
Fax: (614) 791-4235	Total Units:	3457
E-Mail: us_franchise_requests@timhortons.com		
Web Site: www.timhortons.com	**FINANCIAL/TERMS:**	
Franchise Department	Total Investment:	$65-258K
	Fees: Franchise -	$35K

ITEM 19
FINANCIAL PERFORMANCE REPRESENTATIONS

The following table describes the average Gross Sales in 2007 for all franchised Standard Stores with Drive-Thru Shops that were open and operating for at least one year as of December 30, 2007:

State	Average Gross Sales	Number of Shops Above Average	Number of Shops Under Average	Highest Reported Result	Lowest Reported Result
Connecticut	$640,214	2	2	$717,061	$569,354
Kentucky	$673,812	1	1	$725,891	$621,732
Maine	$785,673	5	6	$1,271,286	$426,124
Michigan	$1,002,161	37	43	$1,587,141	$488,000
New York	$1,406,387	43	37	$2,278,766	$462,757
Ohio	$862,891	36	41	$1,635,187	$402,974
Pennsylvania	$699,395	3	2	$857,356	$396,376
Rhode Island	$768,057	N/A (One Store Reporting)			
West Virginia	$955,093	1	2	$1,103,791	$855,578

Notes:

1.   The table reflects the results of 263 franchised Shops, or 73.9% of all franchised Shops. The remaining franchised Shops were not included because they opened after January 1, 2007 (84) or they were not a Standard Store with Drive-Thru Shop (33).

2.   In preparing this table, we relied on the data contained in the unaudited royalty reports submitted to us by our franchisees.

3.   As of December 30, 2007, 89.9% of the Tim Hortons System operated a Standard Store with Drive-Thru Shop, including 90.7% of franchised Shops and 83.3% of Tim Hortons owned Shops.

4.   The information set forth in this table reflects the aggregate Gross Sales results of individual Shops. It should not be considered as the actual or probable sales results that will be realized by any franchisee or Shop. We do not represent that any franchisee or Shop can expect to obtain the results set forth in the table. Actual results vary from Shop to Shop and we cannot estimate the results of any specific Shop. A new franchisee's Shop results are likely to differ from those of established Shops. We recommend that you make your own independent investigation to determine whether or not your Shop may be profitable, and consult with your attorney and other advisors before signing any franchise agreement.

5.   The information contained in the table should not be relied upon as representative of the Gross Sales of a Shop other than a Standard Store with Drive-Thru.

6.   Substantiation for the data set forth in this table will be made available to all prospective franchisees upon reasonable request.

7.   Except for the information contained in this disclosure document, we do not furnish or authorize our salespersons to furnish any oral or written information concerning the actual, average, projected, or forecasted sales, costs, income, or profits of any Tim Hortons Shop.

UNO CHICAGO GRILL
EST. 1943

UNO CHICAGO GRILL

100 Charles Park Rd.
Boston, MA 02132-4985
Tel: (877) 855-8667 (617) 218-5200
Fax: (617) 218-5376
E-Mail: randy.clifton@unos.com
Web Site: www.unos.com
Mr. Jack Crawford, SVP Franchising

A full-service casual theme restaurant with a brand name signature product - UNO's Original Chicago Deep Dish Pizza. A full varied menu with broad appeal featuring steak, shrimp and pasta. A flair for fun including a bar and comfortable décor in a facility that attracts guests of all ages.

BACKGROUND: IFA MEMBER

Established: 1943;	1st Franchised: 1979
Franchised Units:	84
Company-Owned Units:	102
Total Units:	186
Dist.:	US-182; CAN-0; O'seas-4
North America:	32 States, 0 Provinces
Density:	30 in MA, 31 in NY, 15 in VA
Projected New Units (12 Months):	16
Qualifications:	5, 5, 5, 3, 4, 4
Registered:CA,DC,FL,HI,IL,IN,MD,MI,MN,ND,NY,OR,RI,SD,	
	VA,WA,WI

FINANCIAL/TERMS:

Cash Investment:	$500-800K
Total Investment:	$850K-2.5MM
Minimum Net Worth:	$3MM
Fees: Franchise -	$40K
Royalty - 5%;	Ad. - 1%
Earnings Claims Statement:	Yes
Term of Contract (Years):	20/10
Avg. # Of Employees:	40 FT, 40 PT
Passive Ownership:	Allowed
Encourage Conversions:	Yes
Area Develop. Agreements:	Yes
Sub-Franchising Contracts:	No
Expand In Territory:	Yes
Space Needs:	5,800 SF; FS,SC

SUPPORT & TRAINING:

Financial Assistance Provided:	Yes (I)
Site Selection Assistance:	Yes
Lease Negotiation Assistance:	Yes
Co-Operative Advertising:	Yes
Franchisee Assoc./Member:	Yes/Member
Size Of Corporate Staff:	135
On-Going Support:	B,C,D,E,F,G,H,I
Training:	2 Weeks On-Site Staff Training;
	12 Weeks Training Restaurant

SPECIFIC EXPANSION PLANS:

US:	Yes, All United States
Canada:	Yes, All Canada
Overseas:	Yes, Asia, South and Central America, Europe

ITEM 19
FINANCIAL PERFORMANCE REPRESENTATIONS

Except as described below: (a) we do not make any representations about a franchisee's future financial performance or the past financial performance of company-owned or franchised outlets, and (b) we do not authorize our employees or representatives to make any such representations either orally or in writing. If you are purchasing an existing outlet, however, we may provide you with the actual records of that outlet. If you receive any other financial performance information or projections of your future income, you should report it to our management by contacting us at the address and telephone number set out on the cover page of this Disclosure Document, the Federal Trade Commission, and the appropriate state regulatory agencies.

Actual results vary from franchise to franchise, and we cannot estimate the results of a particular franchise. We recommend that prospective franchisees and developers make their own independent investigation to determine whether or not the franchise may be profitable, and consult with an attorney, accountant and other advisors prior to executing the Franchise Agreement or the Development Agreement.

Analysis of Average Sales and Expenses (Unaudited)
For Affiliate-Operated Full-Service Uno Restaurants

Bases and Assumptions

The sales information which follows was aggregated from affiliate-owned and franchised Full Service Uno Restaurants open for the entire fiscal year ended September 30, 2007. The expense information which follows was aggregated from affiliate-owned Full Service Uno Restaurants only, since expense data is not available for franchised Full Service Uno Restaurants. Sales and expense information is not available for Uno Due Go Restaurants. The table included in the analysis contains the number and percentage of affiliate-owned Full Service Uno Restaurants which, during the period October 1, 2006 to September 30, 2007, reported annual net sales of under $2,000,000, between $2,000,000 and $2,500,000, and over $2,500,000. This analysis was constructed using the arithmetic mean (average) annual sales and expenses of all 118 Full Service Uno Restaurants that were open and operated by our affiliates during the entire aforementioned period. However, certain charges which you will be required to pay to us under the Franchise Agreement (see Items 5 and 6) and other differences in the expenses of a franchised Full Service Uno Restaurant are included in the table, as noted below. Our auditors, Ernst & Young LLP, have not performed any procedures on the financial information in the tables below, and assume no responsibility for that information.

The affiliate-owned Full Service Uno Restaurants used in this analysis are substantially similar to the franchised Full Service Uno Restaurants. However, the amount of sales and expenses incurred will vary from restaurant to restaurant. In particular, the sales and expenses of your Full Service Uno Restaurant will be directly affected by factors which include the Full Service Uno Restaurant's geographic location; competition in the market; presence of other Uno Restaurants; the quality of both management and service at the Full Service Uno Restaurant; contractual relationships with lessors and vendors; the extent to which you finance the operation of your Full Service Uno Restaurant; your legal, accounting and other professional fees; federal, state and local income taxes, gross profits taxes or other taxes; cost of any automobile used in the business; other discretionary expenditures; accounting methods used and certain benefits and economies of scale which we may derive as a result of operating Full Service Uno Restaurants on a consolidated basis. A NEW FRANCHISEE'S INDIVIDUAL FINANCIAL RESULTS ARE LIKELY TO DIFFER FROM THE RESULTS DESCRIBED BELOW.

As of our 2007 fiscal year end, the average time in operation of the affiliate-owned Full Service Uno Restaurants included in this analysis is 12 years. The Full Service Uno Restaurants included in this analysis are located in the following states:

	Number of Full Service Uno Restaurants
Colorado	1
Connecticut	5
Florida	6
Illinois	5
Indiana	1
Maine	2
Maryland	10
Massachusetts	31
Missouri	2
New Hampshire	7
New Jersey	2
New York	23
Ohio	2
Pennsylvania	2

Rhode Island	3
Tennessee	1
Vermont	1
Virginia	13
Washington, D.C.	1
Total:	118

Statement of Average Sales for all Full-Service Uno Restaurants for the Fiscal Year ended September 30, 2007		
1) Annual Sales Range	Under $2,235,000	Over $2,235,000
2) Number of Uno Restaurants within the range / % of total affiliate-owned Uno Restaurants within the range	59 / 50%	59 / 50%
3) Number of domestic franchised Uno Restaurants within the range / % of total franchised Uno Restaurants within the range (based on franchisees' reported gross sales)	49 / 62%	30 / 38%

The following paragraphs contain a comparison of certain financial information received from our franchisees along with the average financial results of the 118 affiliate-owned Full Service Uno Restaurants. However, while we suggest that our franchisees utilize a uniform accounting system in reporting, which is consistent with generally accepted accounting principles, it should be expressly noted that we cannot attest to (i) the accuracy of the information received from our franchisees or (ii) whether such information was actually prepared in accordance with generally accepted accounting principles.

The numbers and percents indicated in the table above in lines (2) and (3) relate to the 118 affiliate-owned Full Service Uno Restaurants and 79 domestic franchised Full Service Uno Restaurants open during all of fiscal year 2007 (October 1, 2006 to September 30, 2007). In addition, the average annual sales volume for all affiliate-owned Full Service Uno Restaurants as described above was $2,235,017. This sales volume was attained or surpassed by 59 (or 50%) of the affiliate-owned Full Service Uno Restaurants and 30 (or 38%) of the franchised Full Service Uno Restaurants.

The highest annual sales volume of an affiliate-owned Full Service Uno Restaurant was $3,771,414. The lowest annual sales volume of an affiliate-owned Full Service Uno Restaurant was $1,096,011. The highest annual sales volume of a domestic franchised Full Service Uno Restaurant was $4,386,124. The lowest annual sales volume of a domestic franchised Full Service Uno Restaurant was $941,436.

Uno Restaurant Holdings Corporation Statement of Average Sales and Expenses (Unaudited) of Affiliate-Owned Full Service Uno Restaurants for the Fiscal Year Ended September 30, 2007						
Profit & Loss Period Ended September 30, 2007 Consolidated Financial Performance Representation Disclosure Pro Forma Per Store (Unaudited)						
	Dollars In Thousands	Under $2,000 40 Restaurants		Between $2,000 And 2,500 38 Restaurants		Over $2,500 40 Restaurants	
	SALES						
1	Net Sales	1,753.9	100.0%	2,239.1	100.0%	2,901.0	100.0%

	COST OF SALES						
2	Total Cost of Sales	448.1	25.5%	569.4	25.4%	726.3	25.0%
	LABOR						
3	Total Direct Labor	394.1	22.5%	476.7	21.3%	582.7	20.1%
4	Management	176.7	10.1%	204.0	9.1%	226.2	7.8%
5	Payroll Taxes & Benefits	114.1	6.5%	132.4	5.9%	155.9	5.4%
	Total Labor	684.8	39.0%	813.1	36.3%	964.8	33.3%
	GROSS PROFIT	621.0	35.4%	856.7	38.3%	1,209.9	41.7%
	CONTROLLABLE COSTS						
6	Paper Goods	29.9	1.7%	36.4	1.6%	47.9	1.7%
7	Small Wares	13.0	0.7%	18.4	0.8%	21.7	0.7%
8	Other Controllables	42.9	2.4%	51.1	2.3%	62.8	2.2%
	Total Controllables	85.8	4.9%	105.9	4.7%	132.4	4.6%
	INCOME AFTER CONTROLLABLES	535.2	30.5%	750.7	33.5%	1,077.5	37.1%
	OTHER COSTS						
9	Advertising & Business Coop	42.2	2.4%	48.0	2.1%	61.8	2.1%
10	Royalties	87.7	5.0%	112.0	5.0%	145.1	5.0%
11	Trash, Extermination & Security	13.8	0.8%	16.9	0.8%	20.9	0.7%
12	Other Non- Controllables	38.0	2.2%	44.5	2.0%	54.0	1.9%
	TOTAL OTHER EXPENSES	181.7	10.4%	221.4	9.9%	281.8	9.7%
13	EARNINGS Before R&M, utilities, rent, depr., admin., insurance, interest & taxes.	353.5	20.2%	529.4	23.6%	795.8	27.4%

Each of the 121 affiliate-owned Full Service Uno Restaurants utilized a uniform accounting system and the data pertaining to such Full Service Uno Restaurants was prepared on a basis consistent with generally accepted accounting principles during the covered period. The information contained in this analysis has generally not been audited. The following notes should assist in interpretation of the foregoing table of results.

1.   Net Sales (Line 1). The net sales are based on the average volume of the Full Service Uno Restaurants that fall into each revenue range. Net sales means total gross sales less taxes, employee meals, coupons and house charges.

2.   Total Cost of Sales (Line 2). You will have the opportunity to take advantage of volume discounts on particular items negotiated by us; however, availability of such volume discounts is generally limited to geographic areas in which our affiliates currently operate Uno Restaurants. The cost of items such as produce, which are often purchased locally, may vary according to the location

of the Uno Restaurant. Additionally, freight and shipping costs and the amount of mark-up imposed by suppliers will also vary.

3.   Direct Labor (line 3). Labor for a Full Service Uno Restaurant generally necessitates a range of 40-80 employees, including both full-time and part-time workers.

4.   Management Salary (line 4). This category assumes one designated general manager, 1 manager and 1 assistant manager and includes an amount for bonuses.

5.   Payroll Taxes and Benefits (line 5). This category includes amounts for workers' compensation, group insurance expenses, payroll taxes, and vacation pay. The amounts stated reflect administrative costs incurred by Full Service Uno Restaurants and exclude all other general and administrative costs incurred for payroll matters which are handled by our corporate or regional office. The costs of labor and related payroll expenses may vary substantially depending on the geographic location of the Full Service Uno Restaurant.

6.   Other Controllables (line 8). Other controllable expenses include the following costs: janitorial service; office supplies; entertainment; laundry; telephone; cash shortages; and miscellaneous.

7.   Advertising and Business Coop (line 9). These expenses represent the advertising and business coop contributions you are required to pay to us as described in Item 6. Specifically, you are required to pay a weekly fee of up to 1% of Gross Revenues, for business coop services. This fee includes your share of costs that are incurred by us for the benefit of the Business System. Article 9 of the Franchise Agreement further details and explains this expense. You are also required to expend a minimum of 2% of Gross Revenues on local marketing as described in Item 6. We have not accounted for the impact of a System Wide Marketing and Media Fund Fee of up to 1% of Gross Revenues, because the fee has not yet been implemented.

8.   Royalties (line 10). You will be required to pay a continuing royalty fee equal to the greater of 5% of Gross Revenues or $4,000 per month as described in Item 6.

9.   Other Non-Controllables (line 12). This category of expenses includes amounts for bank processing charges, dues, licenses, subscriptions, guest checks, and recruitment.

10.   Earnings before Repairs and Maintenance, Utilities, Rent, Depreciation, Administration, Insurance, Interest, and Taxes. (line 13). These Earnings do not include the following:

• Repairs & Maintenance: This expense varies depending on the age of the Restaurant and its equipment. Effective preventative programs with timely equipment replacement can reduce these expenses.

• Utilities: The Restaurant's location can result in significantly different heating and cooling requirements and also a wide range in utility costs. We can provide additional substantiating information regarding utility costs upon request.

• Rent, CAM and Property Taxes: These expenses differ for each Restaurant. You will need to estimate these expenses based on your location.

• Administration expense includes bill paying, payroll processing and other typical accounting tasks.

• Insurance: The cost of liability insurance varies widely depending on the State in which the Restaurant is located, the age of the business, its experience rating, the emphasis on bar programs, and whether the Restaurant provides valet parking or delivery.

Due to factors such as quantity discounts for goods and services, franchisor approval costs, reduced training and labor costs, and insurance discounts, your costs of operation may be higher than the costs for our affiliate-owned Full Service Uno Restaurants, and as a result affiliate-owned Full Service Uno Restaurant data is not an indication of how your Full Service Uno Restaurant will perform. Your accountant can help you develop your own estimated operational costs.

Substantiation of the data used in preparing the financial performance representations described above will be made available to you on reasonable request.

The information described in this Item 19 relates solely to Full Service Uno Restaurants. We do not have any information concerning the past, present or potential sales, income, costs or profits of an Uno Due Go Restaurant, nor does any information described in this Item 19 provide a reasonable basis for you to make any estimate about any of these subjects.

WENDY'S	Ms. Mary Schell, VP Corp. & Public Affairs, Issue Management	
1 Dave Thomas Blvd., P.O. Box 256		
Dublin, OH 43017	**BACKGROUND:**	IFA MEMBER
Tel: (800) 443-7266 (614) 764-3100	Established: 1969;	1st Franchised: 1972
Fax: (614) 764-6894	Franchised Units:	6600
E-Mail: mary_schell@wendys.com	Company-Owned Units:	1400
Web Site: www.wendys.com	Total Units:	7000

ITEM 19
FINANCIAL PERFORMANCE REPRESENTATIONS

As of the end of fiscal year 2007 (01/01/2007 to 12/30/2007), there were 1,222 domestic Wendy's Old Fashioned Hamburgers Restaurants owned by Wendy's; and 4,499 domestic Wendy's Old Fashioned Hamburgers Restaurants owned by Wendy's franchisees, which had been open at least 15 months and opened prior to the start of fiscal year 2007[1]. Of those Restaurants owned by Wendy's, the average annual sales volume was $1,421,734, with 532 Restaurants (43.5%) attaining or exceeding this average. 1,129 Restaurants (92.4%) had sales volumes in excess of $1 million; 1,030 Restaurants (84.3%) had sales volumes in excess of $1.1 million; and 881 Restaurants (72.1%) had sales volumes in excess of $1.2 million.

Of those Restaurants owned by Wendy's franchisees, the average annual sales volume was $1,306,452, with 2,055 Restaurants (45.7%) attaining or exceeding this average. 3,671 Restaurants (81.6%) had sales volumes in excess of $1 million; 3,158 Restaurants (70.2%) had sales volumes in excess of $1.1 million; and 2,587 Restaurants (57.5%) had sales volumes in excess of $1.2 million.

In 2007, the highest and lowest annual sales volumes for domestic Restaurants owned by Wendy's were $2,883,743[2] and $507,707[3] respectively; and the highest and lowest annual sales volumes for domestic Restaurants owned by franchisees were $3,360,739[4] and $317,062[5] respectively.

The Restaurant sales volumes for franchised restaurants are based on the monthly unaudited reports Wendy's received from franchisees. Wendy's has not independently verified or audited these unaudited monthly reports, and there are no assurances that generally accepted accounting principles were used by franchisees in preparing them.

As a rule, Wendy's does not furnish or authorize its representatives to furnish any oral or written information concerning the actual or potential sales, costs, income, or profits of any Wendy's Old Fashioned Hamburgers Restaurant, other than that which is presented through this Item 19. The one exception is that, during the fiscal year, Wendy's may furnish current sales volumes for both company and franchised restaurants as part of the local market planning process. This sales information updates and supports the national sales averages provided above, however, it is limited to sales from restaurants in a specific local market.

AS A PROSPECTIVE FRANCHISEE, YOU MUST BEAR IN MIND THAT A NEWLY OPENED BUSINESS CANNOT BE EXPECTED TO ACHIEVE SALES VOLUMES SIMILAR TO THOSE OF AN ESTABLISHED BUSINESS. IN ADDITION, ACTUAL FINANCIAL RESULTS WILL VARY BY RESTAURANT AND TYPE OF RESTAURANT, AND WENDY'S CANNOT ESTIMATE OR PREDICT

THE RESULTS OF ANY PARTICULAR RESTAURANT LOCATION.

IN PROVIDING THIS INFORMATION, WENDY'S DOES NOT REPRESENT THAT YOU CAN EXPECT TO ATTAIN ANY SPECIFIC LEVEL OR RANGE OF ACTUAL OR POTENTIAL SALES, COSTS, INCOME OR PROFIT FROM YOUR WENDY'S RESTAURANT. THE AVERAGE SALES VOLUME STATED IN THIS ITEM 19 SHOULD NOT RE CONSIDERED AS THE ACTUAL OR POTENTIAL SALES THAT MAY OR WILL BE REALIZED BY ANY OTHER FRANCHISEE. WENDY'S DOES NOT REPRESENT THAT YOU CAN EXPECT TO ATTAIN THESE SALES. Wendy's will make available to you, on reasonable request, the data used in preparing the statements listed in this Item 19.

[1] In Item 19, the number of Wendy's Restaurants owned by Wendy's (1,222) and the number owned by Wendy's franchisees (4,499) is different from the number of Wendy's Restaurants stated in item 1. In counting the Wendy's Restaurants for Item 19, Wendy's does not include: (i) new stores that were opened during the fourth quarter of 2006 or during the fiscal year 2007; (ii) stores that were closed for more than a week and reopened during the fourth quarter of 2006 or during the fiscal year 2006; and (iii) stores purchased by franchisees from Wendy's during the fourth quarter of 2006 or during the fiscal year 2007. The Restaurants listed in Item 19 only include those Wendy's Restaurants that were open and in continuous operation for a period of at least 15 months <u>and</u> open prior to the start of fiscal year 2007.

[2] Traditional location (Skokie, IL)

[3] Non-traditional location (El Montez, CA)

[4] Non-traditional location (Milford, CT)

[5] Non-traditional location (Billings, MT)

> *Please note that all of the Item 19s included in the 2009 Edition of "How Much Can I Make?" were taken from the respective company's 2008 Franchise Disclosure Document (FDD)/Uniform Offering Circular (UFOC). Accordingly, all of the financial data in the Item 19s refers to actual operations in 2007. In a very few cases, depending upon the date of the FDD/UFOC, the data might refer to operations in 2006. Because of the need to provide historical data, there is generally a year's lag between the date of the annual FDD/UFOC and the underlying Item 19 data.*

CHOICE HOTELS
INTERNATIONAL®

CLARION HOTELS

10750 Columbia Pike
Silver Spring, MD 20901-4427
Tel: (866) 560-9871 (301) 592-5041
Fax: (301) 592-5058
E-Mail: emerging_markets@choicehotels.com
Web Site: www.choicehotels.com
Mr. Brian Parker, Dir. Emerging Mkts./Bus. Devel

Choice Hotels® is the leading hotel franchisor with over 65 years experience in developing brands and services that optimize hotel performance. Our single focus is on enhancing the return on investment for our owners and growing our brands strategically. Brands include Comfort Inn®, Comfort Suites®, Quality®, Sleep Inn®, Clarion®, MainStay Suites®, Suburban Extended Stay®, Econo Lodge®, Rodeway Inn® and our newest upscale, all-suites brand Cambria Suites®. We offer brands for conversion and new build opportunities. *Source of operating units data: 3rd quarter 2008 internal data *Your fees may fall outside the ranges listed below. Please contact Choice Hotels at (800) 547-0007 to receive the latest FDD for the brand(s) you are interested in or visit choicehotelsfranchise.com for more details.

BACKGROUND: IFA MEMBER
Established: 1940;   1st Franchised: 1940
Franchised Units: 5771
Company-Owned Units: 0
Total Units: 5771
Dist.:   US-4661; CAN-275; O'seas-835
  North America: 50 States, 10 Provinces
  Density: 251 in CA, 205 in FL, 258 in TX

Projected New Units (12 Months):   NR
Qualifications: 4, 4, 4, 2, 1, 1
Registered: CA,DC,FL,HI,IL,IN,MD,MI,MN,ND,NY,OR,
                                         RI,SD,VA,WA,WI

FINANCIAL/TERMS:
Cash Investment: 20-30% Costs
Total Investment: $2.3-12.6M
Minimum Net Worth: Varies
Fees: Franchise - $25-50K
  Royalty - 2.75-5.1%;   Ad. - 1.75% Rev.
Earnings Claims Statement: Yes
Term of Contract (Years):   20/5
Avg. # Of Employees: Varies FT, 0 PT
Passive Ownership: Allowed
Encourage Conversions: Yes
Area Develop. Agreements: 0
Sub-Franchising Contracts: No
Expand In Territory: Yes
Space Needs: 31,000-33,000 SF; FS

SUPPORT & TRAINING:
Financial Assistance Provided: Yes (D)
Site Selection Assistance: Yes
Lease Negotiation Assistance: Yes
Co-Operative Advertising: No
Franchisee Assoc./Member: Yes/Member
Size Of Corporate Staff: 1500
On-Going Support: A,B,C,D,F,G,h,I
Training: NR

SPECIFIC EXPANSION PLANS:
US: Yes, All United States
Canada: Yes, All Canada
Overseas: Yes, All Countries

ITEM 19
FINANCIAL PERFORMANCE REPRESENTATION

TABLE 1: Average Occupancy Rate, Average Daily Room Rate, and RevPAR
For CLARION INN, CLARION HOTEL, CLARION SUITES, CLARION RESORT and CLARION COLLECTION

	For Year Ended December 31, 2007
Average Occupancy Rate	54.8%
Average Daily Room Rate	$80.37
Revenue per Available Room ("RevPAR")	$44.01

As of December 31, 2007, there were 166 open and operating CLARION INN, CLARION HOTEL, CLARION SUITES AND CLARION RESORT and CLARION COLLECTION hotels. Of these 166 hotels, 96 were Stabilized Comparable CLARION Properties.* The data presented in the above table are based on the 96 Stabilized Comparable CLARION Properties. For the 96 hotels that were included in the sample, 56.3% met or exceeded the Average Occupancy Rate; 44.8% achieved or surpassed the average daily room rate; and 54.2% met or exceeded the RevPAR presented.

TABLE 2: Net Reservations Contribution and CRS Average Daily Rate
For CLARION INN, CLARION HOTEL, CLARION SUITES AND CLARION RESORT and CLARION COLLECTION

	For Year Ended December 31, 2007
Net Reservations Contribution	30.4%
CRS Average Daily Rate	$89.39

For the one-year period ending December 31, 2007, reservations generated through the Choice Central Reservations System ("CRS") represented an average of 30.4% of gross room revenue at an Average Daily Rate of $89.39 for the 93 Stabilized Comparable CLARION Properties. For the 93 hotels that were included in the sample, 50.5% met or exceeded the Net Reservations Contribution, and 45.2% exceeded the CRS Average Daily Rate presented in the table above.

TABLE 3: Average Occupancy Rate, Average Daily Room Rate, and RevPAR
For CLARION COLLECTION

	For Year Ended December 31, 2007
Average Occupancy Rate	57.4%
Average Daily Room Rate	$89.99
RevPAR	$51.68

As of December 31, 2007, there were 37 open and operating CLARION COLLECTION hotels in the System. Of these 37 hotels, 15 were "Stabilized Comparable CLARION COLLECTION Properties."** The data presented in the above table are based on the 15 Stabilized Comparable CLARION COLLECTION Properties. For the 15 hotels that were included in the sample, 60% met or exceeded the Average Occupancy Rate; 46.7% achieved or surpassed the average daily room rate; and 40% met or exceeded the RevPAR presented.

** "Stabilized Comparable CLARION COLLECTION Properties" are all CLARION COLLECTION properties that were open and operating as of December 31, 2007, and that were franchised by Choice on or before January 1, 2006, except for properties that: (1) repositioned from one Choice brand to CLARION COLLECTION since January 1, 2006; (2) had reservations suspended by Choice during the year ending December 31, 2007; and/or (3) experienced an interruption in operations (e.g., due to renovation, natural disaster, etc.) of more than 30 days during the year ending December 31, 2007.

TABLE 4: Net Reservations Contribution and CRS Average Daily Rate
For CLARION COLLECTION

	For year ended December 31, 2007

Net Reservations Contribution	36.9%
CRS Average Daily Rate	$84.31

For the one-year period ending December 31, 2007, reservations generated through the Choice Central Reservations System ("CRS") represented an average of 26.9% of gross room revenue at an Average Daily Rate of $84.31 for the 15 Stabilized Comparable CLARION COLLECTION Properties. For the 15 hotels that were included in the sample, 33.3% met or exceeded the Net Reservations Contribution, and 66.7% met or exceeded the CRS Average Daily Rate presented in the table above.

We used the following definitions for Tables 1-4: "**Average Occupancy Rate**" is the average of occupied rooms reported for each hotel divided by its total number of available rooms. "**Average Daily Rate**" is the average of each hotel's gross room revenue reported divided by its total number of occupied rooms reported. "**RevPAR**" is the average of each hotel's gross room revenues reported divided by its number of available rooms. "**Net Reservations Contribution**" is the average of each hotel's revenue generated through the CRS, excluding cancelled reservations, divided by that hotel's gross room revenues. "**CRS Average Daily Rate**" is the Average Daily Rate for reservations generated through the CRS, excluding cancelled reservations.

* * * * *

THE FINANCIAL PERFORMANCE REPRESENTATIONS IN TABLES 1 THROUGH 4 DO NOT REFLECT THE COSTS OF SALES, OPERATING EXPENSES OR OTHER COSTS OR EXPENSES THAT MUST BE DEDUCTED FROM THE GROSS REVENUE, OR GROSS SALES FIGURES TO OBTAIN YOUR NET INCOME OR PROFIT. YOU SHOULD CONDUCT AN INDEPENDENT INVESTIGATION OF THE COSTS AND EXPENSES YOU WILL INCUR IN OPERATING YOUR CLARION BRAND HOTEL. FRANCHISEES OR FORMER FRANCHISEES, LISTED IN THE DISCLOSURE DOCUMENT, MAY BE ONE SOURCE OF THIS INFORMATION.

The data presented in Tables 1 through 4 above represent CLARION System averages. We do not claim that you can expect to achieve the same results. Actual results vary from hotel to hotel and depend on the specific size, location, and seasonality of your hotel, and on factors such as your real estate and construction costs, financing terms and arrangements, the length of time that your hotel has been open and operating, the efficiency with which you operate your hotel, and the competitive factors affecting demand for your hotel. We cannot, therefore, estimate the results of any particular location. Typically, a new hotel requires at least one year of operating experience to reach a stabilized performance.

The data presented in Tables 1 through 4 are based on information that individual CLARION Brand franchise owners provided to us and verified as accurate. We have not audited or otherwise verified the accuracy of the information that the franchisees provided to us. Substantiation of the data used in preparing the statement shown above will be made available to you on reasonable request.

THE INFORMATION ABOVE REFLECTS THE EXPERIENCE OF SPECIFIC HOTEL OWNERS DURING A LIMITED TIME PERIOD AND SHOULD NOT BE CONSIDERED TO BE THE ACTUAL OR PROBABLE, OCCUPANCY, AVERAGE DAILY RATE OR REVPAR THAT YOU WILL ACHIEVE OR NET RESERVATIONS CONTRIBUTION OR CRS AVERAGE DAILY RATE THAT YOUR HOTEL WILL RECEIVE. THE RESULTS FOR YOUR CLARION INN, CLARION HOTEL, CLARION SUITES, CLARION RESORT, OR CLARION COLLECTION HOTEL MAY DIFFER SUBSTANTIALLY FROM THE AVERAGES STATED ABOVE. CHOICE DOES NOT REPRESENT THAT YOU WILL ATTAIN COMPARABLE OCCUPANCY, AVERAGE DAILY RATE OR REVPAR OR RECEIVE COMPARABLE LEVELS OF NET RESERVATIONS CONTRIBUTION OR CRS AVERAGE DAILY RATE.

Except as stated in this Item 19, we do not furnish to you or authorize our salespersons to furnish to you any oral or written information or representation on the actual or potential sales, costs, income or profits of a CLARION INN, CLARION HOTEL, CLARION SUITES, CLARION RESORT, or CLARION COLLECTION hotel franchise.

RI,SD,VA,WA,WI

MOTEL 6

4001 International Pkwy.
Carrollton, TX 75007
Tel: (888) 842-2942 (972) 360-2547
Fax: (972) 360-5567
E-Mail: franchisesales@accor-na.com
Web Site: www.motel6.com
Mr. Dean Savas, SVP Franchising

Accor Hotels is one of the largest owner/operators of economy lodging in the United States. Accor North America is a division of Accor, with 168,000 people in 140 countries, employing approximately 690 people at the corporate offices including the call centers. Approximately 13,000 are employed at Motel 6 and Studio 6 combined.

BACKGROUND: IFA MEMBER
Established: 1962;   1st Franchised: 1996
Franchised Units: 167
Company-Owned Units: 681
Total Units: 848
Dist.:   US-844; CAN-4; O'seas-0
  North America: 50 States, 1 Provinces
  Density: 43 in AZ, 184 in CA, 108 in TX
Projected New Units (12 Months):   50
Qualifications: 4, 4, 1, 1, 1, 3
Registered: CA,DC,FL,HI,IL,IN,MD,MI,MN,ND,NY,OR,

FINANCIAL/TERMS:
Cash Investment: $100-500K
Total Investment: $1.9MM-2.3MM
Minimum Net Worth: $1.5MM
Fees: Franchise - $25K
  Royalty - 4%;   Ad. - 3.5%
Earnings Claims Statement: Yes
Term of Contract (Years):   15/20/9/10
Avg. # Of Employees: 2-4 FT, 4-10 PT
Passive Ownership: Allowed
Encourage Conversions: Yes
Area Develop. Agreements: No
Sub-Franchising Contracts: No
Expand In Territory: Yes
Space Needs: 2.5 Acres SF; FS

SUPPORT & TRAINING:
Financial Assistance Provided: Yes (D)
Site Selection Assistance: No
Lease Negotiation Assistance: No
Co-Operative Advertising: Yes
Franchisee Assoc./Member: Yes/Member
Size Of Corporate Staff: 450
On-Going Support: A,b,C,d,e,h,I
Training: 1 Week On-Site Opening Training;
1 Week Manager Training Dallas, TX; 2 Days Dallas, TX for
Owner's Orientation

SPECIFIC EXPANSION PLANS:
US: Yes, All United States
Canada: Yes, All Canada
Overseas: No

ITEM 19
FINANCIAL PERFORMANCE REPRESENTATIONS

STATEMENT OF AVERAGE REVENUES AND EXPENSES
FOR MOTEL 6 PROPERTIES WITH 70 ROOMS OR LESS OWNF.D OR LEASED BY M6 OLP
DURING THE PERIOD JANUARY 1, 2007 - DECEMBER 31, 2007[1]

NUMBER OF PROPERTIES: 40[2]
AVERAGE PROPERTY SIZE: 60 ROOMS
AVERAGE DAILY RATE: $53.21

AVERAGE OCCUPANCY: 78.16%[4]
REVENUES

Room Rental	MEAN AVERAGE[5]	PERCENTAGE OF MEAN AVERAGE REVENUES[6]	MEDIAN AVERAGE[7]

Revenues	$907,499	98.99%	$872,452
Other Revenues[8]	$9,235	1.01%	$5,769
Total Revenues	**$916,734**	**100.0%**	**$878,221**

OPERATING EXPENSES

Salaries and Wages [9]	$201,273	21.96%	$201,328
Employee Benefits[10]	$60,380	6.59%	$61,363
Supplies[11]	$27,427	2.99%	$ 27,612
Repairs and Maintenance[12]	$37,284	4.07%	$ 35,599
Utilities[13]	$73,287	7.99%	$ 71,889
Billboards/Local Marketing[14]	$4,764	.52%	$782
Security Services[15]	$8,320	.91%	$ -
Travel and Other[16]	$ 25,341	2.76%	$25,010
Total Operating Expenses	**$438,076**	**47.79%**	**$423,583**
Controllable Profit	**$478,658**	**52.21%**	**$454,638**
Overhead & Company Expenses [17]	$ 68,703	7.49%	$65,991
Income from Operations Before Fixed Expenses [18]	**$409,955**	**44.72%**	**$388,647**

THE INFORMATION SET FORTH ABOVE WAS COMPILED FROM DATA FROM MOTEL 6 LOCATIONS OWNED OR LEASED BY M6 OLP AND SHOULD NOT BE CONSIDERED AS THE AVERAGE OR PROBABLE SALES, EXPENSES OR INCOME THAT SHOULD OR WOULD BE REALIZED BY YOU. WE DO NOT REPRESENT THAT YOU CAN EXPECT TO ATTAIN SIMILAR RESULTS. A NEW FRANCHISEE'S RESULTS ARE LIKELY TO DIFFER FROM THE RESULTS SET FORTH IN THIS STATEMENT PRIMARILY BECAUSE "STARTUP" MOTELS TRADITIONALLY EXPERIENCE LOWER REVENUES AND HIGHER COSTS THAN THOSE WHICH HAVE BEEN OPERATING FOR SOME TIME.

OTHER THAN AS SET FORTH IN THIS ITEM 19, WE DO NOT FURNISH, OR AUTHORIZE OUR SALESPERSONS TO FURNISH, ORAL OR WRITTEN INFORMATION CONCERNING ACTUAL OR POTENTIAL SALES, COSTS, INCOME OR PROFITS OF A MOTEL 6 UNIT. ACTUAL RESULTS VARY FROM PROPERTY TO PROPERTY AND WE CANNOT ESTIMATE THE RESULTS OF ANY PARTICULAR FRANCHISE.

1.   No franchised operations are included in the information contained in this Item 19.

2.   This Statement reflects the results of 40 motels owned or leased by M6 OLP and open throughout the entire period January 1 - December 31, 2007 which have a room count of equal to or less than 70 rooms per property. In addition to these motels, during 2007 M6 OLP owned or leased 1 motel which was not open throughout the entire year.

3.   This is the mean average of the rate paid by guests for lodging in all the properties described in note 2 above, for the calendar year 2007. Rate and occupancy are the traditional measures of motel revenue generation, and vary from property to property based on such factors as stay demand in the immediate market, the number and type of competitive properties, the quality and physical condition of the property, service levels, location, visibility and accessibility, brand affiliation (or lack thereof), marketing efforts and effectiveness, prevailing rates in the market, facility repu-

tation, convenience to destinations or generators of motel stays and other factors.

4.   This is the mean average of all room stays in the properties described in note 2 above, and has been calculated by dividing the number of room stays by the number of available room-nights in those same properties.

5.   This is the mean average which has been calculated by aggregating the total revenues or expenses for a given category and thereafter dividing it by the number of properties contributing to such revenues or expenses.

6.   This percentage reflects the relationship between a specific expense or revenue shown in the "mean average" column and the total revenues of the average property.

7.   The "median average" is the point at which half the properties reported higher results, and half the properties reported lower results.

8.   "Other revenues" includes revenue primarily from vending sales and guest laundry. Motel 6 guests are required to pay in advance (check-out is not necessary). Under the Motel 6 System, guests do not pay for local telephone calls and are not permitted to incur "room charges" for long-distance telephone calls and other services. Thus, non-room sales are limited to those which can utilize a point-of-sale payment procedure, as with coin-operated or "card-swipe" machinery; as a result, "other revenue" sources are less significant for Motel 6 properties than in the lodging industry generally.

9.   M6 OLP hires and trains professional managers, who are paid a wage somewhat below industry averages but are generally furnished personal lodging in a "manager's apartment" built into the motel facility. You are not required to construct or furnish a manager's apartment; if you hire a manager to operate your property, but do not provide an apartment, you may pay a higher wage expense, but would save construction and furnishing costs which, in turn, may reduce your financing expenses. In addition to management personnel, a Motel 6 location will require desk clerks to staff the front desk 24 hours per day, as well as a head housekeeper. Variable salary costs, depending upon number of rooms and occupancy, include those for laundry workers, housekeepers and maintenance workers, as necessary.

10.   This expense consists of payroll taxes, workers' compensation expenses and the cost of employee benefits package which includes a 401(k) plan and company-subsidized medical coverage. You are responsible for payroll taxes and worker's compensation expenses which will vary by state. You are not required to offer to your employees any specific level or type of employee benefits. Accordingly, the level and cost of such benefits will be determined by you, and by the requirements of applicable laws.

11.   The largest single expense in this category is for linen and bedding, but this category also includes expendable supplies furnished to guests for their use, cleaning supplies, paper goods and items of a similar nature. Expenditures for such items generally vary with occupancy more than any other factor. M6 OLP is able, by reason of size and purchasing power, to secure advantageous pricing on most supplies, but you may not be able to purchase supplies at similar prices.

12.   This expense includes repairs and maintenance both within guestrooms and in common areas of the property. The extent of needed repairs or maintenance will vary with the quality and durability of construction, furnishings and other materials in the property; occupancy levels; types of guests; unusual climatic conditions; weather and other factors.

13.   This expense includes gas, water, electricity, telephone, trash disposal and expenses of a similar nature. The properties reflected in this Statement are predominantly exterior-door motel designs in which heated or cooled air is lost to the atmosphere whenever an entry door is opened; we believe that an interior-corridor design may experience greater operating efficiencies. Utility charges vary with local suppliers and utility companies, as well as occupancy and climate.

14.   This expense consists primarily of the cost of highway billboards announcing the

proximity of a Motel 6 property, directions for finding it, and the price of a single -occupancy room. Guest surveys indicate that highway billboards are an important tool in attracting guests. The outdoor advertising industry is geographically diverse, as are the laws and regulations which apply to billboard advertising. Costs vary widely among locations, and you should check the availability and costs in the vicinity of your intended location.

15.   This expense consists primarily of third-party security services hired to patrol the Motel grounds and vicinity for the protection of guests, staff and parked automobiles. The necessity or desirability of such services varies from location to location based on such factors as the surrounding neighborhood, guest and visitor demographics, adequate lot lighting and mechanical security devices, whether the location has a history of problems and crime trends in the market area. Such services are usually provided by local companies or agencies, and you should be able to secure cost estimates locally.

16.   This expense includes such items as travel, relocation, training, recruitment, meals, attendance at meetings and miscellaneous smaller categories (losses, legal expense, dues and subscriptions, financial and collection charges and credit card commissions). You will experience some or all such costs, but expenses vary widely among properties. You are obligated to pay any applicable salaries, travel, lodging and meal costs of your employees while undergoing our training programs.

17.   This expense includes costs experienced by M6 OLP for marketing, reservations, administrative and company expenses, field and training expenses, a corporate overhead allocation and some minor management- fee expenses. You are unlikely to experience these costs in the same proportions, and may not experience some such costs at all. However, you will experience expenses not incurred by M6 OLP in its operations or reflected in this Statement, such as marketing contributions, reservations fees and franchise fees (as described in Item 6 of this disclosure document), which, in combination with other "overhead" expenses for accounting, administration and management, will likely exceed the "Overhead and Company Expenses" entry shown.

18.   From "Income from Operations Before Fixed Expenses", you must deduct such capital expenses as interest on mortgages and/or other loans, lease payments, the cost of periodic motel refurbishment, etc. The level of financing-related costs you may experience will be a function of your individual equity and financing structure and, thus, no meaningful estimate can be given here. Periodic refurbishment costs will vary with the quality of original materials used in the construction and furnishing of your Motel, the degree of usage it experiences and factors such as climate and maintenance practices. The Franchise Agreement requires you to replace, refurbish or maintain capital items to ensure continued acceptable quality of the guest experience and conformity with our minimum specifications. You also must deduct fixed expenses such as property taxes, licenses, insurance, etc. These fixed expenses like capital expenses, vary widely by location and individual circumstances.

19.   **WE HAVE WRITTEN SUBSTANTIATION IN OUR POSSESSION TO SUPPORT THE INFORMATION APPEARING IN THIS ITEM 19 AND SUCH SUBSTANTIATION WILL BE MADE AVAILABLE TO YOU ON REASONABLE REQUEST.**

RADISSON HOTELS & RESORTS

701 Carlson Pkwy. MS 8205
Minnetonka, MN 55305
Tel: (800) 336-3301 (763) 212-5660
Fax: (763) 212-3350
E-Mail: bsipple@carlson.com

Web Site: www.radisson.com
Mr. Bill Sipple, VP Development

Radisson Hotels & Resorts® - One of the world's leading full-service hotel companies, Radisson Hotels & Resorts currently encompasses 403 properties with 87,878 guestrooms in 69 countries. Radisson is focused on being the hotel of choice with business and leisure travelers by understanding the independent mindset and changing needs of today's frequent travelers who want more control over their hotel experience. Radisson Hotels & Resorts is continuing to evolve the brand, introducing new product and service standards to address

---

key guest needs and distinguish the hotels within the full-service category.

BACKGROUND: IFA MEMBER

Established: 1983; 1st Franchised: 1983

Franchised Units: 380

Company-Owned Units: 23

Total Units: 403

Dist.: US-148; CAN-21; O'seas-234

North America: 36 States, 7 Provinces

Density: NR

Projected New Units (12 Months): 20

Qualifications: 5, 5, 5, 3, 5, 5

Registered: CA,DC,FL,HI,IL,IN,MD,MI,MN,ND,NY,OR, RI,SD,VA,WA,WI

FINANCIAL/TERMS:

Cash Investment: Varies

Total Investment: $2.6m - $6.2m

Minimum Net Worth: NA

Fees: Franchise - $75K

Royalty - 5%; Ad. - 2%

Earnings Claims Statement: Yes

Term of Contract (Years): 20/NA

Avg. # Of Employees: Varies FT, varies PT

Passive Ownership: Allowed

Encourage Conversions: Yes

Area Develop. Agreements: No

Sub-Franchising Contracts: No

Expand In Territory: No

Space Needs: Varies SF; FS

SUPPORT & TRAINING:

Financial Assistance Provided: No

Site Selection Assistance: No

Lease Negotiation Assistance: No

Co-Operative Advertising: No

Franchisee Assoc./Member: Yes/Member

Size Of Corporate Staff: 24

On-Going Support: C,D,E,G,H,I

Training: NR

SPECIFIC EXPANSION PLANS:

US: Yes, All United States

Canada: Yes, All Canada

Overseas: Yes, Europe, Asia, South and Central America

ITEM 19
FINANCIAL PERFORMANCE REPRESENTATIONS

The following financial performance representation consists of three sections. Section A provides historical data for the Radisson® Reservation System as explained in that Section. Section B lists historical performance figures for certain licensed Hotels as explained in that Section. Section C provides information comparing the average increase in revenue per available room (RevPAR), and the average improvement in RevPAR index, for Hotels that have been participating in the Revenue Optimization Performance Enhancement Services (ROPES) program for at least 60 days to the average increase in RevPAR, and average improvement in RevPAR index, for Hotels that do not participate, or have not been participating for at least 60 days, in the ROPES program during a defined period of time.

We will provide you substantiation of the data used in preparing the Sections of this Item 19 upon reasonable request. **"Base Hotels"** for Sections A and B are defined as Radisson® licensed Hotels located in the United States that had been open as a Radisson® Hotel for twelve full months as of December 31st of the applicable year. The Base Hotels for any given year may include Hotels that are not currently part of the Radisson® System. See Item 20 for details regarding Base Hotels for the year ending December 31, 2007. You should carefully consider the additional information found in the <u>Basis, Sources And Limitations Of Information for each Section as well as the Warnings paragraph at the end of this Item</u> to understand this performance information in the appropriate context.

Section A

1)   Radisson® Reservation System Contribution to Revenue

Radisson® Reservation System Contribution to Revenue	2005	2006	2007
Mean reservation system contribution to total room revenue for Base Hotels	44.6%	50.7%	52.3%

Range of reservation system contribution to total room revenue for individual Base Hotels	13.3% to 87.6%	17.2% to 90%	13.8% to 87.9%
Number and percentage of Base Hotels that met or exceeded the mean reservation system contribution to total room revenue	69/43%	51/38%	61/46%
Total Base Hotels	160	134	134

2)   Room Rate for Radisson® Reservation System Reservations

Room Rate for Radisson® Reservation System Reservations	2005	2006	2007
Mean room rate for reservations booked through the Radisson® Reservation System for Base Hotels	$108.72	$114.62	$121.66
Range of room rates for reservations booked through the Radisson® Reservation System for Base Hotels	$58.40 to $240.13	$66.31 to $257.34	$72.50 to $290.55
Percentage lift in mean room rate for reservations booked through the Radisson® Reservation System over overall mean room rate for Base Hotels	14.1%	13.5%	12.2%
Total Base Hotels	160	134	134

BASIS, SOURCES AND LIMITATIONS OF INFORMATION FOR SECTION A.

The Radisson® Reservation System accepts and transmits reservations to System Hotels through various media including the Technology Systems, toll free numbers, third party Systems using the chain code authorized by us, our Internet website and other means that we may use from time to time. We based the percentages in this Section on records compiled by us and on reports from licensees. Our sales personnel, referrals from other Radisson® Hotels or Resorts and travel companies owned, operated or licensed by an affiliate of ours may have contributed, but they are not included in the figure above. We have not audited or otherwise verified the information reported to us by our franchisees.

We calculated the percentages of our contributions to total Hotel room revenue and differentials in room rates booked shown above based on reservations made through the Radisson® Reservation System for rooms at the Radisson® Hotels in the domestic U.S., reduced by cancellations and adjustments made directly through our Reservation System. Cancellations or no-shows that are not processed through our Reservation System are included in the percentages and would have the effect of overstating the percentage contributions to room revenue and average room rate, in relation to the actual revenue and rate obtained by participating Hotels. Factors such as location and season may significantly influence these rates.

Section B

1)   Average Daily Rate

Average Daily Room Rate	2005	2006	2007
Average daily room rate (ADR) for Base Hotels	$93.38	$99.19	$106.84
Range of daily room rate for Base Hotels	$52.98 to	$53.93 to $223.52	$60.12 to

	$199.54		$250.80
Number and percentage of Base Hotels that met or exceeded ADR	60/38%	49/37%	41/31%
Total Base Hotels	160	134	134

2)   Occupancy Rate

Occupancy Rate	2005	2006	2007
Average occupancy rate for Base Hotels	63.8%	65.5%	65.2%
Range of occupancy rate for Base Hotels	29.7% to 94.8%	31.5% to 90.4%	38.4% to 94.9%
Number and percentage of Base Hotels that met or exceeded the average occupancy rate	79/49%	63/47%	61/46%
Total Base Hotels	160	134	134

3)   Average Revenue Per Available Room ("REVPAR")

Revenue per Available Room (REVPAR)	2005	2006	2007
Average REVPAR	$59.59	$64.97	$69.71
REVPAR range for Base Hotels	$18.80 to $189.25	$27.37 to $202.13	$31.53 to $238.13
Number and percentage of Base Hotels that met or exceeded the average REVPAR	61/38%	52/39%	36/27%
Total Base Hotels	160	134	134

BASIS, SOURCES AND LIMITATIONS OF INFORMATION FOR SECTION B.

All information presented in these System ranges and averages are based principally on information received from independent franchisee owners and has not been audited or otherwise verified by us. In compiling the data, we used the following calculations: First, an average room rate was calculated by dividing the total amount of room revenues reported by franchisees by the total number of guest rooms rented at the licensed Hotels during the study period. Next, an average occupancy rate was calculated by dividing the number of guest room nights reported by franchisees by the total of rooms available for rent. Average Revenue Per Available Room **("REVPAR")** was calculated by multiplying the average room rate for each Hotel by its average occupancy rate.

Section C

Average Increase in RevPAR and RevPAR Index for Hotels Participating In the Revenue Optimization Performance Enhancement Services Program

Participating Hotels had an overall average RevPAR increase of 10.4% for their respective 2007 Measurement Period over the corresponding period for 2006, compared to an overall average RevPAR increase of only 7.6% from 2006 to 2007 for Non-Participating Hotels. Participating Hotels also had an average RevPAR index improvement of 3.1 points for the 2007 Measurement Period over the corresponding period for 2006, compared to an overall average RevPAR index improvement of only 0 points from 2006 to 2007 for Non-Participating Hotels. RevPAR index measures a Hotel's share of the overall RevPAR within its competitive segment.

The 2007 Measurement Period for each Participating Hotel commenced on the sixtieth day after the Hotel signed a ROPES contract and includes all stay nights between that sixtieth day and the end of the year. Consequently, the number of stay nights included in the 2007 Measurement Period is different for each Participating Hotel.

BASIS, SOURCES AND LIMITATIONS OF INFORMATION FOR SECTION C.

"Participating Hotels" include only Radisson Hotels in the U.S. that participated in the ROPES program for more than sixty days during 2007. Non-Participating Hotels include Radisson Hotels in the U.S. that did not participate in the ROPES program, or had been participating in the ROPES program for less than 60 days, in 2007. There were 42 Participating Hotels used in formulating the information set forth in this Section C. All information presented in this Section is based principally on information and data received from independent franchisee owners, or extracted from information in their Hotels' systems, and has not been audited or otherwise verified by us.

In compiling the average increase in RevPAR for Participating Hotels, we used the following methodology: We calculated each Hotels' RevPAR for a given day by multiplying its Average Daily Rate by its occupancy rate. Participating Hotels then were measured on their RevPAR performance for each day of their respective 2007 Measurement Periods over their RevPAR performance for the corresponding week days during the 2006 year. For example, we compared the Hotel's performance on the third Tuesday of July 2007 (July 17, 2007) to the third Tuesday of July 2006 (July 18, 2006). Non-Participating Hotels were measured on their overall average RevPAR performance in 2007 over 2006.

In determining the average improvement in RevPAR index for Participating Hotels, we used data only for those full calendar months following the sixtieth day after the Hotel signed a ROPES contract; we did not include data related to any partial calendar months in which the Hotel participated in the program. The improvement in RevPAR index was determined using information from Smith Travel Research regarding the Hotel's performance as compared to other Hotels that it identified as being in its competitive segment in its market. Smith Travel Research is an independent research firm for the travel industry that compiles RevPAR, rates, index and other relevant information relating to the lodging industry. We relied on the data gathered and reported by Smith Travel Research in providing the information relating to RevPAR index and we have not audited or otherwise verified the information reported by Smith Travel Research.

For all of the calculations relating to RevPAR, we used the Hotels' data regarding consumed stays during each month as extracted from the Hotels' systems on the tenth day of the following month.

WARNINGS FOR SECTIONS A, B AND C:

1.   **Your Radisson® Hotel may likely achieve different, possibly significantly and adversely different, results from operations than the results shown above.**

Many unique factors to each Hotel, including location, physical layout, hotel design and structure, management capabilities, local market conditions and other factors may significantly impact the financial performance of the Hotel, the contribution from our Reservation System and marketing programs, and the average room rates.

We cannot and do not guarantee or promise that you or any Radisson® franchisee will achieve results within the range of percentages set forth above, or any particular level of sales or profitability, or achieve break-even, in any particular year of operation, and we do not authorize our employees, brokers or agents to make any representations, warranties, estimates or predictions regarding actual or anticipated performance of your Hotel, the Reservation System with regard to your Hotel or the effect of the installation of Radisson® Sleep Number® beds at your Hotel. If you receive any other financial performance information or projections of your future income, you should report it to our management by contacting John Sturgess, Radisson Hotels International, Inc., 701 Carlson Parkway, MS 8254, Minneapolis, MN 55305, (763) 212-3393.

We do not offer assurance that your Hotel will receive any level or volume of business from our affiliated travel company.

2.   You have the responsibility of developing your own business plan for your Hotel, including capital budgets, financial statements, projections and other elements appropriate to your particular circumstances. We encourage you to consult with your own accounting, business and legal advisors in doing so. In developing the business plan, we caution you to make necessary allowance for changes in financial results to income, expenses, or both, that may result from operation of your Hotel in an unusual location, in different geographic areas or new market areas, of an unusual size, decor or arrangement, or during periods of or in areas suffering from economic downturns, inflation, unemployment, or other negative economic influences.

Studio 6 EXTENDED STAY

STUDIO 6

4001 International Pkwy.
Carrollton, TX 75007
Tel: (888) 842-2942 (972) 360-2547
Fax: (972) 360-5567
E-Mail: franchisesales@accor-na.com
Web Site: www.staystudio6.com
Mr. Dean Savas, Sr. VP Franchising

Accor Hotels is one of the largest owner/operators of economy lodging in the United States. Accor North America is a division of Accor, with 168,000 people in 140 countries, employing approximately 690 people at the corporate offices including the call centers. Approximately 13,000 are employed at Motel 6 and Studio 6 combined.

BACKGROUND: IFA MEMBER
Established: 1972;   1st Franchised: 1996
Franchised Units: 7
Company-Owned Units: 34
Total Units: 41
Dist.:   US-38; CAN-0; O'seas-3
  North America: 11 States, 0 Provinces
  Density: 4 in GA, 17 in TX
Projected New Units (12 Months):   3
Qualifications: 4, 4, 1, 1, 1, 3
Registered: CA,DC,FL,HI,IL,IN,MD,MI,MN,ND,NY,OR,

RI,SD,VA,WA,WI

FINANCIAL/TERMS:
Cash Investment: $100-500K
Total Investment: $2.7-3.2MM
Minimum Net Worth: $1.5MM
Fees: Franchise - $25K
  Royalty - 5%;   Ad. - 2%
Earnings Claims Statement: Yes
Term of Contract (Years):   15/20/10
Avg. # Of Employees: 2-4 FT, 4-10 PT
Passive Ownership: Allowed
Encourage Conversions: Yes
Area Develop. Agreements: No
Sub-Franchising Contracts: No
Expand In Territory: No
Space Needs: 2.5 Acres Min. SF; FS

SUPPORT & TRAINING:
Financial Assistance Provided: Yes (D)
Site Selection Assistance: No
Lease Negotiation Assistance: No
Co-Operative Advertising: No
Franchisee Assoc./Member: No
Size Of Corporate Staff: 690
On-Going Support: A,b,C,d,e,h,I
Training: 2 Weeks Dallas, TX for Managers' Orientation;
                 2 Days Dallas, TX for Owner's Orientation

SPECIFIC EXPANSION PLANS:
US: Yes, All United States
Canada: Yes, All Canada
Overseas: No

ITEM 19
FINANCIAL PERFORMANCE REPRESENTATIONS

STATEMENT OF AVERAGE REVENUES AND EXPENSES
FOR STUDIO 6 PROPERTIES OWNED OR LEASED BY M6 OLP
DURING THE PERIOD JANUARY 1, 2007 - DECEMBER 31, 2007[1]

NUMBER OF PROPERTIES: 35[2]
AVERAGE PROPERTY SIZE: 129 ROOMS

AVERAGE DAILY RATE: $40.18[3]
AVERAGE OCCUPANCY: 73.30%[4]

REVENUES

	MEAN AVERAGE [5]	PERCENTAGE OF MEAN AVERAGE REVENUES [6]	MEDIAN AVERAGE[7]
Room Rental Revenues	$1,378,678	98.38%	$1,411,431
Other Revenues[8]	$22,712	1.62%	$22,003
Total Revenues	**$1,401,390**	**100.0%**	**$1,433,434**

OPERATING EXPENSES

Salaries and Wages[9]	$233,416	16.66%	$235,311
Employee Benefits[10]	$ 47,745	3.41%	$ 48,281
Supplies[11]	$ 52,190	3.72%	$ 50,759
Repairs and Maintenance[12]	$ 72,912	5.20%	$71,722
Utilitics[13]	$160,036	11.42%	$156,707
Billboards/Local Marketing[14]	$3,341	0.24%	$2,793
Security Services [15]	$ 17,092	1.22%	$546
Travel and Other[16]	$ 34,786	2.48%	$ 35,167
Total Operating Expenses	**$621,518**	**44.35%**	**$601,286**
Controllable Profit	**$779,872**	**55.65%**	**$832,148**
Overhead & Company Expenses[17]	$ 84,628	6.04%	$ 86,162
Income from Operations Before Fixed Expenses [18]	**$695,244**	**49.61%**	**$745,986**

THE INFORMATION SET FORTH ABOVE WAS COMPILED FROM DATA FROM STUDIO 6 LOCATIONS OWNED OR LEASED BY M6 OLP AND SHOULD NOT BE CONSIDERED AS THE AVERAGE OR PROBABLE SALES, EXPENSES OR INCOME THAT SHOULD OR WOULD BE REALIZED BY YOU. WE DO NOT REPRESENT THAT YOU CAN EXPECT TO ATTAIN SIMILAR RESULTS. A NEW FRANCHISEE'S RESULTS ARE LIKELY TO ,DIFFER FROM THE RESULTS SET FORTH IN THIS STATEMENT PRIMARILY BECAUSE "STARTUP" MOTELS TRADITIONALLY EXPERIENCE LOWER REVENUES AND HIGHER COSTS THAN THOSE WHICH HAVE BEEN OPERATING FOR SOME TIME.

THIS ITEM 19 REFLECTS THE RESULTS OF THE 35 STUDIO 6 MOTELS OWNED OR LEASED BY M6, OLP AND OPEN THROUGHOUT THE ENTIRE PERIOD FROM JANUARY 1, 2007 THROUGH DECEMBER 31, 2007. ALTHOUGH THESE ARE ALL OF THE COMPANY-OWNED STUDIO 6 MOTELS OPEN AND OPERATING IN THE UNITED STATES DURING THE ENTIRE ONE-YEAR PERIOD DESCRIBED ABOVE, THE RELATIVELY SMALL NUMBER OF TOTAL PROPERTIES NECESSARILY CREATES A LIMITED AMOUNT OF DATA WHICH MAY OR MAY NOT PROVE TO BE TYPICAL OF A STUDIO 6 MOTEL AS ADDITIONAL MOTELS ARE OPENED AND A MORE EXTENSIVE OPERATING HISTORY IS ESTABLISHED. AS YOU REVIEW THIS ITEM 19, YOU SHOULD CONSIDER THE SMALL AMOUNT OF AVAILABLE DATA, AS WELL AS SUCH ADDITIONAL FACTORS AS (I) THE VARIATIONS AMONG THE SIZE OF THE PROPERTIES INCLUDED IN THIS ITEM 19 (FROM 68 TO 189 ROOMS), (II) THE RELATIVELY SHORT PERIOD OF TIME THAT THE MOTELS HAVE BEEN OPEN AND 1N

OPERATION (7 MOTELS OPENED IN 1999, 4 OPENED IN 2000, 23 OPENED IN 2001 AND 1 OPENED IN 2002), (III) THE LOCATION OF ALL OF THE MOTELS IN OR NEAR LARGE METROPOLITAN AREAS, (IV) THE CONCENTRATION OF TILE MOTELS INCLUDED IN THIS ITEM 19 (29 OF 35) IN THE SOUTHERN, SOUTHEASTERN AND SOUTHWESTERN UNITED STATES AND (V) THAT THE STUDIO 6 SYSTEM HAS BEEN IN OPERATION ONLY SINCE MARCH OF 1999. CERTAIN OF THESE FACTORS ARE ADDRESSED IN MORE DETAIL IN THE FOLLOWING NOTES.

OTHER THAN AS SET FORTH IN THIS ITEM 19, WE DO NOT FURNISH, OR AUTHORIZE OUR SALESPERSONS TO FURNISH, ORAL OR WRITTEN INFORMATION CONCERNING ACTUAL OR POTENTIAL SALES, COSTS, INCOME OR PROFITS OF A STUDIO 6 UNIT. ACTUAL RESULTS VARY FROM PROPERTY TO PROPERTY AND WE CANNOT ESTIMATE THE RESULTS OF ANY PARTICULAR FRANCHISE.

1.   No franchised operations are included in the information contained in this Item 19.

2.   This Statement reflects the results of 35 Studios owned or leased by M6 OLP and open throughout the entire period January 1 - December 31, 2007.

3.   This is the mean average of the rate paid by guests for lodging in all the properties described in note 2 above, for the calendar year 2007. Rate and occupancy arc the traditional measures of motel revenue generation, and vary from property to property based on such factors as stay demand in the immediate market, the number and type of competitive properties, the quality and physical condition of the property, service levels, location, visibility and accessibility, brand affiliation (or lack thereof), marketing efforts and effectiveness, prevailing rates in the market, facility reputation, convenience to destinations or generators of motel stays and other factors.

4.   This is the mean average of all room stays in the properties described in note 2 above, and has been calculated by dividing the number of room stays by the number of available room-nights in those same properties.

5.   This is the mean average which has been calculated by aggregating the total revenues or expenses for a given category and thereafter dividing it by the number of properties contributing to such revenues or expenses.

6.   This percentage reflects the relationship between a specific expense or revenue shown in the "mean average" column and the total revenues of the average property.

7.   The "median average" is the point at which half the properties reported higher results, and half the properties reported lower results.

8.   "Other revenues" includes revenue primarily from vending sales, guest laundry and office services. Studio 6 guests arc required to pay in advance (check-out is not necessary). Under the Studio 6 System, guests do not pay for local telephone calls and are not permitted to incur "room charges" for long-distance telephone calls and other services. Thus, non-room sales arc limited to those which can utilize a point-of-sale payment procedure, as with coin-operated or "card-swipe" machinery; as a result, "other revenue" sources are less significant for Studio 6 properties than in the lodging industry generally.

9.   M6 OLP hires and trains professional managers, who are paid a wage somewhat below industry averages but are generally furnished personal lodging in a "manager's apartment" built into the motel facility. You arc not required to construct or furnish a manager's apartment; if you hire a manager to operate your property, but do not provide an apartment, you may pay a higher wage expense, but would save construction and furnishing costs which, in turn, may reduce your financing expenses. In addition to management personnel, a Studio 6 location will require desk clerks to staff the front desk 24 hours per day. Variable salary costs, depending upon number of rooms occupied, include those for laundry workers, housekeepers and maintenance workers, as necessary.

10.   This expense consists of payroll taxes, workers' compensation expenses and the cost of

M6 OLP employee benefits package which includes a 401(k) plan and company-subsidized medical coverage. You are responsible for payroll taxes and worker's compensation expenses which will vary by state. You are not required to offer to your employees any specific level or type of employee benefits. Accordingly, the level and cost of such benefits will be determined by you, and by the requirements of applicable laws.

11.   The largest single expense in this category is for linen and bedding, but this category also includes expendable supplies furnished to guests for their use, cleaning supplies, paper goods and items of a similar nature. Expenditures for such items generally vary with occupancy more than any other factor. M6 OLP is able, by reason of size and purchasing power, to secure advantageous pricing on most supplies, but you may not be able to purchase supplies at similar prices.

12.   This expense includes repairs and maintenance both within guestrooms and in common areas of the property. The extent of needed repairs or maintenance will vary with the quality and durability of construction, furnishings and other materials in the property; occupancy levels; types of guests; unusual climatic conditions; weather and other factors.

13.   This expense includes gas, water, electricity, telephone, trash disposal and expenses of a similar nature. The properties reflected in this Statement arc predominantly exterior-door motel designs in which heated or cooled air is lost to the atmosphere whenever an entry door is opened; we believe that an interior-corridor design may experience greater operating efficiencies. Utility charges vary with local suppliers and utility companies, as well as occupancy and climate.

14.   This expense consists primarily of the cost of highway billboards announcing the proximity of a Motel 6 property, directions for finding it, and the price of a single-occupancy room. Guest surveys indicate that highway billboards are an important tool in attracting guests. The outdoor advertising industry is geographically diverse, as are the laws and regulations which apply to billboard advertising. Costs vary widely among locations, and you should check the availability and costs in the vicinity of your intended location.

15.   This expense consists primarily of third-party security services hired to patrol the Motel grounds and vicinity for the protection of guests, staff and parked automobiles. The necessity or desirability of such services varies from location to location based on such factors as the surrounding neighborhood, guest and visitor demographics, adequate lot lighting and mechanical security devices, whether the location has a history of problems and crime trends in the market area. Such services are usually provided by local companies or agencies, and you should be able to secure cost estimates locally.

16.   This expense includes such items as travel, relocation, training, recruitment, meals, attendance at meetings and miscellaneous smaller categories (losses, legal expense, dues and subscriptions, financial and collection charges and credit card commissions). You will experience some or all such costs, but expenses vary widely among properties. You are obligated to pay any applicable salaries, travel, lodging and meal costs of your employees while undergoing our training programs.

17.   This expense includes costs experienced by M6 OLP for marketing, reservations, administrative and company expenses, field and training expenses, a corporate overhead allocation and some minor management-fee expenses. You arc unlikely to experience these costs in the same proportions, and may not experience some such costs at all. However, you will experience expenses not incurred by M6 OLP in its operations or reflected in this Statement, such as marketing contributions, reservations fees and franchise fees (as described in Item 6 of this disclosure document), which, in combination with other "overhead" expenses for accounting, administration and management, will likely exceed the "Overhead and Company Expenses" entry shown.

18.   From "Income from Operations Before Fixed Expenses", you must deduct such capital expenses as interest on mortgages and/or other loans, lease payments, the cost of periodic motel refurbishment, etc. The level of financing-related costs you may experience will be a function of your individual equity and financing structure and, thus, no meaningful estimate can be given here. Peri-

odic refurbishment costs will vary with the quality of original materials used in the construction and furnishing of your Motel, the degree of usage it experiences and factors such as climate and mainte-nance practices. The Franchise Agreement requires you to replace, refurbish or maintain capital items to ensure continued acceptable quality of the guest experience and conformity with our minimum specifications. You also must deduct fixed expenses such as property taxes, licenses, insurance, etc. These fixed expenses like capital expenses, vary widely by location and individual circumstances. .

19. WE HAVE WRITTEN SUBSTANTIATION IN OUR POSSESSION TO SUPPORT THE INFORMATION APPEARING IN THIS ITEM 19 AND SUCH SUBSTANTIATION WILL BE MADE AVAILABLE TO YOU ON REASONABLE REQUEST.

> *Please note that all of the Item 19s included in the 2009 Edition of "How Much Can I Make?" were taken from the respective company's 2008 Franchise Disclosure Document (FDD)/Uniform Offering Circular (UFOC). Accordingly, all of the financial data in the Item 19s refers to actual operations in 2007. In a very few cases, depending upon the date of the FDD/UFOC, the data might refer to operations in 2006. Because of the need to provide historical data, there is generally a year's lag between the date of the annual FDD/UFOC and the underlying Item 19 data.*

AARON'S SALES & LEASE OWNERSHIP

309 E. Paces Ferry Rd., N. E.
Atlanta, GA 30305-2377
Tel: (800) 551-6015 (678) 402-3445
Fax: (678) 402-3540
E-Mail: greg.tanner@aaronrents.com
Web Site: www.aaronsfranchise.com
Mr. Greg Tanner, National Director of Franchising

AARON'S SALES & LEASE OWNERSHIP is one of the fastest-growing retail companies in the U.S., specializing in furniture, electronics and appliances. AARON'S SALES & LEASE OWNERSHIP offers franchisees the expertise, advantages and support of a well-established company, plus the opportunity to realize a significant financial return in a booming market segment.

BACKGROUND:	IFA MEMBER
Established: 1955;	1st Franchised: 1992
Franchised Units:	470
Company-Owned Units:	995
Total Units:	1465
Dist.:	US-1456; CAN-9; O'seas-0
North America:	48 States, 6 Provinces
Density:	FL, GA, TX
Projected New Units (12 Months):	80
Qualifications:	5, 5, 1, 4, 5, 5
Registered:	CA,FL,HI,IL,IN,MI,ND,NY,OR,RI,SD,VA,WA,WI

FINANCIAL/TERMS:

Cash Investment:	$300K
Total Investment:	$254-559K
Minimum Net Worth:	$450K
Fees: Franchise -	$35K
Royalty - 6%;	Ad. - 2.5%
Earnings Claims Statement:	Yes
Term of Contract (Years):	10/10
Avg. # Of Employees:	6 FT, 0 PT
Passive Ownership:	Allowed
Encourage Conversions:	Yes
Area Develop. Agreements:	Yes
Sub-Franchising Contracts:	No
Expand In Territory:	Yes
Space Needs:	8,000 SF; FS,SC

SUPPORT & TRAINING:

Financial Assistance Provided:	Yes (D)
Site Selection Assistance:	Yes
Lease Negotiation Assistance:	Yes
Co-Operative Advertising:	No
Franchisee Assoc./Member:	Yes/Member
Size Of Corporate Staff:	3500
On-Going Support:	A,B,C,D,E,F,H,I
Training:	3 Weeks Corporate Headquarters;
	2 Weeks Minimum On-Site; On-Going Varies

SPECIFIC EXPANSION PLANS:

US:	Yes, All United States
Canada:	Yes, All Canada
Overseas:	Yes, All Countries

ITEM 19
FINANCIAL PERFORMANCE REPRESENTATIONS

Exhibit A to this Disclosure Document sets forth certain historical revenue and expense information for ARI operated Aaron's ™ stores. Substantiation of data used in preparing this information is available upon reasonable request. Except as expressly set forth in Exhibit A, neither ARI nor its affiliates furnishes or authorizes any oral or written information of actual, potential, average or projected sales, costs, income or profits of existing or proposed Franchises.

The success of your Franchise will depend largely upon your individual efforts, and the financial results of your franchise are likely to differ, perhaps materially, from the results summarized in Exhibit A.

EXHIBIT A
TO FRANCHISE DISCLOSURE DOCUMENT

<u>Earnings Information</u>
(Attached)
ANALYSIS OF AVERAGE REVENUES AND EXPENSES FOR <u>ARI OPERATED AARON'S SALES & LEASE OWNERSHIP STORES</u>

This Exhibit sets forth certain historical information on revenues and expenses for ARI operated Aaron's Sales & Lease Ownership stores and does <u>not</u> include revenues and expenses for franchisee operated Aaron's Sales & Lease Ownership stores. ARI has not included the information on franchised stores because ARI cannot verify and control the level or type of expenditures made by individual franchisees. However, ARI recommends that you contact the franchisees listed on Exhibit E to the Uniform Franchise Disclosure Document ("UFDD") regarding the operations and financial performance of their Franchised Businesses.

This Exhibit contains two Tables. The Tables reflect the arithmetic mean (average) annual revenues and expenses, as well as the highest, lowest, median, and number and percent of stores higher than the mean, of the stores included therein.

Table 1:

Table 1 contains the average revenues and expenses of ALL ARI operated stores which (i) have opened since January 1, 2001 and operated under the "12 Month Sales & Lease Ownership Plan" since their inception, (ii) were not converted Aaron Rents or Aaron Sells stores, (iii) were not acquired stores and (iv) have been operating one full year (300 stores), two full years (232 stores), three full years (167 stores), four full years (110 stores) or five full years (75 stores), respectively, as of December 31, 2007. ARI has closed some stores or acquired some competitor stores and has merged their revenues into existing revenues with other ARI stores operating in contiguous markets (see item 20). Stores that had not been in operation for at least a full year as of December 31, 2007 are not included, because annual figures were not yet available as of such date. The average revenue and expense information provided in Table 1 by year is also shown by month (by age of store).

Table 2:

Table 2 contains the average revenues and expenses for the year ending December 31, 2007 of ALL ARI operated stores which have been open for at least two full years as of January 1, 2007 and that were still open as of December 31, 2007 (531 stores). Figures are presented for those stores within the following ranges of annual gross revenues: under $800,000 (36 stores); $800,000 to $1,100,000 (132 stores); $1,100,001 to $1,400,000 (152 stores); $1,400,001 to $1,700,000 (131 stores); and over $1,700,000 (80 stores). ARI has closed some stores or acquired some competitor stores and has merged their revenues into existing revenues with other ARI stores operating in contiguous markets. This Table includes stores that were converted at least two full years prior to January 1, 2007 into Aaron's Sales & Lease Ownership stores from Aaron Rents, Aaron Sells or acquired competitor stores (see Item 20).

ARI accrues certain expenses from time to time for internal reporting purposes. Thus, in some instances, all of the expenses reflected in a given month may not have actually been paid as of the end of such month. Also, except for depreciation, the expenses listed in the Tables do not reflect any start-up expenses that you may incur (see Item 7 of the UFDD).

The ARI operated stores for which information is included in this Exhibit are substantially similar to franchisee operated stores in appearance, and in the products and services offered. Most of the ARI operated stores included in this Exhibit are located in metropolitan markets where expenses are frequently higher than non-metropolitan markets and those stores generally have to achieve relatively higher revenues to cover higher expenses. The amount of revenues and expenses incurred will vary from store to store, whether ARI operated or franchisee operated and whether located in a metropolitan market or a non-metropolitan market. In particular, the revenues and expenses of a franchise store will be directly affected by many factors, such as: (a) geographic location; (b) competition from other firms in the market; (c) the presence of other stores opened under ARI's Marks; (d) whether the franchise owner assumes the position of store manager or designates a store manager; (e) lease payments for exterior sign(s); (f) the payment of Continuing License Fees, Ad Production Fees and Regional Media Fees; (g) contractual arrangements with real estate lessors; (h) the extent to which the franchisee borrows working capital and finances inventory purchases, and applicable interest rate(s) on such borrowings; (i) vendor prices or distribution center prices on merchandise; (j) the franchisee's merchandise lease rates and merchandise prices; (k) whether the franchisee purchases or leases a delivery vehicle; (l) the cost of any other vehicles used in the business; (m) other discretionary expenditures; (n) the quality of management and service at the Franchised Business; (o) the franchisee's legal, accounting and other professional fees; (p) federal, state, and local income and other taxes; and (q) accounting methods, particularly the rate of depreciation for lease merchandise. In addition, a franchisee likely will not realize certain benefits and economies of scale that ARI realizes as a result of operating several stores in a single market. Therefore, the information contained in this Exhibit should be used by you **only** as a reference in conducting your own analysis and preparing your own projected income statements, balance sheets and cash flow statements. ARI strongly suggests that you consult your own financial advisor or personal accountant concerning any financial projections and federal, state, local income taxes or any other applicable taxes that you may incur in operating an Aaron's Sales & Lease Ownership franchise.

The revenues and expenses contained in this Exhibit should not be considered to be the actual or potential revenues and expenses that you will realize. ARI does not represent that you can or will attain such revenues and expenses, or any particular level of revenues and expenses. Moreover, ARI does not represent that you will generate income which exceeds the initial payment for, or investment in, the Franchised Business. The success of the franchise will depend largely upon your individual abilities, and the financial results of the franchise are likely to differ, perhaps materially, from the results of ARI operated stores summarized in this exhibit. Substantiation of the data used in preparing the information in this Exhibit will be made available to you upon reasonable request.

The following notes generally define each line item category shown on the attached Tables, identify some of the reasons why your results may differ, and highlight certain factors that you should be aware of. You should review the attached Tables only in conjunction with the following notes, which are an integral part of the numerical information.

Note 1:   Lease Revenue

DEFINED: Lease Revenue is the sum of all revenues received from: all lease fees (for electronics, appliances, furniture, jewelry and other items), renewal fees, damage fees, delivery fees, service plus fees, full lease agreement buyout payments, NSF checks net of NSF collections, and other fees, whether paid in cash, check or credit. Lease Revenue also includes revenue on pager air service, which is pager service income (revenue derived from the service fee for pager airtime only). (ARI no longer carries pagers).

VARIANCES FOR FRANCHISEE: Within ARI guidelines, you will determine the merchandise lease rates, pager service rates and other fees for products and services leased and sold from the Franchised Business. Some states have statutes governing merchandise lease rates and fees. The cost associated with activating and maintaining airtime for pagers varies from market to market.

Note 2:   Other Revenue

DEFINED: Other Revenue consists of revenue for all retail sales of both new and used inventory, revenue from early buyouts of lease agreements, gain or loss on sales of fixed assets, cell phone commissions, pass code and access revenue, and any other miscellaneous charges or fees, whether paid in cash, check or credit.

VARIANCES FOR FRANCHISEE: Within ARI guidelines, you will determine the retail sales price and other fees for products sold from the Franchised Business, as well as the price for early buyouts of lease agreements. Some states have statutes governing early buyout amounts. (ARI no longer carries pagers or cell phones).

Note 3:   Total Revenue

DEFINED: Total Revenue is the sum of Lease Revenue and Other Revenue.

VARIANCE FOR FRANCHISEE: Within ARI guidelines, you will determine the merchandise lease rates and other fees charged by the Franchised Business. Some states have statutes governing merchandise lease rates and fees.

Note 4:   Cost of Sales

DEFINED: Cost of Sales is the net book value of all new and used inventory sold on a retail sale, the net book value of inventory sold on both early and full buyouts of lease agreements, pager service fees and cell phone air time and access fees.

VARIANCES FOR FRANCHISEE: You may elect to depreciate your inventory or fixed assets on a different basis than that used by ARI for tax purposes. Also, certain vendors offer purchase discounts to ARI for quick payment (i.e., a 2% discount on payments made within 10 days). You may not be able to obtain payment terms that are as favorable as those offered to or obtained by ARI. If you are able to obtain quick payment discounts, you must make payments by the early date in order to take advantage of them.

Note 5:   Personnel Cost

DEFINED: Personnel Cost is the sum of all store personnel costs, including: salaries and wages for full-time and part-time employees, employer contributions for F.I.C.A. taxes, federal unemployment taxes, state unemployment taxes, workers' compensation, group health insurance, long term disability, cancer care, 401(k), wages for contracted labor, expense of "help wanted" ads, employment agency fees, employee training expenses, and new hire physical examinations. ARI operated stores generally open with three to six associates.

VARIANCES FOR FRANCHISEE: ARI store managers are compensated on a draw plus bonus program. The draw ranges from $30,000 to $70,000, with an average draw of approximately $48,000 per annum. Personnel Cost also includes ARI's group health insurance cost. These expenses will vary considerably for you, depending on whether you hire a manager and their compensation program, prevailing wage rates in the area of the Franchised Business, and the types and amounts of non-salary benefits, if any, you provide to employees.

Note 6:   Selling Cost

DEFINED: Selling Cost is the sum of all advertising expenses, including: yellow page ads, radio commercials, T.V. commercials, direct mailings, handbills, circulars, brochures, giveaways, sales floor signage, agency fees, exterior sign repairs and exterior sign depreciation.

VARIANCES FOR FRANCHISEE: You will conduct independent advertising programs and will pay an Ad Production Fee of 0.5% of your weekly Gross Revenues (if the Ad Production Fund is established by ARI). You may also pay a Regional Media Fee of $250 or 2% of weekly Gross Revenues, whichever is greater (if the Regional Media Fund is established by ARI). You may be required to spend an amount up to 4.5% of your Gross Revenues on advertising (this includes the payment of any Ad Production Fee and any Regional Media Fee).

ARI purchases the exterior wall sign and any exterior pole sign faces for each of its stores and depreciates its signs on a straight-line basis over 5 years. Therefore, the depreciation of signs is included in the calculation of this expense. ARI will purchase the exterior wall sign and any pole sign faces for the Franchised Business and will lease it to you over the first five years of the Franchise Agreement. See Item 7 of the UFDD for estimated lease payments for the exterior sign(s).

Note 7: Occupancy Cost

DEFINED: Occupancy Cost is the sum of all leased or owned building expenses, including: rent, depreciation of leasehold improvements, depreciation of fixtures and equipment, building maintenance, common area maintenance, real estate commissions, real estate taxes, security systems, real estate insurance and utilities.

VARIANCES FOR FRANCHISEE: The stores used in this Exhibit vary in size from approximately 4,000 to 20,000 square feet. ARI's recommended square footage for the Franchised Business is between 7,000 and 12,000 square feet. ARI's lease rate per square foot varies from $4.00 to $12.00 and ARI's common area maintenance charge (C.A.M.) varies from $1.00 to $4.50 per square foot. The cost per square foot in a strip-type shopping center and freestanding buildings varies considerably, depending on the location and the market conditions affecting commercial property.

ARI operated stores typically pay in full for any portion of leasehold improvements it is responsible for and depreciate the improvements on a straight-line basis over the remaining life of the lease. Therefore, some depreciation of leasehold improvements is included in the calculation of this expense. Occasionally, the landlord will completely build (i.e. carpet, tile, counters, offices, etc.) the space out and increase the rental rate to cover the cost of such build- out. See Item 7 of the UFDD for an estimate of the cost of leasehold improvements.

ARI owns some of the buildings it occupies. In these instances, since no rent is actually paid to a landlord, the rent component of the Occupancy Cost is allocated to the store occupying the facility based on ARI's investment in the land and building associated with that facility. Generally, this expense allocation will reflect the market rent for a company of ARI's credit profile. ARI believes that this arrangement is substantially different from the arrangement you will have with your financial institution(s) if you choose to purchase your building. ARI believes that your interest rate will be substantially higher, depending on the financing source, amount of down payment, and your creditworthiness.

ARI generally negotiates for deferred rental payments. Therefore, the Occupancy Cost may reflect several months with either no rental payments or reduced rental payments. Beginning April 1, 2005, ARI began capitalizing the amount of the deferred rental period and amortizing it as a credit to rent expense over the initial term of the lease.

Note 8: Inventory Carrying Cost

DEFINED: Inventory Carrying Cost is the sum of all of expenses associated with carrying inventory, including: insurance for inventory in the store and in transit, an allocation of personal property tax on store inventory (on hand at year end), interest expense on inventory financing, depreciation of lease merchandise, bedding transfer costs, repair cost and the cost of replacement parts for repairs or refurbishing, clearance center charge backs and freight charges absorbed by the receiving store on inventory redistribution. Also included in this item is depreciation on office furniture, which is depreciated over 36 months with a 0% salvage value.

VARIANCES FOR FRANCHISEE: For internal and SunTrust Bank compliance reporting, ARI uses an eighteen month straight line depreciation (with no salvage value) for franchise calculations. Certain high-end electronics (i.e. big screen TV's) that are normally on twenty-four month lease agreements are depreciated on a twenty-four month straight-line method (with no salvage value). This method is used mostly to reconcile SunTrust disposition book values with SunTrust amortization schedules. For company operated stores (prior to January 1, 2002), ARI paid in full for its lease inventory and generally began depreciating its lease inventory the month after it was received in the store and depreciated most lease inventory over the agreement period, generally 12-24 months, when on lease, and 36 months when not on lease, to a 0% salvage value (a method often referred to as income forecasting in the Sales & Lease Ownership industry). For company owned stores (effective January 1, 2002), ARI continued to pay in full for its lease inventory, but began depreciating its lease inventory upon the earlier to occur of its initial lease to a customer or twelve months after it was acquired from the vendor. ARI continued to depreciate most lease inventory over the agreement period, generally 12-24 months, when on lease, and 36 months when not on lease, to a 0% salvage value.

The depreciation schedules used by ARI are for ARI's internal book purposes and SunTrust compliance reporting only. You should seek advice on depreciation from your financial advisor or personal accountant. ARI makes no recommendation as to the method of depreciation to be used by you for tax purposes.

Prior to January 1, 2002, ARI allocated total interest cost to the ARI operated stores based on the total inventory cost per store. Effective January 1, 2002, ARI allocated an amount equal to 1.44% of the Sales & Lease Ownership division's total revenue to the ARI operated stores on a pro-rata basis based on each store's total inventory cost. ARI believes that this arrangement is substantially different from the arrangement you will have with your financial institution(s) for inventory purchases. ARI believes that your interest rate will be substantially higher, depending on the financing source, the collateral and your credit-worthiness.

Note 9:   Delivery Cost

DEFINED: Delivery Cost is the sum of all expenses incurred in delivering and picking up lease inventory, including: vehicle depreciation or lease payments, rental of extra trucks, pro-rata share of vehicle insurance, truck decals, mechanical repairs, washing expense, parking expense, fuel and oil cost, mileage charged on extra trucks, vehicle repair costs incurred as a result of any accident, including insurance deductibles and taxes and vehicle registrations. Delivery cost also includes payments made to freight companies for the shipment of products from distribution centers operated by ARI.

VARIANCES FOR FRANCHISEE: You may, but are not obligated to, participate in ARI's fleet leasing or fleet purchasing programs. See Item 7 of the UFDD for the estimated cost for a delivery vehicle. ARI depreciates delivery vehicles that it purchases on a straight-line basis over 3 years with a 35% salvage value. Some delivery vehicles are leased and the monthly lease amount appears in this line item. Insurance rates for delivery vehicles will vary depending on the state and type of area (metropolitan or rural) in which the Franchised Business is located, and the amount and types of insurance coverage you maintain.

Note 10:   Inventory Write-Offs

DEFINED: Inventory Write-Offs are the net book value of all inventory write-offs due to: customer skips, inventory shortages, inventory that is not picked up when lease agreements are not renewed and inventory that is damaged beyond repair. All fees paid to outside collection agencies for collections on bad debts and all expenses incurred outside of the normal course of business in collecting extremely delinquent lease fees are included in this line item. When calculating cash flow for its internal purposes, ARI does not consider fees that have been paid to outside collection agencies, which range from $500 to $2,000 per store per year, to be a cash expense (see Note 16).

VARIANCES FOR FRANCHISEE: You may be required to pay to your financial institution any outstanding loan amount on inventory that is written off at the time it is written off, and you may also utilize an outside collection agency more or less frequently than ARI.

Note 11:   General Operating Cost

DEFINED: General Operating Cost is the sum of all operating expenses, including: telephone, office supplies, postage, general liability insurance, bank charges, credit card charges, miscellaneous charges, petty cash shortages, miscellaneous legal expenses, local business licenses and permits, store personnel errand and travel expense and generally a division allocation (beginning February 1996) and generally a regional allocation (beginning July 1995). For company operated stores (prior to April 1, 2000), the division/regional allocation was generally determined by calculating ARI's division/regional cost, and allocating it to ARI's stores pro-rata, based on the respective amount of revenues generated by such stores. For company operated stores (effective April 1, 2000), ARI began allocating the divisional/regional allocation based on 3% of each store's total monthly revenue. Beginning January 1, 2004, for company operated stores, ARI allocated the divisional/regional allocation based on 2% of each store's net revenue (net revenue being defined as total revenue minus cost of sales).

VARIANCES FOR FRANCHISEE: Your general liability insurance coverage will vary depending on the state(s) in which the Franchised Business operates, and the amounts and types of coverage you maintain. See Item 7 of the UFDD for an estimate of insurance costs. You will not be required to pay a division/regional allocation. However, you must pay to ARI a Continuing License Fee of 5% or 6% of weekly Gross Revenues.

Note 12:   General Office Allocation

DEFINED: ARI operated stores are generally charged a General Office Allocation of 4.5% to 6.5% by the ARI home office. The current General Office Allocation is 5%.

VARIANCES FOR FRANCHISEE: You will not be required to pay a General Office Allocation. However, you must pay to ARI a Continuing License Fee of 5% or 6% of your weekly Gross Revenues.

Note 13:   Pre-Tax Earnings

DEFINED: Pre-Tax Earnings is Total Revenue minus the sum of: Cost of Sales, Personnel Cost, Selling Cost, Occupancy Cost, Inventory Carrying Cost, Delivery Cost, Inventory Write-Offs and Collection Fees, General Operating Cost, General Office Allocation and Miscellaneous Other Costs.

Note 14:   Depreciation

DEFINED: Depreciation is the total of all depreciation of lease inventory and fixed assets associated with store operations. The depreciation methods and periods are listed under the note for each expense described above which includes a depreciation component. This item does not include the net book value of inventory write-offs. The depreciation schedules used by ARI are for internal book purposes only. You should seek advice on depreciation from your financial advisor or personal accountant. ARI makes no recommendation as to the method of depreciation to be used by you for tax purposes.

VARIANCES FOR FRANCHISEE: You may elect to amortize intangible and depreciate lease inventory and fixed assets on a basis different than that used by ARI (for tax purposes).

Note 15:   Net Inventory Purchases

DEFINED: Net Inventory Purchases is the sum of all electronics, appliances, furniture and other lease inventory purchased. These items are reflected in the month the merchandise is received in the store, not when the invoice is paid. These numbers also represent the net of book value of inventory transferred between ARI operated stores and inventory transferred from certain ARI operated stores to ARI operated distribution centers or clearance centers for disposal.

VARIANCES FOR FRANCHISEE: You may, but are not obligated to, participate in ARI's combined purchasing power, and to purchase inventory from ARI's furniture manufacturing division, MacTavish, for inventory pricing benefits. Your inventory purchases may vary if you have multiple locations and you transfer inventory to and from those locations.

If you utilize the SunTrust Bank inventory financing program, you will pay one eighteenth or one twenty-fourth (depending on the items being financed) of your monthly inventory purchases as a principal payment, and interest on the total outstanding balance, to your financial institution(s) on a monthly basis (see item 10). These payments should be considered in any pro forma income statements, balance sheets, and cash flows for the Franchised Business.

Note 16:   Pre-Tax Cash Flow

DEFINED: Pre-Tax Cash Flow is the sum of Pre-Tax Earnings, plus Depreciation, less Net Inventory Purchases, plus Cost of Sales, plus Inventory Write-Offs (see Note 10).

VARIANCES FOR FRANCHISEE: Pre-tax cash flow assumes cash purchases of inventory. You may elect to finance your inventory purchases over a period of time through various lenders (including the eighteen-month SunTrust loan program available for qualified franchisees described in Item 10). In determining cash flow, you may consider other cash payments made that are not directly expensed in the period in which the expenditure occurred.

TABLE 1

Statement of Average Revenues and Expenses for All Aaron's Sales & Lease Ownership Company-Operated Stores (As Defined) Opened Under the "12 Month Rental Purchase Plan".
1st, 2nd, 3rd, 4th and 5th Full Years of Operation

	Year 1		Year 2		Year 3		Year 4		Year 5	
	Average	%	Average	%	Average	%	Average	%	Average	%
Lease Revenue (Note 1)	$446,513	88.0%	$865,143	90.9%	$1,006,322	91.2%	$1,080,911	90.8%	$1,159,935	90.3%
Other Revenue (Note 2)	60,686	12.0%	86,599	9.1%	97,287	8.8%	109,380	9.2%	124,494	9.7%
Total Revenue (Note 3)	$507,199	100.0%	$951,742	100.0%	$1,103,609	100.0%	$1,190,291	100.0%	$1,284,429	100.0%
Operating Expenses										
Cost of Sales (Note 4)	$50,856	10.0%	$73,192	7.7%	$85,624	7.8%	$94,502	7.9%	$105,979	8.3%
Personnel Cost (Note 5)	177,745	35.0%	202,073	21.2%	220,497	20.0%	234,563	19.7%	250,630	19.5%
Selling Cost (Note 6)	38,597	7.6%	33,931	3.6%	34,797	3.2%	35,383	3.0%	35,080	2.7%
Occupancy Cost (Note 7)	120,483	23.8%	124,210	13.1%	121,865	11.0%	122,066	10.3%	121,836	9.5%
Inventory Carrying Cost (Note 8)	177,142	34.9%	351,501	36.9%	397,343	36.0%	423,836	35.6%	454,433	35.4%
Delivery Cost (Note 9)	19,789	3.9%	27,931	2.9%	34,267	3.1%	36,946	3.1%	38,761	3.0%
Inventory Write Offs (Note 10)	10,133	2.0%	23,618	2.5%	23,173	2.1%	23,886	2.0%	24,517	1.9%
Gen. Office Allocation (Note 11)	25,340	5.0%	47,464	5.0%	55,075	5.0%	59,422	5.0%	64,129	5.0%
General Operating Cost (Note 12)	37,998	7.5%	45,736	4.8%	51,371	4.7%	53,812	4.5%	56,903	4.4%
Total Operating Costs (Note 12)	$658,083	129.7%	$929,656	97.7%	$1,024,012	92.8%	$1,084,916	91.1%	$1,152,268	89.7%
Pre-Tax Earnings (Note 13)	($150,884)	-29.7%	$22,086	2.3%	$79,597	7.2%	$105,375	8.9%	$132,161	10.3%
Number of Stores within the Range	300		232		167		110		75	
Cash Flow Summary										
Pre-Tax Earnings (Note 13)	($150,884)	-29.7%	$22,086	2.3%	$79,597	7.2%	$105,375	8.9%	$132,161	10.3%
Depreciation (Note 14)	183,822	36.2%	348,632	36.6%	385,219	34.9%	409,463	34.4%	438,592	34.1%
Net Inventory Purchases (Note 15)	(638,193)	-125.8%	(427,673)	-44.9%	(490,439)	-44.4%	(522,106)	-43.9%	(560,196)	-43.6%
Cost of Sales (Note 4)	50,856	10.0%	73,192	7.7%	85,624	7.8%	94,502	7.9%	105,979	8.3%
Inventory Write Offs (Note 10)	10,133	2.0%	23,618	2.5%	23,173	2.1%	23,886	2.0%	24,517	1.9%
* Pre-Tax Cash Flow (Note 16)	($544,266)	-107.3%	$39,855	4.2%	$83,174	7.5%	$111,120	9.3%	$141,053	11.0%

* Assumes Cash Purchase of Inventory - Inventory Financing Available for Qualified Franchisees (See Item 10)

	Month 13	Month 14	Month 15	Month 16	Month 17	Month 18	Month 19	Month 20	Month 21	Month 22	Month 23	Month 24	Year 2	
Lease Revenue (Note 1)	$63,242	$65,062	$67,356	$69,315	$70,036	$72,709	$73,933	$73,812	$75,954	$77,113	$77,801	$78,810	$865,143	90.9%
Other Revenue (Note 2)	6,988	7,263	7,608	7,099	7,553	7,707	7,178	6,523	7,354	7,299	6,784	7,243	86,599	9.1%
Total Revenue (Note 3)	$70,230	$72,325	$74,964	$76,414	$77,589	$80,416	$81,111	$80,335	$83,308	$84,412	$84,585	$86,053	$951,742	100.0%
Operating Expenses														
Cost of Sales (Note 4)	$5,953	$6,087	$6,400	$6,060	$6,324	$6,355	$6,041	$5,602	$6,155	$6,193	$5,660	$6,362	$73,192	7.7%
Personnel Cost (Note 5)	16,049	16,210	16,179	16,614	16,684	16,825	16,634	17,203	17,197	17,297	17,601	17,580	202,073	21.2%
Selling Cost (Note 6)	2,883	2,891	2,866	2,888	2,823	2,867	2,860	2,744	2,768	2,755	2,775	2,811	33,931	3.6%
Occupancy Cost (Note 7)	10,490	10,334	10,154	10,345	10,234	10,135	10,551	10,476	10,315	10,335	10,426	10,415	124,210	13.1%
Inventory Carrying Cost (Note 8)	25,853	26,792	27,398	28,193	28,740	29,421	29,894	30,314	30,717	31,036	31,463	31,680	351,501	36.9%
Delivery Cost (Note 9)	2,034	2,125	2,227	2,142	2,306	2,341	2,367	2,347	2,426	2,481	2,513	2,622	27,931	2.9%
Inventory Write Offs (Note 10)	1,740	1,891	1,830	1,863	2,050	2,003	1,925	2,162	1,991	2,145	2,068	1,950	23,618	2.5%
Gen. Office Allocation (Note 11)	3,506	3,607	3,740	3,813	3,869	4,009	4,044	4,003	4,154	4,211	4,218	4,290	47,464	5.0%
General Operating Cost (Note 12)	3,502	3,505	3,640	3,680	3,762	3,835	3,877	3,863	3,905	3,989	4,087	4,091	45,736	4.8%
Total Operating Costs (Note 12)	$72,010	$73,442	$74,434	$75,598	$76,792	$77,791	$78,193	$78,714	$79,628	$80,442	$80,811	$81,801	$929,656	97.7%
Pre-Tax Earnings (Note 13)	($1,780)	($1,117)	$530	$816	$797	$2,625	$2,918	$1,621	$3,680	$3,970	$3,774	$4,252	$22,086	2.3%
Number of Stores in Sample 232														
Cash Flow Summary														
Pre-Tax Earnings (Note 13)	($1,780)	($1,117)	$530	$816	$797	$2,625	$2,918	$1,621	$3,680	$3,970	$3,774	$4,252	$22,086	2.3%
Depreciation (Note 14)	26,018	26,875	27,474	28,014	28,618	29,258	29,641	29,966	30,215	30,597	30,905	31,051	348,632	36.6%
Net Inventory Purchases (Note 15)	(35,764)	(35,367)	(36,360)	(37,766)	(38,610)	(33,872)	(35,372)	(34,950)	(35,950)	(36,218)	(32,891)	(34,553)	(427,673)	-44.9%
Cost of Sales (Note 4)	5,953	6,087	6,400	6,060	6,324	6,355	6,041	5,602	6,155	6,193	5,660	6,362	73,192	7.7%
Inventory Write Offs (Note 10)	1,740	1,891	1,830	1,863	2,050	2,003	1,925	2,162	1,991	2,145	2,068	1,950	23,618	2.5%
* Pre-Tax Cash Flow (Note 16)	($3,833)	($1,631)	($126)	($1,013)	($821)	$6,369	$5,153	$4,401	$6,091	$6,687	$9,516	$9,062	$39,855	4.2%

* Assumes Cash Purchase of Inventory - Inventory Financing Available for Qualified Franchisees (See Item 10)

	Month 13	Month 14	Month 15	Month 16	Month 17	Month 18	Month 19	Month 20	Month 21	Month 22	Month 23	Month 24	Year 2	
Lease Revenue (Note 1)	$63,242	$65,062	$67,356	$69,315	$70,036	$72,709	$73,933	$73,812	$75,954	$77,113	$77,801	$78,810	$865,143	90.9%
Other Revenue (Note 2)	6,988	7,263	7,608	7,099	7,553	7,707	7,178	6,523	7,354	7,299	6,784	7,243	86,599	9.1%
Total Revenue (Note 3)	$70,230	$72,325	$74,964	$76,414	$77,589	$80,416	$81,111	$80,335	$83,308	$84,412	$84,585	$86,053	$951,742	100.0%
Operating Expenses														
Cost of Sales (Note 4)	$5,953	$6,087	$6,400	$6,060	$6,324	$6,355	$6,041	$5,602	$6,155	$6,193	$5,660	$6,362	$73,192	7.7%
Personnel Cost (Note 5)	16,049	16,210	16,179	16,614	16,684	16,825	16,634	17,203	17,197	17,297	17,601	17,580	202,073	21.2%
Selling Cost (Note 6)	2,883	2,891	2,866	2,888	2,823	2,867	2,860	2,744	2,768	2,755	2,775	2,811	33,931	3.6%
Occupancy Cost (Note 7)	10,490	10,334	10,154	10,345	10,234	10,135	10,551	10,476	10,315	10,335	10,426	10,415	124,210	13.1%
Inventory Carrying Cost (Note 8)	25,853	26,792	27,398	28,193	28,740	29,421	29,894	30,314	30,717	31,036	31,463	31,680	351,501	36.9%
Delivery Cost (Note 9)	2,034	2,125	2,227	2,142	2,306	2,341	2,367	2,347	2,426	2,481	2,513	2,622	27,931	2.9%
Inventory Write Offs (Note 10)	1,740	1,891	1,830	1,863	2,050	2,003	1,925	2,162	1,991	2,145	2,068	1,950	23,618	2.5%
Gen. Office Allocation (Note 11)	3,506	3,607	3,740	3,813	3,869	4,009	4,044	4,003	4,154	4,211	4,218	4,290	47,464	5.0%
General Operating Cost (Note 12)	3,502	3,505	3,640	3,680	3,762	3,835	3,877	3,863	3,905	3,989	4,087	4,091	45,736	4.8%
Total Operating Costs (Note 12)	$72,010	$73,442	$74,434	$75,598	$76,792	$77,791	$78,193	$78,714	$79,628	$80,442	$80,811	$81,801	$929,656	97.7%
Pre-Tax Earnings (Note 13)	($1,780)	($1,117)	$530	$816	$797	$2,625	$2,918	$1,621	$3,680	$3,970	$3,774	$4,252	$22,086	2.3%
Number of Stores in Sample 232														
Cash Flow Summary														
Pre-Tax Earnings (Note 13)	($1,780)	($1,117)	$530	$816	$797	$2,625	$2,918	$1,621	$3,680	$3,970	$3,774	$4,252	$22,086	2.3%
Depreciation (Note 14)	26,018	26,875	27,474	28,014	28,618	29,258	29,641	29,966	30,215	30,597	30,905	31,051	348,632	36.6%
Net Inventory Purchases (Note 15)	(35,764)	(35,367)	(36,360)	(37,766)	(38,610)	(33,872)	(35,372)	(34,950)	(35,950)	(36,218)	(32,891)	(34,553)	(427,673)	-44.9%
Cost of Sales (Note 4)	5,953	6,087	6,400	6,060	6,324	6,355	6,041	5,602	6,155	6,193	5,660	6,362	73,192	7.7%
Inventory Write Offs (Note 10)	1,740	1,891	1,830	1,863	2,050	2,003	1,925	2,162	1,991	2,145	2,068	1,950	23,618	2.5%
* Pre-Tax Cash Flow (Note 16)	($3,833)	($1,631)	($126)	($1,013)	($821)	$6,369	$5,153	$4,401	$6,091	$6,687	$9,516	$9,062	$39,855	4.2%

* Assumes Cash Purchase of Inventory - Inventory Financing Available for Qualified Franchisees (See Item 10)

	Month 25	Month 26	Month 27	Month 28	Month 29	Month 30	Month 31	Month 32	Month 33	Month 34	Month 35	Month 36	Year 3	
Lease Revenue (Note 1)	$81,198	$81,236	$82,533	$83,017	$83,457	$83,903	$83,660	$84,760	$85,399	$84,797	$85,741	$86,621	$1,006,322	91.2%
Other Revenue (Note 2)	8,048	8,311	8,868	8,661	8,346	8,754	7,760	7,288	8,079	7,792	7,562	7,818	97,287	8.8%
Total Revenue (Note 3)	$89,246	$89,547	$91,401	$91,678	$91,803	$92,657	$91,420	$92,048	$93,478	$92,589	$93,303	$94,439	$1,103,609	100.0%
Operating Expenses														
Cost of Sales (Note 4)	$6,908	$7,139	$7,641	$7,518	$7,397	$7,667	$6,986	$6,581	$7,102	$6,981	$6,596	$7,108	$85,624	7.8%
Personnel Cost (Note 5)	17,778	17,708	17,891	18,094	18,274	18,526	18,407	18,545	18,528	18,536	19,354	18,856	220,497	20.0%
Selling Cost (Note 6)	2,794	2,887	3,008	3,011	2,864	3,014	2,962	2,876	2,894	2,863	2,848	2,776	34,797	3.2%
Occupancy Cost (Note 7)	10,092	10,021	10,169	10,190	10,085	10,118	10,006	10,200	10,255	10,275	10,204	10,250	121,865	11.0%
Inventory Carrying Cost (Note 8)	31,986	32,246	32,263	32,469	32,675	32,921	33,180	33,516	33,804	33,910	34,039	34,334	397,343	36.0%
Delivery Cost (Note 9)	2,720	2,681	2,850	2,698	2,783	2,905	2,857	2,868	2,935	2,990	2,911	3,069	34,267	3.1%
Inventory Write Offs (Note 10)	1,883	1,892	1,767	1,789	1,686	1,782	2,049	1,952	2,060	1,893	2,068	2,352	23,173	2.1%
Gen. Office Allocation (Note 11)	4,451	4,466	4,561	4,577	4,584	4,624	4,562	4,589	4,669	4,624	4,655	4,713	55,075	5.0%
General Operating Cost (Note 12)	4,177	4,152	4,234	4,261	4,202	4,316	4,207	4,386	4,382	4,356	4,375	4,323	51,371	4.7%
Total Operating Costs (Note 12)	$82,789	$83,192	$84,384	$84,607	$84,550	$85,873	$85,216	$85,513	$86,629	$86,428	$87,050	$87,781	$1,024,012	92.8%
Pre-Tax Earnings (Note 13)	$6,457	$6,355	$7,017	$7,071	$7,253	$6,784	$6,204	$6,535	$6,849	$6,161	$6,253	$6,658	$79,597	7.2%
Number of Stores in Sample 167														
Cash Flow Summary														
Pre-Tax Earnings (Note 13)	$6,457	$6,355	$7,017	$7,071	$7,253	$6,784	$6,204	$6,535	$6,849	$6,161	$6,253	$6,658	$79,597	7.2%
Depreciation (Note 14)	31,327	31,480	31,433	31,522	31,705	31,907	32,119	32,385	32,630	32,743	32,828	33,140	385,219	34.9%
Net Inventory Purchases (Note 15)	(37,355)	(39,602)	(41,093)	(42,581)	(40,921)	(42,063)	(42,788)	(41,264)	(40,509)	(41,607)	(39,975)	(40,681)	(490,439)	-44.4%
Cost of Sales (Note 4)	6,908	7,139	7,641	7,518	7,397	7,667	6,986	6,581	7,102	6,981	6,596	7,108	85,624	7.8%
Inventory Write Offs (Note 10)	1,883	1,892	1,767	1,789	1,686	1,782	2,049	1,952	2,060	1,893	2,068	2,352	23,173	2.1%
* Pre-Tax Cash Flow (Note 16)	$9,220	$7,264	$6,765	$5,319	$7,120	$6,077	$4,570	$6,189	$8,132	$6,171	$7,770	$8,577	$83,174	7.5%

* Assumes Cash Purchase of Inventory - Inventory Financing Available for Qualified Franchisees (See Item 10)

	Month 37	Month 38	Month 39	Month 40	Month 41	Month 42	Month 43	Month 44	Month 45	Month 46	Month 47	Month 48	Year 4	%
Lease Revenue (Note 1)	$86,019	$87,718	$88,915	$89,151	$89,786	$90,850	$89,589	$91,379	$91,817	$91,559	$91,508	$92,620	$1,080,911	90.8%
Other Revenue (Note 2)	9,111	8,842	9,225	9,265	9,876	10,598	8,767	8,489	9,387	8,893	8,339	8,588	109,380	9.2%
Total Revenue (Note 3)	$95,130	$96,560	$98,140	$98,416	$99,662	$101,448	$98,356	$99,868	$101,204	$100,452	$99,847	$101,208	$1,190,291	100.0%
Operating Expenses														
Cost of Sales (Note 4)	$8,053	$7,875	$7,995	$7,988	$8,514	$9,047	$7,645	$7,569	$7,800	$7,377	$7,258	$7,381	$94,502	7.9%
Personnel Cost (Note 5)	18,766	19,153	19,620	19,033	19,764	19,860	19,324	19,648	19,597	19,708	19,891	20,199	234,563	19.7%
Selling Cost (Note 6)	2,693	2,970	3,176	2,967	2,944	3,161	3,029	3,121	2,943	2,987	2,885	3,007	35,883	3.0%
Occupancy Cost (Note 7)	10,117	9,996	9,863	10,148	10,161	10,111	10,075	10,205	10,289	10,208	10,347	10,546	122,066	10.3%
Inventory Carrying Cost (Note 8)	34,284	34,366	34,605	34,892	34,893	35,070	35,496	35,627	35,856	36,022	36,295	36,430	423,836	35.6%
Delivery Cost (Note 9)	3,063	3,000	3,093	2,992	3,049	3,064	2,974	3,057	3,111	3,097	3,084	3,292	36,946	3.1%
Inventory Write Offs (Note 10)	2,094	1,657	1,880	2,159	1,762	1,871	1,829	1,932	2,270	2,071	1,973	2,388	23,886	2.0%
Gen. Office Allocation (Note 11)	4,747	4,820	4,902	4,912	4,975	5,064	4,911	4,987	5,053	5,016	4,983	5,062	59,422	5.0%
General Operating Cost (Note 12)	4,407	4,484	4,383	4,549	4,491	4,545	4,395	4,544	4,466	4,497	4,538	4,513	53,812	4.5%
Total Operating Costs (Note 12)	$88,224	$98,401	$89,517	$89,640	$90,553	$91,783	$89,678	$90,690	$91,385	$90,983	$91,254	$92,808	$1,084,916	91.1%
Pre-Tax Earnings (Note 13)	$6,906	$8,159	$8,623	$8,776	$9,109	$9,665	$8,678	$9,178	$9,819	$9,469	$8,593	$8,400	$105,375	8.9%
Number of Stores in Sample 110														
Cash Flow Summary														
Pre-Tax Earnings (Note 13)	$6,906	$8,159	$8,623	$8,776	$9,109	$9,665	$8,678	$9,178	$9,819	$9,469	$8,593	$8,400	$105,375	8.9%
Depreciation (Note 14)	33,151	33,191	33,433	33,691	33,766	33,933	34,131	34,423	34,710	34,917	35,047	35,070	409,463	34.4%
Net Inventory Purchases (Note 15)	(45,215)	(44,886)	(43,739)	(43,091)	(42,976)	(45,167)	(44,474)	(46,104)	(44,981)	(39,882)	(40,847)	(40,744)	(522,106)	-43.9%
Cost of Sales (Note 4)	8,053	7,875	7,995	7,988	8,514	9,047	7,645	7,569	7,800	7,377	7,258	7,381	94,502	7.9%
Inventory Write Offs (Note 10)	2,094	1,657	1,880	2,159	1,762	1,871	1,829	1,932	2,270	2,071	1,973	2,388	23,886	2.0%
* Pre-Tax Cash Flow (Note 16)	$4,989	$5,996	$8,192	$9,523	$10,175	$9,349	$7,809	$6,998	$9,618	$13,952	$12,024	$12,495	$111,120	9.3%

* Assumes Cash Purchase of Inventory - Inventory Financing Available for Qualified Franchisees (See Item 10)

	Month 49	Month 50	Month 51	Month 52	Month 53	Month 54	Month 55	Month 56	Month 57	Month 58	Month 59	Month 60	Year 5	%
Lease Revenue (Note 1)	$94,096	$94,232	$95,282	$95,486	$96,806	$97,117	$97,622	$98,041	$96,547	$96,101	$99,062	$97,543	$1,159,935	90.3%
Other Revenue (Note 2)	9,840	9,801	10,294	9,699	10,696	12,262	12,210	9,288	9,229	10,484	10,222	10,469	124,494	9.7%
Total Revenue (Note 3)	$103,936	$104,033	$105,576	$105,185	$107,502	$109,379	$109,832	$107,329	$105,776	$106,585	$109,284	$108,012	$1,284,429	100.0%
Operating Expenses														
Cost of Sales (Note 4)	$8,493	$8,451	$8,698	$8,348	$8,953	$9,825	$10,330	$8,229	$8,205	$8,899	$8,656	$8,892	$105,979	8.3%
Personnel Cost (Note 5)	20,462	20,466	20,809	20,600	21,110	20,822	21,163	21,262	20,576	20,852	21,224	21,284	250,630	19.5%
Selling Cost (Note 6)	2,840	2,883	2,999	2,902	3,033	3,060	3,014	2,997	2,826	2,921	2,920	2,685	35,080	2.7%
Occupancy Cost (Note 7)	10,430	10,201	10,017	10,005	10,337	10,239	10,307	10,093	10,185	9,767	10,253	10,002	121,836	9.5%
Inventory Carrying Cost (Note 8)	37,007	36,862	37,186	37,143	37,429	37,954	38,145	38,245	38,363	38,502	38,860	38,747	454,433	35.4%
Delivery Cost (Note 9)	3,255	3,242	3,293	3,202	3,173	3,157	3,157	3,186	3,256	3,197	3,235	3,399	38,761	3.0%
Inventory Write Offs (Note 10)	2,186	1,890	2,013	1,790	1,966	2,021	2,277	1,914	2,323	2,053	2,092	1,992	24,517	1.9%
Gen. Office Allocation (Note 11)	5,190	5,192	5,272	5,251	5,369	5,463	5,484	5,359	5,260	5,419	5,457	5,393	64,129	5.0%
General Operating Cost (Note 12)	4,647	4,532	4,578	4,727	4,720	4,712	4,836	4,791	4,740	4,779	5,047	4,794	56,903	4.4%
Total Operating Costs (Note 12)	$94,510	$93,719	$94,865	$93,968	$96,090	$97,282	$98,713	$96,056	$95,754	$96,389	$97,734	$97,188	$1,152,268	89.7%
Pre-Tax Earnings (Note 13)	$9,426	$10,314	$10,711	$11,217	$11,412	$12,097	$11,119	$11,273	$10,022	$12,196	$11,550	$10,824	$132,161	10.3%
Number of Stores in Sample 75														
Cash Flow Summary														
Pre-Tax Earnings (Note 13)	$9,426	$10,314	$10,711	$11,217	$11,412	$12,097	$11,119	$11,273	$10,022	$12,196	$11,550	$10,824	$132,161	10.3%
Depreciation (Note 14)	35,805	36,015	36,023	36,089	36,416	36,696	36,764	36,867	37,036	36,931	37,118	36,832	438,592	34.1%
Net Inventory Purchases (Note 15)	(47,600)	(43,502)	(44,434)	(47,666)	(45,749)	(48,352)	(52,773)	(50,738)	(44,707)	(43,509)	(43,509)	(46,514)	(560,196)	-43.6%
Cost of Sales (Note 4)	8,493	8,451	8,698	8,348	8,953	9,825	10,330	8,229	8,205	8,899	8,656	8,892	105,979	8.3%
Inventory Write Offs (Note 10)	2,186	1,890	2,013	1,790	1,966	2,021	2,277	1,914	2,323	2,053	2,092	1,992	24,517	1.9%
* Pre-Tax Cash Flow (Note 16)	$8,310	$13,168	$13,011	$9,778	$12,998	$12,287	$7,717	$7,545	$12,879	$15,427	$15,907	$12,026	$141,053	11.0%

* Assumes Cash Purchase of Inventory - Inventory Financing Available for Qualified Franchisees (See Item 10)

TABLE 1

Statement of Average Revenues and Expenses for All Aaron's Sales & Lease Ownership Company-Operated Stores (As Defined) Opened Under the "12 Month Rental Purchase Plan". 1st, 2nd, 3rd, 4th and 5th Full Years of Operation

	Year 1	Year 2	Year 3	Year 4	Year 5
Sample Size	300	232	167	110	75
Highest Lease Revenue (Note 1)	$1,315,118	$1,552,317	$1,590,804	$1,796,900	$2,228,255
Lowest Lease Revenue	182,565	391,129	528,556	550,654	601,686
Average Lease Revenue	446,513	865,143	1,006,322	1,080,911	1,159,935
Median Lease Revenue	425,317	820,891	978,747	1,044,327	1,101,395
# of Stores Higher than Group Average %	130	101	74	51	34
of Stores Higher than Group Average	43.3%	43.5%	44.3%	46.4%	45.3%
Highest Other Revenue (Note 2)	$354,869	$232,432	$214,229	$252,253	$300,124
Lowest Other Revenue	14,456	25,815	28,314	33,845	47,193
Average Other Revenue	60,686	86,599	97,287	109,380	124,494
Median Other Revenue	52,517	80,357	93,544	106,876	117,255
# of Stores Higher than Group Average %	116	98	78	50	31
of Stores Higher than Group Average	38.7%	42.2%	46.7%	45.5%	41.3%
Highest Total Revenue (Note 3)	$1,540,366	$1,720,768	$1,774,291	$2,008,683	$2,465,580
Lowest Total Revenue	197,021	416,944	572,630	602,530	681,357
Average Total Revenue	507,199	951,742	1,103,609	1,190,291	1,284,429
Median Total Revenue	52,517	80,357	93,544	106,876	117,255
# of Stores Higher than Group Average %	138	101	77	49	32
of Stores Higher than Group Average	46.0%	43.5%	46.1%	44.5%	42.7%
Highest Cost of Sales (Note 4)	$269,110	$173,626	$182,121	$222,335	$243,828
Lowest Cost of Sales	11,061	22,866	29,815	33,574	46,595
Average Cost of Sales	50,856	73,192	85,624	94,502	105,979
Median Cost of Sales	44,749	69,002	82,202	89,120	96,580
# of Stores Higher than Group Average %	118	103	71	47	29
of Stores Higher than Group Average	39.3%	44.4%	42.5%	42.7%	38.7%

187

TABLE 1

Statement of Average Revenues and Expenses for All Aaron's Sales & Lease Ownership Company-Operated Stores (As Defined) Opened Under the "12 Month Rental Purchase Plan". 1st, 2nd, 3rd, 4th and 5th Full Years of Operation

	Year 1	Year 2	Year 3	Year 4	Year 5
Highest Personnel Cost (Note 5)	$318,455	$332,471	$330,273	$369,944	$469,270
Lowest Personnel Cost	119,298	130,151	150,405	149,719	159,679
Average Personnel Cost	177,745	202,073	220,497	234,563	250,630
Median Personnel Cost	172,131	195,947	213,835	222,881	239,079
# of Stores Higher than Group Average %	122	94	68	47	30
of Stores Higher than Group Average	40.7%	40.5%	40.7%	42.7%	40.0%
Highest Selling Cost (Note 6)	$70,504	$48,805	$46,981	$44,136	$42,023
Lowest Selling Cost	25,280	28,259	28,941	30,625	29,290
Average Selling Cost	38,597	33,931	34,797	35,883	35,080
Median Selling Cost	37,961	33,281	34,382	35,870	34,782
# of Stores Higher than Group Average %	136	91	75	55	32
of Stores Higher than Group Average	45.3%	39.2%	44.9%	50.0%	42.7%
Highest Occupancy Cost (Note 7)	$210,385	$189,789	$178,309	$186,358	$194,910
Lowest Occupancy Cost	56,165	58,463	74,388	68,149	61,832
Average Occupancy Cost	120,483	124,210	121,865	122,066	121,836
Median Occupancy Cost	122,298	123,974	122,077	122,201	120,651
# of Stores Higher than Group Average %	157	114	84	55	35
of Stores Higher than Group Average	52.3%	49.1%	50.3%	50.0%	46.7%
Highest Inventory Carrying Cost (Note 8)	$553,734	$687,120	$637,826	$678,262	$829,555
Lowest Inventory Carrying Cost	81,955	183,568	212,004	229,794	260,215
Average Inventory Carrying Cost	177,142	351,501	397,343	423,836	454,433
Median Inventory Carrying Cost	170,393	333,015	382,056	409,931	425,529
# of Stores Higher than Group Average %	131	96	71	48	32
of Stores Higher than Group Average	43.7%	41.4%	42.5%	43.6%	42.7%

TABLE 1

Statement of Average Revenues and Expenses for All Aaron's Sales & Lease Ownership Company-Operated Stores (As Defined) Opened Under the "12 Month Rental Purchase Plan".

1st, 2nd, 3rd, 4th and 5th Full Years of Operation

	Year 1	Year 2	Year 3	Year 4	Year 5
Highest Pre-Tax Earnings (Note 13)	$113,168	$315,607	$357,638	$379,237	$518,826
Lowest Pre-Tax Earnings	(291,617)	(227,618)	(131,172)	(108,004)	(107,259)
Average Pre-Tax Earnings	(150,884)	22,086	79,597	105,375	132,161
Median Pre-Tax Earnings	(154,563)	15,297	79,152	109,413	125,308
# of Stores Higher than Group Average	145	108	83	56	33
% of Stores Higher than Group Average	48.3%	46.6%	49.7%	50.9%	44.0%
Highest Pre-Tax Earnings % (Note 13)	10.1%	19.6%	20.2%	19.9%	21.0%
Lowest Pre-Tax Earnings %	-142.3%	-47.9%	-21.8%	-17.9%	-14.6%
Average Pre-Tax Earnings %	-29.7%	2.3%	7.2%	8.9%	10.3%
Median Pre-Tax Earnings %	-31.0%	1.6%	7.3%	8.8%	10.2%
# of Stores Higher than Group Average	140	109	84	54	36
% of Stores Higher than Group Average	46.7%	47.0%	50.3%	49.1%	48.0%
Highest Depreciation (Note 14)	$533,709	$642,474	$609,376	$641,630	$787,530
Lowest Depreciation	86,678	196,435	213,190	227,679	257,696
Average Depreciation	183,822	348,632	385,219	409,463	438,592
Median Depreciation	176,994	330,767	378,162	393,202	413,778
# of Stores Higher than Group Average	129	98	78	50	30
% of Stores Higher than Group Average	43.0%	42.2%	46.7%	45.5%	40.0%

TABLE 1

Statement of Average Revenues and Expenses for All Aaron's Sales & Lease Ownership Company-Operated Stores (As Defined) Opened Under the "12 Month Rental Purchase Plan". 1st, 2nd, 3rd, 4th and 5th Full Years of Operation

	Year 1	Year 2	Year 3	Year 4	Year 5
Highest Pre-Tax Earnings (Note 13)	$113,168	$315,607	$357,638	$379,237	$518,826
Lowest Pre-Tax Earnings	(291,617)	(227,618)	(131,172)	(108,004)	(107,259)
Average Pre-Tax Earnings	(150,884)	22,086	79,597	105,375	132,161
Median Pre-Tax Earnings	(154,563)	15,297	79,152	109,413	125,308
# of Stores Higher than Group Average %	145	108	83	56	33
of Stores Higher than Group Average	48.3%	46.6%	49.7%	50.9%	44.0%
Highest Pre-Tax Earnings % (Note 13)	10.1%	19.6%	20.2%	19.9%	21.0%
Lowest Pre-Tax Earnings %	-142.3%	-47.9%	-21.8%	-17.9%	-14.6%
Average Pre-Tax Earnings %	-29.7%	2.3%	7.2%	8.9%	10.3%
Median Pre-Tax Earnings %	-31.0%	1.6%	7.3%	8.8%	10.2%
# of Stores Higher than Group Average %	140	109	84	54	36
of Stores Higher than Group Average	46.7%	47.0%	50.3%	49.1%	48.0%
Highest Depreciation (Note 14)	$533,709	$642,474	$609,376	$641,630	$787,530
Lowest Depreciation	86,678	196,435	213,190	227,679	257,696
Average Depreciation	183,822	348,632	385,219	409,463	438,592
Median Depreciation	176,994	330,767	378,162	393,202	413,778
# of Stores Higher than Group Average %	129	98	78	50	30
of Stores Higher than Group Average	43.0%	42.2%	46.7%	45.5%	40.0%

TABLE 1

Statement of Average Revenues and Expenses for All Aaron's Sales & Lease Ownership Company-Operated Stores (As Defined) Opened Under the "12 Month Rental Purchase Plan". 1st, 2nd, 3rd, 4th and 5th Full Years of Operation

	Year 1	Year 2	Year 3	Year 4	Year 5
Highest Net Inventory Purchases (Note 15)	$1,719,626	$806,275	$834,263	$1,051,931	$1,066,814
Lowest Net Inventory Purchases	308,755	172,795	210,975	175,309	231,001
Average Net Inventory Purchases	638,193	427,673	490,439	522,106	560,196
Median Net Inventory Purchases	609,173	417,833	482,015	491,527	514,926
# of Stores Higher than Group Average %	127	108	79	49	31
of Stores Higher than Group Average	42.3%	46.6%	47.3%	44.5%	41.3%
Highest Pre-Tax Cash Flow (Note 16)	($279,048)	$521,897	$313,119	$303,325	$602,886
Lowest Pre-Tax Cash Flow	(921,350)	(196,787)	(143,278)	(148,629)	(84,990)
Average Pre-Tax Cash Flow	(544,266)	39,855	83,174	111,120	141,053
Median Pre-Tax Cash Flow	(537,380)	36,014	79,913	108,083	120,048
# of Stores Higher than Group Average %	158	109	80	52	34
of Stores Higher than Group Average	52.7%	47.0%	47.9%	47.3%	45.3%
Highest Pre-Tax Cash Flow % (Note 16)	-44.9%	30.3%	30.9%	26.6%	26.3%
Lowest Pre-Tax Cash Flow %	-278.7%	-42.4%	-21.9%	-24.7%	-9.4%
Average Pre-Tax Cash Flow %	-107.3%	4.2%	7.5%	9.3%	11.0%
Median Pre-Tax Cash Flow %	-110.3%	3.6%	8.0%	9.2%	10.5%
# of Stores Higher than Group Average %	143	108	86	53	35
of Stores Higher than Group Average	47.7%	46.6%	51.5%	48.2%	46.7%

TABLE 2

Statement of Average Revenues and Expenses of Aaron's Sales & Lease Ownership
Company-Operated Stores for Year Ending December 31, 2007
for ALL Stores (As Defined) Open at Least Two Full Years Before January 1, 2007

	Annual Revenue Under $800,000		Annual Revenue $800,000-$1,100,000		Annual Revenue $1,100,001-$1,400,000		Annual Revenue $1,400,001-$1,700,000		Annual Revenue Over $1,700,000		Annual Revenue All Stores	
	Average	%	Average	%	Average	%	Average	%	Average	%	Average	%
Lease Revenue (Note 1)	$634,179	92.8%	$892,444	93.4%	$1,164,195	93.7%	$1,445,224	93.9%	$1,897,129	93.9%	$1,240,462	93.7%
Other Revenue (Note 2)	49,261	7.2%	62,779	6.6%	78,894	6.3%	93,593	6.1%	122,406	6.1%	83,061	6.3%
Total Revenue (Note 3)	$683,440	100.0%	$955,223	100.0%	$1,243,089	100.0%	$1,538,817	100.0%	$2,019,535	100.0%	$1,323,523	100.0%
Operating Expenses												
Cost of Sales (Note 4)	$42,347	6.2%	$53,648	5.6%	$67,513	5.4%	$82,026	5.3%	$109,990	5.4%	$72,340	5.5%
Personnel Cost (Note 5)	174,186	25.5%	207,714	21.7%	250,748	20.2%	298,311	19.4%	393,964	19.5%	268,170	20.3%
Selling Cost (Note 6)	33,135	4.8%	33,368	3.5%	33,618	2.7%	33,930	2.2%	34,665	1.7%	33,758	2.6%
Occupancy Cost (Note 7)	86,427	12.6%	120,720	12.6%	123,317	9.9%	127,046	8.3%	135,842	6.7%	122,977	9.3%
Inventory Carrying Cost (Note 8)	269,413	39.4%	363,109	38.0%	461,072	37.1%	569,876	37.0%	736,323	36.5%	492,037	37.2%
Delivery Cost (Note 9)	26,233	3.8%	33,981	3.6%	41,012	3.3%	43,338	2.8%	50,736	2.5%	40,301	3.0%
Inventory Write Offs (Note 10)	12,869	1.9%	26,847	2.8%	35,583	2.9%	38,919	2.5%	48,397	2.4%	34,625	2.6%
General Operating Cost (Note 11)	37,689	5.5%	46,561	4.9%	57,357	4.6%	69,233	4.5%	88,420	4.4%	60,950	4.6%
Gen. Office Allocation (Note 12)	34,019	5.0%	47,688	5.0%	62,036	5.0%	76,811	5.0%	100,812	5.0%	66,057	5.0%
Total Operating Costs	$716,318	104.8%	$933,636	97.7%	$1,132,256	91.1%	$1,339,490	87.0%	$1,699,149	84.1%	$1,191,215	90.0%
Pretax Earnings (Note 13)	($32,878)	-4.8%	$21,587	2.3%	$110,833	8.9%	$199,327	13.0%	$320,386	15.9%	$132,308	10.0%
Number of Stores within the Range	36		132		152		131		80		531	
Cash Flow Summary												
Pretax Earnings (Note 13)	($32,878)	-4.8%	$21,587	2.3%	$110,833	8.9%	$199,327	13.0%	$320,386	15.9%	$132,308	10.0%
Depreciation (Note 14)	255,960	37.5%	344,716	36.1%	431,950	34.7%	532,450	34.6%	685,624	33.9%	461,345	34.9%
Net Inventory Purchases (Note 15)	(258,726)	-37.9%	(390,062)	-40.8%	(499,061)	-40.1%	(610,265)	-39.7%	(792,870)	-39.3%	(527,371)	-39.8%
Cost of Sales (Note 4)	42,347	6.2%	53,648	5.6%	67,513	5.4%	82,026	5.3%	109,990	5.4%	72,340	5.5%
Inventory Write Offs (Note 10)	12,869	1.9%	26,847	2.8%	35,583	2.9%	38,919	2.5%	48,397	2.4%	34,625	2.6%
* Pretax Cash Flow (Note 16)	$19,572	2.9%	$56,736	5.9%	$146,818	11.8%	$242,457	15.8%	$371,527	18.4%	$173,247	13.1%

TABLE 2

Statement of Average Revenues and Expenses of Aaron's Sales & Lease Ownership
Company-Operated Stores for Year Ending December 31, 2007
for ALL Stores (As Defined) Open at Least Two Full Years Before January 1, 2007

	Annual Revenue Under $800,000	Annual Revenue $800,000-$1,100,000	Annual Revenue $1,100,001-$1,400,000	Annual Revenue $1,400,001-$1,700,000	Annual Revenue Over $1,700,000	Annual Revenue All Stores
Sample Size	36	132	152	131	80	531
Highest Lease Revenue (Note 1)	$751,638	$1,035,800	$1,326,609	$1,593,792	$3,633,625	$3,633,625
Lowest Lease Revenue	432,832	734,678	991,516	1,275,304	1,573,513	432,832
Average Lease Revenue	634,179	892,444	1,164,195	1,445,224	1,897,129	1,240,462
Median Lease Revenue	640,424	884,807	1,163,764	1,436,961	1,805,162	1,198,517
# of Stores Higher Than Group Avg.	20	65	76	58	30	242
% of Stores Higher Than Group Avg.	55.6%	49.2%	50.0%	44.3%	37.5%	45.6%
Highest Other Revenue (Note 2)	$92,138	$117,767	$172,458	$184,504	$357,587	$357,587
Lowest Other Revenue	23,973	31,704	37,148	30,918	55,803	23,973
Average Other Revenue	49,261	62,779	78,894	93,593	122,406	83,061
Median Other Revenue	49,901	62,763	76,053	92,032	108,745	78,457
# of Stores Higher Than Group Avg.	18	66	68	63	24	229
% of Stores Higher Than Group Avg.	50.0%	50.0%	44.7%	48.1%	30.0%	43.1%
Highest Total Revenue (Note 3)	$787,895	$1,099,918	$1,393,798	$1,694,232	$3,991,212	$3,991,212
Lowest Total Revenue	459,861	803,355	1,102,689	1,405,661	1,715,718	459,861
Average Total Revenue	683,440	955,223	1,243,089	1,538,817	2,019,535	1,323,523
Median Total Revenue	49,901	62,763	76,053	92,032	108,745	78,457
# of Stores Higher Than Group Avg.	22	67	69	60	29	243
% of Stores Higher Than Group Avg.	61.1%	50.8%	45.4%	45.8%	36.3%	45.8%
Highest Cost of Sales (Note 4)	$77,017	$86,295	$128,662	$153,497	$312,435	$312,435
Lowest Cost of Sales	20,156	29,974	40,810	38,805	55,101	20,156
Average Cost of Sales	42,347	53,648	67,513	82,026	109,990	72,340
Median Cost of Sales	40,388	52,759	66,073	78,485	95,702	68,149
# of Stores Higher Than Group Avg.	16	63	70	54	29	221
% of Stores Higher Than Group Avg.	44.4%	47.7%	46.1%	41.2%	36.3%	41.6%

TABLE 2

Statement of Average Revenues and Expenses of Aaron's Sales & Lease Ownership
Company-Operated Stores for Year Ending December 31, 2007
for ALL Stores (As Defined) Open at Least Two Full Years Before January 1, 2007

	Annual Revenue Under $800,000	Annual Revenue $800,000-$1,100,000	Annual Revenue $1,100,001-$1,400,000	Annual Revenue $1,400,001-$1,700,000	Annual Revenue Over $1,700,000	Annual Revenue All Stores
Highest Personnel Cost (Note 5)	$206,465	$281,887	$340,804	$392,451	$729,304	$729,304
Lowest Personnel Cost	135,008	154,442	200,310	238,192	294,229	135,008
Average Personnel Cost	174,186	207,714	250,748	298,311	393,964	268,170
Median Personnel Cost	178,374	205,537	251,170	295,592	379,960	257,173
# of Stores Higher Than Group Avg.	20	59	77	63	32	219
% of Stores Higher Than Group Avg.	55.6%	44.7%	50.7%	46.1%	40.0%	41.2%
Highest Selling Cost (Note 6)	$39,678	$41,305	$39,798	$40,430	$43,400	$43,400
Lowest Selling Cost	29,952	28,933	30,502	30,393	30,567	28,933
Average Selling Cost	33,135	33,368	33,618	33,930	34,665	33,758
Median Selling Cost	32,788	33,021	33,312	33,690	34,130	33,406
# of Stores Higher Than Group Avg.	15	58	65	58	36	224
% of Stores Higher Than Group Avg.	41.7%	43.9%	42.8%	44.3%	45.0%	42.2%
Highest Occupancy Cost (Note 7)	$184,315	$236,191	$228,162	$215,225	$236,191	$236,191
Lowest Occupancy Cost	29,517	46,345	59,228	60,043	79,559	29,517
Average Occupancy Cost	86,427	120,720	123,317	127,046	135,842	122,977
Median Occupancy Cost	85,036	119,347	119,957	124,866	134,912	122,538
# of Stores Higher Than Group Avg.	18	65	69	62	38	261
% of Stores Higher Than Group Avg.	50.0%	49.2%	45.4%	47.3%	47.5%	49.2%
Highest Inventory Carrying Cost (Note 8)	$345,740	$455,815	$564,197	$716,405	$1,381,123	$1,381,123
Lowest Inventory Carrying Cost	191,370	288,424	351,734	458,543	580,574	191,370
Average Inventory Carrying Cost	269,413	363,109	461,072	569,876	736,323	492,037
Median Inventory Carrying Cost	276,668	363,367	462,743	568,674	713,923	475,473
# of Stores Higher Than Group Avg.	19	66	77	64	32	244
% of Stores Higher Than Group Avg.	52.8%	50.0%	50.7%	48.9%	40.0%	46.0%

TABLE 2

Statement of Average Revenues and Expenses of Aaron's Sales & Lease Ownership
Company-Operated Stores for Year Ending December 31, 2007
for ALL Stores (As Defined) Open at Least Two Full Years Before January 1, 2007

	Annual Revenue Under $800,000	Annual Revenue $800,000-$1,100,000	Annual Revenue $1,100,001-$1,400,000	Annual Revenue $1,400,001-$1,700,000	Annual Revenue Over $1,700,000	Annual Revenue All Stores
Highest Delivery Cost (Note 9)	$44,039	$53,963	$51,624	$57,972	$93,132	$93,132
Lowest Delivery Cost	18,868	20,266	20,189	33,899	37,462	18,868
Average Delivery Cost	26,233	33,981	41,012	43,338	50,736	40,301
Median Delivery Cost	24,447	35,815	40,967	42,660	49,042	40,791
# of Stores Higher Than Group Avg.	9	77	75	56	35	283
% of Stores Higher Than Group Avg.	25.0%	58.3%	49.3%	42.7%	43.8%	53.3%
Highest Inventory Write Offs (Note 10)	$33,486	$82,513	$123,727	$123,416	$121,565	$123,727
Lowest Inventory Write Offs	1,726	602	5,625	5,299	11,144	602
Average Inventory Write Offs	12,869	26,847	35,583	38,919	48,397	34,625
Median Inventory Write Offs	11,136	23,722	30,387	35,672	44,849	31,642
# of Stores Higher Than Group Avg.	16	60	65	59	28	232
% of Stores Higher Than Group Avg.	44.4%	45.5%	42.8%	45.0%	35.0%	43.7%
Highest General Operating Cost (Note 11)	$50,933	$58,013	$75,176	$92,001	$185,021	$185,021
Lowest General Operating Cost	24,457	35,170	47,707	57,372	67,576	24,457
Average General Operating Cost	37,689	46,561	57,357	69,233	88,420	60,950
Median General Operating Cost	38,245	46,717	56,143	68,492	85,413	58,233
# of Stores Higher Than Group Avg.	19	71	63	56	30	239
% of Stores Higher Than Group Avg.	52.8%	53.8%	41.4%	42.7%	37.5%	45.0%
Highest Gen. Office Allocation (Note 12)	$39,213	$54,993	$69,701	$84,513	$199,062	$199,062
Lowest Gen. Office Allocation	22,981	39,863	54,882	70,133	85,609	22,981
Average Gen. Office Allocation	34,019	47,688	62,036	76,811	100,812	66,057
Median Gen. Office Allocation	34,605	47,772	61,396	76,444	95,443	63,544
# of Stores Higher Than Group Avg.	22	67	70	61	29	243
% of Stores Higher Than Group Avg.	61.1%	50.8%	46.1%	46.6%	36.3%	45.8%

TABLE 2

Statement of Average Revenues and Expenses of Aaron's Sales & Lease Ownership
Company-Operated Stores for Year Ending December 31, 2007
for ALL Stores (As Defined) Open at Least Two Full Years Before January 1, 2007

	Annual Revenue Under $800,000	Annual Revenue $800,000-$1,100,000	Annual Revenue $1,100,001-$1,400,000	Annual Revenue $1,400,001-$1,700,000	Annual Revenue Over $1,700,000	Annual Revenue All Stores
Highest Pretax Earnings (Note 13)	$84,726	$161,294	$253,299	$330,975	$820,457	$820,457
Lowest Pretax Earnings	(154,580)	(103,792)	(117,554)	16,177	100,797	(154,580)
Average Pretax Earnings	(32,878)	21,587	110,833	199,327	320,386	132,308
Median Pretax Earnings	(28,246)	19,366	121,968	197,705	297,397	128,305
# of Stores Higher Than Group Avg.	20	64	86	65	30	255
% of Stores Higher Than Group Avg.	55.6%	48.5%	56.6%	49.6%	37.5%	48.0%
Highest Pre-Tax Earnings %	12.1%	15.0%	18.7%	21.4%	24.8%	24.8%
Lowest Pre-Tax Earnings %	-19.8%	-12.0%	-9.7%	1.1%	5.1%	-19.8%
Average Pre-Tax Earnings %	-4.8%	2.3%	8.9%	13.0%	15.9%	10.0%
Median Pre-Tax Earnings %	-4.0%	1.9%	9.7%	13.4%	15.7%	9.8%
# of Stores Higher Than Group Avg.	20	61	88	70	39	253
% of Stores Higher Than Group Avg.	55.6%	46.2%	57.9%	53.4%	48.8%	47.6%
Highest Depreciation (Note 14)	$364,760	$428,689	$515,744	$642,318	$1,265,944	$1,265,944
Lowest Depreciation	183,235	264,983	354,790	444,369	520,983	183,235
Average Depreciation	255,960	344,716	431,950	532,450	685,624	461,345
Median Depreciation	262,590	344,219	428,810	531,760	658,422	448,249
# of Stores Higher Than Group Avg.	20	64	71	65	29	244
% of Stores Higher Than Group Avg.	55.6%	48.5%	46.7%	49.6%	36.3%	46.0%
Highest Net Inventory Purchases (Note 15)	$402,277	$597,263	$799,863	$900,247	$1,709,482	$1,709,482
Lowest Net Inventory Purchases	(46,573)	277,770	288,757	402,543	574,621	(46,573)
Average Net Inventory Purchases	258,726	390,062	499,061	610,265	792,870	527,371
Median Net Inventory Purchases	271,581	393,738	493,568	614,242	751,492	503,011
# of Stores Higher Than Group Avg.	21	69	71	71	26	246
% of Stores Higher Than Group Avg.	58.3%	52.3%	46.7%	54.2%	32.5%	46.3%

TABLE 2

Statement of Average Revenues and Expenses of Aaron's Sales & Lease Ownership
Company-Operated Stores for Year Ending December 31, 2007
for ALL Stores (As Defined) Open at Least Two Full Years Before January 1, 2007

	Annual Revenue Under $800,000	Annual Revenue $800,000-$1,100,000	Annual Revenue $1,100,001-$1,400,000	Annual Revenue $1,400,001-$1,700,000	Annual Revenue Over $1,700,000	Annual Revenue All Stores
Highest Pretax Cash Flow (Note 16)	$332,717	$222,235	$400,471	$489,183	$1,043,072	$1,043,072
Lowest Pretax Cash Flow	(127,094)	(109,401)	(75,478)	(27,500)	174,749	(127,094)
Average Pretax Cash Flow	19,572	56,736	146,818	242,457	371,527	173,247
Median Pretax Cash Flow	15,541	57,781	147,867	249,662	339,461	155,822
# of Stores Higher Than Group Avg.	16	67	77	69	33	243
% of Stores Higher Than Group Avg.	44.4%	50.8%	50.7%	52.7%	41.3%	45.8%
Highest Pretax Cash Flow % (Note 16)	48.3%	20.2%	28.9%	30.2%	27.5%	48.3%
Lowest Pretax Cash Flow %	-20.0%	-13.3%	-5.8%	-1.9%	8.9%	-20.0%
Average Pretax Cash Flow %	2.9%	5.9%	11.8%	15.8%	18.4%	13.1%
Median Pretax Cash Flow %	2.7%	5.7%	11.9%	16.3%	17.9%	12.4%
# of Stores Higher Than Group Avg.	18	64	77	70	37	241
% of Stores Higher Than Group Avg.	50.0%	48.5%	50.7%	53.4%	46.3%	45.4%

WA,WI

THE ATHLETE'S FOOT

1346 Oakbrook Dr., # 170
Norcross, GA 30093
Tel: (800) 524-6444 (770) 514-4676
Fax: (770) 514-4903
E-Mail: franchiseinfo@theathletesfoot.com
Web Site: www.theathletesfoot.com
Mr. Martin Amschler, VP Franchise

THE ATHLETE'S FOOT, with more than 600 stores in 45 countries, is the leading international franchisor of name-brand athletic footwear. As a franchisee, you will benefit from headquarters' support, including training, advertising, real estate and product selection.

BACKGROUND: IFA MEMBER

Established: 1971;	1st Franchised: 1972
Franchised Units:	569
Company-Owned Units:	0
Total Units:	569
Dist.:	US-232; CAN-1; O'seas-336
North America:	47 States, 1 Provinces
Density:	NR
Projected New Units (12 Months):	65
Qualifications:	4, 5, 3, 3, 2, 5

Registered:CA,DC,FL,HI,IL,IN,MD,MI,MN,ND,NY,OR,RI,SD,

FINANCIAL/TERMS:

Cash Investment:	$85K
Total Investment:	$200-525K
Minimum Net Worth:	$250K
Fees: Franchise -	$39.9K
Royalty - 5%;	Ad. - 2%
Earnings Claims Statement:	No
Term of Contract (Years):	10/5
Avg. # Of Employees:	2 FT, 6 PT
Passive Ownership:	Allowed, But Discouraged
Encourage Conversions:	Yes
Area Develop. Agreements:	Yes
Sub-Franchising Contracts:	Yes
Expand In Territory:	Yes
Space Needs:	1,200-2,800 SF; FS,SF,SC,RM

SUPPORT & TRAINING:

Financial Assistance Provided:	Yes (I)
Site Selection Assistance:	Yes
Lease Negotiation Assistance:	Yes
Co-Operative Advertising:	Yes
Franchisee Assoc./Member:	Yes/Member
Size Of Corporate Staff:	25
On-Going Support:	C,D,E,f,G,H,I
Training:	Headquarters in Atlanta;
	On-Going Location

SPECIFIC EXPANSION PLANS:

US:	Yes, All United States
Canada:	Yes, All Canada
Overseas:	Yes, All Countries

ITEM 19
FINANCIAL PERFORMANCE REPRESENTATIONS

Of the 238 franchised stores that were open and operating under the Marks in the United States as of December 31, 2007, 150 franchised stores **(i)** were open and operating for all 24 months in calendar years 2006 and 2007 and **(ii)** reported their annual gross sales to us in all 24 months in that period (**"Comparable Stores"**). These Comparable Stores, which represent 63% of the total franchised stores in the United States on December 31, 2007, are the Comparable Stores used in compiling the sales volume data in this Item 19.

In the 2007 calendar year, the annual gross sales volume for Comparable Stores ranged from a low of $64,417.11 to a high of $2,132,285.03. The median gross sales volume of Comparable Stores in 2007 was $751,030.90 meaning that 50% of the Comparable Stores achieved greater than this level of annual gross sales and 50% of the Comparable Stores achieved less than this level of gross sales. The average gross sales volume in 2007 was $819,668.73, with 65 stores above this level of annual gross sales and 85 stores below this level of gross sales. These figures represent gross sales before the deduction of any expenses.

The gross sales volume figures used in this Item 19 are based upon the reports of Gross Sales (as defined in Operating Agreements (our former name for Franchise Agreements) before July 6,

2001) and Net Sales (as defined in Operating Agreements after July 6, 2001) made by franchisees to AFB for purposes of determining royalty payments. Gross Sales and Net Sales are essentially the same sales base, but the term used was changed in 2001. Gross Sales and Net Sales may be accounted for on a cash basis or accrual basis depending upon the accounting method used by each individual franchisee. Upon your written request, we will make available to you written substantiation of the data used in preparing the average sales volume data.

YOUR FINANCIAL RESULTS MAY DIFFER FROM THE AVERAGE SALES VOLUMES STATED IN THIS ITEM 19. You should conduct an independent investigation of the costs and expenses you will incur in operating your Store. Franchisees or former franchisees, listed in this Disclosure Document, may be a source of this information.

We do not make any representations about a franchisee's future financial performance. Except for the disclosure in this Item 19, we do not make any representations about the past financial performance of company-owned or franchised Stores. We also do not authorize our employees or representatives to make any such representations either orally or in writing. If you are purchasing an existing Store, however, we may provide you with the actual records of that Store. If you receive any other financial performance information or projections of your future income, you should report it to the franchisor's management by contacting Legal Counsel at 1346 Oakbrook Drive, Suite 170, Norcross, Georgia 30093 (770) 514-4500, the Federal Trade Commission, and the appropriate state regulatory agencies.

GNC

GENERAL NUTRITION CENTERS

300 Sixth Ave., Fl. 4
Pittsburgh, PA 15222-2514
Tel: (800) 766-7099 (412) 338-2503
Fax: (412) 402-7105
E-Mail: livewell@gncfranchising.com
Web Site: www.gncfranchising.com
Mr. Bruce Pollock, Sr. Dir. Franchise Development

GNC is the leading specialty retailer of vitamins, minerals, herbs and sports nutrition supplements and is uniquely positioned to capitalize on the accelerating self-care trend. As the leading provider of products and information for personal health enhancement, the company holds the largest specialty-retail share of the nutritional supplement market. GNC was ranked America's #1 retail franchise for 17 consecutive years.

BACKGROUND:

Established: 1935;	1st Franchised: 1988
Franchised Units:	2034
Company-Owned Units:	3747
Total Units:	5781
Dist.:	US-3747; CAN-1212; O'seas-822
North America:	50 States, 0 Provinces
Density:	CA, FL, TX
Projected New Units (12 Months):	NR
Qualifications:	5, 5, 1, 1, 1, 4
Registered:CA,DC,FL,HI,IL,IN,MD,MI,MN,ND,NY,OR,RI,SD,	

VA,WA,WI,AB

FINANCIAL/TERMS:

Cash Investment:	$65K
Total Investment:	$133-182K
Minimum Net Worth:	$100K
Fees: Franchise -	$40K
Royalty - 6%;	Ad. - 3%
Earnings Claims Statement:	Yes
Term of Contract (Years):	10/5/5
Avg. # Of Employees:	1 FT, 3-5 PT
Passive Ownership:	Not Allowed
Encourage Conversions:	No
Area Develop. Agreements:	Yes
Sub-Franchising Contracts:	No
Expand In Territory:	Yes
Space Needs:	1,402 (avg.) SF; SF,SC,RM

SUPPORT & TRAINING:

Financial Assistance Provided:	Yes (D)
Site Selection Assistance:	Yes
Lease Negotiation Assistance:	Yes
Co-Operative Advertising:	No
Franchisee Assoc./Member:	No
Size Of Corporate Staff:	600
On-Going Support:	A,D,E,F,G,H,I
Training:	1 Week On-Site in Local Corporate Store

SPECIFIC EXPANSION PLANS:

US:	Yes, All United States
Canada:	Yes, All CAN Exc. PQ
Overseas:	Yes, All Countries

ITEM 19
FINANCIAL PERFORMANCE REPRESENTATION

Except as provided in this Item, we do not furnish or authorize any of our representatives to furnish any oral or written information concerning the actual or potential sales, costs, income, or profits of any franchised GNC Store or GNC Store operated by our affiliate, GNCorp. We do provide information regarding GNC Stores operated by our affiliate GNCorp which are offered for sale as a franchise. We specifically instruct our personnel, agents and employees that they are not permitted to make any claims or statements concerning a specific franchisee's earnings capability, or chances for success, an4any such representations are unauthorized by us. Actual results vary from Store to Store and we cannot estimate the results of any franchisee; therefore, <u>your individual financial results are likely to differ from those reported in this Item.</u>

RESULTS OF OPERATIONS OF FRANCHISED STORES

BASIS OF DATA

This earnings claim is based upon information regarding the actual gross sales of GNC franchised Stores open and operated continuously by our franchisees during our 2007 fiscal year (January 1, 2007 through December 31, 2007). Of the 978 franchise-operated Stores that were open and operating in the United States as of December 31, 2007, 958, or 97.96%, of those participating had been in business continuously throughout the fiscal year 2007. No data has been presented for the franchisees who were terminated, reacquired, not renewed or left our system for other reasons during our last fiscal year. (*See* Item 20 for more information.) None of the information presented in this Item includes data from GNC Stores operated by GNCorp., GNC/Rite Aid, Value Nutrition, or GNC Stores located on military bases.

AVERAGE GROSS RETAIL SALES

The average gross retail sales of the 958 Stores described above during the fiscal year 2007 was $384,336.34. 41% of the 958 Stores (391 Stores) actually attained or surpassed the average gross retail sales of $384,336.34 for the fiscal year 2007. (*See* Note below.) Gross sales is the amount of sales of all products sold in your Store, whether for cash or on a charge, credit or time basis, without reserve or deduction for inability or failure to collect, and including income of every kind related to the franchised business. Gross sales do not include excise or sales taxes paid to the government. To compute gross sales, you should deduct the amount of over-rings, refunds, allowances or discounts to customers. (*See* Attachment E of the Franchise Agreement for our definition of Gross Sales).

OPERATING COSTS AND EXPENSES

The average gross retail sales described in this Item do not include average costs and expenses necessary to operate your GNC Store as experienced by GNC franchisees in certain categories, including but not limited to the following: (1) Fixed Expenses - Occupancy, Local Advertising, National Advertising, Royalties, and POS Maintenance; (2) Variable Expenses - Cost of Sales, Wages, and Benefits, Debt Service, Income Taxes, Depreciation, Supply Expenses, Janitorial Services, Telephone Expenses, Credit Card Expenses, Travel/Entertainment and Discretionary Expenses; and (3) Initial Start-up Expenses - initial franchise fee, Initial Promotional Materials, Construction Handling Fees, Security Deposits, Additional Site Selection Assistance, Initial Training Costs, and Miscellaneous Opening Costs. (*See* Items 7 and 8 of this Disclosure Document for further explanation.)

Actual gross sales and earnings capability will vary depending upon the expenses noted above, as well as a variety of internal and external factors which we cannot estimate, such as: general population of the market, general economic conditions in the market, recognition and brand patronage, the products offered in your Store, competition and price of competitive products and services in the market, your ability to generate repeat customers and create customer loyalty, acquisitions and strategic alliances, competition, e-commerce, new regulations of the supplement industry, taxes, differences in management skills and experience levels, the availability of financing, general economic climate, demographics, Store location, Store size, discounts, and changing consumer preferences. In addition, promotions and discounts we may institute to maintain market share in the increasingly competitive nutritional supplement environment may potentially reduce your earnings capability.

We cannot estimate the results of a particular franchise, and make no guarantee or assertion that you will attain the results set forth in this Item. We strongly recommend that you make your own independent investigation of whether or not the franchise may be "profitable", and confer with your attorney, accountant, or other business advisor before executing any agreement with us.

We will provide you with substantiation for the data set forth in this Item upon reasonable request.

Information specific to California is listed on the Addendum attached to this Disclosure Document.

NOTE:

1.   The figures contained in this Item were compiled by us based upon the reports generated from our franchisees' POS Cash Registers (*See* Item 11). We have not audited this information, nor independently verified this information. Thus, this information has not been separately audited by an independent certified public accountant, and it may not have been prepared on a basis consistent with generally accepted accounting principles.

LEARNING EXPRESS

29 Buena Vista St.
Devens, MA 01434
Tel: (888) 825-3619 (843) 352-4222
Fax: (843) 352-4223
E-Mail: wes@learningexpress.com
Web Site: www.learningexpress.com
Mr. Wes McAden, National Sales Director

Largest franchisor of specialty toy stores in the United states, currently operating in 26 states. Average sales significantly out-performs independent operators. Comprehensive training and turn-key services by franchisor.

BACKGROUND: IFA MEMBER

Established: 1987;	1st Franchised: 1990
Franchised Units:	139
Company-Owned Units:	0
Total Units:	139
Dist.:	US-139; CAN-0; O'seas-0
North America:	26 States, 0 Provinces
Density:	12 in FL, 13 in NJ, 14 in TX
Projected New Units (12 Months):	10-20

Qualifications:	4, 3, 2, 3, 1, 5
Registered:	CA,DC,FL,IL,IN,MD,MI,MN,ND,NY,OR,RI,SD,VA, WA,WI,AB

FINANCIAL/TERMS:

Cash Investment:	$100K-125K
Total Investment:	$207.5K-384.5K
Minimum Net Worth:	$300K
Fees: Franchise -	$35K
Royalty - 5%;	Ad. - NR
Earnings Claims Statement:	Yes
Term of Contract (Years):	10/10
Avg. # Of Employees:	2 FT, 8-10 PT
Passive Ownership:	Allowed, But Discouraged
Encourage Conversions:	NA
Area Develop. Agreements:	No
Sub-Franchising Contracts:	No
Expand In Territory:	Yes
Space Needs:	2,500-3,000 SF; FS,RM, Lifestyle Centers, Grocery Centers, Town Centers

SUPPORT & TRAINING:

Financial Assistance Provided:	No
Site Selection Assistance:	Yes
Lease Negotiation Assistance:	Yes
Co-Operative Advertising:	Yes
Franchisee Assoc./Member:	Yes/Member
Size Of Corporate Staff:	25

On-Going Support:	C,D,E,F,G,H,I	SPECIFIC EXPANSION PLANS:	
Training:	As Needed Certified Store;	US:	Yes, All United States
	8 Days Home Office;4 WeeksOn-Site	Canada:	No
		Overseas:	No

ITEM 19
FINANCIAL PERFORMANCE REPRESENTATIONS

A.   Based upon the performance of Local Store Franchises which were in operation for the entire calendar year reported below, as well as the entire calendar year prior, (Same Store Sales), We are providing a disclosure of the actual Gross Revenues reported to Us by those stores. These revenue figures are of specific operations and should not be considered as the actual or potential sales or earnings figures which any other franchisee could realize. We do not represent that any Local Store Franchise can expect to attain these figures.

It is the nature of the toy industry where some year's sales fluctuate dramatically year over year due to the availability of a certain product that is in high demand by the consumer.

The Average Same Store Sales* for the Past Three Years Are as Follows:

2007 (90 stores)	$ 966,108**
2006 (89 stores)	$ 825,609
2005 (76 stores)	$ 767,893

*We define Same Store Sales as a store open in the same location for the entire year and all of the previous year as well.

** In 2007, these Same Store Sales included Satellite and Temporary Locations.

B.   Based upon the performance of Local Store Franchises for which 2007 was their First Full Year of operation, We are providing a disclosure of the actual Gross Revenues reported to Us by those stores. These revenue figures are of specific operations and should not be considered as the actual or potential sales or earnings figures which any other franchisee could realize. We do not represent that any Local Store Franchise can expect to attain these figures in its First Full Year.

The Average Sales for Stores Open Their First Full Year** Are as Follows:

2007 (11 stores)	$ 828,406
2006 (16 stores)	$ 707,711
2005 (13 stores)	$ 579,974

**We define First Full Year as a store open at the same location for all of 2007.

Of the 133 Stores operating in 2007, We had 32 multiple Store Owners operating 71 Stores in Our system.

Of the 133 Stores, sales per square foot (of retail selling space) ranged between $140.00 sq. ft. to $909.00 sq. ft. and the total store size ranged from 800 sq. ft. to 5,350 sq. ft.

The above figures (which reflect Gross Sales, not profits) were calculated based upon information reported to Us by franchisees in their monthly royalty reports. Accordingly the above figures have not been audited.

The above figures do not reflect the costs of sales, operating expenses or other costs and expenses that must be deducted from the gross revenue or gross sales figures to obtain Your net income or profit. You should conduct an independent investigation of the costs and expenses You will incur in operating Your Learning Express Store.

Actual results vary from store to store, and We cannot estimate the results of any particular Store. Although some stores have achieved the above Gross Sales, the Gross Sales and financial

results of Your Store are likely to differ from the figures stated above, and there is no assurance that You will do as well. If You rely upon the above figures, You must accept the risk of not doing as well. The average unit included in the above calculations for same store sales is a mature unit; accordingly, a new franchisee's individual Gross Sales and financial results are likely to differ from the results stated above. Further, Your Gross Sales and Your financial results will depend upon, among other things, factors including Your location, local and national economic conditions; how much You follow Our methods and procedures; Your management skill, experience and business acumen; whether You personally manage Your Store or hire a manager; the region in which Your Store is located; whether the premises is in a new or existing center; the physical size and location of Your Store; the condition of the premises and the amount and nature of tenant improvements required; the competition in Your local market; the prevailing wage rate; and the sales level reached during the initial period.

Written substantiation of the data used in preparing the earnings claim will be made available to You upon reasonable request.

MERLE NORMAN COSMETICS

9130 Bellanca Ave.
Los Angeles, CA 90045-4710
Tel: (800) 421-6648 (310) 641-3000
Fax: (310) 337-2370
E-Mail: claporta@merlenorman.com
Web Site: www.merlenorman.com
Ms. Carol LaPorta, VP Studio Development

MERLE NORMAN COSMETICS is a specialty retail store, selling scientifically developed, state-of-the-art cosmetic products, using the 'free make over' and 'try before you buy' complete customer satisfaction methods of selling.

BACKGROUND: IFA MEMBER

Established: 1931;	1st Franchised: 1989
Franchised Units:	1936
Company-Owned Units:	4
Total Units:	1940
Dist.:	US-1830; CAN-90; O'seas-20
North America:	50 States, 1 Provinces
Density:	99 in AL, 113 in GA, 260 in TX
Projected New Units (12 Months):	120
Qualifications:	3, 4, 3, 3, 4, 4
Registered:CA,DC,FL,HI,IL,IN,MD,MI,MN,ND,NY,OR,RI,SD, VA,WA,WI	

FINANCIAL/TERMS:

Cash Investment:	NR
Total Investment:	$28.5K
Minimum Net Worth:	NR
Fees: Franchise -	$0
Royalty - 0%;	Ad. - 0%
Earnings Claims Statement:	Yes
Term of Contract (Years):	Unlimited
Avg. # Of Employees:	2 FT, 2-5 PT
Passive Ownership:	Allowed, But Discouraged
Encourage Conversions:	No
Area Develop. Agreements:	No
Sub-Franchising Contracts:	No
Expand In Territory:	Yes
Space Needs:	450-800 SF; SC,RM

SUPPORT & TRAINING:

Financial Assistance Provided:	Yes (I)
Site Selection Assistance:	Yes
Lease Negotiation Assistance:	Yes
Co-Operative Advertising:	Yes
Franchisee Assoc./Member:	No
Size Of Corporate Staff:	630
On-Going Support:	B,C,D,E,F,G,H,I
Training:	2 Weeks Los Angeles, CA

SPECIFIC EXPANSION PLANS:

US:	Yes, All United States
Canada:	Yes, All Canada, except Quebec
Overseas:	No

ITEM 19
FINANCIAL PERFORMANCE REPRESENTATIONS

Except as set forth in this Item 19, MNC does not furnish or authorize its salespersons to furnish any oral or written information concerning the actual or potential sales, costs, income or profits of a Merle Norman Studio. Actual results vary from Studio to Studio and MNC cannot estimate the results of any particular Studio.

MNC does not receive from its Studio Owners any statements regarding the dollar amount of a Studio Owner's retail sales of MN Products, nor does MNC receive from its Studio Owners any statements regarding a Studio Owner's total sales, expenses, costs or profits. Since MNC does not have this information, this financial performance representation only provides information as to the dollar amount of purchases of MN Products by New Design Studios and the retail value of those purchases.

Studio Owners are permitted to sell other merchandise (in addition to MN Products) and to offer other services (in addition to free makeover lessons using the lesson material provided by MNC). While MNC has not formally surveyed its Studio system, MNC believes that virtually all Studios sell merchandise in addition to MN Products and/or offer other services. Accordingly, the dollar amounts listed below as the "Retail Value of Purchases from MNC" are not intended to represent the total sales volume of any New Design Studio(s). MNC is unable to estimate what percentage MN Products comprise of a Studio's total sales.

As mentioned in Item 1, in 1998, MNC completed the development of the New Design, the most significant elements of which include an "open-sell" layout where merchandise is displayed for easy viewing and access; a design that supports either customer self-service or beauty consultant assisted service; perimeter wall fixtures; consultation areas consisting of tables and stools; a tester area; a graphic image display/focal wall; and a cash and wrap area in matching finish.

Existing Studios are not required to implement the New Design; however, as of December 31, 2007, 724 U.S. Studios had implemented the New Design. A total of 395 Studios (111 Studios in regional malls and 284 Studios in non-mall locations) operated in the United States under the New Design during the one-year period from January 1, 2007 through December 31, 2007. This financial performance representation relates only to those 395 New Design Studios.

The following information relates to the 111 U.S. New Design Studios located in regional malls that operated under the New Design for the one-year period January 1, 2007 through December 31, 2007.

REGIONAL MALL LOCATIONS

	PURCHASES FROM MNC PER STUDIO (1)	RETAIL VALUE OF PURCHASES FROM MNC (2)
LOW	$23,055.99	$48,033.31
HIGH	$337,638.67	$703,413.90
AVERAGE	$106,754.05	$222,404.26
MEDIAN	$100,046.72	$208,430.67

The following information relates to the 284 U.S. New Design Studios located in non-mall locations that operated under the New Design for the one-year period January 1, 2007 through December 31, 2007.

NON-MALL LOCATIONS

	PURCHASES FROM MNC PER STUDIO (1)	RETAIL VALUE OF PURCHASES FROM MNC (2)
LOW	$589.35	$1,227.81
HIGH	$257,560.90	$536,585.21
AVERAGE	$47,793.77	$99,570.35

MEDIAN	$40,796.73	$84,993.18

NOTES

(1)   The information in this column represents the purchases from MNC of MN Products by these 395 New Design Studios. MNC sells each of its products to all U.S. Studio Owners at the same wholesale price.

(2)   As noted above, Studio Owners are not required to provide MNC any statements regarding a Studio's sales of MN Products. For each cosmetic product MNC sells to its Studio Owners, MNC establishes a suggested retail price. The wholesale price paid to MNC varies from product to product, ranging from 40% to 50% of the suggested retail price so that the gross profit percentage on individual products ranges from 50% to 60%. The percentage gross profit that a particular Studio will realize during any period of operations from its sales of MN Products will depend on whether the Studio Owner adheres to the suggested retail prices and on the mix of products the Studio sells.

The information in this column is based on the assumption that sales of all MN Products by the 395 New Design Studios included in this financial performance representation were at the suggested retail price, and that the mix of sales of each such Studio was the same as the mix of sales by MNC to its Studios during calendar year 2007. Based on these assumptions, each Studio would have a gross profit percentage of 48%. The information in this column represents the retail value of MN Products purchased by the 395 New Design Studios utilizing this gross profit percentage.

END OF NOTES

In addition to the preceding Notes, the following material factors should be considered in reviewing this financial performance representation:

1.   Studio Owners are not required to purchase any specified amount of MN Products from MNC, other than the initial order of MN Products. (*See* Items 5 and 6.)

2.   As noted above, Studio Owners are not required to provide MNC any statements regarding a Studio's total sales, nor are Studio Owners required to provide MNC any information regarding their expenses, costs or profits. This financial performance representation does not provide any information regarding total sales, expenses, costs or profits.

3.   A small number of Studio Owners who operate multiple Studios may regularly, or frequently, order MN Products for all of their Studios through one Studio, so that the purchases recorded on MNC's records for each of these Studios do not accurately reflect the purchases of MN Products for each Studio. With respect to the New Design Studios included in this financial performance representation, where MNC has determined that such activity is occurring, the purchases of each such Studio are, for purposes of this financial performance representation, calculated by aggregating all purchases by that Studio Owner and allocating purchases of MN Products to each Studio owned by that Studio Owner in the ratio of the purchases of all United States Studios of the same type and location to total purchases of all Studios in the United States.

4.   As noted above, Studio Owners are permitted to sell merchandise (in addition to MN Products) and to offer other services (in addition to free makeover lessons using the lesson material provided by MNC). Accordingly, the percentage of a Studio's business that consists of MN Products can vary widely.

5.   The Studios included in this financial performance representation that are located in regional malls include Studios in super regional malls and regional malls. According to the 2008 definitions of shopping centers published by the International Council of Shopping Centers, a super regional mall has a gross leasable area of at least 800,000 square feet and is built around at least 3 department stores with a primary trade area of 5-25 miles, and a regional mall has a gross leasable area of 400,000 to 800,000 square feet and is built around at least 2 department stores with a primary

trade area of 5-15 miles.

6.   The Studios included in this financial performance representation that are located in non- mall locations operate in a variety of retail settings, including community shopping centers, neighborhood centers, strip centers, office complexes and central business districts.

7.   The New Design Studios included in this financial performance representation are located in the following states:

STATE	NUMBER OF NEW DESIGN STUDIOS	REGIONAL MALL LOCATIONS	NON-MALL LOCATIONS
Alabama	18	3	15
Arizona	5	3	2
Arkansas	16	5	11
California	21	7	14
Colorado	5	4	1
Connecticut	1	0	1
Delaware	1	0	1
Florida	27	7	20
Georgia	27	3	24
Hawaii	1	1	0
Idaho	2	2	0
Illinois	14	3	11
Indiana	17	7	10
Iowa	3	2	1
Kansas	2	1	1
Kentucky	13	5	8
Louisiana	7	4	3
Maryland	4	4	0
Massachusetts	1	0	1
Michigan	6	4	2
Minnesota	4	0	4
Mississippi	10	2	8
Missouri	4	1	3
Montana	1	0	1
Nebraska	1	1	0
Nevada	1	0	1
New Jersey	2	1	1
New Mexico	1	0	1
New York	5	3	2
North Carolina	25	6	19
North Dakota	4	2	2
Ohio	11	2	9
Oklahoma	15	1	14
Oregon	5	1	4
Pennsylvania	6	2	4
South Carolina	15	1	14
Tennessee	20	6	14
Texas	53	14	39

Utah	1	0	1
Virginia	8	0	8
Washington	2	0	2
West Virginia	5	1	4
Wisconsin	5	2	3
Totals:	395	111	284

This financial performance representation was prepared by MNC and was not independently audited. The statements of purchases of MN Products by these 395 New Design Studios were based upon data utilizing a uniform accounting method. Upon your reasonable request, we will make available data substantiating the figures presented in this statement.

The information in this Item does not reflect the cost of sales, operating expenses or other costs or expenses that must be deducted from the gross revenue or gross sales figures to obtain your net income or profit. You should conduct an independent investigation of the costs and expenses you will incur in operating a Studio. Franchisees or former franchisees, listed in this Disclosure Document, may be one source of this information.

THIS FINANCIAL PERFORMANCE REPRESENTATION RELATES TO SPECIFIC MERLE NORMAN STUDIOS THAT HAVE IMPLEMENTED THE NEW DESIGN AND SHOULD NOT BE CONSIDERED AS THE ACTUAL OR POTENTIAL PURCHASES OF MN PRODUCTS OR RETAIL SALES OF MN PRODUCTS THAT WILL BE REALIZED BY ANY STUDIO OWNER WHO IMPLEMENTS THE NEW DESIGN. MNC DOES NOT REPRESENT THAT ANY STUDIO OWNER CAN EXPECT TO ATTAIN SUCH RESULTS WHETHER OR NOT THE NEW DESIGN IS IMPLEMENTED. A STUDIO OWNER'S PURCHASES AND RETAIL SALES ARE LIKELY TO DIFFER FROM THAT STATED IN THIS CLAIM.

PEARLE VISION®
Nobody cares for eyes more than Pearle®

PEARLE VISION

4000 Luxottica Pl.
Mason, OH 45040
Tel: (800) 732-7531 (513) 765-3462
Fax: (513) 492-3462
E-Mail: mlichten@luxotticaretail.com
Web Site: www.pearlevision.com
Mr. Ray Kirmeyer, Manager Franchise Development

PEARLE VISION, the largest optical franchisor, offers the ability for qualified individuals to benefit from PEARLE's strong name recognition and operating systems developed over the past 36 years. We have been franchising for 16 years.

BACKGROUND: IFA MEMBER

Established: 1961;	1st Franchised: 1980
Franchised Units:	402
Company-Owned Units:	499
Total Units:	901
Dist.:	US-813; CAN-103; O'seas-36
North America:	43 States, 2 Provinces

Density:	53 in IL, 65 in PA, 48 in TX
Projected New Units (12 Months):	25
Qualifications:	5, 4, 5, 3, 2, 4
Registered:	DC,FL,HI,IL,IN,MD,MI,MN,ND,NY,OR,RI,SD,VA,WI

FINANCIAL/TERMS:

Cash Investment:	$35-125K
Total Investment:	$250-500K
Minimum Net Worth:	Varies
Fees: Franchise -	$30K
Royalty - 7%;	Ad. - 8%
Earnings Claims Statement:	No
Term of Contract (Years):	10/10
Avg. # Of Employees:	Varies FT, 0 PT
Passive Ownership:	Not Allowed
Encourage Conversions:	Yes
Area Develop. Agreements:	No
Sub-Franchising Contracts:	No
Expand In Territory:	Yes
Space Needs:	1,800-2,400 SF; FS,SC,RM

SUPPORT & TRAINING:

Financial Assistance Provided:	No
Site Selection Assistance:	No
Lease Negotiation Assistance:	No

Co-Operative Advertising:	Yes		
Franchisee Assoc./Member:	Yes/Member	**SPECIFIC EXPANSION PLANS:**	
Size Of Corporate Staff:	250	US:	Yes, All U.S. Except CA
On-Going Support:	a,B,C,D,E,F,G,h	Canada:	No
Training: Varies Dramatically Skill Assessment of Franchisee		Overseas:	No

Item 19
Financial Performance Representations

The information set forth below is based on unaudited financial information for certain Franchised Stores that were operational for all of calendar years 2007 and 2006—specifically, 230 of the 403 stores that were operated by Pearle Vision Franchisees during all of the 2007 calendar year, and 243 of the 439 stores that were operated by Pearle Vision Franchisees during all of the 2006 calendar year. (See Explanatory Notes, for additional information regarding the Franchised Stores that were included) These results are based on unaudited financial statements submitted to us by Pearle Vision Franchisees for the included stores. While we routinely review Franchisee financial statements, we have not investigated or audited them, and we therefore are unable to independently verify the accuracy of this information.

Net Dispensing Sales. The table below shows net dispensing sales for the respective reporting stores in 2007 and 2006. *"Net Dispensing Sales"* for this purpose is net income from sales of prescription and non-prescription eyeglasses, contact lenses, optical goods and services, after all discounts. You should note that this figure may, or may not, be lower than "Gross Revenues" (See Note 2 in the table presented in Item 6 "Other Fees" of this disclosure document for more information regarding how royalties are calculated), depending upon the accounting policies applied by the Franchisee. This figure should give you an idea of the amount of business generated by our stores through the sale of eyeglasses (note that Net Dispensing Sales does not include income from optometric professionals working in the store or in adjoining premises).

Selected Financial Data (Note 1)	2007	2006
Range of Reported Net Dispensing Sales	$115 to $3,084	$117 to $2,782
Average (Mean) Net Dispensing Sales (Note 2)	$747	$732
Median Net Dispensing Sales (Note 3)	$619	$616

Notes:

1.   All dollar amounts are in thousands (000s).

2.   In 2007, a total of 89 stores (39%) reported Net Dispensing Sales in excess of the average Net Dispensing Sales for the year; in 2006, 94 stores (39%) exceeded average Net Dispensing Sales for the year. This analysis includes data for both Express Stores (which include a finishing and surfacing lab) and "mainline" stores (both No-Lab Stores and Finishing Stores). As noted in Item 1, we no longer issue franchise agreements for new Express Stores. If separated out, Express Stores reported average (mean) Net Dispensing Sales of $1,095 in 2007 and $980 in 2006, while mainline stores reported average Net Dispensing Sales of $605 in 2007 and $609 in 2006.

3.   In both years, 50% of the stores (115 in 2007 and 122 in 2006) reported Net Dispensing Sales in excess of the median Net Dispensing Sales for the year.

Gross Margin. The next table shows Gross Margin Percentage for the respective reporting stores in 2007 and 2006. *"Gross Margin Percentage"* for this purpose is the percentage of Net Dispensing Sales (as defined above) remaining after deducting cost of sales (but no other expenses). This will provide you with some information about the amount available to our Pearle Vision Franchisees to pay salaries of their employees, rent, utilities, and other operating expenses they incur.

Selected Financial Data	2007	2006
Range of Reported Gross Margin Percentages	35.9% to 93.6%	38.9% to 89%
Average (Mean) Gross Margin Percentages (Note 4)	66.9%	69.1%
Median Gross Margin Percentages (Note 5)	68.4%	69.8%

Notes:

4.   In 2007, a total of 138 stores (60%) reported Gross Margin Percentage in excess of the average Gross Margin Percentage for the year; in 2006, 132 stores (54%) reported Gross Margin Percentage in excess of the average Gross Margin Percentage for that year. The reported Gross Margin Percentages did not vary substantially for Express Stores and mainline stores.

5.   In both years, 50% of the stores (115 in 2007 and 122 in 2006) reported Gross Margin Percentage in excess of the median Gross Margin Percentage for the year.

Explanatory Notes:

a.   The Franchised Stores included in these calculations are located in 34 states. As of the end of 2007, those Franchised Stores ranged in age from 1 to approximately 25 years; 110 of the Franchised Stores included in the sample had been open for at least ten years, and 48 of the Franchised Stores had been open at least 5 years but less than 10 years. The Franchised Stores were located within a broad range of commercial areas, and included single store markets, suburban communities, and urban population centers.

b.   This analysis is based on the results of 230 of the 403 Franchised Stores that were operated by Pearle Vision Franchisees during all of the 2007 calendar year, and 243 of the 439 Franchised Stores that were operated by Pearle Vision Franchisees during all of the 2006 calendar year. The Franchised Stores included in the analysis for 2007 are not necessarily the same Franchised Stores for which data was included for the analysis in 2006, so the differing results may be an artifact of reports from different Franchised Stores rather than the result of year-over-year changes in performance. The analysis includes data from all Franchised Stores operated during the relevant calendar year except the following Franchised Stores: (i) Franchised Stores that were transferred during the respective years (8 during 2007; 12 during 2006); (ii) Franchised Stores that closed during the respective years (34 during 2007; 39 during 2006); (iii) Franchised Stores that were new openings during the respective years (16 during 2007; 9 during 2006); (iv) Franchised Stores that had a different fiscal year end (26 during 2007; 27 during 2006); or (v) Franchised Stores for which we did not receive financial statements from the Franchisee in time for these calculations (173 during 2007; 105 during 2006).

c.   Factors that could affect financial results at a particular store include size of the store; how closely the Designated Operator of the store follows our methods and procedures; the management skills, experience, and business acumen of the Designated Operator; the extent to which the Franchisee is actively involved in store operations; demographics of the population within the store's trading area; the number of consumers utilizing managed vision care programs within the store's trading area; availability of an on-site professional to perform eye exams; state licensing requirements or prohibitions that may require changes in critical operational aspects of the store; access to the store (including temporary construction of surrounding facilities which may impair visibility of or access to the store); local economic conditions; and the competitive set in the area, such as the number of competitors (including the number of other Company or Franchised Stores) located in or near the Franchised Store.

d.   As compared to the Franchised Stores we are offering pursuant to this Disclosure Document, we provided substantially the same products, services, training, and support to all of the Franchised Stores the results of which were included in this calculation, and the Franchised Stores offered substantially the same products and services to the public, except that Express Stores also have an on-site surfacing lab *(See:* Note 2, above, for a discussion of the effect on average Net Dispensing Sales in Express Stores as compared to mainline stores).

Substantiation of the data used in preparing this calculation will be made available upon reasonable request.

Except for the information in this <u>Item 19,</u> we do not make any representations about a Franchisee's future financial performance or the past financial performance of company-owned or franchised outlets. We also do not authorize our employees or representatives to make any representations either orally or in writing, except as contained in this <u>Item 19.</u> If you are purchasing a Company Conversion Store, however, we may provide you with the actual records of that store. If you receive any other financial performance information or projections of your future income, you should report it to our management by contacting Andra Terrell at 4000 Luxottica Place, Mason, Ohio 45040; telephone number (513) 765-4018, the Federal Trade Commission, and the appropriate state regulatory agencies.

This financial performance data is compiled from the results of specific Franchised Stores and should not be considered as the actual or probable Net Dispensing Sales or Gross Margin Percentage that you will realize. We do not represent that any Franchisee can expect to attain the same or similar actual or average results. Actual results vary from store to store and we cannot estimate the results of any particular franchise. We encourage you to review this material with your attorney or accountant.

SHOEB🌸X
NEW YORK

SHOEBOX NEW YORK

1346 Oakbrook Drive Ste 170
Norcross, GA 30093
Tel: 1-800-524-6444 770-514-4500
Fax: 770-514-4903
E-Mail: franchiseinfo@nexcenfm.com
Web Site: www.shoeboxny.com
Mr. Martin Amschler, Chief Development Officer

Since 1954, Shoebox New York has been New York's top multi-branded women's retailer for luxury and designer footwear, handbags & accessories. Shoebox New York's reputation is built on its vast product assortment & trend-setting styles, offering women the latest fashions from top European & American designers. Shoebox New York's exceptional product offering, personalized customer experience & trendy new store design have gained a dedicated following of sophisticated women worldwide.

North America:	2 States, 0 Provinces
Density:	NR
Projected New Units (12 Months):	70
Qualifications:	5, 5, 4, 4, 4, 3
Registered:	CA,DC,FL,HI,IL,IN,MD,MI,MN,ND,NY,OR,RI,SD, VA,WA,WI,AB

FINANCIAL/TERMS:

Cash Investment:	$150,000
Total Investment:	$390,450-840,900
Minimum Net Worth:	$350,000
Fees: Franchise -	$39,900
Royalty - 5%;	Ad. - 2%
Earnings Claims Statement:	No
Term of Contract (Years):	10/5
Avg. # Of Employees:	10 FT, 5 PT
Passive Ownership:	Allowed, But Discouraged
Encourage Conversions:	NA
Area Develop. Agreements:	Yes
Sub-Franchising Contracts:	No
Expand In Territory:	Yes
Space Needs:	1000-2000 SF; FS,SF,SC

BACKGROUND: IFA MEMBER

Established: 1954;	1st Franchised: 2008
Franchised Units:	10
Company-Owned Units:	0
Total Units:	10
Dist.:	US-9; CAN-0; O'seas-1

SUPPORT & TRAINING:

Financial Assistance Provided:	No
Site Selection Assistance:	Yes
Lease Negotiation Assistance:	Yes
Co-Operative Advertising:	No

Franchisee Assoc./Member:	Yes/Not a Member	**SPECIFIC EXPANSION PLANS:**	
Size Of Corporate Staff:	135	US:	Yes
On-Going Support:	A,B,C,D,E,F,G,H,I	Canada:	Yes
Training:	NR	Overseas:	Yes

ITEM 19
FINANCIAL PERFORMANCE REPRESENTATIONS

The following provides the gross sales and certain cost information for calendar year 2007 for certain of the founder-operated Stores that are owned and operated by SB Holding's predecessor, TSBI, and its subsidiaries. See Item 1 for more information regarding TSBI and its subsidiaries.

The financial performance data included in this Item 19 is based on the actual historic operations of the eight founder-operated Stores that have been operating for a minimum of two years prior to September 22, 2008. Excluded from this data is one founder-operated Store located on 88th Street and Madison Avenue, New York, New York, which has been open for less than two years. The average operating years of the founder-operated Stores included in this Item 19 is 17years.

The founder-operated Stores operate under the mark "THE SHOE BOX" and "SHOE BOX". TSBI and its affiliates founded the SHOEBOX NEW YORK franchise concept and have operated Stores since 1954.

The gross sales and cost information provided in this Item 19 are based upon sales reported to us by TSBI. We have not independently verified the information contained in this Item 19. NEITHER TSBI NOR WE HAVE AUDITED THE INFORMATION CONTAINED IN THIS ITEM 19.

You should take into consideration that seven of the eight Stores upon which this statement is based are founder-operated Stores located in the greater metropolitan New York area, which includes Long Island (the "New York Market"). The New York Market is where the brand was founded in 1954, and has a significant market presence. Because seven of the eight founder-operated Stores used to form the data included in this Item 19 operate in a part of the country in which the SHOE BOX brand has a significant market presence and because, as stated above, all of the founder-operated Stores were operating for at least 2 years prior to September 22, 2008, this Item 19 does not reflect Store operations during start-up. In addition, the New York Market for better footwear, handbags, and accessories is well-developed, and may be more developed than other areas in the United States. The founder-operated Stores are also operated by a management team that has extensive experience in the retail footwear industry and the operation and management of retail footwear stores. In addition, the products offered by the founder-operated Stores may not be the same as the products available and or approved to be offered at a franchised Store.

The Store gross sales and expenses incurred will vary from Store to Store. The total gross sales and expenses of your Stores will be directly affected by many factors such as the Store's size, geographic location, competition in the marketplace, population within trade area, economic demographics, level and quality of marketing expenditures, the presence of other Stores, the quality of management and service at the Store, contractual relationships with lessors and vendors, the extent to which you finance the construction and operation of a Store, your legal, accounting, real estate and other professional fees, federal, state, local gross profits or other taxes, discretionary expenditures, and accounting methods used. Certain benefits and economies of scale that TSBI and its subsidiaries may obtain as a result of operating Stores on a consolidated basis may not be available to you. Therefore, you should use this statement only as a reference to conduct your own analysis.

YOU ARE URGED TO CONSULT WITH APPROPRIATE FINANCIAL, BUSINESS AND LEGAL ADVISERS TO CONDUCT YOUR OWN ANALYSIS WITH THE INFORMATION CONTAINED IN THIS STATEMENT.

The financial performance data does not relate to the performance of any franchisees or any subset of franchisees. The founder-operated stores operate under the terms of a License Agreement dated January 15, 2008.

THIS ITEM 19 <u>IS NOT BASED UPON THE ACTUAL EXPERIENCE OF FRANCHISED SHOE-BOX NEW YORK STORES.</u> NO FRANCHISED STORES ARE IN OPERATION AS OF SEPTEMBER 22, 2008. THE AVERAGE SALES, COSTS, INCOME OR PROFITS REFLECTED IN THIS ITEM 19 <u>ARE OF THE FOUNDER-OPERATED STORES,</u> AND SHOULD NOT BE CONSIDERED AS THE ACTUAL OR POTENTIAL SALES, COSTS, INCOME OR PROFITS THAT YOU WILL REALIZE. WE DO NOT REPRESENT THAT ANY FRANCHISEE CAN EXPECT TO ACHIEVE THE SAME SALES, COSTS, INCOME OR PROFITS OR ANY PARTICULAR LEVEL OF SALES, COSTS, INCOME OR PROFITS. IN ADDITION, WE DO NOT REPRESENT THAT ANY FRANCHISEE WILL DERIVE INCOME THAT EXCEEDS ITS INITIAL INVESTMENT IN A STORE. YOUR SUCCESS LARGELY WILL DEPEND ON YOUR ABILITY, AND THE INDIVIDUAL FINANCIAL RESULTS OF ANY STORE ARE LIKELY TO DIFFER FROM THE INFORMATION DESCRIBED IN THIS ITEM 19. SUB-STANTIATION OF THE DATA USED IN PREPARING THIS ITEM 19 WILL BE MADE AVAILABLE ON REASONABLE REQUEST.

THIS STATEMENT DOES NOT INCLUDE ANY ESTIMATES OF FEDERAL, STATE OR LOCAL INCOME TAXES THAT WOULD BE PAYABLE ON THE TAXABLE INCOME FROM THE STORE OR GROSS PROFITS TAXES THAT MAY BE APPLICABLE TO THE PARTICULAR JURIS-DICTION IN WHICH A STORE MAY BE LOCATED. EACH FRANCHISEE IS STRONGLY URGED TO CONSULT WITH ITS TAX ADVISER REGARDING THE IMPACT THAT FEDERAL, STATE AND LOCAL TAXES WILL HAVE ON THE AMOUNTS SHOWN IN THIS STATEMENT.

CERTAIN OPERATIONAL DATA
(Fiscal Year 2007)(1)

	TOTAL
Number of Stores	8
Total Sales (in thousands):	
High	$3,249,724
Low	$ 546,812
Average	$1,747,924
Average Operating Years	17 years
Number of Stores which equaled or surpassed the Average Total Sales	4
Percentage of Stores which equaled or surpassed the Average Total Sales	50%

(1) Excluded from this data is one founder-operated Store located on 88th Street and Madison Avenue, New York, New York, which has been open for less than two years.

GROSS SALES AND CERTAIN EXPENSES OF FOUNDER-OPERATED STORES
(Fiscal Year 2007)

STORE LOCATION	GROSS SALES (1)	CERTAIN EXPENSES (2)	
Manhasset, New York 2078 Northern Blvd	$3,249,724	Cost of Goods (3)	$1,573,837
		Labor Cost (4)	$536,017
		Rent & Common	$346,450

Plainview, New York 419 S Oyster Bay Rd # B	$2,691,516	Cost of Goods (3)	$1,580,014
		Labor Cost (4)	$479,212
		Rent & Common Charges (5)	$ 160,122
New York, New York 3rd St. Ave. at 77th St.	$2,484,677	Cost of Goods (3)	$1,318,590
		Labor Cost (4)	$426,714
		Rent & Common Charges (5)	$214,262
Greenvale, New York 190 Wheatley Plaza	$1,396,483	Cost of Goods (3)	$ 718,696
		Labor Cost (4)	$ 219,749
		Rent & Common Charges (5)	$ 157,739
New York, New York 3rd St. Ave. at 36th St.	$2,109,253	Cost of Goods (3)	$1,118,570
		Labor Cost (4)	$ 337,453
		Rent & Common Charges (5)	$ 187,822
New York, New York 2151 Broadway	$ 734,190	Cost of Goods(3)	$ 323,076
		Labor Cost (4)	$ 103,781
		Rent & Common Charges (5)	$ 170,131
Boca Raton, Florida 9858 Clint Moore Rd	$770,739	Cost of Goods (3)	$ 382,296
		Labor Cost (4)	$ 124,785
		Rent & Common Charges (5)	$ 71,017
Commack, New York 6401 Jericho Turnpike # A	$ 546,812	Cost of Goods (3)	$ 299,228
		Labor Cost (4)	$ 98,335
		Rent & Common Charges (5)	$ 39,016

NOTES:

(1)   Gross Sales of the founder-operated Stores for 2007 are included in the preceding information. Gross Sales includes coupons and discounts. Excluded from this data is one founder-operated Store located on 88th Street and Madison Avenue, New York, New York, which has been open for less than two years.

(2)   Expenses listed in the chart above are not exclusive. Additional items of cost and expense which you may incur include among others royalties, advertising fund contributions, other discounts and coupons, local promotional and advertising expense, health insurance, occupancy costs, bonus compensation, financing/debt service costs and expenses, credit card fees, utilities, insurance, Store opening expense, costs incurred during training (travel, meals and lodging), short/over expense, interest expense, equipment rental expense, amortization expense, depreciation, state, federal or municipal taxes, other travel expense and professional fees.

213

The earnings claims figure does not reflect costs of sales, operating expenses, or other costs or expenses that you must deduct from the gross revenues to obtain your net income or profit. You should conduct your own investigation of the costs and expenses in operating your Store. Franchisees or former franchisees, listed in the disclosure document, may be once source of the information.

(3)   Cost of goods includes cost of inventory including among others shoes, handbags and related products. Note that we do not guarantee that your Store will carry the same products as the founder-operated Stores. Freight is not included.

(4)   Includes wages and salaries for Store managers, clerks, withholding and social security and certain benefits.

(5)   Includes rent and common charges. Does not include utilities, real estate and other local taxes.

Snap-on

SNAP-ON TOOLS

2801 80th St., P.O. Box 1410
Kenosha, WI 53143
Tel: (800) 786-6600 (877) 476-2766
Fax: (262) 656-5635
E-Mail: franchiseopportunities@snapon.com
Web Site: www.snaponfranchise.com
Mr. Mike Doweidt, Director of Franchising

The premier solutions provider to the vehicle service industry. Premium quality products, delivered and sold with premium service. We are proud of our heritage and are boldly addressing the future needs of our customers with improved efficiency, creating products and services from hand tools to data and management systems. Contact us today for discussion.

BACKGROUND: IFA MEMBER
Established: 1920;   1st Franchised: 1991
Franchised Units: 4490
Company-Owned Units: 51
Total Units: 4541
Dist.:   US-3622; CAN-357; O'seas-814
  North America: 50 States, 12 Provinces
  Density: 373 in CA, 202 in PA, 245 in TX
Projected New Units (12 Months):   682
Qualifications: 3, 4, 2, 2, 5, 5
Registered:CA,DC,FL,HI,IL,IN,MD,MI,MN,ND,NY,OR,RI,SD, VA,WA,WI

FINANCIAL/TERMS:

Cash Investment:	$16.7-52K
Total Investment:	$16.7-278.4K
Minimum Net Worth:	NR
Fees: Franchise -	$5K
Royalty - $50/Mo.;	Ad. - 0%
Earnings Claims Statement:	Yes
Term of Contract (Years):	10/5
Avg. # Of Employees:	1 FT, 0 PT
Passive Ownership:	Not Allowed
Encourage Conversions:	Yes
Area Develop. Agreements:	0
Sub-Franchising Contracts:	No
Expand In Territory:	Yes
Space Needs:	SF

SUPPORT & TRAINING:

Financial Assistance Provided:	Yes (D)
Site Selection Assistance:	NA
Lease Negotiation Assistance:	NA
Co-Operative Advertising:	No
Franchisee Assoc./Member:	No
Size Of Corporate Staff:	NR
On-Going Support:	A,B,C,D,E,F,G,h,I
Training:	1 Week Branch or Regional Office; 1 Week Branch; 3 Weeks On-the-Job

SPECIFIC EXPANSION PLANS:

US:	Yes, All United States
Canada:	Yes, All Canada
Overseas:	Yes, Japan, UK, Germany, Australia, New Zealand, S. Africa

---

ITEM 19
FINANCIAL PERFORMANCE REPRESENTATIONS

Except for the financial performance representations in Appendix H., we do not furnish or authorize our employees to furnish any oral or written information concerning the potential sales, costs, income or profits of a Snap-on franchise. Results vary, and we cannot estimate the results of any particular franchisee.

APPENDIX H

STATEMENT OF "PAID SALES"
REPORTED BY SNAP-ON FRANCHISEES

The following Statement of "Paid Sales" ("Statement") illustrates the various levels of sales reported by numerous franchisees in the Snap-on system for sales activity during the 2007 reporting period. "Paid Sales" are presented in $25,000 increments. This information reflects a number of assumptions and limitations noted after the Statement, and which you should read together with the Statement.

THE NOTES THAT FOLLOW THIS STATEMENT ARE AN INTEGRAL PART OF THE STATEMENT.

REPORTED PAID SALES FOR 2007

	Number of Franchisees Reporting	%
Less than $50,000	2	0.08%
$50,000 to $74,999	2	0.08%
$75,000 to $99,999	1	0.04%
$100,000 to $124,999	9	0.34%
$125,000 to $149,999	16	0.61%
$150,000 to $174,999	19	0.72%
$175,000 to $199,999	45	1.71%
$200,000 to $224,999	72	2.73%
$225,000 to $249,999	91	3.45%
$250,000 to $274,999	135	5.12%
$275,000 to $299,999	154	5.84%
$300,000 to $324,999	181	6.86%
$325,000 to $349,999	225	8.53%
$350,000 to $374,999	217	8.23%
$375,000 to $399,999	219	8.30%
$400,000 to $424,999	194	7.35%
$425,000 to $449,999	189	7.16%
$450,000 to $474,999	164	6.22%
$475,000 to $499,999	121	4.59%
$500,000 to $524,999	127	4.81%
$525,000 to $549,999	108	4.09%
$550,000 to $574,999	71	2.69%
$575,000 to $599,999	58	2.20%
Over $600,000	218	8.26%

TOTAL	2638	100.00%

THE PAID SALES FIGURES USED IN THIS STATEMENT ARE REPORTED BY SPECIFIC FRAN-CHISEES AND SHOULD NOT BE CONSIDERED THE ACTUAL OR PROBABLE PAID SALES THAT MAY BE REALIZED BY ANY FRANCHISEE. YOUR PAID SALES MAY BE AFFECTED BY A NUMBER OF COMMERCIAL VARIABLES AND COMPETITIVE MARKET CONDITIONS. SNAP-ON DOES NOT REPRESENT THAT YOU OR ANY FRANCHISEE CAN EXPECT TO ATTAIN ANY PARTICULAR LEVEL OF PAID SALES.

NOTES

I.   Franchisee Information Included in the Statement.

We compiled the Statement from information reported to us by Snap-on franchisees. We did not verify these reports.

The Statement includes only franchisees in operation for all reporting periods during 2007.

Since the franchisees reporting Paid Sales have, for the most part, operated under a Standard Franchise Agreement the Paid Sales information presented may not be as meaningful to a prospective Gateway Franchisee.

The Statement includes only information received from franchisees who operated for all 12 months of the 2007 reporting period and for which we have received Paid Sales information for the full period. Accordingly, franchisees who began or ended operations during calendar year 2007 are not included in the Statement nor are franchisees who failed to submit all Paid Sales information for 2007. Some franchisees included in the Statement may have operated part of the year as a Trial Franchisee or Gateway Franchisee and part of the year as a Standard Franchisee, but to be included, they must have operated during the entire calendar year as a Trial Franchisee, Gateway Franchisee or a Standard Franchisee or a combination thereof. We have not attempted to verify the information received from franchisees and have no knowledge whether franchisees prepared the information submitted to us in accordance with generally accepted accounting principles.

If a franchisee operated an additional van under one Franchise Agreement, the Paid Sales of that additional van are not included in this Statement, either as sales under the franchise under which that additional van operates or as a separate franchise. If a franchisee operated an additional franchise, that additional franchise is reported as a separate "franchise" on the Statement.

The Statement does not include information on Paid Sales for Snap-on employees who sell tools and equipment to customers that are similar to a franchisee's customers or Paid Sales of Independents.

II.   Definition of "Paid Sales".

Snap-on franchisees do not have to report their total revenue to us. A franchisee's Paid Sales (defined below) should approximate "total revenues," except that a franchisee's sales of tools and equipment purchased from a source other than Snap-on and the value of tools and equipment accepted by a franchisee as a trade-in may not be included in the Paid Sales figure reported to us.

The Statement does not include information about franchisee expenses, or profits and losses; it sets forth Paid Sales only, and a prospective franchisee should discuss the significance of the numbers with an advisor of his choice.

A franchisee's Paid Sales means the sum of: (1) all of the franchisee's cash sales and revolving account collections; (2) all open account and extended credit balances assigned to Snap-on or Snap-on Credit by the franchisee; and (3) all leases assigned to Snap-on or Snap-on Credit by the franchisee. To the extent sales taxes are reported to Snap-on by franchisee, they are included in Paid Sales (each of these terms is defined below). All franchisees included in the Statement were requested to use the same definition of Paid Sales in the reports submitted to Snap-on.

216

Cash Sales – Those sales for which a franchisee receives a cash payment at the time of the sale and any cash down payment received on a revolving account or extended credit sale or a lease.

Revolving Account Collections – As described in Item 7, Revolving Account sales are credit sales between a franchisee and a franchisee's customer where a franchisee extends personal credit, usually at no interest, to finance the customer's purchase of tools and equipment. Revolving account collections are the collections made by a franchisee on revolving account financing extended by the franchisee.

Open Account Balances – Open account sales are short term credit sales made by a franchisee to businesses which the franchisee assigns to Snap-on and for which Snap-on gives the franchisee immediate credit as if the franchisee's customer had paid in cash. (*See* Item 10.) Included in Paid Sales is the dollar amount of the credit (which excludes any down payment and trade-in allowance) given to a franchisee when Snap-on accepted assignment of an open account.

Extended Credit Balances – For certain individual customer purchases a franchisee may assign to Snap-on Credit with Snap-on Credit's consent the purchase money security agreements (also referred to as the "Extended Credit Contracts") for customer purchases (*See* Item 10). Snap-on Credit credits a franchisee the net sales price (which excludes any down payment and trade-in allowance) for the tools or equipment being sold. This credit is included in Paid Sales.

Leases – For certain tools and equipment, Snap-on Credit offers businesses the opportunity to lease the products. Such a lease with a customer of a franchisee may be assigned to Snap-on Credit. Once Snap-on Credit accepts the assignment, the franchisee receives a credit calculated in the same manner as for an Extended Credit contract. This credit is included in Paid Sales (*See* Item 10).

Sales Tax – Most states require that a franchisee collect and pay sales tax on purchases made by franchisee's customers. To the extent sales taxes are reported to Snap-on by franchisee they are included in Paid Sales.

III. Other Notes and Assumptions.

Percentage totals may not equal 100% due to rounding.

Reported Paid Sales are based on franchisee reports submitted weekly and do not correspond exactly with the calendar year. Some weekly reports cover Paid Sales beginning a few days before the start of the calendar year; others end a few days after. In all cases Paid Sales figures in this Appendix reflect no more than one year's Paid Sales.

The Statement reflects the various levels of Paid Sales in all parts of the United States and the prospective franchisee should not assume that the level of sales shown will be reflected in his particular area or in his particular franchise.

Substantiation of the data used in preparing this Statement will be made available to a prospective franchisee upon reasonable request; however, no information that relates to any specific franchise will be made available.

VERLO MATTRESS FACTORY STORES
201 N. Main St. # 5
Fort Atkinson, WI 53538
Tel: (800) 229-8957 + 101 (920) 568-3100

Fax: (920) 568-3140
E-Mail: info@verlofranchise.com
Web Site: www.verlofranchise.com
Ms. Jennifer Roethe, Franchise Administrator

VERLO MATTRESS FACTORY STORES (R) is the nation's largest CRAFTSMAN DIRECT (R) retailer. Each franchise assembles custom-made mattresses to the customer's specifications. Our business model appeals to the multi-unit master because owners can penetrate markets quickly and cost-effectively.

		Avg. # Of Employees:	5 FT, 0 PT
BACKGROUND:	IFA MEMBER	Passive Ownership:	Not Allowed
Established: 1958;	1st Franchised: 1981	Encourage Conversions:	Yes
Franchised Units:	60	Area Develop. Agreements:	Yes
Company-Owned Units:	0	Sub-Franchising Contracts:	No
Total Units:	60	Expand In Territory:	Yes
Dist.:	US-60; CAN-0; O'seas-0	Space Needs:	3,000-10,000 SF; FS,SF
North America:	10 States, 0 Provinces		
Density:	4 in FL, 18 in IL, 29 in WI	**SUPPORT & TRAINING:**	
Projected New Units (12 Months):	6	Financial Assistance Provided:	Yes (I)
Qualifications:	4, 3, 2, 3, 4, 5	Site Selection Assistance:	Yes
Registered:DC,FL,IL,IN,MD,MI,MN,ND,NY,OR,RI,SD,VA,WA,		Lease Negotiation Assistance:	Yes
	WI,AB	Co-Operative Advertising:	No
		Franchisee Assoc./Member:	Yes/Member
FINANCIAL/TERMS:		Size Of Corporate Staff:	8
Cash Investment:	$50-100K	On-Going Support:	C,D,E,G,H,i
Total Investment:	$300-500K	Training:	5-10 Days Corporate Office;5-7 DaysOn-Site
Minimum Net Worth:	$350K		
Fees: Franchise -	$50K	**SPECIFIC EXPANSION PLANS:**	
Royalty - 6%;	Ad. - $400/Mo.	US:	Yes, All United States except CA, HI
Earnings Claims Statement:	Yes	Canada:	No
Term of Contract (Years):	10/10	Overseas:	No

Item 19. FINANCIAL PERFORMANCE REPRESENTATIONS

Except as attached as Exhibit J to this disclosure document, we do not furnish or authorize our salespersons (including any independent franchise broker) to furnish any oral or written information to prospective franchisees concerning the actual or potential sales, costs, income or profits of a VERLO® Mattress Factory Store. Actual results vary from Store to Store and we cannot estimate the results of any particular franchise.

Exhibit J contains a financial performance representation which includes, as qualified in Exhibit J, average annual net sales, gross profits percentage, average EBITDA before franchise owner's salary, inventory data and advertising costs information for affiliate and/or franchisee organizations (as opposed to individual Stores only) that had at least 1 Retail/Assembly Store open for all of calendar years 2004, 2005 and/or 2006. The financial results for your franchise organization are likely to differ from the information for these affiliate and franchisee organizations as described in Exhibit J. Substantiating data used to prepare the financial performance representation will be made available to you upon reasonable written request.

Exhibit J

Financial Performance Representation
Introduction

In this Exhibit, we provide various types of financial performance representations for calendar years 2004, 2005 and 2006, presenting the following information for each year:

· Average Annual Net Sales, Gross Profit Percentage, and Average EBITDA before Franchise Owner's Salary (Tables 1-A through 1-C). As further explained below:

 · For calendar year 2006, this information is presented in 3 groups: Franchise Organizations whose EBITDA dollars based ranking was in the top 26%; those whose EBITDA dollars based ranking was in the middle 48%; and, those whose EBITDA dollars based ranking was in the lower 26%;

 · For calendar year 2005, this information is presented in 3 groups: Franchise Organizations whose EBITDA dollars based ranking was in the top 24%; those whose EBITDA dollars based ranking was in the middle 52%; and, those whose EBITDA dollars based ranking was in the lower 24%;

· For calendar year 2004, this information is presented in 3 groups: Franchisee Organizations whose EBITDA dollars based ranking was in the top 27%; those whose EBITDA dollars based ranking was in the middle 46%; and, those whose EBITDA dollars based ranking was in the lower 27%; and,

· As referenced in the preceding bullets and throughout this Exhibit, "EBITDA dollars based" rankings refer to rankings based on EBITDA dollars before the franchise owner's salary.

· Inventory Turnover Ratio (noted in footers to Tables 1-A through 1-C, respectively). The Inventory Turnover Ratio figure indicates the number of times the entire inventory stock (including showroom) is sold per year by Franchisee Organizations, based on the average of Inventory Turnover Ratios for all Franchisee Organizations.

· Annual Advertising Costs Percentage (Table 1 -D). The Annual Advertising Costs Percentage is calculated by dividing the sum total of the annual advertising costs of all Franchisee Organizations by the sum total of the annual net sales reported by these Franchisee Organizations.

Please note that the following additional definitions apply throughout this Exhibit:

EBITDA:

EBITDA is an abbreviation for "Earnings Before Interest, Taxes, Depreciation and Amortization," and is calculated by taking operating income and adding back depreciation and amortization expenses. EBITDA is used to analyze a company's operating profitability before non-operating expenses and income (such as interest expense or interest income and "other" non-core expenses) and non-cash charges (depreciation and amortization).

EBITDA can be used to analyze the profitability between companies and industries. Because it eliminates the impact of financing and accounting decisions, using EBITDA generally provides a valuable "apples-to-apples" comparison mechanism. For example, the measurement of EBITDA as a percent of sales can be used to find companies that are the most efficient operators (the higher the ratio, the higher the profitability) in an industry.

Franchisee Organization:

For purposes of these financial performance representations, a "Franchisee Organization" consists of the Retail/Assembly Store, and each related Retail Satellite Store, operated under a single VERLO® MATTRESS FACTORY STORES Franchise Agreement. Therefore, a single individual, entity, or investment group might be the owner of more than one Franchisee Organization, assuming that the individual, entity, or investment group entered into more than one VERLO® MATTRESS FACTORY STORES Franchise Agreement. In order for a particular Franchisee Organization's data to be included in the respective 2004, 2005, or 2006 financial performance representations, that Franchisee Organization had to have at least 1 Store open for all of the applicable calendar year. Within some of the Franchise Organizations, however, some of the Stores represented in the financial performance representations were in operation for less than the entire calendar year. Franchisee Organizations that operated at least 1 Store for the entire 12 months in calendar 2004, 2005, or 2006, respectively, may have had 1 or more Stores (*i.e.*, Retail Satellite Stores) open for only a partial year, in which case the partial year data for those Stores is included in the financial performance representations.

Affiliate Organization:

For purposes of these financial performance representations, an "Affiliate Organization" consists of a Retail/Assembly Store, and each related Retail Satellite Store, operated by one of our affiliates in a particular geographic market.

VMFS Organization:

For purposes of these financial performance representations, a "VMFS Organization" consists of either a Franchisee Organization or an Affiliate Organization.

Select Data For Franchisee Organizations

TABLE 1-A (2004)

EBITDA Dollars Before Franchise Owner's Salary Based Ranking	2004 Average Annual Net Sales	Gross Profit Percentage	Average EBITDA Before Franchise Owner's Salary	
			$	%
Top 27% of franchisees *[7 Franchisee Organizations]*	$3,435,505 *[3 out of the 7 Franchisee Organizations exceeded this level]*	51.82% *[5 out of the 7 Franchisee Organizations exceeded this level]*	$328,959 *[4 out of the 7 Franchisee Organizations exceeded this level]*	9.58% *[5 out of the 7 Franchisee Organizations exceeded this level]*
Middle 46% of franchisees *[12 Franchisee Organizations]*	$1,021,651 *[4 out of the 12 Franchisee Organizations exceeded this level]*	50.74% *[6 out of the 12 Franchisee Organizations exceeded this level]*	$104,093 *[4 out of the 12 Franchisee Organizations exceeded this level]*	10.19% *[6 out of the 12 Franchisee Organizations exceeded this level]*
Bottom 27% of franchisees *[7 Franchisee Organizations]*	$1,106,145 *[2 out of the 7 Franchisee Organizations exceeded this level]*	51.42% *[3 out of the 7 Franchisee Organizations exceeded this level]*	($37,533) *[5 out of the 7 Franchisee Organizations exceeded this level]*	(3.39%) *[5 out of the 7 Franchisee Organizations exceeded this level]*
Average of all Franchisee Organizations *[26 Franchisee Organizations]*	$1,694,283 *[8 out of the 26 Franchisee Organizations exceeded this level]*	51.45% *[13 out of the 26 Franchisee Organizations exceeded this level]*	$126,504 *[10 out of the 26 Franchisee Organizations exceeded this level]*	7.47% *[15 out of the 26 Franchisee Organizations exceeded this level]*

2004 Inventory Turnover Ratio of Total Franchise Organization: 8.36 turns per year equates to 6.22 weeks of inventory on hand

TABLE 1-B (2005)

EBITDA Dollars Before Franchise Owner's Salary Based Ranking	2005 Average Annual Net Sales	Gross Profit Percentage	Average EBITDA Before Franchise Owner's Salary	
			$	%
Top 24% of franchisees *[7 Franchisee Organizations]*	$3,367,375 *[3 out of the 7 Franchisee Organizations exceeded this level]*	52.84% *[3 out of the 7 Franchisee Organizations exceeded this level]*	$294,769 *[2 out of the 7 Franchisee Organizations exceeded this level]*	8.75% *[5 out of the 7 Franchisee Organizations exceeded this level]*
Middle 52% of franchisees *[15 Franchisee Organizations]*	$986,193 *[8 out of the 15 Franchisee Organizations exceeded this level]*	52.31% *[7 out of the 15 Franchisee Organizations exceeded this level]*	$91,848 *[7 out of the 15 Franchisee Organizations exceeded this level]*	9.31% *[7 out of the 15 Franchisee Organizations met or exceeded this level]*

Bottom 24% of franchisees [7 Franchisee Organizations]	$1,352,745 [3 out of the 7 Franchisee Organizations exceeded this level]	51.78% [5 out of the 7 Franchisee Organizations exceeded this level]	($50,761) [5 out of the 7 Franchisee Organizations exceeded this level]	(3.75%) [5 out of the 7 Franchisee Organizations exceeded this level]
Average of all Franchisee Organizations [29 Franchisee Organizations]	$1,649,439 [10 out of the 29 Franchisee Organizations exceeded this level]	52.47% [15 out of the 29 Franchisee Organizations exceeded this level]	$106,406 [11 out of the 29 Franchisee Organizations exceeded this level]	6.45% [16 out of the 29 Franchisee Organizations exceeded this level]

2005 Inventory Turnover Ratio of Total Franchise Organization:
7.06 inventory turns per year equates to 7.36 weeks of inventory on hand

TABLE 1-C (2006)

EBITDA Dollars Before Franchise Owner's Salary Based Ranking	2006 Average Annual Net Sales	Gross Profit Percentage	Average EBITDA Before Franchise Owner's Salary $	%
Top 26% of franchisees [7 Franchisee Organizations]	$3,399,006 [3 out of the 7 Franchisee Organizations exceeded this level]	55.85% [5 out of the 7 Franchisee Organizations exceeded this level]	$342,466 [3 out of the 7 Franchisee Organizations exceeded this level]	10.08% [5 out of the 7 Franchisee Organizations exceeded this level]
Middle 48% of franchisees [13 Franchisee Organizations]	$1,256,732 [7 out of the 13 Franchisee Organizations exceeded this level]	55.09% [6 out of the 13 Franchisee Organizations exceeded this level]	$128,657 [7 out of the 13 Franchisee Organizations exceeded this level]	10.24% [7 out of the 13Franchisee Organizations exceeded this level]
Bottom 26% of franchisees [7 Franchisee Organizations]	$981,159 [2 out of the 7 Franchisee Organizations exceeded this level]	56.33% [3 out of the 7 Franchisee Organizations exceeded this level]	$14,900 [6 out of the 7 Franchisee Organizations exceeded this level]	1.52% [5 out of the 7 Franchisee Organizations exceeded this level]
Average of all Franchisee Organizations [27 Franchisee Organizations]	$1,740,692 [10 out of the 27 Franchisee Organizations exceeded this level]	55.66% [14 out of the 27 Franchisee Organizations exceeded this level]	$154,596 [11 out of the 27 Franchisee Organizations exceeded this level]	8.88% [14 out of the 27 Franchisee Organizations exceeded this level]

2006 Inventory Turnover Ratio of Total Franchise Organization:

7.80 inventory turns per year equates to 6.67 weeks of inventory on hand **TABLE 1-D (Annual Advertising Costs Percentage)**

2004	2005	2006
9.5%	9.9%	9.7%

Factual Basis and Material Assumptions (See also "Introduction")

As of July 2007, we had not received financial statements and reports from one Franchisee Organization (Verlo of Raleigh-Durham, Inc.) for the year ending December 31, 2004. This Franchisee Organization closed its VERLO® MATTRESS FACTORY STORES business operations in January 2005 and we do not anticipate receiving these missing statements and reports. Accordingly, any reference to

VMFS or Franchisee Organization statistics, data or other information in these financial performance representations does not include or factor the missing 2004 reports from this particular Franchisee Organization.

For Tables 1-A through 1-C, the data for calendar year 2004 is presented as averages of 3 groups: the average of the 7 Franchisee Organizations who had the highest EBITDA dollars based ranking, the average of the next 12 Franchisee Organizations, in terms of EBITDA dollars based ranking, and the average of the bottom 7 Franchisee Organizations, in terms of EBITDA dollars based ranking. The data for calendar year 2005 is presented as average of the 3 groups: the average of the 7 Franchisee Organizations who had the highest EBITDA dollars based ranking, the average of the next 15 Franchisee Organizations, in terms of EBITDA dollars based ranking, and the average of the bottom 7 Franchisee Organizations, in terms of EBITDA dollars based ranking. The data for calendar year 2006 is presented as averages of 3 groups: the average of the 7 Franchisee Organizations who had the highest EBITDA dollars based ranking, the average of the next 13 Franchisee Organizations, in terms of EBITDA dollars based ranking, and the average of the bottom 7 Franchisee Organizations, in terms of EBITDA dollars based ranking.

For Table 1-D, the data for each of calendar years 2004, 2005 and 2006 was compiled and is presented as the aggregate of data obtained from all Franchisee Organizations. A number of Franchisee Organizations experienced annual advertising costs percentage results substantially different from the system-wide averages provided in Table 1-D.

All of the Stores represented in any given Franchisee Organization were franchised for the period being reported. Each VMFS Organizations' business consisted of the manufacture and retail sale of mattresses, mattress sets, bedding accessories, and futons for calendar years 2004, 2005 and 2006.

We offered substantially the same services to all of the Stores described in the Tables above. These Stores offered substantially the same products and services to the public.

Source of Data

The Annual Net Sales, Gross Profit Percentages, Average EBITDA before Franchise Owner's Salary, Inventory Turnover Ratios and Annual Advertising Costs Percentage of the Franchisee and/or Affiliate Organizations were obtained from the information submitted to us by (or electronically accessed from) the applicable VMFS Organizations. Neither we nor our independent certified public accountant has independently audited or verified the data submitted by (or accessed from) Franchisee Organizations. We have no knowledge whether Franchisee Organizations prepared the information submitted to us in accordance with GAAP.

"Average EBITDA Before Owners' Salary" was calculated by taking the Franchisee Organizations' operating income, and adding back depreciation and amortization, and franchise owners' and officers' salary. "Operating income" does not take into account debt service, income taxes, gain on sale of assets, interest income or expense, or miscellaneous income.

Franchisee Organizations were instructed to calculate operating income by subtracting the following from their annual net sales: cost of sales, labor, royalties, advertising, promotional, warranty expense, bank charges and credit card fees, depreciation & amortization, donations, dues, pension & profit sharing, meals & entertainment, equipment leases, insurance (business and employee), licenses, meetings, office supplies, outside services, payroll taxes, postage, printing, professional fees, property taxes, rent, repair & maintenance, supplies (general), telephone, travel, utilities, vehicle expense and disposal fees.

Substantiation of the data used in preparing the financial performance representations will be made available to you on reasonable written request.

Factors - Varying Results

The average annual net sales, gross profit percentages, and average EBITDA before franchise owner's salary in the above financial performance representations should not be construed as the "profit" which might be experienced by a Franchisee Organization with a similar sales volume. An individual Franchisee Organization will incur various expenses for the items noted above in the third paragraph under "Source of Data." Each of these factors, as well as the actual accounting, operational and management procedures employed by a Franchisee Organization, may significantly affect profits realized in any given operation. The nature of these variables and the economic discretion exercised by individual Franchisee Organizations renders a determination of the profit level you will attain impossible to ascertain.

<u>WARNING</u>

A.   YOU ARE LIKELY TO ACHIEVE RESULTS THAT ARE DIFFERENT, POSSIBLY SIGNIFICANTLY AND ADVERSELY, FROM THE RESULTS AND STATISTICS SHOWN IN THIS FINANCIAL PERFORMANCE REPRESENTATION. MANY FACTORS, INCLUDING LOCATION, MANAGEMENT CAPABILITIES, MOTIVATION AND EFFORT, STORE SIZE AND HOURS, PROMOTIONAL ACTIVITIES, LOCAL MARKET CONDITIONS, PRICING POLICIES, MARKET DEMOGRAPHICS, AND OTHER FACTORS, ARE UNIQUE TO EACH FRANCHISEE ORGANIZATION AND MAY SIGNIFICANTLY IMPACT THE FINANCIAL PERFORMANCE OF YOUR FRANCHISEE ORGANIZATION. NEITHER WE NOR ANY OF OUR AFFILIATES MAKE ANY PROMISES OR REPRESENTATIONS OF ANY KIND THAT YOU WILL ACHIEVE ANY PARTICULAR RESULTS OR LEVEL OF SALES OR PROFITABILITY OR EVEN ACHIEVE BREAK-EVEN RESULTS IN ANY PARTICULAR YEAR OF OPERATION.

B.   YOU ARE RESPONSIBLE FOR DEVELOPING YOUR OWN BUSINESS PLAN FOR YOUR FRANCHISEE ORGANIZATION, INCLUDING CAPITAL BUDGETS, FINANCIAL STATEMENTS, PROJECTIONS AND OTHER ELEMENTS APPROPRIATE TO YOUR PARTIC-ULAR CIRCUMSTANCES. THE EXPENSES IDENTIFIED IN THIS STATEMENT ARE NOT THE ONLY EXPENSES THAT YOU WILL INCUR IN CONNECTION WITH THE OPERATION OF YOUR FRANCHISEE ORGANIZATION. WE ENCOURAGE YOU TO CONSULT WITH YOUR OWN ACCOUNTING, BUSINESS, AND LEGAL ADVISORS TO ASSIST YOU TO IDENTIFY THE EXPENSES YOU LIKELY WILL INCUR IN CONNECTION WITH YOUR STORE, TO PRE-PARE YOUR BUDGETS, AND TO ASSESS THE LIKELY OR POTENTIAL FINANCIAL PER-FORMANCE OF YOUR FRANCHISEE ORGANIZATION. WE ALSO ENCOURAGE YOU TO CONTACT EXISTING FRANCHISEE ORGANIZATIONS, AS DISCLOSED AT EXHIBIT D TO THIS DISCLOSURE DOCUMENT, TO DISCUSS THE VERLO® MATTRESS FACTORY STORES BUSINESS.

C.   IN DEVELOPING THE BUSINESS PLAN FOR YOUR FRANCHISEE ORGANI-ZATION, YOU MUST MAKE NECESSARY ALLOWANCE FOR CHANGES IN FINANCIAL RESULTS TO INCOME, EXPENSES, OR BOTH, THAT MAY RESULT FROM OPERATION OF YOUR FRANCHISEE ORGANIZATION DURING PERIODS OF, OR IN GEOGRAPHIC AREAS SUFFERING FROM, ECONOMIC DOWNTURNS, INFLATION, UNEMPLOYMENT, OR OTHER NEGATIVE ECONOMIC INFLUENCES.

D.   HISTORICAL COSTS DO NOT NECESSARILY CORRESPOND TO FUTURE COSTS BECAUSE OF FACTORS SUCH AS INFLATION, CHANGES IN MINIMUM WAGE LAWS, LOCATION, FINANCING, CONSTRUCTION COSTS, LEASE- RELATED COSTS, AND OTHER VARIABLES. FOR EXAMPLE, COSTS SUCH AS RENT, MAINTENANCE CHARGES, TAXES, INTEREST, INSURANCE AND UTILITIES VARY FROM STORE TO STORE. ALL INFORMATION SHOULD BE EVALUATED IN LIGHT OF CURRENT MARKET CONDITIONS INCLUDING SUCH COST AND PRICE INFORMATION AS MAY THEN BE AVAILABLE.

E.   THE VMFS ORGANIZATION PERFORMANCE RESULTS INCLUDED IN THIS STATEMENT RELATE TO 2006, 2005 AND 2004 PERFORMANCE RESULTS FOR THE FRAN-CHISEE AND AFFILIATE ORGANIZATIONS AND STORES INCLUDED IN THIS FINANCIAL PERFORMANCE REPRESENTATION AND SHOULD NOT BE CONSIDERED AS THE ACTUAL OR PROBABLE PERFORMANCE RESULTS THAT YOU SHOULD EXPECT TO ACHIEVE THROUGH THE OPERATION OF YOUR FRANCHISEE ORGANIZATION. YOU MUST BEAR

IN MIND THAT A NEWLY OPENED VERLO® MATTRESS FACTORY STORES BUSINESS SHOULD NOT BE EXPECTED TO ACHIEVE SALES VOLUMES OR MAINTAIN EXPENSES SIMILAR TO THOSE OF AN ESTABLISHED VERLO® MATTRESS FACTORY STORES BUSINESS.

F.   VERLO® MATTRESS FACTORY STORES FRANCHISEE ORGANIZATIONS OR STORES ARE NOT LOCATED IN ALL STATES OR IN ALL MARKETS. IF YOU ARE CONSIDERING PURCHASING A FRANCHISE TO OPERATE A VERLO® MATTRESS FACTORY STORES FRANCHISEE ORGANIZATION OR STORE IN A MARKET WHERE THERE WERE NO VMFS ORGANIZATIONS OR STORES IN OPERATION THROUGH 2004, 2005 OR 2006, THE TABLES ABOVE DEPICTING RESULTS OF AFFILIATE AND/OR FRANCHISEE ORGANIZATIONS DO NOT INCLUDE SALES OR INCOME OR OTHER RESULTS FOR SUCH MARKETS AND VERLO® MATTRESS FACTORY STORES MAY BE UNKNOWN TO CONSUMERS IN SUCH MARKETS. IN SUCH A CASE THE FOREGOING DATA WILL BE OF LESS RELEVANCE AND YOU SHOULD TAKE THIS INTO CONSIDERATION BEFORE YOU DECIDE TO PURCHASE THE FRANCHISE.

Please note that all of the Item 19s included in the 2009 Edition of "How Much Can I Make?" were taken from the respective company's 2008 Franchise Disclosure Document (FDD)/Uniform Offering Circular (UFOC). Accordingly, all of the financial data in the Item 19s refers to actual operations in 2007. In a very few cases, depending upon the date of the FDD/UFOC, the data might refer to operations in 2006. Because of the need to provide historical data, there is generally a year's lag between the date of the annual FDD/UFOC and the underlying Item 19 data.

Service-Based Franchises | 8

1-800-GOT-JUNK?
THE WORLD'S LARGEST JUNK REMOVAL SERVICE

1-800-GOT-JUNK?

1055 W. Hastings St., 6th Fl.
Vancouver, BC V6E 2E9 Canada
Tel: (866) 920-5865 (800) 468-5865
Fax: (801) 751-0634
E-Mail: franopps@1800gotjunk.com
Web Site: www.1800gotjunk.com
Ms. Colleen Ryan, Franchise Recruitment Manager

1-800-GOT-JUNK? has revolutionized customer service in junk removal for over 10 years. By setting the mark for service standards and professionalism, an industry that once operated without set rates, price lists or receipts, now has top service standards. You will have the expert advice and support that is key to success. Our intensive training program will get you on track; our on-going support and continuing education will keep you there. Centralized call center allows you to focus on your business.

BACKGROUND:	IFA MEMBER
Established: 1989;	1st Franchised: 1999
Franchised Units:	300
Company-Owned Units:	0
Total Units:	300
Dist.:	US-236; CAN-36; O'seas-4
North America:	44 States, 9 Provinces
Density:	45 in CA, 20 in FL, 13 in NY
Projected New Units (12 Months):	100
Qualifications:	5, 5, 1, 2, 4, 5
Registered:CA,DC,FL,HI,IL,IN,MD,MI,MN,ND,NY,OR,RI,SD,	VA,WA,WI

FINANCIAL/TERMS: |
---|---
Cash Investment: | $70-100K
Total Investment: | $90-300K
Minimum Net Worth: | $150K
Fees: Franchise - | $16K
Royalty - 8%; | Ad. - 1%
Earnings Claims Statement: | Yes
Term of Contract (Years): | 5/15
Avg. # Of Employees: | 6 FT, 4 PT
Passive Ownership: | Allowed, But Discouraged
Encourage Conversions: | No
Area Develop. Agreements: | No
Sub-Franchising Contracts: | No
Expand In Territory: | Yes
Space Needs: | 350 SF

SUPPORT & TRAINING: |
---|---
Financial Assistance Provided: | Yes (D)
Site Selection Assistance: | NA
Lease Negotiation Assistance: | NA
Co-Operative Advertising: | Yes
Franchisee Assoc./Member: | Yes/Member
Size Of Corporate Staff: | 100
On-Going Support: | a,B,C,D,G,H,I
Training: | 5-10 Days Vancouver, BC; 3-5 Days Assigned Territory

SPECIFIC EXPANSION PLANS: |
---|---
US: | Yes, All United States
Canada: | Yes
Overseas: | Yes

ITEM 19.   Financial Performance Representations

The following table presents the average gross sales realized by certain 1-800-GOT-JUNK? franchisees as of August 31, 2007. We have provided you with this information to help you make a more informed decision about our franchises. You should not use this information as an indication of how well your specific Franchised Business will do. The actual numbers you experience will vary depending upon several factors, including competition, management and market demographics. You should conduct your own research to assist you in preparing projections for your own Franchised Business.

The information provided below was compiled from our 180 Franchise Partners and Rubbish Boys' 26 Franchise Partners that were in existence during at least the entire 12 month period covered and none of the underlying data supplied to us has been audited. You should note that gross sales will be dependent, among other things, upon the size of the territory in which the Franchised Business operates and number of trucks currently operating in that territory.

<u>Average Gross Sales of 1-800-GOT-JUNK? Franchisees
For the Twelve Months Ending August 31st, 2007</u>

US Franchisees of 1-800-GOT-JUNK? LLC	Total Franchisees	Average Gross Sales (US$)	% of Franchisees at or above Average	Median Gross Sales (US$)	% of Franchisees at or above Median
Franchisees operating for more than 12 months, but less than 24 months	86	$229,822	38%	$193,503	50%
Franchisees operating for more than 24 months, but less than 36 months	31	$371,142	42%	$287,349	52%
Franchisees operating for more than 36 months, but less than 48 months	27	$566,655	37%	$493,236	52%
Franchisees operating for more than 48 months, But less than 60 months	25	$844,709	44%	$822,196	52%
Franchisees operating for more than 60 months, but less than 72 months	4	$947,453	25%	$812,266	50%
Franchisees operating for more than 72 months	7	$1,088,998	71%	$1,150,024	57%

Canadian Franchisees of Rubbish Boys	Total Franchisees	Average Gross Sales (CDN$)	% of Franchisees at or above Average	Median Gross Sales (CDN$)	% of Franchisees at or above Median
Franchisees operating for more than 12 months, but less than 24 months	9	$197,867	33%	$157,903	56%
Franchisees operating for more than 24 months, but less than 36 months	8	$374,898	38%	$324,783	50%
Franchisees operating for more than 36 months, but less than 48 months	1	$410,705	N/A	$410,705	N/A
Franchisees operating for more than 48 months, but less than 60 months	2	$1,466,852	50%	$1,466,852	50%

Franchisees operating for more than 60 months, but less than 72 months	0	N/A	N/A	N/A	N/A
Franchisees operating for more than 72 months	6	$1,833,154	17%	$953,240	50%

THERE IS NO ASSURANCE THAT ANY OTHER 1-800-GOT-JUNK? FRANCHISED BUSINESS WILL PERFORM AS WELL AS, OR ANYWHERE NEAR, THE 206 FRANCHISED BUSINESSES USED IN PREPARING THE AVERAGES SHOWN ABOVE. ANYONE WHO USES THE ABOVE INFORMATION TO PREPARE HIS OWN PRO FORMA STATEMENT MUST ACCEPT THE RISK THAT HIS OWN FRANCHISED BUSINESS MAY PERFORM SUBSTANTIALLY WORSE THAN THOSE INCLUDED IN THE AVERAGES ABOVE.

The earnings claims figures do not reflect the costs of sales or operating expenses that must be deducted from the gross revenue or gross sales figures to obtain your net income or profit. The best source of cost and expense data may be from franchisees and former franchisees, some of whom may be listed in Exhibit A.

Substantiation of the data used in preparing this earnings claim will be made available to you upon reasonable request. Except for the above information, we do not furnish or authorize our salespersons to furnish any oral or written information concerning the actual or potential sales, costs, income, profits or earnings of a 1-800-GOT-JUNK? franchise. Actual results will vary from unit to unit. We cannot estimate the results for any particular franchisee.

alphagraphics®
DESIGN ■ COPY ■ PRINT ▶ COMMUNICATE

ALPHAGRAPHICS

268 S. State St., # 300

Salt Lake City, UT 84111-2048

Tel: (800) 528-4885 (801) 595-7268

Fax: (801) 533-7968

E-Mail: franchiseleads@alphagraphics.com

Web Site: www.alphagraphics.com

Ms. Jenny Langfeld, Franchise Development Support Manager

At AlphaGraphics, we work with people to plan, produce and manage their visual communications, enabling them to achieve their goals more effectively and confidently. Established in 1970 in Tucson, Arizona, the AlphaGraphics network is comprised of nearly 260 business centers located throughout the U.S. and in nine other countries. Our business centers offer complete visual communications solutions. Our trained and experienced team members provide expert consultation for every element of your communication project, including design, copying, printing, digital archiving, finishing, mailing services, oversized printing and promotional items.

BACKGROUND:

		IFA MEMBER
Established: 1970;		1st Franchised: 1980
Franchised Units:		260
Company-Owned Units:		0
Total Units:		260

Dist.:	US-228; CAN-0; O'seas-32
North America:	38 States, 0 Provinces
Density:	19 in CA, 22 in IL, 26 in TX
Projected New Units (12 Months):	30+
Qualifications:	4, 5, 1, 3, 3, 5
Registered:CA,DC,FL,HI,IL,IN,MD,MI,MN,ND,NY,OR,RI,SD, VA,WA,WI	

FINANCIAL/TERMS:

Cash Investment:	$100K
Total Investment:	$415K
Minimum Net Worth:	$450K
Fees: Franchise -	$35K
Royalty - 1.5-8%;	Ad. - 2.5%
Earnings Claims Statement:	Yes
Term of Contract (Years):	15/10
Avg. # Of Employees:	5 FT, 0 PT
Passive Ownership:	Not Allowed
Encourage Conversions:	Yes
Area Develop. Agreements:	No
Sub-Franchising Contracts:	No
Expand In Territory:	Yes
Space Needs:	1,200 SF; FS,SC

SUPPORT & TRAINING:

Financial Assistance Provided:	Yes (D)
Site Selection Assistance:	Yes
Lease Negotiation Assistance:	Yes
Co-Operative Advertising:	Yes

Franchisee Assoc./Member:	No	**SPECIFIC EXPANSION PLANS:**	
Size Of Corporate Staff:	89	US:	Yes, All United States
On-Going Support:	C,D,E,G,H,I	Canada:	Yes, All Canada
Training:	3 Weeks Franchisee's Location	Overseas:	Yes, Spain, Italy, France, Germany, Benelux, Austria

ITEM 19. FINANCIAL PERFORMANCE REPRESENTATIONS

BACKGROUND

This Item sets forth certain historical data as provided by our franchisees. Substantiation of the data used in preparing this information will be made available upon reasonable request.

IMPORTANTLY, THE SUCCESS OF YOUR FRANCHISE WILL DEPEND LARGELY UPON YOUR INDIVIDUAL ABILITIES AND YOUR MARKET, AND THE FINANCIAL RESULTS OF YOUR FRANCHISE ARE LIKELY TO DIFFER, PERHAPS MATERIALLY, FROM THE RESULTS SUMMARIZED IN THIS ITEM.

For purposes of this Item 19 only, "Gross Sales" means all sales a franchisee derives from operating the Business Center. A "Traditional Business Center" is one in which high speed duplicating, basic bindery, design services, hub services and offset printing are performed on the premises. A "Digital Business Center," is a Business Center that does not have an offset press and related equipment. As they have matured, many franchisees included in this section have leased, purchased or obtained access to equipment, which allows them to have greater production capabilities than could otherwise be obtained through the equipment in the new Business Center package.

TOTAL GROSS SALES

The table below shows the combined Gross Sales for all of our Business Centers during our last three fiscal years. Our fiscal year runs from July 1 to June 30. These numbers include Gross Sales for our Traditional and Digital Business Centers located in the U.S. and in foreign countries.

Fiscal Year	Total Gross Sales
2006	$284,401,950 [1]
2007	$295,505,427 [2]
2008	$300,115,271 [3]

Notes to Total Gross Sales Table:

1. During the 2006 fiscal year, we had 239 Business Centers in the United States and 36 foreign Business Centers.

2. During the 2007 fiscal year, we had 235 Business Centers in the United States and 38 foreign Business Centers.

3. During the 2008 fiscal year, we had 225 Business Centers in the United States and 34 foreign Business Centers. This figure does not include gross sales from the month of June for our 6 Business Centers located in Mexico.

COMPARATIVE ANNUAL GROSS SALES

The table below compares annual Gross Sales information reported by U.S. franchisees owning a Traditional Business Center for calendar year 2005, and Gross Sales information reported by U.S. franchisees owning either a Traditional or a Digital Business Center for calendar years 2006 and 2007. The columns in the table for calendar year 2005 exclude data from Business Centers that fall into one or more of the following categories: (i) Business Centers that were not full service Business Centers; (ii) Business Centers that were not operational for the entire calendar year; and (iii) Business Centers that failed to provide us with sales data. The columns for calendar years 2006 and 2007 only exclude data from (i) Business Centers that were not operational for the entire calendar year; and (ii) Business Centers that failed to provide us with sales data.

1. Business Centers Open and Operating for 3 years or more:

Number of Business Centers (U.S.)

GROSS SALES	2007	2006	2005
Under $300,000	2	2	1
$300,000-400,000	4	2	5
$400,000-500,000	9	12	16
$500,000-750,000	50	46	35
$750,000-1,000,000	35	45	53
Over $1,000,000	101	97	82
Total Number of Business Centers open and operating 3 years or more	201	204	192
Average Annual Gross Sales	$1,175,283	$1,173,620	$1,139,620
Percent of Business Centers Meeting or Exceeding Average Annual Gross Sales	32.52%	34.80%	34.8%
Number of Business Centers Meeting or Exceeding Average Annual Gross Sales	67	71	66
Median Annual Gross Sales	$983,098	$967,051	$910,824
Percent of Business Centers Meeting or Exceeding Median Gross Sales	50%	50%	50%
Number of Business Centers Meeting or Exceeding Median Gross Sales	101	102	96

2. Business Centers Open and Operating for 2 years or more:

Number of Business Centers (U.S.)

GROSS SALES	2007	2006	2005
Under $300,000	5	2	1
$300,000-400,000	6	3	5
$400,000-500,000	15	12	16
$500,000-750,000	51	46	43
$750,000-1,000,000	36	45	50
Over $1,000,000	101	97	84
Total of Business Centers open and operating 2 years or more	214	205	202
Average Annual Gross Sales	$1,151,392	$1,169,916	$1,103,820
Percent of Business Centers Meeting or Exceeding Average Annual Gross Sales	32.39%	34.63%	35.15%
Number of Business Centers Meeting or Exceeding Average Annual Gross Sales	69	71	71
Median Annual Gross Sales	$969,165	$965,784	$881,034

229

Percent of Business Centers Meeting or Exceeding Median Gross Sales	50%	50%	50%
Number of Business Centers Meeting or Exceeding Median Gross Sales	107	103	101

3. Business Centers Open and Operating for 1 year or more:

Number of Business Centers (U.S.)

GROSS SALES	2007	2006	2005
Under $300,000	4	7	2
$300,000-400,000	7	5	5
$400,000-500,000	16	14	19
$500,000-750,000	56	48	46
$750,000-1,000,000	37	47	54
Over $1,000,000	101	97	84
Total number of Business Centers open and operating 1 year or more	221	218	210
Average Annual Gross Sales	$1,131,001	$1,125,703	$1,081,292
Percent of Business Centers meeting or Exceeding Average Annual Gross Sales	33.03%	34.4%	34.28%
Number of Business Centers Meeting or Exceeding Average Annual Gross Sales	73	75	72
Median Annual Gross Sales	$917,028	$917,771	$862,517
Percent of Business Centers Meeting or Exceeding Median Gross Sales	50%	50%	50%
Number of Business Centers Meeting or Exceeding Median Gross Sales	111	109	105

Notes to Comparative Annual Gross Sales Table:

1.   As of December 31, 2007, there were 227 U.S. ALPHAGRAPHICS® Business Center franchises, 221 of which were operational for the full calendar year. Of these 221 operational franchised Business Centers, none failed to provide sales information to us. Of the 221 operational franchised Business Centers that had been open and operating for at least one year, 206 had been Business Centers for 3 years or more, 7 had been a franchised Business Center for at least 2 years, but less than 3 years; and 8 had been franchised Business Centers for at least 1 year, but less than 2 years.

2.   As of December 31, 2006, there were 224 U.S. ALPHAGRAPHICS® Business Center franchises, 218 of which were operational for the full calendar year. Of these 218 operational franchised Business Centers, none failed to provide sales information to us. Of the 218 operational franchised Business Centers that had been open and operating for at least one year, 204 had been Business Centers for 3 years or more; 1 had been a franchised Business Center for at least 2 years, but less than 3 years; and 13 had been franchised Business Centers for at least 1 year, but less than 2 years.

3.   As of December 31, 2005, there were 232 U.S. ALPHAGRAPHICS® Business Center franchises, 223 of which were operational for the full calendar year. Of these 223 operational franchised Business Centers, 13 failed to provide sales information to us. Of the 210 operational franchised Business Centers that had been open and operating for at least one year, 192 had been Business Centers for 3 years or more; 10 had been franchised Business Centers for at least 2 years, but less than 3 years, and 8 had been franchised Business Centers for at least 1 year, but less than 2 years.

4.   Average Annual Gross Sales is defined as the sum of Gross Sales of the Business Centers included in a particular financial performance representation divided by the number of Business Centers included.

5.   The figures outlined in the tables above do not reflect the cost of sales, operating expenses, or other costs or expenses that must be deducted from the gross sales figures to obtain your net income or profit. You should conduct an independent investigation of the costs and expenses you will incur in operating your Business Center. Franchisees, or former franchisees, listed in this Disclosure Document, may be one source of this information.

NEW BUSINESS CENTERS MEDIAN SALES FOR THE FIRST TWELVE MONTHS OF OPERATION

The table below sets forth certain sales information for new Digital Business Centers in the U.S. for the period from January 2006 through June 2008. We had a total of 11 new Digital Business Centers open in the U.S. during that period. This table presents data for all 11 new Digital Business Centers.

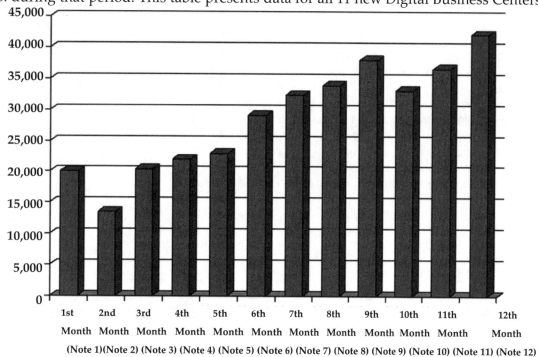

(Note 1)(Note 2) (Note 3) (Note 4) (Note 5) (Note 6) (Note 7) (Note 8) (Note 9) (Note 10) (Note 11) (Note 12)

Notes to New Business Centers Median Sales for the First Twelve Months of Operation Table:

1.   Eleven new Digital Business Centers were open at least one month. Median sales were $19,973 for the first month of operation for these 11 new Digital Business Centers.

2.   Eleven new Digital Business Centers were open at least two months. Median sales were $13,486 for the second month of operation for these 11 new Digital Business Centers.

3.   Eleven new Digital Business Centers were open at least three months. Median sales were $20,441 for the third month of operation for these 11 new Digital Business Centers.

4.   Ten new Digital Business Centers were open at least four months. Median sales were $21,972 for the fourth month of operation for these 10 new Digital Business Centers.

5.   Ten new Digital Business Centers were open at least five months. Median sales were $22,937 for the fifth month of operation for these 10 new Digital Business Centers.

6.   Ten new Digital Business Centers were open at least six months. Median sales were $29,073 for the sixth month of operation for these 10 new Digital Business Centers.

231

7.   Nine new Digital Business Centers were open at least seven months. Median sales were $32,280 for the seventh month of operation for these 9 new Digital Business Centers.

8.   Nine new Digital Business Centers were open at least eight months. Median sales were $33,875 for the eighth month of operation for these 9 new Digital Business Centers.

9.   Nine new Digital Business Centers were open at least nine months. Median sales were $38,022 for the ninth month of operation for these 9 new Digital Business Centers.

10.   Eight new Digital Business Centers were open at least ten months. Median sales were $33,163 for the tenth month of operation for these 8 new Digital Business Centers.

11.   Eight new Digital Business Centers were open at least eleven months. Median sales were $36,594 for the eleventh month of operation for these 8 new Digital Business Centers.

12.   Seven new Digital Business Centers were open at least twelve months. Median sales were $42,049 for the twelfth month of operation for these 7 new Digital Business Centers.

CERTAIN EXPENSE INFORMATION FOR CALENDAR YEAR 2007

The table below sets forth certain median cost and expense information as a percentage of Gross Sales for U.S. franchisees operating a Business Center as of the close of calendar year 2007. This section provides data for 92 of the 227 U.S. Business Centers that were in operation as of December 31, 2007, including both Traditional and Digital Business Centers. The table excludes data from the 135 U.S. Business Centers which fell into one or more of the following categories: (i) multi-location franchises which did not allocate sales and costs accurately to each Business Center; (ii) Business Centers that were missing financial data or that did not provide financial data to us in the proper format; (iii) Business Centers that were not in operation for all 12 months of calendar year 2007; or (iv) Business Centers that were transferred during the calendar year.

Median Costs and Expenses	All 92 Business Centers Reporting[1]	The 51 Business Centers with More than $1,000,000 in Gross Sales[2]	The 41 Business Centers with Less than $1,000,000 in Gross Sales[3]
Offset Printing as a Percentage of Gross Sales	21.6%	21.6%	21.7%
Digital Black & White as a Percentage of Gross Sales	16.8%	16.7%	17.0%
Digital Color as a Percentage of Gross Sales	22.6%	22.7%	22.4%
Bindery (Finishing) as a Percentage of Gross Sales	10.3%	10.3%	10.3%
Graphic Design as a Percentage of Gross Sales	8.0%	8.2%	7.5%
Large Format Color as a Percentage of Gross Sales	1.7%	1.6%	2.0%
Sublet (Outsourced) as a Percentage of Gross Sales	13.8%	14.3%	13.5%
Total Gross Sales	$ 1,056,549	$ 1,398,917	$ 708,166
Gross Margin as a Percentage of Gross Sales[4]	71.7%	71.8%	71.6%
Labor[5] as a Percentage of Gross Sales	31.4%	31.8%	29.9%
Rent[6] as a Percentage of Gross Sales	6.4%	5.0%	8.6%
Labor[5], Equipment[7], and Materials[8] as a Percentage of Gross Sales	59.8%	58.0%	64.5%
EBITDA[9] as a Percentage of Gross Sales	13.9%	16.0%	8.0%
Annual Sales FTE (Full Time Equivalent Person)	$124,649	$135,093	$117,726
Annual Sales Per Square Foot	283	307	263

Notes to the Certain Expense Information for Calendar Year 2007 Table:

1.   All Business Centers Reporting refers to the 92 U.S. Business Centers that were in operation as of December 31, 2007 and that provided us with data.

2.	51 Business Centers reported more than $1,000,000 in Gross Sales for the calendar year ending December 31, 2007.

3.	41 Business Centers reported less than $1,000,000 in Gross Sales for the calendar year ending December 31, 2007.

4.	Gross Margin is defined as Gross Sales less cost of goods sold, which includes Material Costs, Equipment Costs, and vendor services (out-sourced tasks). In the table, Gross Margin is expressed as a percentage of Gross Sales.

5.	Total Labor Costs is defined as the total of direct labor (labor directly employed in the production of product, including benefits) and indirect labor (labor not employed it the production of product, such as administrative or sales personnel), including payroll taxes and group medical, for the Business Center. In the table, Total Labor Costs is expressed as a percentage of Gross Sales.

6.	Rent is defined as the rent paid to the landlord of the premises where the Business Center is located. In the table, Rent is expressed as a percentage of Gross Sales.

7.	Equipment Costs is defined as the expense directly related to the equipment used in the production of product (this does not include depreciation). In the table, Equipment Costs is expressed as a percentage of Gross Sales.

8.	Materials Costs is defined as the expenses directly related to the purchase of materials used in the production of product. In the table, Material Costs is expressed as a percentage of Gross Sales.

9.	EBITDA is defined as Earnings Before Interest, Taxes, Depreciation, and Amortization. In the table, EBITDA is expressed as a percentage of Gross Sales.

CAUTION

THE INFORMATION PRESENTED IN THIS ITEM IS BASED ON SALES AND COST INFORMATION REPORTED TO US BY OUR FRANCHISEES. WE HAVE NOT INDEPENDENTLY INVESTIGATED THE AMOUNTS REPORTED. PROSPECTIVE FRANCHISEES ARE ADVISED THAT NO CERTIFIED PUBLIC ACCOUNTANT HAS AUDITED THESE FIGURES OR EXPRESSED AN OPINION WITH REGARD TO THEIR CONTENT OR FORM.

THE INFORMATION PRESENTED IN THIS ITEM SHOULD NOT BE CONSTRUED AS THE ACTUAL OR POTENTIAL SALES, PROFITS OR EARNINGS THAT YOU WILL REALIZE. WE DO NOT REPRESENT, WARRANT OR OTHERWISE GUARANTEE THAT YOU WILL ATTAIN THESE SALES, PROFITS OR EARNINGS. YOUR INDIVIDUAL FRANCHISE RESULTS ARE LIKELY TO DIFFER FROM THE RESULTS STATED IN THE CHARTS ABOVE.

Assumptions

1.	Your expenses will vary depending upon the location of your Business Center. This analysis does not contain complete information concerning operating costs. Operating costs may vary substantially from Business Center to Business Center.

2.	The above figures exclude finance charges and depreciation. Interest expense, interest income, depreciation, amortization and other income or expenses will vary substantially from Business Center to Business Center, depending on the amount and kind of financing you obtain to establish the Business Center. You should consult with your tax advisor regarding depreciation and amortization schedules and the period over which the assets of the Business Center may be amortized or depreciated, as well as the effect, if any, of recent or proposed tax legislation.

3.	The above figures exclude utilities, advertising, delivery expenses, royalties, telephone, travel and entertainment, training, office supplies and other administrative and miscellaneous expenses.

4.	Expenses and costs, as well as the actual accounting and operational methods employed by a franchisee, may significantly impact profits realized in any particular operation.

CAUTION

Some of our franchisees have sold the amounts provided in this Item 19. Your individual results may differ. There is no assurance you will sell as much. If you rely upon our figures, you must accept the risk of not selling as much. Actual results vary from Business Center to Business Center, and we cannot estimate the result of a particular Business Center. Revenues and expenses may vary depending on whether the business located in a metropolitan market or a non-metropolitan market and on other factors. In particular, the revenues and expenses of your Business Center will be directly affected by factors, such as: (a) geographic location; (b) competition from other firms in the market; (c) advertising effectiveness based on market saturation; (d) whether you assume the sales position as or hire a sales manager; (e) your product and service pricing; (f) vendor prices on materials, supplies and inventory; (g) salaries and benefits to non-business personnel; (h) business personnel benefits (life and health insurance, etc.); (i) weather conditions; and (j) employment conditions in the market.

Importantly, you should not consider the revenues or certain expenses presented above to be the actual potential revenues or expenses that you will realize. We do not represent that you can or will attain these revenues or expenses, or any particular level of revenues or percentage of expenses. We do not represent that you will generate income, which exceeds the initial payment of, or investment in, the franchise.

The financial performance figures included in this Item 19 do not reflect all the costs or expenses that must be deducted from the gross revenues or gross sales figures to obtain your net income or profit. You should conduct an independent investigation of the costs and expenses you will incur in operating your Business Center. Franchisees or former franchisees, listed in the Disclosure Document, may be one source of information.

Therefore, we recommend that you make your own independent investigation to determine whether or not the franchise may be profitable to you. You should use the above information only as a reference in conducting your analysis and preparing your own projected income statements and cash flow statements. We suggest strongly that you consult your financial advisor or personal accountant concerning financial projections and federal, state and local income taxes and any other applicable taxes that you may incur in operating a Business Center.

Disclaimer Regarding Certain Claims:

We specifically instruct our sales personnel, agents, employees and officers that they may not make any claims or statements as to the earnings, sales or profits, or prospects or chances of success of a Business Center other than those identified in this Item 19. They are not authorized to represent or estimate dollar figures as to a Business Center's operation other than as shown above.

ANYTIME FITNESS

12181 Margo Avenue South
Hastings, Minnesota 55033
Tel: 800 704 5004 651 438-5000
Fax: 651 438-5099
E-Mail: leads@anytimefitness.com
Web Site: www.anytimefitness.com
Mr. Mark Daly, National Media Director

Anytime Fitness is the #1 co-ed fitness club chain in the world. We've boiled our business model down to the core essentials which members expect. Our loyal family of preferred vendors supply our franchisees with quality products at the best available prices. Financial and real estate support available. More than half of our franchisees own multiple clubs. Enjoy the freedom of spending time with your friends and family - and the knowledge that you're making your community a better place to live.

BACKGROUND:	IFA MEMBER
Established: 2002;	1st Franchised: 2002
Franchised Units:	1100
Company-Owned Units:	10
Total Units:	1110
Dist.:	US-1087; CAN-11; O'seas-12
North America:	45 States, 2 Provinces

Density:	NR	Expand In Territory:	Yes
Projected New Units (12 Months):	400	Space Needs:	4,000 SF
Qualifications:	3, 2, 2, 2, 3, 4		
Registered:CA,DC,FL,HI,IL,IN,MD,MI,MN,ND,NY,OR,RI,SD, VA,WA,WI,AB		**SUPPORT & TRAINING:**	
		Financial Assistance Provided:	Yes (D)
		Site Selection Assistance:	Yes
FINANCIAL/TERMS:		Lease Negotiation Assistance:	Yes
Cash Investment:	$10K	Co-Operative Advertising:	No
Total Investment:	$35K-$249K	Franchisee Assoc./Member:	Yes/Member
Minimum Net Worth:	$10K	Size Of Corporate Staff:	80
Fees: Franchise -	$18K	On-Going Support:	A,B,C,D,E,F,G,H,I
Royalty - $419/mo;	Ad. - $150/mo	Training:	NR
Earnings Claims Statement:	Yes		
Term of Contract (Years):	5/5	**SPECIFIC EXPANSION PLANS:**	
Avg. # Of Employees:	1 FT, 2 PT	US:	Yes, All 50 states
Passive Ownership:	Allowed	Canada:	Yes, All Canadian provinces
Encourage Conversions:	Yes	Overseas: Yes, India, China, Japan, Australia, Europe, Middle East,	
Area Develop. Agreements:	Yes		Latin America
Sub-Franchising Contracts:	Yes		

ITEM 19.
FINANCIAL PERFORMANCE REPRESENTATIONS

We do not make any representations about a franchisee's future financial performance or the past financial performance of company-owned or franchised outlets, except as disclosed below. We also do not authorize our employees or representatives to make any such representations either orally or in writing. If you are purchasing an existing outlet, however, we may provide you with the actual records of that outlet. If you receive any other financial performance information or projections of your future income, you should report it to the franchisor's management by contacting Jennifer Yiangou at 12181 Margo Avenue south, Hastings, Minnesota 55033, telephone: (800) 704-5004.

Statement of Annual Projected Revenues and Earnings

The following are statements of projected annual revenues and earnings for a franchised Anytime Fitness® center. We have set forth three projections, one based on a center having 400 memberships, one based on 600 memberships and one based on 900 memberships.

We do not require that all our franchisees provide detailed information to us as to the number of memberships in their club, the revenues they receive, and their expenses. Therefore, these projections are not based on the experience of our franchisees, but on our own experience in operating 10 company-owned centers. However, some of these centers are mature centers, as the first one opened in October 2003. Therefore, to project revenues, we did not use the total revenues we received in these centers, but instead used 2007 average per-membership revenues, as the per-membership revenues are not likely to change significantly based on the age of the center or the number of memberships. In compiling the expense projections, we also relied on the experience of our company-owned centers and our knowledge of current economic conditions.

The assumptions we made in compiling these projections are set forth following the projections. Any change in these assumptions would require material alterations to the projections.

Revenues	400 Memberships	600 Memberships	900 Memberships
Membership Fees[1,2,4]	$169,300	$253,900	$383,400

Tanning Revenues[1,2,4]	1,400	2,100	3,100
Vending Revenues[3]	1,200	1,800	2,700
Total Revenues	$171,900	$257,800	$389,200
Operating Expenses			
Rent[5]	63,000	63,000	63,000
Equipment Lease[6]	42,500	42,500	42,500
Royalties	5,028	5,028	5,028
Utilities[7]	10,200	10,200	10,200
Insurance	4,200	4,200	4,200
Proximity Cards[8]	1,600	2,400	3,600
Advertising Fund[9]	3,600	3,600	3,600
Local Advertising[10]	8,000	10,000	12,000
Vending Products[3]	600	900	1,350
Maintenance	600	1,200	1,800
Software/Security	1,100	1,100	1,100
Printing	2,000	3,000	4,500
Miscellaneous[11]	16,000	19,000	22,000
Total Operating Expenses	$158,428	$166,128	$174,870
Income Before Salaries, Depreciation, Interest, Taxes and Debt Expense	$13,472	$91,672	$214,322

THESE PROJECTIONS OF SALES, INCOME, GROSS OR NET PROFITS ARE MERELY ESTIMATES AND SHOULD NOT BE CONSTRUED AS THE ACTUAL OR PROBABLE SALES, INCOME, GROSS OR NET PROFITS THAT WILL BE REALIZED BY ANY FRANCHISEE. WE DO NOT REPRESENT THAT ANY FRANCHISEE CAN EXPECT TO ATTAIN SUCH SALES, INCOME, GROSS OR NET PROFITS. THE FINANCIAL RESULTS FOR A NEW FRANCHISEE ARE LIKELY TO DIFFER FROM THE RESULTS STATED IN THESE PROJECTIONS.

THESE FIGURES WERE PREPARED WITHOUT AN AUDIT. PROSPECTIVE FRANCHISEES OR SELLERS OF FRANCHISES SHOULD BE ADVISED THAT NO CERTIFIED PUBLIC ACCOUNTANT HAS AUDITED THESE FIGURES OR EXPRESSED HIS/HER OPINION WITH REGARD TO THE CONTENT OR FORM.

<u>NOTES AND ASSUMPTIONS</u>

1.   In projecting membership revenues, we had to make certain assumptions regarding the types of memberships you will sell in your center, and the prices you will charge for each type of membership. We assumed that 80% of your memberships are individual memberships, and that 1/3 of those memberships (15% of all memberships) have a tanning membership. We assumed your remaining memberships are couple memberships, and that 1/3 of those memberships have tanning memberships. These assumptions are consistent with our experience in our company-owned centers. It is up to you to set your own prices for your memberships. However, our projections are based on the following prices, which are consistent with what we charge in our centers: Individual memberships

$35; individual memberships with tanning membership $48; couple memberships $53; couple memberships with tanning membership $83.

2.	In determining revenues, we assumed you would have 9% bad debt for membership fees and tanning services. This is actually higher than our experience. We also projected that you would pay a 4.9% monthly billing fee on your remaining membership and tanning revenues.

3.	It is up to you to determine whether you offer vending machines in your center, the products you place in those machines and the vending prices. The amounts we have projected for vending revenue reflect the per membership revenues we receive from vending. We also do not tell you the sources from which you can purchase vending products. We assumed you would purchase your vending products from a warehouse seller such as Sam's Club, and that you pick up these items. If you go to other sources, or have these products delivered, your expenses will likely be higher.

4.	We rounded all revenues and expenses to the nearest $100 (except royalties).

5.	Your rent can vary significantly depending on the size and location of your center. This projection assumes you lease 3,500 square feet at $18.00 per square foot per year. If you have a larger center, or you pay more for rent, your rent expense could increase significantly.

6.	This amount assumes you enter into a three year lease purchase agreement for your equipment, paying approximately 20% down, and financing $100,000. (See Item 7 for additional information about the range of initial investment for equipment and improvements.) Our projection assumes an interest rate of 12% per annum. We also assumed you are required to pay sales tax of 6 1/2% on these lease payments. These numbers will likely be different for each franchisee, as you may decide to make more of a down payment (which would lower your payments), you may decide to finance your equipment over a longer period of time (which will also lower your payments), you may have to pay a higher interest rate (which would increase your payments), and your sales tax may be higher or lower than 6 1/2%. In our company-owned centers, we typically negotiate lower rates than we have projected.

7.	This amount includes gas, electric, water, cable, Internet and telephone.

8.	This amount assumes you signed up each of your members in the current year. In reality, your cost for proximity cards will be less after the first year, because you will not have to issue new proximity cards to each member each year.

9.	This amount is based on our current requirement that you contribute $150 per month to our advertising fund.

10.	We expect you to spend at least $6,000 per year for advertising. However, we recommend you spend more, and our projection assumes you spend at least $8,000, and that your spending increases as you have more members. This amount includes any amount we may require you to contribute to a local marketing fund.

11.	Miscellaneous includes janitorial services, legal and accounting fees, cell phone, supplies, licenses, bank charges, proximity cards, and other similar items. Many of these costs can vary significantly depending on the location of your center and the time you spend looking for the best possible cost on these items. The projections are consistent with the experience of our company owned centers.

Additional Assumptions:

A.	The projections assume you act as manager of your center and do not receive a separate salary. They assume you do not hire any other employees to help you. Because our centers are designed to operate 24 hours a day, without the necessity of having staff on premises, you should not need any other employees. However, some states will require you have an employee on premises whenever your center is open. If you are an absentee-owner, or you operate in a location that requires the center to be staffed at all times, your expenses will increase significantly because you will have to pay salaries and benefits to employees.

B.   We did not provide any allowance for corporate or personal income taxes.

C.   While we did include expenses for a lease/purchase of your equipment, we did not include any other expenses for depreciation, amortization, interest, or the repayment of debt. We anticipate every franchisee will fund its initial investment differently, and we therefore cannot project how you would account for these items.

D.   The projections are based on economic conditions that existed in February 2008, with no consideration in any category for inflation related adjustments or weaknesses in general economic conditions.

E.   The projections assume you follow our guidelines in terms of the products and services you offer and the way you operate your business. If you do not, your results will likely vary dramatically from the results we have projected.

Of the 10 centers we used in compiling these projections, all of them were open during all of 2007. All of those centers had over 400 members, 8 of the 10 had over 600 members, and 4 of the 10 had over 900 members, as of the end of 2007. It does, however, take several months to build your membership, and you should not expect to achieve these levels during your first year. All 10 of the centers exceeded the revenue and income projections in the first (400 members) column, 8 exceeded the revenue and income projections in the second (600 members) column, and 4 exceeded the revenues and income projections in the third (900 members) column. Because our franchisees are not required to give us this level of detail as to their revenues and expenses, we cannot tell you how many of our franchisees exceeded the projected revenues or projected profits.

We recommend a particular accounting method or system to you. This system is consistent with generally accepted accounting principles. All of the centers we used in compiling these projections used this system. We provided substantially the same services to those centers as we will offer to you. All of these centers offered substantially the same products and services as you are expected to offer. If you request, we will provide information to you to substantiate these projections.

We do not furnish or authorize our salespersons to furnish any oral or written information concerning the actual, average or potential sales, costs, income or profits of an Anytime Fitness Express business. Because we did not begin offering Anytime Fitness Express centers until October 2006, we do not have a sufficient operating history for these centers. Actual results will likely vary from one center to another, and we cannot estimate the results of any particular center. If you receive any oral or written information concerning the actual, average or potential sales, income or profits of an Anytime Fitness Express center from any of our representatives, or from a person claiming to act on our behalf, you should immediately report that incident to us, as we have not authorized that information. You should not rely on any oral or written estimate or projection of sales, income or profits, or statement of actual, average, estimated **or** potential sales, income or profits of an existing or future Anytime Fitness Express center, because reliance on that information would not be reasonable in light of the fact that we have not authorized that information to be provided to you or to any other prospective franchisee.

ASSISTING HANDS HOME CARE		
1 N. MacDonald St., # 408		
Mesa, AZ 85201	**BACKGROUND:**	IFA MEMBER
Tel: (877) 974-2637 (480) 850-0110	Established: 2005;	1st Franchised: 2006
Fax: (480) 393-4581	Franchised Units:	8
E-Mail: drennick@assistinghands.com	Company-Owned Units:	0
Web Site: www.assistinghands.com	Total Units:	8
Mr. Dick Rennick, Chief Executive Officer		

ITEM 19
FINANCIAL PERFORMANCE REPRESENTATIONS

The following chart sets forth the actual revenues of Care Corner in Mesa, Arizona, which has been owned and operated by our Director of Training, Gail Silverstein, Ph.D. since its inception in January 2003. (See Item 2) This document is disclosing Care Corner's financial performance, since all systems which have been set up for Assisting Hands™ Business franchises are based on the systems which are used by Care Corner.

Care Corner is located in an office complex and serves a population of approximately 500,000. Care Corner offers substantially the same services to the public as are offered by Assisting Hands™ Business franchisees. Care Corner operates in a manner reasonably comparable to the methods to be used at Assisting Hands™ franchises to be operated by Business franchisees.

The actual gross revenue results for Care Corner shown in the chart are from financial statements furnished by Care Corner. Expenses and net profits have not been included. The accompanying notes are an integral part of the charts.

All years shown in the charts include twelve full months of operating data and include revenues for services provided during that time. Data for the franchised office in Boise, Idaho, has been omitted due to the lack of operating data for at least two full calendar years. The success of your franchise will depend largely upon your individual efforts and the financial results of your franchise are likely to differ, perhaps materially, from the results listed below. Among the reasons why the results listed below may differ materially from yours is the fact that there are no other franchise locations in the region of Care Corner. Therefore, it may have revenue greater than what is possible in the prescribed territories offered by Assisting Hands™ to franchisees.

THE EARNINGS, SALES, PROFITS, OR PROSPECTUS OR CHANCES OF SUCCESS THAT ANY FRANCHISEE CAN EXPECT OR THAT PRESENT OR PAST FRANCHISEES HAVE EXPERIENCED.

THIS INFORMATION WAS PREPARED WITHOUT AN AUDIT. PROSPECTIVE FRANCHISEES OR SELLERS OF FRANCHISES SHOULD BE ADVISED THAT NO CERTIFIED PUBLIC ACCOUNTANT HAS AUDITED THESE FIGURES OR EXPRESSED HIS/HER OPINION WITH REGARD TO THEIR CONTENTS OR FORM.

YOUR FINANCIAL RESULTS ARE LIKELY TO DIFFER FROM. THOSE SHOWN BELOW, AND EACH FRANCHISEE MUST ACCEPT THE RISK OF NOT DOING AS WELL AS THE LISTED BUSINESS. THE REVENUES OF CARE CORNER MAY DIFFER FROM FRANCHISEE-OWNED OUTLETS.

Substantiation of the data used in preparing the following information will be made available to you upon reasonable request.

REVENUES FOR BUSINESS OPERATED BY CARE CORNER[1]						
Year	2002	2003	2004	2005	2006	2007
Gross Revenue	$230,486	$642,851	$1,543,484	$1,692,281	$2,659,944	$3,699,524

Notes:

(1)   At-Home Care, Inc.
d/b/a Care Corner and Care Corner Personal Services
1930 S. Alma School Rd.
Suite B-104

Mesa, Arizona 85210
Telephone: (480) 833-8889
Opened 1996

(2)   In 2007:
Number of Locations: 3
Total Hours: 246,752
Number of unique clients served: 529

AUSSIE PET MOBILE

34189 Pacific Coast Hwy., # 203
Dana Point, CA 92629-2814
Tel: (949) 234-0680
Fax: (949) 234-0688
E-Mail: dlouy@aussiepetmobile.com
Web Site: www.aussiepetmobile.com
Mr. David Louy, VP Franchise Sales

AUSSIE PET MOBILE is an internationally proven franchise system of mobile pet grooming with new U.S. headquarters in Orange County, CA. We pride ourselves on our innovative Mercedes van design, heated hydrobath and a 15-step grooming maintenance process. No experience is required. The AUSSIE PET MOBILE franchise package includes a comprehensive training course. Franchisees enjoy a protected territory with regional and national advertising support. Single unit owner-operator and multi-unit programs available.

BACKGROUND:	IFA MEMBER
Established: 1996;	1st Franchised: 1997
Franchised Units:	448
Company-Owned Units:	13
Total Units:	461
Dist.:	US-425; CAN-3; O'seas-20
North America:	28 States, 1 Provinces
Density:	87 in CA, 25 in FL, 22 in TX
Projected New Units (12 Months):	NR
Qualifications:	4, 4, 1, 3, 4, 5

Registered:CA,DC,FL,HI,IL,IN,MD,MI,MN,NY,OR,RI,SD,VA, WA,WI,AB

FINANCIAL/TERMS:	
Cash Investment:	$62K-125K
Total Investment:	$200K
Minimum Net Worth:	$100K-250K
Fees: Franchise -	$35-75K
Royalty - 5%;	Ad. - 3%
Earnings Claims Statement:	Yes
Term of Contract (Years):	10/10
Avg. # Of Employees:	Varies FT, Varies PT
Passive Ownership:	Allowed
Encourage Conversions:	Yes
Area Develop. Agreements:	No
Sub-Franchising Contracts:	No
Expand In Territory:	Yes
Space Needs:	SF

SUPPORT & TRAINING:	
Financial Assistance Provided:	Yes (D)
Site Selection Assistance:	NA
Lease Negotiation Assistance:	NA
Co-Operative Advertising:	Yes
Franchisee Assoc./Member:	Yes/Member
Size Of Corporate Staff:	40
On-Going Support:	A,B,C,D,E,F,G,H,I
Training:	3 Days Advanced Employees; 3-5 Days Franchisees; 2 WeeksEmployees

SPECIFIC EXPANSION PLANS:	
US:	Yes, All United States
Canada:	Yes, All Canada
Overseas:	Yes, UK, Europe, Mexico, Asia, Worldwide

19.   **FINANCIAL PERFORMANCE REPRESENTATIONS**

IMPORTANT NOTICES

The information provided in Exhibit J is the only information we authorize regarding performance of any Aussie Pet Mobile® Franchise Business. We do not furnish, or authorize our salespersons or anyone else to furnish, any oral or written information concerning the actual or potential sales, costs, income or profits of an Aussie Pet Mobile® Franchise Business. Actual results may vary from business to business and we cannot estimate the results of any particular franchise.

We make no representations, express or implied, regarding potential earnings of your business. We have not suggested, guaranteed or warranted that you will succeed in the operation of a Franchise or provided any sales or income projections of any kind to you. We are unable to reliably predict the operational results of a unit owned by us, and we cannot reliably predict what results you might achieve. How well you might do depends almost entirely on factors outside our control, including your general business ability, how hard and smart you work, your resources, how closely you follow our system, your location, competition, and how good a businessperson you are. The business realities are that no one, including us, can make a reliable estimate of what sort of results you may achieve. We cannot guarantee your success, and we do not authorize any sales, cost or income projections, estimates or otherwise of any kind to you, nor should you rely on any projections or estimates of any type from anyone.

Exhibit J provides information accumulated from a Franchisee Survey sent out over the company intranet in January of 2008. A total of 37 Franchisees operating 96 Pet Mobiles returned their surveys. This represents 45% of all Franchisees who have been operating for at least 6 months and 50% of all Reporting Pet Mobiles operating at least 6 months. The blend of Pet Mobiles in this survey is 77 vans and 19 trailers. We have not independently confirmed the information provided by the franchisees.

The figures presented in Exhibit J do not include <u>any</u> costs to acquire and only certain averages in relation to operational costs of an Aussie Pet Mobile® Franchise Business, and therefore, the information presented is not sufficient to provide any guidance as to profitability (if any) or cash flows. You should obtain estimates (we do not authorize anyone to provide such estimates on our behalf) for costs to acquire and operate an Aussie Pet Mobile® Franchise Business and review them with a professional advisor before buying a franchise.

Exhibit J is our only authorized "financial performance representation" or other statement regarding performance results relating to Aussie Pet Mobile franchises. Exhibit J should be read in its entirety, including the discussion of factual basis and material assumptions and all disclaimers, since all of it is important to your decision. <u>As a new Franchisee, your individual financial results will probably differ from the figures set forth in Exhibit J, particularly during any start up phase and possibly afterwards, as well.</u> Our presentation of the information in Exhibit J is not a representation or guaranty that you will achieve any particular level of results. Perhaps most importantly, note that past performance for any business is no guaranty of future results.

<u>If you believe that any promises, representations or agreements are or have been made to you that are not expressly stated in the Franchise Agreement, the Disclosure Document or this document, you must provide us a written statement describing the same next to your signature on Exhibit J.</u> If any such promises, representations or agreements have been provided to you, you should understand that they are unreliable and unauthorized by us. You shouldn't rely upon them, and we are not bound by them. <u>Please notify us in writing before you buy a franchise if any such promises, representations or agreements have been provided to you by anyone.</u>

Before signing any documents or making any investment, you must make your own independent investigation regarding the possible award of an Aussie Pet Mobile® Franchise, including independent market and industry reviews and comparisons and talking to current and former Aussie Pet Mobile® franchisees. You must consult with your own independent advisors, such as attorneys and accountants, to assist in determining the suitability of this investment for you.

Additional language required by the State of California is contained in the California Addendum in Exhibit 5 of this Disclosure Document.

<u>EXHIBIT J</u>
<u>FINANCIAL PERFORMANCE REPRESENTATIONS</u>

CERTAIN HISTORICAL DATA PROVIDED BY FRANCHISEES

BACKGROUND

This Item sets forth certain historical data provided by our franchisees for their trailers or Sprinter Vans. Substantiation of the data used in preparing this information will be made available upon reasonable request. We do not and will not review or comment on a prospective franchisee's proposed budget, business plan, loan documents or any other plans or documents.

Since June 2005, all new franchisees provide mobile pet grooming services from a customized Sprinter Van rather than a trailer as was required under our original franchise offering. Accordingly the survey results include data with regards to results based on franchisee operated Sprinter Vans and trailers. Except for the change from trailers to customized Sprinter Vans, the Aussie Pet Mobile System and training remained the same.

IMPORTANTLY, THE SUCCESS OF YOUR FRANCHISE WILL DEPEND LARGELY UPON YOUR INDIVIDUAL ABILITIES AND YOUR MARKET, AND THE FINANCIAL RESULTS OF YOUR FRANCHISE ARE LIKELY TO DIFFER, PERHAPS MATERIALLY, FROM THE RESULTS SUMMARIZED IN THIS ITEM.

The information presented in the franchisee survey in this Item is for various periods ranging from six months through 77 months the (the "Measurement Period"). The following represents the percentages of the time periods for which the franchisee operated trailers or Sprinter Vans had been in operation at the date of the survey:

6-12 months	21.5%
13-24 months	48.5%
25-36 months	0%
37-48 months	14%
49-60 months	5%
60+ months	11%
Total	100%

The information in this Item is based on franchisee-operated trailers or Sprinter Vans that operated at least one month during the Measurement Period. In preparing these figures, we relied on information supplied to us solely by our Franchisees, and we have not independently confirmed those figures. The information presented should be read in conjunction with the accompanying notes, which form an integral part of the presentation, together with all other information in this document and the accompanying Disclosure Document, including particularly Item 19.

Some of the franchisees reporting results during the Measurement Period may operate multiple trailers under the franchisors previously offered additional programs: the Silver, Gold and Platinum Programs (all Multi Unit Operators), and therefore the figures reported in this document may not be entirely applicable to prospective franchisees who will operate only one customized Sprinter Van. The Silver Program required a franchisee to acquire and put in service 2 Customized Vehicles and the Platinum Program required a franchisee to acquire and put in service 6 Customized Vehicles. The only Programs offered in this Disclosure are the Single Unit Franchise and Multi Unit Franchise.

You should not use this information as an indication of how well your Franchise Business will do. A number of factors will affect the success of your Franchise Business. These factors include the current market conditions, the type of market in your Protected Area, the location of your Protected Area, the competition and your ability to operate the Franchise Business. A new franchisee's individual financial results will probably differ materially from the figures stated in this document, particularly during any start up phase, and possibly afterwards. Perhaps most importantly, remember that past performance for any business is no guarantee of future results.

The information listed below was accumulated from a Franchisee Survey sent out over the company intranet in January of 2008.

A total of 37 Franchisees operating 96 Pet Mobiles returned their surveys. This represents 45% of all Franchisees who have been operating for at least 6 months and 50% of all Reporting Pet Mobiles operating at least 6 months. The blend of Pet Mobiles in this survey is 77 vans and 19 trailers.

SURVEY QUESTION	PARTICIPATING RESPONSES	AVERAGE RESPONSE
What is your current average cost per call? (advertising spend/number of new inquiries)	87%	28.72 per call
Cost per call is calculated as the amount you have spent in advertising divided by the number of people who respond to your advertising and call to get more information.		
What is your current average cost per sale? (advertising spend/number of new customers)	87%	$57.19 per sale
Cost per sale is calculated as the amount you have spent in advertising divided by the number of people who called on the phone with interest **AND** agreed to sign up for an appointment for service. This number is not incremental to cost per call.		
How much money do you spend per month in advertising?	95%	$3,300
What is your conversion rate? (new calls/appointments)	87%	49%
The conversion rate is the percentage of people who called with interest who actually booked an appointment for service.		
What is your rebooking rate?		
(New customers who booked another appointment)	65%	56%
(Repeat customers who booked another appointment)	70%	80%
How many months would you expect your average repeat customer to stay with you?	81%	22 estimated 29 months
		8 estimated the life of the pet
Have you achieved total revenue of:		
a $1000 day	92%	56% yes
a $1500 day	92%	29% yes
a $2000 day	92%	18% yes

What is your record revenue day?	87%	**Multi unit** averaged $1,518
		Single unit averaged $687
How many days a week do you work?	100%	5.6 days
Are you converting to a 7 day service week?	100%	46% said yes or done
What is your average number of pets per customer?	87%	1.5 pets
How many months have you been in operation?	100%	27 months
Average Groom Price (amount paid for services by a customer)		$77.87

The average groom price is reported from all operating franchisees each month and tabulated on our "Corporate Monthly Report". The groom price reported was taken as an average from 6 monthly reports dating from July 2007 until December 2007.

IMPORTANT NOTICES

Certain figures presented reflect the average number of pets groomed, the average number of repeats and the average price per groom, and do not include any costs to acquire or operate an Aussie Pet Mobile® Franchise Business, and therefore, the information presented is not sufficient to provide any guidance as to profitability (if any) or cash flows. You should obtain estimates for costs to acquire or operate an Aussie Pet Mobile® Franchise Business and review them with a professional advisor before buying a franchise. Also refer to Item 7 of the Offering Circular for information on initial investment costs in establishing an Aussie Pet Mobile® Franchise Business, which are not included here.

Substantiation of the data used in preparing the results stated in this document will be available to you on reasonable request, which may include a requirement to execute a confidentiality document. We do not and will not review or comment on a prospective franchisee's proposed budget, business plan, loan documents or any other plans or documents.

This document is our only authorized "financial performance representations" or other statement regarding financial results relating to Aussie Pet Mobile® Franchises. Any other financial information about Aussie Pet Mobile® Franchises is not authorized and should not be relied upon in any way. We do not authorize our salespersons (or anyone else) to, and have specifically instructed our salespersons, agents, employees, officers and other personnel not to, furnish any other oral or written information concerning actual or potential sales, costs, income or profits, or other financial matters regarding Aussie Pet Mobile® Franchises.

If you believe that any promises, representations or agreements are or have been made to you that are not expressly stated in the Franchise Agreement, the Offering Circular or this document, you must provide us a written statement describing the same next to your signature below. If any such promises, representations or agreements have been provided to you, you should understand that they are unreliable and unauthorized by us. You shouldn't rely upon them, and we are not bound by them. Please notify us in writing before you buy a franchise if any such promises, representations or agreements have been provided to you by anyone.

244

This document should be read in its entirety, including the discussions of factual basis, material assumptions, footnotes and disclaimers, since all of it is important to your decision. Before signing any documents or making any investment, you must make your own independent investigation regarding the possible award of an Aussie Pet Mobile® Franchise, including independent market and industry reviews and comparisons and talking to current and former Aussie Pet Mobile® franchisees. You must consult with your own independent advisors, such as attorneys and accountants, to assist in determining the suitability of this investment for you.

The undersigned hereby confirms that he/she has read and agrees with the contents of this document, including the accompanying notes and Disclosure Document, and will use the data presented for informational purposes only, acknowledging that the results cannot be relied upon in making any decision to purchase, acquire or invest in an Aussie Pet Mobile® Franchise.

THE FIGURES PROVIDED IN THIS <u>FINANCIAL PERFORMANCE REPRESENTATIONS</u> STATEMENT SHOULD NOT BE CONSIDERED AS THE ACTUAL OR PROBABLE RESULTS THAT YOU WILL OR CAN REALIZE. THE EXPERIENCE OF AN INDIVIDUAL FRANCHISEE IS LIKELY TO DIFFER FROM THE INFORMATION SET FORTH ABOVE AND ON THE FOLLOWING STATEMENTS.

BARK BUSTERS - HOME DOG TRAINING

250 W. Lehow Ave. #B
Englewood, CO 80110
Tel: (877) 300-2275 (303) 471-4935
Fax: (720) 283-2819
E-Mail: franchises@barkbusters.com
Web Site: www.barkbusters.com
Ms. Joan Trinka, Director of Franchise Development

Bark Busters is the world's largest, most trusted dog training company, started in Australia in 1989 and came to the United States in 2000. As a world leader in natural home dog training, Bark Busters has trained over 350,000 dogs worldwide using its dog-friendly, natural methods. With 220+ franchised offices in 40 U.S. states and more than 320 offices in nine countries, Bark Busters is continuing its mission to build a global network of dog behavioral therapists to enhance responsible dog ownership and reduce the possibility of maltreatment, abandonment, and euthanasia of companion dogs. Great lifestyle! fulfilling profession! $40+ billion market!

BACKGROUND:

	IFA MEMBER
Established: 1989;	1st Franchised: 2000
Franchised Units:	420
Company-Owned Units:	0
Total Units:	420
Dist.:	US-255; CAN-25; O'seas-80
North America:	40 States, 1 Provinces
Density:	22 in CA, 16 in IL, 17 in TX

Projected New Units (12 Months):	75
Qualifications:	3, 3, 1, 2, 3, 4
Registered:	CA,DC,FL,HI,IL,IN,MD,MI,MN,NY,OR,RI,VA,WA,WI

FINANCIAL/TERMS:

Cash Investment:	$57K-71.1K
Total Investment:	$71.1K-96K
Minimum Net Worth:	$100-150K
Fees: Franchise -	$37.5K
Royalty - 8%;	Ad. - 2%
Earnings Claims Statement:	Yes
Term of Contract (Years):	5/5
Avg. # Of Employees:	1 FT, 0 PT
Passive Ownership:	Not Allowed
Encourage Conversions:	NA
Area Develop. Agreements:	No
Sub-Franchising Contracts:	No
Expand In Territory:	No
Space Needs:	10 x 10 in home office SF; HB

SUPPORT & TRAINING:

Financial Assistance Provided:	Yes (I)
Site Selection Assistance:	NA
Lease Negotiation Assistance:	NA
Co-Operative Advertising:	Yes
Franchisee Assoc./Member:	No
Size Of Corporate Staff:	23
On-Going Support:	A,B,C,D,E,G,h,I
Training:	3 Weeks Denver, CO

SPECIFIC EXPANSION PLANS:

US:	Yes, All United States
Canada:	Yes, All Canada
Overseas:	Yes

ITEM 19
FINANCIAL PERFORMANCE REPRESENTATIONS

Other than as set forth in this ITEM 19, we do not make any representations about a franchisee's future financial performance or the past financial performance of company-owned or franchised outlets. We also do not authorize our employees or representatives to make any such representations either orally or in writing. If you are purchasing an existing outlet, however, we may provide you with the actual records of that outlet. If you receive any other financial performance information or projections of your future income, you should report it to franchisor's management by contacting Joan Trinka at 250 West Lehow Ave., Suite B, Englewood, CO 80110, the Federal Trade Commission, and the appropriate state regulatory agencies.

Substantiation for this data is available for inspection at our corporate headquarters and will be provided upon reasonable request.

CAUTION

Some outlets have sold these amounts. There is no assurance you'll do as well. If you rely upon our figures, you must accept the risk of not doing as well.

The following table shows the average lesson fee per dog trained, average sales of Bark Busters Products for each dog trained, and the average number of lessons with multiple dogs trained for each customer by the 240 franchisees who have been in operation for at least three months during the year ended December 31, 2007. The table also shows the percentage of these franchisees who were above the averages, at the averages, or below the averages state above:

2007 Bark Busters Business Performance

	Average Lesson Fee ($529.12)	Average Product Sales ($20.03)	Average Number of Lessons with Multiple Dog Trained (22.60)	Conversion Rate (44.08)
Above Average	35.83%	32.03%	33.76%	33.33%
Average	33.75%	34.63%	31.65%	35.35%
Below Average	30.42%	33.33%	34.60%	31.31%
Total	100.0%	100.0%	100.0%	100.0%

The earnings claims figures do not reflect the costs of sales, operating expenses, or other costs or expenses that must be deducted from the gross revenue or gross sales figures to obtain your net income or profit. You should conduct an independent investigation of the costs and expenses you will incur in operating your Bark Busters Business. Franchisees or former franchisees, listed in the Franchise Disclosure Document, may be one source of this information.

EXPLANATORY NOTES:

1.   The sales used to compute these averages reflect the sales generated during 2007 by the 223 franchisees who have been in operation for at least three months during the year ended December 31, 2007. We have not audited these amounts but have no reason to doubt the accuracy of the information provided to us by our franchisees. Your revenues may be lower in your first year of business.

2.   These 223 franchised Bark Busters Businesses represent 92% of the total number of franchised Bark Busters Business operating in the United States as of December 31, 2007. These 223 franchised Bark Busters Businesses are located in Arizona, California, Colorado, Connecticut, Delaware, Florida, Georgia, Hawaii, Idaho, Illinois, Indiana, Iowa, Kansas, Kentucky, Louisiana, Maryland, Massachusetts, Michigan, Minnesota, Missouri, Mississippi, Montana, Nevada, New Hampshire,

New Jersey, New Mexico, New York, North Carolina, Ohio, Oregon, Pennsylvania, Rhode Island, South Carolina, Tennessee, Texas, Utah, Virginia, Washington, West Virginia and Wisconsin.

3.	The conversion rate represents the percentage of inquiries for lessons which convert to actual scheduled lessons. The conversion ratio is calculated by dividing the number of inquiries each franchisee receives by the number of times each franchisee actually schedules a lesson.

4.	Substantiation of the data used to prepare these averages will be made available to you upon your reasonable request.

EXCEPT FOR THE INFORMATION IN THIS ITEM, WE DO NOT MAKE ANY REPRESEN-TATIONS OR STATEMENTS OF ACTUAL, AVERAGE, PROJECTED, FORECASTED OR POTEN-TIAL PURCHASES, SALES, COSTS, INCOME OR PROFITS TO YOU. WE DO NOT FURNISH OR MAKE, OR AUTHORIZE OUR SALES PERSONNEL, AGENTS, OFFICERS OR EMPLOYEES TO FURNISH OR MAKE ANY OTHER ORAL OR WRITTEN INFORMATION CONCERNING THE ACTUAL, AVERAGE, PROJECTED, FORECASTED OR POTENTIAL PURCHASES, SALES, COSTS, INCOME OR PROFITS OF A PROPSECIVE FRANCHISEE OR THE CHANCES OF SUCCESS THAT YOU CAN EXPECT OR THAT PRESENT OR PAST FRANCHISEES HAVE HAD, OTHER THAN AS SET FORTH IN THIS ITEM. WE SPECIFICALLY INSTRUCT OUR SALES PERSONNEL, AGENTS, OFFICERS OR EMPLOYEES THAT THEY ARE NOT PERMITTED TO FURNISH OR MAKE ANY OTHER ORAL OR WRITTEN INFORMATION CONCERNING THE ACTUAL, AVERAGE, PRO-JECTED, FORECASTED OR POTENTIAL PURCHASES, SALES, COSTS, INCOME OR PROFITS OF A PROSPECTIVE FRANCHISEE OR THE CHANCES OF SUCCESS THAT YOU CAN EXPECT OR THAT PRESENT OR PAST FRANCHISEES HAVE HAD, OTHER THAN AS SET FORTH IN THIS ITEM. WE RECOMMEND THAT YOU MAKE YOUR OWN INDEPENDENT INVESTIGATION TO DETERMINE WHETHER OR NOT A BARK BUSTERS BUSINESS MAY BE PROFITABLE. WE FUR-THER RECOMMEND THAT YOU CONSULT WITH PROFESSIONAL ADVISORS BEFORE EXE-CUTING ANY AGREEMENT.

COMFORCARE SENIOR SERVICES

2510 Telegraph Rd., # 100
Bloomfield Hills, MI 48302
Tel: (800) 886-4044 (248) 745-9700
Fax: (248) 745-9763
E-Mail: home@comforcare.com
Web Site: www.comforcare.com/franchise
Ms. Brigitte Betser, Director of Sales & Support

Non-medical home care services for seniors and physically chal-lenged individuals of all ages. Turnkey home care franchise opera-tions for aspiring professionals. The broadest array of non-medical home care services in the field. Largest protected territories in the industry - up to 400,000 at no additional cost. Daily support of new franchises.

BACKGROUND:	IFA MEMBER
Established: 1996;	1st Franchised: 2001
Franchised Units:	93

Company-Owned Units:	1
Total Units:	94
Dist.:	US-94; CAN-0; O'seas-0
North America:	26 States, 0 Provinces
Density:	13 in CA, 6 in NJ, 6 in TX
Projected New Units (12 Months):	24
Qualifications:	5, 4, 2, 3, 3, 5
Registered:	CA,DC,FL,HI,IL,IN,MD,MI,MN,NY,OR,VA,WA,WI

FINANCIAL/TERMS:

Cash Investment:	$45.5K-52.5K
Total Investment:	$69.5K-89.5K
Minimum Net Worth:	NR
Fees: Franchise -	$35K
Royalty - 5-3% (Decl.);	Ad. - 0%
Earnings Claims Statement:	No
Term of Contract (Years):	10/10
Avg. # Of Employees:	12 FT, 0 PT
Passive Ownership:	Allowed, But Discouraged
Encourage Conversions:	Yes
Area Develop. Agreements:	Yes
Sub-Franchising Contracts:	No
Expand In Territory:	Yes
Space Needs:	250-450 SF; FS, Office Suite

SUPPORT & TRAINING:		On-Going Support:	A,B,C,D,E,G,H,I
Financial Assistance Provided:	Yes (I)	Training:	1 Week Bloomfield Hills, MI
Site Selection Assistance:	Yes		
Lease Negotiation Assistance:	Yes	**SPECIFIC EXPANSION PLANS:**	
Co-Operative Advertising:	Yes	US:	Yes, All United States
Franchisee Assoc./Member:	No	Canada:	No
Size Of Corporate Staff:	12	Overseas:	No

Item 19
Financial Performance Representations

This Item 19 sets forth certain historical financial performance data as provided by our franchisees; and thus we have a reasonable basis and written substantiation for the representation set forth below. Written substantiation of the data used in preparing this information and for the financial performance representation made in this Item 19 will be made available to you upon reasonable request. The representations made in this Item 19 are based upon the franchise system's outlets existing for the period of time indicated below and are not made up of a subset of those outlets.

IMPORTANTLY, THE SUCCESS OF YOUR FRANCHISE WILL DEPEND LARGELY UPON YOUR PERSONAL ABILITIES, YOUR USE OF THOSE ABILITIES AND YOUR MARKET. THE FINANCIAL RESULTS OF YOUR FRANCHISE WILL LIKELY DIFFER, PERHAPS MATERIALLY, FROM THE RESULTS SUMMARIZED IN THIS ITEM.

The data in the table below contains certain information related to gross sales realized by our franchisees for the period January 1, 2007 through December 31, 2007 and does not include any sales taxes.

The gross sales amounts presented in the table below are based upon information reported to us by the 60 ComForcare franchisees whose offices have been open for at least 12-months for the period ending December 31, 2007, and only for those offices that have reported a full 12 months of gross sales data. We have not audited this information, nor have we independently verified this information.

The information has been extracted from actual financial statements or royalty reports reported to ComForcare. This information may not be relied upon as a projection or forecast of what a new franchisee may experience.

In preparing financial projections for a prospective franchise operation, it is important to keep in mind that each franchisee's experience is unique and their results will most likely vary depending on a number of factors, including the franchisee's personal abilities, use of those abilities, the market in which they operate, the general economic conditions, competition, effectiveness of the franchisee in the management of the office, the size of the individual or combined territories and the overall efficiency of the franchisee's operation. In addition, the population size, density of seniors and number of people over the age of 65 in the exclusive territories for the franchise owners represented in the table below may not be similar to, or representative of, the exclusive territory you may purchase.

TABLE OF GROSS SALES INFORMATION FOR FRANCHISEES OPEN AT LEAST ONE YEAR					
Designation and Franchisee Time in Business	**Total Owners**	**Average Owner's Gross Revenue**	**Median Owner's Gross Revenue**	**Highest Owner's Gross Revenue**	**Lowest Owner's Gross Revenue**
Experienced Franchisees - 49 months and greater	15 (a)	$1,085,152	$980,996	$4,202,086	$216,420

Junior Franchisees - 25-48 months	29	$617,069	$458,730	$3,068,854	$77,437
New Franchisees - 13-24 months	16	$307,489	$272,020	$894,209	$47,203
Total/Average	60 (b)	$651,535 (c)			

(a)   The 15 experienced franchisees listed in this table have been in business for 49 months or greater and this data includes the gross sales totaling $4,202,086 for the 12 months ended December 31, 2007 for the first franchisee who originally began operations on May 1, 1996, which is a sister company to ComForcare and who is affiliated through a common owner.

(b)   The total number of franchised territories on December 31, 2007 was 94 which are comprised of 76 franchise business owners, including the affiliated company franchise. The gross sales data in the table excludes 13 new business owners who did not report gross sales information for a full 12 months and also excludes three inactive offices that are held out for resale. This table includes offices opening in each year from 1996 through January 1, 2006 with the distribution of start dates as follows: 2006 — 16; 2005 — 13; 2004 — 16; 2003 — 10; 2002- 4; and 1996 — 1. The gross sales data presented for the business owners above can and does vary depending on the personal abilities of the owners, use of those abilities, the market in which they operate, competition, effectiveness of the management team in the office, the size of the individual or combined territories and the overall efficiency of the operation. This gross sales data is not necessarily a reflection of, nor comparable to, the actual results you may achieve as a business owner. In addition, the population size, density of seniors and number of people over the age of 65 in the exclusive territories for the franchise owners represented in the table above may not be similar to or representative of the exclusive territory you may purchase

(c)   The average owner's gross sales reported in the table above is $651,535. Eighteen of the 60 franchised business owners, or 30%, met or exceeded this gross sales level for the 12 month period from January 1, 2007 through December 31, 2007.

PRELIMINARY CAUTION

These disclosure figures do not reflect the cost of sales, operating expenses, or other costs or expenses that must be deducted from the gross revenue or gross sales figures to obtain your net income or profit. You should conduct an independent investigation of costs and expenses you will incur in operating your franchise business. Current franchisees or former franchisees listed in the disclosure document may be one source of this information.

There is no assurance that your franchised business will do as well as those offices referenced in the table above. If you rely upon those figures, you do so at your own risk of not doing as well. Actual results vary from business to business, and we cannot reasonably estimate the results of a particular business operation. Gross sales will vary. In particular, the gross sales of your franchised business will be directly affected by many factors, such as: (a) geographic region; (b) competition from other similar businesses in your area; (c) sales and marketing effectiveness based on market saturation; (d) your service pricing; (e) vendor prices on materials and supplies; (f) labor availability and related costs; (g) ability to generate clients; (h) client loyalty; and (i) employment conditions in the market. Any such factor may differ materially from those that may exist for a franchise offered to you.

Importantly, you should not consider the gross sales presented in the above table to be the actual potential that you will realize. We do not represent that you can or will attain those or similar revenues or margins, or any particular level of gross sales. We do not represent that you will generate income, which exceeds the initial payment for, or investment in, your franchise.

Based on all of the matters mentioned in this Item 19, we recommend that you make your own independent investigation to determine whether or not the franchise may be profitable to you and worth the risk. You should use this information only as a reference in conducting your analysis and in preparing your own projected income statements and cash flow statements. We suggest strongly that you consult your financial advisor or personal accountant concerning financial projections and federal, provincial and local income taxes and any other applicable taxes that you may incur in owning and operating a franchised business.

THE SUCCESS OF YOUR FRANCHISE WILL DEPEND LARGELY UPON YOUR INDIVIDUAL ABILITIES, YOUR USE OF THOSE ABILITIES AND YOUR MARKET. THE FINANCIAL RESULTS OF YOUR FRANCHISE OPERATIONS ARE LIKELY TO DIFFER, PERHAPS MATERIALLY, FROM THE RESULTS SUMMARIZED IN ITEM 19.

The above data is the only information, representation or statement of actual gross sales, costs, income or profits of a ComForcare Senior Services franchised business that a ComForcare employee or other representative is authorized to provide to you. ComForcare does not provide any other information regarding actual gross sales, costs, income or profits to any of its employees or representatives and does not authorize any of its employees or other representatives to provide you with any other information, representations or statements.

Actual results vary from franchisee to franchisee and ComForcare cannot estimate the results of any particular franchisee. A new franchisee's financial results may differ from the figures presented. You should make your own investigation and determine whether your franchised business will be profitable. ComForcare does not guarantee that a franchisee will have income.

Disclaimer Regarding Claims made by Agents, Brokers or Employees

We specifically instruct our sales personnel, franchise brokers, agents, employees and officers that they may not make any claims or statements as to the earnings, sales, profits, prospects or changes of success of a ComForcare Senior Service franchised business other than as set forth in this Item 19. They are not authorized to represent or estimate dollar figures as to a franchisee's operation other than as shown above, and if you decide to proceed to own a franchise, you will be required to acknowledge in writing that you have not relied on any such unauthorized representations or estimate in purchasing your franchise.

COMFORT KEEPERS

6640 Poe Ave., # 200
Dayton, OH 45414-2600
Tel: (888) 329-1368 (937) 264-1933
Fax: (937) 264-3103
E-Mail: admin@comfortkeepers.com
Web Site: www.comfortkeepers.com
Mr. Larry France, Manager, Franchise Development, Western USA

COMFORT KEEPERS is the service leader with 95% client satisfaction. We provide non-medical, in-home care, such as companionship, meal preparation, light housekeeping, grocery and clothing shopping, grooming and assistance with recreational activities for the elderly and others who need assistance in daily living.

BACKGROUND:	IFA MEMBER
Established: 1998;	1st Franchised: 1999
Franchised Units:	613
Company-Owned Units:	0
Total Units:	613
Dist.:	US-568; CAN-28; O'seas-17
North America:	47 States, 3 Provinces
Density:	68 in CA, 53 in FL, 43 in OH
Projected New Units (12 Months):	30
Qualifications:	5, 5, 2, 3, 3, 4
Registered:CA,DC,FL,HI,IL,IN,MD,MI,MN,ND,NY,OR,RI,SD,	
	VA,WA,WI,AB

FINANCIAL/TERMS:	
Cash Investment:	$74K

Total Investment:	$74K	**SUPPORT & TRAINING:**	
Minimum Net Worth:	$200K	Financial Assistance Provided:	Yes (I)
Fees: Franchise -	$32.5K	Site Selection Assistance:	No
Royalty - 5/4/3%;	Ad. - 0%	Lease Negotiation Assistance:	No
Earnings Claims Statement:	Yes	Co-Operative Advertising:	No
Term of Contract (Years):	10/10	Franchisee Assoc./Member:	Yes/Member
Avg. # Of Employees:	2 FT, 4-5 PT	Size Of Corporate Staff:	35
Passive Ownership:	Not Allowed	On-Going Support:	C,D,G,h,I
Encourage Conversions:	Yes	Training:	8 Days & Ongoing Dayton, OH
Area Develop. Agreements:	No		
Sub-Franchising Contracts:	No	**SPECIFIC EXPANSION PLANS:**	
Expand In Territory:	Yes	US:	Yes, All United States
Space Needs:400-700 SF; Office Space preferable; Home-Based permitted		Canada:	Yes
		Overseas:	Yes

ITEM 19.
FINANCIAL PERFORMANCE REPRESENTATIONS

The following tables are historical financial performance representations. They represent certain financial information for calendar year 2006 or for calendar year 2007, as applicable, for all franchised units that reported a full twelve months' Gross Revenues during that year. We used the Gross Revenues figures from the royalty reports the franchisees filed with us. While we have not audited this information or independently confirmed the royalty reports, we have no reason to believe that any franchisee would overstate its revenues to us. Because the 2007 table includes Offices that were not included in the 2006 table, you should make no direct comparison of any of the results shown.

"Gross Revenue" means the total amount of money the franchisee and its owners receive for all goods sold and services rendered in connection with the Marks, and all other income of any kind derived directly or indirectly in connection with the operation of an Office, including client deposits and payments for mileage charges but excluding sales tax and client refunds.

Calendar Year 2007

Total Offices (1)	Average Gross Revenue	Number and Percentage of Offices Meeting or Exceeding Average (2)	Median Gross Revenue (3)	Highest Office Gross Revenue	Lowest Office Gross Revenue
489	$496,412	198 / 40%	$409,938	$3,981,065	$0

(1) The total number of franchised Offices that operated during 2007 is 527; we have no company-owned offices. The number in the first column of this table represents all Offices that reported Gross Revenue for each month during calendar year 2007. The table excludes seventeen Offices that closed during 2007 and twenty-one Offices (including Offices that opened in 2007) that did not report revenue for the full twelve months. This chart includes Offices opening in each year from 1998 through January 1, 2007, with the distribution of Start Dates as follows: 1998-1, 1999-2, 2000-36, 2001-86, 2002-142, 2003-76, 2004-48, 2005— 53, 2006-37. 2007-8. Each of the Offices included in the table provides the non-medical, companion care services for seniors and others needing assistance that you must provide under the Franchise Agreement; 419 of those Offices also provided personal care services in 2007 (which are an additional service you may provide), and/or ancillary services such as technology solutions for independence and security.

(2)   Among the 489 Offices included in the Average Gross Revenue calculation are two Offices owned by a single franchisee, and two Offices owned by another franchisee, each of which reports Gross Revenue as a single unit for all of the Offices it owns. Because we are unable to calculate the actual Gross Revenue for those four individual Offices, we have omitted the Offices from the calculation of the number and percentage of Offices meeting or exceeding the Average Gross Revenue figure shown. This means that the calculation in this column is based on 485 Offices, rather than 489 Offices.

(3)   Because we are unable to calculate the actual Gross Revenue by Office for the four Offices mentioned in Note (2), we have omitted the Gross Revenue reported for those Offices from the calculation of the median Gross Revenue.

<u>Calendar Year 2006</u>

Total Offices (1)	Average Gross Revenue	Number and Percentage of Offices Meeting or Exceeding Average	Median Gross Revenue	Highest Office Gross Revenue	Lowest Office Gross Revenue
440	$461,724	166 / 38%	$352,498	$3,095,346	$0

(1)   The total number of franchised Offices that operated during 2006 is 508; we have no company-owned offices. The number in the first column of this table represents all Offices that reported Gross Revenue for each month during calendar year 2006. The table excludes fifty-nine Offices (including Offices that opened in 2006) that did not report revenue for the full twelve months and nine other Offices that closed during 2006. This table includes offices opening in each year from 1998 through January 1, 2006, with the distribution of Start Dates as follows: 1998-1, 1999-2, 2000-34, 2001-88, 2002-143, 2003-75, 2004-49, 2005-46, 2006— 2. Each of the Offices included in the table provides the non-medical, companion care services for seniors and others needing assistance that you must provide under the Franchise Agreement; 374 of those offices also provided personal care services in 2006 (which are an additional service you may provide), and/or ancillary services such as technology solutions for independence and security.

(2)   Among the 440 Offices included in the Average Gross Revenue calculation are two Offices owned by a single franchisee, and two Offices owned by another franchisee, each of which reports Gross Revenue as a single unit for all of the Offices it owns. Because we are unable to calculate the actual Gross Revenue for those four individual Offices, we have omitted the Offices from the calculation of the number and percentage of Offices meeting or exceeding the Average Gross Revenue figure shown. This means that the calculation in this column is based on 436 Offices, rather than 440 Offices.

(3)   Because we are unable to calculate the actual Gross Revenue by Office for the four Offices mentioned in Note (2), we have omitted the Gross Revenue reported for those Offices from the calculation of the median Gross Revenue.

We will make available to you upon reasonable request written substantiation of the information contained in the table above.

THE RESULTS GIVEN IN THESE TABLES ARE HISTORIC REPRESENTATIONS OF FINANCIAL RESULTS ACHIEVED BY CERTAIN COMFORT KEEPERS FRANCHISED OFFICES. A NEW FRANCHISEE'S RESULTS ARE LIKELY TO DIFFER FROM THE RESULTS STATED IN THE TABLES. ACTUAL RESULTS VARY FROM OFFICE TO OFFICE, AND THE SUCCESS OF YOUR OFFICE WILL DEPEND IN LARGE PART UPON YOUR SKILLS AND ABILITIES, COMPETITION FROM OTHER BUSINESSES, AND OTHER ECONOMIC AND BUSINESS FACTORS. WE MAKE NO REPRESENTATION OR WARRANTY THAT YOU WILL, OR ARE LIKELY TO, ACHIEVE THE RESULTS SHOWN IN THE TABLES.

COMPUTER EXPLORERS

COMPUTER EXPLORERS
12715 Telge Rd.
Cypress, TX 77429-2289
Tel: (888) 638-8722 (281) 256-4221
Fax: (281) 256-4178
E-Mail: franchisedevelopment@iced.net
Web Site: www.computerexplorers.com
Ms. Jenny Langfeld, Franchise Dev. Support Mgr.

The newest member of the ICED family of franchises provides educational technology training for childcare centers, preschools and elementary schools. Having taught more than three million classes, we seek entrepreneurs who wish to build a thriving business while providing quality computer education and curriculum for children.

BACKGROUND: IFA MEMBER

Established: 1983;	1st Franchised: 1988
Franchised Units:	107
Company-Owned Units:	0
Total Units:	107
Dist.:	US-101; CAN-1; O'seas-5
North America:	30 States, 1 Provinces
Density:	6 in CA, 6 in IL, 6 in NJ
Projected New Units (12 Months):	NR
Qualifications:	4
Registered:CA,DC,FL,HI,IL,IN,MD,MI,MN,ND,NY,OR,RI,SD, VA,WA,WI	

FINANCIAL/TERMS:

Cash Investment:	$30K
Total Investment:	$62.9K-73.3K
Minimum Net Worth:	$100K
Fees: Franchise -	$35K
Royalty - 8%;	Ad. - 1%
Earnings Claims Statement:	No
Term of Contract (Years):	15/15
Avg. # Of Employees:	1 FT, 5 PT
Passive Ownership:	Not Allowed
Encourage Conversions:	NA
Area Develop. Agreements:	No
Sub-Franchising Contracts:	No
Expand In Territory:	No
Space Needs:	SF

SUPPORT & TRAINING:

Financial Assistance Provided:	No
Site Selection Assistance:	NA
Lease Negotiation Assistance:	NA
Co-Operative Advertising:	No
Franchisee Assoc./Member:	Yes/Member
Size Of Corporate Staff:	0
On-Going Support:	c,d,g,h,I
Training:	2 Weeks Headquarters

SPECIFIC EXPANSION PLANS:

US:	Yes, All United States
Canada:	No
Overseas:	No

ITEM 19. FINANCIAL PERFORMANCE REPRESENTATIONS

AVERAGE ANNUAL GROSS SALES
OF FRANCHISE TERRITORIES
(Territories Reporting for the Full 12 Months in 2005, 2006 and 2007)

	2007	2006	2005
Average for System	$108,737	$113,141	$104,422
Top Franchise Territory	$574,639	$426,337	$318,145
Average for:*			
Top 10% of Territories	$351,303	$309,572	$284,070
Top 25% of Territories	$204,807	$218,628	$208,277
Top 50% of Territories	$168,549	$165,755	$152,638
Top 75% of Territories	$136,407	$138,777	$126,229

*The percentage is based on the total number of reporting territories. (e.g. with 72 reporting territories, the top 10% = 10% of 72, or the top seven reporting territories)

Records show 62 franchise territories reporting gross sales for the full 12 months of 2005, 63 franchise territories reporting gross sales for the full 12 months of 2006 and 72 franchise territories reporting gross sales for the full 12 months of 2007.

Of the 72 territories operating and reporting to us for a full 12 months in the year 2007, 30 (42%) achieved annual gross sales at or above the average annual gross sales of $108,737 for all 72 reporting territories.

Of the 63 territories operating and reporting to us for a full 12 months in the year 2006, 23 (37%) achieved annual gross sales at or above the average annual gross sales of $113,141 for all 63 reporting territories

Of the 62 territories operating and reporting to us for a full 12 months in the year 2005, 20 (32%) achieved annual gross sales at or above the average annual gross sales of $104,422 for all 62 reporting territories.

The results achieved by franchise territories that did not report gross sales for the full 12 months in any year (such as franchise territories that started operations mid-year), and franchise territories that were transferred and assigned new franchise numbers, are not included in this exhibit. For a period of time, a smaller owner-operated territory model was offered. The offering was discontinued in 2004. The above figures do not include these smaller owner-operated model franchise territories.

Gross sales represent the actual revenues collected by franchise territories and are stated before business expenses are paid. While franchise territories carry varying amounts of receivables, receivables are not included in gross sales. Business expenses such as the following must be paid out of gross sales: salaries and benefits; commercial office rent (not required); continuing franchise fees (6% or 8%, subject to monthly minimums), and advertising and promotional contributions; equipment; office supplies and expenses; travel expenses; amortization; depreciation; and taxes.

The gross sales figures stated in this exhibit are substantiated by unaudited reports submitted to us by our franchisees. Relevant portions of those reports are the written substantiations for the financial performance representations in this Item 19 that will be made available to you upon reasonable request.

CAUTION

THE FINANCIAL PERFORMANCE REPRESENTATIONS FIGURES DO NOT REFLECT THE COSTS OF SALES, OPERATING EXPENSES, OR OTHER COSTS OR EXPENSES THAT MUST BE DEDUCTED FROM THE GROSS REVENUE OR GROSS SALES FIGURES TO OBTAIN YOUR NET INCOME OR PROFIT. YOU SHOULD CONDUCT AN INDEPENDENT INVESTIGATION OF THE COSTS AND EXPENSES YOU WILL INCUR IN OPERATING YOUR FRANCHISED BUSINESS. FRANCHISEES OR FORMER FRANCHISEES, LISTED IN THE DISCLOSURE DOCUMENT, MAY BE ONE SOURCE OF THIS INFORMATION.

THE GROSS SALES FIGURES STATED IN THIS ITEM SHOULD NOT BE CONSIDERED AS THE ACTUAL OR POTENTIAL GROSS SALES FIGURES THAT WILL BE REALIZED BY ANY PROSPECTIVE FRANCHISEE.

YOUR RESULTS MAY DIFFER FROM THOSE STATED ABOVE. WE DO NOT REPRESENT THAT YOU CAN EXPECT TO ATTAIN ANY OF THE GROSS SALES FIGURES INDICATED.

Country Place®
LIVING
Do Well While Doing Good.™

COUNTRY PLACE LIVING
1527 W. State Highway 114; Ste. 500-354

Grapevine, TX 76051
Tel: 817-545-5353 817-545-5353
Fax: 866-360-0060
E-Mail: franchise@countryplaceliving.com
Web Site: www.CountryPlaceLiving.com
Ms. Cynthia Gartman, President & COO

Country Place Living offers franchises for assisted living and group home residences. Our residences are places where seniors truly feel at home and maintain their dignity. We specialize in small group residences consisting of either 18 apartments (Country Place Senior Living) or 8 bedrooms (Country Place Home Plus.) Country Place Senior Living is designed for active seniors, while Country Place Home Plus is created especially for those seniors who may need additional specialized care.

BACKGROUND: IFA MEMBER
Established: 1981; 1st Franchised: 2007
Franchised Units: 1
Company-Owned Units: 8
Total Units: 9
Dist.: US-9; CAN-0; O'seas-0
North America: 1 States, 0 Provinces
Density: 7 in KS
Projected New Units (12 Months): 3
Qualifications: 4, 4, 1, 3, 5, 5
Registered: FL,IN,OR

FINANCIAL/TERMS:
Cash Investment: $150K - 500K
Total Investment: $600K - 2.3MM
Minimum Net Worth: $250K
Fees: Franchise - $37,500

Royalty - 5%; Ad. - 1/2%
Earnings Claims Statement: Yes
Term of Contract (Years): 10/10
Avg. # Of Employees: 8 - 13 FT, 0 PT
Passive Ownership: Allowed
Encourage Conversions: No
Area Develop. Agreements: No
Sub-Franchising Contracts: No
Expand In Territory: No
Space Needs: .75 acre to 1.5 acres SF; Near Healthcare

SUPPORT & TRAINING:
Financial Assistance Provided: Yes (I)
Site Selection Assistance: Yes
Lease Negotiation Assistance: NA
Co-Operative Advertising: No
Franchisee Assoc./Member: No
Size Of Corporate Staff: 6
On-Going Support: B,C,D,E,G,h
Training: 5 Days Franchisee Location; 12 Days Wichita, KS;1 1/2 DaysDallas, TX

SPECIFIC EXPANSION PLANS:
US: Yes, All states except for WA, CA, HI
Canada: No
Overseas: No

ITEM 19
FINANCIAL PERFORMANCE REPRESENTATIONS

The following charts include certain relevant information based on the operation of 3 Country Place® Senior Living Residences and 1 Country Place® Home Plus Residence owned by the Country Place Operators. These Residences are all of the Country Place Living Residences opened and in operation for the entire 12 month period from January 2007 through December 2007.

Country Place® Senior Living — 12 Months ending December 31, 2007
18 Apartments

This data represents the results of three Residences which were in operation from January 2007 through December 2007. All Residences are located in Kansas. One Residence opened in 2003, the other two in 2006.

Total Average Occupancy
95.09%

Two Country Place® Senior Living residences are below, and one Country Place® Senior Living Residence is above the occupancy average.

	Gross Revenue One Residence is below and two Residences are above the average.	Total Expenses Two Residences are below and one Residence is above the average.		Net Operating Income[1] One Residence is below and two Residences are above the average.	
Low	$538,289.49	$405,656.34	68.06%	$122,278.47	22.72%
Average	$582,573.06	$423,883.09	72.90%	$158,689.97	27.10%
High	$613,401.07	$416,011.02	77.28%	$190,372.27	31.94%

Expenses - Low, Average, and High[2]

The expenses listed below are the low, average, and high expenses in each category, regardless of the Residence that incurred the expense.

	Low		Average		High	
Administrative	$10,435.46	1.75%	$13,351.95	2.29%	$17,436.23	2.84%
Food Service	$38,173.78	6.40%	$41,399.91	7.15%	$44,765.64	8.32%
Housekeeping	$2,675.37	0.45%	$3,208.02	0.55%	$3,522.27	0.65%
Insurance	$27,928.40	4.69%	$31,632.75	5.43%	$37,110.20	6.05%
Maintenance	$9,536.82	1.60%	$12,848.17	2.20%	$16,719.93	2.73%
Marketing	$4,770.53	0.89%	$6,014.04	1.03%	$7,179.28	1.20%
Property Taxes	$19,681.00	3.30%	$21,330.62	3.68%	$22,505.01	4.18%
Resident Service	$259,986.18	43.62%	$267,399.33	45.97%	$282,877.13	46.12%
Transportation	$0.00	0.00%	$142.80	0.03%	$279.60	0.05%
Utilities	$23,104.70	3.77%	$26,555.50	4.58%	$30,060.05	5.04%

Country Place® Home Plus – 12 Months ending December 31, 2007
8 Bedrooms

This data represents the results of one Residence which was in operation from January 2007 through December 2007. The Residence is located in Kansas and opened in 2005.

Total Average Occupancy
99.84%

Average Gross Revenue	Average Total Expenses		Average Net Operating Income[1]	
$351,407.52	$245,552.79	69.88%	$105,854.73	30.12%

Average Expenses[2]

Administrative	$12,147.47	3.46%
Food Service	$13,911.15	3.96%
Housekeeping	$1,158.99	0.33%
Insurance	$14,703.78	4.18%
Maintenance	$7,449.49	2.12%
Marketing	$7,007.05	1.99%
Property Taxes	$883.05	0.25%
Resident Service	$179,329.22	51.03%
Transportation	$566.63	0.11%
Utilities	$8,395.96	2.39%

NOTES

(1)   "Net Operating Income" is income after deducting for operating expenses but before deducting for interest, taxes, depreciation, and amortization.

(2)   In addition to the expenses listed in this Item, a franchisee will incur a Royalty Fee of 5% of Gross Revenue and IT Support Fee of $100 per month. (See Item 6). Also, due to the required Brand Development Contribution of .5% of Gross Revenues and Local Marketing Activities of 1.5% of Gross Revenues, the marketing expenses for a franchisee will be higher than the marketing expenses listed above. (See Item 6).

THE INFORMATION PRESENTED IN THIS ITEM 19 IS NOT BASED UPON THE ACTUAL EXPERIENCE OF FRANCHISED COUNTRY PLACE LIVING RESIDENCES AND

SHOULD NOT BE CONSIDERED AS THE ACTUAL OR POTENTIAL REVENUES, EXPENSE RATIOS OR OCCUPANCY LEVELS YOU WILL REALIZE. WE DO NOT REPRESENT THAT ANY FRANCHISEE CAN EXPECT TO ATTAIN THE REVENUES, EXPENSE RATIOS OR OCCUPANCY LEVELS DESCRIBED IN THIS ITEM 19, OR ANY PARTICULAR LEVEL OF REVENUES, EXPENSE RATIOS OR OCCUPANCY. IN ADDITION, WE DO NOT REPRESENT THAT ANY FRANCHISEE WILL DERIVE INCOME THAT EXCEEDS THE INITIAL PAYMENT FOR OR INVESTMENT IN THE FRANCHISED BUSINESS. THE INDIVIDUAL FINANCIAL RESULTS OF ANY FRANCHISED RESIDENCE ARE LIKELY TO DIFFER FROM THE INFORMATION DESCRIBED IN THIS ITEM 19, AND YOUR SUCCESS WILL DEPEND LARGELY ON YOUR ABILITY. YOU ARE URGED TO CONSULT WITH YOUR FINANCIAL, BUSINESS AND LEGAL ADVISERS TO CONDUCT YOUR OWN ANALYSIS OF THE INFORMATION CONTAINED IN THIS ITEM 19.

We have written substantiation in our possession to support the information appearing in this Item 19 and such substantiation will be made available to you on reasonable request.

COVERALL
Health-Based Cleaning System℠

COVERALL HEALTH-BASED CLEANING SYSTEM

5201 Congress Ave., # 275
Boca Raton, FL 33487
Tel: (800) 537-3371 (561) 922-2500
Fax: (561) 922-2423
E-Mail: jack.caughey@coverall.com
Web Site: www.coverall.com
Mr. Jack Caughey, Business Development

Commercial cleaning franchise which includes comprehensive training, equipment, billing and collection services, and an initial customer base. With an affordable down payment as low as $3,950, COVERALL HEALTH-BASED CLEANING SYSTEM provides a combination of business programs and support systems that focus on meeting the franchisees and customers alike. Master and territory franchises are also available.

BACKGROUND: IFA MEMBER
Established: 1985; 1st Franchised: 1985
Franchised Units: 9603
Company-Owned Units: 0
Total Units: 9603
Dist.: US-8917; CAN-286; O'seas-400
  North America: 32 States, 3 Provinces
  Density: 1165 in CA, 1083 in FL, 610 in OH
Projected New Units (12 Months): 1736
Qualifications: 3, 3, 2, 2, 3, 5
Registered: CA,FL,HI,IL,IN,MD,MI,MN,NY,OR,RI,VA,WA,WI,AB

FINANCIAL/TERMS:

Cash Investment:	$2,000-$27,200
Total Investment:	$$10,612-$37,345
Minimum Net Worth:	$10,612
Fees: Franchise -	$10,000-$32,200
Royalty - 5%;	Ad. - 0%
Earnings Claims Statement:	No
Term of Contract (Years):	20/20
Avg. # Of Employees:	1-2 FT, 2-3 PT
Passive Ownership:	Allowed
Encourage Conversions:	Yes
Area Develop. Agreements:	No
Sub-Franchising Contracts:	Yes
Expand In Territory:	Yes
Space Needs:	SF

SUPPORT & TRAINING:

Financial Assistance Provided:	Yes (D)
Site Selection Assistance:	NA
Lease Negotiation Assistance:	NA
Co-Operative Advertising:	No
Franchisee Assoc./Member:	No
Size Of Corporate Staff:	90
On-Going Support:	A,B,D,G,H,I
Training:	40 Hours Local Regional Support Center

SPECIFIC EXPANSION PLANS:

US:	Yes, All United States
Canada:	Yes, All Canada
Overseas:	Yes, All Countries

ITEM 19
FINANCIAL PERFORMANCE REPRESENTATION

We do not make any representations about a franchisee's future financial performance or the past financial performance of company-owned or franchised outlets. We also do not authorize our employees or representatives to make any such representations either orally or in writing. If you are purchasing an existing outlet, however, we may provide you with the actual records of that outlet. If you receive any other financial performance information or projections of your future income, you should report it to the franchisor's management by contacting the Compliance Director in the Legal Department at the Global Support Center located at 5201 Congress Avenue, Suite 275, Boca Raton, FL 33487, the Federal Trade Commission, and the appropriate state regulatory agencies.

We sell our franchises as packages. The Franchise Package is described as a specified amount of Initial Business, which we must offer to you within a certain amount of time. For convenience and to be consistent with business practices in the janitorial franchise industry, we describe these Franchise Packages in terms of gross monthly dollar volume (i.e., a P-1500 Franchise Package means $1,500.00 in gross monthly dollar volume). In addition, under the Franchise Agreement, we will guarantee your Franchise Package for up to a maximum of 12 months, subject to the conditions described in Item 11 above.

If we do not offer the Initial Business within the specified time, you may request a refund of a portion of the initial franchisee fee, as described in Item 5, above.

The gross monthly dollar volume of the Initial Business that you purchase should not be considered as the actual or potential income or profit, you will realize. The total gross monthly dollar billings you achieve are affected by many factors such as: the Initial Business may be offered in stages during the specified time period; you may decline an account; you may lose an account for poor service; the account may cancel through no fault of your own and you did not perform the required inspections to earn the extended guarantee; and you may lose an account through no fault of your own and there is a time lag before the replacement account is offered.

Other factors affecting your gross monthly revenue are the quality and efficiency of your cleaning services; the degree to which you finance the purchase and operation of the franchise; and business expenses associated with operating your business, many of which expenses you control, such as wages to employees.

COVERALL'S FULFILLMENT OF FRANCHISE PACKAGES

We analyzed our compliance with the Franchise Agreement concerning the amount, timeliness, and refund requirements for Initial Business provided to our franchisees. We reviewed all franchise sales made during our fiscal year, and determined whether or not as of December 31, 2007 the Initial Business had been offered in compliance with the Franchise Agreement.

During our fiscal year January 1, 2007 to December 31, 2007, we sold 771 franchises. Of those sold, as of the close of the fiscal year: (a) franchisees either had their packages timely filled or have accepted our performance in 482 cases; (b) we and the franchisee made a mutually acceptable adjustment to the franchise package, such as by our recalculation of the franchise fee or an extension of time to provide accounts, in 50 cases; (c) the time for us to provide initial customer accounts under franchise packages had not expired in 239cases; and (d) it is undetermined whether the package has been filled in 0 cases.

Therefore, we complied with the amount, timeliness, and recalculation requirements for Initial Business provided to our franchisees in 100% of the cases. Our compliance could not be determined in less than one percent of the sales. Substantiation of the data used in preparing these statistics will be made available upon request.

The basis for our claim about Initial Business is Paragraph 4 of the Franchise Agreement.

CRUISE HOLIDAYS

6442 City W. Parkway
Minneapolis, MN 55344-3245
Tel: (800) 824-1481 (952) 914-6743
Fax: (763) 219-4182
E-Mail: mwollak@ttfg.com
Web Site: www.cruiseholidays.com
Ms. Megan Wollak, Franchise Development

Cruise Holidays is the largest cruise-specialty franchise in North America offering retail and home-based franchises and career opportunities. Cruise Holidays is also a distinguished provider of all-inclusive resort and land tour vacation packages. It is our carefully crafted standards and brand positioning that set Cruise Holidays apart from the competition. Our name says it all . . . a focus on the cruise experience for our customers. If you are interested in the excitement and allure of the cruise industry, Cruise Holidays has the expertise to help you achieve your entrepreneurial dream.

BACKGROUND: IFA MEMBER

Established: 1984;	1st Franchised: 1984
Franchised Units:	232
Company-Owned Units:	0
Total Units:	232
Dist.:	US-202; CAN-30; O'seas-0
North America:	34 States, 4 Provinces
Density:	11 in CA, 10 in NJ, 20 in ON
Projected New Units (12 Months):	40
Qualifications:	5, 5, 1, 1, 4, 5

Registered:CA,DC,FL,HI,IL,IN,MD,MI,MN,ND,NY,OR,RI,SD, VA,WA,WI,AB

FINANCIAL/TERMS:

Cash Investment:	$30K
Total Investment:	$137K-248K
Minimum Net Worth:	$250K
Fees: Franchise -	$30K
Royalty - $750/mo.;	Ad. - 0%
Earnings Claims Statement:	No
Term of Contract (Years):	3/3
Avg. # Of Employees:	1 FT, 0 PT
Passive Ownership:	Not Allowed
Encourage Conversions:	Yes
Area Develop. Agreements:	No
Sub-Franchising Contracts:	No
Expand In Territory:	Yes
Space Needs:	800-1000 SF; SC, Good Visibility to Traffic

SUPPORT & TRAINING:

Financial Assistance Provided:	No
Site Selection Assistance:	Yes
Lease Negotiation Assistance:	No
Co-Operative Advertising:	Yes
Franchisee Assoc./Member:	Yes/Member
Size Of Corporate Staff:	13
On-Going Support:	C,D,E,G,h,I
Training:	3 weeks New Franchisee training in Minneapolis, MN

SPECIFIC EXPANSION PLANS:

US:	Yes, All United States except Alaska
Canada:	Yes, All Canada except Quebec, New Brunswick, Newfoundland
Overseas:	No

19.   FINANCIAL PERFORMANCE REPRESENTATIONS

Background

This Item sets forth certain historical data related to gross sales and bookings from Stores licensed by us and our Canadian affiliate that are substantially similar to those being offered through this Franchise Disclosure Document and: (a) have been operating more than one year; (b) operate under the CRUISE HOLIDAYS mark; and (c) reported their sales via CruiseWeb 6.0 (our proprietary software). We have not audited this information, nor independently verified this information.

The information is for the period January 1, 2007 through December 31, 2007. In 2007, there were 115 Stores, 81 in the United States and 34 in Canada. 19 Stores were excluded from this Item because 8 had not yet converted to CruiseWeb 6.0 and 11 were not in operation for the full year. The oldest of the Stores presented has been open for 22 years. Written substantiation of the data used in preparing this information will be made available upon reasonable request.

IMPORTANTLY, THE SUCCESS OF YOUR FRANCHISE WILL DEPEND LARGELY UPON YOUR INDIVIDUAL ABILITIES, YOUR MARKET, AND THE FINANCIAL RESULTS OF YOUR FRANCHISE ARE LIKELY TO DIFFER, PERHAPS MATERIALLY, FROM THE RESULTS SUMMA-

RIZED IN THIS ITEM.

You should not use this information as an indication of how well your franchise will do. A number of factors will affect the success of your franchise. These factors include the current market conditions, the type of market in your franchise area, the location of your franchise area, the competition and your ability to operate the franchise.

Stores Open More Than One Year But Less Than Two Years

The following tables set forth Gross Sales[1] and booking information for the period January 1, 2007 through December 31, 2007 for Stores open more than one year but less than two years. During 2007 there were 3 U.S. Stores and 1 Canadian Store that met this criteria. The tables set forth Gross Sales based on two measuring basis, the first column is based on cruises booked in 2007 and the second is for cruises which actually sailed in 2007.

United States

Gross Sales and Bookings for U.S. Licensees
Calendar Year 2007

Range —Booked 2007	Reporting Stores	Range — Sailed 2007	Reporting Stores
$199,000 to $499,999	1	$199,000 to $499,999	1
$500.000 to $749,999	0	$500,000 to 749,999	0
$750,000 to $999,999	0	$750,000 to $999,999	1
Over $1,000,000	2	Over $1,000,000	1
TOTAL	3	TOTAL	3

The average Gross Sales for cruises booked in 2007 was $1,352,658 and the median Gross Sales was $1,172,223. The average Gross Sales for cruises that sailed in 2007 was $816,146 and the median was $807,377. The total number of bookings in 2007 ranged from 100 to 889 with an average of 452 per Licensee and a median of 366 bookings.

Canada

Gross Sales and Bookings for Canadian Licensees
Calendar Year 2007

Range — Booked 2007	Reporting Stores	Range — Sailed 2007	Reporting Stores
$199,000 to $499,999	0	$199,000 to $499,999	0
$500,000 to $749,999	0	$500,000 to 749,999	1
$750,000 to $999,999	0	$750,000 to $999,999	0
Over $1,000,000	1	Over $1,000,000	0
TOTAL	1	TOTAL	1

The Gross Sales for the single Canadian Licensee was $1,145,998 for cruises booked in 2007 and $619,008 for cruises that sailed in 2007. The Licensee had 223 total bookings in 2007.

Stores Open More Than Two Years

The following tables set forth Gross Sales and booking information for the period January 1,

2007 through December 31, 2007 for Stores open more than two years. The tables set forth Gross Sales based on two measuring basis, the first column is based on cruises booked in 2007 and the second is for cruises which actually sailed in 2007.

United States

Gross Sales and Bookings for U.S. Licensees
Calendar Year 2007

Range — Booked 2007	Reporting Stores	Range — Sailed 2007	Reporting Stores
$0 to $999,999	20	$0 to $999,999	25
$1,000,000 to $1,999,999	20	$1,000,000 to $1,999,999	24
$2,000,000 to $2,999,999	20	$2,000,000 to $2,999,999	12
Over $3,000,000	7	Over $3,000,000	6
TOTAL	67	TOTAL	67

The average Gross Sales for cruises booked in 2007 was $2,060,377 and the median Gross Sales was $1,683,633. The average Gross Sales for cruises that sailed in 2007 was $1,655,960 and the median was $1,338,200. The total number of bookings in 2007 ranged from 5 to 3002 with an average of 557 per Licensee and a median of 442 bookings.

Canada

Gross Sales and Bookings for Canadian Licensees
Calendar Year 2007

Range — Booked 2007	Reporting Stores	Range — Sailed 2007	Reporting Stores
$0 to $999,999	5	$0 to $999,999	7
$1,000,000 to $1,999,999	10	$1,000,000 to $1,999,999	10
$2,000,000 to $2,999,999	3	$2,000,000 to $2,999,999	5
Over $3,000,000	7	Over $3,000,000	3
TOTAL	25	TOTAL	25

The average Gross Sales for cruises booked in 2007 was $2,513,069 and the median Gross Sales was $1,734,563. The average Gross Sales for cruises that sailed in 2007 was $2,083,729 and the median was $1,515,896. The total number of bookings in 2007 ranged from 96 to 3240 with an average of 527 per Licensee and a median of 352 bookings.

NOTES

[1] Gross Sales is defined as all revenue a licensee derived from operating its Store, including all amounts it received at or away from the Store from any activities or services including any that are in any way associated with the Marks or the use, leasing, barter or sale of any products or services, and whether from cash, check barter, credit, debit card, or credit transactions, including the redemption value of gift certificates issued by it or someone else. Gross Sales also includes port taxes and NCFs (non-commissionable fares). Gross Sales excludes complimentary products or services actually provided to customers or others by the Store.

[2] Unless otherwise noted, results for United States Stores are given in US Dollars. Canadian results

are given in Canadian Dollars.

[3] Numbers are accurate as of December 31, 2007. The booked figures include adjustments and cancellations that occurred prior to the end of the 2007 fiscal period, but do not include changes that occur after December 31, 2007. It is likely that future cancellations will occur due to nature of the cruise industry's long range booking process.

Average Bookings

In 2007, the average booking for Stores open at least one year located in the United States was $3,674. For Canadian Stores, the average booking was $4,775.

ASSUMPTIONS

(1)   Your results may vary upon the location of your Store.

(2)   This analysis does not contain information concerning operating or other costs and expenses.

CAUTION

There is no assurance you will do as well. If you rely upon our figures, you must accept the risk of not doing as well. Actual results vary from Store to Store, and we cannot estimate the result of a particular franchise. Gross Sales, revenues and expenses may vary. In particular, the revenues and expenses of your franchise will be directly affected by many factors, including: (a) geographic location; (b) competition from other similar businesses in your area; (c) advertising effectiveness based on market saturation; (d) your product and service pricing; (e) vendor prices; (f) labor costs; (g) health and other fringe benefits you provide; (h) ability to generate customers; (i) customer loyalty; and (j) employment conditions in the market.

Importantly, you should not consider the Gross Sales or booking information presented above to be the actual potential revenues or bookings that you will realize. We do not represent that you can or will attain these revenues, bookings, margins, or any particular level of revenues, bookings or expenses. We do not represent that you will generate income, which exceeds the initial payment of, or investment in, the franchise.

Therefore, we recommend that you make your own independent investigation to determine whether or not the franchise may be profitable to you. You should use the above information only as a reference in conducting your analysis and preparing your own projected income statements and cash flow statements. We suggest strongly that you consult your financial advisor or personal accountant concerning financial projections and federal, state and local income taxes and any other applicable taxes that you may incur in operating a franchise.

Disclaimer Regarding Claims Made by Agents, et. al.

We specifically instruct our sales personnel, agents, employees and officers that they may not make any claims or statements as to the earnings, sales or profits, or prospects or chances of success of a franchised Store other than as set forth in this Item 19. They are not authorized to represent or estimate dollar figures as to a franchise's operation other than as shown above. Except as provided by applicable law, we will not be bound by allegations of any unauthorized representation as to earnings, sales, profits, or prospects or chances for success, and you must acknowledge that you have not relied on any representation in purchasing your franchise

DRY CLEANING STATION

8301 Golden Valley Rd., # 230

Minneapolis, MN 55427
Tel: (800) 655-8134 (763) 541-0832
Fax: (763) 542-2246
E-Mail: johnca@franchisemasters.com
Web Site: www.drycleaningstation.com
Mr. John A. Campbell, Chief Executive Officer

A high-quality, lower priced dry cleaner and shirt laundry, offering a special niche in the industry, including environmentally efficient equipment, proprietary unique software/computer systems and attractively designed, high-traffic stores.

BACKGROUND:

Established: 1987;	1st Franchised: 1993
Franchised Units:	48
Company-Owned Units:	0
Total Units:	48
Dist.:	US-48; CAN-0; O'seas-0
North America:	7 States, 0 Provinces
Density:	5 in MN, 4 in NE
Projected New Units (12 Months):	50
Qualifications:	5, 3, 1, 2, 2, 5
Registered:	FL,IL,MI,MN

FINANCIAL/TERMS:

Cash Investment:	$40-120K
Total Investment:	$50-350K
Minimum Net Worth:	$250K
Fees: Franchise -	$22.5K
Royalty - 2-5%;	Ad. - 0%
Earnings Claims Statement:	Yes

Term of Contract (Years):	15/2-5
Avg. # Of Employees:	4 FT, 2 PT
Passive Ownership:	Allowed, But Discouraged
Encourage Conversions:	No
Area Develop. Agreements:	Yes
Sub-Franchising Contracts:	No
Expand In Territory:	Yes
Space Needs:	2,200-4,000 SF; FS,SF,SC

SUPPORT & TRAINING:

Financial Assistance Provided:	Yes (D)
Site Selection Assistance:	Yes
Lease Negotiation Assistance:	Yes
Co-Operative Advertising:	No
Franchisee Assoc./Member:	No
Size Of Corporate Staff:	5
On-Going Support:	B,C,D,E,G,H,I
Training:	10-15 Days Store and Headquarters

SPECIFIC EXPANSION PLANS:

US:	Yes, All United States
Canada:	Yes, All Canada
Overseas:	Yes, All Countries

19.) FINANCIAL PERFORMANCE REPRESENTATIONS

We do not make any representations about a franchisee's future financial performance or the past financial performance of company-owned or franchised outlets, except as disclosed below. We also do not authorize our employees or representatives to make any such representations either orally or in writing. If you are purchasing an existing outlet, however, we may provide you with the actual records of that outlet. If you receive any other financial performance information or projections of your future income, you should report it to the franchisor's management by contacting John Campbell at 8301 Golden Valley Road, Suite 240, Golden Valley, Minnesota 55427, telephone: (800) 655-8134, the Federal Trade Commission, and the appropriate state regulatory agencies.

The following summary contains information relating solely to the revenues for calendar year 2007 of the franchised stores (both full service stores and drop station stores) that were open under current ownership for all of 2007, including revenues from dry cleaning, delivery, alterations, restoration and other services. No inference to cost of goods, expenses or profits for existing or future company or franchised stores should be drawn from this information.

We prohibit our sales persons from furnishing any information concerning actual sales of a Dry Cleaning Station® store other than what is provided below. Actual results vary from unit to unit, and we cannot estimate the results that you will realize. Your revenues will vary significantly depending on a number of factors, including the location of your store and how you operate your business. Substantiation of the data used in preparing the following data will be made available to you upon reasonable request.

<u>Earnings Claim Data</u>

(For stores open under current ownership and reporting completed for the full calendar year 2007)

Annual Gross Revenue:

	2007
Overall Store Average[1]	$238,490
Overall "Most Mature" Store Average[2] (open more than 3 years at December 31, 2007)	$305,977

	Year 1	Year 2
Historical Store Sales Ramp-up Averages Over Their First 24 Months of Operations[3]	$143,648	$227,997

These average revenue numbers should not be considered as the actual or probable revenues or profits that you will realize. We do not represent that you or any franchisee can expect to attain such revenues. Our salespersons, officers, employees and agents are forbidden to give any other information relating to actual or potential revenues, expenses, cost of goods, expenses or profits and no reliance can or should be placed by you on any of such other information that you may learn. All the information contained in this Item 19 was taken from unaudited financial reports provided to us by our individual franchise owners. We are not aware of any reason this information is not accurate, but we have not checked this information for accuracy.

1   45% of the stores that were open during all of 2007 under current ownership and who provided complete reporting to us were above the average and 55% were below the average.

2   41% of the stores that were open during all of 2007 under current ownership and who provided complete reporting to us were above the average and 59% were below the average.

3   Averages for the first 24 months of operation of all stores in our system (dating back to stores opening in 1992) that were open during 2006 and 2007 under their current ownership.

FAST-FIX JEWELRY AND WATCH REPAIRS

1300 NW 17th Ave., # 170
Delray Beach, FL 33445
Tel: (800) 359-0407 (561) 330-6060
Fax: (561) 330-6062
E-Mail: fastfix.ifa@mybrunno.com
Web Site: www.fastfix.com
Mr. Jason Mattes, Director of Franchise Development

With a 25-year track record, Fast-Fix Jewelry and Watch Repairs is the #1 national chain of dedicated jewelry and watch repair stores with more than 160 franchised locations operating in the United States and Canada. Fast-Fix stores operate only in major regional malls that afford customers "while-they-shop" jewelry and watch repair service. Prior jewelry experience is not necessary. Our full training program at Fast-Fix University along with our support system that includes national conventions and regiona

BACKGROUND: IFA MEMBER
Established: 1984;   1st Franchised: 1987
Franchised Units: 157

Company-Owned Units:	3
Total Units:	160
Dist.:	US-153; CAN-2; O'seas-2
North America:	27 States, 2 Provinces
Density:	35 in CA, 23 in FL, 16 in TX
Projected New Units (12 Months):	15
Qualifications:	4, 5, 2, 2, 2, 5
Registered:	CA,DC,FL,IL,MD,MI,MN,NY,OR,RI,VA,WA,WI

FINANCIAL/TERMS:

Cash Investment:	$75K-125K
Total Investment:	$142,750-$307,750
Minimum Net Worth:	$250K
Fees: Franchise -	$40K
Royalty - 5%;	Ad. - 2%
Earnings Claims Statement:	Yes
Term of Contract (Years):	10/10
Avg. # Of Employees:	3 FT, 2 PT
Passive Ownership:	Allowed, But Discouraged
Encourage Conversions:	No
Area Develop. Agreements:	Yes
Sub-Franchising Contracts:	Yes
Expand In Territory:	Yes
Space Needs:	250-850 SF; RM

SUPPORT & TRAINING:

Financial Assistance Provided:	Yes (I)	Training:	5 Days On-Site;
Site Selection Assistance:	Yes		10 Days National Training Center in Delray Beach, FL
Lease Negotiation Assistance:	Yes		
Co-Operative Advertising:	No	**SPECIFIC EXPANSION PLANS:**	
Franchisee Assoc./Member:	Yes/Member	US:	Yes, All United States
Size Of Corporate Staff:	18	Canada:	Yes, All Canada
On-Going Support:	C,D,E,G,H,I	Overseas:	Yes, All Countries

ITEM 19
FINANCIAL PERFORMANCE REPRESENTATIONS

To help you to evaluate our franchise, we have summarized selected historical sales information for our fiscal year ending December 31, 2007. We have compiled the information for each type of franchise we offer, based upon what franchisees have reported to us in the ordinary course of business through our monthly sales reporting system. We assume that the information submitted is accurate, complete and contains no material misrepresentations or omissions. We did not audit this information. **You should not rely on this information to predict the sales or profits you would derive from operating one of our franchises.**

We have included within this data information from franchisees whose franchised businesses were in operation as of December 31, 2007 and had been in uninterrupted operation for at least 24 months. The claim does not include information about businesses that began or discontinued their affiliation with us during 2006 or 2007. The averages and ranges would differ had the results of new and former franchises been included.

The data presented does not reflect the cost of sales, operating expenses or other costs or expenses that must be deducted from the gross sales figures to obtain net income or profit. You should conduct an independent investigation of the costs and expenses you will incur in operating your franchised business. Franchisees or former franchisees listed in the Offering Circular may be one source of this information.

The sales information is presented for periods during which economic conditions may be substantively different from future economic conditions. Competitors may enter or leave the market over time. Brand recognition and awareness and consumer goodwill may vary by market. Market potential and consumer demand may change over time. Each franchisee's managerial skill, experience and resources will differ. **Accordingly, you are urged to consult with appropriate financial, business and legal counsel to conduct your own independent analysis of the information presented.**

	No. of Stores	Average Sales [1]	Range High	Low
Kiosk/Wall Store [2]	48	$298,838	$573,955	$107,617
In-Line Store [3]	79	$430,415	$812,765	$148,098
All Stores	127	$380,685		

[1]   The percentage of stores having attained or surpassed these averages results (Kiosk/Wall Store 48%; In-Line Store 47%; and All Stores 41%).

[2]   Free-standing self contained retail fixture typically located within the exposed aisles (approx. 150-180 sq. ft.).

[3]   In-line store built out within a traditional retail store front setting (approx. 300-800 sq. ft).

THIS ANALYSIS IS BASED UPON THE ACTUAL EXPERIENCE OF FAST-FIX JEWELRY AND WATCH REPAIR FRANCHISED BUSINESSES AND SHOULD NOT BE CONSIDERED AS THE ACTUAL OR POTENTIAL SALES THAT YOU WILL REALIZE. WE DO NOT REPRESENT OR GUARANTY THAT ANY FRANCHISEE WILL ATTAIN THE SALES SHOWN ABOVE OR THAT ANY PARTICULAR LEVEL OF SALES, COSTS, INCOME OR PROFITS WILL BE ACHIEVED BY ANY FRANCHISEE. YOUR SUCCESS LARGELY WILL DEPEND ON YOUR ABILITY, AND THE INDIVIDUAL FINANCIAL RESULTS OF ANY FRANCHISED BUSINESS ARE LIKELY TO DIFFER FROM THE INFORMATION DESCRIBED ABOVE. SUBSTANTIATION OF THE DATA USED IN PREPARING THIS ANALYSIS WILL BE MADE AVAILABLE ON REASONABLE REQUEST.

FASTSIGNS
Sign & Graphic Solutions Made Simple.

FASTSIGNS

2542 Highlander Way
Carrollton, TX 75006-2333
Tel: (800) 827-7446 + 5616 (214) 346-5600
Fax: (972) 248-8201
E-Mail: bill.mcpherson@fastsigns.com
Web Site: franchise.fastsigns.com
Mr. William N. McPherson, VP Franchise Sales

FASTSIGNS centers use state-of-the-art computer technology to create custom signs, graphics, banners, trade show exhibits, vehicle graphics and much more. A pioneer in the sign industry, FASTSIGNS has continued to grow by optimizing our systems and expanding the scope of our products and services. Today, with a growing store network of over 540 centers spanning the globe, FASTSIGNS is an acknowledged leader in one of the world's most dynamic franchised industries. At FASTSIGNS, our primary goal is to help our franchisees build successful centers that achieve and maintain high sales volumes and maximum profits, year after year. And we're accomplishing our goal! Our average per store gross sales have increased 16 of the last 18 years to $612,000 in 2008 (Average gross sales for the period ending 12/31/08 as stated in our FDD).

BACKGROUND: IFA MEMBER

Established: 1985;	1st Franchised: 1986
Franchised Units:	547
Company-Owned Units:	0
Total Units:	547
Dist.:	US-463; CAN-21; O'seas-63
North America:	45 States, 6 Provinces
Density:	41 in CA, 33 in FL, 56 in TX
Projected New Units (12 Months):	20

Qualifications:	5, 5, 2, 3, 4, 5
Registered:CA,DC,FL,HI,IL,IN,MD,MI,MN,ND,NY,OR,RI,SD, VA,WA,WI,AB	

FINANCIAL/TERMS:

Cash Investment:	$75K
Total Investment:	$170,659-$316,673
Minimum Net Worth:	$250K
Fees: Franchise -	$27,500
Royalty - 6%;	Ad. - 2%
Earnings Claims Statement:	Yes
Term of Contract (Years):	20/10
Avg. # Of Employees:	5-6 FT, 0 PT
Passive Ownership:	Not Allowed
Encourage Conversions:	Yes
Area Develop. Agreements:	No
Sub-Franchising Contracts:	No
Expand In Territory:	Yes
Space Needs:1,200-2,000 SF; Business Oriented Retail Strip Center, Mixed Use	

SUPPORT & TRAINING:

Financial Assistance Provided:	Yes (I)
Site Selection Assistance:	Yes
Lease Negotiation Assistance:	Yes
Co-Operative Advertising:	Yes
Franchisee Assoc./Member:	Yes/Member
Size Of Corporate Staff:	93
On-Going Support:	C,D,E,G,H,I
Training:	2 Weeks Dallas, TX ;2 Weeks On-Site

SPECIFIC EXPANSION PLANS:

US:	Yes, All United States
Canada:	Yes, All Canada
Overseas:	Yes, UK, New Zealand, Australia

ITEM 19
FINANCIAL PERFORMANCE REPRESENTATIONS

On December 31, 2007, there were 525 FASTSIGNS Centers open and in operation of which 80 were international. 422 Centers were open and in continuous operation in the US during the entire calendar year ending December 31, 2007. The analysis set forth below is based solely on the average yearly gross sales for those 422 Centers for 2007. The columns are categorized by the year the Center opened.

Based on gross sales reported by the 422 Centers, the average gross sales for such Centers for the year ended December 31, 2007, was $637,170. For purposes of this analysis, gross sales includes cash and credit sales as well as any goods or services received by the franchisee in exchange for goods and services sold at the Center. Gross sales do not include sales or use taxes.

Of the 422 Centers included in this analysis, 171 or 40% of the Centers reported gross sales above the average, ranging from $637,170 to $2,328,448, and 251 or 60% of the Centers reported gross sales below the average, ranging from $80,903 to $637,170. Overall, the Centers included in this analysis reported gross sales in the following ranges for the year:

2007 SALES ENDING DECEMBER 31

Sales Ranges	# of Centers opened in 2006	Percentages	# of Centers in 2005	Percentages	# of Centers opened in 2004	Percentages	# of Centers 2003 or prior	Percentages	Total Centers # of Centers	Percentages
$000,001 - $100,000			1	5.9%						
$100.001 - $200.000	6	31.6%	1	5.9%			7	1.9%	14	3.3%
$200,001 - $300,000	8	42.1%	3	17.6%	4	26.7%	23	6.2%	39	9.2%
$300,001 - $400,000	3	15.8%	4	23.5%	6	40.0%	55	14.8%	68	16.0%
$400,001 - $500,000	1		3	17.6%	5	33.3%	40	10.8%	49	11.6%
$500.001 - $600.000	1	5.3%	1	5.9%			62	16.7%	64	15.1%
$600,001 - $700,000	1	5.3%	2	11.8%			42	11.3%	45	10.6%
$700,001 - $800,000			1	5.9%			40	10.8%	41	9.7%
$800.001 - $900.000			1	5.9%			33	8.9%	34	8.0%
$900.001 - $1,000.000							10	2.7%	10	2.4%
$1,000,001 - $1,100,000							15	4.0%	15	3.5%
$1,100,001 - $1,200,000							9	2.4%	9	2.1%
$1,200,001 - $1,300,000							9	2.4%	9	2.1%
$1,300,001 - $1,400,000							7	1.9%	7	1.7%
$1,400,001 - $1,500,000							7	1.7%	7	1.9%
$1,500,001 - $1,600,000							4	1.1%	4	0.9%
$1,600,001 - $1,700,000							2	0.5%	2	0.5%
$1,700,001 - $1,800,000										
$1,800,001 - $1,900,000							1	0.3%	1	0.2%
$1.900.001 - $2.100.000							2	0.5%	2	0.5%
$2,200,001 - $2,300,000										
$2,300,001 - $2,400,000							1	0.3%	1	
$2,400,001 - $2,500,000							1	0.3%	1	0.2%
$2,500,001 - $2,600,000							1	0.3%	1	0.2%
Totals	20	100%	17	100%	15	100%	371	100.0%	422	100.0%

Of the 171 Centers reporting gross sales above the average, 35 Centers are located in the Southwest Region of the United States, 42 in the West Region, 21 in the Northeast Region, 42 in the Southeast Region and 31 in the Midwest Region. Of the 251 Centers reporting gross sales below the average, 43 are located in the Southwest Region, 38 in the West Region, 53 in the Northeast Region, 42 in the Southeast Region and 75 in the Midwest Region.

On December 31, 2006, there were 501 FASTSIGNS Centers open and in operation of which 76 were international. 404 Centers were open and in continuous operation in the United States during the entire year ended December 31, 2006. The analysis set forth below is based solely on the average gross sales for those 404 Centers for 2006. The columns are categorized by the year the Center opened.

Based on gross sales reported by the 404 Centers, the average gross sales for such Centers for the year ended December 31, 2006, was $620,897. For purposes of this analysis, gross sales includes cash and credit sales as well as any goods or services received by the franchisee in exchange for goods and services sold at the Center. Gross sales do not include sales or use taxes.

Of the 404 Centers included in this analysis, 158 or 39% of the Centers reported gross sales above the average, ranging from $678,897 to $2,378,015, and 246 or 61% of the Centers reported gross sales below the average, ranging from $117,245 to $620,897. Overall, the Centers included in this analysis reported gross sales in the following ranges for the year:

2006 SALES ENDING DECEMBER 31

Sales Ranges			# of Centers opened in 2005	Percentages	# of Centers opened in 2004	Percentages	# of Centers opened in 2003	Percentages	# of Centers opened in 2002 or prior	Percentages	Total Centers # of Centers	Percentages
$000,001	-	$100,000										
$100,001	-	$200,000	4	23.5%	2	13.3%	1	7.7%	3	0.8%	10	2.5%
$200,001	-	$300,000	6	35.3%	5	33.3%	4	30.8%	28	7.8%	43	10.6%
$300,001	-	$400,000	3	17.6%	7	46.7%	1	7.7%	46	12.8%	57	14.1%
$400,001	-	$500,000	3	17.6%	1	6.7%	3	23.1%	47	17.0%	54	13.4%
$500,001	-	$600,000					1	15.3%	66	17.0%	67	15.8%
$600,001	-	$700,000	1	5.9%			1	7.7%	47	13.1%	49	12.1%
$700,001	-	$800,000					1	7.7%	39	10.9%	40	9.9%
$800,001	-	$900,000					1	7.7%	24	6.7%	25	6.2%
$900,001	-	$1,000,000							14	3.9%	14	3.5%
$1,000,001	-	$1,100,000							5	1.4%	5	1.2%
$1,100,001	-	$1,200,000							8	2.2%	8	2.0%
$1,200,001	-	$1,300,000							10	2.8%	10	2.5%
$1,300,001	-	$1,400,000							8	2.2%	8	2.0%
$1,400,001	-	$1,500,000							4	1.1%	4	1.0%
$1,500,001	-	$1,600,000							3	0.8%	3	0.7%
$1,600,001	-	$1,700,000							1	0.3%	1	0.2%
$1,700,001	-	$1,800,000							2	0.6%	2	0.5%
$1,800,001	-	$1,900,000							1	0.3%	1	0.2%
$1,900,001	-	$2,000,000							1	0.3%	1	0.2%
$2,000,001	-	$2,100,000										
$2,100,001	-	$2,200,000										
$2,200,001	-	$2,300,000										
$2,300,001	-	$2,400,000							2	0.6%	2	0.5%
Totals			17	100%	15	100%	13	100%	359	100.0%	404	100.0%

Of the 158 Centers reporting gross sales above the average, 36 Centers are located in the Southwest Region of the United States, 37 in the West Region, 24 in the Northeast Region, 37 in the Southeast Region and 24 in the Midwest Region. Of the 246 Centers reporting gross sales below the average, 42 are located in the Southwest Region, 39 in the West Region, 47 in the Northeast Region, 42 in the Southeast Region and 77 in the Midwest Region.

For purposes of this analysis, the Southwest Region consists of Arkansas, Colorado, Louisiana, New Mexico, Oklahoma and Texas; the West Region consists of Alaska, Arizona, California, Hawaii, Idaho, Montana, Nevada, Oregon, Utah, Washington and Wyoming; the Northeast Region consists of Connecticut, Delaware, Maine, Maryland, Massachusetts, New Hampshire, New Jersey, New York, Pennsylvania, Rhode Island, Vermont, Virginia, Washington, D.C. and West Virginia; the Southeast Region consists of Alabama, Florida, Georgia, Mississippi, North Carolina, South Carolina and Tennessee; and the Midwest Region consists of Illinois, Indiana, Iowa, Kansas, Kentucky, Ohio, Michigan, Minnesota, Missouri, Nebraska, North Dakota, South Dakota and Wisconsin.

We offer substantially the same services to all franchisees. Additionally, advertising and promotional materials developed by the NAC are available to all Franchisees. (See Item 11.) An individual Franchisee is not limited in the amount or type of advertising that it may conduct; provided, however, that all advertising materials developed by Franchisee must be approved in advance by us. (See Item 16.) Consequently, Franchisee's gross sales may be directly affected by the amount, type and effectiveness of advertising conducted by Franchisee.

The Franchise Agreement provides that Franchisees must offer and sell at the Center products and services required by us and may offer and sell such additional products and services approved by us. (See Item 16.) Franchisees offer substantially the same products and services to the public. In certain states, as noted in Item 1, Franchisees may be required to have a contractor's license to perform certain types of sign installation work. In those states, if you do not have, or meet the requirements to obtain a license, then you may not be able to offer those installation services requiring a license. Additionally, although we may suggest prices for the products and services offered at the Center, Franchisees may offer and sell such products and services at any price it chooses. As a result, the products and services offered and the prices at which such products and services are offered to the public at the Centers included in this analysis may vary.

The average gross sales figures included in this analysis are based on sales reports submitted to us by each Franchisee. The figures in the sales reports have not been audited and we have not undertaken to otherwise independently verify (i) the accuracy of such information or (ii) whether such information was prepared in accordance with generally accepted accounting principles.

In addition to the average gross sales analysis, certain expenses, expressed as a percentage of Gross Revenues, have been provided based on the experience of certain of the foregoing FASTSIGNS Centers described below. The expense figures were extracted from the 2007 financial statements submitted by the FASTSIGNS Franchisees included in the 2007 analysis described above. As of the date of this DISCLOSURE DOCUMENT, we have not been provided with expense data from 293 of the 424 Centers open and in continuous operation during 2007. This was primarily due to the close proximity of year-end to the time of compilation of these numbers and such 293 Centers were not included in the expense figures provided herein. Franchisee should note that with respect to the 131 FASTSIGNS Centers included in the compilation of the expense figures, the expense data relates to operations conducted during the one-year period ended 2007. Of the 131 Centers reporting expenses 1 was opened in 1985, 1 was opened in 1987, 5 were opened in 1988, 6 were opened in 1989, 19 were opened in 1990, 13 were opened in 1991, 7 were opened in 1992, 9 were opened in 1993, 9 were opened in 1994, 12 were opened in 1995, 7 were opened in 1996, 8 were opened in 1997, 6 were opened in 1998, 3 were opened in 1999, 1 were opened in 2000, 3 was opened in 2001, 3 were opened in 2002, 3 were opened in 2003 and 2 were opened in 2004, 5 were opened in 2005 and 9 were opened in 2006. These Centers are located in the following regions; 28 in the Southwest region of the United States, 30 in the West region, 22 in the Northeast region, 21 in the Southeast region and 30 in the Midwest region. The information relating to the operations expenses provided by the FASTSIGNS Centers and used by the us in determining the numerical values provided have not been audited and such information has not necessarily been prepared on a basis consistent with generally accepted accounting principles. In particular, we are unable to verify whether the expense data submitted by each FASTSIGNS Center for each separately provided expense item appropriately reflects the types of expenses which are ordinarily incurred by FASTSIGNS Centers and which should be included in the item according to generally acceptable accounting principles.

Each percentage given on this analysis reflects the mean average of the total percentages for the applicable expense item provided by the reporting FASTSIGNS Center (i.e., the aggregate sum of the expense percentages of all reporting FASTSIGNS Centers divided by the number of reporting Centers). The expense percentages for the various expense items provided by each reporting FAST-SIGNS Center reflects that Center's expenses as a percentage of its Gross Revenues. No percentage given on this analysis is the actual expenses percentage experienced by any one FASTSIGNS Center and the actual expense percentages for the reporting FASTSIGNS Centers on any particular expense item may vary significantly. The following expenses represent the major expense items for a FAST-SIGNS Center and should not be considered the only expenses that a FASTSIGNS Center will incur:

Cost of Sales - Includes the cost of consumable raw materials and sub-contracting expense. Average cost of sales is 24.1%.

Advertising - As set forth in Section 5, Advertising, of the Franchise Agreement, this includes yellow page placement, direct mail campaigns and general advertising. This does not include the advertising fee due to the NAC. Average advertising expense is 2.7%.

Salaries and Wages - Includes compensation for production operation, customer service and sales (this does not include employee payroll taxes). Where indicated on the financial statements, the owner's compensation has not been included. Average salary and wage expense is 23.0%.

Rent - Average rent expense of a Center is 6.4%, this is approximately $3,443.54 per month or $41,322.52 a year.

Service Fees - Based upon the current Franchise Agreement, a 6% of gross sales service fee is due to us.

Advertising Fee - Based upon the current Franchise Agreement, a 2% of gross sales advertising fee is due to the NAC.

The franchisor is unable to verify the accuracy of the expense information provided by Fastsigns franchisees and makes no representations or warranties regarding the same.

The average gross sales for all Centers included in the above study was $723,343. The amount of gross sales realized and expenses incurred will vary from unit to unit. In particular, gross sales and expenses at Franchisee's Center will be directly affected by many additional factors not noted above, including, without limitation, the Center's geographic location, competition in the market, the presence of other FASTSIGNS Centers, the quality of management, the effectiveness of sales and marketing and the prices charged for products and services sold at the Center. Further, the franchise agreement to which each franchisee included in this analysis is subject is different from the Franchise Agreement attached to this DISCLOSURE DOCUMENT as Exhibit B. Among other terms, the Franchise Agreement attached to this DISCLOSURE DOCUMENT requires an initial franchise fee of $27,500 and a continuing Service Fee of 6%. Further, Franchisee may be required to participate in an Advertising Cooperative. This analysis, therefore, should only be used as a reference for Franchisee to use in conducting its own analysis.

Finally, Franchisee should particularly note the following:

Each franchisee is urged to consult with appropriate financial, business and legal advisors in connection with the information set forth in this analysis.

The average sales and major expenses reflected in this analysis should not be considered as the actual or potential sales that will be realized by any franchisee. We do not represent that any franchisee can expect to attain such sales. In addition, we do not represent that any franchisee will derive income that exceeds the initial payment for or investment in a FASTSIGNS franchise. No inference as to expenses, cost of goods sold or profits relating to existing or future centers should be drawn from the sales information reflected in this analysis. The success of franchisee will depend largely upon the ability of franchisee, and the individual financial results of a franchisee are likely to differ from the information set forth herein. Substantiation of the data used in preparing this analysis will be made available upon reasonable request.

First Year Center Sales Comparison
2004 Openings vs. 2005/2006 Openings

First full calendar year average gross sales for Centers opened in 2005 and 2006 were 31%

greater than new Centers opened in 2004. 2005 results (for 2004 Center openings) were $222,432 per Center compared to 2006/2007 results (for 2005/2006 Center openings) of $291,824 per Center.

These Centers were opened within each region of the country:

Year Opened	Western Region	SW Region	MW Region	SE Region	NE Region	Total
2004	3	1	5	3	3	15
2005	3	3	5	3	3	17
2006	4	5	1	6	4	20

All Centers were located in markets that met our minimum size criteria of 4,000 businesses or more. All physical locations of the new Centers were reviewed by our Director of Real Estate in accordance with the Franchise Agreement for each franchisee.

Each franchisee is urged to consult with appropriate financial, business and legal advisors in connection with the information set forth in this analysis.

The average sales reflected in this analysis should not be considered as the actual or potential sales that will be realized by any franchisee. We do not represent that any franchisee can expect to attain such sales. In addition, we do not represent that any franchisee will derive income that exceeds the initial payment for or investment in a FASTSIGNS franchise. No inference as to expenses, cost of goods sold or profits relating to existing or future centers should be drawn from the sales information reflected in this analysis. The success of franchisee will depend largely upon the ability of franchisee, and the individual financial results of a franchisee are likely to differ from the information set forth herein. Substantiation of the data used in preparing this analysis will be made available upon reasonable request.

Except for the information contained in this Item 19, we do not furnish or authorize our sales personnel, our employees or the NAC's employees to furnish any oral, visual or written information concerning the actual or potential sales, costs, income or profits of a Center. Actual results vary from unit to unit and we cannot estimate the results of any particular franchise. We do not make any representations that you or any of your principals may or will derive income from any Center, which exceeds the initial payment for or investment in the Center.

FISH WINDOW CLEANING SERVICES
200 Enchanted Pkwy.
Manchester, MO 63021
Tel: (877) 707-3474 (636) 530-7334 +22
Fax: (636) 530-7856
E-Mail: nathan@fishwindowcleaning.com
Web Site: www.fishwindowcleaning.com
Mr. Nathan Merrick, VP Franchise Development

There is no glass ceiling when it comes to the potential you will have to grow your own unique service business in a large protected territory, specializing in year-round commercial and residential low-rise window cleaning. You can have the satisfaction of owning a business that requires no night or weekend work, backed by a franchisor with 29 years of experience.

BACKGROUND: IFA MEMBER

Established: 1978;	1st Franchised: 1998
Franchised Units:	230
Company-Owned Units:	2
Total Units:	232
Dist.:	US-232; CAN-0; O'seas-0
North America:	37 States, 0 Provinces
Density:	NR
Projected New Units (12 Months):	30
Qualifications:	4, 4, 1, 2, 3, 5
Registered:CA,DC,FL,HI,IL,IN,MD,MI,MN,ND,NY,OR,RI,SD,	
	VA,WA,WI

FINANCIAL/TERMS:

Cash Investment:	$57.5-131.5K
Total Investment:	$57.5-131.5K
Minimum Net Worth:	$100-200K
Fees: Franchise -	$20-50K
Royalty - 8-6%;	Ad. - 1%
Earnings Claims Statement:	Yes
Term of Contract (Years):	10

Avg. # Of Employees:	3-12 FT, 0 PT	Co-Operative Advertising:	No
Passive Ownership:	Allowed, But Discouraged	Franchisee Assoc./Member:	Yes/Member
Encourage Conversions:	Yes	Size Of Corporate Staff:	25
Area Develop. Agreements:	No	On-Going Support:	A,B,C,D,E,G,H,I
Sub-Franchising Contracts:	No	Training:	NR Corporate Headquarters;
Expand In Territory:	Yes		NR Franchisee Territory
Space Needs:	SF; SF,SC		
		SPECIFIC EXPANSION PLANS:	
SUPPORT & TRAINING:		US:	Yes, All United States
Financial Assistance Provided:	Yes (D)	Canada:	No
Site Selection Assistance:	Yes	Overseas:	No
Lease Negotiation Assistance:	Yes		

ITEM 19
FINANCIAL PERFORMANCE REPRESENTATIONS

This financial performance information relates to certain financial factors reported to us by our franchisees and the insurance companies who work with many of our franchisees, as further described in the Notes below. The factors include a revenue factor (Average Revenue Generated per "Sales Day") and a number of expense items. These factors can be helpful to you as you evaluate the franchise opportunity and discuss this opportunity with your advisors. The factors do not include annual revenue averages, as the results of a FISH WINDOW CLEANING business depend primarily on you. The factors also do not include all expenses you will incur in operating your Business, as further noted below.

Other than as detailed in this financial performance representation, we do not furnish, or authorize our salespersons (or anyone else) to furnish, and you should not rely on, any oral or written information concerning the actual or potential sales, income or profits of a FISH WINDOW CLEANING business. We have not suggested, and we certainly cannot guarantee, that you will succeed in the operation of your Business, since the most important factors in the success of any FISH WINDOW CLEANING business, including the one to be operated by you, are your personal business, marketing, management, judgment and other skills and your willingness to work hard and follow the System. Actual results vary from business to business, area to area and market to market, and we cannot estimate or project the results for any particular business.

The information included in this financial performance representation is based on information provided to us by 75 franchisees, out of a possible 157 franchisees (or 47.7%), responded to a questionnaire that we sent to our franchisees. Several franchisees did not respond to all the questions, as evident by the numbers noted in the Table below. The information provided has not been audited or submitted as part of a financial statement reporting requirement. It simply was provided to us by our franchisees and two insurance companies, as of December 31, 2007. The FISH WINDOW CLEANING businesses included in this financial performance representation share similar characteristics in that they are in similar locations, have similar degrees of competition, offer similar services, are entitled to receive similar goods and services from us. These FISH WINDOW CLEANING businesses have been in operation an average of 49 months.

The financial performance representation does not include all start-up expenses and development costs for a FISH WINDOW CLEANING Business. See Items 5, 6 and 7 of the Disclosure Document for estimates and other information pertaining to the fees and initial investment required for the development of a FISH WINDOW CLEANING Business. The financial performance representation also does not include certain on-going expenses as noted in Warning E below.

Substantiation of the data contained in this financial performance representation will be made available to you upon reasonable request.

NOTES:

1. **Average Annualized Revenue Generated per "Sales Day."** This is a revenue factor that is somewhat unique to the FISH WINDOW CLEANING System. In order to drive sales results for their Business, we encourage franchisees to use the "Fish System of Selling," as outlined in the Operations Manual. The "Fish System of Selling" is for a person to devote a 6 hour sales day to make approximately 50 contacts with potential customers in a day. The contacts include face-to-face meetings, leaving brochures at businesses and other follow-up. The annualized revenue per person-day of selling is interpreted as the annualized revenue that the franchisee achieved on a daily basis for each salesperson they used in their Business. In other words, if a salesperson was out making sales calls for a full day, for the franchisees reporting this information to us, the customers contacted that day, on average, resulted in annualized revenue of $802.

2. **Labor Cost (Window Cleaners Only).** Franchisees generally pay their window cleaners a percentage of the revenue each cleaner generates from customers for work performed.

3. **Cost of Consumables per Month.** This expense item is similar to cost of goods sold. It includes cleaning supplies, soap and other similar items used in the operation of the Business.

4. **Office Rent per Month.** Most franchisees lease offices in light industrial areas with 300-400 square feet. Utilities generally are included in the lease costs.

5. **Business Phone; Cell Phone.** Franchisees have separate Business and Cell Phone numbers for their Business.

6. **Internet.** Franchisees must have high speed Internet connection for their Business.

7. **Workers' Compensation.** Workers' compensation insurance generally is paid per $100 of payroll. Also, workers' compensation insurance in some states like Florida and California is significantly higher than other states.

8. **Liability Insurance.** Franchisees are required under the Franchise Agreement to maintain comprehensive general liability insurance. Also, liability insurance in some states like Florida and California is significantly higher than other states.

9. **Sales Person.** Salespeople can be hired to generate new accounts through street bidding, to grow the business

10. **Operations Manager.** Typically one full-time Operations Manager is hired. They are paid to generate new accounts, perform cleaning services, and assist in the daily management of the business.

11. **Break-Even Month.** This is the number of months after opening when the business reached the break-even point.

12. **Break-Even Month Production.** This is the average amount of serviced accounts in a single month that led to a break-even point for the business, not including owner income.

13. **Projected Annualized Revenue.** Projected Annualized Revenue (PAR) is the total value of the existing accounts, on a rolling annualized basis.

WARNINGS:

A.   YOU ARE LIKELY TO ACHIEVE RESULTS THAT ARE DIFFERENT, POSSIBLY SIGNIFICANTLY AND ADVERSELY, FROM THE RESULTS SHOWN BELOW. MANY FACTORS, INCLUDING LOCATION OF THE BUSINESS, MANAGEMENT CAPABILITIES, LOCAL MARKET CONDITIONS, AND OTHER FACTORS, ARE UNIQUE TO EACH BUSINESS AND MAY SIGNIFICANTLY IMPACT THE FINANCIAL PERFORMANCE OF THE BUSINESS.

B.   THE ACTUAL RESULTS INCLUDED IN THIS STATEMENT RELATE TO RESULTS FOR THE EXISTING FRANCHISEES WHO REPORTED THE INFORMATION, AND SHOULD NOT BE CONSIDERED AS THE ACTUAL OR PROBABLE PERFORMANCE RESULTS THAT YOU SHOULD EXPECT THROUGH THE OPERATION OF YOUR BUSINESS. WE HAVE NOT AUDITED ANY OF THE INFORMATION REPORTED BY THE FRANCHISEES. WE DO NOT MAKE ANY PROMISES OR REPRESENTATIONS OF ANY KIND THAT YOU WILL ACHIEVE ANY PARTICULAR RESULTS OR LEVEL OF SALES OR PROFITABILITY.

C.   YOU ARE RESPONSIBLE FOR DEVELOPING YOUR OWN BUSINESS PLAN FOR YOUR BUSINESS. WE ENCOURAGE YOU TO CONSULT WITH YOUR OWN ACCOUNTING, BUSINESS, AND LEGAL ADVISORS IN DOING SO. IN DEVELOPING THE BUSINESS PLAN, YOU ARE CAUTIONED TO MAKE NECESSARY ALLOWANCE FOR CHANGES IN FINANCIAL RESULTS TO INCOME, EXPENSES, OR BOTH, THAT MAY RESULT FROM OPERATION OF YOUR BUSINESS IN DIFFERENT GEOGRAPHIC AREAS OR NEW MARKET AREAS, OR DURING PERIODS OF, OR IN AREAS SUFFERING FROM, ECONOMIC DOWNTURNS, INFLATION, UNEMPLOYMENT, OR OTHER NEGATIVE ECONOMIC INFLUENCES.

D.   HISTORICAL COSTS DO NOT NECESSARILY CORRESPOND TO FUTURE COSTS BECAUSE OF FACTORS SUCH AS INFLATION, CHANGES IN MINIMUM WAGE LAWS, LOCATION, FINANCING, REAL ESTATE-RELATED COSTS AND OTHER VARIABLES. ALL INFORMATION SHOULD BE EVALUATED IN LIGHT OF CURRENT MARKET CONDITIONS, INCLUDING SUCH COST AND PRICE INFORMATION AS MAY THEN BE AVAILABLE. PROSPECTIVE FRANCHISEES MUST BEAR IN MIND THAT A NEWLY OPENED BUSINESS CANNOT BE EXPECTED TO ACHIEVE SALES VOLUMES OR MAINTAIN EXPENSES SIMILAR TO THOSE OF AN ESTABLISHED BUSINESS.

E.   THE EXPENSES IDENTIFIED IN THE TABLE ARE NOT THE ONLY EXPENSES THAT YOU WILL INCUR IN CONNECTION WITH YOUR OPERATION OF YOUR BUSINESS. FOR EXAMPLE, YOU WILL PAY ROYALTY AND MARKETING FEES TO US (SEE ITEM 6 OF THIS DISCLOSURE DOCUMENT), ALTHOUGH THESE FEES ARE NOT INCLUDED IN THE TABLE. YOU ALSO MAY INCUR OTHER ADDITIONAL EXPENSES INCLUDING, BUT NOT LIMITED TO, LEGAL AND ACCOUNTING, INTEREST ON DEBT SERVICE, AND TAXES AND LICENSES. YOU AND YOUR ADVISORS SHOULD CONSIDER THIS IN YOUR DUE DILIGENCE AND PREPARATION OF YOUR BUSINESS PLAN.

	Average of Reporting Franchisees	Number of Franchises above average	Percentage of Reporting Franchisees who have actually attained or surpassed the average	Number of Franchisees at or below average	Number of Franchisees that did not provide the requested information
Annual Revenue per person-day of selling	$867	8	15%	45	22
Labor Cost (Percentage Paid to Cleaners)	34%	41	55%	33	1
Cost of consumables per month	$329	20	28%	52	3
Office rent per month	$504	33	44%	42	0
Business phone per month	$158	31	41%	44	0

Cell phone expense per month	$178	32	44%	41	2
Internet expense per month	$51	39	45%	61	14
Workers' compensation insurance rate	6.4%	27	39%	42	6
Liability insurance per year	$3,200	22	29%	53	0
Sales Person Payroll	$345	34	89%	4	37
Operations Manager Payroll	$590	40	85%	7	28
Cash Flow Break Even Months	9.7	10	20%	41	27
Break-Even Month Production	$10,471	25	42%	75	40
Projected Annualized Revenue	$126,188	47	73%	23	36

GLASSDOCTOR.
HOME • AUTO • BUSINESS
We fix your panes!®

GLASS DOCTOR

1020 N. University Parks Dr.
Waco, TX 76707
Tel: (800) 280-9858 (254) 759-5850
Fax: (800) 209-7621
E-Mail: info@servicefranchiseopportunities.com
Web Site: www.servicefranchiseopportunities.com
Ms. Sherri Jurls, Vice President of Franchising

Established in 1962, Glass Doctor is the largest chain of full-service glass replacement providers in the nation. Recognized by Entrepreneur magazine among its "Franchise 500," Glass Doctor franchisees offer complete glass replacement, service and repairs to the automotive, residential and commercial markets at more than 400 locations in the United States and Canada. Glass Doctor is part of The Dwyer Group family of companies, which also includes Rainbow International, Mr. Rooter, Aire Serv, Mr. Electric and Mr. Appliance.

BACKGROUND: IFA MEMBER
Established: 1962;   1st Franchised: 1974
Franchised Units: 162
Company-Owned Units: 0
Total Units: 162
Dist.:   US-162; CAN-0; O'seas-0
  North America: 0 States, 0 Provinces
  Density: NR
Projected New Units (12 Months):   55
Qualifications: 4, 4, 2, 2, 3, 5
Registered:CA,DC,FL,HI,IL,IN,MD,MI,MN,ND,NY,OR,RI,SD,

VA,WA,WI

FINANCIAL/TERMS:
Cash Investment: $50-100K
Total Investment: $109.5-261.5K
Minimum Net Worth: Varies
Fees: Franchise - $22K/100KPop
  Royalty - 4-7%;   Ad. - 2%
Earnings Claims Statement: Yes
Term of Contract (Years):   10/10
Avg. # Of Employees: 4 FT, 0 PT
Passive Ownership: Allowed, But Discouraged
Encourage Conversions: Yes
Area Develop. Agreements: No
Sub-Franchising Contracts: No
Expand In Territory: Yes
Space Needs: 1,500 SF; FS,SF

SUPPORT & TRAINING:
Financial Assistance Provided: Yes (I)
Site Selection Assistance: No
Lease Negotiation Assistance: No
Co-Operative Advertising: No
Franchisee Assoc./Member: Yes/Not a Member
Size Of Corporate Staff: 18
On-Going Support: A,B,C,D,E,F,G,H,I
Training: 1 Week Headquarters in Waco, TX

SPECIFIC EXPANSION PLANS:
US: Yes, All United States
Canada: Yes, All Canada
Overseas: No

ITEM 19
FINANCIAL PERFORMANCE REPRESENTATIONS

Report on Average Sales for Glass Doctor Franchisees
For the Period January 1, 2007 to December 31, 2007

The sales figures listed below are averages derived from historical operating results of the franchised businesses indicated for the time periods covered by license fee reports provided to us by our franchisees from January 1, 2007 through December 31, 2007. Neither we nor our independent certified public accountants have audited or verified any of these sales figures. We make no representations as to the accuracy of sales reported by our franchisees or the extent to which these sales figures were derived using generally accepted accounting principles. Our independent auditors, BDO Seidman, LLP have not audited, reviewed or performed any level of service on the information. Accordingly they provide no form of assurance as to the accuracy of this information.

As of December 31, 2007, we had 147 Glass Doctor franchised businesses in operation in the U.S. Of these, 133 businesses were in operation and reporting sales for the full 12 months of 2007. In order to compare sales for businesses open for the same period, sales results for the other locations were not included in the information provided below. All of the businesses for which sales results are included below were operated by franchisees. We did not operate any of the businesses. All of the businesses are comparable to the franchised businesses offered by this disclosure document and offered substantially the same services to the public.

The sales listed below are an average of the annual gross sales reported by the indicated Glass Doctor franchised businesses. These results are not intended to represent the actual results that would likely have occurred for any specific franchised business during the period indicated. Actual results for a specific location could have differed significantly from the results presented. No adjustments have been made to these reported sales. Because these are gross sales results only, no costs or expenses are taken into account. Profits resulting from any given level of gross sales may differ substantially from one business to another. Sales and profit results are directly impacted by various factors, including: competition from other similar businesses in the area; the quality of management and service in a franchisee's operations; contractual relationships and terms with individual landlords and suppliers; the cost of capital and the extent to which a franchisee might have financed its operations; legal, accounting, and other professional fees; federal, state, and local income and other taxes; and discretionary expenditures. You should therefore use the information in this Report only as a reference to conduct your own analysis.

Except for the information that appears in this report, we do not furnish or authorize our salespersons or affiliates to furnish any oral or written information or representations or statements of actual sales, costs, income or profits. We encourage you to carefully review this material with your attorney and/or accountant.

Substantiation of the data used to prepare this report will be made available to a prospective franchisee on reasonable request.

Caution: this information has been prepared by us without an audit.

Such actual sales are of franchised units and should not be considered as the actual or probable sales that will be realized by any franchisee. The franchisor does not represent that any franchisee can attain such sales. A new franchisee's individual financial results are likely to differ from the results stated herein.

This analysis is based upon the historic experience of businesses in operation for the full 12 months during 2007 and the information has not been adjusted for any factors, including geographic location. The sales reflected in this analysis should not be considered as the actual or potential sales, costs and expenses or operating profits that you will realize. We do not represent that any operator can expect to attain the sales presented in this report, or any other particular level or range of

sales, costs and expenses or operating profits. Your success will depend largely on your ability and efforts.

We do not represent that you will derive income from your franchised business that exceeds your initial payment for or investment in your business. The individual financial results of any franchised business are likely to differ from the information described in this item.

This analysis does not include any cost or expense information and those items may differ substantially from one business or area of the country to another. You should consult with your financial, business, and legal advisors to determine all categories of costs and expenses that you will incur.

You are urged to consult with appropriate financial, business and legal advisors to conduct your own analysis, using the information presented in this report.

Average Annual Sales
for Glass Doctor Franchised Businesses
Open and Reporting Sales for Full 12 Months in 2007

Full Years in Business and Territory Population: Under 400,000 or Over 400,000[1]	Average Annual Sales for 2007 [2]	Number of Businesses in Group Open for Full 12 Months 2007 [3]	Number of Businesses in Group that Attained this Level of Sales or Greater for 2007 [4]	Percentage of Businesses in group that Attained this Level of Sales or greater for 2007 [5]	Number of Businesses in Glass Doctor System Open for full 12 months in 2007 [6]	Number of Businesses in Glass Doctor System that Attained this Level of Sales or Greater for 2007 [7]	Percentage of Businesses in Glass Doctor System that Attained this Level of Sales or greater for 2007 [8]
A. 1-2 Full Years	$523,852	40	13	32.50%	133	74	55.6%
1. Under 400,000	$361,236	19	3	15.80%	133	99	74.4%
2. Over 400,000	$686,467	21	10	46.70%	133	55	41.4%
B. 3-5 Full Years	$1,040,228	53	15	28.30%	133	38	28.6%
1. Under 400,000	$417,282	23	9	39.10%	133	88	66.2%
2. Over 400,000	$1,663,173	30	12	40%	133	23	17.3%
C. 6-7 Full Years	$862,611	21	6	28.60%	133	44	33.1%
1. Under 400,000	$611,067	9	3	33%	133	63	47.7%
2. Over 400,000	$1,114,155	12	4	33%	133	34	25.6%
D. 8-10 Full Years	$1,296,789	7	3	42.90%	133	30	22.6%
1. Under 400,000	n/a	0	n/a	n/a	133	n/a	n/a
2. Over 400,000	$1,296,789	7	3	42.90%	133	30	22.6%
E. 10+ Full Years	$2,186,346	9	4	44.40%	133	13	8.3%
1. Under 400,000	n/a	0	n/a	n/a	133	n/a	n/a
2. Over 400,000	$2,186,346	9	4	44.40%	133	11	8.3%

[1] The franchised businesses are grouped to show the average sales for businesses open for the full years indicated and the groups are further defined by the population in the territory: over 400,000

in population or under 400,000 in population. While territory population and years in business have some impact on level of sales that may be expected, other factors are also important and should be considered.

[2] The average annual sales shows the average sales of all of the businesses in the group based on license fee reports provided to us by our franchisees from January 1, 2007 through December 31, 2007.

[3] This is the number of businesses open for a full 12 months during 2007 that fell within this group. To be included, the business must have been open for the full number of year(s) stated with the indicated territory population level.

[4] This is the number of businesses in the group that achieved the average annual sales level stated for the group during 2007.

[5] This is the percentage of businesses in the group that achieved the average annual sales level stated for the group during 2007.

[6] This is the total number of businesses in the Glass Doctor system open for the full 12 months during 2007.

[7] Of the total number of businesses in the Glass Doctor system open for the full 12 months during 2007, regardless of how long in business or the territory population, this is the number that achieved the indicated level of sales or greater.

[8] Of the total number of businesses in the Glass Doctor system open for the full 12 months during 2007, regardless of how long in business or the territory population, this is the percentage of the total that achieved the indicated level of sales or greater.

[9] The total number of businesses in the Glass Doctor system open for the full 12 months during 2007 includes businesses that may have been counted differently for Item 20 because of the dates that franchisees actually started reporting sales after the franchisee had opened for business.

Great Clips®

Relax. You're at Great Clips.

GREAT CLIPS

7700 France Ave. S., # 425
Minneapolis, MN 55435
Tel: (800) 947-1143 (952) 893-9088
Fax: (952) 844-3443
E-Mail: franchise@greatclips.com
Web Site: www.greatclipsfranchise.com
Mr. Rob Goggins, VP Franchise Development

High-volume haircutting salon, specializing in haircuts for the entire family. What really makes this business concept unique is the fact that it's recession resistant, simple and has steady growth; you will be hard pressed to find a better business that meets all three. Strong, local support to franchisees, excellent training programs.

BACKGROUND:	**IFA MEMBER**
Established: 1982;	1st Franchised: 1983
Franchised Units:	2700
Company-Owned Units:	0
Total Units:	2700

Dist.:	US-2600; CAN-100; O'seas-0
North America:	45 States, 3 Provinces
Density:	190 in CA, 164 in IL, 176 in OH
Projected New Units (12 Months):	200
Qualifications:	5, 4, 1, 3, 3, 5
Registered:	CA,DC,FL,IL,IN,MD,MI,MN,ND,NY,OR,RI,SD,VA, WA,WI,AB

FINANCIAL/TERMS:	
Cash Investment:	$25K
Total Investment:	$109.4-202.5K
Minimum Net Worth:	$300K
Fees: Franchise -	$25K
Royalty - 6%;	Ad. - 5%
Earnings Claims Statement:	Yes
Term of Contract (Years):	10/5
Avg. # Of Employees:	3 FT, 5 PT
Passive Ownership:	Allowed
Encourage Conversions:	No
Area Develop. Agreements:	Yes
Sub-Franchising Contracts:	No
Expand In Territory:	Yes
Space Needs:	1,000-1,200 SF

SUPPORT & TRAINING:		On-Going Support:	A,B,C,D,E,f,G,H,I
Financial Assistance Provided:	Yes (I)	Training:	2.5 Weeks Local Market; 5 Days Minneapolis, MN
Site Selection Assistance:	Yes		
Lease Negotiation Assistance:	Yes	**SPECIFIC EXPANSION PLANS:**	
Co-Operative Advertising:	Yes	US:	Yes, All United States
Franchisee Assoc./Member:	Yes/Member	Canada:	Yes, Western Canada, Toronto
Size Of Corporate Staff:	200	Overseas:	No

Item 19
FINANCIAL PERFORMANCE REPRESENTATIONS

Great Clips provides prospective franchisees with information regarding the average sales, expenses and cash flows of certain franchised GREAT CLIPS® units. Great Clips will substantiate the information set forth in this Item 19, upon reasonable request, provided, however, that such substantiation shall not disclose the sales, expenses or cash flows of any specific franchised unit without the written authorization of the franchisee, except as required by any applicable state or federal registration authorities.

OTHER THAN AS SPECIFICALLY DISCLOSED IN THIS ITEM 19, GREAT CLIPS DOES NOT MAKE ACTUAL, AVERAGE, PROJECTED OR FORECASTED SALES, EXPENSES, PROFITS, CASH FLOW OR EARNINGS INFORMATION AVAILABLE TO PROSPECTIVE FRANCHISEES. THERE IS NO GUARANTY THAT ANY NEW FRANCHISEE WILL ATTAIN THE AVERAGE SALES, EXPENSES, PROFITS, CASH FLOW OR EARNINGS LEVELS ATTAINED BY ANY EXISTING FRANCHISEES.

GREAT CLIPS HAS COMPILED THESE AVERAGE SALES, EXPENSES, PROFITS, CASH FLOW OR EARNINGS FIGURES FROM INFORMATION SUPPLIED BY GREAT CLIPS® FRANCHISEES AND THEY SHOULD NOT BE CONSIDERED AS THE ACTUAL OR POTENTIAL SALES, EXPENSES, PROFITS, CASH FLOW, OR EARNINGS THAT WILL BE REALIZED BY ANY OTHER FRANCHISEE. GREAT CLIPS DOES NOT REPRESENT THAT ANY FRANCHISEE CAN EXPECT TO ATTAIN THESE SALES, EXPENSES, PROFITS, CASH FLOW OR EARNINGS. A NEW FRANCHISEE'S INDIVIDUAL FINANCIAL RESULTS ARE LIKELY TO DIFFER FROM THE AVERAGE FIGURES PRESENTED BELOW. : IF GREAT CLIPS INCLUDED SALONS THAT WERE ONLY OPEN FOR ONE YEAR, THESE NUMBERS WOULD BE SUBSTANTIALLY DIFFERENT.

The average sales, expenses and cash flows of the GREAT CLIPS® units were obtained from operating statements submitted to Great Clips by its franchisees. Most franchisees use a cash versus accrual system for producing their financial statements, which may produce slight differences between the actual date of occurrence of expenses and the date such expenses are reported on the franchisee's financial statements. Neither Great Clips nor its independent certified public accountants have independently audited or verified these franchisee statements.

The information received in these statements, to the best of Great Clips' knowledge, is accurate and complete.

All GREAT CLIPS® units offer substantially the same services and products to the public. The actual sales, expenses, and cash flow results of any franchised GREAT CLIPS® unit may vary substantially from these averages. Sales, expenses and cash flow results depend upon many independently variable factors including, but by no means limited to, the location and visibility of the unit, local traffic patterns, the demographic composition, age of the market and trends of the market area served by the unit, the competitive environment, public awareness of and goodwill associated with the name "GREAT CLIPS®", the region and market area in which the unit is located, the length of time the unit has been in operation, the quality of the management and service at the unit, labor costs, the individual skills of the franchisee and other factors. This information is therefore limited in its usefulness and should only be utilized as a reference for you to use in conducting your own independent analysis of the business.

279

THE FOLLOWING TABLE CONTAINS INFORMATION RELATING SOLELY TO HISTORI-CAL SALES, EXPENSE AND CASH FLOW DATA COMPILED FROM EXISTING FRANCHISED GREAT CLIPS® UNITS. THE TABLE IS QUALIFIED IN ITS ENTIRETY BY ALL THE INFORMA-TION, NOTES, CAUTIONARY STATEMENTS AND QUALIFICATIONS CONTAINED IN THIS ITEM 19.

AVERAGE OPERATING CASH FLOW OF CERTAIN GREAT CLIPS® UNITS
GENERAL DESCRIPTION AND METHODOLOGY

The following statement (referred to in this disclosure document as the "Average Operating Cash Flow Statement") consists of the average sales, expenses and operating cash flow of certain GREAT CLIPS® units. The statement is based on a sample of 938 units that were open two years or longer as of January 1, 2007, and operating as of the date of this disclosure document.

The total eligible sample of units opened for two years or longer, as of January 1, 2007, consisted of 1,943 salons. The sample was reduced by eliminating any unit for which Great Clips had insufficient data to be reasonably assured of having accurate and complete expense information (1,005 units).

The 1,005 units eliminated due to insufficient data were not distributed evenly over the entire database, based on total sales. Of the missing salons, 377 had total sales at or above the median for the total sample and 628 had total sales below the median for the total sample. If all 1,005 of these salons had been included in the sample, it would have reduced the median total sales in the sample by 4.8% and the net operating cash flow by a somewhat larger percent.

The sales and expense data used in the preparation of this table was taken from actual unit operating statements, provided by the franchisee, for each unit in the sample. The time frame or accounting period of these operating statements was the most current available to Great Clips, but, in some cases, did not match the exact time frame from which sales figures were drawn. Therefore some information was annualized to extract a full year worth of data.

The methodology used was to calculate each unit's reported expenses as a percentage of total sales, then to apply this expense percentage to the total sales for 2007 to compute the operating cash flow figure. Great Clips feels that this is the method that produces the fairest representation of the current operating averages for these sample units.

The 938 units included in this sample are located in the following states/provinces:

State/Province	Number of Units
Alberta	5
Arizona	95
British Columbia	8
California	49
Colorado	50
Florida	52
Georgia	35
Idaho	8
Illinois	48
Indiana	70
Iowa	26
Kansas	12
Kentucky	17
Michigan	1
Minnesota	90
Missouri	52
Montana	7
Nebraska	12
Nevada	11
New Mexico	5
North Carolina	53

North Dakota	5
Ohio	78
Oklahoma	1
Oregon	19
Pennsylvania	6
South Carolina	8
South Dakota	4
Tennessee	26
Texas	32
Utah	19
Virginia	5
Washington	24
Wisconsin	3
Wyoming	2

The average annualized total sales for this group of 938 units is $297,535. A total of 388 units, or 41.4%, exceed this average. The average total of all expenses for this group of 938 units is $245,134. A total of 529 units, or 56.4%, have total expenses lower than the average figure of $245,134. The average operating cash flow for this group of 938 units is $52,401. A total of 411 units, or 43.8%, had total average operating cash flow in excess of the average of $52,401.

THE FOLLOWING AVERAGE OPERATING CASH FLOW INFORMATION SHOULD NOT BE CONSTRUED AS ACTUAL OR PROBABLE RESULTS THAT WILL BE REALIZED BY A FRANCHISEE. IT IS BASED ON OPERATING RESULTS OF UNITS IN OPERATION SINCE AT LEAST JANUARY 1, 2005.

AVERAGE OPERATING CASH FLOW STATEMENT

Revenues[1]		
Service Sales	$278, 153	93.49%
Product Sales	19,382	6.51%
Total Revenues	$297,535	100.00%
Expenses		
Labor[2]	$144,839	48.68%
Occupancy[3]	30,674	10.31%
Product[4]	10,790	3.63%
Continuing Franchise Fees[5]	18,285	6.15%
Advertising[6]	16,427	5.52%
Other[7]	24.119	8.10%
Total Expenses	$245,134	82.39%
Operating Cash Flow[8]	$52,401	17.61%

Many GREAT CLIPS® franchisees operate more than one salon. The average number of salons per franchisee who has operated GREAT CLIPS® salons for over five years is 5.2.

AVERAGES BASED ON SALES RANGE

Sales Range ($000)	Salons			Expenses as a % of Sales					
	Number	%	Average Sales in Range	Labor	Occupancy	All Other	Total	Cash Flow (%)	Cash Flow ($)

< $150	11	1.2	$137,997	60.1%	22.2%	27.7%	110.0%	(10.0%)	($13,733)
$150 - $199	103	11.0	$179,017	54.4%	15.6%	25.7%	95.7%	4.3%	$7,782
$200 - $249	209	22.3	$228,367	50.8%	12.8%	24.6%	88.1%	11.9%	$27,236
$250 - $299	234	24.9	$274,101	49.2%	11.1%	23.9%	84.2%	15.8%	$43,428
$300 - $349	152	16.2	$321,567	47.7%	9.5%	23.1%	80.2%	19.8%	$63,552
$350 - $399	105	11.2	$372,945	47.1%	8.7%	22.5%	78.4%	21.6%	$80,543
$400 - $449	61	6.5	$423,445	46.7%	7.8%	21.9%	76.4%	23.6%	$99,815
$450+	63	6.7	$530,077	45.7%	6.8%	22.2%	74.7%	25.3%	$133,973
All Salons in Sample	938	100%	$297,535	48.68%	10.31%	23.40%	82.39%	17.61%	$52,401

Notes:

1. Revenues. Average sales based on actual operating results as reported by franchisees to Great Clips.

2. Labor. Includes all employee-related expenses including: wages, salary, bonus, commission, payroll taxes, insurance benefits, other benefits, and workers' compensation expenses. Includes the cost of salon manager but excludes, if identifiable, any labor expense related to general manager or franchisee.

3. Occupancy. Includes all rent, common area maintenance, real estate taxes plus percentage rent paid, if any. Also includes any other lease-related charges such as maintenance, security, trash removal, merchant association dues or charges or shopping center promotional expenses.

4. Products. Includes the cost of all product purchased for resale or for back bar customer service usage plus all freight or delivery costs associated with this product.

5. Continuing Franchise Fees. All units in the System pay identical Continuing Franchise Fees of 6%. The model is not exactly 6% due to the fact that the franchisees predominately use a cash rather than accrual basis for accounting purposes.

6. Advertising. All units in the System pay identical amounts of 5% of gross sales into the North American Advertising Fund. In addition, virtually all franchisees participate in other discretionary advertising on a local or regional basis.

7. Other. This category includes all other cash expense items and categories not included elsewhere. These would include: travel and entertainment, supplies, dues and subscriptions, telephone, utilities, non-real estate repairs and maintenance, insurance, postage, freight, bad debts, taxes and fees, cash over/short, recruitment expense, laundry, meals, equipment purchase, credit card charges, accounting and legal, employee theft/losses, deposits, bank charges, uniforms, licenses, contributions, meeting expenses, janitorial, bad checks, printing, inventory differences, computer charges, and convention expenses.

8. Operating Cash Flow. This figure does not include any provision for income taxes or for non-cash expenses such as depreciation or amortization. It also does not include any reserve for future capital expenditures.

Newly opened units tend to have average sales and cash flow significantly below the average for the units included in the earnings claim sample above. This is especially true of new units opened by new franchisees in markets that have few existing units. Certain markets have substantially higher real estate costs than others and any prospective franchisee is urged to verify this along with all other expense factors in relation to local market conditions. Markets with many units and correspondingly larger cooperative advertising budgets tend to have units with higher revenues and cash flows than markets with few existing units.

You are responsible for developing your own business plan for your proposed GREAT CLIPS® unit, including capital budgets, pro forma financial statements, sales and expense projections and other elements appropriate to the particular circumstances of the proposed unit. In developing- the business plan, you are cautioned to make necessary allowance for changes in financial results that may occur due to any of the factors listed above, for any and all ranges of general economic conditions that may exist now or in the future, or for any other circumstances that may impact the operation and performance of the business.

No representations or statements of actual, average or projected sales profits or earnings are made to applicants for GREAT CLIPS® franchises, except as stated in this Item 19. Neither Great Clips' sales personnel nor any employee or officer of Great Clips is authorized to make any claims or statements as to the earnings, sales, expenses, cash flows, or profits or prospects or chances of success that any franchisee can expect or that present or past franchisees have had, other than as stated in this Item 19. Great Clips specifically instructs its sales personnel, agents, employees and officers that they are not permitted to make any such claims or statements, nor are they authorized to represent or estimate dollar figures as to existing or future GREAT CLIPS salon operations, other than as stated in this Item 19. Great Clips recommends that applicants for GREAT CLIPS® franchises make their own investigation and determine whether or not existing salons are profitable and whether their Salon is likely to be profitable. Great Clips will not be bound by allegations of any unauthorized representations as to earnings, sales, profits, prospects, or chances of success.

YOU ARE URGED TO CONSULT WITH APPROPRIATE FINANCIAL, BUSINESS AND LEGAL ADVISORS AND EXISTING GREAT CLIPS® FRANCHISEES IN CONNECTION WITH THE USE OF ANY OF THE INFORMATION CONTAINED IN THIS SECTION.

HUNTINGTON LEARNING CENTER

496 Kinderkamack Rd.
Oradell, NJ 07649-1512
Tel: (800) 653-8400 (201) 261-8400
Fax: (800) 361-9728
E-Mail: franchise@huntingtonlearning.com
Web Site: www.huntingtonlearning.com/franchise
Mr. Russell Miller, VP Business Development

Offers tutoring to 5-19 year-olds in reading, writing, language development study skills and mathematics, as well as programs to prepare for standardized entrance exams. Instruction is offered in a tutorial setting and is predominately remedial in nature.

BACKGROUND:	IFA MEMBER
Established: 1977;	1st Franchised: 1985
Franchised Units:	284
Company-Owned Units:	34
Total Units:	318

Dist.:	US-318; CAN-0; O'seas-0
North America:	41 States, 0 Provinces
Density:	31 in CA, 37 in FL, 26 in NY
Projected New Units (12 Months):	80
Qualifications:	5, 3, 1, 3, 1, 5
Registered:	CA,DC,FL,IL,IN,MD,MI,MN,NY,OR,RI,WA,WI

FINANCIAL/TERMS:

Cash Investment:	$60K
Total Investment:	$203-393.75K
Minimum Net Worth:	$250K
Fees: Franchise -	$43K
Royalty - 8%/$1.5K Min.;	Ad. - 2%/$500 Min
Earnings Claims Statement:	Yes
Term of Contract (Years):	10/10
Avg. # Of Employees:	2-4 FT, 12-20 PT
Passive Ownership:	Not Allowed
Encourage Conversions:	Yes
Area Develop. Agreements:	Yes
Sub-Franchising Contracts:	No
Expand In Territory:	No
Space Needs:	2,000-2,500 SF; SF,SC,RM

SUPPORT & TRAINING:		Training:	On-Going Regional;
Financial Assistance Provided:	Yes (I)		5 Weeks Oradell, NJ (Corporate Headquarters)
Site Selection Assistance:	Yes		
Lease Negotiation Assistance:	Yes	**SPECIFIC EXPANSION PLANS:**	
Co-Operative Advertising:	Yes	US:	Yes, Contiguous US
Franchisee Assoc./Member:	No	Canada:	No
Size Of Corporate Staff:	100	Overseas:	No
On-Going Support:	C,D,E,F,G,h,I		

Item 19. Financial Performance Representations

The information in this Item 19 is an historic financial performance representation about the System's existing outlets. This information relates to the performance of franchised and corporate-owned Huntington Learning Centers®. The franchised outlets were in operation and operated by the same franchisee for the entire calendar year. The corporate-owned outlets were in operation for the entire calendar year. Table 19.1 presents this information.

Table 19.1
Average Sales of Huntington Learning Centers® in Operation for 2007
See the note below this table

Center group	Third	Number of centers	Maximum sales of centers in this group	Minimum sales of centers in this group	Average sales of centers in this group	Those centers achieving sales greater than the year's average	
						Number	Percent
Corporate	Top	11	$2,022,677	$964,210	$1,184,228	3	27%
Corporate	Middle	12	$900,300	$656,282	$763,260	4	33%
Corporate	Bottom	11	$651,070	$333,813	$533,752	6	55%
Corporate	All	34	$2,022,677	$333,813	$825,203	15	44%
Franchise	Top	84	$1,578,431	$505,590	$674,260	36	43%
Franchise	Middle	85	$505,214	$337,626	$416,185	38	45%
Franchise	Bottom	85	$336,138	$79,487	$249,255	45	53%
Franchise	All	254	$1,578,431	$79,487	$445,670	112	44%
All	Top	95	$2,022,677	$540,294	$769,342	30	32%
All	Middle	97	$540,115	$357,695	$445,535	48	49%
All	Bottom	96	$350,643	$79,487	$259,924	53	55%
All	All	288	$2,022,677	$79,487	$490,476	123	43%

Note. CAUTION. Not all centers achieved these average sales. There is no assurance you will do as well. If you rely upon our figures, you must accept the risk of not doing as well.

Your individual financial results may, and likely will, differ from the result stated in Table 19.1. Many factors influence the revenue at a Huntington Learning Center®, including the way the manager operates the business, the number of inquiries, conversion of these inquiries to enrolled students, program duration, and tuition rates, as well as factors outside the business, like demographic factors, including the number of school-age children located near the Huntington Learning Center®. Operation of the Huntington Learning Center® may be affected by factors like the curriculum used in the schools attended by students in the area, and the length of the school day and the length of the school year. The presence of competitors, including other Huntington Learning Centers®, may affect your revenue. Factors that determine expenses at a Huntington Learning Center® include the number of teachers and other staff hired and their length of employment; the amount of compensation the franchisee pays himself or herself, as well as staff; and the benefits offered. Another factor includes marketing expenditures; many franchisees spend substantially more on marketing than required under the Franchise Agreement. In addition, the Advertising Cooperative Association can require money for cooperative advertising. Another factor includes the amount of rent for the Huntington Learning Center® premises.

Franchised Huntington Learning Centers® differ from each other in many important ways, including their market area and geographic location and the number of children and population contained thereabout and the economic and financial circumstances of this population. Huntington Learning Centers® also differ from each other in their physical, marketing, employee, and manager's characteristics and in many other factors that may or may not exist or be similar to the factors that exist in any other location or geographic area or market area that you or any prospective franchisee may consider. Actual sales, expenses, profits, and earnings vary from one Huntington Learning Center® to another by significant amounts, and we can not and do not estimate or forecast the sales, expenses, profits, or earnings that you may achieve.

You should conduct an independent investigation of the costs and expenses you will incur in operating the Franchised Center. Franchisees and former franchisees listed in Exhibits K and L, respectively, may be a source of this information. You should consult with financial, business and legal advisors about this Item 19.

We will make the data we used to compile this Item 19 available to you as a prospective franchisee, upon reasonable written request.

We do not authorize anyone, including our officers or sales personnel, to furnish you with any oral or written information about actual or potential sales, expenses, profits, or earnings of Huntington Learning Centers®, other than the information in this Item 19.

If you receive any oral or written information about actual or potential sales, expenses, profits, or earnings of Huntington Learning Centers®, other than the specific information contained in this Item 19, please notify the Chairman of Huntington Learning Centers, Inc. immediately in writing.

How we calculated average actual sales

Franchised and corporate Huntington Learning Centers® in operation for an entire calendar year and for concurrent equal periods of time reported the gross revenues ("sales") in this Item 19. We compiled the data for franchised Huntington Learning Centers® from the monthly income statements our franchisees submitted to us, which they prepare according to a standardized method described in the Manual. We believe these statements are accurate as to sales, because each franchisee must pay us Continuing Royalty and Advertising Fees that are calculated as a percentage of sales. We have not audited nor in any other manner substantiated the truthfulness, accuracy, or completeness of any information supplied by our franchisees. We compiled the data for corporate Huntington Learning Centers® according to a standardized method described in the Manual.

• If a Huntington Learning Center® was transferred from one franchisee to another, its results under the different franchisees are included as the results of one Huntington Learning Center® for the entire period; there were 24 of these centers in 2007.

• Sales of Huntington Learning Centers® owned or operated by us for the entire calendar year are included in this Item 19; there were 34 of these centers in 2007.

• If a Huntington Learning Center® was transferred from a franchisee to us or our affiliate, its results are not included in Table 19.1; there were seven of these centers in 2007.

• If a Huntington Learning Center® was transferred from us or our affiliate to a franchisee, its results were not included in Table 19.1; there were five of these centers in 2007.

The corporate Huntington Learning Centers® operated in New Jersey, New York, and Connecticut.

Table 19.2 lists the states in which franchised Huntington Learning Centers® were in operation.

Table 19,2 States in which Franchised Huntington Learning Centers® Were in Operation during 2007			
Alabama	Indiana	Nebraska	Rhode Island
Arizona	Iowa	Nevada	South Carolina
Arkansas	Kansas	New Hampshire	Tennessee
California	Kentucky	New Jersey	Texas
Colorado	Louisiana	New Mexico	Utah
Connecticut	Maryland	New York	Virginia
Delaware	Massachusetts	North Carolina	Washington
Florida	Michigan	Ohio	Wisconsin
Georgia	Minnesota	Oklahoma	
Idaho	Mississippi	Oregon	
Illinois	Missouri	Pennsylvania	

Expense Items on a Franchise Huntington Learning Centers End-of-Year P&L Statement

Table 19.3 presents the expense items listed on the End-of-Year Profit and Loss Statement franchisees must submit to us. Your profit and loss statement may contain additional or different expense items.

Table 19.3 Expenses Listed on the End-of-Year P&L Statement that Franchisees Must Submit to Us
Gross payroll for franchisee, center director, assistant director
Other full-time staff (like a regional director)
Gross payroll for part-time teachers
Gross payroll for any other part-time staff
Payroll taxes (Employer's portion of FICA, FUTA, etc.)
Advertising center services, including broadcast TV and radio, cable TV, daily and weekly newspaper, magazine, direct mail, free standing insert, yellow pages, Internet, school programs, and marketing
Building, including rent, utilities, janitor, and maintenance
Repairs and maintenance of equipment
Supplies - office and administrative
Exam Prep advertising
ERD fees
Conference Services fees
Supplies - educational
Professional fees (accounting, legal, etc.)
Telephone
Travel and entertainment
Continuing Royalty
Advertising Fee
Insurance (property, liability, health, etc.)
Depreciation and amortization
Debt service

Training (travel, food, lodging, etc.)
Employee benefits
Other expenses
Taxes, other than payroll

INSTANT TAX SERVICE

1 South Main Street, # 1400
Dayton, OH 45402
Tel: 18888701040 18888701040
Fax: 18778229139
E-Mail: franchise@instanttaxservice.com
Web Site: www.instanttaxservicefranchise.com
Mr Brook Wise, VP Franchise Sales

Instant Tax Service is a retail income tax preparation firm serving citizens and residents of the United States in nearly 1,200 offices in 34 states. We specialize in professional tax preparation, expedited refunds, and refund anticipation loans. We're a fast, friendly alternative in the tax business. We pride ourselves on our outstanding customer service, community outreach programs, and the opportunities we give our franchising partners.

BACKGROUND:

Established: 2000;	1st Franchised: 2004
Franchised Units:	1706
Company-Owned Units:	12
Total Units:	1718
Dist.:	US-1718; CAN-0; O'seas-0
North America:	0 States, 0 Provinces
Density:	NR
Projected New Units (12 Months):	NR
Qualifications:	NR

Registered:	NR

FINANCIAL/TERMS:

Cash Investment:	$39K-89K
Total Investment:	$39K-89K
Minimum Net Worth:	NR
Fees: Franchise -	$34K
Royalty - ;	Ad. - NR
Earnings Claims Statement:	No
Term of Contract (Years):	NR
Avg. # Of Employees:	FT, PT
Passive Ownership:	NR
Encourage Conversions:	No
Area Develop. Agreements:	NR
Sub-Franchising Contracts:	No
Expand In Territory:	No
Space Needs:	SF

SUPPORT & TRAINING:

Financial Assistance Provided:	No
Site Selection Assistance:	NR
Lease Negotiation Assistance:	NR
Co-Operative Advertising:	No
Franchisee Assoc./Member:	No
Size Of Corporate Staff:	NR
On-Going Support:	NR
Training:	NR

SPECIFIC EXPANSION PLANS:

US:	NR
Canada:	No
Overseas:	No

ITEM 19
FINANCIAL PERFORMANCE REPRESENTATIONS

This Item 19 contains historical gross sales information for 187 Instant Tax Service locations operated by our Franchisees for the fiscal year ended March 31, 2007 (which we refer to as the "2006 fiscal year").

You should not draw any inference as to the gross sales, net sales, or profits for your future Instant Tax Service location from the information contained in this Item 19. We do not warrant, represent, promise, predict or guarantee that you can or will attain the same financial results. To the contrary, your financial results will vary and probably will vary to a material extent from the results contained in this Item 19.

Your performance will depend upon a variety of factors including (without limitation):

- differences in local competition;

- **demographics;**
- **your marketing efforts and expenditures;**
- **whether you have previous experience in the tax industry;**
- **overall economic conditions;**
- **labor conditions and minimum wage laws;**
- **commodity, transportation, workers' compensation, insurance and utility costs;**
- **real estate acquisition, construction and lease costs;**
- **property and sales tax rates; and**
- **and governmental rules, regulations and interpretations.**

You should consider the following material factors in reviewing and determining whether to rely on the data listed below:

1.   The historical gross revenue information contained in this Item 19 and in <u>Chart #1</u> pertains to 55 Instant Tax Service locations currently operated by our Franchisees and which have been in operation for at least three years. Last fiscal year (year ending March 31, 2006), 27 of these 55 Instant Tax Service locations were owned and operated by our affiliate, TCA Financial, prior to being sold to various Franchisees for the 2006 fiscal year. All of the 59 Instant Tax Service locations are substantially similar to the franchises that are described in this Disclosure Document. For the purposes of this Item 19, we will refer to these locations as the "Seasoned Item 19 Locations." We have excluded from this historical revenue results franchisees that operate at check cashing stores, convenience stores, grocery stores, laundromats, and other venues for which the Instant Tax Service Business is only an ancillary part of the business operation and is not the primary business.

2.   The historical gross revenue information contained in this Item 19 and in <u>Chart #2</u> pertains to 132 Instant Tax Service locations currently operated by our Franchisees and which have been in operation for two years or less. All of these 132 Instant Tax Service locations are also substantially similar to the franchises that are described in this Disclosure Document. For the purposes of this Item 19, we will refer to these locations as the "Unseasoned Item 19 Locations." The Seasoned Item 19 Locations and the Unseasoned Item 19 Locations shall collectively be referred as the "Total Item 19 Locations." We have excluded from this historical revenue results franchisees that operate Instant Tax Service Businesses at check cashing stores, convenience stores, grocery stores, laundromats, and other venues for which the Instant Tax Service Business is only an ancillary part of the business operation and is not the primary business.

3.   We have separated stores with one or two years of operation from those with three to six years because we have found that, generally, it takes several years of operation in a market, with an ongoing physical presence, yearly display of signage, regular marketing and promotion, active involvement by the franchise owner in the community, and other factors to develop name recognition and at least some repeat business. We do not represent or guarantee that any Instant Tax Service Business, or your Instant Tax Service business, will achieve similar results, or will even achieve positive results from year to year.

4.   The Gross Sales information listed below covers the 2006 fiscal year of operation of the Total Item 19 Locations. For purposes of this Item 19, the term "Gross Sales" means the total revenues derived by the Total Item 19 Locations from all sales of all services and merchandise made in, upon, or from the Total Item 19 Locations, whether for cash, check, credit, barter, exchange or otherwise. The term "Gross Sales" does not include rebates or refunds to customers; the amount of any sales taxes or other similar taxes collected from customers and payable to any federal, state or local tax authority; or the amount of any commissions or fees payable to non-affiliated third parties, not directly employed at the location or otherwise providing on-going and continuing services to the location, for the services rendered for outside services or goods provided or sold by the location to its customers.

5.   The earnings claims figures in this Item 19 do not reflect the cost of sales, operating

288

expenses, or other costs or expenses that must be deducted from gross revenues or gross sales figures to obtain your net income or profit. Cost and expense items not included in net sales or annual sales information will affect net income, gross sales, profit, and cash flow of an Instant Tax Service Franchised Business. This earnings claim statement does not include the following costs and expenses, which should be calculated and taken into account for an Instant Tax Service Office:

(a)   Initial franchise fees, royalties and advertising fees charged by us. See Items 5 and 6.

(b)   Operating expenses, such as licenses, permits, and supplies.

(c)   Utilities, including water, gas, electric and sewer.

(d)   Repairs and maintenance, including parking lot repair and landscaping.

(e)   Income and property taxes.

(f)   Depreciation of property and equipment.

(g)   General and administrative costs, including telephone, postage, office supplies, liability insurance, legal, accounting and other professional services.

(h)   Rent, interest or other financing or occupancy costs for land, buildings, equipment and inventory.

(i)   Labor costs, including employee benefits.

(j)   Advertising and marketing expenditures undertaken by the franchisee in addition to the advertising fees required under the Franchise Agreement.

You should conduct an independent investigation of the costs and expenses you might or will incur in operating an Instant Tax Service Office. Franchisees or former franchisees listed in the Disclosure Document may be one source of this information.

6.   While we do consider the figures reliable, we have not had an independent accounting firm audit each Franchisee's gross sales information used in this Item 19.

7.   The Seasoned Item 19 Locations have been open to the public for varying lengths of time ranging from 3 fiscal years to 6 fiscal years. On average, a Seasoned Item 19 Location has been in operation for approximately 4 years. Those Seasoned Item 19 locations that exceeded the average gross sales for all Seasoned Item 19 Locations tended to be the locations that had been in operation for longer periods of time.

CHART #1

The following statements of historical gross sales reflect the operations of the 55 Seasoned Item 19 Locations. You should *not* consider them as the actual or probable gross sales or operating results that you will realize. We do not represent, warrant or promise that you will attain those sales or results. Your financial results will differ from the results stated in this Item 19 and probably will vary to a material extent. If you rely on the information, you must accept the risk that you may not do as well.

Seasoned Item 19 Locations (Fiscal Year 2006) -- 55 Locations

Average Gross Sales:		$182,287
Range of Gross Sales:	High:	$1,115,482
	Low:	$ 41,833
Approximate Percentage of Locations Whose Gross Sales Exceeded the Average:		34%

CHART #2

The following statements of historical gross sales reflect the operations of the 132 Unseasoned Item 19 Locations. You should *not* consider them as the actual or probable gross sales or operating results that you will realize. We do not represent, warrant or promise that you will attain those sales or results. Your financial results will differ from the results stated in this Item 19 and

probably will vary to a material extent. If you rely on the information, you must accept the risk that you may not do as well.

<u>Unseasoned Item 19 Locations (Fiscal Year 2006) -- 132 Locations</u>

Average Gross Sales: $51,721

Range of Gross Sales: High: $291,014
Low: $ 348

Approximate Percentage
of Locations Whose
Gross Sales Exceeded
the Average: 35%

YOU SHOULD REGARD THE ABOVE INFORMATION ONLY AS AN INDICATION OF HISTORICAL PERFORMANCE OF OUR FRANCHISEES, AND NOT AS A PREDICTION OF FUTURE PERFORMANCE. WE WILL PROVIDE SUBSTANTIATION FOR THE DATA USED IN PREPARING THIS ITEM 19 UPON YOUR REASONABLE REQUEST.

Except as disclosed above, we do not make any written or oral representations or statements of actual, average, projected or forecasted sales, profits or earnings to prospective franchisees. We do not furnish any oral or other written information concerning the actual or potential sales, costs or income of your business. We do not authorize any person representing us to furnish such information or to represent or estimate to prospective franchisees any dollar figures relating to a franchisee's operation.

JENNY CRAIG WEIGHT LOSS AND MANAGEMENT CENTRES

VA,WA,WI

5770 Fleet St.
Carlsbad, CA 92008
Tel: (888) 848-8885 (760) 696-4000
Fax: (760) 696-4708
E-Mail: franchising@jennycraig.com
Web Site: www.jennycraig.com/franchise
Ms. Tracy Heiser, Franchise Development Coordinator

We change lives! JENNY CRAIG provides dynamic, safe and effective weight loss and lasting management solutions, tailored to individuals who desire to look better, feel better and live healthier. The JENNY CRAIG program is a long-term solution that helps clients lose weight, create a healthy relationship with food, build an active lifestyle and develop a balanced approach to living.

BACKGROUND: IFA MEMBER

Established: 1983;	1st Franchised: 1983
Franchised Units:	110
Company-Owned Units:	493
Total Units:	603
Dist.:	US-485; CAN-34; O'seas-121
North America:	46 States, 3 Provinces
Density:	NR
Projected New Units (12 Months):	20
Qualifications:	5, 5, 4, 4, 5, 5
Registered:CA,DC,FL,HI,IL,IN,MD,MI,MN,ND,NY,OR,RI,SD,	

FINANCIAL/TERMS:

Cash Investment:	$100-150K
Total Investment:	$165.6-440.5K
Minimum Net Worth:	$300K
Fees: Franchise -	$25K
Royalty - 7%;	Ad. - 10%
Earnings Claims Statement:	Yes
Term of Contract (Years):	10/10
Avg. # Of Employees:	4 FT, 0 PT
Passive Ownership:	Allowed, But Discouraged
Encourage Conversions:	NA
Area Develop. Agreements:	Yes
Sub-Franchising Contracts:	No
Expand In Territory:	Yes
Space Needs:	1,200-1,500 SF; SC

SUPPORT & TRAINING:

Financial Assistance Provided:	No
Site Selection Assistance:	Yes
Lease Negotiation Assistance:	Yes
Co-Operative Advertising:	No
Franchisee Assoc./Member:	No
Size Of Corporate Staff:	250
On-Going Support:	A,B,C,D,E,F,H,I
Training:	2-3 Weeks Corporate Office;
	2 Weeks In-Centre

SPECIFIC EXPANSION PLANS:		Canada:	Yes, All Canada
US:	Yes, All United States	Overseas:	No

ITEM 19. FINANCIAL PERFORMANCE REPRESENTATIONS

Presented below are certain operating results unaudited for the one year period January 1, 2007 through December 31, 2007 for the 96 Weight Loss and Weight Management Centres operated in the United States and Canada by our franchisees and affiliates during that entire time period. The specific operating results reflect mean average revenue and median revenue for these Centres. Please read carefully all of the information in this Item 19, and all of the notes following the data, when you review the historical data.

	Mean Average per Centre	Number of Centres Above Average	Number of Centres Below Average	Range	Median
Franchisee-Owned Centres in the U.S. (excluding Puerto Rico)	$762,465	32	44	$1,650,522 to $313,285	$719,597
Franchisee-Owned Centres in Canada and Puerto Rico	$1,566,507	7	13	$2,779,608 to $735,601	$1,182,501

Notes:

1.   This table represents Gross Sales results (net of discounts) from 96 total Weight Loss and Weight Management Centres that franchisees operated in the United States, and franchisees that operated in Puerto Rico and Canada, for the entire fiscal year ended December 31, 2007. The total number of Weight Loss and Weight Management Centres includes 76 "Franchisee-Owned" Weight Loss and Weight Management Centres that are owned and operated in the United States (excluding Puerto Rico), and 20 Franchisee-Owned Weight Loss and Weight Management Centres that are owned and operated in Canada and Puerto Rico by our franchisees. There were 8 Franchisee-Owned Weight Loss and Weight Management Centres that were only open for part of the fiscal year ended December 3I, 2007, and the Gross Sales for these Weight Loss and Weight Management Centres were not included in the above table.

2.   The information reflecting Franchisee-Owned Centres was obtained from revenue reports that are tracked via the Point-of-Sale system, and are consistent with the reports franchisees submitted to us and from which royalties and advertising contributions are calculated. Therefore, the basis of accounting is on a cash basis accounting method. All results in the tables are reflected in U.S. Dollars. Gross Sales from Weight Loss and Weight Management Centres operated in Canada have been converted to U.S. Dollars at an exchange rate of .9356, which exchange rate represents the average exchange rate reported in our general ledger system during the one year period January 1, 2007 to December 31, 2007. The information presented in this Item 19 has not been audited. Substantiation of the data used in preparing the materials in this Item 19 will be made available to you upon reasonable request.

3.   The above table does not reflect costs that are incurred by a Weight Loss and Weight Management Centre, including, most significantly, the cost of labor and cost of goods sold. Your labor costs will depend on a number of factors, including the size and location of your Weight Loss and Weight Management Centre, the number of employees, and the number of hours that the Centre is open for business. The total amount of salaries for your employees and managers at a particular location will vary according to local wages. You must make labor and wage determinations based on your market, experience, and other factors.

4.   Of the Franchisee-Owned Centres in the U.S. (excluding Puerto Rico), 32 Centres, or 42%, attained the mean average for that sub-group of Centres. Of the Franchisee-Owned Centres in Canada and Puerto Rico, 7 Centres, or 35% attained the mean average for that sub-group of Centres.

5.   **The financial performance figures do not reflect the costs of sales, operating expenses, or other costs or expenses that must be deducted from the Gross Sales figures to obtain your net income or profit. You should conduct an independent investigation of the costs and expenses you will incur in operating your franchised business. Franchisees, or former franchisees, listed in this Franchise Disclosure Document, may be one source of this information.** As a franchisee, you will incur other expenses of doing business which are likely to be significant, and which vary widely among franchisees. You will be required to pay, among other things Royalty Fees, Advertising Contributions, and computer access and support fees on a regular basis. Among the additional categories of expenses which franchisees may incur include, but will not necessarily be limited to, the following: rent and occupancy costs; franchisee compensation over and above that earned from the operations of the Weight Loss and Weight Management Centre (such as a salary that a franchisee may pay to himself/herself); voluntary employee benefits, such as health, vacation, and pension plan contributions; debt service; insurance; facilities and property maintenance (and reserve for future maintenance); business and regulatory fees and licenses; ongoing and supplemental training expenses; recruitment expenses; and bookkeeping and other professional services.

6.   The information in this Item 19 reflects a wide range of aggregate results from 96 Weight Loss and Weight Management Centres. It should not be considered a representation or guarantee that you will or may achieve any level of revenues, sales, or profits, or that you will experience the same or similar expenses or costs in the operation of your Weight Loss and Weight Management Centre. We do not represent that any franchisee can expect to obtain these results. A new franchisee's individual financial results may be lower.

7.   You are strongly advised to perform an independent investigation of this opportunity to determine whether or not the franchise may be profitable and to consult your attorney, accountant, and other professional advisors before entering into a Franchise Agreement.

8.   Actual results vary from franchisee to franchisee and we cannot estimate or predict the results that you may experience as a franchisee. Your individual financial results are likely to differ from the results shown in the charts. Your results will be affected by factors including prevailing economic or market area conditions, demographics, geographic location, interest rates, your capitalization level, the amount and terms of any financing that you may secure, the property values and lease rates, your business and management skills, staff strengths and weaknesses, and the cost and effectiveness of your marketing activities.

9.   Except as disclosed above, we do not make any written or oral representations or statements of actual, average, projected, or forecasted sales, profits, or earnings to prospective franchisees. We do not furnish any oral or other written information concerning the actual or potential sales, costs, or income of your business. We do not authorize any person representing us to furnish that information or to represent or estimate to prospective franchisees any dollar figures relating to a franchisee's operation.

10.   Written substantiation for this financial performance representation will be made available to you upon reasonable request.

Community Begins Here.®

CHILD CARE LEARNING CENTERS

KIDDIE ACADEMY INTERNATIONAL

3415 Box Hill Corporate Center Dr.

Abington, MD 21009

Tel: (800) 554-3343 + 260 (410) 515-0788 + 260

Fax: (410) 569-2729

E-Mail: sales@kiddieacademy.com

Web Site: www.kiddieacademy.com

Mr. Jim Tisack, VP Franchising

We offer comprehensive training and support without additional cost. KIDDIE ACADEMY's step-by-step program assists with staff recruitment, training, accounting support, site selection, marketing, advertising and curriculum. A true turn-key opportunity that provides on-going support so you can focus on running a successful business.

BACKGROUND: IFA MEMBER

Established: 1981;	1st Franchised: 1992
Franchised Units:	83
Company-Owned Units:	6
Total Units:	89
Dist.:	US-89; CAN-0; O'seas-0
North America:	10 States, 0 Provinces
Density:	4 in IL, 15 in MD, 5 in NJ
Projected New Units (12 Months):	100
Qualifications:	4, 4, 2, 3, 2, 4
Registered:	CA,DC,FL,IL,IN,MD,MI,MN,NY,OR,RI,VA,WI

FINANCIAL/TERMS:

Cash Investment:	$60K
Total Investment:	$450K-3.7MM
Minimum Net Worth:	$450K
Fees: Franchise -	$40K
Royalty - 7%;	Ad. - 0%
Earnings Claims Statement:	No
Term of Contract (Years):	10/5
Avg. # Of Employees:	10-20 FT, 2 PT
Passive Ownership:	Allowed, But Discouraged
Encourage Conversions:	No
Area Develop. Agreements:	Yes
Sub-Franchising Contracts:	No
Expand In Territory:	Yes
Space Needs:	6,500-12,000 SF; FS,SF,SC

SUPPORT & TRAINING:

Financial Assistance Provided:	Yes (D)
Site Selection Assistance:	Yes
Lease Negotiation Assistance:	Yes
Co-Operative Advertising:	No
Franchisee Assoc./Member:	No
Size Of Corporate Staff:	30
On-Going Support:	a,B,C,D,E,G,I
Training:	2 Weeks Owner Train., Corp. HQ;
	1 Week Director Train., Corp. HQ; 3-5 Day Staff Training

SPECIFIC EXPANSION PLANS:

US:	Yes, All United States
Canada:	No
Overseas:	No

ITEM 19: FINANCIAL PERFORMANCE REPRESENTATIONS

The information below represents actual historic financial performance representations concerning the franchise system's existing outlets and has been gathered from the financial information reported to us during Kiddie Academy's 2008 fiscal year by our 90 operating franchisees (as of September 28, 2008, the end of our fiscal year) under their reporting requirements. (See Item 9 of this franchise disclosure document). WE HAVE NOT CONDUCTED AN INDEPENDENT INVESTIGATION OR AN AUDIT TO VERIFY THESE FIGURES.

In the charts, all open and operational Kiddie Academy Franchises are divided into two classifications: (1) Mature academies (Kiddie Academy Franchises that have been operational for at least 18 months); and (2) Ramping academies (Kiddie Academy Franchises that have been operational for less than 18 months). The time periods expressed in this chart are not meant to be an indication as to when or if a Kiddie Academy Franchise will reach maturity. Each academy's growth rate will vary by location, programs and the franchisee's marketing efforts and management skills. We have in our possession written substantiation to support the information appearing in this Item 19. Written substantiation of the data used in preparing these financial performance representations will be made available to the prospective franchisee upon reasonable request.

Other than the information presented below we do not furnish or authorize our employees to furnish to anyone, orally or in writing, information concerning the actual historical or potential future sales, costs, income, earnings or profits of any Kiddie Academy Franchise. However, if you are purchasing an existing Kiddie Academy location, you may receive from us actual operating results of the operating business being offered for sale. These actual operating results need not comply with the requirements of the FTC's Franchise Rule.

THE FOLLOWING INFORMATION SHOULD NOT BE CONSIDERED AS THE ACTUAL OR POTENTIAL REVENUE OR RESULTS OF ANY PARTICULAR KIDDIE ACADEMY FRANCHISED LOCATION. THERE IS NO ASSURANCE YOU WILL DO AS WELL. YOUR ACTUAL FINANCIAL RESULTS WILL LIKELY VARY AND YOU MUST ACCEPT THE RISK OF NOT DOING AS WELL.

FOR FISCAL YEAR ENDED SEPTEMBER 30, 2008

MATURE ACADEMIES (open more than 18 months)

	Building Capacity (determined by state regulation)			
	115 Children or fewer	Between 115 and 150 Children	150 Children or more	All Academies
Number of Academies	11	35	30	76
Average Student Capacity of Building	100	133	168	142
Actual Average Annual Gross Revenues during fiscal year 2008	$789,092	$1,144,965	$1,279,154	$1,146,426
Academies operating above Average	6	16	15	37

RAMPING ACADEMIES (open less than 18 months)

	Building Capacity (determined by state regulation)			
	115 Children or fewer	Between 115 and 150 Children	150 Children or more	All Academies
Number of Academies	0	3	11	14
Average Student Capacity of Building	0	142	180	172
Average Weeks Open	0	34	40	39
Average Actual Gross Revenues* during fiscal year 2008	$0	$306,192	$434,735	$407,191
Academies operating above Average	0	1	5	6

* For weeks actually open. Gross Revenues equal the amount of tuition actually charged for enrollment, before costs and expenses are taken into account. Costs vary greatly depending upon the academy's size and location, and other factors.

THE ABOVE DATA WAS PREPARED WITHOUT AN AUDIT. PROSPECTIVE FRANCHISEES SHOULD BE ADVISED THAT NO CERTIFIED PUBLIC ACCOUNTANT HAS AUDITED THESE FIGURES OR EXPRESSED HIS OR HER OPINION WITH REGARD TO THEIR CONTENT OR FORM.

KINDERDANCE INTERNATIONAL

1333 Gateway Dr., # 1003
Melbourne, FL 32901
Tel: (800) 554-2334 (321) 984-4448
Fax: (321) 984-4490
E-Mail: leads@kinderdance.com
Web Site: www.kinderdance.com
Mr. Richard Maltese, Vice President / Franchise Development

KINDERDANCE® is the original Developmental Dance, Motor Skills, Gymnastics, Music and Fitness Program, blended with academics, specifically designed for boys and girls age 2 to 12. KINDERDANCE® franchisees are trained to teach 5 developmentally unique "Education Through Dance and Motor Development" programs: KINDERDANCE®, KINDERGYM®, KINDERTOTS®), KINDERCOMBO™, and KINDERMOTION®, which are designed for boys and girls ages 2-12. Children learn the basics of ballet, tap, gymnastics, motor development and creative dance, as well as learning numbers, colors, shapes and songs. No studio or dance experience required. Franchisees teach at child care centers and other viable locations.

BACKGROUND: IFA MEMBER

Established: 1979;	1st Franchised: 1985
Franchised Units:	114
Company-Owned Units:	1
Total Units:	115
Dist.:	US-109; CAN-2; O'seas-4
North America:	38 States, 1 Provinces
Density:	12 in CA, 14 in FL, 8 in TX
Projected New Units (12 Months):	20

Qualifications:	2, 2, 1, 2, 2, 5
Registered:	CA,DC,FL,HI,IL,MD,MI,MN,NY,OR,VA,WA,AB

FINANCIAL/TERMS:

Cash Investment:	$12-40K
Total Investment:	$14.9-46.1K
Minimum Net Worth:	NA
Fees: Franchise -	$12-40K
Royalty - 6-15%;	Ad. - 3%
Earnings Claims Statement:	Yes
Term of Contract (Years):	5/5
Avg. # Of Employees:	2 FT, 1-2+ PT
Passive Ownership:	Allowed, But Discouraged
Encourage Conversions:	Yes
Area Develop. Agreements:	Yes
Sub-Franchising Contracts:	No
Expand In Territory:	Yes
Space Needs:	HB, Child Care Center, School, Rec. Center, Fitness

SUPPORT & TRAINING:

Financial Assistance Provided:	Yes (D)
Site Selection Assistance:	NA
Lease Negotiation Assistance:	NA
Co-Operative Advertising:	Yes
Franchisee Assoc./Member:	Yes/Member
Size Of Corporate Staff:	8
On-Going Support:	A,B,C,D,E,F,G,H,I
Training:	6 Days Plus Onsite Melbourne, FL and On-Site

SPECIFIC EXPANSION PLANS:

US:	Yes, All United States
Canada:	Yes, All Canada
Overseas:	Yes, Europe, Asia, New Zealand, S. America, Mexico, Australia

Item 19
FINANCIAL PERFORMANCE REPRESENTATIONS

Where to teach	Ages	When operated	Weeks per year	Enrollment	Avg. Fees per Child
Wherever the children are	Children 2-12	Year Round	52	Maximum 12 children per class	$40.00 per month

70% of our Active Full-Time franchisees achieved gross sales that averaged $74,498.00

50% of our Active Full-Time franchisees achieved gross sales that averaged $85,713.00

30% of our Active Full-Time franchisees achieved gross sales that averaged $100,990.00

The information shown above does not show any franchisee that has decided to work on a part time basis.

The information provided is from the current active full-time franchisees that have been open for more than a year (40) from data ending May 31, 2007 and includes tuition and boutique sales. Information on expenses, profits and loss varies widely and we do not have information to report on them.

Our franchisees share the following demographic characteristics in common:

- Each franchisee's trading area consists of approximately 400,000 people.
- Each franchisee's trading area consists of approximately 250 to 400 marketing locations.

Prospective Franchise Owners must understand that they may not achieve results as favorable as presented for a variety of reasons including location of the business, particularly the prospect of competition from present or anticipated competing businesses, your marketing skills, your base fee, the size and number of classes you elect to teach and the amount of time you put into your business.

All franchises offer substantially the same products and services to be offered by you utilizing our MARKS and SYSTEM, and receive the same level of support and service from us.

CAUTION

THERE IS NO ASSURANCE YOU WILL DO AS WELL. IF YOU RELY UPON OUR FIGURES, YOU MUST ACCEPT THE RISK THAT YOUR FRANCHISE WILL NOT DO AS WELL. YOUR ACCOUNTANT CAN HELP YOU DEVELOP YOUR OWN ESTIMATED COSTS FOR YOUR FRANCHISE. FRANCHISE SALES PRESENTED IS NOT AN INDICATION OF HOW YOUR FRANCHISE WILL PERFORM.

ACTUAL RESULTS VARY FROM FRANCHISE TO FRANCHISE, AND WE CANNOT PREDICT THE RESULTS OF ANY NEW OR PARTICULAR FRANCHISE.

WE PRESENT THIS FINANCIAL INFORMATION WITHOUT AUDIT OR REVIEW BY AN INDEPENDENT CERTIFIED PUBLIC ACCOUNTANT. IT IS BASED SOLELY ON THE REPORTS WE RECEIVED FROM OUR FRANCHISEES. ACTUAL SALES FROM THE OPERATION OF A FRANCHISED BUSINESS ARE INHERENTLY SUBJECT TO UNCERTAINTY AND VARIATIONS DEPENDING UPON CHANGING EVENTS AND ECONOMIC CONDITIONS. THERE CAN BE NO GUARANTEE THAT THESE STATEMENTS PREDICT THE SALES OF ANY FRANCHISE OWNER. ANYONE WHO USES THE ABOVE INFORMATION TO PREPARE HIS/HER OWN PROFORMA STATEMENT MUST ACCEPT THE RISK THAT HIS/HER OWN FRANCHISED BUSINESS MAY PERFORM SUBSTANTIALLY WORSE THAN THOSE INCLUDED IN THE AVERAGES ABOVE.

SUBSTANTIATION OF THE DATA PRESENTED IN THIS EARNINGS CLAIM ON GROSS SALES WILL BE MADE AVAILABLE TO YOU UPON REQUEST.

LIBERTY TAX SERVICE

1716 Corporate Landing Pkwy.
Virginia Beach, VA 23454
Tel: (800) 790-3863 (877) 285-4237
Fax: (800) 880-6432

E-Mail: sales@libtax.com
Web Site: www.libertytaxfranchise.com
Ms. Ami Hill, Media Director

We're #1! LIBERTY TAX SERVICE is the fastest-growing international tax service ever, and is ranked as the #1 tax franchise on the latest Entrepreneur magazine "Franchise 500" and #3 overall. Recession or not, there's a growing market of taxpayers, and approximately 63% of them outsource the tax preparation task to paid professionals. LIBERTY's growth is fueled by a proven operating system that has been fine-tuned by the leadership and field support staff's 600 total years of experience. Founder/CEO John Hewitt has worked 40 tax seasons, including 12 years with H&R Block. Accounting Today magazine has named Hewitt one of the accounting profession's top 100 most influential people ten times. The International Franchise Association has honored Hewitt as its "Entrepreneur of the Year." No prior tax experience is required to put this system to work.

BACKGROUND: IFA MEMBER
Established: 1997; 1st Franchised: 1997
Franchised Units: 3055
Company-Owned Units: 62
Total Units: 3117
Dist.: US-2872; CAN-245; O'seas-0
North America: 50 States, 0 Provinces
Density: 350 in CA, 137 in ON
Projected New Units (12 Months): 300-500
Qualifications: 4, 4, 2, 1, 1, 5
Registered: HI,MN,VA,WA,WI

FINANCIAL/TERMS:
Cash Investment: $40K
Total Investment: $56.8-69.9K
Minimum Net Worth: $100K
Fees: Franchise - $40K

Royalty - Varies; Ad. - 5%
Earnings Claims Statement: No
Term of Contract (Years): 5/5
Avg. # Of Employees: 4-6 FT, 2 PT
Passive Ownership: Allowed, But Discouraged
Encourage Conversions: No
Area Develop. Agreements: Yes
Sub-Franchising Contracts: No
Expand In Territory: Yes
Space Needs: 400+ SF; FS,SF,SC,RM, Kiosk

SUPPORT & TRAINING:
Financial Assistance Provided: Yes (I)
Site Selection Assistance: Yes
Lease Negotiation Assistance: Yes
Co-Operative Advertising: No
Franchisee Assoc./Member: No
Size Of Corporate Staff: 407
On-Going Support: A,B,C,D,E,F,G,H,I
Training: 3 Days Various Cities - Intermediate, Advanced;
5 Days Virginia Beach, VA - Initial, Intermediate, Advanced

SPECIFIC EXPANSION PLANS:
US: Yes, All United States
Canada: Yes
Overseas: No

ITEM 19
FINANCIAL PERFORMANCE REPRESENTATIONS

This section contains information regarding the average federal income tax returns prepared or filed by Liberty Tax storefront franchised offices of franchisees who operated one office during the time period May 1, 2007 — April 30, 2008. During this time period we had 2374 franchised offices in the United States and 970 of them met the characteristics for inclusion in this section. Excluded from these figures are offices which did not operate in storefront locations, such as kiosk or Kmart locations, and offices owned by franchisees with multiple offices in operation. The data presented is based largely upon information received from independent franchise owners, and has not been audited or otherwise verified by us. Immediately following the statement is additional information that you should carefully consider in order to understand this performance information in the appropriate context, including the paragraph below entitled "Free Return Policy."

1st year offices

	No of Offices In Category	Avg # tax Returns	% of Offices Which Equaled or Exceeded Avg
Top one-third	99	559	11.15%
Middle third	99	284	50.68%
Bottom third	99	148	85.14%

2d year offices

	No of Offices In Category	Avg # tax Returns	% of Offices Which Equaled or Exceeded Avg

	No of Offices In Category	Avg # tax Returns	% of Offices Which Equaled or Exceeded Avg
Top one-third	70	681	11.43%
Middle third	70	362	50.95%
Bottom third	70	180	85.71%

3d year & older offices

	No of Offices In Category	Avg # tax Returns	% of Offices Which Equaled or Exceeded Avg
Top one-third	155	1113	10.34%
Middle third	155	667	50.22%
Bottom third	154	383	86.42%

Average Price- The average price of paid tax returns in the chart above is $164.20. Free tax returns, as explained below, are not included when calculating this average.

Free Tax Return Policy- We encourage our offices to offer free tax returns during tax season, primarily during the month of March and for select special events, such as offering a free return on President's Day to every person whose last name is the same as that of a United States President. 17.63% of the returns done by offices included in the figures above were prepared free of charge in the hope of gaining future repeat or referral business.

A number of factors will directly affect the performance of your office. These include, but are not limited to, the general market for preparer provided tax preparation in your area, competitive factors from other tax preparers in your market, and the success of your efforts to obtain quality sites, provide recommended tax courses, hire a sufficient number of trained personnel, engage in successful marketing, offer high customer service, and generally follow the Manual and Liberty system. Your individual financial results may differ substantially from the results stated in this financial performance representation. Written substantiation for this financial performance representation is available to you upon reasonable request. We will not disclose the performance data of a specific office without the owner's consent.

STAFFING SERVICES®

LINK STAFFING SERVICES

1800 Bering Dr., # 800
Houston, TX 77057-3151
Tel: (800) 848-5465 (713) 784-4400 + 1065
Fax: (713) 784-4454
E-Mail: franchise@linkstaffing.com
Web Site: www.linkstaffing.com
Mr. Brandon Campbell, Director, Franchise Development

Link Staffing is a sales-driven, relationship-building, community-based industrial temporary labor staffing franchise. Link can provide for a wide range of positions including skilled crafts and trades, light industrial and general labor employees. Link also services positions in office, clerical and administration. Link Staffing provides valued services for its clients such as long and short term assignments, temporary to full time, payroll functions, on-site management, customized new employee orientations for the work site and a comprehensive screening process. Link also offers risk management services like client site evaluations, employee safety programs, and pre-employment, post accident and random drug screening.

BACKGROUND: IFA MEMBER

Established: 1980;	1st Franchised: 1994
Franchised Units:	48
Company-Owned Units:	10
Total Units:	58
Dist.:	US-58; CAN-0; O'seas-0
North America:	13 States, 0 Provinces
Density:	11 in CA, 7 in FL, 24 in TX
Projected New Units (12 Months):	10
Qualifications:	4, 4, 2, 3, 4, 5
Registered:CA,DC,FL,IL,IN,MD,MI,MN,ND,NY,OR,RI,SD,VA, WA,WI	

FINANCIAL/TERMS:

Cash Investment:	$62K-82K
Total Investment:	$85K-158K
Minimum Net Worth:	$150K-200K

Fees: Franchise -	$17K	Site Selection Assistance:	Yes
Royalty - Varies;	Ad. - 0%	Lease Negotiation Assistance:	Yes
Earnings Claims Statement:	Yes	Co-Operative Advertising:	No
Term of Contract (Years):	10/5/5/5/5	Franchisee Assoc./Member:	Yes/Member
Avg. # Of Employees:	2-3 FT, 0 PT	Size Of Corporate Staff:	30
Passive Ownership:	Allowed, But Discouraged	On-Going Support:	A,B,C,D,E,G,H,I
Encourage Conversions:	Yes	Training:	10 Days Field Training;
Area Develop. Agreements:	No	5 Days (Sales) Support Center, TX;5 Days(Operations) Support	
Sub-Franchising Contracts:	No		Center, TX
Expand In Territory:	Yes		
Space Needs:	1,200-1,500 SF; SF,SC, Industrial Office Park	**SPECIFIC EXPANSION PLANS:**	
		US:	Yes, All United States
SUPPORT & TRAINING:		Canada:	No
Financial Assistance Provided:	Yes (D)	Overseas:	No

ITEM 19
FINANCIAL PERFORMANCE REPRESENTATIONS

Except as outlined below, Link does not furnish or authorize its salespersons to furnish any oral or written information concerning the actual or potential sales, costs, income or profits of a franchised Link business. Actual results vary from unit to unit and Link cannot estimate the results of any particular franchise. Link does not make any representations that you or any of your principals may or will derive income from any franchise which exceeds the initial payment for or investment in the franchise.

Listed below is a statement of actual gross sales compiled for Link's franchised and company-operated offices for Link's fiscal year 2007. Gross sales figures are only for those franchisees that were in operation for the entire 2007 fiscal year. There were 30 franchisees that met this criterion. Link has historically awarded franchise territories (designated market areas) that support multiple offices. An office is defined as a separate profit center with a unique office number. If a franchisee had more than one office in its territory (designated market area), the gross sales include revenues from all of the franchisee's offices. Link divided the 30 franchisees into 4 tiers. The franchisees making up the first tier are those with the highest sales averages during 2007 and the franchisees making up the fourth tier are those with the lowest sales averages during 2007. Of the 7 franchisees in the first tier, 3 franchisees had 3 offices each, 2 franchisees had 2 offices each and 2 franchisees had 1 office each. Of the 8 franchisees in the second tier, 5 franchisees had 2 offices each and 3 franchisees had 1 office each. Of the 7 franchisees in the third tier, 3 franchisees had 2 offices each and 4 franchisees had 1 office each. The 8 franchisees in the fourth tier all had one office each.

Franchisees Only in 4 Tiers Sales Averages by Tier	**2007**	**Percentage of Franchisees Exceeding Average**
1st tier average	$5,298,811	28.57%
2nd tier average	$3,087,253	37.50%
3rd tier average	$2,124,816	42.86%
4th tier average	$784,197	37.50%
Average, All Franchisees	**$2,764,566**	**46.67%**

Link Staffing Services had 10 company-operated offices in operation in 2007. Gross sales for these 10 company-operated offices combined equaled $22,210,204. The average gross sales per company-operated office was $2,221,020.

THESE STATEMENTS OF ACTUAL SALES ARE BASED ON HISTORIC RESULTS AND

SHOULD NOT BE CONSTRUED AS THE ACTUAL OR PROBABLE SALES THAT WILL BE REAL-IZED BY ANY FRANCHISEE. LINK DOES NOT REPRESENT THAT ANY FRANCHISEE CAN EXPECT TO ATTAIN THESE ACTUAL SALES. THESE NUMBERS ARE BASED ON ECONOMIC CONDITIONS AS THEY EXISTED IN LINK'S FISCAL YEAR 2007.

The sales, profits and earnings of an individual franchise may vary greatly depending on a wide variety of factors, including the location of the franchise, population demography, competition in the area, the franchisee's business, management and sales expertise, economic and market conditions, labor and product costs. A new franchisee's individual financial results are likely to differ from the results stated in this Item 19.

Link has written substantiation of the data used in preparing this statement of actual sales, and will make it available to franchisees on reasonable request.

THE LITTLE GYM

7001 N Scottsdale Rd #1050
Scottsdale, AZ 85253-3658
Tel: (888) 228-2878 (480) 948-2878
Fax: (480) 948-2765
E-Mail: campaign21482@mail.emaximation.com
Web Site: www.thelittlegym.com
Mr. J. Ruk Adams, SVP Franchise Development

THE LITTLE GYM child development centers are for children 4 months to 12 years, and offer a unique, integrated approach to child development. THE LITTLE GYM'S highly motivational and individualized programs are curriculum-based and provide physical, social and intellectual development. Classes develop motor skills, build self-esteem and encourage risk-taking through gymnastics, karate, dance, cheer and sports skills development.

BACKGROUND: IFA MEMBER

Established: 1976;	1st Franchised: 1992
Franchised Units:	267
Company-Owned Units:	0
Total Units:	267
Dist.:	US-267; CAN-13; O'seas-35
North America:	35 States, 4 Provinces
Density:	25 in CA, 18 in NJ, 24 in TX
Projected New Units (12 Months):	25
Qualifications:	5, 5, 2, 3, 5, 5
Registered:	CA,FL,HI,IL,IN,MD,MI,MN,ND,NY,RI,VA,WA,WI

FINANCIAL/TERMS:

Cash Investment:	$75K
Total Investment:	$127.5-294K
Minimum Net Worth:	$250K
Fees: Franchise -	$69.5K
Royalty - 8%;	Ad. - 1%
Earnings Claims Statement:	Yes
Term of Contract (Years):	10/10/10
Avg. # Of Employees:	2 FT, 2-3 PT
Passive Ownership:	Allowed, But Discouraged
Encourage Conversions:	Yes
Area Develop. Agreements:	Yes
Sub-Franchising Contracts:	No
Expand In Territory:	Yes
Space Needs:	3,800-4,300 SF; SC, Destination

SUPPORT & TRAINING:

Financial Assistance Provided:	Yes (I)
Site Selection Assistance:	Yes
Lease Negotiation Assistance:	Yes
Co-Operative Advertising:	Yes
Franchisee Assoc./Member:	No
Size Of Corporate Staff:	35
On-Going Support:	C,D,G,H,I
Training:	1 Week Internship at Site To Be Determined; 2 Weeks Scottsdale, AZ

SPECIFIC EXPANSION PLANS:

US:	Yes, All United States
Canada:	Yes, All Canada
Overseas:	Yes, Asia, Aus., Europe, Mex., S. America, Middle East

Item 19
Financial Performance Representations

Attached as Exhibit M are unaudited annual gross revenues as reported to us by our franchisees for the year ended December 31, 2007. All franchise locations that opened before January 1, 2007 are included.

YOUR INDIVIDUAL FINANCIAL RESULTS ARE LIKELY TO DIFFER FROM THE RESULTS STATED IN EXHIBIT M. IT WILL TAKE APPROXIMATELY TWO TO THREE YEARS FOR YOU TO ACHIEVE YOUR INCOME POTENTIAL.

SUBSTANTIATION OF THE DATA USED IN PREPARING EXHIBIT M WILL BE MADE AVAILABLE TO YOU ON REASONABLE REQUEST.

The financial performance representation figures do not reflect the costs of sales or operating expenses that must be deducted from the gross revenue or gross sales figures to obtain your net income or profit. The best source of cost and expense data may be from franchisees and former franchisees, some of whom may be listed in Exhibit D.

Other than the unaudited gross revenue numbers in Exhibit M, we do not furnish or authorize our salespersons to furnish any oral or written information concerning the actual or potential sales, costs, income or profits of the franchised business. Actual results vary from unit to unit and we cannot estimate the results of any particular franchise.

EXHIBIT M
THE LITTLE GYM INTERNATIONAL, INC.
FRANCHISE DISCLOSURE DOCUMENT
FINANCIAL PERFORMANCE REPRESENTATION

Annual Gross Revenues year ended Dec. 31, 2007 as reported by Franchisees Unaudited
Opened a minimum of 12 months, listed by year opened, highest to lowest

Opened 2006	Opened 2005	Opened 2004	Opened 2003	Opened Pre 2003
878,260	984,206	744,561	1,033,707	980,366
739,411	566,126	665,616	756,448	918,944
630,054	524,898	551,957	729,993	881,899
603,045	504,747	530,942	699,852	654,242
509,773	502,800	472,510	585,599	647,953
504,017	496,365	471,568	576,866	610,331
486,516	479,310	461,686	557,105	594,331
468,218	472,045	446,078	532,203.	583,513
452,825	455,745	382,418	515,509	554,268
429,627	444,458	379,166	478,845	553,673
400,732	435,046	370,310	444,978	539,791
393,924	434,442	370,003	443,211	529,519
386,261	416,343	353,930	441,309	525,907
365,227	414,274	353,010	435,415	522,184
345,598	390,609	351,916	401,240	516,523
339,624	386,721	348,704	390,247	516,446
325,004	386,403	348,252	386,795	513,724
314,167	378,818	335,646 [7]	384,514	495,356
309,964	344,253	304,059	381,326	474,533
297,838	338,152	295,027	373,505	467,445
295,647	328,748	284,418	351,613	459,892
291,735	324,688	277,186	337,445	458,465
291,327	317,862	273,881	309,656	458,145
281,195 [1]	288,292	263,210	291,970	456,464
267,803	275,328	259,410	272,115	455,023
264,663	272,941	245,995	261,060	454,832
260,631	260,387	226,824	236,091	453,783
260,016	250,588	213,836	232,639	452,494
250,913	237,405	209,716	168,799	448,698
248,679	235,510	206,160	161,474	447,556

247,545	229,444	206,129	128,399	430,285
239,801	221,699	189,956		419,961
237,442	211,649 5	124,619		418,939
201,637	211,279	37,728 8		412,831
189,867	190,932 6			405,963
188,261	190,759			385,878
181,397	147,392			375,849
163,348				371,530
146,802				364,407
145,962 2				364,333
128,268 3				363,125
126,489 4				362,471

1   11 months reported
2   9 months reported
3   11 months reported (closed)
4   8 months reported (closed)
5   10 months reported
6   9 months reported (closed)
7   10 months reported (closed)
8   2 months reported (closed)
9   6 months reported (temp closed during relocation)
10   11 months reported (temp closed during relocation)
11   5 months reported (closed)
12   3 months reported (closed)

352,972
326 113
317,797
308,179
294,650
294,063
291,273
286,962
286,155
285,251
285,066
284,551 5
282,002
278,472
277,894
260,877
258,606
258,596
246,326
233,329
233,076
213,474
213,430
209,661
206,763
205,029
191,684
175,558
163,299
159,893
139,613
116,654
106,107
83,735 9
74,857 10
47,551 11
37,726 12
38,171 8

MaidPro®

MAIDPRO

60 Canal St., 4th Flr.
Boston, MA 02114
Tel: (888) 624-3776 (617) 742-8787 + 222
Fax: (617) 720-0700
E-Mail: chuck@maidpro.com
Web Site: www.maidpro.com
Mr. Chuck Lynch, Director, Strategic Planning

MaidPro is setting the trend in the home and office cleaning industry. MaidPro has a contemporary approach to this high-growth service. With unmatched graphic design and marketing, a completely paperless office and the ability for clients to request service on the Internet, MAIDPRO's franchisees have become successful in running a larger business.

BACKGROUND: IFA MEMBER
Established: 1991; 1st Franchised: 1997
Franchised Units: 105
Company-Owned Units: 1
Total Units: 106
Dist.: US-106; CAN-0; O'seas-0
  North America: 28 States, 0 Provinces
  Density: 6 in CA, 11 in FL, 7 in MA
Projected New Units (12 Months): 20
Qualifications: 3, 3, 1, 2, 4, 5
Registered:CA,DC,FL,HI,IL,IN,MD,MI,MN,ND,NY,OR,RI,SD,VA,WA,WI

FINANCIAL/TERMS:
Cash Investment: $60K
Total Investment: $60-120K
Minimum Net Worth: $100K
Fees: Franchise - $7.9K
  Royalty - 3.5-6.5%; Ad. - 1%
Earnings Claims Statement: No
Term of Contract (Years): 10/5
Avg. # Of Employees: 15 FT, 3 PT
Passive Ownership: Not Allowed
Encourage Conversions: Yes
Area Develop. Agreements: No
Sub-Franchising Contracts: No
Expand In Territory: Yes
Space Needs: 500-1,500 SF; SF, Office Bldg.

SUPPORT & TRAINING:
Financial Assistance Provided: Yes (D)
Site Selection Assistance: Yes
Lease Negotiation Assistance: Yes
Co-Operative Advertising: No
Franchisee Assoc./Member: Yes/Member
Size Of Corporate Staff: 22
On-Going Support: C,D,E,G,h,I
Training: 1 Week Onsite - Boston, MA; 6 Weeks Self-Study

SPECIFIC EXPANSION PLANS:
US: Yes, All United States
Canada: Yes, All Canada
Overseas: No

Item 19
FINANCIAL PERFORMANCE REPRESENTATIONS

Except for the information provided below, we make no actual or projected claims of potential sales, costs, income, profits or earnings of MaidPro franchised businesses.

Along with awarding franchises to others, our affiliate operates 1 business similar to the franchise business opportunity described in this Disclosure Document. Because business maturation can take up to eighteen months or longer we are reporting only on those Businesses open eighteen months or more. All franchised units operate in a defined territory that has within its borders a designated number of Qualified Households. If a franchisee had more than one territory, the Gross Sales include revenues from all of the franchisee's territories. The number of Qualified Households for each franchisee varies, and your territory may have a different number of Qualified Households. The franchisees below all had territories that had in excess of 10,000 Qualified Households at the time they signed their franchise agreements. Some of the franchisees had in excess of 50,000 Qualified Households at the time they signed their franchise agreement, or increased their territory beyond 50,000 Qualified Households by purchasing additional territories after their initial signing. A Qualified Household is a home which has an average annual income of $75,000 or more. The number of Qualified Households in a territory typically increases over time.

There are no other key demographic elements necessary in defining our territory.

303

Based upon the performance of the franchises which were in operation for a minimum of eighteen months as of January 1, 2007, we are providing the following disclosure of the actual Gross Sales which includes both unrelated and affiliate owned franchised units. The Average Same Franchised Unit * sales for the month ending May 31, 2007 is as follows:

*We define "Same Franchise Units" as a franchise business in operations a minimum of eighteen months as of January 1, 2007 and still in operations as of December 31, 2007. Out of the 81 franchise businesses operated by 69 franchisees, that were in operation on January 1, 2007 we are reporting on 55 franchised businesses, operated by 43 franchisees which comply with the definition for Same Franchised Units.

Franchisee	Total Gross Sales for Month Ending 05/31/07	Recurring Service Sales$_1$ Month Ending 05/31/07	OTC Sales$_2$ Month Ending 05/31/07	Job Related Pay-roll$_3$ Month Ending 05/31/07	Job Costing %$_4$ Month Ending 05/31/07	Cost Per Inquiry$_5$ Month Ending 05/31/07	Recurring Custom-ers$_6$ Month Ending 05/31/07
*1	$136,801.50	$115,644.30	$21,157.20	$49,890.24	36.47%	$75.83	687
2	$55,709.77	$47,242.60	$8,467.17	$22,801.48	40.93%	$54.02	306
*3	$80,608.22	$67,133.24	$13,474.98	$30,153.30	37.41%	$71.96	286
4	$46,030.00	$40,798.00	$5,232.00	$14,602.81	31.72%	$49.61	185
5	$32,540.50	$30,199.00	$2,341.50	$12,771.44	39.25%	$63.33	218
6	$22,630.00	$20,770.00	$1,860.00	$7,778.87	34.37%	$66.31	109
7	$41,285.31	$32,786.18	$8,499.13	$14,092.73	34.13%	$72.73	150
8	$56,086.35	$48,816.11	$7,270.24	$17,422.46	31.06%	$31.83	256
*9	$101,782.10	$91,119.20	$10,662.90	$38,796.30	38.12%	$54.71	524
10	$57,259.75	$53,570.75	$3,689.00	$25,264.00	44.12%	$41.75	398
11	$41,734.00	$37,746.50	$3,987.50	$14,842.45	35.56%	$75.21	182
12	$54,263.50	$50,299.00	$3,964.50	$17,638.50	32.51%	$61.49	196
13	$62,351.50	$56,501.25	$5,850.25	$24,242.26	38.88%	$25.51	282
14	$37,568.00	$29,021.36	$8,546.64	$13,073.26	34.80%	$47.01	162
*15	$33,541.61	$30,514.36	$3,027.25	$13,721.36	40.91%	$44.37	174
*16	$61,614.50	$57,043.50	$4,571.00	$22,241.28	36.10%	$86.08	346
17	$31,439.00	$27,817.00	$3,622.00	$13,045.29	41.49%	$57.24	223
18	$49,707.00	$43,343.00	$6,364.00	$18,714.55	37.65%	$24.86	286
19	$25,016.00	$22,941.00	$2,075.00	$10,516.49	42.04%	$66.08	133
20	$42,671.00	$37,297.43	$5,373.57	$15,969.97	37.43%	$39.12	190
*21	$23,540.00	$21,672.00	$1,868.00	$10,207.21	43.36%	$54.94	189
*22	$91,394.47	$72,689.12	$18,705.35	$27,869.78	30.49%	$33.45	386
*23	$104,701.10	$88,112.50	$16,588.60	$48,673.00	46.49%	$35.48	588
24	$63,867.32	$59,078.17	$4,789.15	$26,343.30	41.25%	$60.96	345
*25	$48,330.80	$36,208.50	$12,122.30	$16,284.47	33.69%	$34.04	185
26	$14,642.36	$12,001.36	$2,641.00	$6,339.40	43.29%	$33.77	57
27	$40,856.07	$38,846.07	$2,010.00	$15,256.20	37.34%	$47.06	163
*28	$75,323.39	$63,848.89	$11,474.50	$29,841.86	39.62%	$55.29	348
*29	$49,906.72	$42,968.46	$6,938.26	$23,970.15	48.03%	$72.86	264
30	$50,657.59	$44,911.94	$5,745.65	$18,133.21	35.80%	$39.81	193

*31	$231,195.00	$183,616.55	$47,578.45	$77,199.26	33.39%	$58.05	790
32	$17,132.00	$16,847.00	$285.00	$5,200.00	30.35%	$54.55	54
33	$52,796.92	$50,286.92	$2,510.00	$21,168.77	40.09%	$27.29	239
34	$23,805.00	$20,898.99	$2,906.01	$7,970.73	33.48%	$89.89	118
*35	$98,204.85	$86,346.35	$11,858.50	$37,293.98	37.98%	$44.83	359
36	$51,328.33	$41,285.49	$10,042.84	$20,575.32	40.09%	$45.00	283
37	$58,333.00	$46,096.95	$12,236.05	$25,858.25	44.33%	$40.50	294
38	$43,342.35	$38,936.46	$4,405.89	$9,665.86	22.30%	$48.32	207
39	$68,270.35	$53,656.78	$14,613.57	$28,176.81	41.27%	$44.21	276
40	$53,942.22	$41,850.61	$12,091.61	$13,506.84	25.04%	$53.01	154
41	$35,636.00	$29,608.00	$6,028.00	$15,540.34	43.61%	$53.09	158
42	$39,932.50	$36,460.50	$3,472.00	$15,576.87	39.01%	$88.39	207
43	$47,220.50	$43,670.50	$3,550.00	$18,217.00	38.58%	$91.27	218

* Franchisee with multiple office locations and territories

[1] Sales generated from Recurring Cleaning services

[2] Sales generated from One Time Cleaning services (Non-Recurring)

[3] Cost of direct job related payroll (These figures do not included any insurance, taxes, benefits r incentives paid to your employees)

[4] Percent of direct job related payroll paid to employees based on Gross Sales (These figures do not included any insurance, taxes, benefits or incentives paid to your employees)

[5] Cost in advertising monies spent to get a potential customer to inquire about service

[6] Number of Recurring Customers (weekly, bi-weekly and monthly)

The following averages are based on the chart above:

Average Total Monthly Sales	**$57,092.99**

Average Recurring Sales	**$49,081.44**

Average OTC Sales	**$8,011.55**

Average Job Costing	**$21,312.74**

Average Job Costing %	**37.53%**

Average Cost Per Inquiry	**$53.84**

Average # Recurring Customers	**264**

Average Monthly Sales Per Recurring Customer	**$186**

We believe this month is a representative month out of the year, assuming the franchisees continue to operate in the same manner throughout the year. Monthly Gross Sales, however, will fluctuate somewhat throughout the year. This month represents franchised businesses at various stages of development and in different parts of the country. The locations of the franchised businesses are across the United States (See Item 20), and the franchised businesses are located in both major metropolitan areas, suburban areas and rural areas.

The above figures, which reflects Gross Sales, not profits, were calculated based upon information reported to us by our franchisees in their monthly reports used by us for calculating Royalties. The monthly reports are compiled using Service CEO Software. The above figures have not been audited by us. The figures do not reflect all costs of sales, operating expenses or other costs and expenses that must be deducted from the Gross Sales figures to obtain your net income or profit. You should conduct an independent investigation of the costs and expenses you will incur in operating your MaidPro Franchised Business.

The Gross Sales and financial results of your MaidPro Franchised Business are likely to differ from the figures stated above, and there is no assurance that you will do as well. If you rely upon the above figures, you must accept the risk of not doing as well. The average Franchised Business included in the above calculations is a mature business a minimum of eighteen months; accordingly, a new franchisee's individual Gross Sales and financial results are likely to differ from the results stated above. Further, your Gross Sales and your financial results will depend upon, among other things, such factors as local and national economic conditions; how much you follow our methods and procedures; your sales skills; your management skill, experience and business acumen; whether you personally manage your Franchised Business or hire a manager; the region in which your Franchised Business is located; the competition in your local market; the prevailing wage rate; and the sales level reached during the initial period.

Your analysis of a MaidPro franchised business should include estimates of expenses for all applicable items, including, office rental space, salaries or commissions, your own salary, phone/fax charges, postage, travel, auto expense, insurance, supplies and the costs of marketing. All of these items are based largely on factors within your control, for which you can obtain information through your own research. Since these amounts are to a great degree a matter of personal business decisions and preferences, we have included no estimates for these items, and you should make appropriate assumptions. Please see Items 6 and 7 for a description of certain expense items, which you are likely to incur in operating a Maidpro Franchised Business. However, you should also be aware that the expense items listed above and those listed in Items 6 and 7, taken together, are by no means exhaustive. There are likely to be additional expenses that we have not listed, some of which may be unique to your market or situation. Substantiation of the data used in preparing the earnings claim will be made available to you in writing at our corporate headquarters upon reasonable request.

ADVERTISING AND FINANCIAL ASSUMPTIONS

Advertising Budget: We require that you spend a specified amount on your local advertising, depending on the size of your specific territory. Please refer to Item 8 and Item 11 of this disclosure document for a detailed description of these dollar amounts.

The following figures are based on data compiled from our MaidPro Call Center. Please refer to Item 6 for more information regarding the MaidPro Call Center. All figures are based on 35 franchised businesses that used the MaidPro Call Center in 2007:

Signup percentage as of December 31, 2007
Source: SpirePRO Software, MaidPro Call Center Metrics.

MaidPro Call Center Signup % (includes all leads contacted: internet and phone inquiries)	37%

Recurring Signup percentage as of December 31, 2007
Source: SpirePRO Software, MaidPro Call Center Metrics.
For every customer that signs up for service only a percentage will sign up for recurring service.

MaidPro Call Center Recurring Signup % (includes all signed up leads that were scheduled for recurring service)	80%

MARTINIZING DRY CLEANING

422 Wards Corner Rd.
Loveland, OH 45140-6950
Tel: (800) 827-0345 (513) 351-6211
Fax: (513) 731-0818
E-Mail: cleanup@martinizing.com
Web Site: www.martinizing.com
Mr. Jerald E. Laesser, Vice President

MARTINIZING is the most recognized brand name in dry cleaning. The # 1 Dry Cleaning Franchise: MARTINIZING has been ranked the # 1 dry cleaning franchise 19 out of the last 22 years by Entrepreneur Magazine.

BACKGROUND:

Established: 1949;	1st Franchised: 1949
Franchised Units:	591
Company-Owned Units:	0
Total Units:	591
Dist.:	US-389; CAN-19; O'seas-234
North America:	38 States, 3 Provinces
Density:	67 in CA, 92 in MI, 36 in WI
Projected New Units (12 Months):	25
Qualifications:	5, 4, 1, 3, 1, 5
Registered:CA,DC,FL,HI,IL,IN,MD,MI,MN,ND,NY,OR,RI,SD,	VA,WA,WI

FINANCIAL/TERMS:

Cash Investment:	$125K
Total Investment:	$363K-550.5K
Minimum Net Worth:	$225K
Fees: Franchise -	$35K
Royalty - 4%;	Ad. - 0.5%
Earnings Claims Statement:	Yes
Term of Contract (Years):	20
Avg. # Of Employees:	2 FT, 4 PT
Passive Ownership:	Allowed, But Discouraged
Encourage Conversions:	Yes
Area Develop. Agreements:	Yes
Sub-Franchising Contracts:	Yes
Expand In Territory:	Yes
Space Needs:	1,500-2,000 SF; FS,SC

SUPPORT & TRAINING:

Financial Assistance Provided:	Yes (D)
Site Selection Assistance:	Yes
Lease Negotiation Assistance:	Yes
Co-Operative Advertising:	No
Franchisee Assoc./Member:	Yes/Member
Size Of Corporate Staff:	16
On-Going Support:	C,D,E,G,H,I
Training:	1 Week Classroom; 2 Weeks In-Store

SPECIFIC EXPANSION PLANS:

US:	Yes, All United States
Canada:	Yes, All Except AB, ON
Overseas:	Yes, Europe, Far and Middle East

ITEM 19
FINANCIAL PERFORMANCE REPRESENTATIONS

Class I - Single Location Full Plant Stores

The average gross sales information (without taking into consideration any expenses) reported in Table 1 below was compiled by MFI from monthly gross sales reports received for 36 Martinizing Stores where on-premise dry cleaning is provided ("Full Plant Stores") operating as of December 31, 2007 (under franchise agreements providing for payment of royalties based on a percentage of gross sales in form similar to the Franchise Agreement attached as Exhibit C) and which reported to MFI at least 24 consecutive months of sales activity prior to December 31, 2007 ("Reporting Stores").

Class II - Full Plant Stores Serving Multiple Pick-Up Locations

The average gross sales information (without taking into consideration any expenses) reported in Table 2 below was complied by MFI from monthly gross sales reports received for 13 Full Plant Stores servicing 1 to 4 affiliated pick-up stores that do not provide on-premise dry cleaning ("Pick-Up Stores") operating as of December 31, 2007 (under franchise agreements providing for payment of royalties based on a percentage of gross sales in form similar to the Franchise Agreement attached as Exhibit C) and which the Full Plant Store reported to MFI at least 24 consecutive months of sales activity prior to December 31, 2007. Some of the affiliated Pick-Up Stores have not been operating for 24 months and the sales activity reported for those stores ranges from 8 to 12 consecutive months. Each of the 13 Full Plant Stores in Class II is treated as a Reporting Store in Table 2 below, with the average gross sales information of the Full Plant Store combined with the average gross sales information of the Pick-Up Stores affiliated with the particular Full Plant Store.

The 49 Reporting Stores are all located in the United States. MFI offers substantially the same services to each Reporting Store, but the type and extent of services offered to the public by each Reporting Store may vary depending on the individual franchisee. None of the Reporting Stores are owned or operated by MFI. The Reporting Stores represent approximately 55% of the total Martinizing Stores operating in the United States as of December 31, 2007 under franchise agreements similar to the Franchise Agreement attached as Exhibit C and approximately 15% of the total Martinizing Stores operating in the United States as of December 31, 2007. The balance of the Martinizing Stores operating in the United States as of December 31, 2007, under agreements similar to the Franchise Agreement attached as Exhibit C, did not meet the criteria of Class I or Class II described above. The monthly gross sales reports of the Reporting Stores were prepared by the individual franchisees without an audit and have not been verified by MFI.

In reviewing the average gross sales information reported below, the following should be considered: (a) the gross sales of the Reporting Stores have not been adjusted for factors affecting monthly gross sales of a dry cleaning business, such as seasonality, climate and demographic characteristics of the area in which the business operates; (b) the Reporting Stores have been in operation for varying periods of time ranging from 24 months to 16 years; (c) only the last 12 consecutive months of gross sales reported prior to December 31, 2007 by each Reporting Store were used in compiling the gross sales information reported below; (d) no adjustments have been made for inflation or other economic factors affecting operations over time; (e) the individual franchisee's effectiveness in management, efficiency in operation, and energy, time and dedication to the business greatly impacts gross sales of a particular Martinizing Store and many other factors also impact the gross sales of particular Martinizing Store, including general economic and market conditions, competition and location demographics within the area of operation and the like.

The following reflects: the average gross sales of the Reporting Stores reported to MFI for 12 consecutive months prior to December 31, 2007, divided into four groups ("Groups") by ascending order of sales volume; the number of Reporting Stores falling within each Group; and the percentage of the Reporting Stores attaining or surpassing the average' of gross sales reported in each Group.

TABLE 1 - Class I - Single Location Full Plant Stores

	First Group	Second Group	Third Group	Fourth Group
Sales Range Reported($):	111,375 to 264,826	272,885 to 320,496	320,500 to 367,770	373,721 to 780,454
Averages($):	208,716	299,453	345,660	503,465
No. of Reporting				

Stores in Range:	9 of 36	9 of 36	9 of 36	9 of 36
% of Reporting Stores in Range Attaining or Surpassing Average:	67%	44%	44%	44%

TABLE 2 Class II - Full Plant Stores Servicing Multiple Pick-Up Locations

	First Group	Second Group	Third Group	Fourth Group
Sales Range Reported($):	302,147 to 355,853	368,734 to 506,918	516,893 to 581,377	589,870 to 892,864
Averages($):	323,197	460,297	541,714	740,214
No. of Reporting Stores in Range:	3 of 13	3 of 13	4 of 13	3 of 13
% of Reporting Stores in Range Attaining or Surpassing Average:	33%	67%	50%	33%

The sales information reported above and any calculations derived by use of the above information should not be considered as the actual, probable or potential sales that will be realized by you or any franchisee. MFI is not representing that you or any franchisee can expect to attain the same or similar sales figures shown above. A new franchisee's individual financial results are likely to differ from the average results stated above.

Written substantiation for the information used in compiling the average gross sales information reported above is available to prospective franchisees upon reasonable request, provided it does not require the disclosure of the identity or information leading to the identity of an individual franchisee.

Except for the above sales information, MFI does not furnish or authorize its salespersons (or anyone else) to furnish any oral or written information concerning the actual or potential sales, costs, income or profits of a Martinizing Store. Actual results vary from store to store and MFI cannot estimate the results of any particular franchise.

MASSAGE ENVY
14350 N. 87th St., # 200
Scottsdale, AZ 85260
Tel: (480) 366-4130
Fax: (480) 366-4230
E-Mail: dbennewitz@massageenvy.com

Web Site: www.massageenvy.com
Mr. Dallas Bennewitz, CMO

BACKGROUND:		IFA MEMBER
Established: 2002;		1st Franchised: 2003
Franchised Units:		227
Company-Owned Units:		0
Total Units:		227

ITEM 19
FINANCIAL PERFORMANCE REPRESENTATIONS

Except for the information contained in Item 19 of this Disclosure Document, we do not furnish or authorize our salespersons to furnish any oral or written information concerning the actual or potential revenue, sales, costs, income or profits of a Massage Envy Clinic. Actual results may vary from franchise to franchise, and we cannot estimate the results of any particular franchise. We specifically instruct our sales personnel, agents, employees, and officers that they are not permitted to make such claims or statements as to the earnings, sales or profit, or chances of success, nor are they authorized to represent or estimate dollar figures as to a franchisee's operation. We will not be bound by allegations of any unauthorized representations as to earnings, sales, profits, or chances for success.

See Exhibit L attached to this Disclosure Document for our financial performance representation.

EXHIBIT L

EXCEPT FOR THE INFORMATION CONTAINED IN EXHIBIT l OF THIS DISCLOSURE DOCUMENT, WE DO NOT FURNISH OR AUTHORIZE OUR SALESPERSONS OR REGIONAL DEVELOPERS TO FURNISH ANY ORAL OR WRITTEN INFORMATION CONCERNING THE ACTUAL OR POTENTIAL SALES, COSTS, INCOME, OR PROFITS OF A MASSAGE ENVY CLINIC. ACTUAL RESULTS MAY VARY FROM CLINIC TO CLINIC AND WE CANNOT ESTIMATE THE RESULTS OF ANY PARTICULAR CLINIC.

EARNINGS CLAIM 2008
Analysis of Average Sales

This Analysis of Average Sales (the "Analysis") sets forth average yearly net sales for two hundred thirty six (236) franchised Massage Envy clinics located in the United States. One hundred fifty nine (159) clinics were open for twelve (12) months during the year ended December 31, 2007. The other thirty seventy seven (77) franchised clinics were open for at least six (6) months during that same year. On December 31, 2007, there were 336 Massage Envy clinics open and in operation. However, the averages contained in this Analysis are based solely on the two hundred thirty six (236) clinics that were open and in continuous operation for at least six (6) months during the year ended December 31, 2006. The one hundred six (106) clinics discussed in this Analysis were the only Massage Envy clinics to be open and in continuous operation for at least six (6) months during the year ended December 31, 2007.

For purposes of this Analysis, "Net Sales" equals all cash and credit sales, less massage therapist tips and any sales tax received. "Pro-Rated Net Sales" equals the actual sales for the period of time the clinics were open, divided by the period of time the clinic was open in 2007, multiplied by 12.

Clinics Open for Twelve Months

The one hundred fifty nine clinics open for twelve months during the year ended December 31, 2007 reported average Net Sales of $910,725. Seventy one of these clinics reported Net Sales above the average, ranging from $918,141 to $1,779,621. Eighty eight reported Net Sales below the average, ranging from $309,929 to $907,125.

Clinics Open for At Least Six Months

The seventy seven clinics open for at least six months during 2007 averaged Pro-Rated Net Sales of $554,246. Thirty four reported Pro-Rated Net Sales above the average, ranging from $556,312 to $1,158,343. Thirty four reported Pro-Rated Net Sales below the average, ranging from $242,774 to $552,977.

The average Net Sales and Pro-Rated Net Sales figures included in this Analysis are based on sales reports submitted by each franchisee. The figures have not been audited, and we have not undertaken to independently verify (i) the accuracy of such information or (ii) whether such information was prepared in accordance with generally accepted accounting principles. **Substantiation of the data used in this Analysis will be made available to a prospective franchisee upon reasonable request.** Each franchisee is urged to consult with appropriate financial, business, and legal advisors in connection with the information set forth in this Analysis.

The average sales reflected in this Analysis should not be considered as the actual or potential sales that will be realized by any franchisee. We do not represent that any franchisee can expect to attain such sales. In addition, we do not represent that any franchisee will derive income that exceeds the initial payment for or investment in a Massage Envy franchise. No inference as to expenses, costs of goods sold, or profits relating to existing or future clinics should be drawn from the sales information reflected in this Analysis. The success of any franchisee will depend largely upon the ability of such franchisee, and the individual financial results of a franchisee are likely to differ from the information set forth herein.

Note that the expenses for a Massage Envy clinic will vary depending on many factors, including: local and regional variations in real estate leasing rates; constructions costs and building specifications; local and regional variations in utility and telephone rates; insurance costs; local and state taxes and wage rates; the availability of sufficient labor pool; costs of supplies used; services offered; the efficiency and managerial skills of the franchisee; local economic factors; the type of area in which the clinic is located; and whether the clinic is managed by the owner of the clinic or by an employee manager.

MEINEKE CAR CARE CENTERS
128 S. Tryon St., # 900
Charlotte, NC 28202-5001
Tel: (800) 275-5200 (704) 377-8855
Fax: (704) 372-4826
E-Mail: franchise.info@meineke.com
Web Site: www.meinekefranchise.com
Mr. Dave Schaefers, VP Franchise Development

MEINEKE has been offering superior automotive repair services at discount prices for over 30 years. We are a nationally-recognized brand with a proven system. Brand recognition, comprehensive training and on-going technical and operational support are some of the benefits enjoyed by MEINEKE franchisees.

BACKGROUND: IFA MEMBER

Established: 1972;	1st Franchised: 1972
Franchised Units:	901
Company-Owned Units:	11
Total Units:	912
Dist.:	US-852; CAN-18; O'seas-18
North America:	49 States, 5 Provinces
Density:	69 in NY, 57 in PA, 56 in TX
Projected New Units (12 Months):	69
Qualifications:	4, 3, 3, 2, 2, 5
Registered:CA,DC,FL,HI,IL,IN,MD,MI,MN,ND,NY,OR,RI,SD, VA,WA,WI	

FINANCIAL/TERMS:

Cash Investment:	$60K
Total Investment:	$182.8K-426.8K
Minimum Net Worth:	$150K
Fees: Franchise -	$30K
Royalty - 3-7%;	Ad. - 8%
Earnings Claims Statement:	Yes
Term of Contract (Years):	15/15
Avg. # Of Employees:	4 FT, 0 PT
Passive Ownership:	Not Allowed
Encourage Conversions:	Yes
Area Develop. Agreements:	Yes
Sub-Franchising Contracts:	No
Expand In Territory:	Yes
Space Needs:	2,880-3,880 SF; FS

SUPPORT & TRAINING:

Financial Assistance Provided:	Yes (I)
Site Selection Assistance:	Yes
Lease Negotiation Assistance:	Yes
Co-Operative Advertising:	No
Franchisee Assoc./Member:	Yes/Member
Size Of Corporate Staff:	110
On-Going Support:	A,B,C,D,E,G,H,I
Training:	4 Weeks Charlotte, NC

SPECIFIC EXPANSION PLANS:

US:	Yes, All United States
Canada:	Yes, All Canada
Overseas:	Yes, All Countries

Item 19
FINANCIAL PERFORMANCE REPRESENTATIONS
For Franchised and Company owned Meineke standalone centers
located in the <u>United States</u> only

MEINEKE CENTER AVERAGE BY SERVICE BAY
GROSS SALES FOR FISCAL YEAR END
JUNE 24, 2006 FOR CENTERS OPENED FOR MORE THAN 2 YEARS

Number of Bays	Number of Centers open for more than 2 years as of June 24, 2006	Average sales for fiscal year end June 24, 2006 for centers open more than 2 years
3 Bays	111	$371,587
4 Bays	215	$452,106
5 Bays	191	$500,155
6 Bays	151	$555,919
7 Bays	44	$560,360
8 Bays	34	$700,169
+8 Bays	8	$879,999
Total Centers/Average Sales	**754**	**$495,257**

THIS CHART REFLECTS THE AVERAGE GROSS SALES BY SERVICE BAY FOR FISCAL YEAR END JUNE 24, 2006 FOR MEINEKE CENTERS IN THE <u>UNITED STATES</u> THAT WERE OPEN AS OF JUNE 24, 2006, AND HAVE BEEN OPEN FOR AT LEAST 2 YEARS PRIOR TO JUNE 24, 2006, WHICH NUMBERED 754 CENTERS, AND SHOULD NOT BE CONSIDERED AS THE ACTUAL OR PROBABLE RESULTS THAT WILL BE REALIZED BY YOU OR ANY OTHER FRANCHISEE. WE DO NOT REPRESENT THAT ANY FRANCHISEE CAN EXPECT TO ATTAIN THESE RESULTS. A NEW FRANCHISEE'S RESULTS ARE LIKELY TO DIFFER FROM THESE RESULTS. THESE RESULTS DO NOT REFLECT THE RESULTS OF ANY CO-BRANDED MEINEKE LOCATION, WHICH ARE NOT RELEVANT TO THE OPERATION OF YOUR CENTER.

The chart for the Average Gross Sales by number of service bay for fiscal year end June 24, 2006 statement ("Average Gross Sales Statement") reflects the average gross sales for fiscal year end June 24, 2006 reported by 754 franchised Meineke Centers, all of which are located in the <u>United States, and which</u> had been open and operating for more than 2 years as of June 24. 2006. The Average Sales Statement is based on weekly sales reports submitted by Meineke franchisees and our company owned centers for the purpose of computing royalty fees. These reports have not been audited by certified public accountants nor have we sought to independently verify their accuracy for purposes of the Average Sales Statement.

As of June 24, 2006, there were 958 U.S. Meineke franchises. Of those, 833 centers were already opened, 21 had locations and were awaiting opening, 9 had approved locations that had not yet been secured, and 95 had not yet identified locations. There were 2 company franchise outlets and 4 joint ventures, which are not included in this statement. Of the open centers, 44 have been open less than one year (including 9 that were temporarily closed and re-opened during the fiscal year ending June 24, 2006). 35 have been open more than one year but less than two years, and 754 have been open more than two years.

The above chart breaks down into ranges of gross sales generated at the 754 centers by the number of automotive service bays that are located at a Meineke center location. We require that you open a center that has a minimum of 4 service bays. The column in the chart above designating

312

3 service bays pertains to franchised locations that were developed before we changed the required minimum number of service bays for a Meineke center.

$426,702 represents the average unaudited gross sales figures as reported to Meineke Car Care Centers, Inc., from June 26, 2005, to June 24, 2006, for the 35 centers open for more than one but less than two years as of fiscal year end June 24, 2006.

$495,257 represents the average unaudited gross sales figures as reported to Meineke Car Care Centers, Inc., from June 26, 2005, to June 24, 2006, for the 754 centers open for more then two years as of fiscal year end June 24, 2006.

Exhibit O-1, Part 1 to this document is a list of the franchises together with their geographic locations from which Meineke compiled these figures. All of these franchises, whether or not their results appear in the chart above, are not substantially similar to the co branded location that you will operate pursuant to the terms of the co branded Addendum.

Attached as Exhibit Y is a summary of certain customary and typical expenses of our business shown as a percentage of sales. This exhibit lists expenses by service bays and centers with sales between $400,000 and $600,000, and between $600,000 and up, and which have been open and operating for at least 2 years prior to June 30, 2007. The number of service bays you use in the operation of your center likely will be a material component in calculating the amount of expenses that you incur in your center operations. The listing of expenses is not all-inclusive. Our Meineke franchisees more than likely will incur additional expenses in the operation of their Meineke Centers that do not appear on this listing. The amount of your expenses also will be dictated by the geographic region your Meineke store is located.

We obtained the expense and sales information for these stand alone Meineke centers listed in Exhibit Y from profit and loss statements and tax returns for the year 2006 submitted to us by our franchisees in the ordinary course of business. Since these expenses were as of 2006 they are likely to have increased since that date. Most of the reports have not been audited by certified public accountants nor have we sought to independently verify their accuracy. Not all franchisees supplied us with their profit and loss statements.

Note that sales and expenses vary for Meineke Centers depending on many factors, including local and regional variations in real estate values or rental rates, construction costs and building specifications (including the number of bays). financing terms which the franchisee was able to obtain, local and regional variations in utility and telephone rates (including the number of telephone fines in the center), insurance rates, local and state taxes and wage rates, degree of skilled labor employed and the availability of such labor, cost of parts and supplies used, services offered and the efficiency and managerial skills of the franchisee, local economic factors, the density of vehicle ownership, the number of other automotive after-market outlets in a particular market area and the proximity of such competition to the Meineke center, length of time the center has been in operation and the length of time operating at its current location, type of area (including number of traffic lanes and the type of traffic flow) in which the center is located, and whether the center is managed by the owner or an employee manager.

Substantiation of the data used in preparing the Average Sales Statement and Exhibit Y will be made available to you on reasonable request, provided we will not disclose data that identifies specific locations. Our sales representatives are prohibited from providing you with any further information about actual, average or potential sales, or operating expenses, income, profits or earnings, and are prohibited from commenting on the likelihood of success of any Meineke Center or the business potential of any territory. Any such unauthorized information is inherently unreliable, and you should not rely on it.

THE EXPENSES LISTED IN EXHIBIT Y ARE BASED ON PROFIT AND LOSS STATEMENTS PROVIDED BY MEINEKE FRANCHISEES AND YOU SHOULD NOT CONSIDER THESE AS THE ACTUAL OR POTENTIAL OPERATING EXPENSES THAT WILL BE REALIZED BY YOU OR ANY

OTHER FRANCHISEE. MOREOVER, THESE EXPENSES ARE FROM STAND ALONE MEINEKE CENTERS ONLY. WE DO NOT REPRESENT THAT ANY FRANCHISEE CAN EXPECT TO ATTAIN THESE RESULTS. THE RESULTS FOR A CENTER THAT IS YET TO REACH MATURITY (A NEW CENTER) ARE LIKELY TO DIFFER FROM THOSE CONTAINED IN EXHIBIT Y.

EXHIBIT Y

THE EXPENSES LISTED IN THE FOLLOWING CHARTS ARE BASED ON RESPONSES PROVIDED BY MEINEKE (NON CO-BRANDED) FRANCHISEES AND YOU SHOULD NOT CONSIDER THESE AS THE ACTUAL OR POTENTIAL OPERATING EXPENSES THAT WILL BE REALIZED BY YOU OR ANY OTHER FRANCHISEE. WE DO NOT REPRESENT THAT ANY FRANCHISEE CAN EXPECT TO ATTAIN THESE RESULTS. A NEW FRANCHISEE'S RESULTS ARE LIKELY TO DIFFER FROM THOSE CONTAINED IN THESE CHARTS.

AVERAGE EXPENSE INFORMATION
FOR CENTERS REPORTING FOR CALENDAR YEAR 2006

	EBITDA Quartile ($400,000 - $600,000 only)[1]			
	4th	3rd	2nd	Top
No. of Centers	42	42	41	41
Avg. COGS %	25.50%	24.7%	23.8%	21.8%
Direct Technician Labor	18%	16.4%	14.6%	13.8%
Payroll Taxes	2.0%	1.8%	1.7%	1.6%
Other Center Variables[2]	2.5%	2.2%	2.3%	1.9%
Fixed Expenses[3]	$34,292	$35,165	$32,329	$28,337

	EBITDA Quartile ($600,000 and UP)[1]			
	4th	3rd	2nd	Top
No. of Centers	28	28	28	28
Avg. COGS %	26.60%	24.40%	24.20%	22.40%
Direct Technician Labor	18.7%	17.7%	15.4%	13.7%
Payroll Taxes	1.7%	1.9%	1.6%	1.4%
Other Center Variables[2]	2.2%	2%	1.7%	1.5%
Fixed Expenses[3]	$43,059	$49,506	$41,316	$35,218

		Bay Size				
	All Centers	4	5	6	7	8
No. of Centers	433	119	114	93	31	20
Avg. COGS %	23.9%	23.5%	24.2%	24.2%	23.9%	24.1%
Direct Technician Labor	16.1%	16.2%	15.9%	16.3%	16.9%	15.4%
Payroll Taxes	1.8%	1.8%	1.79%	1.8%	1.9%	1.7%
Other Center Variables[2]	2.1%	2.1%	1.9%	2.3%	1.8%	1.8%
Fixed Expenses[3]	$32,140	$29,245	$33,093	$35,422	$33,432	$37,151

[1]EBITDA is defined as earnings before interest, taxes, depreciation, and amortization. What this means_is that subtracted from your earnings will be the costs of any interest you pay to finance your business as well any taxes you will be required to pay to the federal, state, or local government related to the operation of your Meineke business. Expenses for those centers reporting sales between $400,000 and $600,000, and for $600,000 and up for calendar year end 2006, and which have been open and operating for at least 2 years as of June 30, 2007, are included in this chart.

(2)Other center variables include credit card processing costs and center supplies.

(3)Fixed expenses include property tax, insurance, utilities, telephone, trash, center repairs, monthly computer maintenance, and accounting.

Average royalties and MAF contributions for centers opened in the 2 years to June 30, 2007, are 5.2% and 7.8% respectively (excludes conversion centers). Some centers choose to charge the costs of a vehicle to their business; these expenses have not been included. This analysis does not include the cost of real estate (loan payment or rent). It is assumed that the franchisee will operate the center. THESE AMOUNTS WOULD BE SUBTRACTED FROM THE EBITDA LISTED ABOVE.

EXCEPT AS PROVIDED ABOVE AND IN ITEM 19 OF THIS DISCLOSURE DOCUMENT, WE DO NOT FURNISH OR AUTHORIZE OUR SALESPERSONS TO FURNISH ANY ORAL OR WRITTEN INFORMATION CONCERNING ACTUAL, PROJECTED OR POTENTIAL SALES, COSTS, EXPENSES, INCOME OR PROFITS OF A PROPOSED FACILITY.

MIDAS

1300 Arlington Heights Rd.
Itasca, IL 60143-3174
Tel: (800) 365-0007 (630) 438-3000
Fax: (630) 438-3700
E-Mail: midasfranchise@midas.com
Web Site: www.midasfran.com
Ms. Barbara Korus, Franchise Recruitment Coord.

Globally respected with over 2,500 franchised, licensed and company-owned Midas shops throughout the United States, Canada and the world. Ours is a premier brand name in world-class automotive services, offering repair and maintenance services, as well as tires and batteries. Consider the opportunity. A world-famous brand . . . with a 50-year record of success . . . and a commitment to long-term growth through customer service, customer value and customer relationships.

BACKGROUND: IFA MEMBER

Established: 1956;	1st Franchised: 1956
Franchised Units:	2464
Company-Owned Units:	91
Total Units:	2555
Dist.:	US-1559; CAN-209; O'seas-823
North America:	50 States, 9 Provinces
Density:	NR
Projected New Units (12 Months):	40
Qualifications:	5, 4, 3, 2, 1, 5

Registered: CA,DC,FL,HI,IL,IN,MD,MI,MN,ND,NY,OR,RI,SD, VA,WA,WI

FINANCIAL/TERMS:

Cash Investment:	$75-100K
Total Investment:	$261.6K-350.7K
Minimum Net Worth:	$250-300K
Fees: Franchise -	$20K
Royalty - 10%;	Ad. - Incl. Roy.
Earnings Claims Statement:	Yes
Term of Contract (Years):	20/20
Avg. # Of Employees:	6 FT, 4 PT
Passive Ownership:	Allowed, But Discouraged
Encourage Conversions:	Yes
Area Develop. Agreements:	No
Sub-Franchising Contracts:	No
Expand In Territory:	Yes
Space Needs:	4,000-5,000 SF; FS

SUPPORT & TRAINING:

Financial Assistance Provided:	Yes (I)
Site Selection Assistance:	Yes
Lease Negotiation Assistance:	Yes
Co-Operative Advertising:	No
Franchisee Assoc./Member:	Yes/Member
Size Of Corporate Staff:	197
On-Going Support:	C,D,e,f,G,H,I
Training:	3 Weeks Palatine, IL;
	1-2 Weeks In-Shop Assignment; 1-2 Weeks Self Study

SPECIFIC EXPANSION PLANS:

US:	Yes, All United States
Canada:	Yes, All Canada
Overseas:	Yes, Select Countries

ITEM 19: FINANCIAL PERFORMANCE REPRESENTATIONS

Except as permitted above in (1) and (2) and as provided below, we do not furnish or authorize our salespersons (including officers and directors) to furnish any oral, written or visual representation that states, expressly or by implication, a specific level or range of actual or potential sales, income, gross profits or net profits of a Midas Shop. Any such unauthorized information is inherently unreliable, and you should not rely on it. Actual sales vary from Midas Shop to Midas Shop and we cannot estimate the results of any particular franchised Midas Shop.

The following information is provided for the purpose of helping you evaluate the potential earnings capability of a Midas Shop. Please carefully read all information in this Item 19, including the statements following the table, which explain the information provided in the table below and the limitations on this and the other information contained in this Item 19.

Below are ranges of actual gross sales figures of 1,356 franchised Midas Shops and 72 Midas Shops owned and operated by our affiliate, COSMIC, each in operation in the United States for more than two years as of December 31, 2007. The average actual gross sales of these Midas Shops was $632,990. All of these Midas Shops are generally comparable to the franchise being offered.

Range of Annual Sales	No. of Midas Shops	Percentage
$0 - $399,999	239	16.7%
$400,000 - $899,999	984	68.9%
$900,000 and over	205	14.4%
Total	1,428	100%

We offered substantially the same services to all of these Midas Shops, which offered substantially the same products and services to the public. The figures in the table above are based on actual results of Midas Shops operated by COSMIC and on monthly sales reports submitted by Midas franchisees for the purpose of computing royalty fees. We do not know if the figures reported to us by franchisees were audited. We have not independently audited or verified the accuracy of these numbers, and we do not know if these numbers have been verified or audited on behalf of the franchisees. We have written substantiation of the data used to prepare these figures, and will make available to a prospective franchisee on reasonable request.

Gross sales do not reflect the actual potential net income of a Midas Shop and should not be relied upon in calculating profitability. There are a number of fixed and variable costs associated with a Midas Shop that are not reflected in the table and that vary among individual Midas Shops. These costs, which are likely to be significant, include costs described in Items 6 and 7 of this Disclosure Document, inventory costs, labor costs, rent and other occupancy costs, taxes, utilities, insurance, royalty fees, advertising, supplies, bad debt, warranty expenses, charge card expenses, equipment rental, taxes, debt service, depreciation on equipment and property, legal and accounting fees, regulatory compliance, management costs, general administrative expenses, pre-opening organization costs, employee benefits and repairs and maintenance. We encourage you to consult with your financial advisors in reviewing the information in this Item 19, in particular, in estimating the categories and amount of additional expenses that may be incurred in establishing and operating a Midas Shop.

Furthermore, you should be aware that any particular Midas Shop's financial performance may be affected by numerous factors that may vary due to the individual characteristics of the Midas Shop. These factors include, but are not limited to, competition from car dealers and other auto service centers, appreciation and acceptance of the services and products the Midas Shop offers in its community, a franchisee's experience, business development and managerial skills, advertising programs, personnel and cost controls, geographic and socioeconomic conditions in the Midas Shop's area, business cycles and performance of the economy locally, nationally and world-wide.

Financial Information for Specific Existing Midas Shops

In instances where a prospective franchisee is seeking to buy an existing Midas Shop, whether owned by us, COSMIC or another franchisee, we may provide certain operating results of that Midas

Shop, together with the name and last known address of each owner of the Midas Shop, during the prior three years.

YOUR INDIVIDUAL FINANCIAL RESULTS ARE LIKELY TO VARY FROM THE RESULTS STATED ABOVE. THE FIGURES STATED IN THE TABLE SHOULD NOT BE CONSIDERED THE ACTUAL OR POTENTIAL GROSS SALES THAT YOU WILL REALIZE. WE DO NOT PROVIDE ANY GUARANTEE OR ASSURANCE THAT YOU WILL ATTAIN THESE GROSS SALES, OR AS TO ANY INCOME OR PROFIT THAT COULD BE DERIVED FROM THESE GROSS SALES. IF YOU RELY ON THESE FIGURES, YOU MUST ACCEPT THE RISK OF YOUR RELIANCE.

MONEY MAILER ®
"Like Getting Money In Your Mailbox".

MONEY MAILER

12131 Western Ave.
Garden Grove, CA 92841 (800) 418-3030
Tel: (714) 889-4694 (800) 819-4322
Fax: (714) 265-8494
E-Mail: djenkins@moneymailer.com
Web Site: www.moneymailer.com
Mr. Dennis H. Jenkins, VP Franchise Licensing

MONEY MAILER is one of America's leading direct mail advertising companies with over 300 franchises in the U.S. and Canada. Over its 27 year history, MONEY MAILER has been at the forefront of introducing innovative direct mail advertising products and programs to the marketplace - helping businesses get and keep more customers and helping consumers save money everyday.

BACKGROUND: IFA MEMBER

Established: 1979;	1st Franchised: 1980
Franchised Units:	270
Company-Owned Units:	6
Total Units:	276
Dist.:	US-314; CAN-6; O'seas-1
North America:	0 States, 0 Provinces
Density:	44 in CA, 25 in IL, 21 in NJ
Projected New Units (12 Months):	40
Qualifications:	4, 3, 4, 3, 4, 5
Registered:	CA,FL,IL,IN,NY,VA,WA,WI

FINANCIAL/TERMS:

Cash Investment:	$54K
Total Investment:	$100K
Minimum Net Worth:	Varies
Fees: Franchise -	$37.5-52.5K
Royalty - $1400-1600/mo.;	Ad. - $930/yr.
Earnings Claims Statement:	Yes
Term of Contract (Years):	10/10
Avg. # Of Employees:	1 FT, PT
Passive Ownership:	Allowed, But Discouraged
Encourage Conversions:	NA
Area Develop. Agreements:	No
Sub-Franchising Contracts:	No
Expand In Territory:	Yes
Space Needs:	SF; HB

SUPPORT & TRAINING:

Financial Assistance Provided:	No
Site Selection Assistance:	NA
Lease Negotiation Assistance:	NA
Co-Operative Advertising:	Yes
Franchisee Assoc./Member:	Yes/Member
Size Of Corporate Staff:	300
On-Going Support:	B,C,D,H,I
Training:	13 Days Field Training in Territory; 1 Week Corporate Headquarters

SPECIFIC EXPANSION PLANS:

US:	Yes, All United States
Canada:	No
Overseas:	No

ITEM 19
EARNINGS CLAIMS

We are providing you with the following information to assist you in conducting your own investigation for the purchase of a Money Mailer franchise. We hope that this information will be helpful to you in preparing your own business and future cash flow estimates; however, we want to remind you that it is your sole responsibility to do your own research before purchasing a Money Mailer franchise. Please note that we are not able to provide you with all of the material financial information concerning the operation of a Money Mailer franchise because the results vary significantly among franchisees and because many of the expense items to be considered are largely within your control (such as office, rent, car expenses, employee compensation, etc.). Therefore, we are providing you the selected information set forth below with the understanding that you will do your own research to develop data with which to perform your analysis. We recommend that you contact a number of Money Mailer franchisees to discuss the missing items of information and to compare their experience with the information that we provide. In talking to franchisees about sales prices for advertising, be sure to distinguish between their asking price (also referred to as their "rate card") and their actual selling price for advertising, and to ask what kinds of discounts they provide for volume purchases or annual contracts with advertisers.

You should also keep in mind that the performance of franchisees varies dramatically among markets for a variety of reasons, including, for example, differences in sales and management abilities, demographics, the economic and business environment in a particular market, the history of a particular franchise and the strength of competing advertisers in a given market. Therefore, you cannot assume that the information provided to you by a Money Mailer franchisee is necessarily relevant to your market. If you are buying an existing Money Mailer franchise, you should ask for the seller's historical financial information although you should be aware that we do not review franchisees' financial statements, and we have no responsibility for the accuracy of the same. Accordingly, you should carefully review any financial information received from a selling franchisee with your professional financial advisors.

You should also research the prices charged by competing advertisers in your prospective market to determine the degree of price competition you will face. Even if a selling franchisee has historically sold advertising at above average prices in his or her market, it is not safe to assume that you will be able to charge those same prices in the future, especially if major competitors are providing significant price competition.

Finally, keep in mind that the information below does not address many of the variables that can affect your cash flow. It is intended merely as a starting place for your analysis. Reviewing this limited amount of information cannot substitute for thorough research on your part and a careful evaluation of this franchise opportunity with professional financial and legal advisors. Subject to the foregoing, you may wish to consider the following items:

      1.   For purposes of preparing cash flow projections, you may find it helpful to consider the minimum required mailings per year that you must achieve. You should also take into account that the minimum requirements may be phased in (as described in Item 12, and Paragraphs 2.5 and 7.1 of the franchise agreement). Although under the franchise agreement, you will be required to complete at least 8 shared mailings per year (subject to the initial "ramp up" period and also subject to adjustment from time to time), you should keep in mind that these minimum mailing requirements do not constitute any assurance or representation that you will meet the minimum performance requirements. Information from the mailings of all 328 franchises that mailed from December 1, 2006 to November 30, 2007, was used to calculate the following statistics. The average and median number of mailings completed by our franchisees during the fiscal year ended November 30, 2007 was 7.3 and 8.0, respectively. You should note that many of our existing franchisees are operating under older versions of the franchise agreement that do not have the same minimum mailing requirements as the current version of the franchise agreement.

      2.   The average number of advertising inserts sold by franchisees per envelope (the "average piece count") in fiscal year ended November 30, 2007 was 24.1 pieces per envelope. The median number of advertising inserts sold by franchisees per envelope (the "median piece count") in the fiscal year ended November 30, 2007 was 23.0 pieces. This means that 50% or more of the cooperative advertising envelopes sold by our franchisees had more than 23.0 pieces each. Also, 52.0% percent of our franchisees in operation during this period actually attained or surpassed the average piece count.

      3.   For purposes of the calculation in Paragraph 2, the average piece count was computed by dividing the total number of franchise pieces printed and inserted by us by the total number of

zones mailed during the period between December 1, 2006 and November 30, 2007 ("2007 fiscal year"). Each zone consists of at least 10,000 domiciles and, therefore, one mailing consists of at least 10,000 envelopes mailed per zone. The median piece count was calculated as the number of pieces at which 50% of the envelopes had more pieces and 50% had less pieces. Please also note that the average and median piece counts do not include no fee inserts, regional inserts, chain fee inserts or back of the envelope sales. They also do not take into consideration segmented shared mailings or one to one mailings. The average above only takes into account franchisee inserts into shared mailings.

4.   The average piece count above takes into account that certain franchisees with many years of experience have piece counts significantly higher than the average, while franchisees opening new markets (or franchisees that have ceased mailing for various reasons during the 2007 fiscal year) are likely to have piece counts below this average. If you are purchasing an established franchise, your seller can provide you with important historical information on piece counts. If you are purchasing a franchise in an inactive market, you will need to contact relatively new Money Mailer franchisees in similar markets and make a realistic assessment of your own sales abilities and that of your planned sales staff. Based upon the above, the average piece count does not represent the minimum number that you should expect to sell. Typically, franchisees that meet or exceed this average or median piece counts generally have developed client relationships over a number of years.

5.   The above-referenced calculations relating to "average piece counts" and "median piece counts" were derived from our unaudited books and records as of November 30, 2007.

6.   Because we do not have access to any verifiable average retail sales prices charged for advertising inserts for the franchise network as a whole and since any average could be misleading given the wide disparity of pricing among different markets, you will need to interview the franchisees in and around your territory to determine those prices. Any information you collect does not constitute any representation that you can obtain these prices in your territory. The figures for your market will depend on a variety of factors, including, your product mix, the size and loyalty of the existing customer base, if any, pricing strategies of local competitors, local economic conditions and your own sales and sales management abilities.

7.   You should include in your analysis all applicable taxes, including those required under federal, state and local law. You should consult with your professional advisors regarding applicable taxes.

8.   The average estimated mailing production costs for your shared mailing per zone are as follows:

Fixed cost (per zone) **(Note:** There are 5 zones in a standard territory.)	**$2,204**
Variable cost (per advertisement)	**$116**

The fixed shared mailing production costs include envelopes, inserting and inkjetting charges, mailing list costs and, postage (net of average trucking discounts and costs). These calculations were made on an accrual basis of accounting. The actual fixed costs per zone will vary due to the cost of your postage. The fixed costs do not include the Royalty Fee or Ad Fund costs as these costs will vary. For more information, please see Item 6 and Paragraphs 4.1 and 4.5 of the franchise agreement.

The average variable shared mailing production costs above were determined by dividing our gross printing revenue before any credits or discounts received from franchisees for the 2007 fiscal year divided by the total printed franchisee advertisements for the 2007 fiscal year and adding an estimated average art cost per advertisement of $15 per spot. The gross printing revenues figure was derived from our unaudited books and records as of November 30, 2007.

Although we cannot track the actual, average variable costs per mailing, you can deduce an estimated, average variable cost per mailing by multiplying the average of 24.1 advertisements per mailing times the average variable cost per advertisement of $116. This formula yields an estimated, average variable cost of $2,795.60 per mailing. Please keep in mind that this formula only produces a rough estimate since the multiplier and the multiplicand themselves are "average" calculations. As a start up franchise, your variable costs are likely to be higher (at least initially) since you will not have achieved the economies of scale or operating efficiencies of larger, established Money Mailer franchises.

The term "advertisement," as used above, means each advertisement inserted in a zone. "Franchisee advertisements" do not include no fee inserts, regional inserts, chain fee inserts or advertisements printed on the back of the envelope.

You may also incur additional postage costs if your envelope exceeds the standard weight as contained in the United States Postal Service regulations.

To estimate the total shared mailing production costs of your zone, you must multiply your variable cost by the estimated number of advertisements you insert into the envelope. This amount plus your actual fixed shared Mailing production costs represent the estimated total shared mailing production cost per zone. Again, please be aware that these costs do not include your required Royalty Fee and Ad Fund contributions.

You may determine your estimated gross profit per zone by subtracting the total cost as computed above (plus your Royalty Fee and Ad Fund Contribution) from the estimated total revenue per zone (average sales price multiplied by number of advertisements). Please refer to Paragraph 5 of this item for information on retail sales prices.

The above estimates relate only to typical, cyclical shared mailings and do not reflect the charges and costs associated with other advertising programs, such as any segmented shared mailings or one to one mailings you might offer.

9.   Your analysis of a Money Mailer franchise should include estimates of expenses for all applicable items, including office rent, office staff salaries (including any salespeople you may hire), your own salary, phone/fax charges, postage and courier charges, travel, bad debt expense, auto expense, insurance, advertising expenses and the costs of marketing materials. All of these items are based largely on factors within your control, for which you can obtain information through your own research. Since these amounts are to a great degree a matter of personal preference (for example, if your territory has less than 15 zones, you likely will operate from a home office), we have included no estimates for these items, and you should make appropriate assumptions. Please see Items 6 and 7 (and 10 if you obtain any financing from us) for a description of certain expense items that you are likely to incur in acquiring and operating a Money Mailer franchise. However, you should also be aware that the expense items listed above and those listed in Items 6 and 7, taken together, are by no means exhaustive. There are likely to be additional expenses that we have not listed, some of which may be unique to your market or situation.

10.   Please note that we will make available to you, on your reasonable request, the substantiation of the data that we used in preparing the information contained in this Item 19:

The Plumber You Deserve.

MR. ROOTER CORP.

1020 N. University Parks Dr.
Waco, TX 76707
Tel: (800) 298-6855 (254) 745-5850
Fax: (800) 209-7621

E-Mail: info@servicefranchiseopportunities.com
Web Site: www.servicefranchiseopportunities.com
Ms. Pat Humburg, Lead Development Manager

Established in 1970, Mr. Rooter is the largest all-franchised, full-service plumbing and drain cleaning company in the world with approximately 300 franchises worldwide. Recognized by Entrepreneur magazine among its "Franchise 500" and Franchise Times Top 200, Mr. Rooter franchisees provide services to both residential and commercial customers. Mr. Rooter began franchising in 1974 and is part of The Dwyer Group family of companies, which also includes

Rainbow International, Aire Serv, Mr. Electric, Mr. Appliance and Glass Doctor.

BACKGROUND:	IFA MEMBER
Established: 1968;	1st Franchised: 1974
Franchised Units:	262
Company-Owned Units:	0
Total Units:	262
Dist.:	US-220; CAN-18; O'seas-51
North America:	45 States, 7 Provinces
Density:	32 in CA, 18 in FL, 19 in TX
Projected New Units (12 Months):	50
Qualifications:	5, 3, 3, 2, 3, 5
Registered:CA,DC,FL,HI,IL,IN,MD,MI,MN,ND,NY,OR,RI,SD,	VA,WA,WI

FINANCIAL/TERMS:	
Cash Investment:	$35-75K
Total Investment:	$51-142K
Minimum Net Worth:	$200K
Fees: Franchise -	$23.5K/100KPop
Royalty - 4-7%;	Ad. - 2%
Earnings Claims Statement:	Yes

Term of Contract (Years):	10/10
Avg. # Of Employees:	Varies FT, 0 PT
Passive Ownership:	Not Allowed
Encourage Conversions:	Yes
Area Develop. Agreements:	No
Sub-Franchising Contracts:	No
Expand In Territory:	Yes
Space Needs:	SF; FS,HB

SUPPORT & TRAINING:	
Financial Assistance Provided:	Yes (D)
Site Selection Assistance:	NA
Lease Negotiation Assistance:	NA
Co-Operative Advertising:	No
Franchisee Assoc./Member:	No
Size Of Corporate Staff:	27
On-Going Support:	A,C,D,G,H
Training:	5 Days Waco, TX

SPECIFIC EXPANSION PLANS:	
US:	Yes, Uncovered Areas
Canada:	Yes, All Canada
Overseas:	Yes, Portugal

ITEM 19
FINANCIAL PERFORMANCE REPRESENTATIONS
Report on Average Sales for Mr. Rooter Franchisees
For the Period January 1, 2007 to December 31, 2007

The sales figures listed below are averages derived from historical operating results of the franchised businesses indicated for the time periods covered by franchise service fee reports provided to us by our franchisees from January 1, 2007 through December 31, 2007. Neither we nor our independent certified public accountants have audited or verified any of these sales figures. We make no representations as to the accuracy of sales reported by our franchisees or the extent to which these sales figures were derived using generally accepted accounting principles. Our independent auditors, BDO Seidman, LLP have not audited, reviewed or performed any level of service on the information. Accordingly, they provide no form of assurance as to the accuracy of this information.

Of the Mr. Rooter franchised businesses in operation in the U.S. as of December 31, 2007, 187 businesses were in operation for the full 12 months of 2007. In order to compare sales for businesses open for the same period, sales results for the other locations were not included in the information provided below. All of the businesses for which sales results are included below were operated by franchisees. We did not operate any of the businesses. All of the businesses are comparable to the franchised businesses offered by this offering circular and offered substantially the same services to the public.

The sales listed below are an average of the annual gross sales reported by the indicated Mr. Rooter franchised businesses. These results are not intended to represent the actual results that would likely have occurred for any specific franchised business during the period indicated. Actual results for a specific location could have differed significantly from the results presented. No adjustments have been made to these reported sales. Because these are gross sales results only, no costs or expenses are taken into account. Profits resulting from any given level of gross sales may differ substantially from one business to another. Sales and profit results are directly impacted by various factors, including: competition from other similar businesses in the area; the quality of management and service in a franchisee's operations; contractual relationships and terms with individual land-lords and suppliers; the cost of capital and the extent to which a franchisee might have financed its operations; legal, accounting, and other professional fees; federal, state, and local income and other taxes; and discretionary expenditures. You should therefore use the information in this Report only as a reference to conduct your own analysis.

Except for the information that appears in this report, we do not furnish or authorize our salespersons or affiliates to furnish any oral or written information or representations or statements of actual sales, costs, income or profits. We encourage you to carefully review this material with your attorney and/or accountant.

Substantiation of the data used to prepare this report will be made available to a prospective franchisee on reasonable request.

Caution: this information has been prepared by us without an audit.

Such actual sales are of franchised units and should not be considered as the actual or probable sales that will be realized by any franchisee. The franchisor does not represent that any franchisee can attain such sales. A new franchisee's individual financial results are likely to differ from the results stated herein.

This analysis is based upon the historic experience of businesses in operation for the full 12 months during 2007 and the information has not been adjusted for any factors, including geographic location. The sales reflected in this analysis should not be considered as the actual or potential sales, costs and expenses or operating profits that you will realize. We do not represent that any operator can expect to attain the sales presented in this report, or any other particular level or range of sales, costs and expenses or operating profits. Your success will depend largely on your ability and efforts.

We do not represent that you will derive income from your franchised business that exceeds your initial payment for or investment in your business. The individual financial results of any franchised business are likely to differ from the information described in this exhibit.

This analysis does not include any cost or expense information and those items may differ substantially from one business or area of the country to another. You should consult with your financial, business, and legal advisors to determine all categories of costs and expenses that you will incur.

You are urged to consult with appropriate financial, business and legal advisors to conduct your own analysis, using the information presented in this report.

Average Annual Sales for Mr. Rooter Franchised Businesses Open Full 12 Months in 2007

Full Years in Business and Territory Population [1]: 1. Under 400,000 2. Over 400,000	Average Annual Sales for 2007 [2]	Number of Businesses in Group Open for Full 12 Months 2007 [3]	Number of Businesses in Group that Attained this Level of Sales or Greater for 2007 [4]	Percentage of Businesses in group that Attained this Level of Sales or greater for 2007 [5]	Number of Businesses in Mr. Rooter System Open for full 12 months in 2007 [6]	Number of Businesses in Mr. Rooter System that Attained this Level of Sales or Greater for 2007 [7]	Percentage of Businesses in Mr. Rooter System that Attained this Level of Sales or greater for 2007 [8]
A. 1-2 Full Years	$494,475	68	19	28%	187 [9]	110	59%

1.	Under 400,000	$339,101	43	16	37%	187	137	73%
2.	Over 400,000	$761,718	25	8	32%	187	79	42%
B.	3-5 Full Years	$894,680	45	16	36%	187	72	39%
1.	Under 400,000	$558,516	22	11	50%	187	104	56%
2.	Over 400,000	$1,216,228	23	9	39%	187	59	32%
C.	6-7 Full Years	$1,478,152	38	16	42%	187	48	26%
1.	Under 400,000	$746,855	11	4	36%	187	81	43%
2.	Over 400,000	$1,776,088	27	10	37%	187	34	18%
D.	8-10 Full Years	$1,655,220	22	7	32%	187	39	21%
1.	Under 400,000	$750,417	8	3	38%	187	80	43%
2.	Over 400,000	$2,172,250	14	4	29%	187	23	12%
E.	10+ Full Years	$3,093,496	14	5	36%	187	12	6%
1.	Under 400,000	$1,186,271	2	1	50%	187	59	32%
2.	Over 400,000	$3,411,367	12	5	42%	187	11	6%

[1] The franchised businesses are grouped to show the average sales for businesses open for the full years indicated and the groups are further defined by the population in the territory: over 400,000 in population or under 400,000 in population. While territory population and years in business have some impact on level of sales that may be expected, other factors are also important and should be considered.

[2] The average annual sales shows the average sales of all of the businesses in the group based on franchise service fee reports provided to us by our franchisees from January 1, 2007 through December 31, 2007.

[3] This is the number of businesses open for a full 12 months during 2007 that fell within this group. To be included, the business must have been open for the full number of year(s) stated with the indicated territory population level.

[4] This is the number of businesses in the group that achieved the average annual sales level stated for the group during 2007.

[5] This is the percentage of businesses in the group that achieved the average annual sales level stated for the group during 2007.

[6] This is the total number of businesses in the Mr. Rooter system open for the full 12 months during 2007.

[7] Of the total number of businesses in the Mr. Rooter system open for the full 12 month during 2007, regardless of how long in business or the territory population, this is the number that achieved the indicated level of sales or greater.

[8] Of the total number of businesses in the Mr. Rooter system open for the full 12 months during 2007, regardless of how long in business or the territory population, this is the percentage of the total that achieved the indicated level of sales or greater.

[9] The total number of businesses in the Mr. Rooter system open for the full 12 months during 2007 includes one business that started the year as two separate businesses but was consolidated into one business during the year.

The One You Can Trust.℠

OIL CAN HENRY'S INTERNATIONAL

1200 Naito Pkwy. NW, # 690

Portland, OR 97209

Tel: (800) 765-6244 (503) 243-6311

Fax: (503) 228-5227

E-Mail: georges@oilcanhenry.com

Web Site: www.oilcanhenry.com

Mr. George Steinfurth, VP Franchise Development

Automotive lubrication and filter specialist. We work hard, blending the best of yesterday with the best of today to provide unbeatable service. The distinctive design of our crew uniforms and service centers evoke memories of days past when the neighbor service station provided friendly, quality service. While our centers may remind you of yesteryear, our focus is on the future. Our technicians are well-trained to provide a wide variety of valuable maintenance and safety services.

BACKGROUND: IFA MEMBER

Established: 1978;	1st Franchised: 1989
Franchised Units:	70
Company-Owned Units:	12
Total Units:	82
Dist.:	US-82; CAN-0; O'seas-0
North America	9 States, 0 Provinces
Density:	11 in CA, 41 in OR, 19 in WA
Projected New Units (12 Months):	15

Qualifications:	5, 4, 3, 3, 4, 5
Registered:	CA,FL,MN,OR,WA

FINANCIAL/TERMS:

Cash Investment:	$150-250K
Total Investment:	$816-1259K
Minimum Net Worth:	$500K
Fees: Franchise -	$25K
Royalty - 5.5%;	Ad. - 1%
Earnings Claims Statement:	No
Term of Contract (Years):	15/5+
Avg. # Of Employees:	4-6 FT, 5-9 PT
Passive Ownership:	Not Allowed
Encourage Conversions:	Yes
Area Develop. Agreements:	Yes
Sub-Franchising Contracts:	No
Expand In Territory:	Yes
Space Needs:	15,000 SF; FS

SUPPORT & TRAINING:

Financial Assistance Provided:	Yes (I)
Site Selection Assistance:	Yes
Lease Negotiation Assistance:	Yes
Co-Operative Advertising:	Yes
Franchisee Assoc./Member:	No
Size Of Corporate Staff:	15
On-Going Support:	A,B,C,D,E,F,G,H,I
Training:	NA Ongoing;
	2 Weeks On-Site;5 Weeks Portland, OR

SPECIFIC EXPANSION PLANS:

US:	Yes, WA,OR,CA,AZ,NV,ID,MN,CO
Canada:	No
Overseas:	No

19. FINANCIAL PERFORMANCE REPRESENTATIONS

Once an individual becomes a franchisee, we will help the franchisee project costs and revenue based on a projected site.

Except as outlined below, we do not provide nor do we authorize our salespersons to furnish any oral or written information concerning the actual or potential sales, costs, income or profits of a Center. Actual results vary from unit to unit and we cannot estimate the results of any particular Franchise.

The following composite of a cash flow breakeven analysis and pre-tax cash flow were prepared by taking an average of the expenses incurred by us and reported to us by our Franchisees in the operation of Centers, which had been operating for at least one full year as of October 2007, over the period from January through October 31, 2007 and projected through December 31, 2007. It reflects an average based on our experience and the experience of our franchisees in operating numerous Oil Can Henry's® Service Centers, not on the actual operating experience of any one particular Center. The expenses projected in the cash flow breakeven analysis are those which, on average, can be expected to occur when our operating systems and procedures are followed as outlined in our training program and the Operations Manuals and other management guidance. The analysis is followed by notes explaining the material assumptions used in the preparation of this item.

Information concerning the actual operating results of our franchised and company-owned Centers open and operating for the period covered by this item follows.

The following breakeven and pre-tax cash flow analyses are examples only and should not be considered the actual costs, expenses, sales, revenues and earnings that will be realized by any specific franchisee. Be aware that the sales, profits, expenses and earnings of an individual Franchise may vary greatly depending on a wide variety of factors, including adherence to the System, the location of the Franchise, the real estate lease/purchase/financing terms, the demographic characteristics of the population within the Center's market area, competition in the area, the franchisee's business and management expertise, economic and market conditions, labor and product costs, and many others.

We will provide substantiation of the data used in preparing this item to the prospective franchisee on reasonable request.

Oil Can Henry's®
Breakeven Analysis
$950,000 Real Estate Capital Investment
(Example)

	VARIABLE EXPENSES	FIXED EXPENSES
Cost of Goods Sold*	26%	
Labor**	19%	$40,950 (Manager)
Controllables	7%	
Occupancy:(1) Rent CAM/Taxes/Ins.		$85,500 $16,245
Royalties	5.5%	
Advertising Fund Trust Account Fee	1%	
Local Center Marketing	7%	
Accounting		$6,000
Other	1.5%	
TOTALS:	67%	$148,695 (33%)

Cash Flow Breakeven	**$450,591**
Average Ticket (2)	**$61.00**
Cars per day (3)	**22.28**

* Castrol financing impact

** Labor is fully loaded and includes payroll taxes and worker's compensation insurance. As revenues increase the variable labor expenses generally decrease as a percentage of total revenue.

Notes:

1.   This rental rate is based on a leased project with real property and improvement costs (land and building) of $950,000 and a capitalization return for the development costs of 9% on a fifteen-year lease. The Common Area Maintenance (CAM), Taxes and Insurance are computed as 19% of the rent.

2. See System Average Ticket below.

3. Our Centers are open 6.5 days a Week (open for half a day on Sundays) and 51 Weeks a year (closed for the five major holidays).

Pre-Tax Cash Flow*

REVENUE	$$	% OF REVENUE
$450,591	- 0 -	- 0 -
$800,000	$114,305	14%
$1,000,000	$180,305	18%
$1,200,000	$246,305	21%

*Before taxes, debt service and interest. Based on cash flow break even of $450,591.

The following actual GROSS SALES, ticket average and daily car count information is for system centers (franchised and company-owned) open the full year of 2006 (based on sales January 1, 2007 through October 31, 2007):

	GROSS SALES	DAILY CAR COUNTS	AVERAGE TICKET
Average	$862,464	42	$61.54
Range	$370,591 - $1,677,104	19 - 80	$47.75 - $71.08

Of these Centers, 44% met or exceeded the average GROSS SALES, 51% met or exceeded the average ticket, and 43% met or exceeded the average daily car count. These centers are one, two and three bays.

We have written substantiation in our possession to support the information appearing in this Item 19. This substantiation will be made available by us to all prospective franchisees upon reasonable request.

We do not make any representations about a franchisee's future financial performance or, except for the information appearing in the tables in this Item, the past financial performance of company-owned or franchised outlets. We also do not authorize our employees or representatives to make any such representations either orally or in writing, other than for the information described in this Item or for information which supplements these tables with respect to performance at particular locations or under particular circumstances. If you are purchasing an existing Center, however, we may provide you with the actual records of that Center.

If you receive any other financial performance information or projections of your future income, you should report it to our management by contacting our President, John Ayres at 503-243-6311, the Federal Trade Commission, and the appropriate state agencies.

PAK MAIL

7173 S. Havana St., # 600

Centennial, CO 80112-3891

Tel: (800) 833-2821 (303) 957-1000

Fax: (800) 336-7363

E-Mail: sales@pakmail.org

Web Site: www.pakmail.com

Mr. Evan Lasky, President/CEO

PAK MAIL is a convenient center for packaging, shipping and business support services, offering both residential and commercial customers air, ground, and ocean carriers, custom packaging and crating, private mailbox rental, mail services, packaging and moving supplies, copy and fax service and internet access and related services. We ship anything, anywhere.

BACKGROUND:

	IFA MEMBER
Established: 1983;	1st Franchised: 1984
Franchised Units:	430
Company-Owned Units:	0
Total Units:	430
Dist.:	US-421; CAN-8; O'seas-22
North America:	42 States, 0 Provinces
Density:	22 in CA, 91 in FL, 41 in GA
Projected New Units (12 Months):	50
Qualifications:	3, 2, 2, 2, 2, 5
Registered:CA,DC,FL,HI,IL,IN,MD,MI,MN,ND,NY,OR,RI,SD, VA,WA,WI,AB	

FINANCIAL/TERMS:

Cash Investment:	$50K
Total Investment:	$130-164K
Minimum Net Worth:	$100K
Fees: Franchise -	$29,950
Royalty - 5% Sliding;	Ad. - 2%
Earnings Claims Statement:	Yes
Term of Contract (Years):	10/10
Avg. # Of Employees:	1 FT, 1 PT
Passive Ownership:	Allowed, But Discouraged
Encourage Conversions:	Yes
Area Develop. Agreements:	Yes
Sub-Franchising Contracts:	No
Expand In Territory:	Yes
Space Needs:	1,200 SF; SC

SUPPORT & TRAINING:

Financial Assistance Provided:	Yes (D)
Site Selection Assistance:	Yes
Lease Negotiation Assistance:	Yes
Co-Operative Advertising:	No
Franchisee Assoc./Member:	Yes/Member
Size Of Corporate Staff:	22
On-Going Support:	B,C,D,E,F,G,H,I
Training:	10 Days Englewood;
3 Days Existing Center;3 Days New Center at Opening	

SPECIFIC EXPANSION PLANS:

US:	Yes, All United States
Canada:	Yes, All Canada
Overseas:	Yes, All Countries

ITEM 19
FINANCIAL PERFORMANCE REPRESENTATIONS
REPORT OF GROSS SALES OF FRANCHISED PAK MAIL CENTERS

CAUTION: THE FOLLOWING DATA SHOULD NOT BE CONSIDERED AS THE ACTUAL OR POTENTIAL INCOME OR RESULTS OF OPERATIONS OF ANY PARTICULAR FRANCHISE. WE DO NOT REPRESENT THAT YOU CAN EXPECT TO ATTAIN THESE GROSS SALES LEVELS. **A FRANCHISEE'S FINANCIAL RESULTS ARE LIKELY TO DIFFER FROM THE FIGURES PRESENTED. SEE ATTACHED NOTES.**

	NO. OF CENTERS	AVERAGE SALES
AVERAGE ANNUAL SALES: TOP 10%	31	$571,851
AVERAGE ANNUAL SALES: TOP 30%	92	$409,427
AVERAGE ANNUAL SALES: TOP 50%	154	$344,758
AVERAGE ANNUAL SALES: ALL CENTERS	307	$240,223

EXPLANATORY NOTES
(Containing Summary of Factual Data and Significant Assumptions)

1.   As of November 30, 2006, there were a total of 372 PAK MAIL Centers and as of November 30, 2007 there were a total of 355 PAK MAIL Centers located in the United States. The above data

represents the historical reported gross sales of 307 franchised PAK MAIL Centers that were in operation at least two years before the reporting period of December 1, 2006 through November 30, 2007.

2.	Aside from geographical and demographic differences and managerial emphasis, there are no material differences in the products, services, training or support offered to you. Differences in sales volumes are attributable to the amount of time a PAK MAIL Center has been open, geographical and demographic differences, and your ability and willingness to follow system guidelines.

3.	The sales of products and services by franchised PAK MAIL Centers include those which reflect higher revenue margins such as freight, business services, custom packaging, etc. and those which reflect little or no revenue margins such as postage stamp sales. The mix of products and services varies at the discretion of each franchisee.

4.	We prepared the above information from royalty reports provided by each individual franchisee. A franchisee pays us a royalty based on sales. However, we know of no instance, and have no reason to believe, that any franchisee would overstate its level of sales receipts in its royalty report.

5.	This information represents aggregate results of sales reported to us and you must not consider this information the actual or probable sales while you will achieve. We do not represent that you can expect to attain these results. A franchisee's results are likely to be lower in its first year of business. We recommend that you make your own independent investigation to determine whether or not a franchise may be profitable. We further recommend that you consult with professional advisors before signing any agreement.

6.	Actual results may vary from franchise to franchise and depend on a variety of internal and external factors, many of which neither we nor you can estimate, such as competition, economic climate, demographics, changing consumer demands, etc. Your ability to achieve any level of gross sales or net income will depend on these factors and others, including your level of expertise and ability to follow the System, none of which are within our control. Accordingly, we cannot, and do not, estimate the results of your franchise.

Substantiation for this data will be made available for inspection at our headquarters and will be provided to all prospective franchisees upon request.

EXCEPT FOR THE INFORMATION IN THIS ITEM AND EXCEPT FOR SUPPLEMENTAL FINANCIAL PERFORMANCE REPRESENTATIONS DESCRIBED ABOVE IN THIS ITEM WHICH ARE AUTHORIZE BY US, NO REPRESENTATIONS OR STATEMENTS OF ACTUAL, AVERAGE, PROJECTED, FORECASTED OR POTENTIAL SALES, INCOME OR PROFITS ARE MADE TO YOU BY US. WE DO NOT FURNISH OR MAKE, OR AUTHORIZE OUR SALES PERSONNEL TO FURNISH OR MAKE, ANY ORAL OR WRITTEN INFORMATION CONCERNING THE ACTUAL, AVERAGE, PROJECTED, FORECASTED OR POTENTIAL SALES, INCOME OR PROFITS OF A FRANCHISE OR YOUR PROSPECTS OF CHANCES OF SUCCESS THAT YOU CAN EXPECT OR THAT PRESENT OR PAST FRANCHISES HAVE HAD, OTHER THAN AS SET FORTH IN THIS ITEM. WE DISCLAIM AND WILL NOT BE BOUND BY ANY UNAUTHORIZED REPRESENTATIONS.

POSTAL ANNEX+

7580 Metropolitan Dr., # 200

San Diego, CA 92108-4417

Tel: (800) 456-1525 (619) 563-4800

Fax: (619) 563-9850

E-Mail: ryan@postalannex.com

Web Site: www.postalannex.com

Mr. Ryan Heine, Director of Franchising

Retail business service center, providing: packaging, shipping, copying, postal, mail box rental, printing fax, notary, office supplies and more.

BACKGROUND:	IFA MEMBER

Established: 1985;	1st Franchised: 1986	Encourage Conversions:	Yes
Franchised Units:	375	Area Develop. Agreements:	Yes
Company-Owned Units:	0	Sub-Franchising Contracts:	No
Total Units:	375	Expand In Territory:	Yes
Dist.:	US-374; CAN-0; O'seas-1	Space Needs:	1,200 SF; Supermarket Anchored
North America:	25 States, 0 Provinces		
Density:	130 in CA, 17 in MI, 20 in OR	**SUPPORT & TRAINING:**	
Projected New Units (12 Months):	36	Financial Assistance Provided:	Yes (D)
Qualifications:	5, 3, 1, 1, 3, 3	Site Selection Assistance:	Yes
Registered:	CA,DC,FL,IL,MD,MI,NY,OR,WA,WI	Lease Negotiation Assistance:	Yes
		Co-Operative Advertising:	No
		Franchisee Assoc./Member:	Yes/Member
FINANCIAL/TERMS:		Size Of Corporate Staff:	21
Cash Investment:	$50K	On-Going Support:	c,d,E,G,H,I
Total Investment:	$128.8-190.1K	Training:	2 Weeks San Diego, CA;
Minimum Net Worth:	$200K		1 Week On-Site
Fees: Franchise -	$29.95K		
Royalty - 5%;	Ad. - 2%		
Earnings Claims Statement:	Yes	**SPECIFIC EXPANSION PLANS:**	
Term of Contract (Years):	15/15	US:	Yes, All United States
Avg. # Of Employees:	1 FT, 2 PT	Canada:	Yes, All Canada
Passive Ownership:	Allowed	Overseas:	Yes, All Countries

Item 19
FINANCIAL PERFORMANCE REPRESENTATIONS

GROSS SALES OF POSTALANNEX+
AND SUNSHINE PACK & SHIP FRANCHISED UNITS
IN OPERATION AT LEAST 1 YEAR
AS OF FISCAL YEAR END SEPTEMBER 30, 2007

NUMBER OF UNITS IN SAMPLE:	283		
AVERAGE ANNUAL SALES:	$250,000		
MEDIAN ANNUAL SALES:	$217,000		
RANGE OF SALES FOR TOP 10 STORES:	$862,000	to	$522,000
RANGE OF SALES FOR BOTTOM 10 STORES:	$74,000	to	$60,000

The data above represents the actual operating results of 283 PostalAnnex+ and Sunshine Pack & Ship franchised businesses that were in operation at least 1 year as of September 30, 2007. These 283 franchised businesses represent all of the franchised businesses that were in operation at least 1 year as of September 30, 2007. Of these businesses, 40% achieved the average annual sales level and 50% achieved the median annual sales level.

GROSS SALES OF HANDLE WITH CARE PACKAGING STORE FRANCHISED UNITS
IN OPERATION AT LEAST 1 YEAR
AS OF CALENDAR YEAR ENDED DECEMBER 31, 2006

NUMBER OF UNITS IN SAMPLE:	61		
AVERAGE ANNUAL SALES:	$251,000		
MEDIAN ANNUAL SALES:	$189,000		
RANGE OF SALES FOR TOP 10 STORES:	$1,603,000	to	$404,000
RANGE OF SALES FOR BOTTOM 10 STORES:	$119,000	to	$10,000

The data above represents the actual operating results of 61 HANDLE WITH CARE PACK-AGING STORE franchised businesses that were in operation at least 1 year as of December 31, 2006. These 61 franchised businesses represent all except 7 of the franchised businesses that were in operation at least 1 year as of December 31, 2006. Information for those 7 units was incomplete and could not be used. Of the 61 businesses, 35% achieved the average annual sales level and 50% achieved the median annual sales level.

<u>Explanatory Notes:</u>

The sales of services and products made by franchised businesses include those that reflect high margins such as shipping services, facsimile and copies, and those that reflect lower margins such as postage stamps sales. Money order sales, electronic transfer of funds sales and utility collections are not included in the sales figures presented here (however, the low margin generated by these sales is included). The mix of postal, printing and copying, packaging and shipping, and business support services offered to the public by each individual franchised business varies at the discretion of each franchisee. The sales volume attainable by a franchisee is largely dependent on the type and quality of service offered to the public, individual sales and marketing efforts.

We prepared the information above from unit sales reports submitted by each franchised business. Franchisees pay a royalty based on their "Gross Receipts", as defined in Item 6. We know of no instance in which, and have no reason to believe that, any franchised business overstated its level of Gross Receipts in any royalty report.

There are no material differences between the operations of, or the services or products offered by, the franchised businesses whose results are reported above, and the franchises we currently offer.

Your individual financial results likely will be lower initially. We recommend that you make your own independent investigation to determine whether or not a franchised business may be profitable, and consult with your advisors before signing our franchise agreement.

We will substantiate the information above available to you on reasonable request.

Beyond the information contained in this Item, we do not furnish or authorize our salespersons to furnish any oral or written information on the actual or potential sales, costs, income or profits of a franchised business. Actual results may vary from unit to unit, and we cannot estimate the results of any particular franchised business.

CAUTION

THE EARNINGS CLAIMS FIGURES DO NOT REFLECT THE COSTS OF SALES, OPERATING EXPENSES OR OTHER COSTS OR EXPENSES THAT MUST BE DEDUCTED FROM THE GROSS REVENUE OR GROSS SALES FIGURES TO OBTAIN YOUR NET INCOME OR PROFIT. YOU SHOULD CONDUCT AN INDEPENDENT INVESTIGATION OF THE COSTS AND EXPENSES YOU WILL INCUR IN OPERATING YOUR FRANCHISED BUSINESS. FRANCHISEES OR FORMER FRANCHISEES, LISTED IN THE FRANCHISE DISCLOSURE DOCUMENT, MAY BE ONE SOURCE OF THIS INFORMATION.

THE SALES FIGURES ABOVE SHOULD NOT BE CONSIDERED AS THE ACTUAL OR POTENTIAL FIGURES THAT WILL BE REALIZED BY ANY PROSPECTIVE FRANCHISEE. WE DO NOT REPRESENT THAT YOU CAN EXPECT TO ATTAIN ANY OF THE FIGURES INDICATED.

PRECISION TUNE AUTO CARE CENTER

748 Miller Dr. SE

Leesburg, VA 20175

Tel: (800) 438-8863 (703) 669-2311

Fax: (703) 669-1539

E-Mail: lee.oppenheim@precisionac.com

Web Site: www.precisiontune.com

Mr. Lee Oppenheim, VP Franchise Development

PRECISION TUNE AUTO CARE is America's largest engine performance car care company, specializing in tune-up, quick oil and lube and brake services. Our work is backed by certified technicians and a nationwide warranty. We are your one stop shop for all your auto care needs. We offer a variety of automotive services to fit your cars needs, including services for air conditioning, brake systems, fuel injection, air induction systems, cooling systems, fluid maintenance, tune-ups, as well as other scheduled maintenance services. We provide quality support in site selection, training, marketing, operations, management, business profitability and much more.

BACKGROUND: IFA MEMBER

Established: 1975;	1st Franchised: 1976
Franchised Units:	401
Company-Owned Units:	1
Total Units:	407
Dist.:	US-286; CAN-2; O'seas-106
North America:	29 States, 1 Provinces
Density:	41 in CA, 33 in GA, 32 in NC
Projected New Units (12 Months):	25

Qualifications:	4, 5, 2, 2, 3, 5
Registered:	CA,DC,FL,IL,IN,MD,MI,MN,ND,NY,OR,RI,SD,VA, WA,WI,AB

FINANCIAL/TERMS:

Cash Investment:	$75-100K
Total Investment:	$123-208K
Minimum Net Worth:	$150K
Fees: Franchise -	$10-25K
Royalty - 6-7.5%;	Ad. - 1.5%
Earnings Claims Statement:	Yes
Term of Contract (Years):	10/5
Avg. # Of Employees:	6 FT, 1-2 PT
Passive Ownership:	Allowed, But Discouraged
Encourage Conversions:	Yes
Area Develop. Agreements:	Yes
Sub-Franchising Contracts:	Yes
Expand In Territory:	Yes
Space Needs:	3,000 SF; FS,SF,SC

SUPPORT & TRAINING:

Financial Assistance Provided:	Yes (I)
Site Selection Assistance:	Yes
Lease Negotiation Assistance:	No
Co-Operative Advertising:	Yes
Franchisee Assoc./Member:	Yes/Member
Size Of Corporate Staff:	26
On-Going Support:	A,B,C,D,E,F,G,H,I
Training:	2 Weeks Leesburg, VA

SPECIFIC EXPANSION PLANS:

US:	Yes, All United States, except Hawaii
Canada:	Yes, All Canada
Overseas:	Yes, All Countries

ITEM 19
FINANCIAL PERFORMANCE REPRESENTATIONS

We do not authorize our salespersons to furnish any oral information concerning the actual or potential sales, costs, income or profits of a Precision Tune Auto Care Center. Except as provided in this Item 19, we do not provide any written information concerning the actual or potential sales, costs, income or profits of a Precision Tune Auto Care center. The information presented does not represent the actual performance of any single center.

THE GROSS SALES ARE A COMPILATION OF THE RESULTS OF INDIVIDUAL PRECISION TUNE AUTO CARE CENTERS OPERATED BY OUR FRANCHISEES AND SHOULD NOT BE CONSIDERED AS THE ACTUAL OR PROBABLE GROSS WEEKLY SALES THAT YOU WILL ACHIEVE. ACTUAL RESULTS VARY FROM CENTER TO CENTER, AND WE CANNOT ESTIMATE THE RESULTS OF YOUR CENTER OR ANY PARTICULAR FRANCHISEE. YOUR EXPERIENCE IS LIKELY TO DIFFER.

ACTUAL SALES AND EARNINGS OF THE CENTER ARE AFFECTED BY MANY FACTORS, INCLUDING YOUR OWN EFFORTS, ABILITY AND CONTROL OF THE CENTER, AS WELL AS OTHER FACTORS OVER WHICH YOU DO NOT HAVE ANY CONTROL.

WE DO NOT REPRESENT THAT ANY CENTER YOU ESTABLISH WILL BE PROFITABLE.

If we wish to disclose to a prospective franchisee additional information, or average sales, profits, or earnings of other franchisees or the projected sales, profits, or earnings for a prospective franchisee, we will comply with the requirements of applicable federal and state laws and regulations before making such disclosure, which will be in writing.

CAUTION: THERE IS NO ASSURANCE YOU WILL DO AS WELL AS THESE CENTERS. IF YOU RELY ON THESE FIGURES, YOU MUST ACCEPT THE RISK OF NOT DOING AS WELL.

AVERAGE CENTER SALES BY QUARTILE*

*Results ***

52 WEEKS Ended June 24, 2007

	Total	**1st Quartile (top 25%**)**	Stratified by Sales Ranking		**4th Quartile (bottom 25%**)**
			2nd Quartile (2nd highest 25%)**	**3rd Quartile (3rd highest 25%**)**	
# of centers in survey	276	69	69	69	69
Total annual sales	146,929,909	56,345,622	38,999,518	30,619,265	20,965,504
Average sales per center	532,355	816,603	565,210	443,757	303,848
Total Stores Above Avg	117	24	31	34	43
Total Stores Below Avg	159	45	38	35	26
Median	500,309	762,472	555,902	443,292	318,635
Average number of bays	5.8	6.5	5.7	5.4	5.3

AVERAGE SALES BY BAY
52 WEEKS ENDED JUNE 24, 2007

Number of Bays	Number of Shops that reported 52 Weeks from 07/02/06 to 06/24/07	Average Sales for fiscal year end June 30, 2007 For shops that reported 52 Weeks
2 Bays	1	454,963
3 Bays	17	405,802
4 Bays	54	512,266
5 Bays	21	415,864
6 Bays	129	504,825
7 Bays	12	649,286
8 Bays	31	644,453
+8 Bays	11	935,353
Total Shops/Average Sales	276	532,355

Footnotes:

1. The above tables reflects gross sales as reported by 276 Precision Tune Auto Care centers located in the United States wahich reported their weekly sales figures to us for all 52 weeks ended June 24, 2007. These 276 centers in the survey represent 92.62% of the 298 Precision Tune Auto Care centers open and in operation in the United States on June 26, 2007.

2. The data is not audited.

3. Although we believe the data to be reliable, we have not independently verified its accuracy.

4. On your reasonable request, we will make available to you substantiation of the data used in preparing the tables shown above.

5. During the reporting period, our affiliate, PTAC Operating Centers, Inc., acquired one franchised center and continued to operate that center as a Precision Tune Auto Care Center. Data for this center is included in the above tables. In addition, data from some of the centers used to compile the above tables are owned and operated by our area developers under franchise agreements with us.

6. Due to rounding, the numbers may not add up.

7. We do not provide expense information because the data may vary significantly from one location to another. Examples of expenses that vary materially from location to location include salaries and owner's draw, rent, marketing, refunds and allowances, and interest expenses.

8. The tables shown above do not reflect expenses or debt service costs. If you finance the initial franchise fee, development and constructions costs, costs to purchase furniture, fixtures and equipment, or costs to acquire the Center, you will incur costs to pay back the money you borrow.

9. The Center may face competition from other auto repair centers, including dealerships, independents and other franchised chains.

10. You may not have comparable automotive experience to that of the existing franchisees and their employees reflected in the tables shown above. While we will provide certain assistance to you (see Item 11), you and your staff will be primarily responsible for the daily operations of your Center in accordance with the terms of your Franchise Agreement.

11. The quality and effectiveness of your managerial skills will affect, positively or negatively, the sales results of the Center. Decisions made with respect to location, implementation of marketing programs, personnel, cost controls and other factors may impact the results of your Center.

12. Factors including those bearing upon business cycles and performance of the national and world economy may affect the results of the Center.

WE RECOMMEND THAT YOU MAKE YOUR OWN INDEPENDENT INVESTIGATION TO DETERMINE WHETHER THE FRANCHISE MAY BE PROFITABLE, AND THAT YOU CONSULT WITH YOUR ATTORNEY AND OTHER ADVISORS PRIOR TO SIGNING THE FRANCHISE AGREEMENT.

PRIMROSE SCHOOLS FRANCHISING COMPANY

3660 Cedarcrest Rd.
Atworth, GA 30101
Tel: (800) 774-6767 (770) 529-4100
Fax: (770) 529-1551
E-Mail: kmusso@primroseschools.com
Web Site: www.primroseschools.com
Ms. Kim Musso, Dir. Franchise Recruitment

Educational child-care franchise, offering a traditional pre-school curriculum and programs while also providing quality childcare services. Site selection assistance, extensive training, operations manuals, building plans, marketing plans and on-going support.

BACKGROUND: IFA MEMBER

Established: 1982;	1st Franchised: 1989
Franchised Units:	200
Company-Owned Units:	1
Total Units:	201
Dist.:	US-201; CAN-0; O'seas-0
North America:	15 States, 0 Provinces
Density:	37 in GA, 10 in NC, 37 in TX
Projected New Units (12 Months):	15
Qualifications:	5, 5, 1, 4, 5, 5
Registered:	CA,DC,FL,IL,IN,MD,MI,MN,NY,OR,SD,VA

FINANCIAL/TERMS:

Cash Investment:	$350-500K
Total Investment:	$2.8-4.2MM
Minimum Net Worth:	$500K
Fees: Franchise -	$70K
Royalty - 7%;	Ad. - 1%
Earnings Claims Statement:	Yes
Term of Contract (Years):	11/10/10
Avg. # Of Employees:	25 FT, 5 PT
Passive Ownership:	Not Allowed
Encourage Conversions:	NA
Area Develop. Agreements:	0
Sub-Franchising Contracts:	No
Expand In Territory:	No
Space Needs:	8,500 SF; FS

SUPPORT & TRAINING:

Financial Assistance Provided:	Yes (D)
Site Selection Assistance:	Yes
Lease Negotiation Assistance:	Yes
Co-Operative Advertising:	No
Franchisee Assoc./Member:	Yes/Member
Size Of Corporate Staff:	35
On-Going Support:	A,C,D,E,f,G,h,I
Training:	1 Week Home Office;
	1 Week Existing School; 1 Week Franchisee's New School

SPECIFIC EXPANSION PLANS:

US:	Yes, SW, SE, TX, OH, CO
Canada:	No
Overseas:	No

19. FINANCIAL PERFORMANCE REPRESENTATIONS

PSFC does not furnish or authorize its salespersons to furnish to prospective franchisees any oral or written information concerning the actual or potential sales, costs, income or profits of a PRIMROSE franchise except as presented in this Item 19. Actual results vary from unit to unit and PSFC cannot estimate the results of any particular franchise.

SUMMARY OF REVENUE OF COMPANY AND FRANCHISED SCHOOLS DURING THE PERIOD JANUARY 1, 2007 THROUGH DECEMBER 31, 2007

This summary sets forth the average school revenue achieved by 17 136 to 144 capacity franchised PRIMROSE facilities ("Smaller Facilities"), and 125 145 to 222 capacity franchised PRIMROSE facilities ("Larger Facilities"), for the year ended December 31, 2007. Revenues are calculated based on gross receipts less any allowable credits or discounts and the data is based on revenue reported to PSFC by its franchisees. On December 31, 2007, there were 177 PRIMROSE facilities open and in operation for at least one month of the year. Of these 177, 17 Smaller Facilities and 160 Larger Facilities were open. However, the average revenue reported in this Item 19 is based solely on the 17 Smaller Facilities and 125 Larger Facilities that were opened and in operation for at least 24 months. Accordingly, the revenues of schools, opened after March 1, 2006, are not included. All of the PRIMROSE facilities opened and in operation are located in Alabama, Arizona, Colorado, Florida, Georgia,

Kansas, Minnesota, Missouri, Nebraska, North Carolina, Ohio, Tennessee, Texas and Virginia.

The average revenue for the year ending December 31, 2007, was $1,133,340 for the Smaller Facilities, and $1,471,017 for the Larger Facilities. The high revenue produced by a Smaller Facility was $1,417,291, and the low revenue for a Smaller Facility was $858,716. The high revenue for a Larger Facility was $2,225,234, and the low revenue for the Larger Facility was $557,768. This data has not been audited.

Average Revenues		High and Low Annual Revenue	
Franchised Smaller Facilities	$ 1,133,340	High, Smaller Facilities	$ 1,417,291
Franchised Larger Facilities	1,471,017	High, Larger Facilities	2,225,234
		Low, Smaller Facility	858,716
		Low, Larger Facility	557,768

RANGE OF ANNUAL REVENUE
SMALLER FACILITIES

Annual Revenue	Number of Schools Within Ranges	Percentage of Franchised PRIMROSE Facilities Within Ranges	Aggregate Percentage of Franchised PRIMROSE Facilities Equaling or Exceeding Revenue Ranges
More than $1,300,000	4	23.5%	23.5%
Between $1,000,000 and $1,299,999	7	41.2%	64.7%
Between $800,000 and $999,999	5	29.4%	94.1%
Less than $900,000	1	5.9%	100%

RANGE OF ANNUAL REVENUE
LARGER FACILITIES

Annual Revenue	Number of Schools Within Ranges	Percentage of Franchised PRIMROSE Facilities Within Ranges	Aggregate Percentage of Franchised PRIMROSE Facilities Equaling or Exceeding Revenue Ranges
More than $1,700,000	29	23.2%	23.2%
Between $1,400,000 and $1,699,999	47	37.6%	60.8%
Between $1,100,000 and $1,399,999	32	25.6%	86.4%
Less than $1,100,000	17	13.6%	100%

All PRIMROSE facilities included in this Item 19 are located in free-standing buildings.

Explanatory Notes to Summary:

1. You are responsible for developing your own business plan for your PRIMROSE facility, including capital budgets, financial statements, projections and other appropriate factors, and you are encouraged to consult with your own accounting, business and legal advisors

in doing so. The business plan should make necessary allowances for economic downturns, periods of inflation and unemployment, and other negative economic influences.

2. This Item 19 should not be considered to be the actual or probable revenues that you will experience. PSFC does not represent that you can expect to obtain the results provided in this Summary. Actual results vary from franchisee to franchisee, and PSFC cannot estimate the results of any particular franchisee. Significant variations in revenues and expenses exist among franchisees for a variety of reasons, such as the length of time the PRIMROSE facility has been open, location, the franchisee's prior business experience, the owner's or Principal's active involvement in the management of the facility, competition, and other factors.

3. Historical revenues may not correspond to future revenues due to a variety of factors. **AS WITH MOST BUSINESSES, THE INITIAL FINANCIAL PERFORMANCE OF YOUR PRIMROSE FACILITY IS LIKELY TO BE LESS FAVORABLE THAN THOSE REPRESENTED HEREIN.**

4. Substantiation for the data contained in Item 19 will be made available to you by PSFC upon reasonable request.

PROSHRED

PROSHRED
6790 Century Blvd., # 200
Toronto, ON LN5 2V8 Canada
Tel: (877) PROSHRED (416) 849-3490
Fax: (905) 812-9448
E-Mail: craig.aris@proshred.com
Web Site: www.proshred.com
Mr. Craig Aris, VP Development

PROSHRED invented mobile shredding. The Proshred onsite professional shredding system is the most secure method of destroying confidential documents and other proprietary materials. Government legislation passed to protect customers and the environment has made it imperative that all companies, big and small, as well as home-based employees and businesses, find convenient and effective ways to discard all types of documents and materials containing sensitive information. Proshred is a powerful, long-standing brand supported by an experienced management team.

BACKGROUND: IFA MEMBER

Established: 2002;	1st Franchised: 2002
Franchised Units:	18
Company-Owned Units:	0
Total Units:	18
Dist.:	US-18; CAN-0; O'seas-0
North America:	10 States, 0 Provinces
Density:	NR
Projected New Units (12 Months):	9
Qualifications:	5, 4, 1, 3, 1, 5

Registered:	CA,DC,FL,MD,MI

FINANCIAL/TERMS:

Cash Investment:	$250K
Total Investment:	$178.5K-499.5K
Minimum Net Worth:	$750K
Fees: Franchise -	$35K
Royalty - 6.5%;	Ad. - 1-3%
Earnings Claims Statement:	Yes
Term of Contract (Years):	10/5/5
Avg. # Of Employees:	5 FT, 2 PT
Passive Ownership:	Allowed
Encourage Conversions:	Yes
Area Develop. Agreements:	Yes
Sub-Franchising Contracts:	No
Expand In Territory:	Yes
Space Needs:	2,000 SF; SF,SC,RM, Industrial Commercial

SUPPORT & TRAINING:

Financial Assistance Provided:	Yes (I)
Site Selection Assistance:	Yes
Lease Negotiation Assistance:	Yes
Co-Operative Advertising:	Yes
Franchisee Assoc./Member:	Yes/Member
Size Of Corporate Staff:	11
On-Going Support:	B,C,D,E,F,G,H,I
Training:	10 Days Toronto, ON;
	10 Days Local

SPECIFIC EXPANSION PLANS:

US:	Yes, All United States
Canada:	No
Overseas:	No

Item 19
FINANCIAL PERFORMANCE REPRESENTATIONS

We have compiled the following information regarding actual sales

1. by service type per customer
2. generated from recycling of shredded paper and
3. generated by franchisees during the fiscal years ended March 31, 2007, and March 31, 2008.

Revenue per Customer by Service Type

	April 1, 2006 to March 31, 2007			April 1, 2007 to March 31, 2008 [4]		
Highest Franchisee	Scheduled Revenue per Customer per Month[1]	Un-Scheduled Revenue per Customer [2]	Price per Ton of Recycled Paper[3]	Scheduled Revenue per Customer per Month[1]	Un-Scheduled Revenue per Customer [2]	Price per Ton of Recycled Paper[3]
	$ 209	$ 378	$ 119	$ 185	$ 812	$ 162
System-wide Average	$ 133	$ 242	$ 70	$ 127	$ 277	$ 131
Lowest Franchisee	$ 49	$ 135	$ 43	$ 57	$ 126	$ 85

Notes:

(1) Scheduled revenue is the revenue associated with customers that procure shredding service on a regular schedule (i.e. once per week, once per month, once per quarter). Scheduled Revenue per Customer per Month is calculated by taking the revenue from scheduled customers and dividing by the number of customers with regularly scheduled service.

(2) Un-Scheduled revenue is the revenue associated with customers that procure shredding service on an ad hoc basis or to do annual purging of documents. Un-Scheduled Revenue per Customer is calculated by taking the revenue from unscheduled customers and dividing by the number of customers without regular service.

(3) Franchisees sell the shredded paper to recyclers. The Price per Ton of Recycled Paper is the price received from recyclers for the paper.

The above figures reflect the 9 franchised operations that were opened and operating for at least 12 months. The figures shown are the highest franchisee, the system wide average and the lowest franchisee. 56% of the franchisees exceeded the system wide average during the fiscal year ended March 31, 2008.

YOUR RESULTS ARE LIKELY TO DIFFER FROM THOSE CONTAINED IN THIS ITEM 19. WE DO NOT REPRESENT THAT YOU WILL ATTAIN COMPARABLE SALES OR INCUR COMPARABLE EXPENSES. Your business will be located in a different market where there may be little or no brand awareness. Your revenues may also be affected by factors that include the number of businesses within a market, the number of competitors within a market and state and local legislation regarding document destruction and recycling.

The figures above should not be considered as potential revenue figures that may be realized by you. We do not represent that you can expect to achieve these revenue figures. Actual results will vary from franchise to franchise and we cannot estimate the results of any particular franchise. You should not rely on these figures. You must accept the risk that your franchise will not perform as well.

These figures are based upon information submitted to us by our franchisees which we have not audited. On reasonable written request, we will provide you with written substantiation of the above sales figures.

Except for the information contained in this Item 19, we do not furnish or authorize our salespersons (including officers and directors) to furnish any oral, written or visual representation that states, expressly or by implication, a specific level or range of actual or potential sales, income or profits of a *Proshred* franchise.

RIGHT AT HOME

11949 Q St., # 100
Omaha, NE 68137
Tel: (877) 697-7537 (402) 697-7537
Fax: (402) 697-0289
E-Mail: dcarlson@rightathome.net
Web Site: www.rightathome.net
Ms. Sharon Thomsen, Franchise Development Coordinator

RIGHT AT HOME offers one of the most exciting opportunities in franchising today. RIGHT AT HOME offers in-home senior care and supplemental staffing for the healthcare industry. You double your opportunity with the same franchise system.

BACKGROUND: IFA MEMBER
Established: 1995; 1st Franchised: 2000
Franchised Units: 150
Company-Owned Units: 1
Total Units: 151
Dist.: US-151; CAN-0; O'seas-0
North America: 35 States, 0 Provinces
Density: NR
Projected New Units (12 Months): 50
Qualifications: 3, 4, 1, 1, 1, 5
Registered: CA,DC,FL,IL,IN,MD,MI,MN,NY,OR,SD,VA,WA,WI

FINANCIAL/TERMS:
Cash Investment: $50K-60K
Total Investment: $40K-70K
Minimum Net Worth: $100K
Fees: Franchise - $30K
Royalty - 5%; Ad. - 0%
Earnings Claims Statement: Yes
Term of Contract (Years): 10/5/5/5
Avg. # Of Employees: FT, 0 PT
Passive Ownership: Allowed, But Discouraged
Encourage Conversions: No
Area Develop. Agreements: No
Sub-Franchising Contracts: No
Expand In Territory: Yes
Space Needs: 700 SF; FS

SUPPORT & TRAINING:
Financial Assistance Provided: No
Site Selection Assistance: Yes
Lease Negotiation Assistance: No
Co-Operative Advertising: Yes
Franchisee Assoc./Member: No
Size Of Corporate Staff: 18
On-Going Support: C,D,G,H,I
Training: 2 Weeks Omaha, NE

SPECIFIC EXPANSION PLANS:
US: Yes, All United States except RI, ND, HI
Canada: No
Overseas: No

ITEM 19.   FINANCIAL PERFORMANCE REPRESENTATIONS

BACKGROUND

This Item 19 sets forth certain historical financial performance data as provided by our franchisees; and thus we have a reasonable basis and written substantiation for the representation set forth below.

Written substantiation of the data used in preparing this information and for the financial performance representation made in this Item 19 will be made available to you upon reasonable request. The representations made in this Item 19 are based upon the franchise system's outlets existing for the period of time indicated below and are not made up of a subset of those outlets.

IMPORTANTLY, THE SUCCESS OF YOUR FRANCHISE WILL DEPEND LARGELY UPON YOUR PERSONAL ABILITIES, YOUR USE OF THOSE ABILITIES AND YOUR MARKET. THE FINANCIAL RESULTS OF YOUR FRANCHISE WILL LIKELY DIFFER, PERHAPS MATERIALLY, FROM THE RESULTS SUMMARIZED IN THIS ITEM.

AVERAGE NET BILLINGS

The table presented below contains certain information related to Net Billings realized by our franchisees for the period beginning January 1, 2007 and ending December 31, 2007. For the purpose of this Item, "Net Billings" means the total of all revenues from the operation of the Franchised Business whether received in cash, in services in kind, from barter and/or exchange, on credit (whether or not payment is received therefore) or otherwise. Net Billings does not include the amount of all sales tax receipts or similar tax receipts which, by law, are chargeable to clients, if such taxes are separately stated when the client is charged and if such taxes are paid to the appropriate taxing authority. In addition, Net Billings does not include the amount of any documented refunds, chargebacks, credits and allowances given in good faith to clients by franchisee.

The figures presented below are based upon information reported to us by Right at Home franchisees whose offices have been open for at least 12-months for the period ending December 31, 2007, which is 78 Franchised Businesses. NOTE: Right at Home has not audited this information, nor have we independently verified this information. The information is for the period commencing January 1, 2007 through December 31, 2007.

The information has been extracted from actual franchise reports made to Right at Home as required by the Franchise Agreement. The information may be used to evaluate the experience of existing Right at Home offices, but the information may not be relied upon as a projection or forecast of what a new franchisee may experience.

In preparing financial projections for a prospective franchise operation, it is important to keep in mind that each franchisee's experience is unique and their results will most likely vary depending on a number of factors, including the franchisee's personal abilities, use of those abilities, the market in which they operate, the general economic conditions, competition, effectiveness of the franchisee Fri the management of the office, and the overall efficiency of their operation.

Net Billings Information For Franchisee Offices Open At Least One Year

Right at Home Franchises Time in Business	Total Offices	Average Net Billings	Median Net Billings	Highest Office Net Billings	Lowest Office Net Billings	Average Percent Increase over 2006
73 To 84 Months	8	$1,487,081.28	$1,286,415.59	$3,078,656.73	$659,217.50	18.7%
61 To 72 Months	9	$1,251,464.18	$1,152,145.70	$2,182,299.98	$241,883.81	13.4%
49 To 60 Months	16	$819,052.67	$800,762.91	$2,238,516.78	$197,909.22	28.5%
37 To 48 Months	16	$1,303,916.44	$1,274,921.11	$2,061,469.01	$182,180.73	24.1%
25 To 36 Months	14	$724,344.30	$586,766.96	$2,140,739.20	$126,920.16	73.9%
13 To 24 Months	15	$500,891.00	$385,855.52	$1,913,891.47	$70,232.92	*
All Offices Open One Year or More Ending 2007	78	$976,307.70	$898,673.22			27.3%

* Percent not included because the offices were open less than 12 months in 2006.

For the period ending December 31, 2007, there were 78 Right at Home franchisee offices that had been open more than 12 months. The average amount of Net Billings reported from those offices that had been open more than 12 months was $976,307.70. This represented an average of 27.3% growth in Net Billings from these offices over the year ending December 31, 2006.

For the 8 Right at Home offices open for 73 to 84 months for the period ending December 31, 2007, the average amount of Net Billings was $1,487,081.28 with a median amount of Net Billings being $1,286,415.59. The highest amount of Net Billings in this group of 8 offices was $3,078,656.73 and the lowest amount of Net Billings was $659,217.50. These figures represent an average of 18.7% growth in Net Billings from these 8 offices over the amount of their Net Billings in 2006.

For the 9 Right at Home offices open for 61 to 72 months for the period ending December 31, 2007, the average amount of Net Billings was $1,251,464.18 with a median amount of Net Billings being $1,152,145.70. The highest amount of Net Billings in this group of 9 offices was $2,182,299.98 and the lowest amount of Net Billings was $241,883.81. These figures represent an average of 13.4% growth in Net Billings from these 9 offices over the amount of their Net Billings in 2006.

For the 16 Right at Home offices open for 49 to 60 months for the period ending December 31, 2007, the average amount of Net Billings was $819,052.67 with a median amount of Net Billings being $800,762.91. The highest amount of Net Billings in this group of 16 offices was $2,238,516.78 and the lowest amount of Net Billings was $197,909.22. These figures represent an average of 28.5% growth in Net Billings from these 16 offices over the amount of their Net Billings in 2006.

For the 16 Right at Home offices open for 37 to 48 months for the period ending December 31, 2007, the average amount of Net Billings was $1,303,916.44 with a median amount of Net Billings being $1,274,921.11. The highest amount of Net Billings in this group of 16 offices was $2,061,469.01 and the lowest amount of Net Billings was $182,180.73. These figures represent an average of 24.1% growth in Net Billings from these 16 offices over the amount of their Net Billings in 2006.

For the 14 Right at Home offices open from 25 to 36 months for the period ending December 31, 2007, the average amount of Net Billings was $724,344.30 with a median amount of Net Billings being $586,766.96. The highest amount of Net Billings in this group of 14 offices was $2,140,739.20 and the lowest amount of Net Billings was $126,920.16. These figures represent an average of 73.9% growth in Net Billings from these 14 offices over the amount of their Net Billings in 2006.

For the 15 Right at Home offices open from 13 to 24 months for the period ending December 31, 2007, the average amount of Net Billings was $500,891.00 with a median amount of Net Billings being $385,855.52. The highest amount of Net Billings in this group of 15 offices was $1,913,891.47 and the lowest amount of Net Billings was $70,232.92. These figures represent an average of 646.8% growth in Net Billings from these 15 offices over the amount of their Net Billings in 2006.

CAUTION

There is no assurance that your Franchised Business will do as well as those offices referenced in the above table. If you rely upon those figures, you do so at your own risk of not doing as well. Actual results vary from business to business, and we cannot reasonably estimate the result of a particular business operation. Gross revenues and Net Billings will vary. In particular, the gross revenues and Net Billings of your Franchised Business will be directly affected by many factors, such as: (a) geographic location; (b) competition from other similar businesses in your area; (c) sales and marketing effectiveness based on market saturation; (d) your product and service pricing; (e) vendor prices on materials, supplies and inventory; (f) labor costs; (g) ability to generate clients; (h) client loyalty; and (i) employment conditions in the market. Any such factor may differ materially from those that may exist for a franchise offered to you.

Importantly, you should not consider the Net Billings presented in the above table to be the actual potential Net Billings that you will realize. We do not represent that you can or will attain those or similar revenues or margins, or any particular level of Net Billings. We do not represent that you will generate income, which exceeds the initial payment for, or investment in, your franchise.

Based on all of the matters mentioned in this Item 19, we recommend that you make your own independent investigation to determine whether or not the franchise may be profitable to You and worth the risk. You should use this information only as a reference in conducting your analysis and in preparing your own projected income statements and cash flow statements. We suggest strongly that you consult your financial advisor or personal accountant concerning financial projections and federal, state and local income taxes and any other applicable taxes that you may incur in owning and operating a franchised business.

THE SUCCESS OF YOUR FRANCHISE WILL DEPEND LARGELY UPON YOUR INDIVID-UAL ABILITIES, YOUR USE OF THOSE ABILITIES, AND YOUR MARKET. THE FINANCIAL RESULTS OF YOUR FRANCHISE OPERATIONS ARE LIKELY TO DIFFER, PERHAPS MATERI-ALLY, FROM THE RESULTS SUMMARIZED IN THIS ITEM 19.

Disclaimer Regarding Claims Made by Agents, et. al.

We specifically instruct our sales personnel, franchise brokers, agents, employees and officers that they may not make any claims or statements as to the earnings, sales, profits, prospects, or chances of success of a Right at Home franchised business other than as set forth in this Item 19, They are not authorized to represent or estimate dollar figures as to a franchisee's operation other than as shown above, and if you decide to proceed to own a franchise you will be required to acknowledge in writing that you have not relied on any such unauthorized representation or estimate in purchasing your franchise.

Sir Speedy
Printing **and** Marketing Services

SIR SPEEDY

26722 Plaza Dr.
Mission Viejo, CA 92691-6390
Tel: (800) 854-3321 (949) 348-5000
Fax: (949) 348-5010
E-Mail: success@sirspeedy.com
Web Site: www.sirspeedy.com
Mr. Robert Miller, Director Franchise Development

We are the world's largest franchised network of printing and marketing service providers. We target the communication needs of small- and medium-sized businesses by partnering with them to help them achieve their business growth objectives. Whether acquiring, retaining, or reactivating customers, or maintaining brand integrity and increasing ROI, Sir Speedy can assist them with a full range of print communications and marketing support.

Density:	50 in CA, 46 in FL, 21 in IL
Projected New Units (12 Months):	20
Qualifications:	5, 4, 1, 3, 3, 5
Registered:	CA,FL,IL,IN,MD,MI,MN,ND,NY,RI,SD,VA,WA,WI

FINANCIAL/TERMS:

Cash Investment:	$100-175K
Total Investment:	$275-300K
Minimum Net Worth:	$300K
Fees: Franchise -	$25K
Royalty - 4-6%;	Ad. - 1-2%
Earnings Claims Statement:	Yes
Term of Contract (Years):	20/10
Avg. # Of Employees:	5+ FT, 0 PT
Passive Ownership:	Allowed, But Discouraged
Encourage Conversions:	Yes
Area Develop. Agreements:	No
Sub-Franchising Contracts:	No
Expand In Territory:	Yes
Space Needs:	1,500 to 2,500 SF; FS,SC, Business Park

BACKGROUND: IFA MEMBER

Established: 1968;	1st Franchised: 1968
Franchised Units:	463
Company-Owned Units:	0
Total Units:	463
Dist.:	US-428; CAN-4; O'seas-31
North America:	42 States, 2 Provinces

SUPPORT & TRAINING:

Financial Assistance Provided:	Yes (D)
Site Selection Assistance:	Yes
Lease Negotiation Assistance:	Yes
Co-Operative Advertising:	No
Franchisee Assoc./Member:	No
Size Of Corporate Staff:	62

On-Going Support:	C,D,E,F,G,H,I	US:	Yes, All United States
Training:	6 Weeks Franchisee's Site;	Canada:	Yes, ON
	2 Weeks Mission Viejo, CA	Overseas:	Yes, Most Countries
SPECIFIC EXPANSION PLANS:			

ITEM 19
FINANCIAL PERFORMANCE REPRESENTATIONS

SIR SPEEDY MAKES NO REPRESENTATIONS AS TO ACTUAL, AVERAGE, PROJECTED, OR FORECASTED PROFITS, EARNINGS, OR SALES YOU MAY EXPECT FROM THE OPERATIONS OF A SIR SPEEDY CENTER.

United States Sir Speedy Centers in business over 1 year averaged $887,065 in gross sales for the 12-month period ended December 31, 2007. This average is based on 341 reporting franchises.*

The 2007 figures reveal that 27% or 92 of the 341 reporting Centers actually attained or surpassed $887,065; 23% or 79 Centers exceeded $950,000; 21% or 72 Centers exceeded $1,000,000; 10% or 34 Centers exceeded $1,500,000; and 5% or 17 Centers exceeded $2,000,000, and 9 Centers exceeded $3,000,000**

Of the 341 Centers in this report, 2 had been opened and operating for 1 to 5 years; 19 Centers had been opened and operating for 6 to 10 years; and 318 Centers had been opened and operating for over 10 years.**

The sales figures, although unaudited, are based upon the actual reported sales volumes of Franchisees. The earnings claim figure(s) does (do) not reflect the costs of sales or operating expenses that must be deducted from the gross revenues or gross sales figures to obtain your net income or profit. The best source of cost and expense data may be from franchisees and former franchisees, some of whom may be listed in Item 20.

Sir Speedy offers substantially the same services to each of its Franchisees. The type and extent of services offered to the public by each individual Franchisee may vary somewhat with each Franchisee. The sales volume attainable by a Franchisee is largely dependent on the type and quality of service offered to the public as well as individual sales and marketing efforts.

*   Reported as of February 20, 2008, the average in this report represents approximately 70% of the domestic Sir Speedy Centers, in business for more than 1 year as of December 31, 2007. Those Centers not included were either in business less than 1 year, non-domestic Centers, Copies Now Centers, or Sir Speedy Centers that did not report the total years' information as of February 20, 2008.

**   Specific locations available upon reasonable request.

THESE SALES ARE AVERAGES OF SPECIFIC FRANCHISES AND SHOULD NOT BE CONSIDERED AS THE ACTUAL OR POTENTIAL SALES THAT YOU WILL ACHIEVE. SIR SPEEDY DOES NOT REPRESENT THAT YOU CAN EXPECT TO ATTAIN THESE SALES. SUBSTANTIATION OF THE ABOVE AVERAGES IS AVAILABLE UPON REQUEST TO PROSPECTIVE FRANCHISEES.

Assumptions That May Be Used in Developing Projections
(Percentages given for cost of sales and for salaries and wages are recommended ranges)

Cost of Sales - Consumable raw materials and supplies for the production of digitally printed material (where applicable), copying, preparation, large format printing, mailing services and bindery, the cost of goods purchased for resale such as business cards, offset printing and rubber stamps. Cost of sales optimally should range from **28% to 32%** for efficiency.

Accounting and Legal - Expenses required for basic monthly bookkeeping and financial statement preparation. Fees may increase as sales volumes increase.

Selling and Advertising - 1% of gross sales for network Advertising Fee for the first year of operation and **2%** of gross sales after first year, plus costs associated with traditional yellow page advertisement, online yellow page advertisement, search engine marketing, direct mail and a dedicated full-time salesperson each year.

Automobile - Based upon estimated business miles, expensed according to the appropriate IRS regulation.

Depreciation - Original equipment cost depreciated over a 3-7 year period using the straight-line method with additional equipment added as necessary to meet sales demands.

Insurance - Average cost of coverage under Sir Speedy's group business liability offered to all Franchisees is approximately $1,000 to $1,500 per year.

Office Supplies - Cost of miscellaneous supplies used in operating the business.

Rent - Approximate monthly rent of a new Center ranges from $1,200 to $4,500 per month depending on the location of the Center. Some areas may be higher.

Repairs and Maintenance - Costs associated with operating presses and cameras at various sales volumes, approximately **1%** (Offset Equipment Upgrade Option only). Monthly costs of copier maintenance agreements.

Continuing Franchise Fees - 4% of gross sales for the first year of operation and **6%** of gross sales after the first year. (See <u>Exhibit "B"</u> of the Franchise Agreement for Continuing Franchise Fee rebates).

Salaries and Wages - Salary figures should reflect the staffing requirements for counter sales, and a production and/or binding person, and optimally should range from **20% to 25%** of sales for efficiency, including employer's share of FICA, FUTA, and SUTA taxes. Owner's compensation is not included.

Taxes - Personal Property - Varies depending on individual state, county and city laws.

Telephone - Expenses associated with having two business lines, an internet connection, plus increases related to levels of sales activity.

Utilities - Expenses associated with operating the various equipment, etc.

SPHERION

925 North Point Pkwy., # 100
Alpharetta, GA 30005
Tel: (800) 903-0082 (678) 867-3702
Fax: (678) 867-3190
E-Mail: robertamarcantonio@spherion.com
Web Site: www.spherion.com
Ms. Roberta Marcantonio, VP Market Expansion

SPHERION franchise opportunities provide individuals a chance to join an exciting and rewarding industry: temporary staffing. We placed millions of workers in flexible and full-time jobs during our nearly 60 years in business. Continuous innovation and decades of growth have helped SPHERION become an industry leader. Entrepreneur Magazine ranked SPHERION Best Staffing Service for five straight years. Our franchisees contribute their talent, commitment and passion to building our brand.

BACKGROUND:	IFA MEMBER
Established: 1946;	1st Franchised: 1956
Franchised Units:	<u>155</u>
Company-Owned Units:	523
Total Units:	678
Dist.:	US-646; CAN-32; O'seas-0
North America:	46 States, 8 Provinces
Density:	29 in CA, 29 in FL, 27 in OH
Projected New Units (12 Months):	10
Qualifications:	5, 4, 1, 3, 4, 4
Registered:	CA,DC,FL,HI,IL,IN,MD,MI,MN,ND,NY,OR,RI,SD, VA,WA,WI

FINANCIAL/TERMS:		SUPPORT & TRAINING:	
Cash Investment:	$100-170K	Financial Assistance Provided:	No
Total Investment:	$98-164K	Site Selection Assistance:	Yes
Minimum Net Worth:	$100K	Lease Negotiation Assistance:	Yes
Fees: Franchise -	$25K	Co-Operative Advertising:	Yes
Royalty - 3-6%/25%;	Ad. - 0.25%	Franchisee Assoc./Member:	No
Earnings Claims Statement:	Yes	Size Of Corporate Staff:	525
Term of Contract (Years):	10/5	On-Going Support:	A,B,C,D,E,G,H,I
Avg. # Of Employees:	3 FT, 0 PT	Training:	Addl. Self-Paced Instruction;
Passive Ownership:	Not Allowed		Over 112 Hours In-Office Instruction
Encourage Conversions:	Yes		
Area Develop. Agreements:	No	SPECIFIC EXPANSION PLANS:	
Sub-Franchising Contracts:	No	US:	Yes, Targeted Cities in US.
Expand In Territory:	Yes	Canada:	No
Space Needs:	1,500 SF; SF,RM, Office Bldg.	Overseas:	No

ITEM 19
FINANCIAL PERFORMANCE REPRESENTATIONS

Spherion believes that it will be helpful for a prospective franchisee to know the average Gross Profit percentage, the average per Franchise Agreement annual Sales, and the average per franchise agreement annual Gross Profit of its franchisees for FY 2007. "Gross Profit" and "Sales" have the meanings given them in the Franchise Agreement.

The average Gross Profit percentage of our franchisees for FY 2007 was 20.6%. The average annual Sales per Franchise Agreement of our franchisees for FY 2007 were $4,341,608. And, the average annual Gross Profit per Franchise Agreement of our franchisees for FY 2007 was $786,160.

The information for the average Gross Profit percentage, and annual Gross Profit and Sales is only for our franchisees which were in operation for all of FY2007. It does not include information on 2 franchised offices transitioned to us during the course of FY2007 which were operated for the balance of FY2007 by our Franchise Division. Those 2 offices performed slightly below the average numbers stated and would have affected the averages as follows: the average Gross Profit would have been 20.4%, the average Sales $4,226,526, and the average Gross Profit $764,243. The information for Sales and Gross Profit is that for franchisees on a per Franchise Agreement basis. That is, if a franchisee has more that one Franchise Agreement with us, then the numbers achieved under each Franchise Agreement are considered separately. If a franchisee has more than one office under the same Franchise Agreement, then these offices are aggregated for the purposes of determining the average number for agreements. One tenured franchisee has been divided into three separate markets and been included in the average Sales and Gross Profit numbers as multiple markets are under one agreement. Multiple markets under one agreement is not currently permitted, so we believe breaking out the information as to that tenured franchisee provides a more accurate picture for future agreements.

You should note that, on balance, this information is that of mature franchisees, as we have only had eight franchisees who started up a new office under a new Franchise Agreement in Fiscal Years 2005-2007. Other new franchisees in that time period bought existing offices, either from us or from a franchisee, as opposed to starting a new office. The information is for all of our franchised operations for FY 2007 (other than Today's franchised offices), including Spherion branded franchised offices operating under the Norrell agreement. The information does not include the area based program franchises (refer back to Item 1), which operate under a fundamentally different agreement.

In FY 2007, twenty-one of our fifty franchises that were in operation for all of FY 2007 attained or surpassed the average Gross Profit percentage stated above, nineteen attained or surpassed the average annual Sales stated above and twenty-one attained or surpassed the average annual Gross Profit stated above.

Your results will likely differ from the results of those franchisees whose results are included in the information presented above, depending on your efforts and those of your staff, your particular market size and makeup, your competition, general economic conditions locally, regionally, nationally and internationally, the business mix you achieve (temporary staffing vs. permanent placement, and clerical vs. light industrial, and the amount of professional staffing you do, if you are offered the right to do professional staffing), and other factors.

The financial performance representations above do not reflect the costs of sales, operating expenses, or other costs or expenses that must be deducted from the gross revenues or gross sales figures to obtain your net income or profit. As stated below, you should conduct an independent investigation of the costs and expenses you will incur in operating your (franchised business). Franchisees or former franchisees listed in the disclosure document may be one source of information. To help you analyze what your expenses might be on a monthly basis, we have set forth below what we believe to be your normal monthly expense items.

Salaries and Wages
Commission/bonus accrual
Employee Benefits (including payroll taxes and health, life and disability insurance)
Franchise Data Processing Allocation (MISTEF fee-paragraph 8 of the Franchise Agreement)
Insurance (see, for example, the required insurances in paragraph 7(q) of the Franchise Agreement)
National Advertising
Local Advertising
Classified and yellow page advertising
Meetings/seminars/courses/conventions
Office supplies
Equipment/software repair/maintenance
Bank/credit card fees
Rent (premises lease)
Rent (equipment)
Repairs and maintenance
Depreciation and amortization expense
Utilities
Interest Expense (includes interest on AR over 60 days charged by Spherion)
Professional fees
Telecommunications
Automobile & parking
Other Travel
Customer relations/development
Bad debt expense
Taxes & franchises
Miscellaneous

This expense listing may not be a complete listing for you, and we do not make any representations to you as to what the actual expenses in each category will be. The answers to those questions will depend on your market and how you set up your business. You should consult with your financial advisor, as well as discuss the list and the expenses involved with our other franchisees, and former franchisees, which are listed in an exhibit to this disclosure document.

Substantiation of the data used in the preparation of this Item 19 will be made available to you upon reasonable request.

SportClips HAIRCUTS

SPORT CLIPS

110 Briarwood
Georgetown, TX 78628
Tel: (800) 872-4247 +240 (512) 868-4601
Fax: (512) 868-4699
E-Mail: beth@sportclips.com
Web Site: www.sportclips.com
Ms. Beth Boecker, Director of Franchise Recruitment

Sports-themed haircutting salons, appealing primarily to men and boys. Unique design, proprietary haircutting system and complete support at the unit level. Retail sale of Paul Mitchell & American Crew hair care products, sports apparel and memorabilia.

BACKGROUND: IFA MEMBER

Established: 1993;	1st Franchised: 1995
Franchised Units:	558
Company-Owned Units:	14
Total Units:	572
Dist.:	US-572; CAN-0; O'seas-0
North America:	28 States, 0 Provinces
Density:	42 in FL, 34 in IL, 128 in TX
Projected New Units (12 Months):	150
Qualifications:	4, 5, 1, 1, 3, 5
Registered:	CA,FL,IL,IN,MD,MI,OR,SD,WA,WI

FINANCIAL/TERMS:

Cash Investment:	$100K
Total Investment:	$150-200K
Minimum Net Worth:	$300K
Fees: Franchise -	$49.5K for 3pk
Royalty - $300;	Ad. - $250/Wk.
Earnings Claims Statement:	Yes
Term of Contract (Years):	5/5
Avg. # Of Employees:	8 FT, 4 PT
Passive Ownership:	Allowed
Encourage Conversions:	No
Area Develop. Agreements:	Yes
Sub-Franchising Contracts:	No
Expand In Territory:	Yes
Space Needs:	1,200 SF; SC

SUPPORT & TRAINING:

Financial Assistance Provided:	Yes (D)
Site Selection Assistance:	Yes
Lease Negotiation Assistance:	Yes
Co-Operative Advertising:	Yes
Franchisee Assoc./Member:	No
Size Of Corporate Staff:	60
On-Going Support:	C,D,E,F,G,H,I
Training:	1 Week Locally;
5 Days Georgetown, TX for Franchisee; 1 Week Locally for Manager	

SPECIFIC EXPANSION PLANS:

US:	Yes, All United States
Canada:	No
Overseas:	No

ITEM 19
FINANCIAL PERFORMANCE REPRESENTATIONS

At the end of calendar year 2007, there were 501 franchised Sport Clips stores. The two Statements of Gross Sales below do not include four stores in Rochester, New York, which are not typical Sport Clips stores and operate under a special limited services license agreement that is not offered to new franchisees. Although we do not have complete sales data for the stores in Rochester, New York, we know that their gross sales are, on average, less than other stores in the System.

Except for the stores in Rochester, New York, all stores included in the Statements of Gross Sales did not receive any services that were not generally available to other Sport Clips stores, and each store offered similar products and services as would generally be offered by a typical Sport Clips store.

The gross sales figures included in the first Statement of Gross Sales below are based upon all 201 Sport Clips franchise stores and Company-owned stores that were in continual operation for the entire calendar years of 2005, 2006 and 2007. The gross sales figures are taken directly from gross sales reports made by the stores to the Company.

STATEMENT OF GROSS SALES
YEAR 2007 GROSS SALES AS REPORTED TO THE COMPANY
(201 Stores In Continual Operation During 2005, 2006 and 2007)

Gross Sales	Number of Stores	Percentage of Stores/Cumulative % of stores at each level or higher
Over $450,000	14	7%/7%
$400,001-$450,000	14	7%/14%
$350,001-$400,000	34	17%/31%
$300,001-$350,00	39	19%/50%
$250,001-$300,000	47	23%/73%
$200,001-$250,000	38	19%/92%
$150,001-$200,000	12	6%/98%
Less than $150,000	3	1+%/100%
Total	**201**	**100%**

The gross sales figures included in the second Statement of Gross Sales below are based upon all 290 Sport Clips franchise stores and Company-owned stores that were in continual operation for the entire calendar years of 2006 and 2007. The gross sales figures are taken directly from gross sales reports made by the stores to the Company.

STATEMENT OF GROSS SALES YEAR 2007 GROSS SALES AS REPORTED TO THE COMPANY (290 Stores in Continual Operation During 2006 and 2007)		
Gross Sales	Number of Stores	Percentage of Stores/ Cumulative % of stores at each level or higher
Over $450,000	17	6%/6%
$400,001-$450,000	17	6%/12%
$350,001-$400,000	39	14%/26%
$300,001-$350,000	50	17%/43%
$250,001-$300,000	73	25%/68%
$200,001-$250,000	64	22%/90%
$150,001-$200,000	24	8%/98%
Less **than $150,000**	6	1+%/100%
Total	290	100%

The earnings claims figures above do not reflect the costs of sales, operating expenses, or other costs or expenses that must be deducted from gross revenue or gross sales figures to obtain your net income or profit. You should conduct an independent investigation of the costs and expenses you will incur in operating your Sport Clips franchise. Franchisees or former franchisees, listed in

the Disclosure Document, may be one source of this information.

Expense Reports for Company-Owned Stores During 2007

The Expense Report below shows the average expenses at each store's sales level and those expenses as a percentage of total revenue in each column. It is based on 11 stores owned and operated by the Company in Austin, Texas during the year 2007. The managers of the Company-owned stores included in the Expense Report did not receive any services that were not generally available to other Sport Clips stores. Each store offered similar products and services as would generally be offered by a typical Sport Clips store, except for limited tests of procedures, products and/or services that may or may not be eventually incorporated into the system, depending on the success of the tests.

We owned and operated 11 stores in Austin for the entire year 2007. One Company- owned store that we closed in October 2007 is not included in the data below. We also acquired one store in Rogers, Arkansas (that opened in September 2003) when the franchisee (Clete Brewer) became President of Sport Clips, Inc. on February 1, 2006. We have not included annualized results for the Rogers, Arkansas store in the data below because it was being managed remotely and is not typical of store operations. This store was sold to a new franchisee in March 2008.

	Sales $250,000 to $300,000	Sales $300,001 to $350,000	Sales > $350,001	Average of all stores
Number of Stores	6	2	3	11
Gross Sales	$278,668	$328,719	$475,266	$341,386
	100%	100%	100%	100%
Variable Costs (Note 1)	$22,654	$26,886	$36,546	$27,212
	8%	8%	8%	8%
Payroll (Note 2)	$146,742	$165,603	$237,250	$174,855
	53%	50%	50%	51%
Occupancy (Note 3)	$56,456	$57,841	$58,915	$57,379
	20%	18%	12%	17%
Advertising (Note 4)	$15,201	$14,540	$15,223	$15,087
	5%	4%	3%	4%
Miscellaneous (Note 5)	$2,718	$2,405	$2,687	$2,653
	1%	1%	1%	1%
Operating Profit (Note 6)	$34,897	$61,444	$124,644	$64,200
	13%	19%	26%	19%

Note 1. Variable Costs include operating supplies, cost of goods sold, bank service charges, credit card discounts, and classified ads to recruit Stylists.

Note 2. Payroll includes direct payroll, including payroll for an on-site full time manager, payroll taxes and fringe benefits except for 401K and medical insurance costs.

Note 3. Occupancy includes rent, pass-through expenses from the landlord, utilities, phone charges, repairs and maintenance.

Note 4. Advertising includes the weekly payments to the Ad Fund plus other advertising and marketing expenses for the store.

Note 5. Miscellaneous expense includes magazine subscriptions, store insurance and overages and/or shortages from the cash drawer.

Note 6. Operating Profit does not include an amount paid for royalties or weekly training fees. The numbers in the Expense Report are unaudited, but we believe that these numbers are substantially correct.

A NEW FRANCHISEE'S INDIVIDUAL FINANCIAL RESULTS ARE LIKELY TO DIFFER FROM THE RESULTS STATED IN THE STATEMENTS OF GROSS SALES AND THE EXPENSE REPORT.

THESE SALES ARE AVERAGES OF SPECIFIC STORES OWNED AND OPERATED BY THE COMPANY, AND BY SPECIFIC FRANCHISEES, AND SHOULD NOT BE CONSIDERED AS THE ACTUAL OR POTENTIAL SALES OR EXPENSES THAT WILL BE REALIZED BY A FRANCHISEE. THE COMPANY DOES NOT REPRESENT THAT ANY FRANCHISEE CAN EXPECT TO ATTAIN THESE SALES, PROFITS, OR EARNINGS.

Substantiation of the information contained in this Item is made available to prospective franchisees at the Company's office at 110 Briarwood, Georgetown, Texas 78628.

SPRING-GREEN.
America's *Neighborhood* Lawn Care Team.

SPRING-GREEN LAWN CARE
11909 Spaulding School Dr.
Plainfield, IL 60544-9501
Tel: (800) 777-8608 (815) 436-8777
Fax: (815) 436-9056
E-Mail: franinfo@spring-green.com
Web Site: www.springgreenfranchise.com
Mr. Mark Potocki, Franchise Development Manager

SPRING-GREEN delivers lawn and tree care services nationwide. Our service is centered on the beautification of middle class and affluent neighborhoods and communities. Our customers include both residential and commercial establishments. SPRING-GREEN services include lawn, tree and shrub fertilization as well as disease and perimeter pest control. SPRING-GREEN has been beautifying the environment for more than 30 years as your national lawn care team.

BACKGROUND: IFA MEMBER

Established: 1977;	1st Franchised: 1977
Franchised Units:	95
Company-Owned Units:	21
Total Units:	116
Dist.:	US-116; CAN-0; O'seas-0
North America:	25 States, 0 Provinces
Density:	29 in IL, 10 in NC, 15 in WI
Projected New Units (12 Months):	15
Qualifications:	4, 3, 1, 3, 2, 4
Registered:	IL,IN,MD,MI,MN,OR,SD,VA,WA,WI

FINANCIAL/TERMS:

Cash Investment:	$30K
Total Investment:	$165K
Minimum Net Worth:	$125K
Fees: Franchise -	$40K
Royalty - 10-8%;	Ad. - 2%
Earnings Claims Statement:	Yes
Term of Contract (Years):	10/10
Avg. # Of Employees:	5 FT, PT
Passive Ownership:	Not Allowed
Encourage Conversions:	Yes
Area Develop. Agreements:	No
Sub-Franchising Contracts:	No
Expand In Territory:	No
Space Needs:	HB

SUPPORT & TRAINING:

Financial Assistance Provided:	Yes (I)
Site Selection Assistance:	NA
Lease Negotiation Assistance:	NA
Co-Operative Advertising:	Yes
Franchisee Assoc./Member:	Yes/Member
Size Of Corporate Staff:	22
On-Going Support:	A,B,C,D,E,F,G,h,i
Training:	Min. 2 Days Each 3 Annual On-Site Visits; 1 Week Training at Corp. HQ; Ongoing On-Line Pre-Training

SPECIFIC EXPANSION PLANS:

US:	Yes, All Exc. AK,AZ,CA,CT,NY,NV,ND,HI,MA,ME,MS,NM, RI,VT
Canada:	No
Overseas:	No

Item 19
FINANCIAL PERFORMANCE REPRESENTATIONS

We use financial information submitted by our franchisees to compile the information contained in these Tables. The financial information submitted by our franchisees is also used for calculating the Royalty described in Item 6. We did not independently verify the accuracy of the information. Franchised Businesses did not typically submit copies of all of the invoices for each customer or list each customer in their period reports to us. The information contained in these Tables is based upon the financial information and other data entered by each Franchised Business into the software system described in Item 11.

EXCEPT FOR INFORMATION CONTAINED IN THIS ITEM 19, WE DO NOT AUTHORIZE OUR SALESPERSONS TO FURNISH ANY ORAL OR WRITTEN INFORMATION CONCERNING THE ACTUAL OR POTENTIAL SALES, COSTS, INCOME, OR PROFITS OF A FRANCHISE. ACTUAL RESULTS VARY FROM FRANCHISE TO FRANCHISE, AND WE CANNOT AND DO NOT ESTIMATE THE RESULTS WHICH ANY PARTICULAR FRANCHISE MAY EXPECT TO ACHIEVE. YOU ARE ENCOURAGED TO OBTAIN ADDITIONAL FINANCIAL AND OPERATING INFORMATION FROM FRANCHISEES AND OTHER INDUSTRY SOURCES. NEW FRANCHISEES' FINANCIAL RESULTS ARE LIKELY TO DIFFER FROM THE FINANCIAL INFORMATION CONTAINED IN THIS ITEM 19.

Upon reasonable request, we will provide you with substantiation of the data used to prepare the tables.

Table A
Statement of the Average of Average Revenue Per Customer for Calendar year 2007 for 64 Franchised Businesses in Operation for Two Full Calendar Years or More as of December 31, 2007, Categorized by Quartiles in Descending Order

Category	Average	Number of Franchised Businesses in the Quartile That Attained or Surpassed the Average
Top Quartile of Franchisees[2]	$570	6 of 16
Second Quartile of Franchisees[2]	$369	7 of 16
Third Quartile of Franchisees[2]	$293	8 of 16
Lowest Quartile of Franchisees[2]	$237	8 of 16

Notes:

(1)   We compiled information contained in Table A from information for 64 Franchised Businesses that were in business for two full calendar years or more as of December 31, 2007. To compute the average per customer we totaled all invoices for all services for each Franchised Business for 2007 calendar year that was in business for two full calendar years or more for calendar year ended December 31, 2007 and divided by the number of customers invoiced during the 2007 calendar year for a spring lawn care service application. Each Franchised Business reports its revenue on an aggregate basis for all franchise territories covered by the Franchised Business. Thus, in this Item 19 we do not include financial information for franchise territories.

(2)   The lowest revenue per customer and the highest average revenue per customer in each quartile is as follows: Top Quartile - $429 and $965; Second Quartile - $339 and $420; Third Quartile - $264 and $319; and Lowest Quartile - $200 and $261.

Table B
Statement of the 2007 Average Gross Sales Results for 64 Franchised Businesses in Operation for Two Full Calendar Years or More as of December 31, 2007, Categorized by Quartiles in Descending Order

Category	Average	Number of Franchised Businesses in the Quartile That Attained or Surpassed the Average
Top Quartile of Franchisees[2]	$1,148,013	4 of 16
Second Quartile of Franchisees[2]	$345,374	7 of 16
Third Quartile of Franchisees[2]	$159,488	7 of 16
Lowest Quartile of Franchisees[2]	$85,639	7 of 16
All Quartiles	$434,629	18 of 64

Notes:

(1)   We compiled information contained in Table B from information for 64 Franchised Businesses that were in business for two full calendar years or more as of December 31, 2007. Each Franchised Business reports its revenue on an aggregate basis for all franchise territories covered by the Franchised Business. Thus, in this Item 19 we do not include financial information for franchise territories. A Franchisee may own and operate multiple franchises as one Franchised Business each under a separate franchise agreement with us. Each Franchised Business reports its revenue on an aggregate basis for all franchise territories covered by the Franchised Business. Thus, in this Item 19 we do not include separate financial information for each individual franchise territory. Due to various demographic factors such as population changes, differences in climate, and the need for the services in the territory, the Gross Sales among territories will vary. Further, the number of franchised territories within a Franchised Business does not necessarily correlate with the Gross Sales of that Franchised Business.

(2)   To compute Average Gross Sales per Franchised Business, we totaled the Gross Sales for each Quartile and divided by the number of Franchised Businesses in the Quartile.

(3)   The top quartile includes the 4 Franchised Businesses operated by our affiliate.

(4)   The lowest Gross Sales of a Franchised Business and the highest Gross Sales of a Franchised Business in each quartile is as follows: Top Quartile - $537,182 and $3,894,358; Second Quartile - $245,076 and $508,273; Third Quartile - $115,854 and $243,543; and Lowest Quartile - $32,830 and $114,185.

(5)   This information is based upon the Gross Sales of Franchised Businesses for each Franchised Business that was in business for two full calendar years or more for the calendar year ended December 31, 2007. Franchisees pay us royalty based on Gross Sales. Franchised Businesses typically use the accrual method of accounting.

Table C
Statement of 2007 Gross Profit Margin Results as a Percentage of Gross Sales For 38 Franchised Businesses in Operation One Full Year or More As of December 31, 2007

Line Item	Average %	Number of Franchised Businesses That Attained or Surpassed the Average
Material Costs (See Note3)	17.49%	22 of 38 had lower than average Material Costs
Direct Labor Costs (See Note 4)	12.36%	14 of 38 had lower than average Direct Labor Costs
Cost of Sales (See Note 5)	29.85%	17 of 38 had lower than average Cost of Sales
Gross Profit Margin (See Note 6)	70.15%	18 of 38 had higher than average Gross Profit Margin

Notes:

(1)   As of December 31, 2007, 116 franchise territories were in operation, 109 of

351

which had been in operation for at least the full calendar year. These 109 franchise territories were owned by 70 Franchised Businesses (including 4 Franchised Businesses operated by Superior Lawns, Incorporated, our affiliate) which for reporting purposes, consolidated their financial information for all franchise territories operated by such Franchised Business. As of December 31, 2007, Superior Lawns, Incorporated operated 4 Franchised Businesses, and there were 21 franchise territories covered by those 4 Franchised Businesses. Certain franchisees also own multiple franchise territories, but aggregate the reporting of their financial information as one Franchised Business.

(2)   38 Franchised Businesses included in Table C operated 64 of the 109 franchise territories that were operational during the 2007 calendar year. Data concerning the remaining 32 Franchised Businesses that were in operation for at least one full year as of December 31, 2007 was not included in Table C due to insufficient information from the franchisees that owned them. We do not know whether the inclusion of such data, if available, would have a material effect on the gross profit margin percentages.

(3)   We attribute variances in material costs to franchisee variances in pricing of lawn and tree care applications. Additionally, we believe that inconsistency in the manner in which franchisees account for their inventory purchases may contribute to the variances. We believe that inconsistency in the manner in which franchisees account for their inventory purchases may contribute to the variances. Some franchisees use the "last in first out" method of accounting for inventory, and others use the "first in first out" method.

(4)   Direct Labor includes compensation (excluding payroll taxes, medical insurance, and fringe benefits) for employees who perform lawn and tree care services and excludes compensation for franchisee and other administrative and office personnel. We attribute the variance in Direct Labor primarily to the extent to which franchisees employed others to perform application services. Franchisees who performed all application services themselves incurred no direct labor costs and franchisees that employ others to perform some or all of the application services incurred higher Direct Labor cost. We also believe that some franchisees may have employees who perform administrative functions as well as application functions, but charged those employees' entire payroll to Direct Labor rather than splitting out that portion more appropriately charged to administration.

(5)   Cost of Sales is the Sum of Material Costs and Direct Labor Costs. However, in the High Percentage column, the Material Costs percentage added to the Direct Labor Costs percentage will not equal the Cost of Sales because the franchisee who reported the highest Material Costs is different than the franchisee who reported the highest Direct Labor Cost. The stated High Percentage Cost of Sales is based on the number reported by the franchisee with the highest combined Material Costs and Direct Labor Costs.

(6)   We obtained the stated Gross Profit Margin percentages by subtracting the Cost of Sales from the 100% Gross Sales. Therefore, the Low Percentage column reflects the Gross Profit Margin of the most profitable of these 38 franchisees, which means that the highest Gross Profit Margin percentage is reported in the "Low Percentage" column. Likewise, the Gross Profit Margin of the least profitable of these 38 franchisees is stated in the "High Percentage" column, because it related to the franchisee with the highest costs.

(7)   THE RESULTS DESCRIBED IN TABLE C INCLUDE CERTAIN COST INFORMATION FOR 38 OUT OF 70 FRANCHISED BUSINESSES OPEN FOR ATLEAST ONE FULL YEAR AS OF DECEMBER 31, 2007. THE RESULTS ARE FOR CALENDAR YEAR 2007. FRANCHISED BUSINESSES TYPICALLY USE THE ACCRUAL METHOD OF ACCOUNTING.

Table D

**Statement of Average Gross Sales and Average Revenue Per Customer for the
First Year of Operation for 19 Franchised Businesses**

First Full Year of Operation	Average	Number of Franchises That Attained or Surpassed the Average
Average Gross Sales	$52,183	9 of 19 had higher gross sales than the average of the group
Average Revenue per Customer	$343	5 of 19 had higher avg. rev. per customer than the average of the group

Notes:

(1)   Table D contains information regarding the first year of full time operation for 19 Franchised Businesses that had one full calendar year of full time operations during 2005, 2006 or 2007. Due to the Flex Start Program 5 of the 19 Franchised Businesses included in Table D began operating part time before their first full calendar year of full time operation.

(2)   To compute the average revenue per customer we totaled all invoices for all services for each Franchised Business for the calendar year in which their first year of full time operations occurred and divided by the number of customers invoiced for a spring lawn care service application in that year. Each Franchised Business reports its revenue on an aggregate basis for all franchise territories covered by the Franchised Business. Thus, in this Item 19 we do not include separate financial information for each individual franchise territories.

SUPERCUTS
every time

SUPERCUTS

7201 Metro Blvd.
Minneapolis, MN 55439-2103
Tel: (888) 888-7008 (952) 947-7777
Fax: (952) 947-7900
E-Mail: franchiseleads@regiscorp.com
Web Site: www.regisfranchise.com
Mr. Alan Storry, VP Franchise Development

Our strategy is simple: give men and busy families what they want. That's why SUPERCUTS Salons offer a contemporary and comfortable atmosphere that appeals to those in search of current hairstyles at affordable prices.

BACKGROUND:	IFA MEMBER
Established: 1975;	1st Franchised: 1975
Franchised Units:	1010
Company-Owned Units:	1122
Total Units:	2132
Dist.:	US-2066; CAN-50; O'seas-16
North America:	48 States, 1 Provinces
Density:	397 in CA, 188 in FL, 164 in TX
Projected New Units (12 Months):	78
Qualifications:	5, 5, 1, 3, 4, 5
Registered:CA,DC,FL,HI,IL,IN,MD,MI,MN,ND,NY,OR,RI,SD, VA,WA,WI	

FINANCIAL/TERMS:

Cash Investment:	$111-239.7K
Total Investment:	$97-208K
Minimum Net Worth:	$300K/100K Liq
Fees: Franchise -	$22.5K
Royalty - 4% Yr. 1/6% succ. Yrs.;	Ad. - 4
Earnings Claims Statement:	No
Term of Contract (Years):	Evergreen
Avg. # Of Employees:	5 FT, 4 PT
Passive Ownership:	Allowed
Encourage Conversions:	Yes
Area Develop. Agreements:	Yes
Sub-Franchising Contracts:	No
Expand In Territory:	Yes
Space Needs:	1,000 SF; SC

SUPPORT & TRAINING:

Financial Assistance Provided:	Yes (I)
Site Selection Assistance:	Yes
Lease Negotiation Assistance:	Yes
Co-Operative Advertising:	Yes
Franchisee Assoc./Member:Yes/Member	NR
Size Of Corporate Staff:	900
On-Going Support:	C,D,E,G,H
Training:	Outstanding support in all areas; 4-5 Days Minneapolis, MN

SPECIFIC EXPANSION PLANS:

US:	Yes, All United States
Canada:	Yes, All Canada
Overseas:	No

ITEM 19
FINANCIAL PERFORMANCE REPRESENTATIONS

The following information addresses average salon gross sales during the 12-month period ending June 30, 2008 for 809 franchised SUPERCUTS salons operating throughout the United States. The salons whose gross sales were included in order to calculate the average were open for at least 2 full years as of July 1, 2007, the beginning of the period for which the numbers were calculated (meaning that they were open for at least 3 full years as of June 30, 2008). As of June 30, 2008, there were an additional 176 franchised SUPERCUTS salons operating throughout the United States. However, their gross sales were not included in this calculation because they either were not open at all as of July 1, 2007, the beginning of the period for which the numbers were calculated, or had not been open for 2 full years as of that date.

The following information has been compiled from the figures reported by the franchisees of these 809 salons on sales and royalty statements. While SUPERCUTS believes this information to be accurate and complete, SUPERCUTS has not audited this information or otherwise verified its accuracy. The numbers reported do not include the operating results of any of the 1,091 SUPERCUTS salons owned and operated by SUPERCUTS, the franchisor. The average total sales for 934 SUPERCUTS owned and operated Stores that have been open and operating for at least two years, as of July 1, 2007, is $258,559.

The 809 salons included in this sample are located in the following states:

1.	Alabama (8)	21.	Minnesota (7)
2.	Arkansas (7)	22.	Missouri (5)
3.	Arizona (28)	23.	Mississippi (4)
4.	California (224)	24.	Nebraska (8)
5.	Connecticut (3)	25.	New Hampshire (16)
6.	Delaware (4)	26.	New Jersey (10)
7.	District of Columbia (2)	27.	New Mexico (14)
8.	Florida (34)	28.	New York (6)
9.	Georgia (5)	29.	North Carolina(8)
10.	Idaho (8)	30.	North Dakota (3)
11.	Illinois (31)	31.	Oklahoma (45)
12.	Indiana (9)	32.	Oregon (11)
13.	Iowa (2)	33.	Pennsylvania (54)
14.	Kansas (4)	34.	South Carolina (5)
15.	Kentucky (7)	35.	Tennessee (8)
16.	Louisiana (13)	36.	Texas (104)
17.	Maine (5)	37.	Vermont (1)
18.	Maryland (1)	38.	Virginia (3)
19.	Massachusetts (44)	39.	Washington (55)
20.	Michigan (1)	40.	Wisconsin (2)

The average total sales for this group of 809 salons was $331,952 for the fiscal year ending June 30, 2008. A total of 337 salons, or 42%, exceeded this average. The average total sales for both franchised and SUPERCUTS owned and operated Stores that have been open for at least two years is $292,624.

AVERAGE SALES FOR FRANCHISED STORES BASED ON SALES RANGES

SALES RANGE ($000)	SALONS	%	AVG. SALES IN RANGE
<$150	29	3.58%	$132,626

>=$150 - <$200	94	11.62%	$179,066
>=$200 - <$250	137	16.93%	$226,455
>=$250 - <$300	136	16.81%	$275,836
>=$300 - <$350	115	14.22%	$325,096
>=$350 - <$400	87	10.75%	$372,868
>=$400 - <$450	71	8.78%	$422,424
>=$450 - <$500	43	5.32%	$471,122
>=$500	97	11.99%	$610,894
ALL SALONS	809	100.0%	$331,952

The products and services offered by each franchised SUPERCUTS salon are essentially the same. These franchised salons are substantially similar to the franchises SUPERCUTS currently offers in all states. These salons receive substantially the same services from SUPERCUTS.

The gross sales information listed above should not be used as a measure of profitability. Your salon's actual performance will be affected by the specific conditions in your salon's market. These conditions include location, competition within the immediate market area, amount of time in business, lease terms, financing costs, taxes, labor costs, supply costs, local economic and regulatory conditions, your management skills, the quality of the services provided to the salon's customers, and the salon's own marketing and sales efforts. Units opened less than two years tend to have lower average sales than those included in the averages above, particularly when developing units in a new market or one with few stores.

THE INFORMATION IN THIS ITEM IS TO HELP YOU AND YOUR PROFESSIONAL ADVISORS EVALUATE THE SUPERCUTS FRANCHISE OPPORTUNITY. THE SALES FIGURES ABOVE ARE AVERAGES OF HISTORICAL DATA OF SPECIFIC FRANCHISES. THEY SHOULD NOT BE CONSIDERED AS POTENTIAL SALES THAT MAY BE REALIZED BY YOU. SUPERCUTS DOES NOT REPRESENT THAT YOU CAN EXPECT TO ATTAIN THESE SALES LEVELS. YOUR ACTUAL FINANCIAL RESULTS ARE LIKELY TO DIFFER FROM THE FIGURES PRESENTED. ACTUAL RESULTS VARY FROM SALON TO SALON, AND SUPERCUTS CANNOT ESTIMATE THE RESULTS OF ANY PARTICULAR FRANCHISE.

THE EARNINGS CLAIMS FIGURES DO NOT REFLECT THE COSTS OF SALES, OPERATING EXPENSES, OR OTHER COSTS OR EXPENSES THAT MUST BE DEDUCTED FROM THE GROSS REVENUE OR GROSS SALES FIGURES TO OBTAIN YOUR NET INCOME OR PROFIT. YOU SHOULD CONDUCT AN INDEPENDENT INVESTIGATION OF THE COSTS AND EXPENSES YOU WILL INCUR IN OPERATING YOUR SUPERCUTS SALON. FRANCHISEES OR FORMER FRANCHISEES, LISTED IN THE DISCLOSURE DOCUMENT, MAY BE ONE SOURCE OF THIS INFORMATION. SUPERCUTS WILL NOT BE BOUND BY INFORMATION RECEIVED FROM ANY UNAUTHORIZED THIRD PARTY REGARDING EARNINGS, SALES, PROFITS, OR THE LIKELIHOOD OF SUCCESS.

SUBSTANTIATION OF THE ABOVE AVERAGES IS AVAILABLE TO YOU AT SUPERCUTS' OFFICES IF YOU REQUEST, PROVIDED IT DOES NOT REQUIRE THE DISCLOSURE OF THE IDENTITY OF ANY SALON OWNER.

OTHER THAN THE ABOVE INFORMATION, SUPERCUTS DOES NOT FURNISH OR AUTHORIZE ITS SALESPERSONS TO FURNISH ANY ORAL OR WRITTEN INFORMATION CONCERNING THE ACTUAL OR POTENTIAL SALES, INCOME, OR PROFITS OF A SUPERCUTS SALON.

TWO MEN AND A TRUCK

"Movers Who Care."

3400 Belle Chase Way
Lansing, MI 48911
Tel: (800) 345-1070 (517) 394-7210
Fax: (517) 394-7432
E-Mail: franchiseinfo@twomenandatruck.com
Web Site: www.twomenandatruck.com
Ms. Pamela Batten, Franchise Sales Coordinator

TWO MEN AND A TRUCK is the nation's first and largest local moving franchise. Known as the "Movers Who Care," TWO MEN AND A TRUCK is committed to exceeding customers' expectations. They offer a full range of residential and commercial moving services, as well as boxes and packing supplies.

BACKGROUND:
IFA MEMBER

Established: 1985;	1st Franchised: 1989
Franchised Units:	205
Company-Owned Units:	3
Total Units:	208
Dist.:	US-202; CAN-5; O'seas-1
North America:	29 States, 1 Provinces
Density:	20 in FL, 14 in GA, 18 in MI
Projected New Units (12 Months):	32
Qualifications:	3, 4, 1, 3, 5, 5
Registered:	CA,FL,IL,IN,MI,MN,NY,OR,RI,WA,WI

FINANCIAL/TERMS:

Cash Investment:	$50K
Total Investment:	$150-412.9K
Minimum Net Worth:	$300K+
Fees: Franchise -	$37K
Royalty - 6%;	Ad. - 1%
Earnings Claims Statement:	Yes
Term of Contract (Years):	5/5
Avg. # Of Employees:	5 FT, 3 PT
Passive Ownership:	Allowed, But Discouraged
Encourage Conversions:	Yes
Area Develop. Agreements:	Yes
Sub-Franchising Contracts:	No
Expand In Territory:	Yes
Space Needs:	800+ SF; Varies

SUPPORT & TRAINING:

Financial Assistance Provided:	No
Site Selection Assistance:	No
Lease Negotiation Assistance:	No
Co-Operative Advertising:	Yes
Franchisee Assoc./Member:	Yes/Member
Size Of Corporate Staff:	55
On-Going Support:	C,D,G,h,I
Training:	3 Weeks Lansing, MI at Stick Men University

SPECIFIC EXPANSION PLANS:

US:	Yes, All United States, 30 units
Canada:	Yes, All Canada, 1 unit
Overseas:	Yes, South Africa, 1 unit

Item 19
FINANCIAL PERFORMANCE REPRESENTATION

The financial performance information provided in this Item 19 is an historic financial performance representation about all of the Franchisees existing in our system for the relevant period based upon financial information those Franchisees reported to us.

The chart below reflects **average annual sales and expenses** for each of the first four years a new Franchisee operated its business as reported to us by the new Franchisees for the years 2003 through 2007.

Sales/Expense Category	Year 1 of Operation	Year 2 of Operation	Year 3 of Operation	Year 4 of Operation	Average Expense as % of Sales During First Four Years
Average Annual Gross Sales	$486,889	$758,132	$891,141	$1,133,789	
Average Direct Labor Expense	$160,962	$261,547	$311,308	$386,649	34%

356

Average Cost of Supplies/Damages	$22,333	$32,664	$34,965	$46,241	4%
Average Moving Truck Expenses	$76,072	$111,795	$132,348	$173,664	15%
Average Advertising Expenses	$26,558	$30,797	$35,718	$41,102	4%
Average Operating Fees	$41,222	$65,716	$76,837	$94,030	8%
General Ad./ Support Staff Exp.	$140,998	$168,078	$186,472	$220,798	22%
Total Average Annual Expenses	**$468,145**	**$670,597**	**$777,647**	**$962,483**	**88%**

The chart below reflects **average annual sales and expenses** for our Franchisees with five or more years of experience in the franchise system as reported to us by them for the years 2003 through 2007.

Sales/Expense Category	Dollar Amount of Sales/ Expenses	Expense as % of Sales	% of Franchises Performing Better Than the Average for Sales or Expense Categories
Average Gross Sales	**$1,899,994**		31%
Average Direct Labor Expenses	$665,649	35%	53%
Average Cost of Supplies/Damages	$70,069	4%	55%
Average Moving Truck Expenses	$273,750	14%	48%
Average Advertising Expenses	$70,441	4%	56%
Average Operating Fees	$153,838	8%	55%
General Ad./ Support Staff Expenses	$407,250	21%	47%
Total Average Expenses	**$1,640,997**	**86%**	48%

THESE CHARTS ARE BASED ON ACTUAL FINANCIAL INFORMATION REPORTED TO US BY OUR FRANCHISEES. THIS INFORMATION HAS NOT BEEN AUDITED OR VERIFIED BY US. THESE CHARTS SHOULD NOT BE VIEWED AS ASSURANCE THAT YOU WILL ACHIEVE ANY PARTICULAR SALES VOLUME OR INCUR ANY PARTICULAR COSTS OR EXPENSES. THEY SHOULD NOT BE CONSIDERED THE ACTUAL, POTENTIAL OR PROBABLE GROSS SALES OR COSTS OR EXPENSES THAT WILL BE EXPERIENCED BY YOUR FRANCHISE, IF YOU CHOOSE TO BECOME A FRANCHISEE. YOUR VOLUMES WILL BE AFFECTED BY THE CONDITION OF THE ECONOMY, BOTH LOCALLY AND NATIONALLY, THE STATUS OF THE COMPETITION, YOUR DILIGENCE AND EXPERIENCE AND MANY OTHER FACTORS BEYOND OUR CONTROL. YOUR INDIVIDUAL FINANCIAL RESULTS ARE LIKELY TO DIFFER FROM THE RESULTS STATED IN THE CHARTS. EVEN SO, SUBSTANTIATION OF THE DATA USED IN PREPARING THESE CHARTS WILL BE MADE AVAILABLE TO YOU

UPON REASONABLE REQUEST.

GROSS SALES DO NOT REFLECT THE ACTUAL POTENTIAL INCOME OF A FRAN-CHISE AND SHOULD NOT BE RELIED UPON IN CALCULATING POTENTIAL PROFIT-ABILITY. THE PROFITABILITY OF INDIVIDUAL FRANCHISE UNITS IS DEPENDENT ON A NUMBER OF FACTORS, WHICH CAN VARY DUE TO THE INDIVIDUAL CHARACTERISTICS OF THE FRANCHISE BUSINESS. THIS INCLUDES, FOR EXAMPLE, ECONOMIC OR MARKET CONDITIONS AND COSTS AND EXPENSES, SUCH AS THE COST OF OBTAINING TRUCK-ING LICENSES OR AUTHORITIES TO PERFORM LONG DISTANCE MOVES, LABOR COSTS INCURRED TO PROVIDE MOVING AND RELATED SERVICES, THE COST OF PURCHAS-ING AND/OR FINANCING TRUCKS, PAYMENT OF ROYALTY AND ADVERTISING FEES TO US AND OVERHEAD COSTS INCURRED AT YOUR BUSINESS LOCATION, INCLUDING LEASE, UTILITY AND INSURANCE EXPENSES. THESE AND OTHER VARIABLE COSTS AS DESCRIBED IN ITEMS 6 AND 7 SHOULD BE CONSIDERED.

WE DO NOT PROVIDE ANY GUARANTY OR ASSURANCE THAT ANY FRANCHISEE WILL ATTAIN THE SALES OR INCUR THE COSTS AND EXPENSES REFLECTED IN THESE CHARTS, OR ANY INCOME OR PROFIT THAT COULD BE DERIVED FROM SUCH SALES. IF ANYONE RELIES ON THESE FIGURES, THEY MUST ACCEPT THE RISK OF NOT DOING AS WELL.

ACTUAL RESULTS VARY FROM UNIT TO UNIT AND WE CANNOT ESTIMATE THE RESULTS OF ANY PARTICULAR FRANCHISE. WE WILL NOT BE BOUND BY ALLEGATIONS OF ANY UNAUTHORIZED REPRESENTATION AS TO EARNINGS, SALES, PROFITS OR PROSPECTS OR CHANCES OF SUCCESS.

WSI
we simplify the Internet

WSI

5580 Explorer Dr., #600
Mississauga, ON L4W 4Y1 Canada
Tel: (888) 678-7588 (905) 678-7588
Fax: (905) 678-7242
E-Mail: wsileads@wsicorporate.com
Web Site: www.wsicorporate.com
Franchise Development Team

Now in its 11th year of business, WSI is the world's leading internet services franchise with 1500 franchisees in 87 countries! You can be part of this successful franchise and profit from the Internet! Own the #1 rated internet franchise. Proven business system. Comprehensive training and support is provided. Home- or office-based. Complete training and support. The WSI Formula is simple: Successful Franchise Owners + Successful Clients - Successful Franchise Opportunity.

BACKGROUND: IFA MEMBER

Established: 1995;	1st Franchised: 1996
Franchised Units:	1743
Company-Owned Units:	20
Total Units:	1763
Dist.:	US-804; CAN-69; O'seas-890

North America:	1 States, 1 Provinces
Density:	NR
Projected New Units (12 Months):	400
Qualifications:	2, 2, 3, 3, 4, 5
Registered:	CA,DC,FL,HI,IL,IN,MD,MI,MN,ND,NY,OR,RI,SD, VA,WA,WI,AB

FINANCIAL/TERMS:

Cash Investment:	$49.7K
Total Investment:	$49.7K
Minimum Net Worth:	$100K
Fees: Franchise -	$49.7K
Royalty - 10%;	Ad. - NA
Earnings Claims Statement:	No
Term of Contract (Years):	5/5
Avg. # Of Employees:	3 FT, 1 PT
Passive Ownership:	Not Allowed
Encourage Conversions:	NA
Area Develop. Agreements:	No
Sub-Franchising Contracts:	No
Expand In Territory:	Yes
Space Needs:	1,600-1,900 SF; HB

SUPPORT & TRAINING:

Financial Assistance Provided:	No
Site Selection Assistance:	NA
Lease Negotiation Assistance:	NA
Co-Operative Advertising:	No

Franchisee Assoc./Member:	Yes/Member	**SPECIFIC EXPANSION PLANS:**	
Size Of Corporate Staff:	100	US:	Yes, All United States
On-Going Support:	a,b,c,e,G,H,I	Canada:	Yes, All Canada
Training:	1 Week Mississauga, ON	Overseas:	Yes, All Countries

ITEM 19
FINANCIAL PERFORMANCE REPRESENTATIONS

ANALYSIS OF CERTAIN SALES INFORMATION

This analysis contains average sales and related information for certain WSI franchisees who began their operations in the US between January 1, 2007 and December 31, 2007.

The analysis is based on sales of WSI internet marketing systems delivered within the first 3 to 4 months after beginning operations (the "Measurement Period") by 65 of the 76 franchisees who began operating in the US in 2007. [1] Commencement of operations is measured from the date a franchisee successfully completes our mandatory initial training program and opens its business.

All 65 of the franchisees included in this analysis completed our Quick Start Program ("QSP") of coaching for new franchisees during the Measurement Period. The QSP is a 90 day coaching program that was made available to all new franchisees following completion of our mandatory initial training program. Franchises who elect to participate typically enroll in the program within one month following the completion of initial training. The QSP offers coaching in the WSI System, and in sales and marketing and business start-up. The goal is to expedite a Franchisee's start-up phase of their business by providing one on one coaching to the specific needs of the Franchisee.

Average Sales Information and Assumptions Of the 65 franchisees included in this analysis:

· **Average Sales Price:** The average sale price[2] for the Quadrant 1[3] internet solutions sold was $779.71. The average sale price for the Quadrant 2[4] internet solutions sold was $5,172.43. 28 franchisees exceeded this average and 56 franchisees were below the average.

· **Average Mark-Up:** The average mark-up above the development costs for the internet solution was 443%.[5] 53 franchisees exceeded this average and 12 franchisees were below the average.

· **Recurring Revenue:** 79% of sales made by this group during the Measurement Period included recurring revenue.[6]

Notes:

(1)   All franchisees regardless of which one of the territorial licenses held are included in the above number (the type of license held does not restrict the type of internet solutions that a franchisee can sell).

(2)   The average sales figure indicates the one time cost for the sale of the internet solution.

(3)   The Quadrant 1 solution is a small project aimed at allowing a company to create an internet presence at a low initial cost. We have special products with very low production costs aimed at this market.

(4)   The Quadrant 2 solution is a solution with a higher development cost that also brings a higher value to the end client. These are higher value solutions.

(5)   The mark-up is the sales price amount divided by development cost. The cost of web development equals cost of goods sold.

(6)   Certain sales made during the Measurement Period by the group included in this analysis may also include an additional recurring monthly amount for services rendered following the initial sale and charged on a monthly basis. Recurring revenue is derived from services and hosting and from other related technology requirements. Sales that do not have recurring revenue may be due

to client budget or lack of client need for these services. The length of time during which recurring revenues are earned varies considerably.

These statistics are based on QSP Reports and other information submitted by the franchisees included in this analysis as well as information drawn from our enterprise system, a system that tracks and supports a Franchisee's orders as they are placed with our production center network. The information contained in this analysis has not been audited.

During the period from January 1, 2007 through December 31, 2007, gross sales revenues generated by WSI franchisees located in the United States ranged from zero (for franchisees who have not completed Initial Training) to $1,092,467.

The amount of sales realized and associated development and other costs incurred in sales of WSI internet solutions will vary from sale to sale. Your sales and costs will be directly affected by many factors, such as competition in the marketplace, client requirements, and your skills. You should, therefore, use this information only as a reference to conduct your own analysis.

YOU ARE URGED TO CONSULT WITH APPROPRIATE FINANCIAL, BUSINESS AND LEGAL ADVISERS TO CONDUCT YOUR OWN ANALYSIS OF THE INFORMATION CONTAINED IN THIS ITEM 19.

SOME FRANCHISEES HAVE ACHIEVED THE AVERAGE SALES, MARK—UP AND RECURRING REVENUE REFLECTED IN THIS ANALYSIS BUT THESE FIGURES SHOULD NOT BE CONSIDERED AS THE ACTUAL OR POTENTIAL SALES, INCOME OR PROFITS THAT YOU WILL REALIZE. THERE IS NO ASSURANCE YOU'LL DO AS WELL, AND WE DO NOT REPRESENT THAT ANY FRANCHISEE CAN EXPECT TO ATTAIN THE SALES, INCOME OR PROFITS DESCRIBED IN THIS ITEM 19, OR ANY PARTICULAR LEVEL OF SALES, INCOME OR PROFITS. IN ADDITION, WE DO NOT REPRESENT THAT ANY FRANCHISEE WILL DERIVE INCOME THAT EXCEEDS THE INITIAL PAYMENT FOR OR INVESTMENT IN THE FRANCHISED BUSINESS. IF YOU RELY UPON OUR FIGURES, YOU MUST ACCEPT THE RISK OF NOT DOING AS WELL. THE INDIVIDUAL FINANCIAL RESULTS OF ANY FRANCHISED BUSINESS ARE LIKELY TO DIFFER FROM THE INFORMATION DESCRIBED IN THIS ITEM 19, AND YOUR SUCCESS WILL DEPEND LARGELY ON YOUR ABILITY.

THIS ANALYSIS DOES NOT INCLUDE ANY ESTIMATES OF THE FEDERAL INCOME TAX THAT WOULD BE PAYABLE ON THE NET INCOME FROM A FRANCHISED BUSINESS OR STATE OR LOCAL NET INCOME OR GROSS PROFITS TAXES THAT MAY BE APPLICABLE TO THE PARTICULAR JURISDICTION IN WHICH YOUR FRANCHISED BUSINESS IS LOCATED. EACH FRANCHISEE IS STRONGLY URGED TO CONSULT WITH ITS TAX ADVISER.

THE FINANCIAL PERFORMANCE REPRESENTATIONS FIGURES DO NOT REFLECT THE COSTS OF SALES, OPERATING EXPENSES OR OTHER COSTS OR EXPENSES THAT MUST BE DEDUCTED FROM THE GROSS REVENUE OR GROSS SALES FIGURES TO OBTAIN YOUR NET INCOME OR PROFIT. YOU SHOULD CONDUCT AN INDEPENDENT INVESTIGATION OF THE COSTS AND EXPENSES YOU WILL INCUR IN OPERATING YOUR FRANCHISED BUSINESS. FRANCHISEES OR FORMER FRANCHISEES, LISTED IN THE DISCLOSURE DOCUMENT, MAY BE ONE SOURCE OF THIS INFORMATION.

WE HAVE WRITTEN SUBSTANTIATION IN OUR POSSESSION TO SUPPORT THE INFORMATION APPEARING IN THIS ITEM 19, AND SUCH SUBSTANTIATION WILL BE MADE AVAILABLE TO YOU ON REASONABLE REQUEST.

Please note that all of the Item 19s included in the 2009 Edition of "How Much Can I Make?" were taken from the respective company's 2008 Franchise Disclosure Document (FDD)/Uniform Offering Circular (UFOC). Accordingly, all of the financial data in the Item 19s refers to actual operations in 2007. In a very few cases, depending upon the date of the FDD/UFOC, the data might refer to operations in 2006. Because of the need to provide historical data, there is generally a year's lag between the date of the annual FDD/UFOC and the underlying Item 19 data.

Listing
of Franchisors

The Definitive Franchising Directory

Bond's Franchise Guide
2009 (20th) Edition

Key Features:
- The Most Comprehensive and Up-To-Date Directory of Franchise Listings
- All New Data Every Edition
- Over 900 Detailed Franchisor Profiles
  - ~750 American Franchisors
  - ~150 Canadian Franchisors
- Profiles of Franchise Attorneys, Consultants and Service Providers
- 29 Distinct Business Categories
- Detailed Industry Statistics by Category
- 528 Pages
- Direct Comparability Between Franchise Listings

PUBLISHED ANNUALLY

Yes, I want to order _____ copy(ies) of *Bond's Franchise Guide* at $34.95 each ($45.50 Canadian). Please add $8.50 per book for shipping & handling ($12.00 Canada; international shipments at actual cost). California residents add appropriate sales tax.

Name_____ Title_____

Company_____ Telephone No. (_____) _____

Address _____

City _____ State/Prov. _____ Zip _____

Email Address_____

☐ Check Enclosed or

Charge my: ☐ American Express ☐ MasterCard ☐ Visa

Card #:_____ Expiration Date: _____

Signature:_____ Security Code _____

Please send to: **Source Book Publications**, 1814 Franklin Street, Suite 603, Oakland, CA 94612

* Note: All books shipped by USPS Priority Mail.
Satisfaction Guaranteed. If not fully satisfied, return for a prompt, 100% refund.

For faster service, please call (800) 841-0873 or fax (510) 839-2104

Now's the time to be **in business for yourself,** but **not by yourself**. Own a Franchise.

The West Coast Franchise Expo

Los Angeles Convention Center
October 2–4, 2009

Visit: WCFExpo.com

With today's unpredictable economy, and uncertain job market, there's never been a better time to take control of your financial future – by being in business for yourself

When you own a proven franchise, you have the support of a professional team to help you carry the load. That's why a franchise is a safer way to be in business for yourself.

At the West Coast Franchise Expo, you'll be able to see hundreds of the top franchises. Sample their products. Attend educational seminars. And get all the information you need to choose the right franchise for your interests, skills and investment level – all in one place.

Don't miss this opportunity to take control of your financial future.

SPONSORED BY

IFA Franchising
INTERNATIONAL FRANCHISE ASSOCIATION **Building** local businesses, one **opportunity** at a time.

Produced by MFV Expositions
For Exhibitor Info Call: Maryjane at 201.881.1666
or exhibit@mfvexpo.com

DEFINITIVE FRANCHISOR DATABASE
AVAILABLE FOR RENT

SAMPLE FRANCHISOR PROFILE

Name of Franchise:	EXPRESS EMPLOYMENT PROFESSIONALS
Address:	8516 NW Expressway
City/State/Zip/Postal Code:	Oklahoma City, OK 73162-5145
Country:	U.S.A.
800 Telephone #:	(877) 652-6400
Local Telephone #:	(405) 840-5000
Fax #:	(405) 717-5665
E-Mail:	franchising@expresspros.com
Internet Address:	www.expressfranchising.com
# Franchised Units:	592
# Company-Owned Units:	4
# Total Units:	596
Company Contact:	Ms. Diane Carter
Contact Title/Position:	Manager of Franchise Admin.
Contact Salutation:	Ms. Carter
President:	Mr. Robert A. Funk
President Title:	Chief Executive Officer
President Salutation:	Mr. Funk
Industry Category (of 48):	17/ Personnel Services
IFA Member:	International Franchise Association
CFA Member:	Canadian Franchise Association

KEY FEATURES

• Number of Active North American Franchisors	~ 3,000
% US	~90%
% Canadian	~10%
• Data Fields (See Above)	29
• Industry Categories	48
• % With Toll-Free Telephone Numbers	64%
• % With Fax Numbers	94%
• % With Name of Preferred Contact	95%
• % With Name of President	81%
• % With Number of Total Operating Units	92%
• Guaranteed Accuracy — $0.50 Rebate/Returned Bad Address	
• Converted to Any Popular Database or Contact Management Program	
• Initial Front-End Cost	$1,500
• Quarterly Up-Dates	$150
• Mailing Labels Only — One-Time Use	$600

For More Information, Please Contact
Source Book Publications
1814 Franklin Street, Suite 603, Oakland, CA 94612
(800) 841-0873 • (510) 839-5471 • FAX (510) 839-2104

An In-Depth Analysis of Today's Top Franchise Opportunities

Bond's Top 100 Franchises

2009 (3rd) Edition

Key Features:

In response to the constantly asked question, *"What are the best franchises?"*, this book focuses on the top 100 franchises broken down into four major segments — food-service, lodging, retail and service-based franchises. Within each group, a rigorous, in-depth analysis was performed on over 500 systems. Many of the companies selected are household names. Others are rapidly-growing, mid-sized firms that are also strong national players. Still others are somewhat smaller systems that demonstrate sound concepts, exceptional management and an aggressive expansion system. Companies were analyzed on the basis of historical performance, brand identification, market dynamics, franchisee satisfaction, the level of training and on-going support, financial stability, etc. This book includes detailed four to five page profiles on each company, as well as key statistics and industry overview. All companies are proven performers and most have a national presence.

Yes, I want to order _____ copy(ies) of *Bond's Top 100 Franchises* at $24.95 each ($32.50 Canadian). Please add $8.50 per book for shipping & handling ($12.00 Canada; international shipments at actual cost). California residents add appropriate sales tax.

Name_____Title_____

Company_____Telephone No. (_____) _____

Address_____

City_____ State/Prov. _____ Zip _____

Email Address_____

☐ Check Enclosed or

Charge my: ☐ MasterCard ☐ Visa

Card #:_____ Expiration Date: _____

Signature:_____ Security Code:_____

Please send to: **Source Book Publications**, 1814 Franklin Street, Suite 603, Oakland, CA 94612

* Note: All books shipped by USPS Priority Mail.
Satisfaction Guaranteed. If not fully satisfied, return for a prompt, 100% refund.

For faster service, please call (800) 841-0873 or fax (510) 839-2104